PRENTICE-HALL INTERNATIONAL SERIES IN MANAGEMENT

Baumol	*Economic Theory and Operations Analysis, 2nd ed.*
Boot	*Mathematical Reasoning in Economics and Management Science*
Brown	*Smoothing, Forecasting, and Prediction of Discrete Time Series*
Churchman	*Prediction and Optimal Decision: Philosophical Issues of a Science of Values*
Coffey, Athos, and Raynolds	*Behavior in Organizations: A Multidimensional View, 2nd ed.*
Cohen and Cyert	*Theory of the Firm: Resource Allocation in a Market Economy, 2nd ed.*
Ewart, Ford, and Lin	*Probability for Statistical Decision Making*
Fabrycky and Torgersen	*Operations Economy: Industrial Applications of Operations Research*
Frank, Massy, and Wind	*Market Segmentation*
Green and Tull	*Research for Marketing Decisions, 2nd ed.*
Hadley and Whitin	*Analysis of Inventory Systems*
Holt, Modigliani, Muth, and Simon	*Planning Production, Inventories, and Work Force*
Ijiri	*The Foundations of Accounting Measurement: A Mathematical, Economic, and Behavioral Inquiry*
Kaufmann	*Methods and Models of Operations Research*
Mantel	*Cases in Managerial Decisions*
Massé	*Optimal Investment Decisions: Rules for Action and Criteria for Choice*
McGuire	*Theories of Business Behavior*
Miller and Starr	*Executive Decisions and Operations Research, 2nd ed.*
Montgomery and Urban	*Management Science in Marketing*
Montgomery and Urban	*Applications of Management Science in Marketing*
Morris	*Management Science: A Bayesian Introduction*
Muth and Thompson	*Industrial Scheduling*
Nelson (ed.)	*Marginal Cost Pricing in Practice*
Nicosia	*Consumer Decision Processes: Marketing and Advertising Decisions*
Peters and Summers	*Statistical Analysis for Business Decisions*
Pfiffner and Sherwood	*Administrative Organization*
Simonnard	*Linear Programming*
Singer	*Antitrust Economics: Selected Legal Cases and Economic Models*
Vernon	*Manager in the International Economy*
Wagner	*Principles of Operations Research with Applications to Managerial Decisions*
Zangwill	*Nonlinear Programming: A Unified Approach*
Zenoff and Zwick	*International Financial Management*
Zionts	*Linear and Integer Programming*

SECOND EDITION

THEORY OF THE FIRM

RESOURCE ALLOCATION
IN A MARKET ECONOMY

KALMAN J. COHEN

Distinguished Bank Research Professor
Graduate School of Business Administration
Duke University

RICHARD M. CYERT

Professor of Economics and
Industrial Administration and
President, Carnegie-Mellon University

Prentice-Hall, Inc., Englewood Cliffs, New Jersey

Library of Congress Cataloging in Publication Data

COHEN, Kalman J
    Theory of the firm.

    (Prentice-Hall international series in management)
    Includes bibliographies and index.
    1.   Microeconomics.   I.   Cyert, Richard Michael,
        joint author.   II. Title.
HB171.5.C78 1975   338'.001   75-2284
ISBN 0-13-913798-X

TO JOAN AND MARGARET

© 1975, 1965 by Prentice-Hall, Inc., Englewood Cliffs, New Jersey

Printed in the United States of America

10 9 8 7 6 5 4 3 2 1

PRENTICE-HALL INTERNATIONAL, INC., *London*
PRENTICE-HALL OF AUSTRALIA, PTY. LTD., *Sydney*
PRENTICE-HALL OF CANADA, LTD., *Toronto*
PRENTICE-HALL OF INDIA PRIVATE LIMITED, *New Delhi*
PRENTICE-HALL OF JAPAN, INC., *Tokyo*

PRENTICE-HALL, INC.
PRENTICE-HALL INTERNATIONAL, INC., *United Kingdom and Eire*
PRENTICE-HALL OF CANADA, LTD., *Canada*
DUNOD PRESS, *France*
MARUZEN COMPANY, LTD., *Far East*
HERRERO HERMANOS, SUCS., *Spain and Latin America*
R. OLDENBOURG VERLAG, *Germany*
ULRICO HOEPLI EDITORS, *Italy*

Contents

11. Monopolistic Competition, 211

12. Duopoly and Oligopoly, 233

13. Imperfection in the Factor Markets, 267

PART 3

New Approaches to the Theory of the Firm, 287

14. Decision Making for an Uncertain Future, 289

15. The Cost of Capital and Investment Decisions, 313

Preface to
First Edition

The focus of this book is on the role of business firms in the resource allocation process. In any market economy in which decision making is decentralized, the actions of business firms critically affect the welfare of the society. Business firms are both the major sources of employment and the major producers of goods and services in a market economy. In order to determine whether improvements are possible in the pattern of resource allocation, it is important for citizens to obtain an understanding of the impact of business decisions on the efficiency of an economy. This book aims at providing such an understanding in a technical and rigorous manner.

In most discussions of resource allocation, the emphasis tends to be on the functioning of markets rather than the operations of individual firms. We have attempted to present a more balanced analysis by exploring in some detail the decision-making processes of firms in a variety of market structures. The decision-making processes of consumers have been investigated only to the extent necessary for understanding the influence of consumer preferences on the pattern of resource allocation.

It has been necessary to expound a considerable amount of microeconomic theory to develop an understanding of how business firms affect the resource allocation process. However, we have attempted to indicate the empirical relevance of economic theory by providing numerous illustrations of the manner in which theoretical propositions correspond to and are testable by actual events in the economy. This book emphasizes the use of economic theory to explain the actual functioning of a market economy, rather than economic theory for its own sake.

While teaching courses in "The Economics of the Firm" for several years at Carnegie Institute of Technology, we were unable to find any existing textbook that we felt was appropriate for the type of course we wished to teach and the backgrounds of our students. As a result, we began to write and distribute our own "Classnotes" for these courses. After several revisions, these "Classnotes" have become the manuscript for this book.

As prerequisites for this book, it is assumed that the reader possesses an elementary knowledge of economics and a working knowledge of calculus. Although calculus is used whenever we feel that it is the most natural technique for conveying an understanding of particular economic concepts, this is not a book in mathematical economics. Our attitude has been pragmatic. Where it seemed most appropriate, we have used calculus. Where graphical, literary, or computer simulation analyses seemed most appropriate, they have been used. Our primary interest has been in the economic content of this book rather than the use or non-use of any particular mode of analysis.

Professors Geoffrey P. E. Clarkson, Otto A. Davis, John R. Meyer, Michael B. Nicholson, Daniel Orr, and Leonard A. Rapping have made many helpful suggestions on the basis of their reading earlier drafts of parts of this book. Bruce P. Fitch and Dale T. Mortensen carefully read the "final" version of the manuscript and helped us produce a better final document. We wish to thank these people, as well as those colleagues and students at Carnegie Institute of Technology who have encouraged us during the gestation period of this book. We are grateful to Virginia C. Bloom for organizing the secretarial staff of the Graduate School of Industrial Administration to type the manuscript under the usual time pressures. We wish to thank Lynn Anne Cyert for her help in typing and correcting the manuscript. Kenneth H. Fagerhaugh, Melva E. Raynovich, and Mary T. Scarlott of Carnegie Tech's Hunt Library have been especially helpful and considerate.

It is customary to add that any defects which remain in this book are the sole responsibility of the authors. However, we wish to state that some of the defects are the fault of the entire economics profession, since the theory of the firm has not been perfected to the point where it can provide complete and unambiguous answers to all important microeconomic public policy questions. As economists, we share in this guilt. More research is needed, by others as well as ourselves, to extend the power of economic theory so that it can eventually provide a more adequate guide to public policy. We hope that some readers of this book will feel motivated to join us in this task.

KALMAN J. COHEN
RICHARD M. CYERT

Preface to Second Edition

The focus, style of, and prerequisites for this book remain the same for the Second Edition as they were for the First Edition.

The Second Edition includes a substantial amount of entirely new material, in particular, Chapters 15, 16, and 19, and the Appendix. The remaining chapters have, with some revisions, been retained from the First Edition, although the numbering of some of the latter chapters has been changed.

Upon request to the publisher, a *Teacher's Manual* is available to teachers adopting this book as a text for their courses. This *Teacher's Manual* contains discussion questions, comments, and problems relevant to various chapters of the book; detailed answers to all the problems are included as well.

In addition to the people noted in the First Edition, we would especially like to thank Randall G. Chapman who initially drafted Section I of Chapter 16 and Marie-Thérèse Flaherty who wrote the Appendix. As authors, of course, we assume complete responsibility for any unknown errors which might exist.

KALMAN J. COHEN
RICHARD M. CYERT

Acknowledgments

We wish to thank the following copyright holders for their kindness in permitting us to quote or adapt material from some of their publications:

The American Economic Association: from the *American Economic Review, Papers and Proceedings*, "Technological Progress in Some American Industries," by W. R. Maclaurin (May, 1954); and from the *American Economic Review*, Vol. 63, No. 1, "An Analysis of Cooperation and Learning in a Duopoly Context," by R. M. Cyert and H. M. DeGroot (1973).

The Brookings Institution: from *Pricing in Big Business: A Case Approach*, by A. D. H. Kaplan, J. B. Dirlam and R. F. Lanzillotti (1958).

Cambridge University Press: from *The Analysis of Family Budgets*, by S. J. Prais and H. S. Houthakker (1955).

The Canadian Journal of Economics and Political Science: from "Size of Firm, Oligopoly, and Research: The Evidence," Vol. 30, No. 1, by D. Hamberg (February, 1964).

The University of Chicago Press: from *The Economics of Discrimination*, by G. S. Becker (1957); from the *Journal of Political Economy*, Vol. 70, No. 5, "The Costs of Automobile Model Changes Since 1949," by F. M. Fisher, Z. Griliches and C. Kaysen (1962); from *Essays in Positive Economics*, by M. Friedman (1953); and from the *Journal of Political Economy*, Vol. 67, "Reply," by H. H. Villard (1959).

Consumer's Reports (September, 1956) material reprinted in *Business Economics: Principles and Cases*, 3rd ed., by M. R. Colberg, D. R. Forbush and G. R. Whitaker, Jr., Richard D. Irwin, Inc. (1964).

Harper & Row, Publishers: from *A Textbook of Econometrics*, by L. R. Klein (1953).

Harvard University Press: from *The Theory of Monopolistic Competition*, E. H. Chamberlain (1948); from the *Quarterly Journal of Economics*, Vol. 65, No. 3, "Relation of Profit Rate to Industry Concentration: American Manufacturing" (1951); from the *Quarterly Journal of Economics*, Vol. 84, "Multiperiod Decision Models with Alternating Choice as a Solution of the Duopoly

Problem," by R. M. Cyert and M. H. DeGroot (1970); and from *Foundations of Economic Analysis*, by P. A. Samuelson (1947).

Holt, Rinehart & Winston, Inc.: from *Pricing, Distribution, and Employment*, by J. S. Bain (1953).

University of Illinois: from Studies in Business Expectations and Planning No. 4, *The Role of Anticipations and Plans in Economic Behavior and Their Use in Economic Analysis and Forecasting*, by F. Modigliani and K. J. Cohen.

The Iowa State College Press: from *Econometric Analysis for Public Policy*, by K. A. Fox (1958).

The Macmillan Company: from *The Structure of American Industry*, 3rd ed., ed. by W. Adams (1961); from *Readings in Economics*, ed. by W. Adams and L. E. Traywick (1948); from *Business Behavior, Value and Growth*, by W. J. Baumol (1959); from *The Theory of Price*, by G. J. Stigler (1946); and from *Five Lectures on Economic Problems*, by G. J. Stigler (1949).

Macmillan & Company, Ltd.: from *Economic Essays*, by R. F. Harrod, reprinted by Harcourt, Brace & World, Inc.; from *Principles of Economics*, by A. Marshall (with permission of St. Martin's Press); and from *Mathematical Economics*, by R. G. D. Allen (with permission of St. Martin's Press).

McGraw-Hill Book Company, Inc.: from *Statistical Cost Analysis*, by J. Johnson (1960).

Oliver & Boyd, Ltd.: from *Review of Economic Studies*, Vol. 29, "Chamberlain *versus* Chicago," by G. C. Archibald (1961–1962).

Oxford University Press: from *Towards a More General Theory of Value*, "The Chicago School," by E. H. Chamberlain (1957); and from *A Revision of Demand Theory*, by J. R. Hicks (1956).

Prentice-Hall, Inc.: from *A Behavioral Theory of the Firm*, by R. M. Cyert and J. G. March (1963).

United States Government Printing Office: from the T.N.E.C. Hearing, Part 5, 76 Congress, First Session (1939) reprinted in *Business Economics: Principles and Cases*, 3rd ed., ed. by M. R. Colberg, D. R. Forbush, and G. R. Whitaker, Jr., Richard D. Irwin, Inc. (1964); and from *Price Behavior and Business Policy*, T.N.E.C. Monograph No. 1, 76 Congress, Third Session (1940) reprinted in *Business Economics: Principles and Cases*, rev. ed., ed. by M. R. Colberg, W. C. Bradford, and R. M. Alt, Richard D. Irwin, Inc. (1957).

John Wiley & Sons, Inc.: from *Studies in Econometric Methods*, Cowles Commission Monograph No. 14, by W. C. Hood and T. C. Koopermans, from the article "Statistical Analysis of the Demand for Food: Examples of Simultaneous Estimation of Structural Equations," by M. A. Girshick and T. Haavelmo (1953); from *Economic Fluctuations in the United States*, Cowles Commission Monograph No. 11, by L. R. Klein (1950); from *Interindustry Economics*, by H. B. Chenery and P. G. Clark (1959); and from *Demand Analysis*, by H. Wold and L. Jureen (1953).

The Williams and Wilkins Company: from *Statistical Cost Analysis*, by J. Johnson (1960).

Part 1

Business Firms,
Decision Making,
and Economic Models

Chapter One

Some Reasons for Studying
Business Behavior

This book concentrates on the most significant institution in our economic system—the business firm—and the most important function of our economic system—resource allocation. It is impossible to have a clear understanding of the functioning of the modern American society without knowing a great deal about the firm and the role it plays in the economy's resource allocation process.

I. Four Allocation Functions

An *economic resource* is either a good or service which is valued by consumers for its own sake or an element which is used in producing goods or services for consumers. Unfortunately, almost all economic resources are scarce. Therefore each society must devise some system for allocating them.

In the process of allocating its scarce economic resources, each society must perform four main functions. First, it must decide *what goods and services will be produced*. Because its productive resources are scarce, no society can make unlimited amounts of everything. It must decide whether it will produce guns or butter. If it wants to produce both guns and butter, then it must decide how much of each it will produce. In any modern economy there are literally hundreds of thousands of different types of goods and services produced. Somehow each economy must determine exactly what will be produced and in what quantities.

Second, each society must determine *how its goods and services will be produced*. There generally are several different ways by which any product can be made. For example, suits of clothes can be made from wool, cotton, rayon, dacron, silk, and a variety of other materials, including blends. Houses can be built from bricks, stone, wood, cement, steel, and a variety of other materials. Automobiles may be produced in a highly automated plant using very little labor, or they may be produced in a less automated plant employing relatively more men and fewer machines. In any modern society there are almost endless combinations of productive resources which can be used to produce the goods and services desired. Some methods of producing goods and services may be more efficient than others. The more efficient methods may differ from society to society, however, depending both upon the availability of various resources and upon local customs. Which particular ways (or which particular combinations of ways) will be chosen to produce a society's goods and services is a fundamental resource allocation question which must be answered.

Third, each society must determine *who will get the goods and services which are produced*. Since economic resources are scarce, some people—perhaps everybody—must get fewer goods and services than they would wish to have. Food which the Jones family consumes is not available for the Smiths. Automobiles which are owned by the Browns cannot be owned by the Blacks. A barber can cut only one man's hair at a time. The resource allocation task of determining "who gets what" is staggering in a country like the United States, where it must be decided which of several hundred million people will receive how much of several hundred thousand types of goods and services.

Finally, each society must decide *how much of its economic resources to devote to future growth and how much to satisfy current consumption desires*. An economy can grow larger only by using some of its productive resources to increase its capacity to meet future needs. Only by curtailing current consumption can a society provide higher standards of living for future generations. Steel and labor which are used to make automobiles and refrigerators for current use cannot be used to build factories and automatic machinery that may increase future production capabilities. The time which engineers spend designing appliances for today, they cannot use for basic research which may create new products and new production techniques for the future. The choice between current consumption and economic growth is a fundamental resource allocation problem which every society must somehow face.

II. Sketch of a Hypothetical Free-Market Economy

Let us consider how the four allocation functions are handled in a hypothetical free-market economy, which we call the *perfectly competitive* model. This type of economy is characterized by five important assumptions.

A. THE ASSUMPTIONS OF PERFECT COMPETITION

First, we assume that all firms in an industry produce a homogeneous product. Thus, the properties of any one firm's product are neither superior nor inferior to the products made by other firms in the same industry. Any one farmer's wheat is considered equivalent to any other farmer's wheat. If this is not strictly true, then we assume that suitable price differentials are established to compensate for different quality grades of the product.

A second assumption is that business firms and consumers possess perfect knowledge of relevant alternatives. It follows that all firms have access to the same types of production technology, and that potential buyers and sellers are familiar with prevailing market prices. The perfect knowledge assumption, combined with our previous assumption of homogeneous products, means that no buyer will be willing to pay a premium above the going market price for the product of any specific producer. Therefore, producers will be unable to sell their products unless they price them at the prevailing market price.

Third, we assume that firms attempt to maximize their profits and consumers try to maximize their utilities (i.e., their satisfactions from spending their money as they choose). This implies that a consumer having a choice between two alternative patterns of consumption will choose that one which will provide him with the greater amount of satisfaction. This also implies that a business firm will seek to make that product in the way which will provide it with the maximum possible profit.

Fourth is the assumption of atomistic competition. This assumption implies that the number of buyers and sellers in each market is so large that any one individual firm or household has only a negligible effect on market price. A further aspect of the atomistic competition assumption is that the buyers and sellers in each market act independently. No collusive action on the part of either buyers or sellers which might permit them collectively to control market prices is permitted.

The fifth assumption of our free-market model is that there is free entry and exit in every market. This means that if any firm thinks that it can earn higher profits by moving from its present industry to some other industry, it is free to do so; there are no barriers or hindrances to prevent it. This also implies that whenever a firm is incurring losses, it will be free to go out of business. There must be no barriers, legal, institutional, or informational, which prevent economic resources from flowing freely from industry to industry in pursuit of their own private gain.

B. Equilibrium Price Determination

In such a hypothetical free-market economy (the perfectly competitive model), the price system, in conjunction with supply and demand considerations, determines what is produced. At any specific market price, households wish to buy some particular amount of a product. At the same market price, there is a certain amount of the product which firms are willing to sell. Unless the quantities demanded and supplied are the same, the market price is not in equilibrium, and it will change accordingly. According to the law of supply and demand, the price in any market will tend to be that equilibrium price for which the quantity supplied equals the quantity demanded. The reasoning behind the law can be understood by analyzing the situations in which price is not at its equilibrium value.

Suppose, for example, that the market price is below its equilibrium level. Then the quantity demanded of the product will be larger than the quantity supplied; i.e., consumers would like to buy more of the product than the sellers are willing to let them have. As long as the market price remains below its equilibrium level, some would-be purchasers will be left out. Most of these purchasers feel that they would be better off paying a slightly higher price for the product than doing completely without it. Hence these buyers will compete with each other for the limited quantity of the product available. This competition will force the market price up toward its equilibrium level.

Suppose, on the other hand, that the market price starts out above its equilibrium level. Then the quantity supplied of the product will be larger than the quantity demanded; i.e., suppliers would be willing to sell more of this product than purchasers are willing to take at such a high price. This time it is some suppliers that will be left out, but some of these suppliers would prefer to receive a somewhat lower price and sell more of their product. Competition of this kind among the suppliers to sell their products will force the market price downward toward its equilibrium level.

If the equilibrium price level is below the average cost of production for some firms, then these firms will be suffering losses. As soon as they are able to find more profitable opportunities elsewhere, these firms will leave this industry. There is a long-run tendency for the equilibrium market price to equal the lowest possible average cost that is consistent with known technology. Excess economic profits tend to be eliminated by competition in the long run. If at any time high profits are obtainable in some industry, new competitors will be drawn in thus reducing market price and profits for all firms.

C. DETERMINING WHAT WILL BE PRODUCED

In a perfectly competitive economy, it is the consumers who ultimately determine what will be produced and in what quantities. The pricing process just described provides a way for consumers to register their preferences for goods and services. The more consumers want some product, the more money they will spend on it; and the higher the price which they will be willing to pay for it. The comparative strength of consumer demand for different products is reflected in the relative prices of, and expenditures on, these products. Thus the price system, reflecting consumer preferences, tells firms which goods and services are the most important (i.e., the most profitable) to produce.

The process by which consumers determine what will be produced is a form of voting in which dollars rather than people count. Thus it is a "one dollar, one vote" scheme rather than a "one man, one vote" procedure. No matter how much some consumers may wish to have particular products, unless they have the money to back up their desires they will not be effective in determining what is produced. No matter how badly a poor family may want to have champagne, caviar, and Cadillacs, its desires are effective in the market place only when, and to the extent that, they are backed up by the economic means to pay for these products. The price mechanism is impersonal. It produces what people who have money are willing to pay for, not necessarily what is most desirable from a social viewpoint. The price system may bring about the production of yachts and mansions for millionaires while poor children do not have enough food to maintain an adequate level of health. Market prices reflect how much people are willing and able to pay for goods and services, not how much consumers really "need" them.

D. DETERMINING HOW IT WILL BE PRODUCED

In our hypothetical perfectly competitive economy, the goods which are produced will be made at the lowest possible total cost. This results from the desire of businessmen to maximize their profits. Since profit is the difference between total revenue and total cost, firms will try both to increase their revenue and decrease their costs wherever possible. Assuming that a certain final output is going to be produced and sold in the market place, a firm will then try to minimize its total costs in order to maximize profits. This determines the factors of production, i.e., the productive resources, that each firm will use in producing its output.

The firm will use a productive resource up to the point where the value of the contribution of the last unit of the resource equals its hiring price. The equilibrium prices for productive resources will be the same for all users. No firm will have to pay more for resources than other firms pay, because under perfect competition any firm can buy all the resources that it wants at the going market prices. No firm can get a factor for less than the market price, because under perfect competition, the owners of the factors could sell all that they wish at the prevailing market prices.

In our model all productive resources will be used in those industries where they contribute most in fulfilling consumer demands. This property is easily established. If any productive factor were employed where its contribution to fulfilling consumer demand was not as great as possible, some other firm in seeking to increase its own profits would bid this resource away to an industry where it would contribute more to satisfying consumer demands. Its productivity in the latter industry would be greater than the price paid for the factor in the original industry. It follows then that all owners of productive resources will be earning the maximum return consistent with consumer demands for final products and consistent with the resource owners' preferences.

In seeking to increase their own profits, entrepreneurs may move into industries where consumer demand bids up prices or where costs may be reduced because of changes in technology or the entrepreneurs' special skills. Insofar as they are motivated by pay, workers and the owners of other productive resources will move their resources away from lower-paying opportunities into industries which offer higher pay. To the extent that motivations other than pay are important, the economic system adjusts to the preferences of resource owners for working in lower-paying but otherwise more attractive industries. The over-all interactions of consumer demand, workers' job preferences, and businessmen's desire for profits get those goods and services that consumers want most produced at the lowest possible cost. In this process business firms undertake the vital social function of organizing productive activity in the lowest-cost (i.e., the most efficient) possible manner and of channeling productive resources toward those industries where consumer demand runs strongest. The entrepreneurs do this primarily because they are seeking profits, rather than trying to perform a vital social function; however, they also accomplish the latter at the same time, although perhaps involuntarily.

E. Determining Who Gets What Is Produced

To see how our hypothetical perfectly competitive economy determines who gets the goods and services that are produced, it is necessary briefly to review some of the mechanisms we have already examined. Business firms, in seeking to maximize profits, try to produce at the lowest possible cost the commodities and services that they think will sell best on the market. Consumers express their preferences for what should be produced by their purchasing behavior. The interaction of supply and demand determines the market prices of each commodity and service. The resource owners decide in what industries they will utilize the resources at their disposal. Each resource owner, faced with many different employment possibilities, balances each alternative's relative attractiveness at the margin in terms of income return and other considerations, such as the value he places on leisure when allocating his labor. Thus the income of each household is determined. Most consumers earn their incomes primarily by selling productive services to businessmen. Competition tends to force the businessmen to pay each resource owner about what he contributes to the revenue of the firm. The incomes received in this way by consumers largely determine what they can afford to buy.

The demand of each household for any commodity depends upon the prices of all commodities, the household's income, and the household's tastes or preferences. In these decisions households are constrained by their budgets. Each household's budget constraint states that the total amount of money it can spend on buying goods and services (or saving for future purchases of goods and services) cannot exceed its already accumulated wealth plus its income from selling its productive services. In effect, each household allocates its spendable income over the various commodities available (including saving) so as to maximize the total satisfaction it receives. An equilibrium point is reached when the household cannot increase its satisfaction by reallocating a dollar from any one commodity or service to any other.

The demand for, and purchase of, each good and service is determined in the foregoing framework. Those households with the largest money incomes have the greatest potential to purchase commodities. Each household gets a share of what is produced, although not necessarily a share of each product produced. There are some commodities, such as steaks, which almost all people will buy, although poor people buy many fewer steaks than rich households. Some other commodities, such as mink coats, yachts, and mansions, will be purchased only by wealthy households. And some commodities, such as inexpensive clothing, may be bought only by poor families.

When an equilibrium set of market prices has been reached, the total quantities of all goods and services which are distributed to households for consumption and to firms for purposes of production will equal the total amount of goods and services produced. This is true individually in each market, as well as for all commodities and services collectively.

F. Deciding between the Present and the Future

Through the functioning of a price system, the perfectly competitive economy determines how much of its resources should be used for present consumption and how much for future growth. Each household, in deciding what products it will buy in order to maximize its satisfactions, simultaneously decides how much of its income it wants to save for its future consumption. Each business firm makes the same type of decision. A business man will decide to accumulate capital in the form of a larger plant or new equipment if he feels that he can earn greater profits in the long run by doing so. For example, if a firm foresees an increase in consumer demand for its product, it will probably wish to invest in enlarged facilities to expand its productive capacity. The more that households and firms decide to save of their current income, the easier it is for entrepreneurs to obtain funds for new investment expenditures.

One particular price, the interest rate for borrowing or lending money, is an important factor in determining how much both households and firms will consume today rather than save for future use. The interest rate, because of its relation to the cost of capital, is also a key element in business firms' perceptions of the profitability of new investment. Thus, the interest rate functions as an equilibrating price which helps balance the amount of income consumers wish to save and the amount of investment funds that firms wish to provide for future facilities. In our hypothetical free-enterprise economy, the balance between current consumption and future capital accumulation depends on the many individual decisions of consumers and business firms.

G. Interdependencies

The four fundamental types of resource allocation questions—what is produced; how it is produced; who gets what is produced; and what resources are devoted to future consumption—are answered interdependently rather than separately in our hypothetical free-market economy. Such an economic system consists of an interconnected set of markets, each with its own set of buyers and sellers. Many individuals, however, function as buyers in some markets and sellers in others. Consumers, for example, are buyers in the final products markets and sellers in the labor services markets. Business firms are buyers in the resources markets and sellers in the finished goods and services markets. Since most buyers operate in many different markets, their purchases of one commodity affect what they are able to buy of others. Similarly most sellers must compete with many other sellers in buying and hiring productive resources, such as labor, raw materials, and capital. While the production process is making goods and services to meet consumer demands, it is generating incomes for workers to enable them to implement their demands as consumers. Each household is always faced with the choice between buying something or saving money for future needs.

The hypothetical free-market economy answers all four of its major resource allocation questions simultaneously. Each of these answers arises from millions of individual decisions being made at the same time by consumers, businessmen, bankers, workers, and other participants in the economic process. The manner in which all these complex decisions are simultaneously and continuously made and the way they interact to determine whether the resulting resource allocation pattern is desirable is one of the key features of economic life on which this book focuses.

In reviewing this brief summary of a hypothetical perfectly competitive economy, we can see that consumer sovereignty and economic freedom are two of its key attributes. Consumer sovereignty essentially means that the goods and services that people most want and can afford to buy are the ones that will be produced. Economic freedom means that individuals will be able to trade in whatever markets they please, to buy whatever they wish and can afford, and to sell their services wherever they can; the only restrictions on this freedom are financial limitations. Business firms, in pursuit of private profits, play a vital catalytic role in the economic process.

III. The American Economy

Our discussion of the ways in which a hypothetical free-market economy solves the four fundamental problems of resource allocation is useful in providing insight into the working of the American economy. In many respects the present-day American economy closely resembles the hypothetical economy we have just examined. There are, however, some major departures from perfect competition in the American economy. One significant difference is that in the United States, some individual business firms are large enough in their industries so that they can exert a significant influence on market prices. A second major difference is that the role of the government in the United States is not completely neutral, as was implicitly assumed in our discussion of a perfectly competitive economy.

Whenever market prices are influenced by individual firms, these prices become ineffective in directing the flow of resources in accordance with the dollar votes of consumers. The power to influence market prices is the power to affect in some significant sense the resource allocation pattern which results. As we shall see in later chapters of this book, firms which can control market prices, and thereby gain larger profits for themselves, distort the resource allocation patterns.

Our survey (Section II) of the way a perfectly competitive economy would allocate resources did not mention any role for the government. This was intentional, because in the type of economy we assumed there is little need for government to interfere with the resource-allocation mechanisms. In the American economy, this is not the case. Governments at all levels—Federal, state, and local—obtain command over economic resources by their abilities to impose taxes and borrow money. When they do this, governments remove economic resources which consumers might otherwise control. In deciding how they will spend their revenues, governmental units increase the demand for particular types of goods and services. Since this is effective demand which is backed up by funds, governments exert a definite influence on what will be produced in the economy. Since many goods and services are themselves produced by governmental enterprises, part of the answer to the question of how things will be produced also is provided by government. In levying taxes governmental units may not be neutral, since they sometimes redistribute purchasing power. Thus the government also influences who gets the goods and services that are produced. Finally, because of its power to affect interest rates (i.e., the prices that determine the amount of our economic resources that will be consumed today rather than set aside to meet future needs), government plays a vital role in this area of resource allocation.

Despite these two types of departures from the perfectly competitive economy, the behavior of individual economic units (consumers and business firms) plays a significant role in the resource-allocation process in the American economy. Although prices may unduly reflect the influence of large firms and be distorted by governmental actions, nevertheless the price system plays an important and fundamental role in the resource-allocation process in the United States. Most of this book focuses on how price systems function in our economy and on the influence of individual economic units in the resource allocation process.

There have been periods in history when the American economy has not relied primarily on actions of individual business firms and consumers, working through a price system, to allocate its resources. For example, in recent major wars (such as the two World Wars) governmental decrees and regulations, rather than individual economic actions, were most important in determining how resources would be allocated. During World War II the Federal government established direct controls over the prices at which almost all commodities could be traded. Since prices were then no longer able to equilibrate supply and demand, the government also had to establish a system of rationing—to determine which consumers would obtain scarce consumer goods and services—and a priority system for allocating raw materials and labor to producers—to determine which firms would be able to produce final products. In wartime the mobility of labor was also curtailed. Workers were not entirely free to move from job to job in response to the lure of higher wages, since if they left jobs that were essential to the war effort, they lost their draft-deferment status. The construction of some types of new plants was largely financed by the government, in order to assure a supply of essential war materials and munitions. Some of these wartime commodities were even directly produced by governmental enterprises.

Clearly the measures which the American economy has accepted during times of all-out war are much more severe than we are generally willing to adopt. Even in peacetime, however, many aspects of the resource allocation process are directly controlled by the actions of Federal, state, and local governments. Military, police, and fire protection are almost exclusively provided by governmental units in this country, not by private enterprises. Roads and highways, airports, schools, and dams are generally constructed, operated, and maintained by various governmental units, rather than by private business firms. Expenditures for space research and travel, for foreign economic aid, and for foreign military aid fall under the province of our Federal government, rather than the private sector.

There are, to be sure, exceptions to the roles that governments in the United States play in these areas. For example, some police protection is provided by private detectives; some schools may be privately financed and operated; some power dams may be built by private firms, etc. By and large, however, the decisions as to what and how much to spend for these and other areas are generally made by governmental units. These decisions may indirectly reflect the wishes of consumers, but if so this comes about by a political, rather than a market, process. In the political arena, the "one man, one vote" maxim rules, rather than the "one dollar, one vote" procedure that generally governs the resource allocation pattern in a free-enterprise economy. In the political arena the poor man has relatively more power compared to the rich man than he does in the economic market place—although even in politics rich people, through their ability to contribute to party campaign funds, etc., may command more power than do poor people.

Governments in the United States exert some peacetime control over the resource allocation process in other ways which are questionable reflections of consumer desires. For example, the way in which the Federal government controls the resource-allocation pattern in agriculture is the result of a fairly complex political process which could not reasonably be said to be in accordance with the wishes of most American citizens who are consumers of farm products. As consumers we certainly would like to have more farm goods available at lower prices. The effects of the Federal government's farm program is to make farm goods available to us only at prices higher than would otherwise be necessary. Resale price maintenance legislation is another area where the effects of governmental actions of the resource allocation process can hardly be said to be in accordance with our desires as consumers. Such laws attempt to prevent store operators from lowering their prices on some items in an attempt to gain more patronage. It is hard to see that consumers in general would knowingly favor economic measures which result in their paying higher prices for the goods and services which they buy.

Many other approaches to answering the four fundamental questions of resource allocation have been attempted in other countries during various periods. Central planning is one approach which is the polar extreme of our hypothetical free-market economy. Such communist countries as the U.S.S.R. and China are striking examples of centrally planned economies. Between the two extremes of free-market economies and centrally planned economies are the so-called mixed economies, represented by India, Israel, and Sweden. In these latter countries resources are allocated by a combination of some free-market mechanisms and some of the procedures used in planned economies.

IV. Aims of This Book

In the rest of this book we shall examine in considerably greater detail the manner in which economic resources are allocated in a free-market economy. The individual actions of many millions of economic units—consumers and business firms—play a crucial role in this process. We shall consider this role in some detail, seeing how economic incentives may provide some of the motivations for this behavior. Households will be viewed as trying to earn and spend their incomes in those ways that make their satisfactions as large as possible. Business firms will be viewed as trying to produce and sell goods in those ways that earn the largest possible profits. In an economy of the market type, a price system functions to influence the actions of individual consumers and firms. An elaborate system of markets has developed in order to facilitate transactions between economic units. When one firm offers products for sale, this is done in some type of market where goods of a similar nature produced by other firms may also be offered for sale. Many different consumers come to these markets in order to buy commodities. Without market institutions, economic transactions between various consumers and business firms would be difficult.

Although most individual consumers and business firms accept market prices as being beyond their control, in the aggregate the results of their individual actions actually determine the market prices which will prevail. The set of market prices which results, and consequently the final pattern of resource allocation in an economy, are influenced by the type of market structure present in that society. When we use the term *market structure,* we refer to such considerations as the number and size of buyers and sellers in the market, the restrictions that may prevent firms and households from entering or leaving particular markets, and the availability of information about potential buyers and sellers. One of the key topics that we consider in this book is the way in which market structures influence the resulting market prices and patterns of resource allocation. In particular, we shall try to determine which types of market organization may be desirable from the standpoint of society as a whole.

Government regulations, which in the modern world commonly interact with the economic system, will also partially determine the set of market prices and the pattern of resource allocation which exists in a society. Some types of governmental intervention in the economy may be justified to redress what would otherwise be malfunctions resulting from structural defects in the system. Other types of governmental regulations may be designated to counter socially undesirable activities of individual firms or households. Still other kinds of governmental interferences in the market place may be entirely unjustifiable on either economic or social grounds. In this book we hope to develop some criteria which may be used to determine when government interactions with the economy result in better or worse over-all patterns of resource allocation.

Our greatest emphasis in this book, however, will be on the behavior of business firms. We feel that in the American economy the extent to which the resulting resource allocation pattern is desirable or not depends much more on the ways in which business firms organize and interact than on consumer behavior. Governmental units may also be important, but in order to understand their effects it is first necessary to develop a good understanding of business behavior. Because of the great variety of business behavior which is present in the American economy, it is important to know whether some patterns of business behavior are socially more desirable than others. Business firms also are much larger than households, so that any individual business firm necessarily plays a larger role in the resource allocation process than does any single household. Finally, business firms are important in any economy of the market type because of their critical role as agents in the production and distribution process.

Our hope is that the reader who perseveres will attain a technical understanding of a significant aspect of our society—resource allocation. At the same time he should achieve an understanding of the way in which the modern economist studies the firm and also some feeling for the empirical side of economics. We hope also that the reader will gain insight into new problems for research and will be stimulated to do further work on the business firm.

SUGGESTED READINGS

ALCHIAN, A. A., AND H. DEMSETZ, "Production, Information Costs, and Economic Organization," *American Economic Review*, LXII, No. 5 (December, 1972), 777–95.

MARSHALL, ALFRED, *Principles of Economics*, 8th ed., chaps. 1–2. London: Macmillan & Co., Ltd., 1920.

PHELPS BROWN, E. H., "The Underdevelopment of Economics," *Economic Journal*, LXXXII (March, 1972), 1–10.

RADFORD, R. A., "The Economic Organization of a P.O.W. Camp," *Economica*, IXX (November, 1945), 189–201.

SCHUMPETER, JOSEPH, "The Nature and Necessity of a Price System," *Readings in Economic Analysis*, R. V. Clemence, ed., Vol. II. Cambridge: Addison-Wesley Press, 1950.

SCHWARTZ, HARRY, *Russia's Soviet Economy*, 2nd ed., chap. 5. Englewood Cliffs, N.J.: Prentice-Hall, Inc., 1961.

STIGLER, GEORGE J., AND PAUL A. SAMUELSON, "A Dialogue on the Proper Economic Role of the State," *Selected Papers No. 7*. Chicago: University of Chicago Graduate School of Business, 1963.

Chapter Two

The Methodology of
Model Building

In beginning our study of the theory of the firm and the process of resource allocation in a market economy, it is important to examine the basic methodology used by professional economists. This methodology is the one which is used in all scientific analyses. Certain difficulties arise in the conduct of any science, be it natural or social, when laboratory experimentation is not possible. Contrary to some opinions, however, the possibility of using the laboratory is not a valid basis for distinguishing between natural and social sciences.[1] The distinctive feature of any science lies in the subject matter with which it deals, not in its methods for studying this material.

---

[1] For example, laboratory experimentation is commonplace in chemistry but virtually absent in meteorology, yet both are natural sciences. Furthermore, although psychology and cultural anthropology are both social sciences, laboratory experiments are frequently conducted by psychologists but almost never by cultural anthropologists.

I. Nature of Models

A. Fundamental Concepts

The basic procedure which is used by scientists in their efforts to increase our understanding of the world is the formulation of models. A *model* is a set of assumptions from which a conclusion or a set of conclusions is logically deduced. In deriving the conclusions from the assumptions, a set of subject-matter definitions may also be used.

Consider the following simple example of a model widely used in economic theory:[2]

Assumptions
1. All firms attempt to maximize profits.
2. The marginal revenue curve of any firm intersects its marginal cost curve from above.
3. The marginal revenue and marginal cost curves of any firm are continuous.

Conclusion

Each firm will produce that output corresponding to the point of intersection of its marginal revenue and marginal cost curves.

Implicit in this model are the definitions of such subject-matter terms as *profits, marginal cost,* and *marginal revenue.*[3]

Using this model as an example, the first point we discuss is the relation of a model to the real world. One obvious connection of a model with reality is, of course, through its assumptions. These assumptions characterize the type of world to which the model is intended to apply. It is important to realize that the assumptions need not be *exact representations* of

----

[2] George J. Stigler, *The Theory of Price* (New York: The Macmillan Company, 1946), p. 4.

[3] In this book we shall use the terms *model* and *theory* as synonyms. In technical discussions of scientific methodology, a distinction is sometimes made between these terms. As Geoffrey P. H. Clarkson has pointed out to us, a *theory* is the general statement which contains the hypotheses, postulates, assumptions, etc.; a specific instance of that theory is a *model* of the theory. Models, according to this definition, must have a one-to-one structural correspondence with the theory. Most, if not all, theories contain certain general hypotheses. Since a general hypothesis cannot be tested against general data, to test a theory, one tests a specific instance of it against a specific set of data. To perform this operation one may have to add a number of special constraints and this is where we introduce the model. A theory is tested by constructing a specific model which is then used as the vehicle against which the test data are compared.

An excellent description of this process is given in May Brodbeck, "Models, Meaning, and Theories," chap. 12 in *Symposium on Sociological Theory,* ed. Llewellyn Gross (Evanston, Ill.: Row, Peterson and Company, 1959). In this article, Brodbeck is critical of the use of the terms *model* and *theory* as synonyms, although she points out that this usage is prevalent in the social sciences.

reality, but they may instead be *reasonable abstractions* of reality. By reasonable abstractions we mean that only certain aspects of reality are contained in the assumptions, namely, those aspects considered to be relevant. Thus in the example, the first assumption is that all firms attempt to maximize profits. In reality this assumption may not be literally true, at least not for all types of firms in every conceivable situation. Nevertheless if over a reasonably interesting range of circumstances most firms generally do attempt to maximize profits, then the assumption that "all firms attempt to maximize profits" may be a reasonable abstraction for certain purposes.

To restate this point in more general terms, even though the assumptions of a model may not be literally exact and complete representations of reality, if they are realistic enough for the purposes of the analysis we may be able to draw conclusions which can be shown to apply to the world. A good example is provided by plane geometry. Certain geometrical objects are assumed which in a strict sense do not exist in the world; for example, there are no physical embodiments of angles exactly 90 degrees and lines possessing zero width. Nevertheless, these postulated geometrical objects correspond sufficiently closely to existing physical objects so that for certain purposes, e.g., surveying, the conclusions obtained about the properties of these abstract geometrical objects are valid for the corresponding real world objects.

Some scientific models with intentionally unrealistic assumptions are developed for special types of analysis, as, for example, the model of a frictionless world in physics. The situations characterized by these models are admittedly hypothetical. Nonetheless, such hypothetical models are important in any science. These models are intended to be intellectual experiments. They are created for the purpose of isolating and determining the nature of certain crucial variables. Sometimes they may also be used as criteria against which the current state of the real world is evaluated. Thus the economist's perfectly competitive model may be used as a standard for judging the performance of real agricultural markets. The one warning that must always be kept in mind, however, is that conclusions which are logically deduced from a set of assumptions which do not correspond to the real world do not necessarily apply to the real world. More will be said about this shortly.

Another point that should be recognized about assumptions is that they often contain so-called hypothetical constructs. Some assumptions may refer to elements that are not directly observable, as the concept of the field in electrical theory or the concept of a consumer utility function in economic theory. Even though they may be artificial, such constructs are extremely useful. The real test of such concepts is whether they lead to conclusions which help to further our scientific objectives of explanation, prediction, and control. The major point we are making is that all assumptions need not necessarily refer or correspond to observable elements.

A model may have a number of conclusions; it is not limited to one. The structure of the model includes the conclusions as well as the assumptions. In addition, models in economic theory usually implicitly assume an institutional framework. Thus the example of a model from the theory of the firm implicitly assumes a private-enterprise economy. Finally, we frequently may formulate a hierarchy of theories, so that an assumption in one theory may at the same time be a conclusion of a higher-level theory. This hierarchical structure of models is, in fact, the basis on which a discipline such as economics is systematically developed.

B. Relation Between Assumptions and Conclusions

The derivation of conclusions of a model from the assumptions is a deductive process in which questions of empirical truth or realism of either assumptions or conclusions are irrelevant. A first test of a model, therefore, is logical consistency. The test of logical consistency is distinct from the empirical truth of the conclusion. Deductive validity in no way guarantees empirical truth or even empirical significance.

In the deductive process, a number of different languages can be used to derive conclusions from assumptions. The same variety of languages can be used to state the assumptions. In the past economists have commonly used three types of languages: ordinary prose, pictorial geometry, and mathematics. There is now a fourth type of language which is being increasingly used by economists: computer programming languages.[4]

There is no particular honorific ranking of theories on the basis of the language used. The scientist chooses his language primarily as a matter of convenience both in terms of the requirements of the problem and of his facility in handling the language. Some languages are not suitable for analyzing the simultaneous interactions of a large number of variables, but a model involving a large number of variables is not necessarily more valuable than a model involving only a few variables. The value of a model is directly related to the significance of the questions it is intended to answer and the quality of the answers it gives.

To clarify the way in which the value of a model depends upon the questions it is intended to answer (i.e., to the intended purposes of the model), let us draw an analogy between models and maps. Actually this is more than an analogy, since maps are one particular type of model, expressed in a pictorial or diagramatic language. There are various maps, each of which in a sense depicts New York City, that a person might want

---

[4] For a discussion of the emerging importance of computer programming languages for deriving the conclusions of economic models, see Kalman J. Cohen and Richard M. Cyert, "Computer Models in Dynamic Economics," *Quarterly Journal of Economics*, 75, No. 1 (February, 1961), 112–27.

Chapters 17 and 18 of this book contain examples of two economic models which have been analyzed in a computer programming language.

for different purposes. To plan an automobile trip from San Francisco to New York, a highway map of the United States would be appropriate, and on this map New York City would be represented in a high degree of abstraction. As the person approaches New York, he would find it appropriate to use a detailed street map of New York City to enable him to drive to the hotel where he plans to stay. When he is ready to go from his hotel to the New York World's Fair by subway, the person would find that still another map, showing the details of the subway system, would be appropriate. Finally, when he arrives at the entrance to the World's Fair, the person would find it appropriate to use a map showing the details of the fair grounds in order to find his way among the exhibits he plans to visit.

Thus we see that four different maps, all of which in some sense represent New York City, are appropriate for different purposes. Each of these maps is designed to answer particular types of questions. The map of the World's Fair would be useless for determining how to drive from San Francisco to New York. Similarly, the highway map of the United States would be useless for determining how to walk from the United States Pavilion to the IBM Pavilion at the World's Fair. It is not appropriate to say that any one of these maps is more realistic than any other. Each map is a reasonable abstraction of reality, but since each is intended for a different purpose, it abstracts from the world in a different way.

It is the same with models as it is with maps. It may be appropriate to have various models of the same general part of the world because each model is intended to answer different questions about the world. We cannot say that one model is more realistic or more appropriate than another model unless we specify the questions we wish to use the model to answer.

To talk about a model answering a question, however, involves a number of considerations relating to the meaning of scientific *explanation, prediction,* and *control.* What does it mean, for example, to say that a particular phenomenon is explained by a particular model? What is the relationship between explanation and prediction? If a model predicts, does it also explain? And if a model predicts, can it also be used for control?

Attention has been called to the importance of these questions by Friedman's essay on the methodology of economics.[5] He has made a strong argument against the notion of testing a theory on the basis of the realism of its assumptions. Friedman maintains that the empirical validity of the

---

[5] Milton Friedman, "The Methodology of Positive Economics," *Essays in Positive Economics* (Chicago: The University of Chicago Press, 1953), pp. 3–43. Friedman's essay has stimulated a number of articles. See, for example, R. M. Cyert and E. Grunberg, "Assumption, Prediction, and Explanation in Economics," appendix A in Richard M. Cyert and James G. March, *A Behavioral Theory of the Firm* (Englewood Cliffs, N.J.: Prentice-Hall, Inc., 1963); and the session on Problems in Methodology, held at the December, 1962, meetings of the American Economic Association in Pittsburgh, published in the *American Economic Review, Papers and Proceedings,* 53, No. 2 (May, 1963), 204–36. See also the references cited in the preceding publications.

assumptions themselves is irrelevant, since if the conclusion is verified by accurate predictions, then the theory as a whole is valid. The essence of his argument is summed up in the following example:

> Consider the problem of predicting the shots made by an expert billiard player. It seems not at all unreasonable that excellent predictions would be yielded by the hypothesis that the billiard player made his shots *as if* he knew the complicated mathematical formulas that would give the optimum directions of travel, could estimate accurately by eye the angles, etc., describing the location of balls, could make lightning calculations from the formulas, and could then make the balls travel in the direction indicated by the formulas. Our confidence in this hypothesis is not based on the belief that billiard players, even expert ones, can or do go through the process described; it derives rather from the belief that, unless in some way or other they were capable of reaching essentially the same result, they would not in fact be *expert* billiard players.[6]

It is possible to argue that you could not get good predictions from such a theory. Let us, however, assume that you could. Even then would such a theory be satisfactory? It predicts, but does it explain? To answer this question, we need to look more closely at the meaning of explanation and prediction in science.

II. The Role of Models in Scientific Explanation, Prediction, and Control

To speak about explanation and prediction it is necessary to introduce some additional terminology.[7] The *explanandum* is the phenomenon or the observation which is to be explained; the *explanans* is the set of assumptions intended to explain this phenomenon. Since a model of some kind is used for explanation, it is necessary to determine when a model constitutes an adequate explanation.

The following *logical conditions of adequacy* have been proposed by Hempel and Oppenheim:

1. The explanandum must be logically deducible from the explanans. Clearly if the explanandum does not logically follow from the explanans, there can be no explanation.

2. The explanans, i.e., the assumptions of the model, must contain general laws which are required for the logical derivation of the explanandum. When we refer to a law we mean a relationship that has been sub-

---

[6] Friedman, *op. cit.*, p. 21. Note that Friedman uses the term *hypothesis* as a synonym for what we have called *assumption*.

[7] This terminology and the resulting discussion on the adequacy conditions for explanation is based on Carl G. Hempel and Paul Oppenheim, "Studies in the Logic of Explanation," *Philosophy of Science*, 15 (1948), 135–75.

jected to empirical testing, has not been rejected, and is generally agreed upon in the literature as having empirical validity. Notice that in order for a model to be accepted for explanatory purposes, it is necessary that some of its assumptions have been tested and converted into laws. Thus without laws one has at best only proposed explanations, not actual explanations.

3. The explanans must have empirical content; i.e., there must be at least one proposition deducible from the explanans which is at least in principle testable by experimentation or observation. Note that this condition is implicit in (1), since the explanandum must describe an empirical phenomenon.

4. The empirical propositions in the explanans must be highly confirmed by all available relevant evidence. Loosely speaking, this means that the empirical propositions in the explanans must be "true."

Hempel and Oppenheim characterize the notion of explanation in the manner shown in Figure 2–1. To clarify the meaning of this diagram, let us consider a simple example. In the immediate period following World War II after automobile production resumed in the United States, recently manufactured automobiles which were sold as "used" cars had higher prices than similar automobiles which were sold as "new" cars; i.e., the price of a 1946 automobile in a used car lot was higher than the price of a similar 1946 automobile in a new car dealer showroom. We are interested in explaining this phenomenon because it is contrary to normal price patterns.

The explanandum, therefore, is a used 1946 car selling for a higher price than a new 1946 car of similar make and model. The explanans consists of the following:

C_1. Manufacturers set prices on new automobiles but not on used automobiles.

C_2. Evidence indicated that at the prices set on new automobiles, the quantity demanded was greater than the quantity supplied.[8]

C_3. Dealers were able to transform new cars into used cars by having them driven a short distance.

C_4. New car dealers also have used car lots.

L_1. Firms (dealers) exploit known opportunities for increasing their profits.

L_2. The Law of Demand indicates that at any particular price there are some consumers willing to pay a higher price if necessary to obtain the product.

} Explanans

---

[8] This evidence was independent of the explanandum. It consisted, in part, of data on back orders and reports of dealers receiving side-payments for selling new cars to some people "out-of-turn."

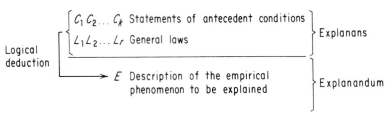

FIGURE 2-1. Diagram of scientific explanation.

C_1, C_2, C_3, and C_4 are statements of antecedent conditions, since they describe facts about the world which are relevant in explaining the observed phenomenon. L_1 and L_2 are general laws of economics which form the core of the model used to explain the observed phenomenon. The explanandum can be logically derived from the propositions in the explanans.

It is easy to distinguish between explanation and prediction. In Figure 2-1, if E has been observed and if the C's and L's are provided afterwards, then we have explanation. If E is deduced from the C's and L's before E is observed, then we have prediction. Thus the requirements for explanation are also appropriate for prediction. We do not mean to imply by this statement that it is impossible to make correct predictions unless the four logical conditions for adequacy are fulfilled. If correct predictions can be made when these conditions are not fulfilled, however, then this is prediction without explanation.

Friedman's position may lead to prediction without explanation. Referring again to the billiard player example, it is clear that requirement (4) is violated since the explanans is not true, as Friedman himself indicates. Therefore the model has no explanatory power. Any predictive power that the model may have would arise from some unknown relationship between variables in the model and some unknown variables not included in the model. If our scientific standards require a model which can provide explanation as well as prediction, then the billiard player model is unsatisfactory.

To use a model for purposes of control, it is necessary to determine how the values of one or more variables must be altered to bring about some desired change in the world. It is clear that this use of a model involves the process of prediction, for we must predict that *if* we change particular control variables, *then* some other changes will occur. It is generally preferable for purposes of control to use a model which provides valid explanations as well as accurate predictions. If we were to use a model which provides accurate predictions without explanations, the changes to be introduced in the control variables may alter some of the unknown underlying relationships that had previously led to the accurate predictions, thus causing future predictions to be less accurate.

To understand the role of models in scientific explanation, prediction, and control, it is necessary to understand some of the limits of their applicability. There is always in any science a great desire to formulate models that are general. The economist, for instance, is much more interested in a model that he thinks has relevance for all the firms in the economy than he is in a model that pertains only to a particular firm. At the same time, it must be realized that the more general a model is, the less detailed are its implications about anything in particular. In other words, a general model must abstract from a great many variables which account for differentiation among units in order to arrive at conclusions which apply to all the relevant units. Thus in order to answer the many questions that are asked in any science, it is usually necessary to develop a number of models of varying generality, as our previous discussion of the map analogy indicated.

The test as to how general a model must be can be answered only by referring to the generality of the questions asked of the particular model. The drive for generality comes from two sources—science and aesthetics. From the scientific view, we are interested in generality because we want to know all the characteristics that the units under study have in common. Thus we would like a theory of the firm which answers questions about all firms regardless of size or market structure. From the aesthetic point of view, there is a drive toward generality just because it is intellectually satisfying to be able to say a great deal about the world with an economy of effort. In this respect, social scientists have probably been influenced by mathematicians who seem always to be aiming a a single equation which summarizes all that is worth knowing about the world.

III. The Construction and Testing of Models

Up to this point we have talked in general terms about the nature of theory, but we have said little about the way that scientists develop models. In many respects it is difficult to be definitive about such a subject because each man may operate differently. The choice of problems and the specific ways each man approaches his problem are, in a sense, the part of science that is "art." However, some things of general relevance can be said. We shall try to describe the major steps involved in model building.

1. DEFINE THE PROBLEM. Defining the problem covers three phases. The first relates to isolating the observable phenomena of interest in the world. There are some regularities of behavior which are observed and which the scientist is interested in understanding. The observations may be made

as a result of the interest in a particular unit or, as frequently happens, the phenomena may actually have been observed by someone else and been recorded in the literature. Frequently interest is stimulated by the need to control some phenomena in the interest of society. The second stage is concerned with formulating questions which one wants his model to answer. The most obvious and usual questions relate to the causes of the phenomena and the manner in which they occur. There are generally many more questions, such as the relations of the proposed model to other models of the discipline. In the third phase, the scientist, after establishing some framework for beginning his research, attempts to identify the major variables of interest.

2. FORMULATE PRELIMINARY MODEL. Having some idea of the major variables involved, the scientist then attempts to develop a model. He constructs the set of assumptions that seem to be necessary to explain the observed phenomena. The preliminary conclusions that are derived generally concern the nature of the relationships among the variables.

3. COLLECT EMPIRICAL DATA. Once tentative relations are established among the variables, the problem is to collect the relevant data for estimating the constants and parameters in the functional forms derived. Data collection cannot be performed before the establishment of a model, since some theoretical framework is required in order to determine the data that need to be obtained.

4. ESTIMATE THE PARAMETERS. After the data have been collected, the parameters of the model are estimated. A variety of quantitative techniques are available for making such estimates, but nonquantitative estimates may also be used. In many of the computer models, for instance, estimation may be made by interviews and direct observations.

5. PRELIMINARY TESTS OF THE MODEL. The same data that have been used for the estimation of the functional forms are generally used to make a rough test of the model. Obviously, the chances of invalidating the model's implications are somewhat reduced by this procedure; hence such a procedure must not be viewed as a final test. On the other hand, if the model is not confirmed under these relatively favorable circumstances, time can be saved by making revisions in the model immediately.

6. FURTHER TESTS OF THE MODEL. On the basis of the model, predictions are then made about the phenomena under study. New data must be collected to test these predictions. The data should not include any of the observations utilized in making the original estimates or first revisions of the model. Frequently the data gathering takes place all at once, but the scientist utilizes only part of the data in making his parameter estimates. The remaining portion is then used to test the model's predictions. This procedure is generally followed when the data collection is time-consuming and there are definite costs of beginning and stopping. The actual test

procedure, which is both interesting and involved, will not be discussed here.[9]

7. ACCEPT OR REVISE THE MODEL. If the predictions of the model are consistent with the available empirical evidence, the model cannot be rejected. This means that the model becomes part of the knowledge of the discipline until further evidence becomes available which shows that the model is inadequate. If the model is rejected on the basis of the test in step 6 or at some later point, then the cycle begins again with step 2.

These seven steps summarize the procedures which a scientist follows in the development of a model.

IV. Summary

Our objective in this chapter has been to understand the methodology used by economists in studying business firms. We first discussed the nature of models. We defined a *model* as a set of assumptions and conclusions which are logically derived from these assumptions. We showed that even though the assumptions of a model are abstractions of reality, it is possible to derive conclusions from them which have relevance to the real world.

Economists use four types of languages for obtaining the conclusions of a model from its assumptions: ordinary prose, pictorial geometry, mathematics, and computer programs. The choice of language to be used depends upon the complexity of the model and the tastes of the scientist. The generality of a model depends upon the types of questions which the model is intended to answer. This point was illustrated by analogy to a set of maps of differing degrees of detail. Each map is appropriate for a different purpose.

Models may be used in economics for explanation, prediction, or control. The concept of explanation was discussed in terms of Hempel and Oppenheim's four logical conditions of adequacy. This discussion was related to Friedman's billiard player model, and it was shown that it is conceptually possible to have a model which predicts without providing an adequate explanation of the phenomena.

We concluded this chapter by describing the seven steps involved in developing a model: (1) define the problem; (2) formulate preliminary

[9] Econometric techniques are frequently used in estimating the parameters of a model and in testing the accuracy of the model's predictions. For a nontechnical survey of the field, see Lawrence R. Klein, *An Introduction to Econometrics* (Englewood Cliffs, N.J.: Prentice-Hall, Inc., 1962). More advanced discussions of parameter estimation and model testing are contained in J. Johnston, *Econometric Methods* (New York: McGraw-Hill Book Company, Inc., 1963); and Alexander M. Mood and Franklin A. Graybill, *Introduction to the Theory of Statistics*, 2nd ed. (New York: McGraw-Hill Book Company, Inc., 1963).

model; (3) collect empirical data; (4) estimate the parameters; (5) subject the model to preliminary tests; (6) test the model further; (7) accept or revise the model.

SUGGESTED READINGS

These recommendations are in addition to the footnote references cited in this chapter.

DIESING, PAUL, *Patterns of Discovery in the Social Sciences.* Chicago, Ill.: Aldine-Atherton, Inc., 1971.

DRÈZE, J. H., "Econometrics and Decision Theory," *Econometrica*, XL (January, 1972), 1–17.

GONCE, R. A., "Frank H. Knight on Social Control and Scope and Method of Economics," *Southern Economic Journal*, XXXVIII, No. 4 (April, 1972), 547–58.

GRUNBERG, E., "Notes on the Verifiability of Economic Laws," *Philosophy of Science*, XXIV (1957), 337–48.

LESOURNE, JACQUES, *Economic Analysis and Industrial Management*, Scripta Technica, Inc., trans. chaps. 1–2. Englewood Cliffs, N.J.: Prentice-Hall, Inc., 1963.

MORGENSTERN, O., "Descriptive, Predictive and Normative Theory," *Kyklos*, XXV, No. 4 (1972), 669–714.

NAGEL, ERNEST, *The Structure of Science*, chaps. 2–3, 13–14. New York: Harcourt, Brace & World, Inc., 1961.

ROBBINS, LIONEL, *The Nature and Significance of Economic Science*, 2nd ed. New York: The Macmillan Company, 1935.

SAMUELSON, PAUL ANTHONY, *Foundations of Economic Analysis*, chaps. 1–2. Cambridge: Harvard University Press, 1955.

Chapter Three

Decision Making by
Marginal Analysis

The concept of marginalism forms the core of the traditional theory of the firm. As we shall presently see, this theory assumes that decision making within firms is carried out by means of marginal analysis. Whether the decision processes actually used in most business firms correspond to the canons of marginalism is a question to which we shall subsequently return (see Chapters 14–19). For analyzing market behavior, the purposes for which we shall use the theory of the firm, it is proper to assume that firms operate as though they used marginal analysis.

I. The Concept of Marginal Analysis

Before providing a precise definition of marginalism, we present an elementary example which illustrates this notion. Let us consider the decision-making problem faced by John Jones, in determining how many of his waking hours he should devote to working for a living, and how many he should devote to the pursuit of leisure. Let us suppose that John does not regard his work as an end in itself, but rather works so that he may earn enough money to engage in more desirable activities during his leisure time. The more John works, the more income he earns, and the more interesting pastimes he can provide to occupy his remaining leisure hours. The more John works, however, the fewer hours he will have free for pursuing these pleasurable activities. John must resolve this conflict in determining how many hours to work each week, and hence how many hours to spend in leisure.

A rational way for John Jones to approach this decision problem is to ask himself the following questions: If I work one additional hour per week, how much extra money will I earn? With this extra income, how will I spend my remaining hours of leisure? Would I rather have one additional hour of leisure filled with the types of activities which I can now afford, or would I rather have one less hour of leisure and have my remaining free hours filled with a more expensive level of activity? By repeatedly asking himself these questions, John can allocate his total waking hours between work and leisure until he has arrived at the most satisfactory balance for himself, given his earning potential and his tastes regarding leisure time activities.

This example illustrates two aspects of any decision problem. The example involves the choice of a combination of two alternatives: work or leisure. Without the existence of at least two or more alternative courses of action, there can be no decision problem, because there is no choice to be made. Second, a decision problem is conceptually solvable by considering the effect on the decision maker's total "satisfaction" of small changes in the pursuit of each alternative. An appropriate question to ask is: "Would slightly increasing my pursuit of one alternative contribute more to my over-all satisfaction than the corresponding loss in satisfaction resulting from the required decrease in my pursuit of the other alternative?"

With this discussion in mind, we can now define the concept of marginal analysis.

In the example, the increase in John Jones' satisfaction from working one additional hour is the increase in his satisfaction during his remaining hours of leisure made possible by the additional money earned during the extra hour of work. The decrease in John Jones' satisfaction from the extra hour of work is the amount of satisfaction at his old level of activities given up by having one less hour of leisure.

By the concept of *marginal analysis*, then, we mean the process of making a choice between alternatives by considering small changes in total satisfaction resulting from small changes in the combination of alternatives. Carried to its logical limit, marginal analysis deals with infinitesimal changes associated with a continuous function. If we consider any continuous total value function, then we can define the marginal value as the rate of change in the total value with respect to the change in the independent variable; i.e., the marginal value is equal to the derivative of the total value. When the total value is not a continuous function, but is defined only for a discrete set of values of the independent variable, then the incremental change in the total value corresponding to a unit change in the independent variable would be the discrete analog of the marginal value.

In the type of decision-making problem where the decision maker must allocate some scarce resource between two or more alternatives, it is rational to use a marginal approach to reach the optimal allocation. Pursuing one alternative means that the decision maker is thereby prevented from pursuing the other alternatives, at least to a matter of degree. We can, therefore, examine the marginal increase in satisfaction stemming from an increased pursuit of one alternative and compare this with the resulting marginal losses in satisfaction from the decreased pursuit of other alternatives. It is rational to expand the degree to which one alternative is pursued as long as the marginal gain in satisfaction from pursuing this alternative is greater than the marginal losses in satisfaction from not pursuing to the same extent as previously the other possible alternatives. One should continue allocating effort to the pursuit of any one alternative up to the point where the marginal increase in satisfaction from this alternative just equals the marginal loss in satisfaction by giving up the pursuit of some of the other alternatives. At this point, no reallocation of effort among the alternatives can increase total satisfaction.[1]

II. An Advanced Treatment of an Elementary Decision Problem

In order to examine in greater detail how marginal analysis can be used in decision making, we shall provide an advanced treatment for an elementary decision problem. In our initial discussion of this problem, we shall not use the calculus, in order to illustrate both verbally and diagrammatically the rationale underlying the marginal approach to decision making, a rationale which is sometimes overlooked by students in their mechanical attempts at maximizing or minimizing a function by setting its derivative equal to zero.

Our illustrative problem can be stated as follows: *Suppose that a farmer has 2000 linear ft of fencing material, and that he wishes to use this material*

---

[1] To test his understanding, the reader may wish to consider how the concept of marginal analysis could be used to solve some simple decision problems. For example, in driving to a distant city, should a family proceed as quickly as possible or stop to rest en route? In eating dinner, should a person eat more sirloin steak or save room for apple pie?

to enclose the largest possible rectangular field. How long and how wide should the field be?

The farmer has only two parameters to choose, the length and the width of the rectangle. He is not free to choose any arbitrary combination of length and width, because he must observe the restriction that the total perimeter of the rectangle cannot exceed 2000 ft. Although strictly speaking this restriction has the form of an inequality, it is easy to see that if the farmer is trying to fence in the *maximum* rectangular area, then the total perimeter must exactly equal 2000 ft. Hence the farmer's decision alternatives are either simultaneously to increase the length of the rectangle and decrease the width, or else simultaneously to increase the width of the rectangle and decrease the length.

The farmer could appropriately reason as follows: "Let me first find any rectangle that is feasible; i.e., for which the total perimeter equals 2000 ft. Let me then ask if it is possible to increase the area by increasing the length of the rectangle and simultaneously decreasing its width? If it is, then I should lengthen the rectangle. If it is not, let me then ask if it is possible to increase the total area by widening the rectangle and simultaneously shortening it? If it is, then I should widen the rectangle. If it is not, then since it is not desirable either to lengthen it or to widen it, I must have the best possible rectangular field."

As the initial feasible configuration, suppose the farmer selects a length of 750 ft and a width of 250 ft. This field is illustrated in Figure 3–1; it is feasible because the total perimeter equals 2000 ft. The area resulting from this initial configuration is 187,500 sq ft.

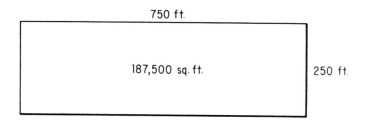

750 ft.

187,500 sq. ft.

250 ft.

FIGURE 3–1.   Initial area.

The farmer now considers whether there is any advantage to lengthening the field. If he lengthens the field by 1 ft, then in order to maintain the restriction on total perimeter, he must narrow the field by 1 ft. What will be the resulting change in area? Figure 3–2 shows exactly what is involved in this process. In Figure 3–2, the original area of 187,500 sq ft is represented by the sum of the areas B_1 and B_2.

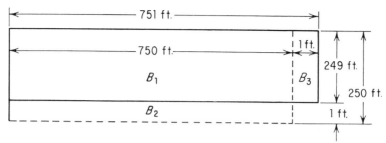

FIGURE 3–2.   Changes in area from lengthening.

By adding 1 ft to the length, it is increased to 751 ft, but at the same time we must subtract 1 ft from the width, decreasing it to 249 ft. This amounts to decreasing the area of the rectangle by B_2 (750 sq ft) and at the same time increasing the area of the rectangle by B_3 (249 sq ft). It will be desirable to lengthen the rectangle if and only if the area B_3 is greater than the area B_2. In our example, this is clearly not the case.

The farmer then should consider the effects of widening the rectangle by 1 ft, and hence also shortening it by 1 ft to observe the restriction on total perimeter. As can be seen from Figure 3–3, this change will increase the total area. The farmer can continue this general procedure, gradually widening the rectangle by 1 ft at a time, until he finds that there is no longer any advantage to be gained by continuing to widen the rectangle. This will occur when the width and the length of the rectangle are equal; i.e., when the rectangle is a square, of side 500 ft.

We shall now present a formal mathematical statement of the incremental approach to the farmer's problem. Let L represent the length of the

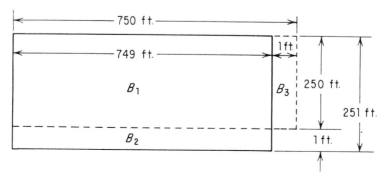

FIGURE 3–3.   Changes in area from widening.

field; W, the width of the field; and A, the area of the field. The farmer wants to maximize

$$A = LW. \tag{3-1}$$

The restriction that the farmer must observe on total perimeter may be represented formally as

$$2L + 2W = 2000 \text{ ft.} \tag{3-2}$$

Equation (3–1) states that the area is a continuous function of both the length and the width of the rectangle. Because of the restriction, Eq. (3–2), it is not permissible to treat both the length and the width of the rectangle as independent variables; the choice of a value for either the length or the width automatically determines the other. Therefore, in applying the differential calculus to Eq. (3–1) in order to find a maximum value for A, we must choose either L or W as the independent variable.

Suppose we consider L to be the independent variable. Then we can maximize A by equating its derivative with respect to L to zero.

$$\frac{dA}{dL} = W + L\frac{dW}{dL} = 0. \tag{3-3}$$

From Eq. (3–2),

$$W = 1000 - L. \tag{3-4}$$

Hence,
$$\frac{dW}{dL} = -1. \tag{3-5}$$

Substituting Eq. (3–5) in Eq. (3–3), we have

$$\frac{dA}{dL} = W - L = 0. \tag{3-6}$$

It is worth pausing before obtaining the trivial solution to Eq. (3–6) to explore one implication of this equation for the analysis we have developed earlier.

From Eq. (3–6), $$dA = W\,dL - L\,dL. \tag{3-7}$$

Equation (3–7) shows that the marginal change in area stemming from changes in the length of the field consists of two terms: The first term, $W\,dL$, is the marginal gain in area from lengthening the rectangle; the second term, $-L\,dL$, is the marginal loss in area from simultaneously being forced to narrow the rectangle.

The solution to Eq. (3–6) yields, of course, the result that

$$W = L. \tag{3-8}$$

To insure that this solution results in maximum rather than minimum area, we can find the second derivative of A with respect to L from Eq. (3–6):

$$\frac{d^2A}{dL^2} = \frac{dW}{dL} - 1. \tag{3-9}$$

Substituting Eq. (3–5) in Eq. (3–9),

$$\frac{d^2A}{dL^2} = -2. \tag{3-10}$$

Since the second derivative is negative, the solution we have found maximizes A. Therefore, the optimal configuration for the field is a square. Substituting Eq. (3–8) in Eq. (3–2) yields $W = 500$ and $L = 500$.[2]

III. Some Useful Quantitative Relations

There are a number of formal relations between total values, average values, and marginal values which it is useful to state and prove in general terms. Specific instances of these relations will frequently arise in later chapters.[3]

---

[2] An alternative method of solution is by use of the Lagrange multiplier as follows:

$A = L \cdot W$

$L + W = 1000$

$A = L \cdot W + \lambda (1000 - L - W)$

$\frac{\partial A}{\partial L} = W - \lambda = 0$

$\frac{\partial A}{\partial W} = L - \lambda = 0$

Thus

$W = \lambda$

$L = \lambda$

$\therefore W = L$

We shall make frequent use of the Lagrange multiplier. If the reader is not already familiar with the technique, it will be worthwhile for him to investigate it. Almost any calculus text will discuss the Lagrange multiplier; e.g., see R. Courant, *Differential and Integral Calculus*, vol. II (New York: Interscience Publishers, 1953) pp. 190–99.

[3] If the reader wishes to have a specific example in mind to help him see some economic significance in these general relations, he can substitute the word "cost" for the word "value" in the statement and discussion of Theorems 1, 2, and 3 below, regarding x then as the rate of production.

Suppose that $T(x)$, which we shall call the *total value*, is a continuous and differentiable function of the variable x. Then as already indicated, the marginal value, $M(x)$, is defined by

$$M(x) = \frac{d}{dx} T(x). \tag{3-11}$$

Theorem 1. The marginal value is unchanged by adding a constant to the total value.

In formal terms, this theorem states

$$\frac{d}{dx} [T(x) + K] = \frac{d}{dx} T(x) \tag{3-12}$$

where K is an arbitrary constant. Since the derivative of a constant is zero, the proof of the theorem is evident.

Two more terms, *fixed value* and *variable value* need to be defined. The total value can always be written in the following form:

$$T(x) = f(x) + K \tag{3-13}$$

where K is a constant, and

$$f(0) = 0. \tag{3-14}$$

Then we define the fixed value as K and the variable value as $f(x)$.

There are three notions of average values corresponding to the concepts of total value, variable value, and fixed value. The average total value is $T(x)/x$. The average variable value is $f(x)/x$. Finally, the average fixed value is K/x.[4]

Several important general relations hold between the marginal and the average values.

Theorem 2. The marginal value intersects the average total value at any turning points of the latter; the marginal value also intersects the average variable value at any turning points of the latter.

This theorem is easily proved using some elementary differential calculus. Consider the first part of the theorem. Saying that the average total value has a turning point means, of course, that the derivative of the average

---

[4] Note that the definition of "average fixed value" does not conform to the normal mathematical definition of the average value of a function. If $Q(x)$ is a continuous function of x, the standard definition of the average value, $\overline{Q}$, is: $\overline{Q} = \int_a^b Q(x)\,dx/\int_a^b dx$. When $Q(x)$ is identically equal to a constant value, K, this results in $\overline{Q} = K$. In contrast, we have defined the average fixed value to be K/x. The difference, of course, is that the normal mathematical definition of average value gives, in effect, the average *height* of the function. In the concept of average costs, the averaging is done per unit of output. Thus, our concept of average value is not the average height of a function, but rather the height of the function divided by the value of the abscissa.

total value equals zero; i.e.,

$$\frac{d}{dx}\left[\frac{T(x)}{x}\right] = 0. \tag{3-15}$$

Applying the rule for differentiating a quotient to Eq. (3–15),

$$\frac{x\left[\dfrac{d}{dx}T(x)\right] - T(x)}{x^2} = 0. \tag{3-16}$$

In order for Eq. (3–16) to be satisfied, the numerator of the left-hand side must equal zero. Hence Eq. (3–11, 3–16) imply that

$$xM(x) - T(x) = 0 \tag{3-17}$$

or

$$M(x) = \frac{T(x)}{x}. \tag{3-18}$$

Equation (3–18), which states that the marginal value equals the average total value, was derived from the assumption that x is a turning point for the average total value. Hence the first part of Theorem 2 is proved.

The second part of Theorem 2 is analogously proved. Note that from Eq. (3–11) and (3–13),

$$M(x) = \frac{df(x)}{dx} \tag{3-19}$$

Theorem 3. If the average (total or variable) value is rising, then the marginal value lies above it; if the average (total or variable) value is falling, then the marginal value lies below it; if the average (total or variable) value is neither rising nor falling, then the marginal value is equal to it.

When the average (total or variable) value is neither rising nor falling, then its derivative must equal zero. Hence the method used to prove Theorem 2 establishes that in this case, the marginal value equals the average (total or variable) value.

Continuing with the proof of Theorem 3, the average total value is rising if and only if the derivative of the average total value is positive. Hence, we must prove that when

$$\frac{d}{dx}\left[\frac{T(x)}{x}\right] > 0, \tag{3-20}$$

then

$$M(x) > \frac{T(x)}{x}. \tag{3-21}$$

To establish this, note that

$$\frac{d}{dx}\left[\frac{T(x)}{x}\right] = \frac{x\left[\dfrac{d}{dx}\,T(x)\right] - T(x)}{x^2}. \tag{3-22}$$

Using Eq. (3–20) and (3–22) together implies that

$$x\left[\frac{d}{dx}\,T(x)\right] - T(x) > 0. \tag{3-23}$$

Substituting Eq. (3–11) in (3–23), and solving,

$$M(x) > \frac{T(x)}{x}. \tag{3-24}$$

This establishes the first part of Theorem 3 for average total value. An analogous proof holds for average variable value.

To complete the proof of Theorem 3, reverse the direction of the inequality sign in Eq. (3–20) and (3–21). This will reverse the direction of the inequality in Eq. (3–23) and (3–24), so the preceding proof is readily modified.

It is useful to illustrate Theorem 3 for a cubic total value function: $x^3 - 2x^2 + 3x + 60$. The fixed value is 60, and the variable value is $x^3 - 2x^2 + 3x$. The total value, variable value, and fixed value are all graphed in Figure 3–4.

The corresponding marginal value is $3x^2 - 4x + 3$. The average total value is $x^2 - 2x + 3 + (60/x)$. The average fixed value is $60/x$. Finally, the average variable value is $x^2 - 2x + 3$. The marginal and the average values are all graphed in Figure 3–5. It may be verified that Figure 3–5 is consistent with Theorems 2 and 3.

The last concept that we wish to introduce in this chapter is the notion of elasticity. The elasticity of a function is the relative change in the value of the function corresponding to a given relative change in the independent variable.[5] Suppose, for example, that we have a function

$$q = D(p). \tag{3-25}$$

Then we define the elasticity of q with respect to p as

$$\eta = \frac{dq/q}{dp/p} = \frac{dq}{dp}\frac{p}{q}. \tag{3-26}$$

---

[5] The commonest economic example of elasticity is the price elasticity of demand, which is the relative change in the quantity demanded of a commodity divided by the relative change in the price of that commodity. In terms of this example, in Eq. (3–25) and (3–26) we can regard q as the quantity demanded and p as the price of a commodity; i.e., Eq. (3–25) can be regarded as a simple demand function.

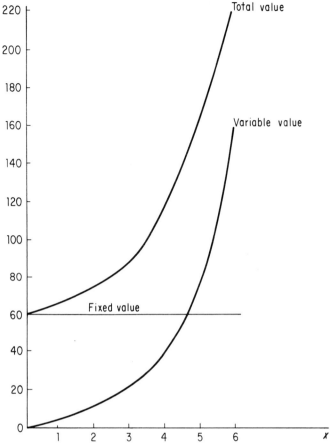

FIGURE 3–4. Total, variable, and fixed values.

The concept of elasticity provides a measure of the responsiveness of a function to changes in the independent variable.[6] It is superior in this respect to the slope of the function, because the elasticity is entirely independent of units of measurement whereas the slope is not.

Theorem 4. If p is positive, then:

$$\frac{d}{dq}\,(p \cdot q) < 0 \qquad \text{if } \eta > -1 \tag{3–27}$$

$$\frac{d}{dq}\,(p \cdot q) = 0 \qquad \text{if } \eta = -1 \tag{3–28}$$

$$\frac{d}{dq}\,(p \cdot q) > 0 \qquad \text{if } \eta < -1. \tag{3–29}$$

---

[6] In terms of the example used in the preceding footnote, the price elasticity of demand is a measure of the percentage change in quantity which will result from a small percentage change in the price of the commodity.

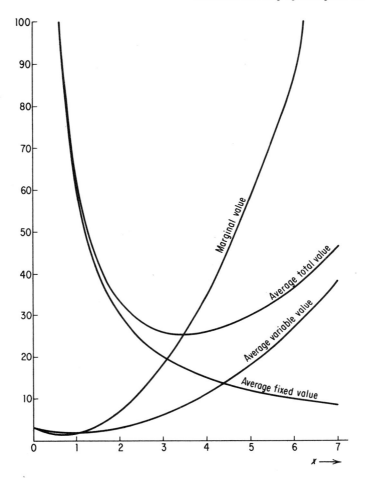

FIGURE 3–5.   Marginal and average values.

If in the foregoing expressions p is interpreted as price and q as quantity demanded, then this theorem states the relationship between changes in total revenue and price elasticity of demand. In view of this theorem, an elasticity equal to -1 plays a critical role, and is therefore given the special name *unitary elasticity*.

The proof of Theorem 4 proceeds as follows:

$$\frac{d}{dq}\,(p \cdot q) = p + q\,\frac{dp}{dq} = p\left(1 + \frac{1}{\dfrac{p}{q}\dfrac{dq}{dp}}\right). \qquad (3\text{–}30)$$

Substituting Eq. (3–26) in Eq. (3–30), we obtain

$$\frac{d}{dq}(p \cdot q) = p\left(1 + \frac{1}{\eta}\right). \qquad (3-31)$$

From Eq. (3–31), it is readily seen that if p is positive, then the assertions stated in Eq. (3–27), (3–28), and (3–29) necessarily hold.

IV. Summary

In this chapter, we have introduced the most important approach used in microeconomic theory: marginal analysis. We first showed how this concept relates to everyday decision problems. We found that when a problem involves choosing a combination of two or more alternatives, the marginal approach consists in analyzing the effects on total satisfaction of small changes in the level of each alternative. We found that this type of reasoning is applicable both to problems involving discrete changes and to problems involving continuous changes. Once it was established that marginal analysis is appropriate for problems involving continuous changes, it was logical to identify marginal changes with derivatives, and hence to utilize the calculus in solving many decision problems. By using both verbal reasoning and the calculus to solve a specific problem, it became clear that mathematics can be a useful language for economics.

Given any continuous total value function, we defined six related functions: total variable value, total fixed value, average total value, average variable value, average fixed value, and marginal value. We demonstrated some important relationships between the average and marginal values. The marginal approach was also used to define the concept of elasticity. The elasticity of a function is a dimension-free measure of the relative responsiveness of the function to small relative changes in its independent variable. This concept, as well as its relationship to changes in the product of the independent and dependent variables, will become important in subsequent chapters.

SUGGESTED READINGS

These recommendations are in addition to the footnote references cited in this chapter.

ALLEN, R. G. D., *Mathematical Analysis for Economists*, chaps. 8, 10, 14. London: Macmillan & Co., Ltd., 1938.

MARSCHAK, J., "Demand Elasticities Reviewed," *Econometrica*, XI (1943), 25–34.

RUGGLES, RICHARD, "Methodological Developments," *A Survey of Contemporary Economics*, B. F. Haley, ed., Vol. II, pp. 408–53. Homewood, Ill.: Richard D. Irwin, Inc., 1952.

SAMUELSON, PAUL ANTHONY, *Foundations of Economic Analysis*, chap. 3. Cambridge: Harvard University Press, 1955.

WICKSTEED, PHILIP H., "The Scope and Method of Political Economy," in *Readings in Price Theory*, George J. Stigler and Kenneth E. Boulding, eds., pp. 3–26. Homewood, Ill.: Richard D. Irwin, Inc., 1952.

YAMANE, TARO, *Mathematics for Economists: An Elementary Survey*, chaps. 3, 5. Englewood Cliffs, N.J.: Prentice-Hall, Inc., 1962.

Part 2

Market Structures and the
Theory of the Firm

Chapter Four

Price Determination in a Perfectly Competitive Market

The major question on which microeconomic analysis focuses is the manner in which resources are allocated in a private-enterprise economy. We shall see in later chapters that this depends in large part upon a free price mechanism. In a capitalist society, prices serve as signals which help guide the flows of productive factors and final outputs. As a starting point for examining the resource allocation process, we shall attempt in this chapter to explain the behavior of price and output in a single market. Our aim is to discover the significant explanatory variables which interact to determine market price and output and the resulting effects of changes in these explanatory variables.

I. Elementary Concepts

A. THE NOTION OF A MARKET

The concept of a market, as with many other concepts in economics, is not amenable to a clear-cut, operational definition. Alfred Marshall, the great English economist, took eight pages to discuss the concept over forty years ago,[1] and since then many complexities have been added.

In its simplest form, a *market* may be thought of as a physical location in which buying and selling take place, and in which at any instant of time there is only one price at which a particular product is traded. Such a concept might cover markets like the produce markets in any large city, as well as the major commodity and stock exchanges. This simple notion does not, however, cover the modern firm's idea of a market. A large firm may well consider the whole geographical area of the United States as its market, and it may have one price at which it sells a particular product anywhere in the market.

For our purposes, it is most convenient to define a market as the general area or region in which a single price for a product will prevail and in which the product will be bought and sold. This means that the market of the corner grocery store may be measured in blocks, whereas the market of a modern firm may be measured in terms of the number of countries in which it sells (and perhaps some day by the number of planets in which it does business).

The precise definition of the geographical area constituting a market has become an important problem in the law. In an industry where two firms merge, for example, the courts are interested in determining the effect of the merger on the competitive structure of the industry. Operationally this means that the market in which the merged firms are selling must be defined so that the effect of the merger on competition can be measured. A merger of two cement companies which was brought to trial by the Federal Trade Commission (FTC) illustrates the importance and the difficulty of an operational definition of a market.[2]

The major firm in the merger was Diamond Alkali, a large chemical company which has a cement division. The Bessemer Limestone and Cement Company was purchased by Diamond in 1961. The FTC argued that a 23-county area in Ohio and Pennsylvania in which Diamond had sold almost all of its cement for several years constituted the relevant economic market.

Diamond, on the other hand, argued that the geographic market for a commodity is that area which includes all those sellers whose changes in

---

[1] Alfred Marshall, *Principles of Economics*, 8th ed. (London: Macmillan and Co., Ltd., 1920), pp. 323–30.

[2] Diamond Alkali Company, Federal Trade Commission Docket No. 8572.

output or price will affect every other producer selling or potentially selling to a group of buyers. Thus their geographical market included all the cement plants located in a 5-state area because those plants had been established as actual or potential sources of supply to the 23-county area and a broader surrounding area. Diamond also argued that their definition was substantiated by evidence which showed a substantial conformity of movement of prices over time by the mills in this area as well as a strong trend toward uniformity in the actual price level.

This example is typical of many cases now being heard before the FTC and the courts. Unfortunately the tendency in these hearings is to use opinion rather than empirical evidence. The blame for this should, however, not be placed solely on lawyers, since economists have not provided as much help as they might in translating economic theory into operational terms.

B. Market Supply and Demand Curves

In order to deal with the problem of price and output determination in the market, economists have invented two concepts: the market demand and the market supply curves. The essential nature of both these concepts is similar. Both will be discussed briefly in this chapter. The assumptions and conceptual bases behind both of these curves will be discussed in the following two chapters.

The market demand curve is an *ex ante* concept.[3] It indicates the amount of a product that consumers in a specified market would be willing to buy during a given period of time at particular selling prices. The demand curve (in the sense in which it is used in economic theory) is *not* an empirically determined curve showing what people have done in the past. The demand curve is a hypothetical construct which is intended as an aid in reasoning about a particular problem. Similarly, the market supply curve is an *ex ante* concept. It indicates the amount of a product that sellers in a specified market would be willing to sell during a given period of time at particular selling prices.

In most of this chapter we shall assume negatively sloping demand curves and positively sloping supply curves, as shown in Figure 4–1.[4] There is no

---

[3] An *ex ante* concept is an anticipatory concept; i.e., it refers to the *anticipated* future values of economic variables or the future behavior of economic agents. An *ex post* concept, in contrast, refers to the *actual* values of economic variables or behavior of economic agents.

[4] In order to conform to the type of graphical supply and demand curve analysis which is now traditional in economics, we have measured price on the vertical axis and quantity on the horizontal axis. This represents a reversal of the usual mathematical convention of using the horizontal axis to represent the independent variable and the vertical axis to represent the dependent variable. Price is the independent variable for both the supply and the demand curves, with quantity being the dependent variable in each case.

particular reason why both the demand and the supply curves should be
straight lines, other than that this simplifies geometrical and mathematical
analyses.

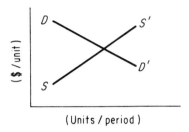

FIGURE 4–1. Market supply and
demand curves.

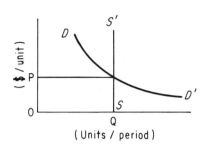

FIGURE 4–2. The perishable commodity case.

C. TEMPORARY EQUILIBRIUM OF SUPPLY AND DEMAND

Economists apply supply and demand concepts to a wide variety of
market situations. The simplest case is one in which the sellers bring a
perishable commodity to market for sale at the best possible price. If a
given quantity of the perishable commodity has already been produced and
if there are no storage possibilities, then supply is not dependent upon
price, and the market supply curve is a vertical line. By assuming an
arbitrary market demand curve, the analysis of this case can proceed with
the help of Figure 4–2.

The intersection of the demand and supply curves in Figure 4–2 establishes an equilibrium price of *OP*.[5] Note that no individual buyer or
seller has sufficient knowledge to determine that *OP* is the price which will
clear the market. Each buyer and seller is trying to trade the commodity
on terms which are most favorable to himself.

The literature of economics lacks a completely satisfactory analysis of
the process by which an equilibrium price is reached. Early economists,

---

[5] By *equilibrium price* we mean a price which simultaneously satisfies all buyers and
sellers in the market (i.e., a price which clears the market). This implies that, when the
price is at its equilibrium level, every buyer who wishes to purchase the commodity at
that price can buy all that he wishes and that furthermore every seller who wishes to
sell the commodity at that price can sell all that he wishes. In graphical terms, the
equilibrium price is determined by the intersection of the market demand and supply
curves. (In those pathological cases in which there may be two or more intersections of
the demand and supply curves, each of these intersections would determine an equilibrium price.)

such as Walras and Edgeworth, assumed "re-contracting."[6] This assumption meant that all transactions could be renegotiated until the equilibrium price was reached. Marshall, in describing the market, envisages many price changes:

> So the price may be tossed hither and thither like a shuttlecock, as one side or the other gets the better in the "higgling and bargaining" of the market. But unless they are unequally matched; unless, for instance, one side is very simple or unfortunate in failing to gauge the strength of the other side, the price is likely to be never very far from 36s. [the equilibrium price]; and it is nearly sure to be pretty close to 36s. at the end of the market.[7]

Marshall's description implies that there is enough knowledge on the part of both buyers and sellers so that even the first prices established in the market will be close to the equilibrium price. Thus he sees this market as one in which the equilibrium price probably is the actual price for most of the transactions and the prices of the other transactions deviate only slightly from the equilibrium price. The equilibrium price in this type of market might also be viewed as a weighted average that, in fact, never actually prevails in the market. Thus some transactions take place at a price above the equilibrium and some below it. If at the end of the market period an average of the transaction prices were computed, with each price weighted by the quantity sold at that price, this average should be close to the equilibrium price. For repetitive markets it is likely that Marshall's interpretation is correct.

Economists refer to several types of market equilibria. These vary according to the length of time assumed to be necessary for the equilibrium price to be established. The type of market equilibrium we have just analyzed is called *temporary equilibrium* because it is quickly achieved and short-lived; a new temporary equilibrium position will be established when market conditions change.

D. PERFECTLY COMPETITIVE MODEL

Now we shall examine price determination over two longer periods of time. The first such period, the *short run*, is defined as the length of time for which the basic production facilities must remain fixed. Obviously the lengths of time will be different for various industries. Accordingly, the *long run*, which is the second time period we are interested in, is defined as the length of time necessary for a new plant to be built. We shall explore the determination of price for these two periods within the context of a particular market structure: perfect competition.

---

[6] For a comprehensive review of the processes by which the market equilibrium price may be reached and of the stability of the market equilibrium, see Takashi Negishi, "The Stability of a Competitive Economy: A Survey Article," *Econometrica*, 30, No. 4 (October, 1962), 635–69.

[7] Marshall, *op. cit.*, p. 333.

Although the perfectly competitive model is the most commonly analyzed form of market structure in economics, the assumptions which underlie it are often not made completely explicit. In this section we specify and describe the five basic assumptions, which were mentioned briefly in Chapter 1.

1. HOMOGENEOUS PRODUCT. To insure that no seller has a special advantage and that no buyer has any reason to favor a particular seller, it is assumed that the product is homogeneous in every dimension. The purpose of this assumption is to have the product and the conditions under which it is sold completely uniform, at least uniform enough so that selling price is the only factor which determines a buyer's purchases. This assumption limits the power of any supplier to sell his product at a price which is even slightly above the market price.[8]

2. PERFECT KNOWLEDGE. This assumption has been much discussed and frequently misunderstood. This assumption should be interpreted as meaning that all buyers and sellers in the market are aware of all current opportunities. As Marshall wrote: "But though everyone acts for himself, his knowledge of what others are doing is supposed to be generally sufficient to prevent him from taking a lower or paying a higher price than others are doing. This is assumed provisionally to be true both of finished goods and of their factors of production, of the hire of labour and of the borrowing of capital."[9] We do not assume perfect ability to forecast the future, but only perfect knowledge of current opportunities. Furthermore it is not necessary to assume that everyone possesses the same technical knowledge or specialized abilities (even though it is true that faulty knowledge may result in early exit from an industry and inferior ability will result in fewer resources to command).

3. UTILITY AND PROFIT MAXIMIZATION. This is, perhaps, the most controversial of the assumptions necessary to define the model of perfect com-

---

[8] This assumption is stated in stricter terms than is absolutely necessary. It is permissible to allow certain systematic differences in the products of different sellers and still have a perfectly competitive market. In particular, both quality differentials and location differentials may exist, provided, however, that these are effectively neutralized by corresponding price differentials. For example, if two sellers are located in different places, the selling prices of each for products of a standard quality must differ only by the differential in the costs of transporting their products to market. Further, if two sellers at the same location have products of different quality, the selling prices of each must differ by only a standard amount which reflects the differential in quality. In this way, all winter wheat which is traded on the Chicago Commodity Exchange can be considered as a homogeneous product, and the market for winter wheat on this exchange can be considered perfectly competitive, even though there are considerable differences in the quality and location of this wheat. Because of the standard quality and transportation price differentials, any buyer of wheat is not concerned about these differences, since they are adequately reflected in the selling prices.

[9] Marshall, *op. cit.*, p. 341.

petition. It means basically that households make decisions which will maximize their utilities (i.e., satisfactions), and that firms make decisions which will maximize their profits. Many economists argue that this is completely unrealistic and that, for example, the decision makers in firms are trying to do something else, such as maximize their own security or power. Perhaps, as Herbert A. Simon argues, they are interested only in "satisficing."[10] The basic defense that we can make for this assumption should be clear from our discussion of methodology in Chapter 2. The utility and profit maximizing assumption is a gross one, but we intend here to apply it to an analysis that fundamentally is concerned with markets and industries rather than with households and firms. At this level of generality, we think that the results deduced from a set of assumptions which include utility and profit maximization are perfectly acceptable. If we wish to predict how a *particular* household or firm will behave, then assumptions this general will not be satisfactory.

4. ATOMISTIC COMPETITION. A basic requirement of perfect competition is that no buyer or seller possesses sufficient market power to affect price. This implies that there must be limitations on the size of individual buyers and sellers, as well as large numbers of buyers and sellers in the market. The assumption of atomistic competition specifies that each seller must be so small that his transactions have no noticeable effect on market price no matter how much or how little he sells. In the same way, each buyer must be so small that any variation in his purchases has no noticeable effect on the market price. Finally, there can be no collusive agreements among the buyers or among the sellers.

5. FREE ENTRY AND EXIT OF RESOURCES. This assumption guarantees that productive resources, including land, labor, capital, and entrepreneurship, can enter or leave any industry whenever their owners wish. Thus if the owners of any productive resources perceive that a higher return is available in another industry, they will shift some of these resources to the industry with higher returns. Thus, if the returns in any one industry are higher than the returns available for comparable opportunities elsewhere, then additional productive resources will quickly enter that industry since it is assumed that no barriers exist to prevent this. Free entry and exit implies that resources are relatively unspecialized and, therefore, can easily be transferred to other uses.

II. Market Price Determination

The five assumptions—homogeneous product, perfect knowledge, utility and profit maximization, atomistic competition, and free entry and exit—

[10] Herbert A. Simon, "A Behavioral Model of Rational Choice," *Quarterly Journal of Economics*, 69 (1955), 99–118. For a review of criticisms made of the profit-maximizing assumption, see Richard M. Cyert and James G. March, *A Behavioral Theory of the Firm*, (Englewood Cliffs, N.J.: Prentice-Hall, Inc., 1963), chap. 2.

define the model which we shall now use to gain an understanding of market price determination. Although this model is not a literal description of the American economy, it should not be dismissed for this reason.[11] We do not maintain that every proposition deduced from this model is a valid description of the behavior of individual households and firms. We regard the perfectly competitive model as a tool for analyzing the effects of certain variables on market price and output; through such analysis we gain some insight into the way such variables function in the real world—even in markets which are not perfectly competitive.

A. Short-Run Equilibrium

Our first application of the perfectly competitive model will be an analysis of short-run market equilibrium. In the short run the productive facilities of the industry are fixed. Figure 4–3 portrays the prevailing demand and supply curves for the market. The market supply curve is not a vertical line because firms will adjust their production to the prices that prevail. The higher the selling price, the greater the amount firms will offer to supply.

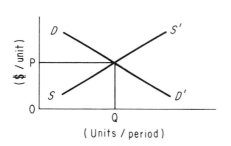

(Units / period)

FIGURE 4–3. Short-run market equilibrium.

In Figure 4–3, OP is the equilibrium price and OQ is the equilibrium output. Basically this diagram indicates that during a short-run period, the firms in the market will adjust to the demand situation with which they are presented. After some trial-and-error experimentation during which price and output will fluctuate, both will tend to settle at their equilibrium levels.

The short-run equilibrium position may not, however, be maintained indefinitely. If there are no shifts in the demand curve, the duration of the equilibrium solution depends upon the state of profits in the industry. It is not possible to determine from Figure 4–3 whether there are profits in the industry, since Figure 4–3 contains no cost information. We can, however, deduce from the assumptions of profit maximization, perfect knowledge, and free entry and exit that unless the returns to the productive resources are at the level that could be derived from alternative uses elsewhere in the

[11] There are markets in the United States which do satisfy the assumptions of perfect competition. Some examples are the organized auction exchanges on which securities and commodities are traded, and also certain dealer markets (such as the market for United States government securities) where trading is done by individual negotiation rather than public auction.

economy, there will be resources entering or leaving this industry. Such movements will shift the supply curve, altering the equilibrium price and output.

In order to illustrate the manner in which mathematics can be applied to economic theory, we shall obtain the short-run market equilibrium solution mathematically. By gaining some familiarity with the analysis in this relatively uncomplicated case, the reader will be in a better position to exploit the power of mathematics in more complex cases.

If we let p denote the market price and q the quantity demanded or supplied in the market, then the market demand and supply curves can be expressed as[12]

$$p = D(q) \quad \text{(demand curve)} \tag{4-1}$$

$$p = S(q) \quad \text{(supply curve).} \tag{4-2}$$

The equilibrium level of market price and output is the simultaneous solution of Eq. (4–1) and (4–2). In most cases, a unique solution to these equations will exist, so the equilibrium price, $\bar{p}$, and the equilibrium output, $\bar{q}$, are constants.

We can analyze the effects of shifts in the demand curve on the equilibrium solution by incorporating a shift parameter, t, into the demand function. The demand curve might shift as the result of change in consumers' tastes or incomes or in the prices of related commodities. We wish to determine the effects on equilibrium price and output of a change which shifts the demand curve upward and to the right.[13]

In place of Eq. (4–1), we shall now represent the demand function by

$$p = D(q, t). \tag{4-3}$$

Since increases in t represent shifts in the demand curve upward and to the right,

$$\frac{\partial D(q,t)}{\partial t} > 0. \tag{4-4}$$

---

[12] We have adopted this method for writing the demand and supply equations to conform with the graphical convention generally used by economists of measuring price along the vertical axis and quantity along the horizontal axis. As we have already pointed out, p represents the independent variable and q the dependent variable. Therefore, from the standpoint of economic causality, it would be more appropriate to write the demand curve in the form $q = D^{-1}(p)$, and the supply curve in the form $q = S^{-1}(p)$, where D^{-1} and S^{-1} are the inverse functions of D and S, respectively. As long as both the demand curve and the supply curve are single-valued functions, however, either approach leads to the same market solutions.

[13] This analysis parallels an example given in Paul Samuelson, *Foundations of Economic Analysis* (Cambridge, Mass.: Harvard University Press, 1947), pp. 17–19.

The equilibrium values for market price and quantity, which result from the simultaneous solution of Eq. (4–2) and (4–3), depend upon the specific value of the shift parameter t. Hence we can write

$$\bar{p} = f(t) \tag{4–5}$$

and

$$\bar{q} = g(t). \tag{4–6}$$

To determine the effects of shifts in the demand curve on the equilibrium values of price and output, we have to evaluate $d\bar{p}/dt$ and $d\bar{q}/dt$. As a first step, it is convenient to write Eq. (4–2) and (4–3) in implicit form:[14]

$$D(\bar{q},t) - \bar{p} = 0. \tag{4–7}$$

$$S(\bar{q}) - \bar{p} = 0. \tag{4–8}$$

Differentiating Eq. (4–7) and (4–8) with respect to t,

$$\frac{\partial D}{\partial \bar{q}}\frac{d\bar{q}}{dt} + \frac{\partial D}{\partial t} - \frac{d\bar{p}}{dt} = 0. \tag{4–9}$$

$$\frac{dS}{d\bar{q}}\frac{d\bar{q}}{dt} - \frac{d\bar{p}}{dt} = 0. \tag{4–10}$$

To solve Eq. (4–9) and (4–10) simultaneously for $d\bar{q}/dt$, we substitute $d\bar{p}/dt$, as determined by Eq. (4–10), into Eq. (4–9). Rearranging terms,

$$\frac{\partial D}{\partial \bar{q}}\frac{d\bar{q}}{dt} - \frac{dS}{d\bar{q}}\frac{d\bar{q}}{dt} = -\frac{\partial D}{\partial t} \tag{4–11}$$

or

$$\frac{d\bar{q}}{dt} = \frac{-(\partial D/\partial t)}{(\partial D/\partial \bar{q}) - (dS/d\bar{q})}. \tag{4–12}$$

Solving for $d\bar{p}/dt$ in a similar manner, we have

$$\frac{\partial D}{\partial \bar{q}} \cdot \frac{d\bar{p}/dt}{dS/d\bar{q}} - \frac{d\bar{p}}{dt} = -\frac{\partial D}{\partial t} \tag{4–13}$$

or

$$\frac{d\bar{p}}{dt} = \frac{-(dS/d\bar{q})(\partial D/\partial t)}{(\partial D/\partial \bar{q}) - (dS/d\bar{q})}. \tag{4–14}$$

Equations (4–12) and (4–14) indicate how shifts in demand affect the equilibrium levels of market quantity and market price. These equations show that under normal supply and demand conditions, an increase in demand leads to an increase in both price and quantity. Normal conditions of supply and demand mean that the short-run demand curve is negatively

---

[14] We use $\bar{p}$ and $\bar{q}$ in Eq. (4–7) and (4–8) to emphasize that we are investigating the effects of changes in t on the equilibrium solution. In contrast, in Eq. (14–15) and (14-16) we use q to emphasize that we are concerned with the slopes of the demand and supply curves throughout their domains.

sloping whereas the short-run supply curve is positively sloping, as drawn in Figure 4–3. Mathematically, this means that

$$\frac{\partial D}{\partial q} < 0 \tag{4-15}$$

and
$$\frac{dS}{dq} > 0. \tag{4-16}$$

When Eq. (4–15) and (4–16) hold, the denominator on the right-hand sides of Eq. (4–12) and (4–14) is negative. Equation (4–4) implies that the numerator on the right-hand side of Eq. (4–12) is also negative. Hence, it follows that under normal conditions an increase in demand will cause an increase in the equilibrium level of market output; i.e.,

$$\frac{d\bar{q}}{dt} > 0. \tag{4-17}$$

In a similar fashion, it is easy to see that under these same conditions the right-hand side of Eq. (4–14) is positive, so that

$$\frac{d\bar{p}}{dt} > 0. \tag{4-18}$$

Hence, an increase in demand will also cause an increase in the equilibrium level of market price.[15]

The mathematical analysis used is, of course, consistent with the results of the simple geometrical analysis which would be used in this case. For this simple example, it is solely a matter of taste which of these approaches is preferred. There are many more complicated situations, however, in which a mathematical approach is considerably easier to use than a geometrical approach.[16]

---

[15] This mathematical analysis can be used to derive the effects of the imposition of a sales tax on the market equilibrium solution. We may analyze this situation by considering that the effect of the sales tax is to shift the demand curve downward by the unit amount of the tax; i.e., that $\partial D/\partial t < 0$. Equations (4–12) and (4–14) then imply that the market equilibrium quantity and price will both decrease.

[16] For example, suppose that we have a normal, i.e., a negatively sloping, demand curve, together with an abnormal, negatively sloping, supply curve. A correct graphical analysis of this situation must consider both the case where the supply curve is more steeply sloping than the demand curve, and the case where the supply curve is less steeply sloping than the demand curve. Frequently a student trying graphically to analyze this situation will consider only one of these two cases. In contrast, no new equations need be derived to analyze this situation mathematically. It is apparent from Eq. (4–12) and (4–14) that the results in this situation depend upon the relative magnitudes of the slopes of the demand and supply curves, which are $\partial D/\partial q$ and dS/dq, respectively. When the supply curve is negatively sloping but less negatively sloping than the demand curve (i.e., when $dS/dq > \partial D/\partial q$), then an increase in demand will decrease the market price and increase the market output. In contrast, when the supply curve is more negatively sloping than the demand curve (i.e., when $dS/dq < \partial D/\partial q$), then an increase in demand has precisely the opposite effect, increasing the market price but decreasing the market output.

B. Long-Run Equilibrium

Two distinct processes may cause changes in the short-run market equilibrium position—shifts in the demand curve or shifts in the supply curve. Since the supply curve is fixed in the short run, the preceding mathematical analysis indicates the effect on the equilibrium solution of shifts in demand. Over longer periods of time, however, the supply curve may shift as resources enter or leave the industry. The long-run equilibrium analysis assumes a time period of sufficient duration for productive facilities in the industry to be increased or decreased, as firms react to changing market conditions.

The first case to be analyzed is a situation in which the firms in an industry are making a greater than normal return in the short run. It follows from the assumptions of perfect knowledge, profit maximization, and free entry that new resources will then be attracted to the industry. The effect of these new productive resources will be to increase the supply curve, i.e., to move it to the right. Assuming a fixed and downward-sloping market demand curve, the market price will tend to fall. Hence the profit margins of firms in the industry will begin to decrease. Resources will continue to flow into the industry, and prices and profit margins will continue to fall, until the rate of return in the industry equals the rate of return available from comparable opportunities elsewhere in the economy. At this point, a long-run equilibrium position will have been reached, and there will be no further incentives for resources to enter the industry. This long-run equilibrium solution will prevail indefinitely, unless there are changes in demand, costs, or technology.

The next case to consider is one in which the firms in the industry are earning abnormally low profits in the short run. The process by which long-run equilibrium is established is analogous to the first case, except that now productive resources will leave the industry. The final equilibrium position would again be one in which the return to firms in the industry is equal to the normal return in the economy.

We have analyzed the problem of price determination in the market by viewing firms in the aggregate, rather than individually. The process by which the decisions of individual firms contribute to the establishment of an equilibrium position will be clarified in Chapters 6–8. There are, however, two major points which need emphasis at this stage of our discussion.

First, we have used a "partial equilibrium" approach in our analysis. We have concentrated on one industry only, assuming that all demand and supply curves elsewhere in the economy are fixed. For this to be possible it is necessary that any movements of resources into or out of the one industry will be of such small magnitudes as not to affect the rest of the economy. The partial equilibrium approach is exceedingly useful in many kinds of analyses, and it has been a traditional way for economists to study problems involving many related variables. In Chapter 9, however, we shall examine the nature of a general equilibrium approach.

Second, our approach to market price determination has utilized the method of comparative statics. In analyzing the effect of shifts in demand on the short-run equilibrium levels of market price and output, for example, we have considered the end effect of the movement from one short-run equilibrium position to another short-run equilibrium position without attempting to trace the exact time path by which the system has moved. A more complete analysis which would indicate the nature of the time paths traced by market price and output in this situation requires a precise specification of the dynamic mechanisms which are involved. This would belong to the field of economics known as *dynamics*. In general, in this book we shall use primarily static or comparative static analyses. The following section, however, gives an example of the way in which a dynamic analysis might be carried out.

C. COBWEB MODEL

One of the simplest examples of dynamic analysis in economics is the so-called cobweb model. This model was originally proposed by Tinbergen as a possible explanation for the corn-hog production cycle.[17] The basis of this model is the assumption that supply is a function of price in the previous period whereas demand is a function of price in the current period. That is,

$$D_t = D(p_t) \tag{4-19}$$

$$S_t = S(p_{t-1}) \tag{4-20}$$

A geometric illustration of the cobweb model is provided in Figure 4–4. Suppose that p_0 is the price in the previous period; then in period 1 the firms produce q_1 on the assumption that p_0 will prevail. With a supply of q_1 however, price will be bid up to p_1 in the first period. This new price brings forth a higher supply, q_2, in the second period. In order to sell this entire quantity, the price will have to fall to p_2. As a result of this lower price, output in the next period will be reduced to q_3, which will sell at a higher price, p_3, etc.

---

[17] The theoretical framework of this model was worked out independently by three different economists: Jan Tinbergen in Holland, Henry Schultz in the United States, and Umberto Ricci in Italy. Tinbergen's analysis was the most complete, and it was offered as an explanation of the pattern of hog prices in Germany. The name *cobweb theorem* was first suggested by the English economist, Nicholas Kaldor. Specific references to this work, as well as an excellent discussion of the extent to which the cobweb theorem is adequate to explain observed commodity price cycles, are found in Mordecai Ezekiel, "The Cobweb Theorem," *Quarterly Journal of Economics*, 52 (1938), 255–80.

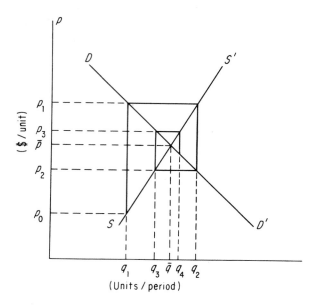

FIGURE 4-4. Cobweb model.

Figure 4-4 portrays a convergent process, leading eventually to the equilibrium solution $(\bar{p}, \bar{q})$. By varying the slope of one of the curves, we could portray an explosive process; i.e., a market in which the discrepancies between the amounts supplied and demanded in a given period grow successively larger. This model has been studied, and the conditions for convergence, divergence, or continued oscillation have been clearly determined.[18]

In order to see exactly what these conditions are, let us for simplicity assume the following linear demand and supply curves:

$$p_t = a - bq_t \tag{4-21}$$

$$p_{t-1} = c + dq_t \tag{4-22}$$

where a, b, c, and d are all positive constants.

From Eq. (4-22), the short-run value of the quantity supplied in period t is

$$q_t = \frac{1}{d} p_{t-1} - \frac{c}{d}. \tag{4-23}$$

---

[18] For an excellent mathematical presentation of the cobweb model, see R. G. D. Allen, *Mathematical Economics* (London: Macmillan and Company, Ltd., 1956), pp. 2–6. The following discussion has been adapted from Allen.

Substituting Eq. (4–23) into equation (4–21) and simplifying, the short run value of the price in period t is

$$p_t = a + \frac{bc}{d} - \frac{b}{d} p_{t-1}. \tag{4–24}$$

Equations (4–23) and (4–24) allow the possibility that the values of price and output may change from period to period, since these both depend upon the previous period's price, which itself may vary from period to period. To determine the conditions under which this variation will occur and the pattern of changes in quantity and price, some further mathematical analysis is necessary.

If $\bar{p}$ is the equilibrium value of price, then Eq. (4–24) must remain valid when we replace both p_t and p_{t-1} by $\bar{p}$. Making this replacement,

$$\bar{p} = a + \frac{bc}{d} - \frac{b}{d} \bar{p}. \tag{4–25}$$

Solving Eq. (4–25) for $\bar{p}$,

$$\bar{p} = \frac{ad + bc}{b + d}. \tag{4–26}$$

Equation (4–26) indicates that a unique equilibrium level for price exists.

To determine the equilibrium level of quantity, $\bar{q}$, in Eq. (4–23) we can replace q_t and p_{t-1} by $\bar{q}$ and $\bar{p}$, respectively. Doing so, and using the value for $\bar{p}$ found in Eq. (4–26), we obtain

$$\bar{q} = \frac{a - c}{b + d}. \tag{4–27}$$

Thus, a unique equilibrium level for quantity also exists.

Since the equilibrium values of price and quantity must lie on the market demand and supply curves, we can substitute $\bar{q}$ and $\bar{p}$ for q_t, p_t, and p_{t-1} in Eq. (4–21) and (4–22) to obtain

$$\bar{p} = a - b\bar{q}. \tag{4–28}$$

$$\bar{p} = c + d\bar{q}. \tag{4–29}$$

From Eq. (4–21) and (4–23), we have

$$q_t = \frac{a}{b} - \frac{1}{b} p_t = \frac{1}{d} p_{t-1} - \frac{c}{d}. \tag{4–30}$$

Similarly, from Eq. (4–28) and (4–29), we have

$$\bar{q} = \frac{a}{b} - \frac{1}{b} \bar{p} = \frac{1}{d} \bar{p} - \frac{c}{d}. \tag{4–31}$$

Subtracting Eq. (4–31) from Eq. (4–30), and introducing the abbreviations

$$p'_t = p_t - \bar{p} \tag{4–32}$$

and

$$q'_t = q_t - \bar{q} \tag{4–33}$$

we have

$$q'_t = -\frac{1}{b} p'_t = \frac{1}{d} p'_{t-1}. \tag{4–34}$$

An analysis of the behavior of the market over time is most conveniently conducted in terms of the deviations of market price in each period from its equilibrium value, i.e., in terms of the p'_t. The conclusions that we shall reach are immediately applicable to the behavior of the deviations of quantity in each period from its equilibrium value, in view of Eq. (4–34). In particular, whenever price is above, equal to, or below its equilibrium level, quantity will be below, equal to, or above its equilibrium level.

Solving the two right-hand members of Eq. (4–34) for p'_t, we have

$$p'_t = -\frac{b}{d} p'_{t-1}. \tag{4–35}$$

It is convenient to introduce the abbreviation

$$r = \frac{b}{d}. \tag{4–36}$$

Then Eq. (4–35) may be written more simply as

$$p'_t = -rp'_{t-1}. \tag{4–37}$$

Equation (4–37) indicates that the deviation from equilibrium of the market price in period t depends solely upon the deviation from equilibrium of the market price in period $t - 1$. This is a first-order difference equation, with a boundary condition that the deviation of market price from its equilibrium value is a known value in period $t = 0$, p'_0. By substituting a few specific values for t (e.g., $t = 0, 1, 2, \ldots$) it can be seen that the solution to Eq. (4–37) is simply:

$$p'_t = (-1)^t r^t p'_0. \tag{4–38}$$

Equation (4–38) can be used to trace the specific course of prices in successive time periods. Unless the initial price is in equilibrium; i.e., unless $p'_0 = 0$, prices will trace a fluctuating pattern around their equilibrium level. In fact, for $t = 0, 1, 2, 3, \ldots$, we get $p'_0, -rp'_0, r^2p'_0, -r^3p'_0, \ldots$.

The exact pattern of this series of price fluctuations depends upon the magnitude of r. There are three qualitatively different situations:

1. $r < 1$. This means that $b < d$. Since $-b$ is the slope of the demand curve and d is the slope of the supply curve (both relative to the quantity

axis), this is equivalent to saying that the supply curve is more nearly vertical than is the demand curve. In this case r^t approaches 0 as t increases, so that the fluctuations of price in successive periods converge toward the equilibrium price level. This is the situation where the equilibrium level is stable.

2. $r = 1$. This means that $b = d$, so that the demand and supply curves have numerically equal slopes. In this case, the price each period alternates above and below its equilibrium level by a constant amount, and this alternation of prices is repeated indefinitely.

3. $r > 1$. This means that $b > d$, so that the demand curve is more nearly vertical than is the supply curve. In this case r^t increases without bound as t grows larger, so that the fluctuations of price in successive periods become further and further removed from the equilibrium price level. This is the explosive case. If $p_0' = 0$, then the system will remain in equilibrium; if $p_0' \neq 0$, equilibrium will never be attained.

The cobweb model has been presented here primarily to illustrate one possible way of introducing dynamic mechanisms into the analysis of price and output determination in a perfectly competitive model. A variety of alternative dynamic mechanisms could have been adopted, and many of these would have led to essentially different results.[19] A complete dynamic analysis of market equilibria is beyond the scope of this book, but we shall occasionally find it useful to employ simple dynamic analysis to obtain insights which cannot be obtained from static and comparative static approaches.

III. Summary

This chapter focused on the behavior of price and output in a single market. In simplest terms, a *market* may be thought of as the general area or region in which a price that is determined for a product will prevail and in which the product will be bought and sold. Some of the complex issues involved in operationally defining a market were illustrated by our discussion of the Diamond Alkali Company's merger with the Bessemer Limestone and Cement Company.

The market demand and the market supply curves are useful hypothetical constructs in dealing with the problem of market price and output determination. The market demand curve indicates the amount of a product that consumers in a particular market would be willing to buy during a given period of time at specific selling prices. Similarly, the market supply curve indicates the amount of a product that sellers in a particular market would be willing to sell during a given period of time at specific selling prices.

---

[19] See Allen, *op. cit.*, chap. 1.

The first case we analyzed using supply and demand concepts was one in which the sellers bring a perishable commodity to market for sale at the highest price which will clear the market. In this case the market supply curve is a vertical line. A temporary equilibrium price is established where the market supply curve intersects the market demand curve. This temporary equilibrium solution is quickly achieved and usually short-lived, changing whenever a different quantity of the commodity is brought to market.

The perfectly competitive model is the most commonly analyzed form of market structure in economics. It is characterized by five basic assumptions: (1) the product is homogeneous in every dimension; (2) all buyers and sellers in the market are aware of all current opportunities; (3) households make decisions which will maximize their utilities and firms make decisions which will maximize their profits; (4) no single buyer or seller possesses sufficient market power to affect price; (5) productive resources can enter or leave any industry whenever their owners wish.

The perfectly competitive model was used to analyze both short-run and long-run market equilibria solutions. In the short run, the productive facilities of the industry are fixed, but the firms in the market can vary their output according to the demand situation. The short-run equilibrium values for market price and quantity are determined by the intersection of the supply and demand curves. Even in the absence of shifts in the demand curve, the short-run equilibrium solution may not be maintained indefinitely. Unless the returns to the productive resources in the industry are at the same level that could be derived from alternative uses of these resources elsewhere in the economy, resources will enter or leave this industry, shifting the supply curve and altering the short-run equilibrium values of price and output. This process will continue until a long-run equilibrium position is reached, in which there is no longer any incentive for resources to enter or leave the industry. Under "normal" conditions, i.e., when the demand curve is negatively sloping and the supply curve is positively sloping, an increase in demand will raise the short-run equilibrium values of both price and output, whereas a decrease in demand will reduce the short-run equilibrium values of both price and output.

The cobweb model was presented to illustrate one possible way of introducing dynamic considerations into the analysis of price and output determination in a perfectly competitive market. This model assumes that the quantity supplied in the market depends upon the price prevailing in the previous period, and that any quantity supplied will be sold at whatever price clears the market. Whether the market equilibrium solution in this case is stable or unstable was shown to depend upon the relative slopes of the demand and the supply curves.

In this chapter, we have utilized market supply and demand curves to analyze the process of price determination in perfectly competitive markets. We shall now look behind these curves to investigate the ways in which they are determined by the decisions of individual households and firms. In Chapter 5 we shall see that the market demand curve arises from the consumption decisions of individual households. Similarly, in Chapter 6 we shall find that the market supply curve results from the production decisions of individual business firms.

SUGGESTED READINGS

These recommendations are in addition to the footnote references cited in this chapter.

CHIPMAN, J. S., "External Economies and Economies of Scale and Competitive Equilibrium," *Quarterly Journal of Economics*, LXXXIV (August, 1970), 347–85.

GORDON, R. A., "Short-Period Price Determination in Theory and Practice," *American Economic Review*, XXXVIII, No. 3 (June, 1948), 265–88.

REILLY, E. E., "The Use of the Elastic Concept in Economic Theory (with Special Reference to Some Economic Effects of a Commodity Tax)," *Canadian Journal of Economics and Political Science*, VI (1940), 39–55.

SMITH, VERNON L., "An Experimental Study of Competitive Market Behavior," *Journal of Political Economy*, LXX (April, 1962), 111–37.

USHER, D., "The Effects of Distribution Cost on Elasticities of Demand and Supply," *Canadian Journal of Economics*, III (August, 1970), 432–47.

Chapter Five

Derivation of the Market
Demand Curve

In Chapter 4, we saw that on the basis of the market demand and the market supply curves it is possible to analyze the manner in which the equilibrium price is determined in a perfectly competitive market. Here and in Chapter 6, we shall deepen our understanding of price determination in perfect competition by considering the economic forces which are summarized in the notions of market supply and demand curves. In this chapter we investigate the manner in which the market demand curve is determined, focusing our attention on the major variables which give shape and form to this curve.

I. The Individual Household's Demand Curve for a Commodity

In order to understand the properties of the market demand curve, it is useful to decompose it into a series of smaller segments. There are obviously a large number of ways in which this decomposition might be made. It could, for example, be done on the basis of individual firms, showing the segment of the market demand which would be supplied by each firm. It could also be done by groups of consumers characterized by their income levels, to show the demand stemming from each income class. The fundamental criterion for choosing the manner of the decomposition, however, is that it should enrich our understanding of the market demand curve. From this standpoint, it seems reasonable to perform the decomposition in terms of the individual consumer and to deal with as small a segment of demand as possible. The individual consumer demand curves show the amount of the commodity that an individual consumer will demand at each possible price during a given period. Hence we shall now focus our attention on the behavior of individual households.

A. THE UTILITY FUNCTION

As a first step in the analysis of household demand, it is useful to specify the assumptions we make about consumer behavior. We assume that consumer behavior is the result of neither purely random chance nor habit and custom. Instead, we assume that the consumer is rational in allocating his income to consumption. The actual behavior of consumers does exhibit some characteristics of randomness and habit. These characteristics may be extremely important to the marketing manager of a firm. For the purpose of understanding the role that consumers play in the resource allocation process, however, these departures from consumer rationality are of minor importance.

In trying to gain some insights into consumer behavior, it quickly becomes apparent that a measuring device representing the inherent value of commodities to households is necessary. Consumers must make choices among such different commodities as, for example, food, refrigerators, and automobiles. There must be some basis for making comparisons among commodities having widely different characteristics. The concept of *utility* is used by economists for this purpose. Utility is a measure by which consumers are able to make comparisons among the different commodities that the rationality assumption requires. A utility function indicates the amount of utility (or satisfaction) a consumer receives from various amounts of different commodities. The utility function is an example of a hypothetical construct, a notion we discussed in Chapter 2.

We shall not assume that we can measure utility in a *cardinal* fashion; i.e., that we can assign an actual number of utils (the unit in which utility might be measured) to any point on a utility function. Rather, we assume only that the utility function enables the consumer to order his preferences, i.e., to indicate the relative ranking of various bundles of commodities. This type of ordering measure is referred to as *ordinal*. We assume only that any household has an ordinal utility function. Ordinal utility functions, of course, make interpersonal comparisons of utility impossible, a point we shall elaborate in Chapter 20, which discusses welfare economics.

Purely as an illustration, however, let us suppose that we have an actual cardinal utility function of the form

$$U = xy \tag{5-1}$$

where x and y are the rates of consumption of two different commodities. If U is now given a fixed value, say U_0, and we divide both sides of Eq. (5–1) by x, we have

$$y = \frac{U_0}{x}. \tag{5-2}$$

Many different combinations of values for x and y correspond to the same value of U_0. These are graphed in Figure 5–1.

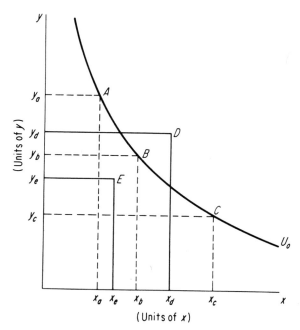

FIGURE 5–1. A consumer indifference curve.

A number of inferences can be drawn from Figure 5–1. First, each point of the curve (e.g., A) represents a different combination of the two commodities (e.g., x_a and y_a) enjoyed by the consumer. He is indifferent as to which of the combinations of x and y represented by the curve he actually obtains (e.g., A, B, or C), since they all lead to the same level of utility, U_0. Second, assuming that more of a commodity is always preferred to less, the consumer prefers all points above U_0 to all points on U_0 (e.g., D is preferred to A, B, or C). The reason is that given any point above U_0 (e.g., D), by moving southwest it is always possible to find some point on U_0 (e.g., B) representing smaller amounts of both x and y (i.e., $x_b < x_d$ and $y_b < y_d$). Hence the consumer prefers D to B. Since the consumer is indifferent among A, B, and C, it follows that he prefers D to either A or C. Third, the consumer prefers all points on U_0 (e.g., A, B, or C) to any point below U_0 (e.g., E). The reasoning is analogous to the second case, except now by moving northeast from any point below U_0 (e.g., E), it is always possible to find some point on U_0 (e.g., B) representing larger amounts of both x and y.

For obvious reasons, the curve U_0 is called an *indifference curve*. Our brief analysis shows that an indifference curve can be considered as a boundary between points preferred and points not preferred. Thus we would never expect indifference curves to intersect. We also would never expect indifference curves to be positively sloping because of the assumption made that more is always preferred to less.

As can be seen from the utility function defined in Eq. (5–1), an infinite number of indifference curves can be drawn. Each curve is determined by a different value of U. These numbers, however, should be used only for ranking purposes. In other words, the only thing we should assume about a curve that has $U = 400$ is that the points on it are preferred to the points on all curves for which $U < 400$.

B. THE BUDGET CONSTRAINT

The indifference map portrays the consumption preferences of the consumer. If there were no constraints on his consumption behavior, he would continually move to a higher indifference curve. Since no consumer has unlimited resources to spend, he cannot choose any arbitrary consumption bundle.

For convenience in exposition, we shall continue to assume a two-commodity world. The necessary modifications for n commodities will be indicated in the following section. We also assume that the consumer's resources are represented by his income. His achievable opportunities, in terms of possible bundles of commodities, will then be described by

$$p_x x + p_y y = M \qquad (5\text{–}3)$$

where p_x is the price of commodity X, x is the number of units of commodity X consumed per period, p_y is the price of commodity Y, y is the number of units of commodity Y consumed per period, and M is the income of the consumer (measured in dollars per period). This equation is called the *budget constraint*. Since in a perfectly competitive market (the assumption of atomistic competition) no consumer is able to affect market prices, the budget constraint is a straight line, as shown in Figure 5–2.

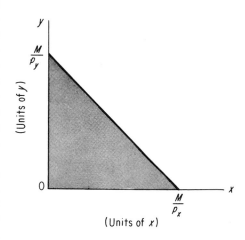

FIGURE 5–2. Budget constraint.

All points within the shaded area and on the budget line in Figure 5–2 are feasible points; i.e., they represent commodity bundles that the consumer could buy. Every point above the line represents an opportunity too expensive for the consumer's resources. Thus the budget line can be considered as a boundary line between attainable and unobtainable commodity bundles.

C. THE CONSUMPTION CHOICES OF A HOUSEHOLD

When the indifference map corresponding to the consumer's utility function is superimposed on the budget line, the optimal consumption decision is obtained, as shown in Figure 5–3. Since the consumer is assumed to be maximizing his utility, he will move to a point on the highest indifference curve in the set of feasible points. This is A in Figure 5–3, the point of tangency between the budget line and the indifference curve U_1. A represents a consumption of x_1 units per period of X and y_1 units per period of Y. The slope of the budget line, $- p_x/p_y$, is equal to the slope of the indifference curve U at the point (x_1, y_1), i.e. $- (\partial U/\partial x)/(\partial U/\partial y)$.

We can derive the same relationship using the calculus. This is an example of the marginal approach to decision making discussed in Chapter 3. We want to maximize the consumer's utility function,

$$U = U(x, y) \qquad (5\text{–}4)$$

subject to his income constraint, specified by Eq. (5–3). This constrained maximization problem can be solved by the use of a Lagrange multiplier.

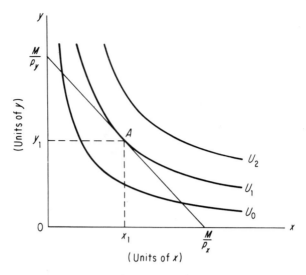

FIGURE 5–3.   Optimal consumption choices of a household.

First form the Lagrangian function:

$$L = U(x, y) - \lambda(M - p_x x - p_y y).\qquad(5\text{–}5)$$

Then take the partial derivatives of L with respect to the variables x and y (M, p_x, and p_y are all assumed fixed), and equate each to zero:

$$\frac{\partial L}{\partial x} = \frac{\partial U}{\partial x} + \lambda p_x = 0.\qquad(5\text{–}6)$$

$$\frac{\partial L}{\partial y} = \frac{\partial U}{\partial y} + \lambda p_y = 0.\qquad(5\text{–}7)$$

We can solve Eq. (5–6) and (5–7) for λ, obtaining:

$$\lambda = -\frac{\partial U/\partial x}{p_x}.\qquad(5\text{–}8)$$

$$\lambda = -\frac{\partial U/\partial y}{p_y}.\qquad(5\text{–}9)$$

Equating the right-hand sides of Eq. (5–8) and (5–9), and rearranging terms:

$$-\frac{\partial U/\partial x}{\partial U/\partial y} = -\frac{p_x}{p_y}.\qquad(5\text{–}10)$$

Equation (5–10) can be interpreted as stating that the slope of an indifference curve equals the slope of the budget constraint. This is the same relationship already obtained using the language of geometry.

The concept of marginal utility plays an important role in the analysis of consumer behavior. As indicated in Chapter 3, a marginal value in effect is a derivative. Thus $\partial U/\partial x$ is the marginal utility of X, i.e., the increase in utility resulting from a small increase in the amount of X consumed. Similarly, $\partial U/\partial y$ is the marginal utility of Y. Let us write U_x and U_y in place of $\partial U/\partial x$ and $\partial U/\partial y$. We can then rewrite Eq. (5–10) in the form:

$$\frac{U_x}{p_x} = \frac{U_y}{p_y}. \tag{5–11}$$

Equation (5–11) can be interpreted as stating that the marginal utility obtained from the last penny spent on commodity X must equal the marginal utility obtained from the last penny spent on commodity Y. This result is a necessary consequence of utility maximization, since the marginal utility obtained per penny of X cannot be greater than the marginal utility obtained per penny of Y; otherwise the consumer could obtain a higher utility level without increasing his total expenditures by spending one penny more for X and one penny less for Y.

Since the generalization to n commodities follows a similar path, it will merely be sketched. Suppose that the amounts the household consumes of these n commodities each period are $x_1, x_2, \ldots x_n$. The household's utility function is

$$U = U(x_1, x_2, \ldots, x_n). \tag{5–12}$$

Letting p_i denote the price per unit of the ith commodity, the household's budget constraint is

$$\sum_{i=i}^{n} p_i x_i = M. \tag{5–13}$$

The household's decision problem is the constrained maximization of its utility function, Eq. (5–12), subject to its budget constraint, Eq. (5–13). By equating the partial derivatives of the Lagrangian function,

$$L = U(x_1, x_2, \ldots, x_n) - \lambda(M - \sum_{i=1}^{n} p_i x_i) \tag{5–14}$$

with respect to each of the x_i to zero, the reader can verify that Eq. (5–11) generalizes to

$$\frac{U_1}{p_1} = \frac{U_2}{p_2} = \ldots = \frac{U_n}{p_n} \tag{5–15}$$

where $U_i = \dfrac{\partial U}{\partial x_i}$ $(i = 1, 2, \ldots, n)$.

D. Derivation of the Household's Demand Curve for a Commodity

Equation (5–11)—or its generalization in the form of Eq. (5–15)—can be regarded as a decision rule which the household follows in determining its consumption expenditures. To see the implications of this decision rule for the household's demand curves, let us return to the special form of the utility function which we presented in Eq. (5–1). Substituting the partial derivatives of Eq. (5–1) into Eq. (5–11), we can obtain the relations:

$$\frac{y}{p_x} = \frac{x}{p_y} \tag{5-16}$$

or

$$y = x \frac{p_x}{p_y}. \tag{5-17}$$

Substituting Eq. (5–17) into the budget relation Eq. (5–3), we have:

$$xp_x + xp_x = M. \tag{5-18}$$

Solving (Eq. 5–18) for x, we get:

$$x = \frac{M}{2p_x}. \tag{5-19}$$

Equation (5–19) can be interpreted as the household's demand curve for commodity X.[1] It indicates the number of units of commodity X which the household will consume each period for various prices of X, when the household's income, M, and the price of the other commodity, p_y, are fixed. Since in deriving Eq. (5–19) we have assumed a given utility function, we have also implicitly assumed that the household's tastes are fixed.

More generally, we can derive a household's demand curve for any commodity in the n-commodity case. This has the form,

$$x_i = D_i (p_i; p_1, \ldots, p_{i-1}, p_{i+1}, \ldots, p_n, M). \tag{5-21}$$

From Eq. (5–21), it can be seen that a household's demand for any commodity depends upon the price of that commodity, when the prices of all

---

[1] By analogous reasoning, the household's demand curve for commodity Y is

$$y = \frac{M}{2p_y}. \tag{5-20}$$

other commodities as well as the household's income are fixed.[2] The household's tastes are automatically incorporated in the functional form of D_i, since in deriving Eq. (5–21) a particular utility function is assumed.

It is instructive to find the elasticity of demand for the demand curve defined by Eq. (5–19). In Chapter 3 we defined the price elasticity of demand:

$$\eta = \frac{dx}{dp_x}\frac{p_x}{x}.$$ (5–24)

From Eq. (5–19) and (5–24);

$$\eta = -\frac{M}{2p_x^2}\frac{p_x}{(M/2p_x)} = -\frac{M}{2p_x^2}\frac{2p_x^2}{M} = -1.$$ (5–25)

Equation (5–25) shows that the demand curve Eq. (5–19) has unit elasticity (-1) at every point.[3] As noted in Chapter 3, saying that a demand curve is unit elastic is equivalent to asserting that as the price of the commodity varies, the total amount of expenditures the consumer devotes to that commodity is unchanged. That this is true for Eq. (5–19) is immediately evident if we rewrite it in the form:

$$xp_x = \frac{M}{2}.$$ (5–28)

---

[2] The only reason that p_y does not appear in Eq. (5–19) is that an extremely special form of utility function was assumed in Eq. (5–1). For most two-commodity utility functions, the price of the other commodity would enter as a parameter in the demand for one commodity. For example, if the household's utility function were

$$U = xy + x + y$$ (5–22)

the reader can verify that the demand curve for commodity X would be

$$x = \frac{M}{2p_x} + \frac{p_y}{2p_x} - \frac{1}{2}.$$ (5–23)

[3] The geometric form of the demand curve Eq. (5–19) is a rectangular hyperbola. Our proof in effect has shown that every demand curve which is a rectangular hyperbola, i.e., for which xp_x is constant, has unit elasticity at every point on it.

The converse proposition is also true. If a demand function is unit elastic at every point, it must have the form:

$$x = \frac{k}{p_x}$$ (5–26)

where k is a constant. This follows by solving the differential equation:

$$\frac{dx}{dp_x}\frac{p_x}{x} = -1.$$ (5–27)

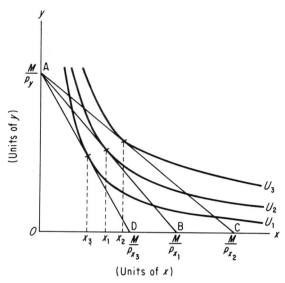

FIGURE 5–4. Derivation of the household's demand curve for commodity X.

We can derive the household's demand curve geometrically as well as mathematically. Start from a position of equilibrium and allow price to vary, as shown in Figure 5–4. At a price p_{x_1}, the consumer buys x_1 units of commodity X, since the budget line AB is tangent to an indifference curve at that point. His income, M, and the price of commodity Y are assumed fixed. The line AC represents the budget line when the price of X has fallen to p_{x_2}. At this point the quantity x_2 is purchased. The line AD represents the budget line when the price has increased to p_{x_3}. At this point x_3 is purchased. In a similar fashion all the points on the demand curve could be determined. Note that in determining the demand curve, money income, M, has been held constant.

II. The Market Demand Curve for a Commodity

We have shown in the preceding section how the utility-maximizing behavior of a single household leads to its demand curve for any commodity. The market demand curve for any commodity can be obtained from the individual demand curves of all households for that same commodity by a lateral addition of all of these individual demand curves. This manner of deriving the market demand curve is intended to be of conceptual rather than of practical importance. It is obviously not the way to estimate market demand curves empirically. On the theoretical level, however, we can argue that the same economic variables which influence the individual household's demand for a commodity should also affect the market demand. Thus, we would expect to find that the market demand for a commodity depends not only upon the price of that commodity alone, but also upon the prices of other commodities, consumer income, and those variables which influence consumer tastes.

III. Some Applications of Utility Theory

A. INCOME-CONSUMPTION CURVES

In order to obtain a richer understanding of the properties of both individual household and market demand curves, it is useful to pursue somewhat further the implications of consumer utility maximization. In deriving geometrically the individual consumer's demand curve for commodity X, we kept his income, M, and the price of commodity Y, p_y, constant, and we allowed the price of commodity X, p_x, to vary. Let us now investigate the effect on the household's consumption decisions of holding both p_x and p_y constant and allowing M to vary. Since the slope of the budget line is $-(p_x/p_y)$, variations in M alone will not change the slope of the budget line. Thus, changes in the household's income will represent parallel shifts of the budget line. This situation is portrayed in Figure 5–5.

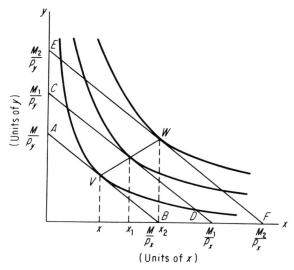

FIGURE 5–5.   Income-consumption curve.

Figure 5–5 shows that as income increases, the consumption of commodity X also increases. This characteristic defines a *normal* commodity. If the consumption of X decreases as income increases, then commodity X is defined as *inferior*. The line VW which connects the equilibrium points is the *income-consumption* curve. If X were an inferior commodity, VW would have a negative slope as income increased.

B. Income and Substitution Effects

In developing a framework for understanding consumer behavior, it is important to examine the effects of price changes on consumption. Start from a situation in which the consumer is at equilibrium (point F in Figure 5–6) and consuming x_1 units per period of X and y_1 units per period of Y. At point F, the budget line AB is tangent to the indifference curve I_1. Income is M, and the prices of X and Y are p_{x_1} and p_{y_1}, respectively. Assume now that the price of X falls to p_{x_2}. The new budget line is AC, and the consumption of X and Y changes to x_3 and y_3, respectively.

In Figure 5–6, a fall in the price of X has led to an increase in the consumption of X and a decrease in the consumption of Y. This result is not general, since it depends upon the specific way in which the indifference curves have been drawn. It is necessary to analyze further the movement

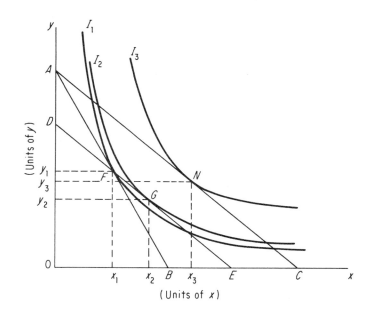

$$OA = M/p_{y_1}; \ OB = M/p_{x_1}; \ OC = M/p_{x_2}; \ OD = M'/p_{y_1}; \ OE = M'/p_{x_2}$$

Figure 5–6.   Income and substitution effects.

from point F to point N in order to understand the conditions under which the particular result shown in Figure 5–6 will be obtained.

The first step in understanding the changes in the consumption of X and Y is to determine what consumption would be if, after the price change, the consumer's money income was adjusted so that it was just sufficient to allow the original consumption (x_1 and y_1) at the new prices. Initially the consumer had enough income to purchase x_1 of X and y_1 of Y. His income was

$$M = p_{x_1}x_1 + p_{y_1}y_1. \tag{5–29}$$

After the price of X has fallen to p_{x_2}, the adjusted money income, M', which is just adequate to buy x_1 and y_1, is

$$M' = p_{x_2}x_1 + p_{y_1}y_1. \tag{5–30}$$

Graphically, the budget line with the adjusted income M' is the line DE in Figure 5–6. It passes through the original equilibrium position and is tangent to the indifference curve I_2 at point G. G represents an increase in consumption of X to x_2 and a decrease in consumption of Y to y_2. In moving from F to G, the consumer would substitute X for Y because of the lower relative price of X.[4]

We have conceptually moved the consumer from F to G by reducing his money income so that at the new prices he can just buy the initial consumption bundle. If we now conceptually restore his money income to its original level, M, and keep the new prices, p_{x_2} and p_{y_1}, then his budget line is AC in Figure 5–6, which is parallel to DE. The new budget line leads to the equilibrium position N, representing the consumption bundle x_3 and y_3. The increase from x_2 to x_3 and from y_2 to y_3 must therefore be due solely to the increase in income from M' to M. Thus we have decomposed the movement from F to N into two segments, F to G and G to N. The movement from F to G is the *substitution effect,* and the movement from G to N is the *income effect.*

There is an alternative to decomposing the movement from F to N into substitution and income effects. This alternative is depicted in Figure 5–7. Note that the essential difference between Figures 5–6 and 5–7 stems from the notion of adjusted money income. In the case of Figure 5–6, we have defined in Equation (5–30) an adjusted money income, M', to be that money income which will just allow the consumer to purchase his original quantities of x and y at the new prices. In Figure 5–7, an alternative adjusted money income, M'', is defined to be that amount of money which

---

[4] Note that in fact the consumer does not move from F to G, but only from F to N. Since we know his entire indifference map, we can safely predict that, with a money income of M' and prices p_{x_2} and p_{y_1} for X and Y, his optimal consumption bundle would be point G.

is just adequate at the new prices to maintain the consumer's initial level of utility. In Figure 5–7, $D'E'$ represents the budget line corresponding to the adjusted money income M''; it is tangent to the initial indifference curve I_1, and its slope reflects the lower price of X. Clearly

$$M'' = p_{x_2}x_2' + p_{y_1}y_2'. \qquad (5\text{—}31)$$

According to this alternative approach, the movement from F to G' represents the substitution effect, and the movement from G' to N represents the income effect. Note that the final equilibrium position, N, is the same in both Figures 5–6 and 5–7. However, the intervening points, G and G', are different because different definitions of adjusted money income are used; i.e., the M' defined in Eq. (5–30) is not the same as the M'' defined in Eq. (5–31).

We can state unambiguously that the substitution effect will lead to an increase in the consumption of the commodity which has become relatively cheaper and a decrease in the consumption of the commodity which has become relatively more expensive. The new budget line must intersect the original budget line from below, since money income is lower ($M' < M$), and must have a flatter slope than the original budget line, since the price of X has fallen ($p_{x_2} < p_{x_1}$). Since indifference curves cannot intersect, the new budget line's point of tangency with some indifference curve must be below and to the right of the original equilibrium point. It is therefore

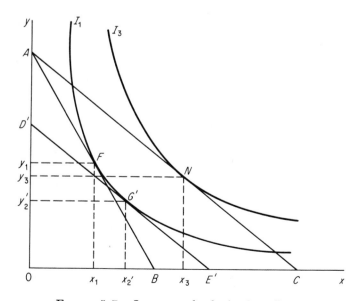

FIGURE 5–7.   Income and substitution effects.

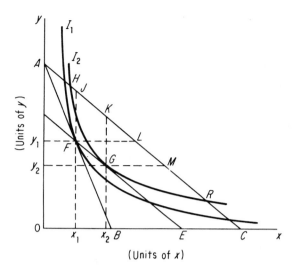

FIGURE 5–8. Possibilities for the income effect.

necessarily the case that the consumption of X will increase and the consumption of Y will decrease.

The results of the income effect are not unambiguous, however; N, the point of tangency between the new budget line AC and an indifference curve I₃, is not necessarily to the right of x_2, nor is it necessarily above y_2. The range of possibilities is shown in Figure 5–8.[5] All that we can say is that the income effect will move the household from point G to a point N on the budget line AC somewhere between H and R. Exactly where between H and R the equilibrium point N lies depends upon the degree of curvature of the indifference curve I₃. The income effect alone will tend to increase the consumption of both X and Y only if N lies somewhere between K and M. If N is between H and K, then the income effect tends to increase the consumption of Y but decrease the consumption of X; in this case, X would be an inferior commodity. If N is between M and R, then the income effect tends to increase the consumption of X but decrease the consumption of Y; in this case, Y would be an inferior commodity. It is clear that not all commodities can be inferior commodities, for the movement from G to N must increase the consumption of either X or Y or both.

The over-all result of the decrease in the price of X on the consumption of X and Y depends upon both the substitution and the income effects.

---

[5] Figure 5–8 is essentially the same as Figure 5–6, except that the indifference curve I₃ has not been drawn in Figure 5–8. From the general properties of indifference curves, we know that I₃ may be tangent to the budget line AC anywhere between H and R.

The substitution effect definitely increases the consumption of X and decreases the consumption of Y. In extreme cases, the income effect may be strong enough to overpower the substitution effect completely, as would be the case if N lies between H and J in Figure 5–8. In this case the consumption of X would be decreased (and the consumption of Y increased) even though the price of X had fallen. This is the only situation which could lead to a positively sloping individual demand curve for commodity X.[6] Note, however, that not all inferior commodities lead to positively sloping demand curves. If N were to lie between J and K, X would be an inferior commodity, but the decrease in the price of X would nevertheless lead to an increased demand for X.

Since the market demand curve for a commodity is the lateral sum of the individual demand curves of all buyers in the market for that commodity, the market demand curve must be negatively sloping as long as the underlying individual demand curves are all negatively sloping. Even if some of the individual demand curves are positively sloping, however, there may be enough buyers in the market with negatively sloping individual demand curves so that the resulting market demand curve is negatively sloping.

C. Indifference Diagrams With Money as One of the Commodities

Up to this point we have used only two commodities in our indifference curve diagrams. It is, however, possible to introduce money as one of the commodities, as shown in Figure 5–9. We have allowed the indifference curves I_1 and I_2 to intersect the money axis at points C and D. At these points of intersection the consumer would hold only money and no units of commodity X.

Introducing money into the indifference map enables us to determine visually whether the demand for commodity X is elastic or inelastic between two particular prices. Suppose the consumer's income is M. In Figure 5–9 the intercept of the budget line on the money axis is M, since the price of a unit of money is 1. If the price of X is p_{x_1}, the consumer will hold OA of money and buy x_1 of X. If the price of X decreases to p_{x_2}, the consumer will hold OB of money and buy x_2 of X. The amount of money spent on commodity X is measured downward from M, and since more money is spent when the price of X falls to p_{x_2}, the demand curve for X is elastic between p_{x_1} and p_{x_2}.

---

[6] This statement implicitly rests on the assumption that indifference curves are not functions of prices; i.e., that the indifference map is fixed regardless of prevailing market prices. The so-called *snob effect*, in which some people value a commodity solely because of its high price (e.g., diamonds), may lead to a positively sloping demand curve. This snob effect assumes that the preference map is a function of prices.

It is also possible to develop some work-money diagrams which give us some insight into behavior. If we measure a person's hours of work per day along the abscissa, there is, of course, an upper limit at 24 hours. If we drew the indifference curves in the conventional form, i.e., convex to the origin, we would be implying that the person would be as satisfied with a combination of less money and more work as he would be with a combination of more money and less work. This is clearly nonsense—at least for most cultures. Therefore, we must draw the work-money indifference curves with a positive slope. We would not expect the work-money indifference curves to intersect the horizontal work axis (no money) or the vertical 24-hour per day work line. Thus, the work-money indifference curves have the shapes shown for curves I, II, and III in Figure 5–10. The work-money opportunity line would be positively sloping (the slope equals the hourly wage rate) and would begin at the origin, as shown for lines *OA* and *OD*.

The work-money diagram in Figure 5–10 illustrates two propositions. First, a higher hourly wage rate may result in fewer hours of labor supplied by the worker each day. The line *OD* represents a higher hourly wage rate than *OA*, but w_2 is less than w_1. Second, in order to get more hours of work beyond a certain point, it may be necessary to offer a marginal wage rate (such as an overtime premium) which is higher than the average wage

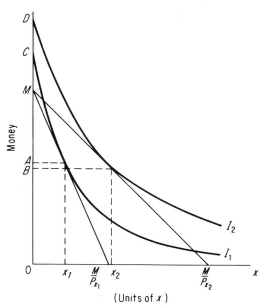

FIGURE 5–9. Indifference diagram with money as one commodity.

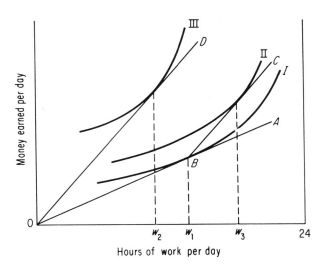

FIGURE 5–10. Work-money diagram.

rate paid up to that point. Hence, after w_1 hours of labor have been supplied during a day by the worker, he would be willing to work an additional w_3-w_1 hours that day if he were paid a higher wage rate for the incremental work. The worker's opportunity line then becomes OBC, and curve II is the highest work-money indifference curve which is tangent to it.

These few examples have been offered to show the versatility of the indifference curve technique. A large number of additional examples which throw light on observed phenomena could be given.

IV. Some Recent Developments in Demand Theory

We have discussed the theory of demand in a relatively elementary form. The primary aim of demand theory is to determine through the study of consumer behavior the variables that affect the shape and position of the market demand curve. Economists studying consumer behavior have been moving in two different directions. Some recent work has attempted to formalize the foundations of this theory. Its orientation has been toward determining the least restrictive set of assumptions necessary to derive the important propositions of demand theory. A second area of interest has centered on the empirical investigation of consumer behavior by modern econometric techniques. We briefly examine each of these areas to indicate what is involved.

A. Improving the Analytical Foundations

J. R. Hicks, an English economist, has attempted to specify the underlying postulates for the theory of demand.[7] The three basic assumptions are:

1. Consumers behave according to a scale of preferences.
2. The preference ordering is a weak ordering.
3. More of a commodity is always preferred to less of it.

To understand the second assumption, it is necessary to discuss the concept of *ordering*. A *weak* ordering can best be understood by contrasting it with an alternative, *strong* ordering. The latter is the kind of ordering with which we are familiar. It is an ordering of a group of items in which each item has a specific place. The alphabet is an example of a strong ordering. Although a weak ordering may have some individual items which are equivalent to one another, all the items in a weak ordering can be put into groups that are themselves strongly ordered. For instance, suppose we ordered people on the basis of birthdays (without regard to years). In a large enough population there would be some people whose birthdays were the same. Thus the groups of birthdays could be strongly ordered, but within a group there would be no ordering. Consumer preferences are clearly an example of weak, rather than strong, ordering since all commodity bundles on the same indifference curve are not ordered although the indifference curves themselves are strongly ordered.

Weak ordering is examined by Hicks and shown to depend upon two conditions: (a) the two-term consistency condition; (b) the transitivity condition. The two-term consistency condition may be stated as:

(a) If P is not right of Q, Q is not left of P.
(b) If P is not left of Q, Q is not right of P.

These conditions probably seem like obvious nonsense to the reader who has not been exposed to the logical problems of ordering. To get a better understanding of the use of these conditions in an ordering problem and to show the necessity of adding the transitivity condition, let us examine one of Hicks' illustrations.

Suppose we are ordering a group of people with respect to a person P. We use the rule that people to the left of P are older siblings and people to the right of P are younger siblings. The two-term consistency condition is then met. It tells us that if P is not a younger sibling of Q, Q is not an older sibling of P; and if P is not an older sibling of Q, Q is not a younger

---

[7] J. R. Hicks, *A Revision of Demand Theory* (Oxford: The Oxford University Press, 1956). This approach to analyzing consumer behavior is known as the theory of *revealed preferences*.

sibling of P. This leaves a group that is neutral to P. This neutral group may include both twins and people not related by the sibling relationship. Thus we need a means of separating out twins from people who are not siblings of each other. This is done by the transitivity condition.

The transitivity condition states that if Q is not right of P, and R is not right of Q, then R is not right of P (and similarly for the other direction, not left of). It can also be shown that if P is neutral to Q and Q is left of R, then P is left of R (and similarly for the other direction).

Now it is possible to show that unordered items (as previously occurred for the possibility of both twins and unrelated people) can be excluded. Thus in the previous ordering it was not possible to say that if Q is not a younger sibling of P and R is not a younger sibling of Q, then R will not be a younger sibling of P. R could well be a younger sibling of P even though Q is unrelated to either P or R. But if we insist on the transitivity condition holding for a population, then we know that the population can consist only of siblings (including the possibility of twins). Thus these complicated, but common-sense, logical rules (the two-term consistency condition and the transitivity condition) guide in establishing a proper ordering relationship.

Hicks has shown that the Law of Demand, which states that demand curves are negatively sloping, can be derived on the basis of his three fundamental postulates. His derivation indicates that in order to have

> ...an exception to the rule that consumption tends to increase, when price falls and other things remain equal, three things are necessary
> (i) the commodity must be an inferior good, with a negative income-elasticity of significant size,
> (ii) the substitution effect must be small,
> (iii) the proportion of income spent upon the inferior good must be large.[8]

It can also be shown that any consumer whose behavior is consistent with Hicks' three postulates necessarily possesses a complete indifference map with all the properties usually ascribed to indifference curves. Furthermore, it can be shown that such a consumer's indifference curves can be empirically determined by confronting him with various appropriately chosen sets of prices and incomes and observing his purchases; the greater the number of sets of prices and incomes that are used, the more accurately will the indifference curves be approximated.[9]

B. Empirical Investigations of Consumer Behavior

In the present century, economists have utilized modern econometric techniques to obtain a rich empirical understanding of consumer behavior.

---

[8] *Ibid.*, pp. 66–67.

[9] The proofs of the assertions in this paragraph are found in H. S. Houthakker, "Revealed Preference and the Utility Function," *Economica*, new ser., 17 (May, 1950), 159–74.

TABLE 5–1

PERCENTAGES OF INCOME SPENT BY BRITISH FAMILIES ON VARIOUS CATEGORIES*

	Working-Class Families	Middle-Class Families
Food	39	23
Housing	12	12
Clothing	9	9
Fuel and light	6	6
Tobacco	3	2
Newspapers and books	1.5	1.5

* These data are adapted from S. J. Prais and H. S. Houthakker, *The Analysis of Family Budgets* (Cambridge: Cambridge University Press, 1955), table 19, pp. 104–105. Since we have not provided an exhaustive classification of expenditures, the percentages shown do not add to 100.

By applying statistical estimation procedures to both aggregate market transactions data and data on the purchases of individual households, it has been possible to obtain empirical estimates of the market demand curves for particular commodities and groups of commodities, to measure empirically various types of demand elasticities, and to make empirically validated predictions about the behavior of specific groups of consumers in particular circumstances. In this section we present brief illustrations of some types of econometric investigations of consumer behavior.

By analyzing data on the budgets of individual families, it is possible to establish a number of important empirical relationships about consumer behavior. As an example, we shall discuss some work which has been done on the relationship between the income of a family and its expenditures on a particular commodity. In the nineteenth century an English economist, Ernst Engel, published the proposition: " . . . the proportion of expenditure devoted to food decreases as the standard of living of the household increases." This assertion is known as Engel's law.[10]

Some recent empirical research by Prais and Houthakker has enriched the original investigations of Engel by taking into account the size of the consuming unit and the curvature of the expenditure-income relationship. In their study, which was conducted in the United Kingdom, Prais and Houthakker classified families according to their economic status. Some summary comparisons of the percentages of their total income that working-class and middle-class families allocated to various categories are given in Table 5–1. The percentages of income spent on food provide evidence for the validity of Engel's law.

[10] For an extensive discussion of Engel's law, see S. J. Prais and H. S. Houthakker, *The Analysis of Family Budgets* (Cambridge: Cambridge University Press, 1955), chap. 7; the quotation is from p. 79.

TABLE 5-2

FOOD CONSUMPTION BY SWEDISH FAMILIES IN DIFFERENT SOCIAL STRATA

| | | Food Expenditure | |
Social Stratum	Average Income per Household (crowns)	Average per Household (crowns)	Per Cent of Income
1. Farm and forestry workers	1704	862	50.6
2. Small farmers	1952	833	42.7
3. Industrial workers and low-grade employees	4079	1382	33.9
4. Middle-class families	7725	1732	22.4

Prais and Houthakker's results are in close agreement with the conclusions of a study of Wold and Jureen which utilized budget data on Swedish families.[11] These results, summarized in Table 5-2, where the social strata are arranged in order of increasing income levels, provide additional empirical evidence for Engel's law. As income rises, the percentage spent on food declines. One point of interest is the similarity in the percentage of income spent on food by the middle-class families in both the British and the Swedish surveys.

Wold and Jureen also computed the income elasticity for food. Income elasticity is similar to the concept of price elasticity, except that income rather than price is regarded as the independent variable. More specifically, income elasticity is the ratio of the relative change in consumption to the relative change in income. Wold and Jureen found that the income elasticity of food shows a clear tendency to decrease as income increases. The average income elasticity for all family strata in the Swedish study was approximately 0.50. If this income elasticity can be regarded as constant, then a 10 per cent increase in income will be accompanied by a 5 per cent increase in expenditures on food.[12]

One question that arises is whether social factors affect consumer habits independently of income and cause the fall in the income elasticity or whether rising income is the causal variable. Wold and Jureen present evidence which suggests that income is the causal variable. Their evidence

---

[11] Herman Wold and Lars Jureen, *Demand Analysis* (New York: John Wiley & Sons, Inc., 1953), chap. 16. Table 5-2 has been adapted from Wold and Jureen's table 16.4.1, p. 258.

[12] It is interesting to note that Fox obtained virtually the same result; in an analysis based on budget data for urban families in the United States during the spring of 1948, he estimated that the income elasticity for food was 0.51. See Karl A. Fox, *Econometric Analysis for Public Policy* (Ames, Iowa: Iowa State College Press, 1958), p. 127.

results from constructing an artificial stratum by merging strata 1, 2, and 4. This gives a stratum with an average income only slightly smaller than the average income of stratum 3. The income elasticities are the same for the artificial stratum as for stratum 3, a fact which leads Wold and Jureen to "... the conclusion that the income level is the factor of primary importance behind the differences in the income elasticity for food, and that the social factors have only a small or negligible influence on this elasticity."[13]

Market demand curves for particular commodities or groups of commodities have been estimated using aggregate market data. Using annual data for the United States during the period 1922 through 1941, Girshick and Haavelmo have analyzed the market demand function for food. Their empirical work rested, in part, on the following type of theoretical reasoning:

> If one divides total consumption into two groups, food and nonfood, one could say, by analogy from the microtheory of consumers' choice, that the per capita demand for food is a function of the price of food, the price of nonfood, and the per capita disposable income.... The demand for food may be subject to a trend due to changes in taste, eating habits, etc.... Still another alternative would be that the consumption of food also depends, to some extent, on past income....[14]

Girshick and Haavelmo translated this theoretical reasoning into a particular mathematical equation representing the demand function for food. Using refined statistical procedures, they obtained the following estimate for this function:

$$F = 97.677 - 0.246 \frac{p_f}{p} + 0.247\, Y + 0.051\, Y_{-1} - 0.104\, t. \quad (5\text{--}32)$$

In this demand function, F is per capita food consumption in constant prices; p_f is an index of retail food prices; p is the consumer price index; Y is per capita disposable income during the current year; Y_{-1} is per capita disposable income during the past year, and t is a time trend. Equation (5–32) provides some empirical evidence for the Law of Demand, which states that market demand curves are negatively sloping. According to (5–32), the demand for food in the United States between 1922 and 1941 decreased as the price of food increased. Furthermore, the income effect was positive (i.e., food was not an inferior good), since the demand for food increased as income increased. Finally, food and nonfood expenditures were partially substitutable for each other, since an increase in the price of nonfood items relative to food items (i.e., a decrease in p_f/p) led to an increased demand for food.

---

[13] Wold and Jureen, *op. cit.*, p. 259.

[14] M. A. Girshick and Trygve Haavelmo, "Statistical Analysis of the Demand for Food: Examples of Simultaneous Estimation of Structural Equations," in *Studies in Econometric Methods*, Cowles Commission Monograph No. 14, ed. William C. Hood and Tjalling C. Koopmans (New York: John Wiley & Sons, Inc., 1953), pp. 100–101.

Statistical techniques have also often been used to estimate the price elasticities of demand for different commodities and groups of commodities. For example, using annual data for the period 1922 through 1941 in the United States, Fox has obtained the following interesting results:

> First, it will be noted that the demand elasticities for livestock products at the retail price level are all less (in absolute value) than unity. For food livestock products as a group, elasticity of demand during 1922–41 seems to have been slightly more than −.5. The elasticity of demand for all meat appears to have been slightly more than −.6. Demand elasticities for individual meats, assuming that supplies of other meats remain constant, ranged from −.8 for pork and beef to at least −.9 for lamb. It is possible that the true elasticity of demand for lamb (with supplies of other meats held constant) was somewhat more than −1.0.
>
> ...it seems likely that the elasticities of consumer demand for chicken and turkey were approximately −1.0. The elasticity of demand for eggs is estimated at −.26.[15]

A great many additional examples could be provided to illustrate the type of empirical research on consumer behavior that is being done by combining the type of theoretical analysis contained in this chapter with modern econometric techniques. This research has demonstrated the operational relevance of microeconomic theory for understanding the ways in which the decisions of consumers affect the allocation of resources in the economy.

V. Summary

In this chapter we have shown that the shape and position of the market demand curve for any commodity is determined by the consumption decisions of individual households. In making these decisions, households need to make comparisons among commodities having diverse characteristics. We assumed that they used a utility function for this purpose. A *utility function* indicates the amount of utility (or satisfaction) that a consumer receives from various amounts of different commodities. It was not necessary to assume that utility is cardinally measurable; all the properties of utility functions and demand curves that we have derived in this chapter require only the weaker assumption that utility is ordinally measurable.

In discussing consumer behavior, it was convenient to represent a utility function by means of indifference curves. Each point on an indifference curve is a consumption bundle, i.e., a specification of the amounts of each commodity that the consumer has. All consumption bundles located on the same indifference curve provide the same degree of utility to the consumer. Hence an indifference curve is a boundary between points preferred and

---

[15] Fox, *op. cit.*, p. 115. Fox used the words "more" and "less," when talking about demand elasticities, to refer to absolute values. Thus an "elasticity of demand...slightly more than −.5" should be regarded as between −.5 and −.6.

points not preferred; any point above an indifference curve is preferred to any point on the curve, whereas any point on the indifference curve is preferred to any point below the curve. Indifference curves may never intersect. As long as the commodities represented along the axes are positively desired goods, then indifference curves will be negatively sloping.

Since no consumer has unlimited resources to spend, he cannot choose any arbitrary consumption bundle. His achievable consumption opportunities are limited by his budget constraint, which states that a consumer may not buy more than his income permits. The budget line is the boundary between attainable and unobtainable consumption bundles. As long as the decisions of an individual consumer have no effect on market prices, his budget line will be a negatively sloping straight line.

The particular commodity bundle (i.e., consumption decision) which is optimal for a household can be determined by maximizing its utility function subject to its budget constraint. The result of this constrained maximization problem indicates that the optimal consumption decision for a household is to buy that commodity bundle represented by the point of tangency between his budget line and an indifference curve. At this optimal point, the marginal utility obtained from the last penny spent on any one commodity purchased must equal the marginal utility obtained from the last penny spent on every other commodity purchased.

Any household's demand curve for any particular commodity can be derived with the help of the preceding analysis. For any particular set of commodity prices and income level, the household's optimal consumption pattern is determined by the solution to a constrained maximization problem. To trace the relationship between the price of a particular commodity and the amount of that commodity demanded by the household, it is only necessary to vary the price of that particular commodity while holding constant the prices of all other commodities and the household's income, and to observe how the optimal consumption pattern changes as a result. In this way we showed that a household's demand for any commodity is a function not only of the price of that commodity but also of the prices of all other commodities, the household's income, and the household's tastes.

The market demand curve for any commodity can be obtained by laterally adding the individual households' demand curves for that same commodity, where this summation extends over all households actually or potentially in the market. The market demand for a commodity depends not only upon the price of that commodity but also upon the prices of other commodities, consumer income, and those variables which influence consumer tastes.

In addition to using utility theory as the basis for deriving demand curves, we also applied it to discussions of income-consumption curves, income and substitution effects, and indifference diagrams with money as one of the commodities. An income-consumption curve shows the manner in which the consumption of any commodity varies as income varies, while prices remain constant. In graphical terms, an income-consumption curve is determined by the locus of points of tangency between a parallel set of budget lines and the set of indifference curves. If the consumption of a commodity decreases as income increases, then that commodity is called an *inferior commodity*.

To determine the effects of a price change on consumption, it is useful to decompose this effect into two parts: the income effect and the substitution effect. Conceptually this is done in the following manner. Suppose that we wish to determine the effects on consumption of a fall in the price of one commodity. We first determine the effect on consumption if after the price change the consumer's income were adjusted so that it was just sufficient to allow purchase of the original commodity bundle at the new prices. We showed that the consumer would then increase his consumption of the one commodity whose price had fallen and decrease his consumption of some other commodities. The effect of this price change on consumption is called the *substitution effect*. We next determine the effect on consumption of increasing the consumer's income by the difference between his original income and the adjusted income used in the first step. The effect of this income change on consumption is called the *income effect*. Although we can state unambiguously that the substitution effect leads to an increase in the consumption of the commodity which has become relatively cheaper and a decrease in the consumption of some commodities which have become relatively more expensive, we are not certain what result the income effect will have, since the latter depends on whether any of the commodities involved are inferior goods. The over-all result of the decrease in the price of one commodity on consumption depends upon both the substitution and the income effects. This analysis indicates that for most commodities, each household's individual demand curves (and hence also the market demand curves) will be negatively sloping; i.e., that greater quantities of these commodities will be demanded at lower prices. It is logically possible, however, that there are a few commodities which are so strongly inferior and for which the income effect so overwhelms the substitution effect that they have positively sloping demand curves.

Introducing money as one of the commodities in the indifference map enables us to determine visually whether the demand for a commodity is elastic or inelastic between two particular prices. The supply curve for labor can also be investigated by means of a work-money diagram, in which one axis represents money and the other axis represents hours worked per day. By this means we have seen that the supply curve for labor is not necessarily upward sloping, since a higher hourly wage rate may result in fewer hours of labor supplied by the worker each day. Furthermore, we have seen why offering an overtime premium may be more effective than a higher average wage in obtaining additional hours of work each day beyond a particular point.

To conclude this chapter, we have briefly considered two different directions in which economists have recently been going in their study of consumer behavior. One of these directions has led to an improved formalization of the analytical foundations by determining the least restrictive set of assumptions necessary to derive the important propositions of demand theory. On the basis of only three assumptions (that consumers behave according to a scale of preferences, that this preference ordering is a weak ordering, and that more of a commodity is always preferred to less of it), it can be shown that most demand curves are downward sloping, that indifference maps exist, and that a consumer's indifference curves can be empirically approximated by confronting him with various appropriately chosen sets of prices and incomes and observing his purchases.

The second direction taken in recent economic research into consumer behavior has been econometric investigations using both aggregate market transactions data and family budget data. By analyzing family budget data, it has been possible to establish the empirical validity of Engel's law; i.e., the proportion of income spent on food decreases as family income increases. Econometric techniques permit the measurement of both the income elasticities and the price elasticities of demand for various commodities. Finally, we have seen that market demand curves for particular commodities or groups of commodities can be estimated by statistical techniques. These types of econometric investigations have demonstrated the operational relevance of microeconomic theory for understanding the ways in which consumers' decisions affect the economy-wide allocation of resources.

SUGGESTED READINGS

These recommendations are in addition to the footnote references cited in this chapter.

BECKER, GARY S., "Irrational Behavior and Economic Theory," *Journal of Political Economy*, LXX (February, 1962), 1–13.

CLARKSON, GEOFFREY P. E., *The Theory of Consumer Demand: A Critical Appraisal.* Englewood Cliffs, N.J.: Prentice-Hall, Inc., 1963.

CRAGG, J. G., AND R. S. UHLER, "The Demand for Automobiles," *Canadian Journal of Economics*, III (August, 1970), 386–406.

HICKS, J. R., *Value and Capital*, chaps. 1–3, and Mathematical Appendix. Oxford: Clarendon Press, 1948.

JOHNSON, W. R., "The Supply and Demand for Scrapped Automobiles," *Western Economic Journal,* IX (December, 1971), 441–43.

MOSTELLER, F., AND P. NOGEE, "An Experimental Measurement of Utility," *Journal of Political Economy,* LIX (1951), 371–404.

ROSETT, R. N., AND L. HUANG, "The Effect of Health Insurance on the Demand for Medical Care," *Journal of Political Economy,* LXXXI (March/April, 1973), 281–305.

SAMUELSON, PAUL ANTHONY, *Foundations of Economic Analysis,* chap. 5. Cambridge: Harvard University Press, 1955.

STIGLER, GEORGE J., "The Limitations of Statistical Demand Curves," *Journal of the American Statistical Association,* XXXIV (1939), 469–81.

Chapter Six

Derivation of the Short-Run
Market Supply Curve

In Chapter 4, we saw that the equilibrium price and output in a perfectly competitive market are determined by the intersection of a market demand curve and a market supply curve. In Chapter 5, we established the dependence of the market demand curve on the behavior of individual households. In this chapter, we shall establish the dependence of the market supply curve on the production decisions of individual firms. These decisions, motivated by entrepreneurs' attempts to maximize profits, determine the allocation of resources to the production of particular goods and services.

I. The Short-Run Cost Curves of a Firm

To understand the production decisions of a firm, it is necessary to investigate the firm's cost structure. Our analysis in this chapter applies exclusively to a short-run period, i.e., a time period during which a firm's plant and equipment remain fixed. Chapter 8 will generalize this analysis to include long-run considerations.

A. THE TOTAL COST FUNCTION

The starting point for our investigation of the firm's cost structure is its total cost function. This function specifies the total costs which the firm incurs for producing a given output during a particular time period. Let us denote these total costs by $TC(q)$, where q is the rate of output.

Economists define costs in terms of *alternative costs* or *opportunity costs*. The alternative cost doctrine states that the cost of a productive factor is the maximum value that this factor could produce in an alternative use. An equivalent definition is that the cost of using a productive factor to produce any commodity is the value of the best opportunity which is foregone by not using this factor in another way.

Economic costs cannot directly be determined from accounting figures. Major differences arise because the accountant measures cost on an historical basis, whereas the economist measures cost on an opportunity cost basis. Hence such items as depreciation, inventories, and the entrepreneur's services and capital will be valued differently by the two approaches.

B. SHORT-RUN COST FUNCTIONS DERIVED FROM THE TOTAL COST FUNCTION

1. TOTAL FIXED COST FUNCTION. Total fixed cost, $TFC(q)$, is defined as the value of total cost at a zero rate of output. Thus $TFC(q)$ is a function of q only in a trivial sense, since it is constant for all possible values of q:

$$TFC(q) = TC(0). \tag{6-1}$$

2. TOTAL VARIABLE COST FUNCTION. Total variable cost, $TVC(q)$, equals the difference between the total cost of producing q and the total fixed cost:

$$TVC(q) = TC(q) - TFC(q). \tag{6-2}$$

Thus total variable cost is that portion of total cost which varies with the rate of output.

The relations among the three types of total cost functions are illustrated graphically in Figure 6–1.

3. AVERAGE FIXED COST FUNCTION. Corresponding to the three types of total costs, there are three notions of average costs. Each average is simply an ordinary arithmetic mean.

Average fixed cost, $AFC(q)$, is the fixed cost per unit of output:

$$AFC(q) = \frac{TFC(q)}{q}. \tag{6-3}$$

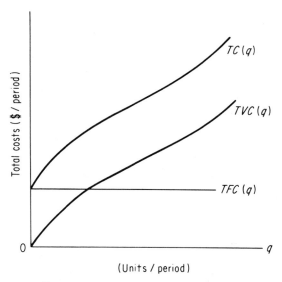

FIGURE 6–1.   Three total cost functions.

4. AVERAGE VARIABLE COST FUNCTION. Average variable cost, $AVC(q)$, is the variable cost per unit of output:

$$AVC(q) = \frac{TVC(q)}{q}. \tag{6-4}$$

5. AVERAGE TOTAL COST FUNCTION. Average total cost, $ATC(q)$, is the total cost per unit of output:

$$ATC(q) = \frac{TC(q)}{q}. \tag{6-5}$$

6. MARGINAL COST FUNCTION. The marginal cost function, $MC(q)$, is the rate of change in total cost with respect to changes in output:

$$MC(q) = \frac{d}{dq}[TC(q)]. \tag{6-6}$$

The general concept of marginal value has already been explained in Chapter 3; marginal cost is a special case of this concept. Since the total fixed cost is constant, the marginal cost also equals the derivative of total variable cost:

$$MC(q) = \frac{d}{dq}[TVC(q)]. \tag{6-7}$$

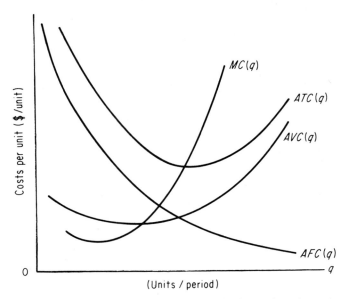

FIGURE 6–2. Average and marginal cost functions.

The relations among the three types of average cost curves and the marginal cost curve are illustrated graphically in Figure 6–2.

C. SOME PROPERTIES OF THE COST FUNCTIONS

Some general relations between marginal values and average values were proved in Chapter 3. These relations can be stated in terms of marginal and average costs. It is unnecessary to provide any additional proofs of them, however, since the original proofs remain valid under this new interpretation.

> *Theorem 1. When average (total or variable) cost is at its minimum, marginal cost equals average (total or variable) cost.*

> *Theorem 2. When average (total or variable) cost is increasing, marginal cost is greater than average (total or variable) cost. When average (total or variable) cost is decreasing, marginal cost is less than average (total or variable) cost. When average (total or variable) cost is neither increasing nor decreasing, marginal cost is equal to average (total or variable) cost.*

Figure 6–2 illustrates these theorems. There is one additional theorem of interest which relates the marginal cost function and the total variable cost function:

> *Theorem 3. The numerical value of the area under the marginal cost function from an output of 0 to an output of Q equals the numerical value of the height of the total variable cost curve at an output of Q.*

Symbolically, Theorem 3 states:

$$\int_0^Q MC(q) \, dq = TVC(Q). \tag{6-8}$$

To establish Eq. (6-8) integrate both sides of Eq. (6-6):

$$\int_0^Q MC(q) \, dq = \int_0^Q \frac{d}{dq} TC(q) \, dq. \tag{6-9}$$

Since integration and differentiation are inverse operations, Eq. (6-9) simplifies to

$$\int_0^Q MC(q) \, dq = TC(q) \Big]_0^Q. \tag{6-10}$$

Inserting the limits in the right-hand side of Eq. (6-10), we obtain the difference between the total cost of producing Q and the total cost of producing 0. The latter is, by Eq. (6-1), simply the total fixed cost for producing a rate of output Q; i.e.,

$$\int_0^Q MC(q) \, dq = TC(Q) - TFC(Q). \tag{6-11}$$

By Eq. (6-2), however, the right-hand side of Eq. (6-11) is the total variable cost of producing Q. Hence, Eq. 6-8 follows, proving Theorem 3.

II. The Short-Run Supply Curve of an Individual Firm

We now consider the role of costs in determining the output of a firm in a perfectly competitive market. It is first necessary to consider the shape of the demand function which such a firm faces.

A. THE INDIVIDUAL FIRM'S DEMAND CURVE IN PERFECT COMPETITION

In a perfectly competitive market, the demand curve for the output of any individual firm must be infinitely elastic, i.e., a horizontal line at the prevailing market price, $\bar{p}$, as illustrated in Figure 6–3. To establish this, suppose that an individual firm tried to sell its product at a price higher

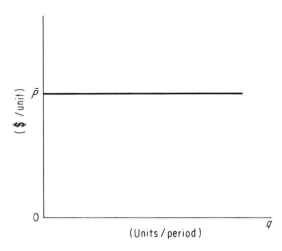

FIGURE 6–3.   Demand curve for an individual firm in perfect competition.

than that prevailing in the market. Since all buyers possess perfect information about the terms of trade other sellers are offering and since the
buyers are trying to maximize their own satisfaction, they would refuse
to trade with the higher-priced firm. Hence any seller who tried to price
his commodities above the prevailing market price would find no takers.
On the other hand, there is no reason for any individual firm to sell its
product below the prevailing market price. If it tried to do so, it would, of
course, find a horde of buyers flocking to its doors. Since, however, it could
sell at the prevailing market price any amount of its product that it could
economically produce, the firm would be irrational to charge a lower price.

In perfect competition, the demand curve for any individual firm's
output coincides with both its average revenue curve and its marginal
revenue curve. Average revenue is defined as the total revenue received
per unit of product sold. Since the firm is able to sell as much of its product
as it wishes at the prevailing market price without affecting that price, the
total revenue from selling q units is simply $\bar{p}q$. Hence the average revenue
obtained from selling q units is simply $\bar{p}$. Thus, the individual firm's demand
curve in Figure 6–3 is also its average revenue curve. Marginal revenue is
the derivative of total revenue with respect to quantity sold. Since total
revenue is $\bar{p}q$, where $\bar{p}$ is constant, marginal revenue equals $\bar{p}$. Hence the
individual firm's demand curve in perfect competition is also its marginal
revenue curve.[1]

In Chapter 10, we shall see that the demand curve, the average revenue
curve, and the marginal revenue curve for an individual firm are all coinci-

[1] Note that this result follows immediately from Theorem 3 in Chapter 3, since the
average revenue curve is a horizontal line.

dent only under perfect competition. When a firm's actions can affect the prevailing market price, then that price cannot be treated as a constant and the marginal and average revenue curves are not coincident.

B. The Short-Run Supply Curve of an Individual Firm

It is easy to determine the most profitable rate of output for a firm operating in a perfectly competitive market. Let $\pi(q)$ be the profits a firm obtains from producing and selling q:

$$\pi(q) = \bar{p}q - TC(q). \qquad (6\text{--}12)$$

For any positive rate of output to result in maximum profits (or minimum losses) for the firm, it is necessary that the derivative of profits with respect to output equals zero:[2]

$$\frac{d\pi(q)}{dq} = \bar{p} - \frac{d}{dq}[TC(q)] = 0. \qquad (6\text{--}13)$$

Substituting Eq. (6–6) into Eq. (6–13) and solving,

$$MC(q) = \bar{p}. \qquad (6\text{--}14)$$

In order for a firm to be maximizing its profits, Eq. (6–14) states that it should be producing an output for which its marginal cost equals the prevailing market price.[3]

In order to insure that Eq. (6–14) leads to a point of maximum profits, instead of minimum profits or a turning point in profits, the second derivative of profits must be negative:

$$\frac{d^2\pi(q)}{dq^2} = -\frac{dMC(q)}{dq} < 0 \qquad (6\text{--}15)$$

i.e.,

$$\frac{d}{dq}MC(q) > 0. \qquad (6\text{--}16)$$

---

[2] We can use the differential calculus to find the rate of output, q, which will maximize the firm's profits, $\pi(q)$, provided that π is a continuous and differentiable function of q. From Eq. (6–12), this will be the case if TC is a continuous and differentiable function of q. In reality this is probably not the case. Our purpose in conducting this investigation is not to describe in detail the behavior of individual firms *per se*, but rather, to focus on industry-wide and market-wide behavior. The simplifying assumptions conventionally made in the theory of the firm lead to implications which are generally useful in answering questions about resource allocation among industries and markets. Therefore, we shall assume that TC is a continuous and differentiable function of q for all positive values of q.

[3] There is no guarantee, of course, that the firm will in fact be able to earn positive profits. Since losses are negative profits, a firm which is maximizing its profits is also minimizing its losses. Although it may be more appropriate to speak of minimizing losses when a firm is unable to earn positive profits, for convenience we shall usually speak in terms of maximizing profits.

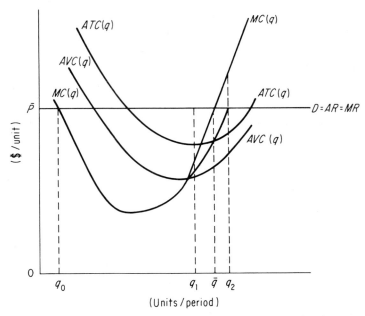

FIGURE 6–4. Conditions when a positive output is optimal.

Hence for a firm to achieve maximum profit levels, it is both necessary and sufficient that it operate at a rate of output where its marginal cost equals the prevailing market price, and also in a region of output where its marginal costs are increasing.[4]

These results are illustrated graphically in Figure 6–4, where $\bar{q}$ is the optimal rate of production for the firm, i.e., the level of output for which marginal cost is upward sloping and equal to the prevailing market price $\bar{p}$. At a rate of output q_0, marginal cost also equals market price; but since at that point marginal cost is decreasing, q_0 is an operating level which would result in minimum, rather than maximum, profits for the firm.

The geometric language can also be used to verify that $\bar{q}$ is the output level where profits are maximized. Consider a rate of output q_1, slightly less than $\bar{q}$. At q_1, the firm's marginal cost curve lies below its marginal revenue curve. Hence if output is increased by one unit, total revenue will be increased by $\bar{p}$, while total costs will be raised by $MC(q_1)$. Since

$$\bar{p} > MC(q_1), \tag{6–17}$$

total profits will be increased. Thus any lower rate of output than $\bar{q}$, e.g., q_1, could not be a rate of output which maximizes profits because a slight increase in production will raise profits.

Similarly a slightly larger rate of output than $\bar{q}$, e.g., q_2, can be shown to be nonoptimal. At a rate of output q_2, the marginal cost curve is above the marginal revenue curve. Hence if production is decreased by one unit, total costs will be reduced by $MC(q_2)$, while total revenue will be decreased by only $\bar{p}$. Since

$$MC(q_2) > \bar{p}, \tag{6-18}$$

reducing output one unit will increase profits. Hence any rate of output larger than $\bar{q}$, e.g., q_2, could not be optimal.

Thus it is easy to see that a production level can be optimal only if its marginal cost equals the market price. Similar geometric reasoning applied to the other point of intersection of marginal cost and market price, q_0, shows that it is a point of minimum profits (i.e., maximum losses).

One important limitation of our analysis must be noted. In order to find the rate of output for a firm which maximizes profits, we have used the differential calculus. The procedure locates the turning points, i.e., the relative maximum or relative minimum points, of continuous functions. Although a relative maximum is often the absolute maximum, there is one particular case in connection with the production decisions of a firm when a relative maximum profit position may not be the absolute maximum profit position. This case arises when the optimal output of the firm is zero. Because a firm's production rate cannot be negative, its problem of maximizing profits should really be formulated as a constrained maximization problem:

$$\left\{ \begin{array}{l} \text{maximize } \pi(q) \\ \\ \text{subject to } q \geq 0. \end{array} \right. \tag{6-19}$$

In deriving Eq. (6–14) and Eq. (6–16) as necessary and sufficient conditions for maximizing profits, we have ignored the constraint in Eq. (6–19). A correct procedure for taking the constraint into account is to compare $\pi(\bar{q})$, where $\bar{q}$ satisfies Eq. (6–14) and Eq. (6–16), with $\pi(0)$. Only when

$$\pi(\bar{q}) \geq \pi(0) \tag{6-20}$$

will $\bar{q}$ in fact be the optimal output.

We need not, however, make the comparison shown in Eq. (6–20) because it is easier to test the equivalent condition that total revenue is greater than, or equal to, total variable cost. This equivalence may be shown by substituting Eq. (6–12) and (6–1) in Eq. (6–20):

$$\bar{p}\,\bar{q} - TC(\bar{q}) \geq -\,TFC(\bar{q}). \tag{6-21}$$

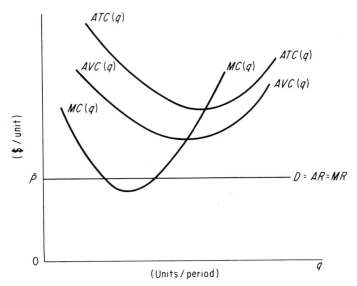

FIGURE 6–5. Conditions when zero output is optimal.

Eq. (6–2) and Eq. (6–21) together imply:

$$\bar{p}\,\bar{q} \geq TVC(\bar{q}) \tag{6–22}$$

or, equivalently, $\bar{p} \geq AVC(\bar{q}).$ (6–23)

Our discussion has shown that the firm should produce a positive output if and only if Eq. (6–23) holds. Hence when the average variable cost curve lies everywhere above the prevailing market price, as illustrated in Figure 6–5, the firm should produce nothing.[5]

The short-run supply curve of an individual firm indicates the amount that firm will produce and offer for sale in any period as a function of the prevailing market price. The preceding analysis has demonstrated that the upward sloping portion of a firm's marginal cost curve lying above its average variable cost curve is the short-run supply function of a firm selling

---

[5] A minor qualification of this last result should be noted. If the prevailing market price should fall below the average variable cost curve only temporarily, then even though in a steady state situation the firm would have greater profits (i.e., smaller losses) by shutting down rather than operating at any positive rate, it might be the case that the firm should still produce something. This would occur when the shut-down and start-up costs which a firm would incur by first discontinuing its operations and later resuming them are greater than the total out-of-pocket losses which the firm would incur by operating at some positive rate. When a firm expects the prevailing market price to remain below its average variable cost curve for a protracted period, however, then the firm should definitely discontinue its operations.

in a perfectly competitive market, and that the short-run supply function has a value of zero for all levels of market price below the minimum point on the average variable cost curve.

III. The Short-Run Market Supply Curve

We have just seen that the short-run supply curve for any individual firm selling in a perfectly competitive market has a point of discontinuity at that level of price equal to the minimum point on its average variable cost curve. The short-run supply curve for an entire market is obtained, of course, by adding laterally the short-run supply curves for each firm. In Chapter 4 we drew the short-run market supply curve as a continuous function of market price. How can we obtain a continuous function by adding together a large number of discontinuous functions?

This outcome can be rationalized by recalling that any perfectly competitive market consists of an extremely large number of individual sellers. It is unlikely that the minimum points on the average variable cost curves for each firm occur at the same level of market price. If they should so occur, then the short-run market supply curve would necessarily possess a point of discontinuity at that minimum level, for if the market price were any lower, nobody would produce anything for sale. As long as the height of the minimum point on each firm's average variable cost curve differs from firm to firm, the short-run market supply curve which results from the lateral addition of all the individual short-run supply curves will be much smoother than any of the individual curves. In minute detail, the short-run market supply curve would have points of discontinuity at each level of market price which corresponds to a minimum point on some firm's individual average variable cost curve. Since there are an extremely large number of sellers in any perfectly competitive market, however, these discontinuities do not significantly affect the construction of the short-run market supply curve. Hence for convenience we always treat the short-run market supply curve as though it were a continuous function.

Because the short-run market supply curve is obtained by a lateral addition of the individual firm's short-run supply curves, and since each of these individual functions is upward sloping, it necessarily follows that the short-run market supply curve must be upward sloping.[6]

The general notion of elasticity which we defined in Chapter 3 is applicable to our various supply curves. The elasticity of supply is defined as the relative change in quantity supplied divided by a relative change in price. The larger the value of this elasticity, the more responsive are the producers to changes in price. An infinitely elastic supply curve is a hori-

---

[6] We shall see in Chapter 8, however, that the *long-run* market supply curve is not necessarily upward sloping.

zontal line. A completely inelastic supply curve is a vertical line. Most supply curves are neither infinitely elastic nor completely inelastic.

Since the short-run market supply curve results from the horizontal addition of the short-run supply curves for a large number of individual firms, it is obvious that the exact short-run market supply curve which results depends upon the number of firms there are in the market. So far, we have said nothing about how this number is determined. Changes in the number of firms in a market occur because of the entry or exit of firms. The considerations governing this phenomenon will be discussed in Chapter 8.

IV. Empirical Studies

We have presented in this chapter the theoretical framework for the derivation of short-run cost curves for the firm and the derivation of the short-run market supply curve. In our derivation we have assumed a U shape for our average total cost and average variable cost curves. This shape is the traditional one assumed in the theory. A number of economists have, however, done a great deal of work directed toward using statistical techniques to determine actual cost curves. Statistical techniques have also been used to estimate market supply functions.

A. STATISTICAL COST FUNCTIONS

Johnston has provided a comprehensive review of the extant studies of statistical cost curves. He concludes "... that the various short-run studies more often than not indicate constant marginal cost and declining average cost as the pattern that best seems to describe the data that have been analyzed."[7] An example of this pattern of cost curves is given in Figure 6–6.

The implication of this set of curves has not been completely analyzed. One problem arises because the range of output for which the marginal costs are constant is not known. There is some evidence that the condition is true over wide ranges of output. Perhaps the most important theoretical implication of this result is that it increases the importance of new approaches, such as those described in Chapter 17, in which the internal decision-making processes are analyzed. This follows because cost curves such as those in Figure 6–6 do not give a unique profit-maximizing solution. Thus knowledge of the firm's decision-making techniques becomes of increasing importance. We are not prepared at this time, however, to argue that the classical theory should be completely discarded because of these empirical results. Insights into the operation of the economy are still the main advantages to be gained from a study of this book. These insights are

---

[7] J. Johnston, *Statistical Cost Analysis* (New York: McGraw-Hill Book Company, Inc., 1960), p. 168.

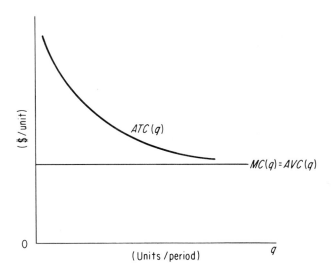

FIGURE 6-6. Declining average total cost and constant average variable and marginal cost curves.

not necessarily dependent upon the empirical validity of the set of cost curves utilized.

It is also useful to look at some of the empirical data on cost curves. One of the earliest studies was conducted by T. O. Yntema at U.S. Steel.[8] In preparation for a government hearing on its price behavior, U.S. Steel had Yntema make an intensive study of its operations. Yntema concluded that the total cost curve for U.S. Steel between 1927 and 1938 was

$$TC(q) = 182.1 + 55.73q, \tag{6-24}$$

where $TC(q)$ is measured in millions of dollars and q in millions of tons. Such a total cost curve leads to the set of curves shown in Figure 6-6. The AVC and MC are constant (55.73) and

$$ATC = 55.73 + \frac{182.1}{q}. \tag{6-25}$$

Johnston studied data from firms generating electricity in England.[9] In twelve of seventeen cases the best-fitting total cost function was a linear equation containing only a linear term in the output. A typical example is

$$TC(q) = 3.9 + 2.048q, \tag{6-26}$$

---

[8] Yntema's study is summarized in *ibid.*, pp. 143–44.

[9] *Ibid.*, pp. 44–73

where $TC(q)$ is measured in thousands of £'s and q in millions of kilowatt-hours. These curves were derived by use of a statistical technique, regression analysis. There are other forms for some of the cost functions and certain statistical problems involved in the work which will not be discussed here. In our opinion this kind of empirical research is of critical importance to the theory of the firm, and the results must be incorporated into the body of classical theory.

B. MARKET SUPPLY FUNCTIONS

As part of their analysis of the demand for food in the United States between 1922 and 1941 (see Chapter 5, Section IV.B), Girshick and Haavelmo also estimated the market supply functions for two different segments in the distribution chain. Realizing that there was an independent commercial sector lying between the consuming public and the farmers, they found it useful to develop one supply function describing the supply of food from the commercial sector to the retail market and a second supply function describing the supply of food from farmers to the commercial sector.

Girshick and Haavelmo's estimates of these two supply functions rested on sound theoretical reasoning. For example, they felt that the supply of finished food products at retail would be positively related to the retail price, i.e., that the market supply curve would be upward sloping. Furthermore, they reasoned that the quantity of food supplied at retail would be positively related to the ". . . farm output of foodstuff, assuming that the farmer *has to sell* once the foodstuff has been produced."[10] Finally, they expected a time trend in the retail supply function to reflect the gradual change in processing and marketing techniques.

This theoretical reasoning was translated into a particular mathematical equation representing the supply function for food in the retail market. Using refined econometric techniques, Girshick and Haavelmo obtained the following estimate of the retail supply function for food in the United States between 1922 and 1941:

$$F = 13.319 + 0.157 \frac{p_f}{p} + 0.653A + 0.339t. \qquad (6\text{--}27)$$

In this retail supply function, F is per capita food consumption in constant prices; p_f is an index of retail food prices; p is the consumer price index; A is per capita food production in constant prices; and t is a time trend. Note that all the variables in Eq. (6–27) have the algebraic signs expected from theoretical considerations.

___

[10] M. A. Girshick and Trygve Haavelmo, "Statistical Analysis of the Demand for Food: Examples of Simultaneous Estimation of Structural Equations," in *Studies in Econometric Methods*, Cowles Commission Monograph No. 14, ed. William C. Hood and Tjalling C. Koopmans (New York: John Wiley & Sons, Inc., 1953), p. 103.

The theoretical foundation Girshick and Haavelmo provided for the market supply function of food from farmers to the commercial sector was, in part, the following:

> For many farm products one might consider current output as a result of decisions based on *past* prices and other variables not related to the current market situation, such as weather, pasture conditions, available acreage, etc. The farmers have, on the other hand, undoubtedly some possibilities of almost instantaneous adjustment to the current price situation. They can speed up or slow down the feeding of livestock, put more labor, or less labor, into harvesting crops, etc. Other products, such as vegetables or poultry, may have a period of production much shorter than a year. When we use annual data it would, therefore, seem necessary to include current prices as a variable influencing farm output of food. A trend might account for certain technological changes in technique of production, changes in the farm population, etc.[11]

Girshick and Haavelmo translated this theoretical reasoning into a particular mathematical equation representing the market supply function for food by farmers to the commercial sector. Using refined statistical procedures, they obtained the following estimate for this function:

$$A = 81.250 + 0.556 \frac{p_a}{p} - 0.300 \left(\frac{p_a}{p}\right)_{-1} - 0.190t. \qquad (6\text{--}28)$$

The new variable introduced in Eq. (6–28) is p_a, an index of food prices received by farmers; $(p_a/p)_{-1}$ is last year's value of the ratio of the index of food prices received by farmers to the consumer price index. By rewriting Eq. (6–28) in the equivalent form,

$$A = 81.250 + 0.556 \left[\frac{p_a}{p} - \left(\frac{p_a}{p}\right)_{-1}\right] + 0.256 \left(\frac{p_a}{p}\right)_{-1} - 0.190t, \qquad (6\text{--}29)$$

it is seen that the supply of food by farmers in the United States between 1922 and 1941 was positively related to the change in the relative prices farmers received. This market supply curve was upward sloping, it had a downward time trend, and it was shifted upward by positive changes in the relative prices received by farmers.

A great many additional examples could be provided to illustrate the type of empirical research on cost functions and market supply curves that is being done by combining the type of theoretical analysis contained in this chapter with modern econometric techniques.

V. Summary

The shape and position of the short-run market supply curve for any product depends upon the production decisions of individual firms. This

---

[11] *Ibid.*, pp. 103–104.

dependence was established by first starting with an investigation of the firm's cost structure. In this chapter we considered only a short-run period, when the firm's plant and equipment are fixed. Changes in the firm's production then result from changes in the degree of intensity with which the fixed plant and equipment are utilized.

The total cost function specifies the total costs which the firm incurs in producing a given output during a particular time period. Economists measure costs on an alternative cost or opportunity cost basis. This means that we consider the cost of using a productive factor to produce any commodity as the value of the best opportunity which is foregone by not using this factor in any other way.

Six other short-run cost functions were defined in terms of the total cost function. The total fixed cost function (which is really a constant) is the value of total cost at a zero rate of output. The total variable cost function is the difference between the total cost of producing some output and the total fixed cost. The average fixed cost function is the fixed cost per unit of output. The average variable cost function is the variable cost per unit of output. The average total cost function is the total cost per unit of output. The marginal cost function is the derivative of the total cost function.

Some general relations between marginal values and average values that were proved in Chapter 3 were stated in terms of marginal and average costs. In particular, the marginal cost curve intersects the average total or variable cost curves at their minimum points. Furthermore, when average (total or variable) cost is increasing (or, alternatively, decreasing), the marginal cost lies above (or, alternatively, below) the average (total or variable) cost. Finally, we proved that the area under the marginal cost curve between the origin and some output rate is equivalent to the height of the total variable cost curve at that output rate.

We showed that the demand curve for the output of any individual firm in a perfectly competitive market is a horizontal line at the prevailing market price. This implies that under perfect competition the demand curve, the average revenue curve, and the marginal revenue curve for an individual firm all coincide.

The optimal output for a firm can be determined by maximizing its profit function subject to the constraint that its output must be non-negative. If the constraint is ignored, a necessary and sufficient condition for the firm to maximize profits is that it produce at the point where the marginal cost curve equals the prevailing market price and is increasing. To consider the constraint, however, the firm must determine whether a zero rate of output would be more profitable (i.e., result in lower losses) than the positive rate of output which satisfies the necessary and sufficient condition just stated. It has been shown that the firm should shut down (i.e., produce no output) if and only if its average variable cost curve is entirely above the prevailing market price. If the firm can recover at least its variable production costs, then it should produce at a rate of output where its marginal cost equals the market price and where marginal costs are increasing.

The short-run supply curve of a firm was shown to be the upward sloping portion of its marginal cost curve lying above its average variable cost curve. For prices below the minimum point on its average variable cost curve, the firm's short-run supply curve coincides with the vertical (price) axis. The short-run supply curve for the market is obtained by adding laterally the short-run supply curves for each firm. We discussed the reasons why we generally treat the market supply curve as though it were a continuous function. The short-run market supply curve for any product is necessarily upward sloping.

To conclude this chapter, we briefly reviewed some of the econometric work that has been done in estimating the cost functions of firms and the market supply functions for products. The studies of cost functions raise some questions about the specific shapes of the cost curves that have been assumed in economic theory. Econometric estimates of market supply functions display the properties expected on the basis of economic theory.

SUGGESTED READINGS

These recommendations are in addition to the footnote references cited in this chapter.

BARZEL, G., AND R. S. McDONALD, "Assets, Subsistence and the Supply Curve of Labor," *American Economic Review*, LXIII (September, 1973), 621–33.

BISHOP, R. L., "Cost Discontinuities, Declining Costs and Marginal Analysis," *American Economic Review*, XXXVIII (1938), 607–17.

COWLING, K., AND A. S. RAYNES, "Price, Quality and Market Share," *Journal of Political Economy*, LXXVIII (November/December, 1970), 1292–1309.

KLEIN, LAWRENCE R., *An Introduction to Econometrics*, pp. 111–29. Englewood Cliffs, N.J.: Prentice-Hall, Inc., 1962.

MEYER, J. R., "Some Methodological Aspects of Statistical Costing as Illustrated by the Determination of Rail Passenger Costs," *American Economic Review, Papers and Proceedings*, XLVIII, No. 2 (May, 1958), 209–22.

NATIONAL BUREAU OF ECONOMIC RESEARCH, *Cost Behavior and Price Policy*, chaps. 2, 4, 5. New York: The Bureau, 1943.

STAEHLE, HANS, "The Measurement of Statistical Cost Functions: An Appraisal of Some Recent Contributions," in *Readings in Price Theory*, ed. George J. Stigler and Kenneth E. Boulding, chap. 13. Homewood, Ill.: Richard D. Irwin, Inc., 1952.

Chapter Seven

Production Decisions and the
Utilization of Resources

In deriving the short-run market supply function from the production decisions of firms, we assumed that the total cost functions for the firms were known. In this chapter we shall discuss the factors which lie behind the total cost function.

I. The Firm's Optimal Production Decisions

A. THE SHORT-RUN PRODUCTION FUNCTION OF A FIRM

In the short run, any particular firm possesses a given stock of plant and equipment. This available capital equipment, together with the present state of technology, imposes a set of technical relations which govern the possible transformations of inputs into outputs. In particular, we can view these technical relations as defining a number of constraints.

Suppose that there are M possible outputs which a firm could produce and N possible inputs which it could use. Let $q_1, q_2 \ldots , q_M$ be the amounts the firm produces of each output during a period, and let $v_1, v_2, \ldots , v_N$ be the amounts that the firm uses of each input during the same period.[1] With this notation, we can say that the constraints which limit the firm's transformations of inputs into outputs can be summarized by the mathematical relation

$$F(q_1, \ldots , q_M) = G(v_1, \ldots , v_N). \tag{7-1}$$

To interpret Eq. (7–1), suppose that we consider the quantities of all the outputs to be fixed except for output i, and that we consider the quantities of all the inputs to be fixed. Equation (7–1) then becomes

$$F(\bar{q}_1, \ldots , \bar{q}_{i-1}, q_i, \bar{q}_{i+1}, \ldots , \bar{q}_M) = G(\bar{v}_1, \ldots , \bar{v}_N). \tag{7-2}$$

The functions F and G in Eq. (7–2) determine the maximum possible amount of output i which could be produced when $\bar{v}_1, \ldots , \bar{v}_N$ units of the inputs are used and $\bar{q}_1, \ldots , \bar{q}_{i-1}, \bar{q}_{i+1}, \ldots , \bar{q}_M$ units of the other outputs are made.

A further interpretation of Eq. (7–1) is provided if we consider the quantities of all the inputs to be fixed except for input j. Equation (7–1) then becomes

$$F(\bar{q}_1, \ldots , \bar{q}_M) = G(\bar{v}_1, \ldots , \bar{v}_{j-1}, v_j, \bar{v}_{j+1}, \ldots , \bar{v}_N). \tag{7-3}$$

The functions F and G in Eq. (7–3) determine the minimum possible amount of input j which could be used if we are to produce $\bar{q}_1, \ldots , \bar{q}_M$ units of the outputs and if we are to use only $\bar{v}_1, \ldots , \bar{v}_{j-1}, \bar{v}_{j+1}, \ldots , \bar{v}_N$ units of the other inputs.

The functions F and G in Eq. (7–1) constitute the short-run *production function* of a firm. As the foregoing interpretations indicate, the production function is a boundary relationship which indicates the present limits of the firm's technical production possibilities. The production function states that a firm cannot achieve a higher rate of output without using more inputs, and that a firm cannot use fewer inputs without decreasing its rate of output. Further, the production function indicates the manner in which

---

[1] It is necessary, of course, that

$$q_i \geq 0 \qquad i = 1, 2, \ldots , M$$

and

$$v_j \geq 0 \qquad j = 1, 2, \ldots , N.$$

The dimensions of the q_i and the v_j are physical units per time period.

the firm can substitute one input for another without reducing the total amount of output, and also the manner in which the firm can substitute one output for another without altering its total usage of inputs.

Points on the production function reflect technically efficient operations on the part of the firm. If a firm is not operating on its production function, then it can produce its present output with a smaller volume of one or more inputs, or else use its present inputs to produce a larger volume of one or more outputs. In other words, a firm cannot be maximizing profits unless it is operating on its production function.

B. THE LAW OF DIMINISHING RETURNS

The "law of diminishing returns" is a frequently quoted, often misunderstood general economic principle that is sometimes treated with as much hushed reverence as is the "law of supply and demand." The law of *diminishing marginal returns* states that as equal increments of one input (e.g., iron ore) are added, the inputs of the other productive services (e.g., coke, limestone, furnace, labor) being held constant, beyond some point the resulting increments of product (e.g., pig iron) will decrease; i.e., the marginal product will diminish. Another version, the law of *diminishing average returns*, states that under exactly the same conditions the resulting average product will decrease.

Several points should be noted about the law of diminishing returns. First, a given state of technology is assumed. The law of diminishing returns says nothing about the effect of adding additional units of any one input factor, holding constant the amounts used of other input factors, when the technological processes are also being changed. Second, there must be at least one productive service whose quantity is being held constant. The law of diminishing returns says nothing about the effect on either marginal or average product of a proportional increase in the quantities used of all productive factors. Third, it must be possible to vary the proportions in which the different input factors are combined. Finally, the law of diminishing returns is intended to be an empirical generalization. In most production processes which we can observe in the real world, the law of diminishing returns seems to hold.

In Chapter 6, we usually drew U-shaped short-run average variable cost curves. Under conditions of perfect competition, when the prices which a firm pays for productive services are unrelated to the amounts purchased of these services, U-shaped short-run average variable cost curves are a consequence of the law of diminishing average returns. In the short run, the plant and productive equipment of a firm are fixed factors. With constant factor prices, the average variable cost is inversely related to the average product of the variable factors.[2] Hence U-shaped average variable cost curves are implied by the law of diminishing average returns.

C. A Special Short-Run Production Function: One Output and Two Inputs

1. ISOPRODUCT CURVES. We shall consider two special types of production functions, and for each of these special cases we shall indicate the optimal mix of inputs and outputs for the firm. The first special case is a production function consisting of one output and two inputs:

$$q = G(v_1, v_2). \tag{7-4}$$

This production function is shown in Figure 7–1.

The horizontal and the vertical axes represent the rates of usage of the first and the second input factors. In order to graph the resulting maximum rate of production, a third dimension could be used. It is more convenient, however, to use contour lines to represent particular heights of the production function surface, as illustrated in Figure 7–1. Each of the curved lines labeled q', q'', q''', and q'''' represents specific output rates. The contour q', for example, indicates all possible combinations of the two input factors which result in a rate of production q'. Without any loss of generality, we can assume that productive factors are defined and measured in such a way that as a larger quantity is used of any productive factor, a larger total output will result. With this convention, it follows that $q' < q'' < q''' < q''''$.

The contour lines in Figure 7–1 are called *isoproduct curves* or *isoquants*. An isoproduct curve is a curve along which the maximum achievable rate of production is constant. All of the isoproduct curves in Figure 7–1 are downward sloping, because output is constant along any curve and the

---

[2] For purposes of exposition, we assume that there is only one variable factor, and that v units of this factor are used. Let w be the (constant) price at which the variable factor can be purchased. We know that

$$AVC = \frac{TVC}{q} = \frac{wv}{q}.$$

Since the average product of the variable factor is defined as

$$AP = \frac{q}{v}$$

it follows that

$$AVC = \frac{w}{AP}.$$

factors are substitutable.[3] The slope of an isoproduct curve, dv_2/dv_1, is called the *rate of technical substitution* between the two factors. It is generally assumed that the rate of technical substitution (numerically) decreases as we move to the right along an isoproduct curve and (numerically) increases as we move to the left; i.e., the isoproduct curves are convex to the origin.[4]

---

[3] A more formal proof of this proposition is easily constructed. The equation for any isoquant is

$$q = G(v_1, v_2) = \text{constant}.$$

The total differential of this equation is

$$dq = \frac{\partial G}{\partial v_1} dv_1 + \frac{\partial G}{\partial v_2} dv_2 = 0.$$

Solving for the slope of an isoquant, we have

$$\frac{dv_2}{dv_1} = -\frac{\partial G/\partial v_1}{\partial G/\partial v_2}.$$

As long as the marginal product of each factor is positive, i.e., as long as

$$\frac{\partial G}{\partial v_1} > 0 \quad \text{and} \quad \frac{\partial G}{\partial v_2} > 0$$

it follows that the slope of an isoquant is negative.

[4] In formal terms, we generally assume that along an isoproduct curve,

$$\frac{d^2 v_2}{dv_1^2} = \frac{d}{dv_1}\left(\frac{dv_2}{dv_1}\right) > 0.$$

Let us now investigate the conditions under which this assumption will be valid. To simplify the analysis, the following abbreviated notation will be used:

$$G_i = \frac{\partial G}{\partial v_i}; \; G_{ii} = \frac{\partial^2 G}{\partial v_i^2}; \; G_{ij} = \frac{\partial^2 G}{\partial v_i \, \partial v_j} \quad \text{for all } i \text{ and } j.$$

The preceding footnote established that

$$\frac{dv_2}{dv_1} = -\frac{G_1}{G_2}.$$

We must determine the conditions under which the derivative with respect to v_1 of this expression will be positive. To obtain this derivative, the formula for differentiating a quotient yields

$$\frac{d}{dv_1}\left[\frac{dv_2}{dv_1}\right] = -\frac{1}{G_2^2}\left[G_2\left(\frac{dG_1}{dv_1}\right) - G_1\left(\frac{dG_2}{dv_1}\right)\right].$$

Because G_1 and G_2 may in general be functions of both v_1 and v_2, we must take the *total* (rather than just the partial) derivatives with respect to v_1 of G_1 and G_2 in the

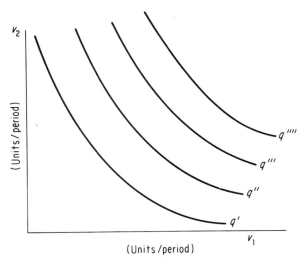

v_2

(Units/period)

q''''

q'''

q''

q'

v_1

(Units/period)

FIGURE 7–1. A one-output, two-input production function.

Figures 7–2 and 7–3 illustrate two extreme cases of factor substitutability. An example of Figure 7–2, no substitutability between the factors, would be the chemical electrolysis of water, since two atoms of hydrogen must be combined with exactly one atom of oxygen to produce one molecule of water. An example of Figure 7–3, complete substitutability between the factors, would be some types of electrical wiring in which it is completely

---

above equation. This results in

$$\frac{d^2v_2}{dv_1^2} = -\frac{1}{G_2^2}\left\{G_2\left[G_{11}\left(\frac{dv_1}{dv_1}\right) + G_{12}\left(\frac{dv_2}{dv_1}\right)\right] - G_1\left[G_{12}\left(\frac{dv_1}{dv_1}\right) + G_{22}\left(\frac{dv_2}{dv_1}\right)\right]\right\}$$

$$= -\frac{1}{G_2^2}\left\{G_2\left[G_{11} + G_{12}\left(-\frac{G_1}{G_2}\right)\right] - G_1\left[G_{12} + G_{22}\left(-\frac{G_1}{G_2}\right)\right]\right\}$$

$$= -\frac{1}{G_2^3}\left(G_{11}G_2^2 - 2G_{12}G_1G_2 + G_{22}G_1^2\right).$$

In the preceding footnote, we have already assumed that G_1 and G_2 are both positive. Furthermore, if the firm is operating under conditions of diminishing marginal returns, G_{11} and G_{22} are both negative. If we make the further assumption that G_{12} is positive, then it can readily be seen that the entire right-hand side of the above expression is positive.

Hence a set of sufficient conditions for the slope of the isoproduct curves to be convex to the origin (i.e., for $d^2v_2/dv_1^2 > 0$) is that:

a. the marginal product of each factor is positive (i.e., $G_1 > 0$ and $G_2 > 0$);

b. the firm is operating under conditions of diminishing marginal returns (i.e., $G_{11} < 0$ and $G_{22} < 0$);

c. the marginal product of each factor is an increasing function of the amount of the other factor that is used (i.e., $G_{12} = (\partial/\partial v_1)(\partial G/\partial v_2) = (\partial/\partial v_2)(\partial G/\partial v_1) > 0$).

The above set of conditions is only sufficient, rather than necessary and sufficient, for the isoproduct curves to be convex to the origin.

116

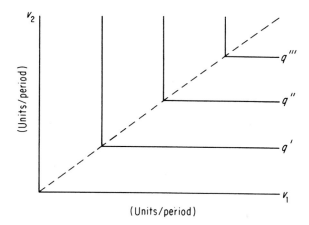

FIGURE 7-2.   A one-output, two-input production function—no substitutability.

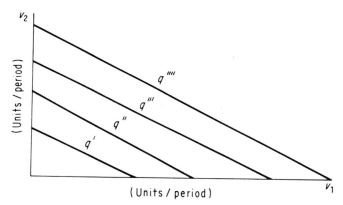

FIGURE 7-3.   A one-output, two-input production function—complete substitutability.

immaterial whether aluminum wire or copper wire is used, as long as a certain electrical conductivity is present.

2. THE OPTIMAL INPUT MIX. The production function alone does not determine the optimal input mix for the firm. The firm should choose that particular combination of inputs which will enable it to produce any chosen level of output at the minimum possible total cost. If w_1 and w_2 are the market prices of the factors, then the total cost the firm incurs in using v_1 and v_2 units of the two factors is

$$TC = w_1v_1 + w_2v_2 + A, \qquad (7-5)$$

where A represents total fixed costs.

Figure 7–4 is a graphical representation of Eq. (7–5) for various values of v_1 and v_2. The straight lines represent different levels of total cost. They are called *isocost curves*, and they represent the locus of all combinations of the two input factors which result in the same total cost. $TC_1 < TC_2 < TC_3 < TC_4$.

In Figure 7–5, we have superimposed on the isocost curves from Figure 7–4 one of the isoproduct curves from Figure 7–1 representing an arbitrary rate of production. The point of tangency between the isoproduct curve q

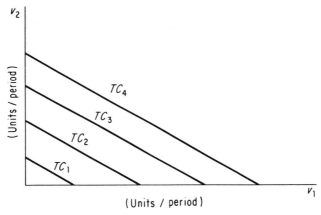

FIGURE 7–4.   Isocost curves.

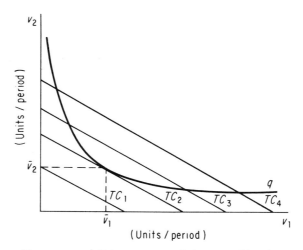

FIGURE 7–5.   Tangency condition for an efficient combination of input factors.

and the isocost curve TC_2 represents the most efficient combination of input factors: $\bar{v}_1$ units of the first factor and $\bar{v}_2$ units of the second factor produce the desired output q at minimum total cost. At any other point on the isoproduct curve in Figure 7–5, q can be produced only at a higher level of total cost. No other isoproduct curve need be considered, since it would not represent an output q. Hence the point of tangency (with co-ordinates $\bar{v}_1$ and $\bar{v}_2$) is the best combination of input factors for producing a rate of output q.

It is conceivable that the optimal mix of factors would result in only one factor being used. One such case is illustrated in Figure 7–6, where w_2, the market price of the second factor, is so much less relative to w_1 that only the second factor is used.

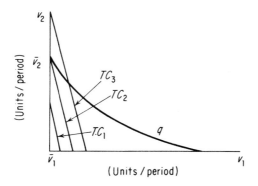

FIGURE 7–6. Corner condition for an efficient combination of input factors—only factor two used.

D. A SPECIAL SHORT-RUN PRODUCTION FUNCTION: TWO OUTPUTS AND ONE INPUT

1. PRODUCT TRANSFORMATION CURVES. The second special case we consider is a production function which consists of two outputs and one input:

$$v = F(q_1, q_2). \tag{7–6}$$

Equation (7–6) is the minimum quantity, v units per time period, which is required of the single input factor in order to produce q_1 units per time period of the first output and q_2 units per time period of the second output. This production function is represented graphically in Figure 7–7.

The interpretation of Figure 7–7 is similar to the interpretation of Figure 7–1, except that the roles of inputs and outputs are reversed. In Figure 7–7 the horizontal and vertical axes represent the rates of output of the first and second product, respectively. Instead of using a third dimension to represent the rate of utilization of the single input factor, contour lines are used. Each of the curved lines labeled v', v'', v''', and v'''' represents specific input rates. The contour v', for example, indicates all possible combinations of the two outputs which could be produced when v' units of the input factor are used. As more units of input are used, a greater total output can be produced. Hence, $v' < v'' < v''' < v''''$.

The contour lines in Figure 7–7 are called *product transformation curves*. Each product transformation curve is the locus of output combinations which can be obtained from a given amount of input. All the product transformation curves are downward sloping, because an increase in output one must be accompanied by a decrease in output two.[5] The slope of a product transformation curve, dq_2/dq_1, is the *rate of product transformation* between the two outputs. It is generally assumed that the rate of product transformation (numerically) increases as we move to the right along a product transformation curve and (numerically) decreases as we move to the left; i.e., the product transformation curves are concave to the origin.[6]

---

[5] The slope of a product transformation curve is dq_2/dq_1. In view of Eq. (7–6),

$$\frac{dq_2}{dq_1} = -\frac{\partial F/\partial q_1}{\partial F/\partial q_2}.$$

Since the marginal inputs required to produce small increases in outputs one and two, $\partial F/\partial q_1$ and $\partial F/\partial q_2$, are the reciprocals of the marginal products (as long as it is possible to vary the production of one output without varying the production of the other output), it is reasonable to assume that they are positive. Hence dq_2/dq_1 must be negative. Note that this proof is symmetrical to the proof given in footnote 3, except that the roles of inputs and outputs are reversed.

[6] In formal terms, we generally assume that along an isoproduct curve,

$$\frac{d^2q_2}{dq_1^2} = \frac{d}{dq_1}\left(\frac{dq_2}{dq_1}\right) < 0.$$

Let us now investigate the conditions under which this assumption will be valid. To simplify the analysis, the following abbreviated notation will be used:

$$F_i = \frac{\partial F}{\partial q_i} \; ; \; F_{ii} = \frac{\partial^2 F}{\partial q_i^2} \; ; \; F_{ij} = \frac{\partial^2 F}{\partial q_i\, \partial q_j} \qquad \text{for all } i \text{ and } j.$$

The preceding footnote established that

$$\frac{dq_2}{dq_1} = -\frac{F_1}{F_2}.$$

We must determine the conditions under which the derivative with respect to q_1 of this expression will be negative. To obtain this derivative, the formula for differentiating a quotient yields

$$\frac{d}{dq_1}\left[\frac{dq_2}{dq_1}\right] = -\frac{1}{F_2^2}\left[F_2\left(\frac{dF_1}{dq_1}\right) - F_1\left(\frac{dF_2}{dq_1}\right)\right].$$

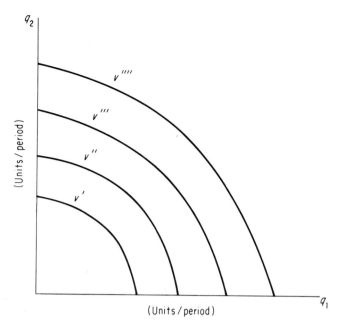

FIGURE 7–7. A two-output, one-input production function.

Since F_1 and F_2 may in general be functions of both q_1 and q_2, we must take the *total* (rather than just the partial) derivatives with respect to q_1 of F_1 and F_2 in the above equation. This results in

$$\frac{d^2 q_2}{dq_1^2} = -\frac{1}{F_2^2} \left\{ F_2 \left[F_{11} \left(\frac{dq_1}{dq_1}\right) + F_{12} \left(\frac{dq_2}{dq_1}\right) \right] - F_1 \left[F_{12} \left(\frac{dq_1}{dq_1}\right) + F_{22} \left(\frac{dq_2}{dq_1}\right) \right] \right\}$$

$$= -\frac{1}{F_2^2} \left\{ F_2 \left[F_{11} + F_{12} \left(-\frac{F_1}{F_2}\right) \right] - F_1 \left[F_{12} + F_{22} \left(-\frac{F_1}{F_2}\right) \right] \right\}$$

$$= -\frac{1}{F_2^3} (F_{11} F_2^2 - 2 F_{12} F_1 F_2 + F_{22} F_1^2).$$

In the preceding footnote, we have already assumed that F_1 and F_2 are both positive. Furthermore, if the firm is operating under conditions of diminishing marginal returns, F_{11} and F_{22} are both positive. If we make the further assumption that F_{12} is negative, then it can readily be seen that the entire right-hand side of the above expression is negative.

Hence a set of sufficient conditions for the slope of the isoproduct curves to be concave to the origin (i.e., for $d^2 q_2 / dq_1^2 < 0$) is that:

a. The reciprocal of the marginal product of each factor is positive (i.e., $F_1 > 0$ and $F_2 > 0$).

b. The firm is operating under conditions of diminishing marginal returns (i.e., $F_{11} > 0$ and $F_{22} > 0$).

c. The reciprocal of the marginal product of each factor is a decreasing function of the amount of the other factor that is used (i.e., $F_{12} = (\partial/\partial q_1)(\partial F/\partial q_2) = (\partial/\partial q_2)(\partial F/\partial q_1) < 0$).

The above set of conditions is only sufficient, rather than necessary and sufficient, for the isoproduct curves to be concave to the origin.

121

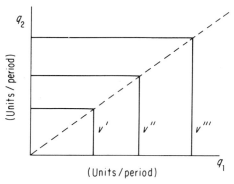

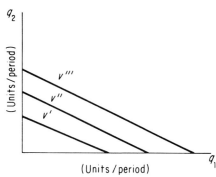

FIGURE 7–8. A two-output, one-input production function—no substitutability.

FIGURE 7–9. A two-output, one-input production function—complete substitutability.

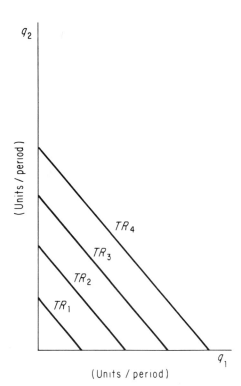

FIGURE 7–10. Isorevenue curves.

There are, however, two special cases where the product transformation curves are not concave. One is the situation in which no substitutability between the outputs exists, for example the case of joint products produced in rigidly fixed proportions. The second is the situation in which complete substitutability between the outputs exists, for example the case of the same commodity being produced but packaged in different sized containers. These two extreme cases are shown in Figures 7–8 and 7–9. Our subsequent analysis will chiefly apply to the case of imperfect or limited substitutability, where the product transformation curves are concave to the origin.

2. THE OPTIMAL OUTPUT MIX. Let us now determine the optimal mix of outputs which the firm should produce if it is going to use v units of input per time

period. If p_1 and p_2 are the selling prices of the two outputs, then the firm's total revenue is

$$TR = p_1q_1 + p_2q_2. \tag{7-7}$$

Figure 7–10 is a graphical representation of Eq. (7–7) for various values of q_1 and q_2. The straight lines represent different levels of total revenue. They are called *isorevenue curves*, and they represent the locus of all possible combinations of the two outputs which result in the same total revenue. $TR_1 < TR_2 < TR_3 < TR_4$.

In Figure 7–11, we have superimposed on the isorevenue curves from Figure 7–10 one of the product transformation curves from Figure 7–7, representing an arbitrary rate of factor utilization. The point of tangency between the product transformation curve v and the isorevenue curve TR_2 determines the combination of outputs ($\bar{q}_1$ and $\bar{q}_2$) which gives the firm the highest total revenue when v units of input are used. Any other combination of outputs on the product transformation curve in Figure 7–11 can also be produced with v units of input, but they represent lower levels of total revenue. No other product transformation curve need be considered, since it would not represent an input v. Hence the point of tangency (with co-ordinates $\bar{q}_1$ and $\bar{q}_2$) is the best combination of outputs which can be produced using v units of input.

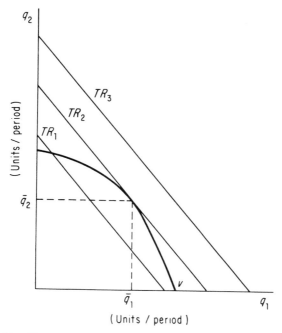

FIGURE 7–11.   Tangency condition for an efficient combination of outputs.

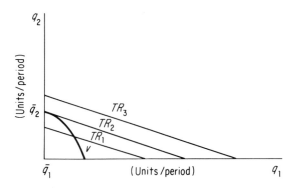

FIGURE 7-12. Corner condition for an efficient combination of outputs—only output two produced.

It is conceivable that the optimal mix of outputs would result in only one product being produced. One such case is illustrated in Figure 7–12, where p_1, the selling price of the first product, is so much less relative to p_2 that only the second product is produced.

E. THE GENERAL SHORT-RUN PRODUCTION FUNCTION: *M* OUTPUTS AND *N* INPUTS

The two specialized short-run production functions analyzed in Section D provide the background for considering the general short-run production function defined earlier:

$$F(q_1, \ldots, q_M) = G(v_1, \ldots, v_N). \qquad (7\text{--}1)$$

Our objective in this section is to determine the combination of outputs and inputs which will maximize the firm's short-run profits. In the two preceding sections we did not completely solve the firm's production problem. In Section C we did not find the most profitable value for q, and in Section D we did not find the most profitable value for v, since these are not conveniently discovered graphically. In order to determine the firm's optimal production decisions, in this section we must use a mathematical approach.

1. THE OPTIMAL PRODUCTION DECISIONS. The firm's short-run profit function is

$$\pi = \sum_{i=1}^{M} p_i q_i - \sum_{j=1}^{N} w_j v_j - A, \qquad (7\text{--}8)$$

where p_i is the (constant) price at which output i can be sold, w_j is the (constant) price at which input j can be bought, and A represents fixed costs. The production function Eq. (7–1) constrains the firm's ability to choose any combination of inputs and outputs in its attempt to maximize profits. Hence a constrained maximization problem must be solved to determine the most profitable production decisions.

In order to solve this constrained maximization problem using the differential calculus, form the Lagrangian function:[7]

$$L = \sum_{i=1}^{M} p_i q_i - \sum_{j=1}^{N} w_j v_j - A - \lambda [F(q_1, \ldots, q_M) - G(v_1, \ldots, v_N)]. \quad (7\text{–}9)$$

Differentiating Eq. (7–9) with respect to the q_i and the v_j and equating the results to zero:

$$\frac{\partial L}{\partial q_i} = p_i - \lambda \frac{\partial F}{\partial q_i} = 0 \qquad i = 1, \ldots, M. \qquad (7\text{–}10)$$

$$\frac{\partial L}{\partial v_j} = -w_j + \lambda \frac{\partial G}{\partial v_j} = 0 \qquad j = 1, \ldots, N. \qquad (7\text{–}11)$$

Solving the system of Eq. (7–10) and (7–11) for $1/\lambda$:

$$\frac{\partial F/\partial q_1}{p_1} = \cdots = \frac{\partial F/\partial q_M}{p_M} = \frac{\partial G/\partial v_1}{w_1} = \cdots = \frac{\partial G/\partial v_N}{w_N} = \frac{1}{\lambda}. \qquad (7\text{–}12)$$

Each of the partial derivatives in Eq. (7–12) may be functions of the $q_1, \ldots,$ q_M and $v_1, \ldots, v_N$. Therefore the $M + N$ independent equations in Eq. (7–12) plus the constraint represented by Eq. (7–1) can be solved for the $M + N + 1$ values $\bar{q}_1, \ldots, \bar{q}_M, \bar{v}_1, \ldots, \bar{v}_N, \bar{\lambda}$ which maximize the firm's profits.[8]

The economic meaning of $\partial G/\partial v_j$ is best explained on the basis of our

---

[7] We are implicitly assuming that the components of the production function, F and G, are continuous and differentiable, so that the calculus approach is legitimate.

[8] Implicit in this statement is the assumption that this solution results in nonnegative values for all the $\bar{q}_i$ and $\bar{v}_j$. This corresponds to a generalization of the tangency conditions portrayed in Figures 7–5 and 7–11. It is, however, logically possible for the solution to this system of equations to result in negative values for one or more of the $\bar{q}_i$ or $\bar{v}_j$. This, of course, is not permissible economically, for negative inputs cannot be used and negative outputs cannot be produced. In this case, any negative $\bar{q}_i$ or $\bar{v}_j$ would be replaced by a zero value. This would correspond to a generalization of the corner solutions portrayed in Figures 7–6 and 7–12, indicating that a zero utilization of one or more inputs or a zero production of one or more outputs would be optimal.

A further assumption implicit in the text is that when the values thus obtained for $\bar{q}_1, \ldots, \bar{q}_M, \bar{v}_1, \ldots, \bar{v}_N$ are substituted into Eq. (7–8) the resulting value of π is not less than $-A$. If $\pi < -A$, then it would be optimal for the firm to shut down its operations, thereby making $\pi = -A$. For the special case discussed in Chapter 6, where we considered a firm producing a single output, $\pi < -A$ corresponds to the situation where market price was below the minimum point of the firm's average variable cost curve.

discussion in Section I.C. There $\partial G/\partial v_1$ and $\partial G/\partial v_2$ clearly were the marginal products of the first and second inputs, respectively, since only one product was produced. Now, however, there are M outputs produced, so that a marginal increase in input j (all other inputs being held constant) may result in an increase in all the outputs rather than in just a single output. Therefore $\partial G/\partial v_j$ should be interpreted as an index of the marginal increase in outputs resulting from a small increase in input j; for convenience, however, we shall continue to call $\partial G/\partial v_j$ the *marginal product* of input j.

Similarly, the economic meaning of $\partial F/\partial q_i$ is best explained on the basis of our discussion in Section I.D. There $\partial F/\partial q_1$ and $\partial F/\partial q_2$ clearly were the marginal inputs required to produce an extra unit of the first and second products, respectively, since only one input was used. Now, however, there are N inputs used, so that a marginal increase in output i (all other outputs being held constant) may require an increase in all the inputs rather than in just a single input. Therefore $\partial F/\partial q_i$ should be interpreted as an index of the marginal increase in inputs required to produce a small increase of output i; for convenience, however, we shall continue to call $\partial F/\partial q_i$ the *marginal input* required for output i.

Further economic interpretations of the conditions in Eq. (7–12) will result from the statements and proofs of nine formal theorems.

2. THEOREM 1. *The marginal product of the last dollar spent on purchasing an input must be equal for every input.*

To prove Theorem 1, note that $(\partial G/\partial v_j)/w_j$ is the marginal product of the last dollar spent on input j. Hence Theorem 1 is an immediate consequence of Eq. (7–12).

3. THEOREM 2. $\lambda(\partial G/\partial v_j)$ *is equal to the value of the marginal product resulting from a change in any one input.*

To prove Theorem 2, we shall show that

$$\lambda\left(\frac{\partial G}{\partial v_j}\right) = \frac{dTR}{dv_j}. \tag{7–13}$$

The right-hand side of Eq. (7–13) is clearly the value of the marginal product of input j, i.e., the incremental revenue obtained by selling the extra output mix produced when a small additional amount of input j is used.

To establish the validity of Eq. (7–13), note that the total revenue function is

$$TR = \sum_{i=1}^{M} p_i q_i. \tag{7–14}$$

The total differential of Eq. (7–14) is

$$dTR = \sum_{i=1}^{M} p_i \, dq_i. \tag{7-15}$$

The total differential of Eq. (7–1) is

$$\sum_{i=1}^{M} \frac{\partial F}{\partial q_i} \, dq_i = \sum_{j=1}^{N} \frac{\partial G}{\partial v_j} \, dv_j. \tag{7-16}$$

Since we are considering the marginal revenue resulting from a change in only one input factor, input j, we can assume that

$$dv_k = 0 \qquad \text{if } k \neq j. \tag{7-17}$$

Equations (7–16) and (7–17) together imply

$$dv_j = \frac{1}{\partial G/\partial v_j} \sum_{i=1}^{M} \frac{\partial F}{\partial q_i} \, dq_i. \tag{7-18}$$

Substituting Eq. (7–12) into Eq. (7–18):

$$dv_j = \frac{1}{\partial G/\partial v_j} \sum_{i=1}^{M} \left(\frac{p_i}{\lambda}\right) dq_i. \tag{7-19}$$

Dividing Eq. (7–15) by Eq. (7–19),

$$\frac{dTR}{dv_j} = \frac{\displaystyle\sum_{i=1}^{M} p_i \, dq_i}{[\displaystyle\sum_{i=1}^{M} p_i \, dq_i]/\lambda(\partial G/\partial v_j)}. \tag{7-20}$$

Equation (7–20) implies Eq. (7–13), thus completing the proof of Theorem 2.

4. THEOREM 3. *Any input will be utilized in such a manner that its market price equals the value of its marginal product*

This can be established by looking at one of the equations in (7–12):

$$\frac{\partial G/\partial v_j}{w_j} = \frac{1}{\lambda}. \tag{7-21}$$

Hence,

$$\lambda \left(\frac{\partial G}{\partial v_j}\right) = w_j. \tag{7-22}$$

By Theorem 2—see Eq. (7–13)—the left-hand side of Eq. (7–22) is the value of the marginal product, and Theorem 3 follows.

5. THEOREM 4. *The marginal revenue received from the last unit of input must be equal for every output.*

To prove Theorem 4, note that p_i is the marginal revenue received from selling one additional unit of output i, and $\partial F/\partial q_i$ is the marginal increase in inputs required to produce an additional unit of output i. Hence the marginal revenue received from the last unit of input is $p_i/(\partial F/\partial q_i)$ when the marginal inputs are used to produce output i. In mathematical terms, Theorem 4 is thus equivalent to

$$\frac{p_1}{\partial F/\partial q_1} = \cdots = \frac{p_i}{\partial F/\partial q_i} = \cdots = \frac{p_M}{\partial F/\partial q_M}. \tag{7-23}$$

The validity of Eq. (7–23), and hence of Theorem 4, follows immediately from Eq. (7–12).

6. **THEOREM 5.** $\lambda(\partial F/\partial q_i)$ *is equal to the marginal cost resulting from a change in any one output.*

To prove Theorem 5, we shall show that

$$\lambda\left(\frac{\partial F}{\partial q_i}\right) = \frac{dTC}{dq_i}. \tag{7-24}$$

The right-hand side of Eq. (7–24) is clearly the marginal cost incurred in changing the production of output i.

To establish the validity of Eq. (7–24), note that the total cost function is

$$TC = \sum_{j=1}^{N} w_j v_j + A. \tag{7-25}$$

The total differential of Eq. (7–25) is

$$dTC = \sum_{j=1}^{N} w_j \, dv_j. \tag{7-26}$$

Since we are considering the marginal cost incurred by a change in only one output, output i, we can assume that

$$dq_k = 0 \qquad \text{if } k \neq i. \tag{7-27}$$

Equations (7–16) and (7–27) together imply

$$dq_i = \frac{1}{\partial F/\partial q_i} \sum_{j=1}^{N} \frac{\partial G}{\partial v_j} \, dv_j. \tag{7-28}$$

Substituting Eq. (7–12) into Eq. (7–28):

$$dq_i = \frac{1}{\partial F/\partial q_i} \sum_{j=1}^{N} \left(\frac{w_j}{\lambda}\right) dv_j. \tag{7-29}$$

Dividing Eq. (7–26) by Eq. (7–29):

$$\frac{dTC}{dq_i} = \frac{\sum\limits_{j=1}^{N} w_j \, dv_j}{\dfrac{1}{\lambda(\partial F/\partial q_i)} \sum\limits_{j=1}^{N} w_j \, dv_j} . \tag{7-30}$$

Equation (7–30) implies Eq. (7–24), thus completing the proof of Theorem 5.

7. THEOREM 6. *Any output will be produced in such a manner that its selling price equals its marginal cost.*

This can be shown by looking at one of the equations in Eq. (7–12):

$$\frac{\partial F/\partial q_i}{p_i} = \frac{1}{\lambda} . \tag{7-31}$$

Hence,
$$\lambda\left(\frac{\partial F}{\partial q_i}\right) = p_i. \tag{7-32}$$

By Theorem 5, the left-hand side of Eq. (7–32) is the marginal cost of output i, and Theorem 6 follows.

8. THEOREM 7. *The rate of product transformation between every pair of outputs, holding all other outputs and inputs constant, is numerically equal to the inverse ratio of their prices.*

To prove Theorem 7 for any arbitrary pair of outputs i and k, we want to show that

$$\left|\frac{dq_k}{dq_i}\right| = \frac{p_i}{p_k} . \tag{7-33}$$

Equation (7–12) implies that

$$\frac{p_i}{p_k} = \frac{\partial F/\partial q_i}{\partial F/\partial q_k} . \tag{7-34}$$

From Eq. (7–16), by setting all the differentials equal to zero except for dq_i and dq_k (i.e., holding all other outputs and inputs constant), we have

$$\frac{dq_k}{dq_i} = -\frac{\partial F/\partial q_i}{\partial F/\partial q_k} \tag{7-35}$$

Equations (7–34) and (7–35) together imply Eq. (7–33), thus establishing the validity of Theorem 7.

9. THEOREM 8. *The rate of technical substitution between every pair of inputs, holding all other inputs and outputs constant, is numerically equal to the inverse ratio of their prices.*

To prove Theorem 8 for any arbitrary pair of inputs j and k, we want to show that

$$\left| \frac{dv_k}{dv_j} \right| = \frac{w_j}{w_k} . \tag{7-36}$$

Equation (7–12) implies that

$$\frac{w_j}{w_k} = \frac{\partial G/\partial v_j}{\partial G/\partial v_k} . \tag{7-37}$$

From Eq. (7–16), by setting all the differentials equal to zero except for dv_j and dv_k (i.e., holding all other inputs and outputs constant), we have

$$\frac{dv_k}{dv_j} = - \frac{\partial G/\partial v_j}{\partial G/\partial v_k} . \tag{7-38}$$

Equations (7–37) and (7–38) together imply Eq. (7–36), thus establishing the validity of Theorem 8.

10. THEOREM 9. *The rate at which any input can be transformed into any output, holding all other inputs and outputs constant, is equal to the inverse ratio of their prices.*

To prove Theorem 9 for any arbitrary output i and any arbitrary input j, we want to show that

$$\frac{dq_i}{dv_j} = \frac{w_j}{p_i} . \tag{7-39}$$

Equation (7–12) implies that

$$\frac{\partial G/\partial v_j}{\partial F/\partial q_i} = \frac{w_j}{p_i} . \tag{7-40}$$

From Eq. (7–16), by setting all the differentials equal to zero except for dq_i and dv_j (i.e., holding all other inputs and outputs constant), we have

$$\frac{dq_i}{dv_j} = \frac{\partial G/\partial v_j}{\partial F/\partial q_i} . \tag{7-41}$$

Equations (7–40) and (7–41) together imply Eq. (7–39), thus establishing the validity of Theorem 9.

Theorems 7 and 8 represent generalizations of the tangency conditions portrayed in Figures 7–11 and 7–5. It is possible that instead of the tangency type of solutions for all inputs and outputs there may be some corner solutions of the types indicated in Sections I.C. and I.D. Should this occur, then the statements of Theorems 1 to 9 must be modified so that they refer only to those inputs actually utilized and to those outputs actually produced. For example, Theorem 3 could be modified to state: Any input actually used will be utilized in such a manner that its market price equals the value of its marginal product; the market price is greater than the value of the marginal product of any input which is not actually used.

II. Some Effects of Product and Factor Price Changes

We now wish to explore some of the effects which changes in product or factor prices will have on the firm's utilization of resources and production of products. At this stage, we shall consider only the relatively simple situations which occur when there is a change in any one product or factor market price, with the prices of all other inputs and outputs remaining constant. Hence this analysis must be interpreted as a partial equilibrium analysis. The more complex analyses required when several prices change simultaneously will be presented in Chapter 9.

Assume a change in p_i, with all other prices remaining constant. Thus the price ratios, p_i/p_k, will change for every output $k \neq i$. According to Eq. (7-33), there must then be a corresponding change in the rate of product transformation between each other output k and output i. Since the rate of product transformation is the slope of a product transformation curve, it is necessary to reach a new equilibrium position by moving along the same product transformation curve to a point whose slope equals the new price ratio. Since product transformation curves are concave to the origin (as in Figure 7-7), if p_i increases the movement will be to the right and if p_i decreases the movement will be to the left.[9] Hence, *ceteris paribus*, a rise in the price of output i will lead to an increase in its production.

Assume next a change in w_j, with all other prices remaining constant. Thus the price ratios, w_j/w_k, will change for every input $k \neq j$. According to Eq. (7-36) there must then be a corresponding change in the rate of technical substitution between each other input k and input j. Since the rate of technical substitution is the slope of an isoproduct curve, it is necessary to reach a new equilibrium position by moving along the same isoproduct curve to a point whose slope equals the new price ratio. Since isoproduct curves are convex to the origin (as in Figure 7-1), if w_j decreases the movement will be to the right and if w_j increases the movement will be to the left. Hence, *ceteris paribus*, a rise in the price of input j will lead to a decrease in its utilization.

---

[9] The slope of a product transformation curve is dq_k/dq_i. This means that product k is measured along the ordinate and product i is measured along the abcissa. Since we have shown in Eq. (7-33) that the absolute value of this slope equals p_i/p_k, it follows that an increase in p_i must make the slope steeper; i.e., that there is a movement to the right along the product transformation curve.

III. Market Determination of Factor Prices

In the preceding analysis, we have assumed that the factor prices at which a firm can purchase productive services are constant. For the individual firm operating in perfect competition, this assumption is appropriate. We are, however, now ready to look beyond the individual firm to the entire market and ask how the prices of productive factors are determined in the market.

Assume that the market prices of the final outputs produced by any one firm are constant and that the prices of all productive factors other than input j are fixed. It is clear from the analysis of the preceding sections that under these conditions we can determine the firm's utilization of input j for various values of w_j, i.e., the firm's demand curve for input j. From Theorems 7 to 9 it follows that this demand curve depends upon the prices assumed for the inputs other than input j and for all the outputs; i.e., $w_1, \ldots, w_{j-1}, w_{j+1}, \ldots, w_N$ and $p_1, \ldots, p_M$ are parameters in the firm's demand function for input j.

It is conceptually possible to derive the individual demand curves for factor j for all firms in the market. The market demand curve for factor j is then the lateral sum of all the individual firm's demand curves for this input. This market demand curve shows the total demand for the jth productive factor at various prices w_j.

Correspondingly a market supply curve for factor j can be constructed. If factor j is supplied by firms (e.g., steel), then its market supply curve results from the lateral addition of portions of marginal cost curves, as discussed in Chapter 6. If factor j is supplied by households (e.g., labor), then its market supply curve results from work-leisure considerations, as briefly discussed in Chapter 5.

The intersection of the market demand curve and the market supply curve for factor j determines the equilibrium price for this factor. Similarly, supply and demand considerations determine equilibrium prices for all other factors in the market.

We can see from the analysis that the quantity produced and the selling price of any final product depend upon a set of markets for each factor. These markets can be represented by a simultaneous system of equations which determines both the demands of every firm for all productive services and the amounts of final products which each firm and household supplies as a function of both the prices of the final products and of all the factors of production. The full details of this system of simultaneous equations will be explored in Chapter 9, which deals with general equilibrium analysis.

IV. Empirical Production Functions

We have spent much time developing a theoretical framework for the analysis of a firm's production decisions. The discussion has been highly abstract. Economists have, however, done a great deal of empirical work utilizing this framework. Using econometric techniques, they have obtained estimates of the production functions for particular firms, industries, and entire economies. To illustrate the type of results obtained, we shall concentrate on a study (conducted by Klein) of the short-run production function for railroads in the United States in 1936.[10]

Railroads produce two major outputs: they carry freight and they carry passengers. Let q_1 denote the net ton-miles of freight carried per year, and let q_2 denote the net passenger miles carried per year. In transporting freight and passengers, railroads use three major variable factors of production: manpower, fuel, and trains. Let v_1 denote man-hours of employment per year, let v_2 denote tons of fuel consumed (coal equivalents) per year, and let v_3 denote train hours utilized per year. Since this study obtained a short-run production function, it assumed that the railroads' plants (e.g., tracks, stations, yards, etc.) were fixed. Different amounts of freight-miles or passenger-miles could then result only from changes in the utilization of manpower, fuel, and/or trains.

Adding a subscript i to each variable to denote a specific railroad, and letting u_i denote a random disturbance (accounting for the effects of missing variables, purely chance effects, etc.), the production function for the ith railroad was assumed to be

$$q_{1i}\, q_{2i}^{\delta} \;=\; A v_{1i}^{\alpha}\, v_{2i}^{\beta}\, v_{3i}^{\gamma}\, u_i. \tag{7-42}$$

Note that Eq. (7–42) is a specific form for the general production function defined by Eq. (7–1). The parameters A, α, β, γ, and δ are constants whose values must be estimated.

Since railroads do not operate under identical geographical conditions, Klein found it necessary to incorporate two additional variables to explain productivity differentials among railroads. The first such variable, z_1, is the average length of haul for the railroad. Klein justified this approach in the following manner:

> One of the more important regional differences affecting productivity is average length of haul. The Western transcontinental roads are obviously in a different position in this respect from that of New England roads. Short hauls are less economical in the use of many production factors.[11]

The second variable used to explain productivity differentials among railroads, z_2, is the percentage of freight which consists of the products of mines. The argument for using this variable was:

> Freight ton-miles means different things to different roads. Compared with

---

[10] This study was sponsored by the National Bureau of Economic Research. It is summarized in Lawrence R. Klein, *A Textbook of Econometrics* (Evanston, Ill.: Row, Peterson and Company, 1953), pp. 226–36.

[11] *Ibid.*, p. 229.

the outputs of other industries, ton-miles seem to be composed of rather homogeneous units, yet coal carriers have quite different operating characteristics from other types of roads. A five-fold classification into manufactures, agricultural products, livestocks, lumber and mineral products would be adequate for much empirical work, but we have, for simplicity, confined our attention to the distinction between mineral products and all others, since this is the striking difference affecting productivity.[12]

Adding a subscript i to denote a specific railroad to the two productivity variables, Klein incorporated them into the production function by replacing Eq. (7–42) with

$$q_{1i}\, q_{2i}^{\delta} \;=\; A v_{1i}^{\alpha}\, v_{2i}^{\beta}\, v_{3i}^{\gamma}\, z_{1i}^{\epsilon}\, z_{2i}^{\eta}\, U_i. \tag{7–43}$$

Applying advanced econometric techniques to data pertaining to the operations of Class I railways within the continental United States during 1936, Klein estimated the values of the parameters in Eq. (7–44), obtaining the following production function:

$$q_{1i}\, q_{2i}^{0.16} \;=\; 5.62\, v_{1i}^{0.89}\, v_{2i}^{0.12}\, v_{3i}^{0.28}\, z_{1i}^{0.34}\, z_{2i}^{0.25}. \tag{7–45}$$

All the coefficients in Eq. (7–45) have the theoretically expected algebraic signs. The two outputs, freight and passengers, are imperfect substitutes for each other, so that the product transformation curves have the general concave shape shown in Figure 7–7. The three inputs, manpower, fuel, and trains, are imperfect substitutes for each other, so the isoproduct curves have the general convex shape shown in Figure 7–1. An interesting property of the production function Eq. (7–45) is that it displays increasing returns to scale, since increasing each input by r per cent can result in more than an r per cent increase in each output.[13]

---

[12] *Ibid.*, p. 229.

[13] To prove this, let $\bar{q}_{1i}\bar{q}_{2\,i}^{0.16}$ be the output resulting from an r per cent increase in each of the three inputs. Then,

$$\bar{q}_{1i}\bar{q}_{2\,i}^{0.16} \;=\; (5.62 z_{1\,i}^{0.34} z_{2\,i}^{0.25})\left[v_{1i}\left(1 + \frac{r}{100}\right)\right]^{0.89}\left[v_{2i}\left(1 + \frac{r}{100}\right)\right]^{0.12}\left[v_{3i}\left(1 + \frac{r}{100}\right)\right]^{0.28}$$

$$=\; (5.62 z_{1\,i}^{0.34} z_{2\,i}^{0.25}) v_{1\,i}^{0.89} v_{2\,i}^{0.12} v_{3\,i}^{0.28}\left(1 + \frac{r}{100}\right)^{0.89+0.12+0.28}$$

Hence, $\bar{q}_{1i}\bar{q}_{2\,i}^{0.16} \;=\; q_{1i}q_{2\,i}^{0.16}\left(1 + \frac{r}{100}\right)^{1.29}$

This last equation indicates that an r per cent increase in each of the three inputs results in more than an r per cent increase in the outputs. Therefore the production function Eq. (7–45) displays increasing returns to scale.

V. Summary

The major objective of this chapter has been to discuss the factors which determine the total cost function of the firm. In the first section we introduced the concept of a production function and showed that this function indicates the limits of the firm's technical production possibilities. Points on the production function reflect the best possible operations of the firm, given the state of technology. Thus a firm cannot be maximizing its profits if it is not operating on the production function.

Both the laws of diminishing marginal and average returns were defined. It was shown that U-shaped cost curves are a consequence of the law of diminishing average returns when the prices of inputs are constant for the individual firm.

Two special short-run production functions were discussed. The first case assumed one output and two inputs. The second case assumed two outputs and one input. These cases were introduced to illustrate some of the economic considerations involved in the choice of an optimal factor mix. In the first case the production function was graphically portrayed by letting the two axes represent the rates of usage of the two different input factors and using a family of contour lines to represent various rates of output. Each of these contour lines is called an *isoproduct curve* (or an *isoquant*), and it represents a curve along which the same maximum rate of output can be produced from different mixes of the two inputs. When the two input factors are imperfectly substitutable, the isoproduct curves are convex to the origin. The slope of an isoproduct curve is called the *rate of technical substitution* between the two inputs.

We showed that the production function alone does not determine the optimal input mix for the firm. In order to determine the particular combination of inputs which will enable the firm to produce any particular amount of output at the minimum possible total cost, it is necessary to consider the market prices of the inputs. For any given set of factor market prices, the isocost curves are a family of straight lines; each isocost line represents the locus of all combinations of the two inputs which result in the same total cost. The point of tangency between some isocost line and the isoproduct curve representing some particular rate of output determines the most efficient combination of the inputs for producing the specified rate of output.

The second special short-run production function we considered had two outputs and one input. The graphic portrayal of the production function in this case uses the two axes to represent the rates of output of the two different products and a family of contour lines to represent various rates of utilization of the input factor. Each of these contour lines is called a *product transformation curve*, and it represents the locus of output combinations which can be obtained from some given amount of input. When the products are imperfectly substitutable, the product transformation curves are concave to the origin. The slope of a product transformation curve is called the *rate of product transformation* between the two products.

We showed that the production function alone does not determine the optimal output mix for the firm. In order to determine the most profitable combination of outputs which the firm can produce from any particular amount of the input, it is necessary to consider the selling prices of the products. For any given set of product market prices, the isorevenue curves are a family of straight lines; each isorevenue line represents the locus of all combinations of the two outputs which result in the same total revenue. The point of tangency between some isorevenue line and the product transformation curve representing some particular amount of input determines the most profitable combination of the outputs which can be produced from the specified amount of input.

The general production function, allowing M different outputs to be produced from N different inputs, was analyzed mathematically. The production function constrains the firm's ability to choose any combination of inputs and outputs in its attempt to maximize profits. Hence we solved a constrained maximization problem to determine the most profitable production decisions for a firm. The partial derivatives of the production function with respect to both inputs and outputs play important roles in this solution. $\partial G/\partial v_j$ is an index of the marginal increase in outputs resulting from a small increase in input j; more simply, we regard $\partial G/\partial v_j$ as the marginal product of input j. Similarly, $\partial F/\partial q_i$ is an index of the marginal increase in inputs required to produce a small increase of output i; more simply, we regard $\partial F/\partial q_i$ as the marginal input required to produce an additional unit of output i.

The most important properties of the profit-maximizing production decisions for a firm are contained in nine formal theorems, which we stated and proved.

Using partial equilibrium analysis, we considered the effects of changes in product or factor market prices on the firm's utilization of resources and production of products. We showed that, *ceteris paribus*, a rise in the price of one output will lead to an increase in its production, whereas a decline in the price of one output will lead to a decrease in its production. We also showed that, *ceteris paribus*, a rise in the price of one input will lead to a decrease in its utilization, whereas a decline in the price of one input will lead to an increase in its utilization.

In analyzing the production decisions of a single firm, we assumed that factor market prices are given constants. In this chapter, however, we also considered the manner in which the prices of factors are determined in the market. The production function analysis determines the firm's demand function for input j, i.e., the firm's utilization of input j at various values of w_j. In this demand function, the prices of all other inputs and ᴜᵣ prices of all outputs enter as parameters. By laterally summing all the individual firms' demand curves for an input, the market demand curve for this input can be obtained. A market supply curve for the input can be constructed from the individual firms' or households' supply curves for that factor (depending whether the input is supplied by firms or by households). The intersection of the market demand curve and the market supply curve for the input factor determines its equilibrium price. Thus the quantity produced and the selling price of any final product depend upon a set of markets for each factor, as well as a set of markets for each product.

To conclude this chapter, we briefly considered the type of empirical research on production functions being done by econometricians. A short-run production function for railroads in the United States was discussed, in which two outputs, freight and passengers, were functions of three inputs: manpower, fuel, and trains. Two additional variables, average length of haul and percentage of freight consisting of the products of mines, were added to reflect productivity differentials among railroads. The empirical results were in accordance with the theoretical framework developed in this chapter.

SUGGESTED READINGS

These recommendations are in addition to the footnote references cited in this chapter.

DEMSETZ, H., "The Private Production of Public Goods," *Journal of Law and Economics*, XIII (October, 1970), 293–306.

DIAMOND, P. A., AND J. A. MIRRLEES, "Optimal Taxation and Public Production: I," *American Economic Review*, LXI (March, 1971), 8–27.

GORDON, W. J., "The Short-Run Cost Function in Manufacturing," *Quarterly Review of Economics and Business*, X (Autumn, 1970), 55–67.

KLEIN, LAWRENCE R., *An Introduction to Econometrics*, pp. 83–111. Englewood Cliffs, N.J.: Prentice-Hall, Inc., 1962.

MOORE, F. T., "Economics of Scale—Some Statistical Evidence," *Quarterly Journal of Economics*, LXXIII (May, 1959), 232–45.

NATIONAL BUREAU OF ECONOMIC RESEARCH, *Cost Behavior and Price Policy*, chaps. 6–8. New York: The Bureau, 1943.

OHLS, J. C., "Marginal Cost Pricing, Investment Theory, and CATV," *Journal of Law and Economics*, XIII (October, 1970), 439–60.

REDER, MELVIN W., "Wage Differentials: Theory and Measurement," in National Bureau of Economic Research, *Aspects of Labor Economics*, pp. 257–317. Princeton: Princeton University Press, 1962.

SAMUELSON, PAUL ANTHONY, *Foundations of Economic Analysis,* chap. 4. Cambridge: Harvard University Press, 1955.

SMITH, VERNON L., "Engineering Data and Statistical Techniques in the Analysis of Production and Technological Change: Fuel Requirements of the Trucking Industry," *Econometrica,* XXV (April, 1957), 281–301.

Chapter Eight

Entry and Exit in a Perfectly Competitive Market

We are now ready to consider how the short-run analysis of Chapter 7 must be modified when we adopt a long-run view of affairs and realize that given sufficient time, firms can alter the amounts of plant and equipment which they use. In brief, we now want to discuss the long-run production decisions of a firm and their impact on the market-wide allocation of resources. For this purpose, it is convenient to assume that each firm produces only one final product, as this considerably simplifies the analysis. The basic propositions would, however, be unaltered if we were to generalize the analysis to multiproduct firms.

Throughout this chapter we shall continue to assume that the firms purchase all inputs and sell all outputs in perfectly competitive markets. In particular, this means that any firm can purchase as much as it desires of any productive factor at a constant price, and it can also sell as much as it desires of its final product at a constant price.

I. The Long-Run Production Decisions of a Firm

A. The Long-Run Total Cost Function

We can write the production function of a firm which produces only a single output as

$$q = G(v_1, \ldots, v_N, V_1, \ldots, V_H). \tag{8-1}$$

In Eq. (8-1), q is the rate of output produced by the firm; $v_1, \ldots, v_N$ are the rates of utilization by the firm of the variable input factors $1, \ldots, N$; $V_1, \ldots, V_H$ are the amounts of the fixed input factors $1, \ldots, H$ which are held by the firm. In the short run, the firm's stock of each type of fixed input is given, so that $V_1, \ldots, V_H$ have some specific numeric values, say $\bar{V}_1, \ldots, \bar{V}_H$. Substituting these values into Eq. (8-1),

$$q = G(v_1, \ldots, v_N, \bar{V}_1, \ldots, \bar{V}_H). \tag{8-2}$$

Equation (8-2) is a short-run production function; it is a special case of Eq. (8-1), since the firm's stock of fixed factors is constant in the short run.

By definition, the long run is a period of time in which the firm can alter its plant and equipment in any way it desires. Thus in the long run the only technological constraint on the firm's production decisions is the long-run production function, Eq. (8-1). Once a stock of fixed factors has been selected, then the short-run production function, Eq. (8-2), becomes the binding constraint. We shall now investigate the manner in which a firm determines its stock of fixed productive factors.

The criterion for the firm's production decisions is still profit maximization. We assume that the firm expects to operate indefinitely in a perfectly competitive market and that current factor market prices will continue to prevail. Then the firm's long-run production decisions involve the determination of both its rate of output and the manner of combining variable and fixed input factors to produce this rate of output. Thus the firm must decide both the optimal rate of utilizing expendable input factors (such as labor and raw materials) and its optimal stock of plant and equipment.

Since we are assuming that the firm produces only one final product, one approach to the long-run profit-maximization problem is first to find the long-run total cost function of the firm; i.e., the function $LTC(q)$ indicating the minimum possible costs at which the firm can produce any rate of output q. A problem arises in the definition of the long-run total cost function, however. What should be the costs attributed to long-lived productive factors used in production? It is clear that if a short-lived factor is entirely consumed during a particular production period, the quantity of that factor, when multiplied by its unit price, equals the cost incurred in using that factor. Long-lived inputs to the production process, such as plant and equipment, are not generally consumed in a single production period, but instead provide a stream of services over many periods.

The extreme case of a long-lived productive input is a factor which could go on producing a stream of productive services forever. Land is the closest approximation to such an input. If V_i is the number of units of a permanent productive factor and if W_i is the price per unit of this factor, then $W_i V_i$ is the total "once-and-for-all" expenditure which the firm makes for this factor. Such an expenditure will produce services in every future period, and hence it cannot be directly added to the rates of expenditures on the short-lived inputs to determine the total costs of the firm for any one period.

The way out of our dilemma is to utilize the concept of opportunity cost. As an alternative to purchasing one unit of the long-lived productive factor, the firm could have invested W_i dollars in some form that would have paid a return of rW_i dollars each period, where r is the rate of return. Thus the opportunity cost of using one unit of the long-lived productive factor is rW_i dollars per period. If all the long-lived input factors were permanent, then the firm's long-run total costs in each period are

$$LTC = \sum_{j=1}^{N} w_j v_j + \sum_{i=1}^{H} rW_i V_i. \qquad (8\text{--}3)$$

A more general case is to assume that each long-lived input does not necessarily last forever, but instead that it has some definite, finite life. Suppose that input i has a lifetime of L_i periods. Then if a stock of V_i units of this input is permanently maintained, expenditures of $W_i V_i$ dollars must be made every L_i periods. We must convert this stream of expenditures into an appropriate cost per period.

Again the concept of opportunity cost is invoked. To do so, it is necessary to utilize the concept of the *present value* of an expenditure. Consider the case where $1.00 is put into a savings account which pays interest at the rate of 6 per cent per year. At the end of one year, the initial deposit has increased in value to $1.06. Therefore, the value today of $1.06 one year from now is $1.00. Clearly only $(1/1.06)$ would need to be invested at 6 per cent per year in order to have $1.00 at the end of one year. Hence the present value of $1.00 one year hence is $(1/1.06)$. Similarly, the present value of $1.00 two years hence is $[\$1/(1.06)^2]$, and the present value of $1.00 n years hence is $[\$1/(1.06)^n]$.

Thus the present value of an expenditure of W_i dollars which is to be made at the end of L_i periods is $W_i/[(1 + r)^{L_i}]$, assuming that the rate of interest is r. Letting S denote the present value of the expenditures required for the firm always to have one unit of the input, we have

$$S = W_i + \frac{W_i}{(1 + r)^{L_i}} + \frac{W_i}{(1 + r)^{2L_i}} + \frac{W_i}{(1 + r)^{3L_i}} + \cdots \qquad (8\text{--}4)$$

The right-hand side of Eq. (8–4) is an infinite geometric series, with constant ratio $1/[(1 + r)^{L_i}]$. Applying the formula for the sum of an infinite geometric series, we then have[1]

$$S = \frac{W_i}{1 - [1/(1 + r)^{L_i}]} = \frac{W_i}{1 - (1 + r)^{-L_i}} . \qquad (8\text{–}5)$$

The present value in Eq. (8–5) can be converted into an equivalent opportunity cost per period by multiplying S by the interest rate r. Therefore U_i, the opportunity cost which is incurred each period when one unit is purchased every L_i periods is

$$U_i = \frac{rW_i}{1 - (1 + r)^{-L_i}} . \qquad (8\text{–}6)$$

The right-hand side of Eq. (8–6) reduces to rW_i when L_i is infinite. Thus the present case includes the case where i is a permanent input.

As a generalization of Eq. (8–3), the firm's long-run total costs in each period are

$$LTC = \sum_{j=1}^{N} w_j v_j + \sum_{i=1}^{H} U_i V_i. \qquad (8\text{–}7)$$

In order to derive the firm's long-run total cost function, we need to find the values of the v_j and the V_i which would be used to produce each rate of

---

[1] If A is the first term and if r is the constant ratio, then the formula for the sum of the first n terms in a geometric series is

$$S_n = A\left(\frac{1 - r^n}{1 - r}\right),$$

and the formula for the sum of all the terms in a convergent infinite geometric series (i.e., a series for which $0 < r < 1$) is

$$S_\infty = \frac{A}{1 - r} .$$

These formulas are derived in the following way:

$S_n = A + Ar + Ar^2 + \ldots + Ar^{n-1}$	(by definition).
$rS_n = Ar + Ar^2 + Ar^3 + \ldots + Ar^n$	(multiply the previous equation by r).
$S_n - rS_n = A(1 - r^n)$	(subtract the foregoing two equations).
$S_n = A\left(\dfrac{1 - r^n}{1 - r}\right)$	(solve the preceding equation for S_n).
$\lim_{n\to\infty} r^n = 0$	(S_∞ converges only when $0 < r < 1$).
$S_\infty = \lim_{n\to\infty} S_n = \dfrac{A}{1 - r}$	(from the foregoing two relations).

output q. Since the firm wishes to produce each rate of output at the lowest possible total cost, we can solve this problem by finding the values of the v_j and the V_i which minimize Eq. (8–7) subject to the constraint Eq. (8–1).

To solve this constrained minimization problem, we form the Lagrangian function:

$$L = \sum_{j=1}^{N} w_j v_j + \sum_{i=1}^{H} U_i V_i - \lambda[G(v_1, \ldots, v_N, V_1, \ldots, V_H) - q]. \qquad (8\text{–}8)$$

Equating to zero the derivatives of Eq. (8–8) with respect to each v_j and each V_i:

$$\frac{\partial L}{\partial v_j} = w_j - \lambda \frac{\partial G}{\partial v_j} = 0 \qquad j = 1, \ldots, N. \qquad (8\text{–}9)$$

$$\frac{\partial L}{\partial V_i} = U_i - \lambda \frac{\partial G}{\partial V_i} = 0 \qquad i = 1, \ldots, H. \qquad (8\text{–}10)$$

From these equations, together with the production function, Eq. (8–1), it is possible to determine the optimum mix of inputs for producing each rate of output q. Letting $\bar{v}_j(q)$ and $\bar{V}_i(q)$ denote the optimum inputs for a given q, these values can be substituted into Eq. (8–7) to yield the firm's long-run total cost function:

$$LTC(q) = \sum_{j=1}^{N} w_j \bar{v}_j(q) + \sum_{i=1}^{H} U_i \bar{V}_i(q). \qquad (8\text{–}11)$$

We have explicitly written $\bar{v}_j(q)$ and $\bar{V}_i(q)$ as functions of q, since the optimum mix of inputs will vary for each output. For any given q, Eq. (8–11) indicates the minimum total cost at which that output may be produced when both the v_j and the V_i are permitted to vary. Hence the long-run total cost curve shows the minimum total cost at which each output can be produced.

The theorems proved in Chapter 7 also apply in the long run when appropriate costs are assigned to long-lived inputs. Note that the cost of a long-lived input will change if there are changes in the following variables: (a) the market price, W_i; (b) the interest rate, r; (c) the length of life, L_i. If we regard "labor" as a short-lived input and "capital" as a long-lived input, then (*ceteris paribus*) capital will be substituted for labor whenever the market price of capital goods decreases, the interest rate declines, or capital goods become more durable, for these all are ways in which the cost of capital can fall relative to the cost of labor. The demand function for long-lived inputs for an individual firm, and hence for the market as a whole, can also be seen to depend not only upon the market prices but also upon the interest rate and the durability of the factors.

B. The Long-Run Average Cost Function

On the basis of a firm's long-run total cost function, two additional long-run cost functions can be defined. The long-run average cost function, LAC, is the long-run total cost per unit of output:

$$LAC(q) = \frac{LTC(q)}{q}. \qquad (8\text{--}12)$$

The long-run marginal cost function, LMC, is the rate of change in long-run total cost with respect to changes in output:

$$LMC(q) = \frac{d}{dq} LTC(q). \qquad (8\text{--}13)$$

The preceding section derived the firm's long-run total cost function mathematically. It is useful to provide an alternative graphical interpretation of this process. This is most conveniently done in terms of the long-run average cost function rather than the long-run total cost function. In view of Eq. (8–12), finding that combination of short-lived and long-lived input factors which minimizes $LTC(q)$ for a given output is equivalent to finding that combination of factors which minimizes $LAC(q)$.

For any given stock of the long-lived inputs, i.e., any particular scale of plant, there is a corresponding short-run average total cost curve. Consider for the moment six different scales of plants, i.e., six different stocks for all long-lived input factors. The short-run average total cost curves which correspond to each of these six plants are shown in Figure 8–1.

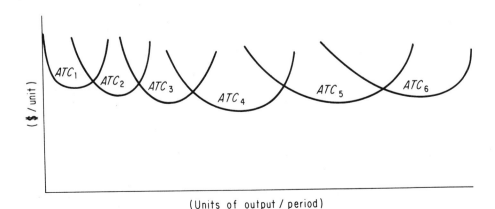

FIGURE 8–1.   Average total cost curves for six plants.

We regard Figure 8–1 as a representative selection from the set of possible short-run average total cost curves which a firm can obtain, for we shall assume that all input factors are completely divisible. Thus, we can conceptually divide the long-lived inputs into infinitesimal units, and thereby make one plant only infinitesimally larger than another. Therefore, in actuality, there are an infinite number of plants between each of the cost curves portrayed in Figure 8–1.

The discrete set of curves drawn in Figure 8–1 illustrates two propositions. The first (and least important) is that, as we build larger plants, each has an increasing range of outputs over which it can operate. Second, to each plant there corresponds a particular set of outputs which can be produced most economically by that plant. If we added the additional plants that it is possible to build, we would find that there is one rate of output which each of the plants can produce at the least cost, a rate of output which in general does not occur at the minimum point of that plant's average total cost curve.

This may be seen most clearly if we consider the short-run average total cost, ATC, to be a function of both the rate of output, q, and the scale of plant, s. The scale of plant for which a given rate of output q can be most economically produced is determined by finding that s for which $ATC(q, s)$ is minimal, and this is the way in which the long-run average cost curve is defined. In contrast, the minimum point on a given plant's average total cost curve is determined by finding that q for which $ATC(q, s)$ is minimal. In general,

$$\min_{s} ATC(q, s) \neq \min_{q} ATC(q, s). \tag{8–14}$$

The one exception occurs for that scale of plant for which the corresponding average total cost curve is tangent at its minimal point to the long-run average cost curve. Economists call this particular scale of plant the *optimal scale of plant*. The minimum possible cost per unit of output can be produced by the optimum scale of plant, for

$$\min_{q} \min_{s} ATC(q, s) = \min_{s} \min_{q} ATC(q, s). \tag{8–15}$$

On the basis of our assumptions, it is possible to draw a continuous curve which is tangent to each of the short-run average total cost curves at the rate of output for which a plant of that size is most efficient. Such a curve is the long-run average cost curve, LAC; it is shown in Figure 8–2, along with some representative short-run average total cost curves.

The long-run average cost curve in Figure 8–2 is drawn with a positive slope after its minimum point is passed. The basis for increasing average costs must be some form of diminishing returns. These arise because of the increasing problems of management. The costs of coordination and control

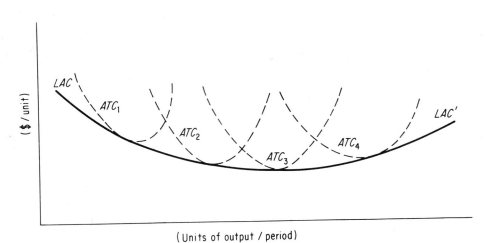

FIGURE 8–2.   Long-run average cost curve.

increase proportionately more than output as plants get larger and larger. Eventually the increased management costs offset the gains from the lower production costs of larger-scale operations. In technical terms, we say that economies of scale are limited, and that after some point decreasing returns to scale will begin. The optimum scale of plant, that is the plant having the lowest possible average total cost, as illustrated in Figures 8–1 and 8–2, will not be the largest possible plant.[2]

The long-run average cost curve sometimes is called a *planning curve*. This terminology is descriptive because the long-run average cost curve exhibits the alternative cost-volume production opportunities for a particular firm at a given time. We specify at a given time because the state of technology is assumed known and fixed in determining the long-run average cost curve in such a manner that its minimum point moves downward and to the right.

It is important to determine the relationships among the long-run average cost curves of different firms. Since some managers are more efficient and generally more capable than others, we would expect the better managers

---

[2] It should be noted that, as an empirical proposition, not all economists agree that the long-run average cost curve must be U-shaped. Some economists argue that, on the basis of available empirical evidence, this curve should frequently be thought of as L-shaped, as in Figure 8–3, rather than U-shaped. For example: "The empirical results on long-run costs seem to us to confirm the widespread existence of economies of scale. The evidence on diseconomies is much less certain for, while there is in some studies a suggestion of an upturn at the top end of the size scale, it is usually small in magnitude and well within the range of variation displayed by the data." J. Johnston, *Statistical Cost Analysis* (New York: McGraw-Hill Book Company, Inc., 1960), p. 193.

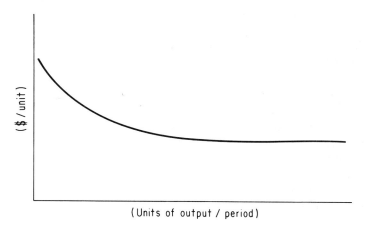

FIGURE 8–3. L-shaped long-run average cost curve.

to be able to coordinate and control larger amounts of factors and, therefore, operate efficiently at larger scales of output. Hence the minimum point on the *LAC* curve need not necessarily occur at the same output rate for every firm. We shall, however, show that the minimum point of the *LAC* curve will be at the same cost per unit for all firms in the industry at long-run equilibrium, even though these common minimum costs per unit may occur at different output rates.

First consider the case of a firm whose minimum point on its *LAC* curve represents a higher cost per unit than the minimum points of other firms. If this firm is considering entrance into the industry, it will be discouraged since its higher costs will lead to lower profits or higher losses than other firms in the industry obtain. If this firm is in the industry, it will eventually be driven out by competition from the lower-cost firms, as we shall prove in Section II.

Next consider the case of a firm which, because of an efficient manager, has a minimum cost that is lower than the minima of the other firms in the industry. Let us assume that this efficient manager is not the owner, but that he has been hired at some stated salary. Since his superior ability accounts for the lower cost, it is worthwhile for another firm to offer a higher salary to bid him away. In this way, by the process of other salary bids, we would expect the manager's salary to rise to the point where the minimum costs for the firm hiring him exactly equal the minimum costs of other firms, although each firm might be operating at a different scale of output. On the other hand, if the efficient manager were the owner, then the use of opportunity costs (the salary he could earn elsewhere) would raise the minimum costs of this firm to equality with those of other firms. Similarly, if the lower unit cost were due to cheap rent on the land because of an old lease or some other special arrangement with another type of resource, then the use of opportunity costs would equalize the minimum costs.

C. A Relationship Between the Short-Run and Long-Run Marginal Cost Curves

It is necessary to establish a relationship between the short-run and the long-run marginal cost curves. The long-run marginal cost curve intersects the short-run marginal cost curve corresponding to each possible scale of plant at the same rate of output for which the short-run average total cost curve of that plant is tangent to the long-run average cost curve. This relationship is illustrated in Figure 8–4.

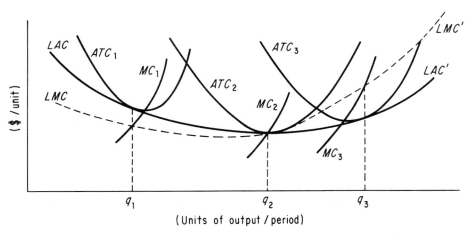

Figure 8–4. Relationship between the short-run and long-run marginal cost curves.

Let Q_i be the rate of output for which the ith scale of plant is most economical relative to any other scale of plant. Hence the short-run average total cost curve corresponding to the ith scale of plant must be tangent to the long-run average cost curve at an output Q_i. Using a subscript i to designate the short-run cost curves corresponding to the ith scale of plant, the tangency condition may be expressed as

$$LAC(Q_i) = ATC_i(Q_i) \qquad (8\text{–}16)$$

$$\frac{d}{dq}[LAC(q)]_{q=Qi} = \frac{d}{dq}[ATC_i(q)]_{q=Qi}. \qquad (8\text{–}17)$$

In order to establish the relationship we asserted between the short-run and long-run marginal cost curves, we need to prove that whenever Eq. (8–16) and Eq. (8–17) hold, then

$$LMC(Q_i) = MC_i(Q_i) \tag{8–18}$$

necessarily also holds.

To prove this, note that

$$LMC(Q_i) = \frac{d}{dq}[LTC(q)]_{q=Q_i} = \frac{d}{dq}[q \cdot LAC(q)]_{q=Q_i}$$

$$= LAC(Q_i) + Q_i \frac{d}{dq}[LAC(q)]_{q=Q_i}. \tag{8–19}$$

Similarly,

$$MC_i(Q_i) = \frac{d}{dq}[TC_i(q)]_{q=Q_i} = \frac{d}{dq}[q \cdot ATC_i(q)]_{q=Q_i}$$

$$= ATC_i(Q_i) + Q_i \frac{d}{dq}[ATC_i(q)]_{q=Q_i}. \tag{8–20}$$

If we multiply both sides of Eq. (8–17) by Q_i and add the resulting equation to Eq. (8–16), we obtain

$$LAC(Q_i) + Q_i \frac{d}{dq}[LAC(q)]_{q=Q_i} = ATC_i(Q_i) + Q_i \frac{d}{dq}[ATC_i(q)]_{q=Q_i}. \tag{8–21}$$

From Eq. (8–19), we see that the left-hand side of Eq. (8–21) is $LMC(Q_i)$. From Eq. (8–20), we see that the right-hand side of Eq. (8–21) is $MC_i(Q_i)$. Hence Eq. (8–18) must be valid, thus completing the proof.

D. A SPECIFIC ILLUSTRATION

A specific example is useful to illustrate some of the concepts which we have been developing. Suppose that the set of possible short-run average total cost curves for a firm is defined by

$$ATC(q, s) = (q - s)^2 + (s - a)^2 + b, \tag{8–22}$$

where s is a variable which represents the firm's scale of plant, and a and b are constants.

To derive the long-run average cost curve from the family of possible short-run average total cost curves in Eq. (8–22), for each q we must find the particular s which minimizes $ATC(q, s)$. This can be done by setting the partial derivative of $ATC(q, s)$ with respect to s equal to zero and solving the resulting equation for s. Thus

$$\frac{\partial}{\partial s} ATC(q, s) = -2(q - s) + 2(s - a) = 0, \qquad (8\text{–}23)$$

or
$$s = \frac{q + a}{2}. \qquad (8\text{–}24)$$

Equation (8–24) indicates the most efficient scale of plant for producing an output rate q. The larger the rate of output which is to be produced, the larger the corresponding plant should be.

To determine the long-run average cost function, substitute Eq. (8–24) into Eq. (8–22), obtaining

$$LAC(q) = \left(q - \frac{q + a}{2}\right)^2 + \left(\frac{q + a}{2} - a\right)^2 + b, \qquad (8\text{–}25)$$

which simplifies to

$$LAC(q) = \tfrac{1}{2}(q - a)^2 + b. \qquad (8\text{–}26)$$

Because of the manner in which $LAC(q)$ has been derived, it is necessarily true that $LAC(q)$ is tangent to $ATC(q, s)$ when s is defined by Eq. (8–24). Hence the long-run average cost curve in Eq. (8–26) is the envelope to the family of short-run average total cost curves in Eq. (8–22).

To verify that the relationship established in the preceding section holds for the long-run and short-run marginal cost curves in this example, we proceed as follows. First find the long-run and the short-run total cost curves by multiplying Eq. (8–26) and (8–22) by q:

$$LTC(q) = \tfrac{1}{2}q(q - a)^2 + bq. \qquad (8\text{–}27)$$

$$TC(q, s) = q(q - s)^2 + q(s - a)^2 + bq. \qquad (8\text{–}28)$$

Next obtain the long-run and short-run marginal cost curves by differentiating Eq. (8–27) and (8–28) with respect to q, obtaining

$$LMC(q) = q(q - a) + \tfrac{1}{2}(q - a)^2 + b. \qquad (8\text{–}29)$$

$$MC(q, s) = 2q(q - s) + (q - s)^2 + (s - a)^2 + b. \qquad (8\text{–}30)$$

Substituting Eq. (8–24) into Eq. (8–30), we have

$$MC(q) = 2q\left(q - \frac{q + a}{2}\right) + \left(q - \frac{q + a}{2}\right)^2 + \left(\frac{q + a}{2} - a\right)^2 + b. \quad (8\text{–}31)$$

Simplifying the right-hand side of Eq. (8–31),

$$MC(q) = q(q - a) + \tfrac{1}{2}(q - a)^2 + b. \qquad (8\text{–}32)$$

Equations (8–29) and (8–30) imply that

$$LMC(q) = MC(q) \tag{8-33}$$

verifying the relationship established in Section C.

II. Long-Run Equilibrium of a Perfectly Competitive Market

With the understanding of the long-run production decisions of individual firms gained in Section I, we can now consider the manner in which these decisions collectively determine the long-run supply function for the market. We shall show that a perfectly competitive market is in long-run equilibrium if and only if the following conditions hold for every firm in the market:

$$MC = ATC = LMC = LAC = \text{price.} \tag{8-34}$$

Thus a necessary condition for market equilibrium is that the demand curve for each firm be tangent to its LAC curve at the minimum point. This implies that every firm in the industry is driven to the optimum-sized plant in the long run (recall that the optimum-sized plant is the plant whose ATC curve is tangent to the LAC curve at the minimum point). Figure 8–5 illustrates the long-run equilibrium conditions, Eq. (8–34).

Let us now prove that the conditions in Eq. (8–34) are necessary and sufficient for the long-run equilibrium of a perfectly competitive market. We shall show that if these conditions are not satisfied, then forces will be set in motion which will drive the firms in the market to positions where Eq. (8–34) is satisfied. Furthermore, we shall show that when the con-

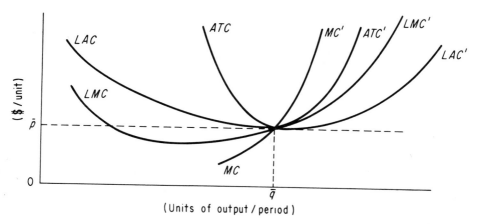

FIGURE 8–5.   Long-run equilibrium conditions for the firm.

ditions in Eq. (8–34) are satisfied, there will be no tendency for any firm to alter its output or enter or leave the industry. The particular dynamic process through which long-run equilibrium is reached will depend upon the initial position of the market. Since the same types of arguments can be made regardless of the initial position, we shall illustrate only one such movement.

Let the industry be in long-run equilibrium initially; i.e., suppose Eq. (8–34) is satisfied. For ease of exposition, assume that all firms in the industry have the same LAC curve and the same sized plant. The market price is $\bar{p}$ and each firm produces an output $\bar{q}$, as illustrated in Figure 8–5. If there are N firms in the industry, then the total industry output is $N\bar{q}$, and the market equilibrium position occurs at the intersection of the market demand curve, DD, and the short-run market supply curve, SS, as shown in Figure 8–6.

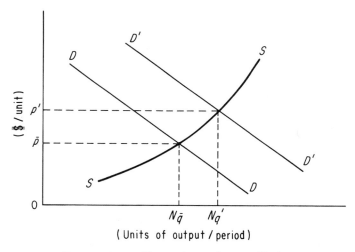

FIGURE 8–6. Change in market equilibrium.

Now assume an increase in market demand from DD to $D'D'$. The shift in demand will result in a new short-run equilibrium price p', after the firms complete their short-run output adjustments to the new demand situation. Total industry output is now Nq'. Each firm produces an output q' and earns positive profits as shown by the shaded area in Figure 8–7. These profits will attract new firms into the industry.

The new firms entering the industry must decide what size plants they will build. The rational decision for them would be to build the optimum-sized plant, i.e., the same size of plant shown in Figure 8–5, since this

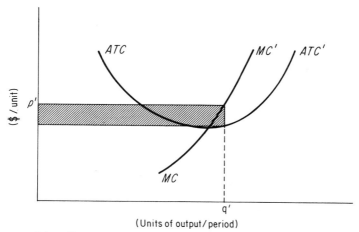

FIGURE 8–7. Short-run equilibrium of the firm after the shift in demand.

would enable them eventually to attain the minimum long-run average cost. If the new firms behave this way, then the new long-run equilibrium position can be attained with the minimum number of adjustments. For generality, however, we shall deal with a slightly more complex case and assume that the new firms decide to build that scale of plant for which price equals long-run marginal cost; i.e., that scale of plant which will enable them to maximize long-run profits if the current price prevails forever. Suppose then that the new firms build the scale of plant shown in Figure 8–8. At the current price p', each of the new firms will produce an output of q_0, and each will earn positive profits.

The effect of the entry of new firms into the industry is to shift the industry's short-run supply curve to the right. If we assume that n firms have entered the industry and built the plants shown in Figure 8–8, then the short-run market supply curve will shift from SS to $S'S'$, as shown in Figure 8–9. At the price p', the total amount supplied would now be $Nq' + nq_0$. Since this amount exceeds the amount demanded at the price p', the market price will fall until a new short-run equilibrium price is established at p''.

Suppose that at p'' the plants shown in Figure 8–8 are earning zero profits, as shown in Figure 8–8. It is clear that the optimum-sized plants in Figure 8–5 are still earning positive profits. Thus there are still incentives for new firms to enter the industry. If they behaved as the previous entrants, each new firm would build the plant for which price equals long-run marginal cost. In this case the new plants would be between the two existing plant sizes. The result would be to shift the supply curve farther to the right and lower price still further. This reduction in price would result in

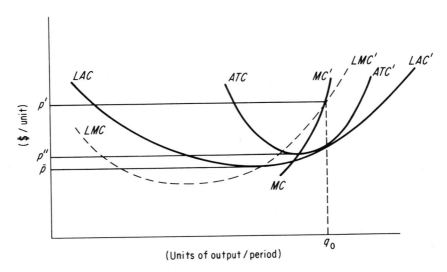

FIGURE 8–8.   New plant size.

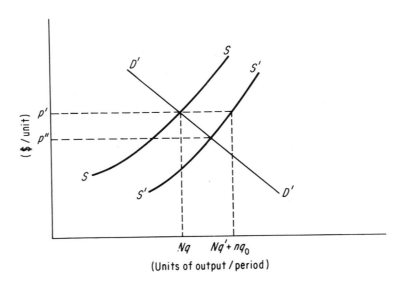

FIGURE 8–9.   Market with new firms.

the gradual elimination of the n firms that had entered earlier. Similarly the second group of entrants will eventually leave the industry when price falls below their average total cost curve, while the optimum-sized plants in Figure 8–5 will still be earning positive profits. This indicates why we had said earlier that the rational decision for a new firm is to build an optimum-sized plant. Thus we would continue to get a repetition of the same situation until all firms in the industry have optimum-sized plants and the short-run market supply curve shifts far enough to the right so that it intersects the market demand curve, $D'D'$, at the initial long-run equilibrium price p. At this point, the conditions in Eq. (8–34) will again prevail, but now there will be more than N firms in the industry. Again all firms in the industry are earning zero profits, and there is no incentive for further entry or exit to occur.

This illustrates the way in which the entry and the exit of firms modify the supply curve and affect price, moving the industry toward its point of long-run equilibrium. Thus if the demand curve falls, a similar adjustment process would occur, except that now firms would have to leave the industry. The supply curve would shift to the left until price is reestablished at the long-run equilibrium level, p, as shown in Figure 8–5. Now, however, there will be fewer than N firms in the industry.

III. Constant-, Increasing-, and Decreasing-Cost Industries

In our illustration of long-run equilibrium adjustments, we have assumed that the position of the long-run average cost curve is unaffected by the entry or exit of firms. This implies that the prices of inputs used by this industry remain the same regardless of the amounts of each input demanded, and the long-run equilibrium price is independent of the number of firms in the industry and the total industry output. An industry having these characteristics is called a *constant-cost* industry.

An *increasing-cost* industry is an industry in which the long-run equilibrium price is directly related to the number of firms in the industry and the total industry output. Thus if demand increases in such an industry, some factor prices will rise as the industry expands output, the long-run average cost curve will move upward, and therefore the long-run equilibrium price will increase. Conversely, if demand falls in such an industry, the net effect of the various adjustments will be a lower long-run equilibrium price.

A *decreasing-cost* industry is an industry in which the long-run equilibrium price is inversely related to the number of firms in the industry and the total industry output. Thus an increase in demand in such an industry will lead to a lower long-run equilibrium price.

The *long-run supply curve* for an industry is the locus of long-run equilibrium points. Each point on the long-run supply curve represents a possible long-run equilibrium combination of price and output for the

industry. It is clear that the long-run supply curve is horizontal for a
constant-cost industry, upward-sloping for an increasing-cost industry,
and downward-sloping for a decreasing-cost industry.

We shall now show how we can algebraically derive the long-run supply
curve for a perfectly competitive industry in sufficient generality to include
the cases of increasing-cost and decreasing-cost industries. Let us initially
assume that all the actual and potential firms in the industry have the same
long-run total cost function; this assumption will later be relaxed. Under
this simplifying assumption, in long-run equilibrium all firms in the industry
will have the same output, which we denote by q, and the same scale of
plant, which we denote by k. Let Q be the total industry output, N the
number of firms in the industry, and P the market price.

Increasing-cost and decreasing-cost industries differ from constant-cost
industries in that the total cost function for any firm is a function of the
total industry output and the number of firms in the industry, as well as
of the individual firm's output and scale of plant. Thus the total cost function of any firm in the industry can be represented as follows:

$$TC = TC(q, k, Q, N). \tag{8-35}$$

The average total cost function for a firm is:

$$ATC(q, k, Q, N) = \frac{TC(q, k, Q, N)}{q}. \tag{8-36}$$

The long-run average cost function for a firm is determined by utilizing
the scale of plant that is most efficient for any particular output level; this
may be expressed as:

$$LAC(q, Q, N) = \min_k ATC(q, k, Q, N). \tag{8-37}$$

Let us now define $m(Q, N)$ as the minimal height on a firm's long-run
average cost function when industry output is Q and there are N firms in
the industry. Thus

$$m(Q, N) = \min_q LAC(q, Q, N). \tag{8-38}$$

When the industry is in long-run equilibrium, the number of firms in the
industry must be constant. Hence the minimal height of a firm's long-run
average cost function must be the long-run equilibrium price, because only
at that price will a firm have zero profits in the long run and there will be
no incentives for firms to enter or leave the industry. That is,

$$P = m(Q, N) = \min_q LAC(q, Q, N). \tag{8-39}$$

The equilibrium condition $P = m(Q, N)$ determines one point on the
long-run supply function of the industry. In order to determine other points

on the industry's long-run supply function, we must first derive this function by suitably aggregating the long-run supply functions of the firms in the industry. To derive a firm's long-run supply function, we must first start with its long-run total cost and marginal cost functions.

A firm's long-run total cost function is:

$$LTC(q, Q, N) = q \cdot LAC(q, Q, N). \tag{8-40}$$

A firm's long-run marginal cost function is:

$$LMC(q, Q, N) = \frac{d[LTC(q, Q, N)]}{dq}. \tag{8-41}$$

The long-run supply function of a firm is the upward-rising portion of its long-run marginal cost curve which intersects or lies above its long-run average cost curve. Hence, we can determine the long-run supply function of a firm,

$$q = s(P, Q, N) \tag{8-42}$$

by solving the equation,

$$P = LMC(q, Q, N) \tag{8-43}$$

for q as a function of P, Q, and N, verifying that the resulting q is a point which maximizes the firm's profits, and imposing the condition that

$$P \geq m(Q, N). \tag{8-44}$$

Note that

$$s(P, Q, N) = 0 \text{ if } P < m(Q, N) \tag{8-45}$$

because the firm cannot then cover its costs. Thus the firm's long-run supply function, expressing q as a function of P, with Q and N appearing as parameters, is determined in Eq. (8–42) by the type of analysis embodied in Eq. (8–43) through (8–45).

When there are exactly N firms in the industry, the long-run quantity supplied by these N firms is:

$$Q = Nq = N \cdot s(P, Q, N). \tag{8-46}$$

Equation (8–46) is not the form in which we wish to express the industry's long-run supply function, because the right-hand side of Eq. (8–46) is not expressed as a function of P alone. In order to eliminate Q and N from the right-hand side of Eq. (8–46), we must utilize the zero profits condition that must hold in long-run equilibrium, and that is expressed in Eq. (8–39).

Thus, our next step is simultaneously to solve the following pair of equations:

$$\left. \begin{array}{l} Q = N \cdot s(P, Q, N) \\ P = m(Q, N) \end{array} \right\}. \tag{8-47}$$

This solution then will express both Q and N as functions of P:

$$Q = S(P) \tag{8-48}$$

and

$$N = F(P). \tag{8-49}$$

Note that Eq. (8–48) is the desired long-run industry supply function, expressing long-run equilibrium industry output as a function of price. Equation (8–49) is a function that indicates the long-run equilibrium number of firms in the industry as a function of price.

Although the preceding analysis was general enough to accommodate the cases of increasing-cost and decreasing-cost industries, it did utilize an assumption that all firms in the industry are identical. This assumption is merely convenient, but not essential, as we shall now show. Suppose that different firms in the industry have different cost functions. For any pair of firms, i and j, which are in the industry at long-run equilibrium, we must have

$$P = \min_{q_i} LAC_i(q_i, Q, N) = \min_{q_j} LAC_j(q_j, Q, N) = m(Q, N). \tag{8-50}$$

In Eq. (8–50), subscripts to the individual firm's output and long-run average cost function have been added to denote the particular firm.

The reason that Eq. (8–50) must hold is that when the industry is in long-run equilibrium, each firm in the industry must have zero profits. Any firm for which the minimum height on its long-run average cost curve was greater than price would be losing money, and hence would leave the industry. Similarly, any firm for which the minimum height on its long-run average cost curve was lower than price would be earning positive profits, and this would attract the entry of other firms to the industry.

Because various firms in the industry may have different cost functions, the long-run supply function for a firm must be derived individually for each firm. This development will be entirely analogous to the derivations in Eq. (8–40) through (8–45) above, except that now there will be subscripts added to denote the output and cost functions for a specific firm. Thus, analogous to Eq. (8–42), we will derive the long-run supply function for firm i as

$$q_i = s_i(P, Q, N). \tag{8-51}$$

To determine the long-run supply function of the industry, note that (8–46) now becomes

$$Q = \sum_{i=1}^{N} q_i = \sum_{i=1}^{N} s_i(P, Q, N). \tag{8-52}$$

We now simultaneously solve the following pair of equations, derived from Eq. (8–52) and the zero profits equilibrium condition, Eq. (8–50):

$$
\left.
\begin{aligned}
Q &= \sum_{i=1}^{N} s_i(P,\, Q,\, N) \\
P &= m(Q,\, N)
\end{aligned}
\right\} . \tag{8–53}
$$

The simultaneous solution to Eq. (8–53) then expresses both Q and N as functions of P, analogously to the expressions Eq. (8–48) and (8–49). We thus have shown how the long-run supply function of the industry, $Q = S(P)$, and the number of firms in the industry in long-run equilibrium, $N = F(P)$, can be algebraically derived when various firms in the industry may have different cost functions, and when we may be dealing with an increasing-cost or a decreasing-cost, instead of a constant-cost industry.

In general, whether an industry will display constant or increasing costs depends upon the industry's demand for the factors it uses relative to the total demand for these factors. For example, the needle industry could expand without its increased demand for steel raising steel prices; but a rise in the automobile industry's demand for steel might well force an increase in the price of steel.

Decreasing costs are difficult to analyze in a perfectly competitive economy. It is difficult to see how a decreasing-cost industry can exist unless there are imperfect markets or external economies. For example, if an input used by a competitive industry was supplied by a monopolist, then an increase in the demand for this input might push the monopolist toward a more economical size of plant and thereby lower his costs, allowing him to sell the input to the competitive industry at a lower price. The concept of external economies may help explain a decreasing-cost industry. *External economies* are reductions in costs which occur when the industry as a whole expands. Consider, for example, a coal mine's costs in pumping out water. When the number of mines expands in a neighborhood, it is less costly for each individual mine to pump out the water. Another example of external economies might arise when an industry expands in a particular region. More labor might tend to move into the region, resulting in lower labor costs either because of lower wages or because of increased productivity from improved labor.

IV. Entry and Exit in Two Competitive Industries

On the basis of the theory presented in this chapter, we are particularly interested in examining the relationship between changes in prices and profits and the entry and exit of firms. In this connection we shall examine developments in two industries: bituminous coal and cotton textiles.

A. THE BITUMINOUS COAL INDUSTRY

The bituminous coal industry can reasonably be described by the perfectly competitive model. The number of bituminous coal mines in

TABLE 8–1

AVERAGE PRICE AND NUMBER OF MINES IN OPERATION IN THE UNITED STATES
BITUMINOUS COAL INDUSTRY (1910–57)

Year	Average Price (per ton)	Number of Mines	Year	Average Price (per ton)	Number of Mines
1910	$1.12	5,818	1935	1.77	6,315
1911	1.11	5,887	1936	1.76	6,875
1912	1.15	5,747	1937	1.94	6,548
1913	1.18	5,776	1938	1.95	5,777
1914	1.17	5,592	1939	1.84	5,820
1915	1.13	5,502	1940	1.91	6,324
1916	1.32	5,726	1941	2.19	6,822
1917	2.26	6,939	1942	2.36	6,972
1918	2.58	8,319	1943	2.69	6,620
1919	2.49	8,994	1944	2.92	6,928
1920	3.75	8,921	1945	3.06	7,033
1921	2.89	8,038	1946	3.44	7,333
1922	3.02	9,299	1947	4.16	8,700
1923	2.68	9,331	1948	4.99	9,079
1924	2.20	7,586	1949	4.88	8,559
1925	2.04	7,144	1950	4.84	9,429
1926	2.06	7,177	1951	4.92	8,009
1927	1.99	7,011	1952	4.90	7,275
1928	1.86	6,450	1953	4.92	6,671
1929	1.78	6,057	1954	4.52	6,130
1930	1.70	5,891	1955	4.50	7,856
1931	1.54	5,642	1956	4.82	8,520
1932	1.31	5,427	1957	5.08	8,539
1933	1.34	5,555			
1934	1.75	6,258			

SOURCE: James B. Hendry, "The Bituminous Coal Industry," in *The Structure of American Industry*, 3rd ed., ed. Walter Adams (New York: The Macmillan Company, 1961), table 1, pp. 78–79.

operation in the United States (which is not the same as the number of firms, since some firms operate more than one mine) has varied between 5,000 and 9,000 during the past half-century.[3] The product itself is highly standardized, because of the existence of a grading system.

[3] The information about the bituminous coal industry presented in this section is drawn from James B. Hendry, "The Bituminous Coal Industry," in *The Structure of American Industry*, 3rd ed., ed. Walter Adams (New York: The Macmillan Company, 1961), chap. 3.

Despite the general similarities between the bituminous coal industry and the perfectly competitive model, bituminous coal has been viewed as a "sick" industry; i.e., an industry that is unable to attain a long-run competitive equilibrium position when demand declines. It has been the object of much legislation aimed at maintaining profits in the industry. As we shall see, this inability to reach equilibrium arises because exit is difficult whereas entry is relatively easy.

The difficulty of exit stems from two factors. First, it is expensive to shut down a mine and then later reopen it for production. In terms of our earlier theory, this means that price may be below average variable costs and firms will still be better off to operate the mines rather than to shut down. Second, it is difficult to keep a mine closed for longer than a two-year period unless it is to be abandoned entirely, because of corrosion and water damage. This means that even mines which are shut down are likely to resume operations within a two-year period as soon as price equals average variable costs.

Because of the relative ease of entry and difficulty of exit, we would expect to see a marked increase in the number of bituminous coal mines in operation following an increase in price but only a small number of firms actually abandoning mines following a decrease in price. Table 8–1 shows some of the relationships between price and the number of mines in operation between 1910 and 1957. Notice that the column headed "Number of Mines" refers to mines in actual operation; therefore a decrease in the number of mines does not necessarily mean that firms have actually left the industry, since firms may have temporarily closed some of their mines.

The actual workings of competition in the bituminous coal industry can be best understood from the following description of events:

> The heavy demand of World War I, operating with accelerated impact on coal operators, brought new mines into operation quickly, jumped output and employment, and more than doubled the average price per ton (1915–18). High average prices continued into the postwar period, and, although production dropped in 1921–22, it climbed again to wartime levels in 1923. Prices started to decline after 1922 as industry began to enter a more "normal" period and the demand for coal underwent a shift downward.
>
> Market forces had thus brought about an allocation of coal reserves, labor, and capital into the coal industry through the lure of high prices and rising demand. Railroad rates had also encouraged opening distant mine fields by offering low ton-mile rates on long hauls. The demand shift of the early twenties, therefore, left more resources committed to coal production than consumers required at the old level of prices. The adjustment process required by the market was neither easy nor rapid. Operators faced strong incentives to maintain production, even in the face of declining demand; labor faced severe difficulties in moving into alternative kinds of employment, even, in fact, in leaving the mining communities. Operators could do little to alter their fixed costs, which in some cases reflected investments made during boom times, but they could try to do something about their variable

costs, of which labor cost was the most important. Their efforts to force wages down resulted in a breakdown of collective bargaining agreements in unionized areas. The nonunion areas had already reduced wages and were expanding sales. Competition was therefore "working," and it signaled a re-allocation of resources by bankruptcy, falling wages, and unemployment. This was the "excess capacity" problem which drew increasing attention as the decade of the twenties wore on. The onset of the depression in 1929 accelerated the decline in demand, now essentially a cyclical force rather than an adjustment of changing technology and the competition of other fuels. The coal industry continued to reflect the pressures on it as hourly wage rates, annual earnings, and average number of days worked declined for employees; production, average prices, and the number of mines declined for the operators. Industry operators as a whole showed a net loss in income from 1925 to 1940.[4]

B. The Cotton Textile Industry

The cotton textile industry has been described as an industry providing " . . . a closer approximation to perfect competition than any other manu-facturing industry in the United States . . . ."[5] In our discussion of this industry, we shall specifically focus on its principal product, grey cotton print cloth. The product can be regarded as homogeneous, since print cloth is sold in a few standard grades which are based on weight and closeness of weave; no brand names or advertising expenditures are used to differentiate the print cloth produced by one mill from that produced by another mill. There are a large number of buyers and sellers of print cloth, no one of whom is large enough to exercise any control over market price. The optimum scale of plant is small relative to total demand for the product, and entrance to the industry is relatively easy. "All in all, then, the industry conforms sufficiently well to the requirements of perfect competition that its operations may reasonably be compared with the results of theoretical reasoning."[6]

From 1924 through 1936 there appears to have been substantial excess capacity in the cotton textile industry. An indirect confirmation of the existence of this excess capacity can be obtained by comparing the profit ratios for all manufacturing firms in general with the profit ratios for all cotton textile firms, as shown in Table 8–2. During the periods 1924–28 and 1933–36, the profits of all manufacturing firms averaged 8.0 per cent of their capitalization, whereas the profits of all textile firms averaged 3.7 per cent of their capitalization; this " . . . is strong *prima facie* evidence

---

[4] *Ibid.*, pp. 101–102.

[5] The information about the cotton textile industry which we present in this section is drawn from Lloyd G. Reynolds, "Competition in the Cotton-Textile Industry: A Case Study," in *Readings in Economics*, ed. Walter Adams and Leland E. Traywick (New York: The Macmillan Company, 1948). The quotation in the text is from p. 147.

[6] *Ibid.*, p. 148.

TABLE 8–2

PROFITS AS A PERCENTAGE OF CAPITALIZATION FOR ALL MANUFACTURING FIRMS AND
FOR COTTON TEXTILE FIRMS IN THE UNITED STATES (1919–36)

Year	All Manufacturing Firms	Cotton Textile Firms		
		All	Northern	Southern
1919	18.3	32.5	n.a.*	n.a.
1920	12.3	12.1	n.a.	n.a.
1921	2.9	9.4	n.a.	n.a.
1922	10.2	11.4	n.a.	n.a.
1923	11.2	11.0	n.a.	n.a.
1924	10.0	1.3	n.a.	n.a.
1925	12.1	4.3	−1.6	5.2
1926	12.4	3.2	−0.4	3.7
1927	9.5	10.2	3.2	10.4
1928	11.0	4.7	2.9	5.7
1929	n.a.	n.a.	2.4	4.1
1930	n.a.	n.a.	n.a.	n.a.
1931	n.a.	n.a.	n.a.	n.a.
1932	n.a.	n.a.	n.a.	n.a.
1933	0.7	6.6	3.8	10.2
1934	3.0	1.3	−3.1	4.0
1935	5.7	−1.0	n.a.	n.a.
1936	7.9	2.6	n.a.	n.a.

* n.a., not available.

SOURCE: Lloyd G. Reynolds, "Competition in the Cotton-Textile Industry: A Case Study," in *Readings in Economics*, ed. Walter Adams and Leland E. Traywick (New York: The Macmillan Company, 1948), table I, p. 149.

that average profits in the [cotton textile] industry were below 'normal.' It is virtually certain that in every year from 1923 through 1938 the least efficient mills remaining in the industry had negative earnings."[7]

More direct evidence of the excess capacity in the cotton textile industry from 1924 through the late 1930's is available: "The consumption of cotton goods increased very little over this period, due in part to the development and cheapening of rayon fabrics. At the same time the productive capacity of the industry was increased by longer hours of plant operation and by the building of new plants in the southern states."[8]

As a result of their desires to spread fixed costs over larger volumes of

[7] *Ibid.*, p. 150.
[8] *Ibid.*, p. 148.

output, cotton textile mill operators found it desirable to operate their plants on more than a single-shift basis. Institutional changes during this period made it possible for the mill operators to implement their desires, so that the hours of operation of active spindles increased from 55 hours per week in 1923 to 75 hours per week in 1936. This increase in multiple-shift operations was equivalent to an increase of almost one-third in industry capacity during this period.

Wage rates, raw cotton costs, construction costs, and local tax rates were all lower in the South than in New England. Hence the profit ratios of Southern textile mills were substantially higher than the profit ratios of Northern textile mills during this period, as shown in Table 8–2. During the years for which data are available, the profits of Southern textile firms averaged 6.2 per cent of their capitalization, whereas the profits of Northern textile firms averaged 1.0 per cent of their capitalization. "The relative profitableness of cotton textiles in the South caused plant capacity to increase from 16 million spindles in 1923 to 18.5 million spindles in 1937. These additional plants intensified the problem of excess capacity in the industry as a whole."[9]

Starting in 1924 and lasting at least through 1936 the cotton textile industry was characterized by chronic excess capacity. Furthermore higher profits were earned during this period in Southern mills than in Northern mills. For both of these reasons it is clear that the industry was not in a state of long-run equilibrium. For long-run equilibrium to be established in the cotton textile industry, it was necessary not only for total industry capacity to be reduced by the exit of many mills, but also for this capacity reduction to be considerably more marked among Northern than among Southern mills. The theoretical analysis that we have presented in this chapter predicts that in such a situation many firms would leave the industry and other firms would relocate their plants until a long-run equilibrium situation was established. This is what actually happened in the cotton textile industry. Writing in 1940, Reynolds found that in fact competition did perform as expected on the basis of economic theory:

> The experience of the industry from 1923–38 may now be summarized. The development of excess capacity in the early twenties brought low earnings, which could be increased only by controlling production or by reducing plant capacity. For reasons already indicated, control proved impossible and events took the latter course. Under the pressure of shrinking processors' margins, elimination of marginal mills went steadily forward. The total number of spindles in place fell from a peak of 38 millions in 1925 to 27 millions in 1938. Available estimates indicate that the process of liquidation is nearing its end; and that the capacity of the industry is now only slightly in excess of probable future sales. Competition has thus performed, though tardily and haphazardly, its traditional function of adjusting productive

---

[9] *Ibid.*, p. 149.

capacity to effective demand. The process of adjustment, of course, has been painful for many of those connected with the industry. The chief losers have not been the owners of New England mills, whose investments had in most cases been thoroughly amortized from previous earnings, but the New England textile workers. The closing of the mills has thrown some 100,000 New England workers out of employment, and large numbers of these workers were still unemployed in 1937.[10]

V. Summary

In the long run firms can alter their rates of output both by changing the intensities with which any existing plants are used and by changing the scales of their plants. This chapter considered how the long-run production decisions of firms are made and the effects of these decisions on the pattern of resource allocation. The long-run production function of a firm relates the firm's rate of output to its rates of utilization of short-lived inputs and to its stocks of long-lived inputs. The short-run production function is determined when the actual value of the firm's stock of long-lived inputs is inserted in its long-run production function. In the long run, a firm chooses its rates of utilization of the variable inputs and its stock of fixed inputs to enable it to maximize profits by producing its chosen rate of output at the minimum possible total cost.

The long-run total cost function indicates the minimum possible cost at which the firm can produce any particular rate of output. In determining the least-cost combination of inputs, it is necessary to specify the costs attributed to long-lived inputs in the production process. The concept of opportunity cost is used for this purpose. The opportunity cost of using one unit of a permanent input was shown to be rW_i dollars per period. The opportunity cost of using one unit of an input that needs to be replaced every L_i periods was shown to be $rW_i/[1 - (1 + r)^{-L_i}]$ dollars per period.

Once the opportunity costs of using long-lived inputs were determined, we saw that the firm then solves a constrained minimization problem in order to find the points on its long-run total cost function. The analysis involved in solving this problem is similar to the analyses of short-run production functions that were undertaken in Chapter 7. When appropriate opportunity costs are assigned to long-lived productive factors, then the theorems proved in Chapter 7 also apply in the long run. In particular, we saw that capital will be substituted for labor, *ceteris paribus*, whenever the market price of capital goods decreases, the interest rate declines, or

---

[10] *Ibid.*, p. 151. The original version of Reynold's paper was published in 1940. [Lloyd G. Reynolds, "Cut-Throat Competition," *American Economic Review*, 30, No. 4 (December, 1940), 736–47.] Our quotations are drawn from the slightly modified version of this paper in Adams and Traywick, *op. cit.*

capital goods become more durable, for these are all ways in which the cost of capital can fall relative to the cost of labor.

The long-run average and marginal cost functions were defined in terms of the long-run total cost function. We showed that the long-run average cost curve is composed of points belonging to various short-run average total cost curves. The long-run average cost curve is tangent to a short-run average total cost curve at that point which is common to both curves. This point of tangency does not occur at the minimum point of the short-run average total cost curve except for the one short-run average total cost curve which corresponds to the optimum scale of plant. By definition, the optimum scale of plant is that plant size which enables the firm to produce at the minimum possible long-run average cost.

Although the minimum point on the long-run average cost curve for each firm may correspond to a different rate of output from firm to firm, we showed that the minimum attainable long-run average cost will be the same cost per unit for all firms in an industry when the industry is in long-run equilibrium. One reason is that any firm whose minimum attainable cost per unit is higher than that of other firms will eventually be driven out of the industry by competitive forces. The other reason is that any firm which temporarily is able to produce at a lower cost per unit than other firms because it possesses an unusually skillful manager will find that its opportunity cost of retaining the services of that manager will increase until its cost per unit equals that of other firms in the industry.

We proved that the long-run marginal cost curve intersects the short-run marginal cost curve corresponding to each possible scale of plant at the same rate of output for which the short-run average total cost curve of that plant is tangent to the long-run average cost curve. This result indicates that when a plant is built to maximize long-run profits at a given market price, then as long as price is unchanged, the most profitable output for the firm is the same in both the short run and the long run.

A necessary and sufficient condition for long-run equilibrium in a perfectly competitive market is that each firm in the industry must have that size of plant and be operating at that rate of output for which short-run marginal cost, short-run average total cost, long-run marginal cost, long-run average cost, and price are all equal. This implies that the demand curve for each firm will be tangent to its long-run average cost curve at the minimum point. Hence every firm in the industry has an optimum-sized plant. These conditions for long-run equilibrium were established by showing that whenever they do not hold, then the entry or exit of firms in response to profits or losses will change market conditions until the long-run equilibrium conditions once more hold. We illustrated one such movement toward long-run equilibrium by considering in detail how an industry responds to an increase in market demand. The initial result is an increase in price, as the existing firms expand their output to equate the new market demand curve with the original short-run market supply curve. At the higher price, there will be positive profits in the industry. These profits will attract new firms to the industry, thus shifting the short-run market supply curve to the right and causing a decrease in price. This process continues until enough new firms have entered with optimum-sized plants so that the demand curve for each firm is once more tangent to each firm's long-run average cost curve.

A constant-cost industry was defined as an industry in which the long-run equilibrium price is independent of the number of firms in the industry and the total industry output. An increasing-cost industry was defined as an industry in which the long-run equilibrium price is directly related to the number of firms in the industry and the total industry output. Finally, a decreasing-cost industry was defined as an industry in which the long-run equilibrium price is inversely related to the number of firms in the industry and the total industry output. A decreasing-cost industry can exist only if there are imperfect markets or external economies in the system.

To indicate the applicability of the theoretical analysis of long-run equilibrium adjustments in a perfectly competitive industry to industries in the real world, we concluded this chapter by examining the bituminous coal and the cotton textile industries. Each of these industries can reasonably be described as perfectly competitive. There are a large number of buyers and sellers, none of whom can control market price, standardized products, and relatively free entry in both industries. Exit is relatively free in cotton textiles but comparatively difficult in bituminous coal. Each of these industries suffered from overcapacity in the United States during the twentieth century. The overcapacity in bituminous coal resulted from a decline in the demand for coal (primarily stemming from the increased usage of substitute fuels) and the comparative difficulty of exit. In cotton textiles the overcapacity resulted from a stable demand combined with increased industry capacity due to a change to multishift operations and increased plant construction in the South (where costs were lower than in New England). Eventually the exit of firms, primarily in New England, was able to eliminate the excess capacity problem so that a long-run equilibrium position was attained in the cotton textile industry. The difficulty of exit prevented the attainment of long-run equilibrium in bituminous coal, however, and that industry still is plagued with overcapacity.

SUGGESTED READINGS

These recommendations are in addition to the footnote references cited in this chapter.

CAIRNCROSS, A. K., "The Optimum Firm Reconsidered," *The Economic Journal*, LXXXII (March, 1972), 312–20.

ELLIS, HOWARD S., AND WILLIAM FELLNER, "External Economies and Diseconomies," in *Readings in Price Theory*, George J. Stigler and Kenneth E. Boulding, eds., chap. 13. Homewood, Ill.: Richard D. Irwin, Inc., 1952.

HOFFMAN, A. C., "Changing Competition in the Food Trade," *Journal of Farm Economics*, LXI (December, 1959), 1185–96. (See also the discussion by R. W. Gray and S. N. Whitney in the same issue, 1207–12.)

PYATT, F. G., "Profit Maximization and the Threat of New Entry," *The Economic Journal*, LXXXI (June, 1971), 242–55.

ROBINSON, JOAN, "Rising Supply Price," in *Readings in Price Theory*, Stigler and Boulding, chap. 11.

RUBIN, P. H., "The Expansion of Firms," *Journal of Political Economy*, LXXXI (July/August, 1973), 936–49.

SHERMAN, R., "Entry Barriers and the Growth of Firms," *Southern Economic Journal*, XXXVIII (October, 1971), 238–47.

VINER, JACOB, "Cost Curves and Supply Curves," in *Readings in Price Theory*, Stigler and Boulding, chap. 10.

WHITIN, T. M., AND M. H. PESTON, "Random Variations, Risks, and Returns to Scale," *Quarterly Journal of Economics*, LXVIII (November, 1954), 603–12.

Chapter Nine

General Equilibrium Analysis

In preceding chapters, we have traced the determinants of the prices of consumer goods and productive factors in perfectly competitive markets. In doing this, we used a partial equilibrium approach, in which single competitive markets were viewed in isolation. For example, when we analyzed the manner in which the price of one particular consumer good is determined in a perfectly competitive market, we assumed that the prices of all other consumer goods, consumers' incomes, and factor prices were all given. Similarly, when we considered the determination of the selling price of a particular factor of production, we assumed that the prices of all other productive factors and of all consumer goods were given.

I. The Framework of General Equilibrium Analysis

The insights we have gained into the processes by which prices are determined and resources allocated in an economy justifies the use of partial equilibrium analysis. It is clear, however, that there are complex interactions among various markets. To answer some questions about the resource allocation process, it is necessary to focus attention upon market interrelationships. We can learn a great deal about how the price of butter is determined by using a partial equilibrium analysis which assumes that the price of oleomargarine is fixed. We also, however, need to be able to analyze the behavior of the price of butter under conditions which allow the price of oleomargarine to change simultaneously.

An approach which permits us to study the simultaneous determination of prices in several markets is general equilibrium analysis. There is little point in trying to undertake an elaborate verbal exposition of general equilibrium analysis. Verbal reasoning indicates that any departure from a previously obtained equilibrium position in any one market, e.g., a change in consumer tastes which increases the demand for beef, will have not only its direct effects, e.g., increasing both the price and quantity sold of beef, but also many secondary effects on the markets for pork, lamb, grazing land, feed grains, farm labor, etc. However, any attempts to trace in prose the entire set of ramifications of such a change will inevitably bog down because what in fact is a consistent, determinate set of simultaneous relations appears in verbal dress as an unending sequence of circularities. Since mathematics provides a convenient language for the analysis of a system of simultaneous relations, we shall now turn to a mathematical presentation of general equilibrium theory.[1]

A. THE TWO-SECTOR ECONOMY

For convenience of exposition, we assume an economy consisting of only two sectors, a consumer sector and a business sector. A simplified representation of such an economy, in terms of a circular flow diagram, is shown in Figure 9–1. All production is undertaken by firms, and all productive services originate in households. We assume that there is no involuntary unemployment of factors of production; i.e., that any owners of productive resources who wish to sell them to firms at the prevailing market prices are in fact able to do so. Finally, we assume that all income received by households comes from the sale of productive services to firms and that this entire income is spent purchasing final products from the firms.

Although we are admittedly dealing with a simple economy, it is complex enough to portray many of the essential features of the interrelations among the various product and factor markets in the real world. It is beyond the scope of this book to discuss the types of modifications which are necessary when other sectors (e.g., a government sector or a foreign sector) are added, when savings are allowed, and when there are intermediate

---

[1] The original, and now classical, formulation of general equilibrium analysis was published in 1874 in Lausanne, Switzerland, by Léon Walras. For an English translation of this work, see Léon Walras, *Elements of Pure Economics*, William Jaffé, trans. (Homewood, Ill.: Richard D. Irwin, Inc., 1954).

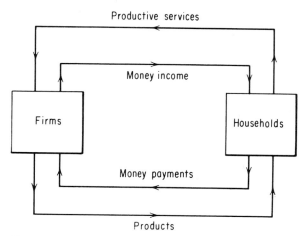

Figure 9–1. Circular flows in a two-sector economy.

products (industrial goods) which are made by some firms solely for the use of other firms in manufacturing consumer goods.[2]

When this two-sector economy is in equilibrium, the magnitude of the money income flow from firms to households will equal the magnitude of the money payment flow from households to firms. Both streams, in fact, represent ways of measuring this economy's total income, the former stream representing the income approach and the latter stream representing the product approach.

Throughout this chapter we shall use only static analysis. Hence we are concerned only with the properties exhibited by the economy in equilibrium, and we shall not consider the dynamics involved when the economy is in transition toward equilibrium.[3]

B. Notation

Let the economy consist of H households and F firms. The subscript h ($h = 1 \ldots, H$) is used to denote a particular household. Similarly, the

[2] The interested reader can find more complete treatments of general equilibrium analysis in the following references: R. G. D. Allen, *Mathematical Economics*, 2nd ed. (London: Macmillan & Co., Ltd., 1960), chap. 10; J. R. Hicks, *Value and Capital*, 2nd ed. (Oxford: Clarendon Press, 1946), chaps. 4–8; Jacob L. Mosak, *General Equilibrium Theory in International Trade* (Bloomington, Ind.: Principia Press, 1944); Don Patinkin, *Money, Interest, and Prices* (New York: Harper & Row, Publishers, Inc., 1956).

[3] Discussions of the conditions for the dynamic stability of multimarket equilibrium are found in Allen, *op. cit.*, chap. 13; Paul A. Samuelson, *Foundations of Economic Analysis* (Cambridge, Mass.: Harvard University Press, 1948), chap. 9.

For an excellent survey of the literature, see Takashi Negishi, "The Stability of a Competitive Economy: A Survey Article," *Econometrica*, 30 (October, 1962), 635–69.

superscript f ($f = 1, \ldots, F$) is used to denote a particular firm. We suppose that there are M consumer products and N types of factors of production. A subscript or a superscript m ($m = 1, \ldots, M$) is used to denote a particular product; n ($n = 1, \ldots, N$) is used to denote a particular factor of production. The price of product m is denoted by p_m; w_n denotes the price of factor n. Since we assume that all markets in our economy are perfectly competitive, the same price confronts all firms and households in any particular market. The symbol q, with appropriate subscripts or superscripts, denotes a flow of consumer goods. Similarly, the symbol v, with appropriate subscripts or superscripts, denotes a flow of factors of production. (Note that f or m written in superscript position after q or v is always used as a superscript, not as an exponent.)

C. Equations of the Model

In Chapter 5 we showed that the demand of each household for any commodity is determined by the prices of all commodities, the household's income, and the household's tastes (the latter, in effect, being the household's utility function). In the partial equilibrium analysis used there, it was appropriate to regard the household's income as given. In the general equilibrium approach, however, the income of the household is determined by its sale of productive services. The amounts of productive services that any household sells to firms will be simultaneously determined with the amounts of commodities which the household buys from firms. This determination is the result of utility-maximizing behavior by the household. The household's utility function is a function of $M + N$ variables, namely, the amounts consumed of the M commodities and the quantities provided of the N productive services. When the household's utility-maximizing problem is solved, the amounts of commodities demanded and the quantities of services supplied are functions of the prices in all markets and the household's tastes. The household's tastes, i.e., the particular form of its utility function, are implicit in the functional forms in the right-hand sides of Eq. (9–1) and (9–2), which are the household's demand equations for commodities and supply equations for productive services.

$$q_{mh} = q_{mh}(p_1, \ldots, p_M, w_1, \ldots, w_N) \qquad m = 1, \ldots, M$$
$$h = 1, \ldots, H. \qquad (9\text{–}1)$$

$$v_{nh} = v_{nh}(p_1, \ldots, p_M, w_1, \ldots, w_N) \qquad n = 1, \ldots, N$$
$$h = 1, \ldots, H. \qquad (9\text{–}2)$$

The next step is to determine the amounts of commodities supplied and the quantities of productive services used by business firms. We shall allow for the possibility that any firm produces all commodities, without excluding the possibility that any particular firm produces only one or a few commodities. In case a firm does not produce a particular commodity, then its supply of that commodity and its demand for productive services to produce that commodity are identically zero.

The demand by firm f for productive service n in manufacturing commodity m (denoted by v_n^{fm}) depends upon the prices of all factors of production, the quantity of commodity m manufactured by firm f, and the particular production function of the firm:

$$v_n^{fm} = v_n^{fm}(q_m^f, w_1, \ldots, w_N) \qquad \begin{aligned} m &= 1, \ldots, M \\ n &= 1, \ldots, N \\ f &= 1, \ldots, F. \end{aligned} \qquad (9\text{--}3)$$

In Eq. (9–3), q_m^f is the quantity of commodity m produced by firm f. The particular form of the function in the right-hand side of Eq. (9–3) depends upon the production function of firm f.[4]

From the long-run equilibrium conditions established in Chapter 8, we have

$$p_m q_m^f = \sum_{n=1}^{N} w_n v_n^{fm} \qquad \begin{aligned} m &= 1, \ldots, M \\ f &= 1, \ldots, F. \end{aligned} \qquad (9\text{--}4)$$

Equation (9–4) indicates that firm f's total revenues from selling commodity m equal its total costs of producing that product; i.e., firm f is earning zero profits.[5]

In order for each commodity market to be in equilibrium, it is necessary for the total demand of households for that product to equal the total

---

[4] The relatively simple form of Eq. (9–5) is valid only under the convenient assumption that the multiproduct production function for firm f,

$$\Phi^f(q_1^f, \ldots, q_m^f) = G^f(v_1^f, \ldots, v_n^f)$$

(where v_n^f is the total amount of productive service n used by firm f) is separable into a set of M single-product production functions for firm f, of the form

$$q_1^f = G_1^f(v_1^{f1}, \ldots, v_n^{f1})$$
$$\vdots$$
$$q_M^f = G_M^f(v_1^{fM}, \ldots, v_n^{fM}).$$

[5] Since we have assumed in the two-sector economy that all productive services originate in households, there are no stocks of long-lived productive factors which are held by firms, so there is no problem of converting infrequent purchases of input stocks into equivalent periodic rates of cost. Hence,

$$\sum_{n=1}^{N} w_n v_n^{fm}$$

is firm f's total cost of producing commodity m. Note that if firm f does not produce commodity m, then $q_m^f = v_1^{fm} = \ldots = v_N^{fm} = 0$, so that Eq. (9–4) remains valid.

supply by firms of that product. Hence, we have the following "clearing of the commodity market" equations:

$$\sum_{h=1}^{H} q_{mh} = \sum_{f=1}^{F} q_m^f \qquad m = 1, \ldots, M. \tag{9-5}$$

Similarly, for each factor market to be in equilibrium, the total demand by firms for that factor must equal the total supply by households of that factor. Thus, we have the following "clearing of the factor market" equations:

$$\sum_{f=1}^{F} \sum_{m=1}^{M} v_n^{fm} = \sum_{h=1}^{H} v_{nh} \qquad n = 1, \ldots, N. \tag{9-6}$$

D. Solution of the Model

Equations (9–1)–(9–6) describe the general equilibrium model. A solution of the model exists if and only if a feasible and consistent set of values can be assigned to all variables so that Eq. (9–1)–(9–6) are simultaneously satisfied. If a solution exists, then each firm and each household is in a long-run equilibrium position, and hence all commodity and factor markets are also in long-run equilibrium. One step in determining whether a solution exists is to compare the number of equations with the number of variables which are to be determined. Before this is done, however, it is necessary to eliminate any equation from (9–1)–(9–6) which is not independent of the rest of the equations.

We shall now show that one of the equations in (9–1)–(9–6) is redundant. Suppose that all the equations in (9–4) except the one for firm F and commodity M are written as follows:

$$p_1 q_1^1 = \sum_{n=1}^{N} w_n v_n^{11}$$

$$p_2 q_2^1 = \sum_{n=1}^{N} w_n v_n^{12}$$

$$\vdots \tag{9-7}$$

$$p_M q_M^1 = \sum_{n=1}^{N} w_n v_n^{1M}$$

$$\vdots$$

$$p_{M-1} q_{M-1}^F = \sum_{n=1}^{N} w_n v_n^{F,M-1}$$

Eq. (9–7) contains $FM - 1$ equations. The one equation in (9–4) which is not contained in Eq. (9–7) is

$$p_M q_M^F = \sum_{n=1}^{N} w_n v_n^{FM}. \tag{9–8}$$

We shall show that whenever all the equations in (9–1), (9–2), and (9–7) are satisfied, then Eq. (9–8) is necessarily satisfied, and that Eq. (9–8), therefore, is a redundant equation. Let the variables assume any values which simultaneously satisfy all the equations in (9–1), (9–2), and (9–7). Suppose that both sides of (9–1) are multiplied by p_m, and that the resulting equation is summed over all commodities and all households. This results in

$$\sum_{h=1}^{H} \sum_{m=1}^{M} p_m q_{mh} = \sum_{h=1}^{H} \sum_{m=1}^{M} p_m q_{mh}(p_1, \ldots, p_M, w_1, \ldots, w_N). \tag{9–9}$$

Similarly, suppose that both sides of Eq. (9–2) are multiplied by w_n, and that the resulting equation is summed over all productive services and all households. This results in

$$\sum_{h=1}^{H} \sum_{n=1}^{N} w_n v_{nh} = \sum_{h=1}^{H} \sum_{n=1}^{N} w_n v_{nh}(p_1, \ldots, p_M, w_1, \ldots, w_N). \tag{9–10}$$

Since the total expenditures by households for commodities must equal the total receipts of firms, the left-hand side of Eq. (9–9) must equal the sum of the left-hand sides of the equations in (9–7) and (9–8). Using $l(i)$ as an abbreviation for the left-hand side of Eq. (9–i), this relation can be written in the equivalent form:

$$l(9) - \sum l(7) = l(8). \tag{9–11}$$

Similarly, the total incomes received by households from the sale of productive services must equal the total payments by firms for productive services; i.e., the left-hand side of Eq. (9–10) must equal the sum of the right-hand sides of the equations in (9–7) and (9–8). Using $r(i)$ as an abbreviation for the right-hand side of Eq. (9–i), this relation can be written in the equivalent form:

$$l(10) - \sum r(7) = r(8). \tag{9–12}$$

We know by the definition of the two-sector economy in Section A that the total magnitude of the money payment flow from households to firms in payment of commodities purchased must equal the total magnitude of the money income flow from firms to households in payment for productive services. This is equivalent to

$$\sum_{h=1}^{H} \sum_{m=1}^{M} p_m q_{mh} = \sum_{h=1}^{H} \sum_{n=1}^{N} w_n v_{nh}. \tag{9–13}$$

Equation (9–13) indicates that the left-hand side of Eq. (9–9) equals the left-hand side of Eq. (9–10):

$$l(9) = l(10). \tag{9–14}$$

Subtracting the sum of the equations in (9–7) from (9–14), we have

$$l(9) - \sum l(7) = l(10) - \sum r(7). \tag{9–15}$$

Equations (9–11), (9–12), and (9–15) together imply:

$$l(8) = r(8), \tag{9–16}$$

i.e., Eq. (9–8) must be satisfied.

Thus we have shown that whenever Eq. (9–1), (9–2), and (9–7) are simultaneously satisfied, then Eq. (9–8) must necessarily also be satisfied. Hence Eq. (9–8) is a redundant equation. This means that Eq. (9–4) contains only $FM - 1$ independent equations.

The count of the independent equations in the general equilibrium model is summarized in Table 9–1. The count of the variables determined by the model is summarized in Table 9–2. The number of variables to be determined exceeds the number of equations by one. Thus the entire system is underdetermined in the sense that the set of supply and demand forces represented in Eq. (9–1)–(9–6) are not sufficient to determine unique values for all commodity and factor prices and for all commodity and factor flows. We can, however, obtain an exactly determined system if we arbitrarily select any one commodity or factor as the *numéraire*, i.e., as the standard in terms of which all other prices are measured. Suppose, for definiteness, that we arbitrarily select the first commodity as *numéraire*. This means that the price of that commodity will be 1, just as the price of one dollar is 1. Hence there is now one fewer variable to be determined by the model.

The set of equations (9–1)–(9–6) forms an exactly determined system once the *numéraire* has been chosen. The values this system assigns to the

TABLE 9–1

COUNT OF INDEPENDENT EQUATIONS

Equation Number	Number of Independent Equations
(9–1)	HM
(9–2)	HN
(9–3)	FMN
(9–4)	$FM - 1$
(9–5)	M
(9–6)	N

Table 9–2

Count of Variables

Form of Variable	Number of Variables
q_{mh}	HM
v_{nh}	HN
v_n^{fm}	FMN
q_m^f	FM
p_m	M
w_n	N

remaining commodity and factor prices, $p_2, \ldots, p_M$ and $w_1, \ldots, w_N$, in effect may be interpreted as multiples of the price of the first commodity, which we arbitrarily selected as *numéraire*. We call such a model a *real* model, because prices are stated in terms of a commodity which is itself consumed (e.g., pounds of butter, if commodity 1 is butter) instead of being stated in terms of money (e.g., dollars).

The general equilibrium system of equations thus has a solution which uniquely determines all price ratios, but not the absolute level of prices. Despite the indeterminacy of absolute prices in the general equilibrium model, all real flows of commodities and productive services are uniquely determined. The price level itself can be determined by adjoining to the real general equilibrium model defined by Eq. (9–1) to (9–6) at least one (and possibly several) additional relation(s) pertaining to the market for money. In the two-sector economy, the workings of the money market serve to determine the absolute level of prices but have no effect on the allocation of real goods and services.[6]

We have assumed up to this point that equality in the number of independent equations and the number of variables to be determined guarantees the existence of a unique solution to the model. In fact, however, we cannot be sure that this solution is unique without more detailed specification of the functional forms. We have also assumed that the solution to the model is economically meaningful, i.e., that all prices and flows are nonnegative. To guarantee that this will be the case, some nonnegativity constraints on the variables must be added to Eq. (9–1) to (9–6). When these constraints are added, we cannot be sure that any solution exists to the model. It has been shown, however, that adding some further conditions requiring diminishing marginal utility for all commodities for all households and

---

[6] For a very readable discussion of some reasons why and the extent to which this conclusion must be modified in more realistic economic systems, see William J. Baumol, *Economic Theory and Operations Analysis* (Englewood Cliffs, N.J.: Prentice-Hall, Inc., 1961), chap. 12. The standard and considerably more complete reference on this topic is Patinkin, *op. cit.*

diminishing marginal productivity for all factors in all uses guarantees a unique and economically meaningful solution.[7]

II. Applications of General Equilibrium Analysis

A. Market Aggregations and the General Equilibrium System

For a general equilibrium system of equations to have any empirical usefulness, it is necessary to restructure it to eliminate all references to individual firms and households, since there are too many firms and households in a real-world economy to treat them individually. One way in which this restructuring can be done is to define market demand and market supply variables for all commodities and factors. The market demand for commodity m is defined as

$$Q_m^D = \sum_{h=1}^{H} q_{mh} \qquad m = 1, \ldots, M. \tag{9-17}$$

The market supply of commodity m is defined as

$$Q_m^S = \sum_{f=1}^{F} q_m^f \qquad m = 1, \ldots, M. \tag{9-18}$$

The market supply of factor n is defined as

$$V_n^S = \sum_{h=1}^{H} v_{nh} \qquad n = 1, \ldots, N. \tag{9-19}$$

Finally, the market demand for factor n is defined as

$$V_n^D = \sum_{f=1}^{F} \sum_{m=1}^{M} v_n^{fm} \qquad n = 1, \ldots, N. \tag{9-20}$$

In order to eliminate all reference to individual households and firms, the right-hand sides of Eq. (9-17)–(9-20) are in practice replaced by particular functions of market prices and market quantities:

$$Q_m^D = Q_m^D (p_1, \ldots, p_m, w_1, \ldots, w_n) \qquad m = 1, \ldots, M. \tag{9-21}$$

$$Q_m^S = Q_m^S (p_m, w_1, \ldots, w_n) \qquad m = 1, \ldots, M. \tag{9-22}$$

$$V_n^S = V_n^S (p_1, \ldots, p_m, w_1, \ldots, w_n) \qquad n = 1, \ldots, N. \tag{9-23}$$

$$V_n^D = V_n^D (Q_1^S, \ldots, Q_m^S, w_1, \ldots, w_n) \qquad n = 1, \ldots, N. \tag{9-24}$$

---

[7] The reader interested in a rigorous treatment of this point is referred to Kenneth J. Arrow and Gerard Debreu, "Existence of an Equilibrium for a Competitive Economy," *Econometrica*, 22 (July, 1954), 265–90; Gerard Debreu, *Theory of Value: An Axiomatic Analysis of Economic Equilibrium*, Cowles Foundation Monograph 17 (New York: John Wiley & Sons, Inc., 1959).

Additional relations which must be added to Eq. (9–21)–(9–24) are the "clearing of the commodity market" and the "clearing of the factor market" equations. In terms of the market variables, these are:

$$Q_m^D = Q_m^S \qquad m = 1, \ldots, M. \tag{9–25}$$

$$V_n^D = V_n^S \qquad n = 1, \ldots, N. \tag{9–26}$$

Although Eq. (9–21)–(9–26) together contain $3M + 3N$ equations, one of them is redundant. This redundancy can be established in a manner analogous to that used in Section I.D.

Equations (9–21)–(9–26) can be regarded as an aggregate form of a general equilibrium system. It contains $3M + 3N - 1$ independent equations. There are, however, $3M + 3N$ variables in the system. This model is thus undetermined by exactly one equation, as was the earlier model. The solution is similar: arbitrarily select any one commodity or factor as *numéraire*, and then solve for all prices in terms of the *numéraire*.

B. Input-Output Analysis

Input-output analysis is an attempt to render operational the type of general equilibrium system contained in Eq. (9–21)–(9–26). Even though all reference to individual firms and households has been eliminated, there still may be many equations in the system if M and N are large numbers. The problems of finding the solution to the system are reduced to manageable proportions by a number of simplifying assumptions made in input-output analysis. Two assumptions are especially important. The first assumption is that the consumer demand for all commodities is exogenously specified. The second assumption is that inputs are used in constant and known proportions in producing any particular product and that the production functions display constant returns to scale (i.e., there are no external economies or diseconomies). When these assumptions are made, then prices no longer explicitly appear as variables in the input-output equations. The primary variables which this type of model is designed to determine are the amounts of output that will be sold by each industry to every other industry as well as the total amounts of output that will be produced by each industry.

An example of an input-output model which is a simplification of an actual model for the Italian economy will now be presented. There are four sectors in this model: services, agriculture, basic industry, and finished goods. Let Q_S, Q_A, Q_B, and Q_F be the total outputs of the four sectors. Table 9–3 shows the production coefficients in the economy. For example, in order to produce 1 unit of output from the agricultural sector, it is necessary to use 0.1 unit of output from the agricultural sector and 0.3 unit of output from the finished goods sector, along with the primary inputs (such as land and labor) that are required. If we assume that the consumer demand (measured in monetary units at constant prices) is 30 units of

TABLE 9–3

PRODUCTION COEFFICIENTS

Producing Sector	Using Sector			
	S	A	B	F
Services (S)	0.1	0.1	0.1	0.2
Agriculture (A)	0.0	0.1	0.0	0.3
Basic Industries (B)	0.0	0.1	0.3	0.1
Finished Goods (F)	0.0	0.0	0.0	0.2

SOURCE: Adapted from Hollis B. Chenery and Paul G. Clark, *Interindustry Economics* (New York: John Wiley & Sons, Inc., 1959), p. 27.

services, 120 units of agriculture, 60 units of basic industries, and 400 units of finished goods, then the equations of the input-output model are:

$$Q_S = 0.1Q_S + 0.1Q_A + 0.1Q_B + 0.2Q_F + \quad 30. \tag{9–27}$$

$$Q_A = \qquad\qquad 0.1Q_A \qquad\qquad + 0.3Q_F + 120. \tag{9–28}$$

$$Q_B = \qquad\qquad 0.1Q_A + 0.3Q_B + 0.1Q_F + \quad 60. \tag{9–29}$$

$$Q_F = \qquad\qquad\qquad\qquad\qquad\qquad 0.2Q_F + 400. \tag{9–30}$$

The solution to Eq. (9–27)–(9–30) is easily found by the method of successive substitutions. First solve Eq. (9–30) to obtain $Q_F = 500$. Next substitute this value for Q_F into Eq. (9–28) and solve for Q_A, obtaining $Q_A = 300$. Then substitute these values for Q_F and Q_A into Eq. (9–29) and solve for Q_B, obtaining $Q_B = 200$. Finally, substitute these values for Q_F, Q_A, and Q_B into Eq. (9–27) and solve for Q_S, obtaining $Q_S = 200$. By combining the production coefficients in Table 9–3 with the solution just obtained for total outputs, we can obtain the complete set of intersector flows shown in Table 9–4. From Table 9–4, we see that although only 30 units of output

TABLE 9–4

INTERSECTOR FLOWS

Producing Sectors	Using Sectors				Total Intermediate Use	Final Use	Total Use (Q_i)
	S	A	B	F			
Services (S)	20	30	20	100	170	30	200
Agriculture (A)		30		150	180	120	300
Basic Industry (B)		30	60	50	140	60	200
Finished Goods (F)				100	100	400	500

from the services sector are demanded by consumers, it is necessary for the services sector to produce 200 units of output. The remaining 170 units of output from the services sector are required to produce the goods and services needed to satisfy consumer demand. For this purpose the services, agricultural, basic industries, and finished goods sectors use 20, 30, 20, and 100 units of output, respectively, from the services sector.

Equations (9–27)–(9–30) resulted from a particular specification of consumer demand. No matter what specification of consumer demand is assumed, it is possible to formulate and solve a similar set of equations. In this manner input-output analysis can be used to obtain results of a comparative statics nature. This type of analysis allows us to determine how a change in consumer demand for the output of one sector will affect intersector flows and total outputs for all sectors.

The value of input-output analysis as a practical tool of analysis depends in part upon the stability of the production coefficients. Although the model assumes that the production coefficients are constant, there are two reasons why they may in fact not be constant in the real world. First, if there are changes in the relative prices of inputs, then firms may alter the combinations of inputs used, leading to changes in the production coefficients. Second, changes in technology may lead to changes in the production coefficients as firms alter the mix of inputs used in response to new opportunities for profits. Chenery and Clark conclude that:

> ...technological change seems to have been the most important source of variation in input functions [i.e., production coefficients] in the American economy, which is the only one which has been studied over any considerable period of time from this point of view. In the long run, technological change is also responsible for most of the changes in relative prices that take place, and it is therefore very difficult to distinguish between the effects of... [changes in relative prices and technological change].[8]

The two critical assumptions that were made in our discussion of input-output analysis, that consumer demand for all commodities is known and that inputs are used in constant and known proportions, are consistent with the assumption that prices in the economy are constant. It is possible to use the specification of intersector flows and the total outputs of all sectors which is obtained in a solution of the input-output model to determine the long-run equilibrium prices. These are the prices at which the total revenues received by each sector equal the total costs (including an allowance for normal profits) of each sector. In this manner it is possible to incorporate prices into an input-output model.

The example of an input-output model has been simplified to give some insights into one way of applying general equilibrium analysis to real-world problems. Considerably more complex input-output models containing

---

[8] Hollis B. Chenery and Paul G. Clark, *Interindustry Economics* (New York: John Wiley & Sons, Inc., 1959), p. 42.

between 12 and 450 sectors have been formulated for many different countries for various purposes, as indicated in the following summary by Chenery and Clark:

> Most academic research in this field has been designed to reveal the quantitative significance of various types of interdependence. This kind of study is invaluable for the validation and improvement of these techniques, but it is not directly concerned with economic policy. Other work in the interindustry field, both in the United States and abroad, has been stimulated primarily by the prospects for developing a technique which would have practical value in guiding decisions in government and business. The United States government research program of 1950–1954 was designed to analyze problems of mobilization. A principal aim of government-sponsored interindustry research in Denmark, Norway, Italy, the Netherlands, and Japan has been to determine the relation of imports and exports to domestic production and to guide policy affecting them. In the less developed countries— Argentina, Colombia, Mexico, Peru, Puerto Rico, India, Yugoslavia, and others—work on input-output analysis has been undertaken as an aid to planning economic development.[9]

C. MACROECONOMETRIC MODELS

We have seen that input-output analysis represents one approach to introducing enough simplifying assumptions into general equilibrium analysis so that it becomes a practical tool for answering many types of empirical questions. An alternative approach, which is useful for answering other types of empirical questions, is to simplify general equilibrium analysis by performing suitable aggregations until there are few enough aggregate variables and equations in the resulting model so that functional forms can be specified and parameters can be statistically estimated. This type of econometric model is typically formulated in terms of such aggregate variables as total consumption expenditures, total profits, total investment expenditures, etc., for an entire economy.

To illustrate the approach used in developing macroeconometric models from a general equilibrium framework, we shall review a simple model of the United States developed by Klein and estimated on the basis of annual data for the period 1921–41.

> The macroeconomic system will be considered to be made up of consumer goods and two factors of production: (1) producer goods, and (2) human labor power. Our three equations will thus be the three demand schedules for the three goods in the system. The fact that our three-equation system is composed entirely of three demand schedules does not mean that the supply side is neglected. The equations of demand for factors of production determine the supply of commodities. The supply schedules are merely the production function at its equilibrium value of profit maximization. But the equations of profit maximization are the demand schedules for factors of production;

---

[9] *Ibid.*, p. 7. For a comprehensive survey and bibliography of input-output models that have been formulated for various countries, see *ibid.*, chap. 7.

hence we have not neglected the supply side if we have included the demand for labor and capital.[10]

The first equation in Klein's model is the demand relationship for consumer goods. This states that total consumption expenditures are a function of consumer income; income, however, is divided into two components, wages and profits, since income received from wages may affect consumption expenditures differently than income received from profits. The consumption function is:

$$C = \alpha_0 + \alpha_1 W + \alpha_2 \Pi + u_1, \qquad (9\text{-}31)$$

where C is total consumption expenditures, W is total wages, and Π is profits (i.e., nonwage income). α_0, α_1, and α_2 are constants whose values must be statistically estimated, and u_1 is a random term.

The second equation in the model is the demand relationship for producer goods. This states that aggregate investment expenditures (net of depreciation) are a function of profits during the current year, profits during the previous year, and the stock of capital at the beginning of the year. According to Klein, "... this equation expresses the heuristic principle ... that profits are the mainspring of economic action in a capitalist society. Entrepreneurs expand when profits are anticipated to be high and contract when profits are anticipated to be low. However, not only the absolute size of profits but also their relation to the existing stock of capital is important. ..."[11] The investment function is:

$$I = \beta_0 + \beta_1 \Pi + \beta_2 \Pi_{-1} + \beta_3 K_{-1} + u_2, \qquad (9\text{-}32)$$

where I is aggregate investment expenditures (net of depreciation), Π is profits during the current year, Π_{-1} is profits during the previous year, and K_{-1} is the stock of capital at the beginning of the year. β_0, β_1, β_2, and β_3 are constants whose values must be statistically estimated, and u_2 is a random term.

The demand relationship for human labor power is the third equation in the model. This states that total wages are a function of the total output produced in the economy both during the current and the previous years and of a time trend. The demand for labor equation is:

$$W = \gamma_0 + \gamma_1 Y + \gamma_2 Y_{-1} + \gamma_3 t + u_3, \qquad (9\text{-}33)$$

where W is total wages, Y is total output during the current year, Y_{-1} is total output during the previous year, and t is a time trend variable. γ_0, γ_1, γ_2, and γ_3 are constants whose values must be statistically estimated,

---

[10] Lawrence R. Klein, *Economic Fluctuations in the United States*, Cowles Commission Monograph 11 (New York: John Wiley & Sons, Inc., 1950), p. 58.

[11] *Ibid.*, p. 60.

and u_3 is a random term. Klein's theoretical rationale for Eq. (9–33) is:

> Equations of this type have ... been developed ... by setting the derivative of profits with respect to labor input equal to zero. This particular form of the marginal-productivity equation follows if the production function is of the constant-elasticity type, a form of the production function which is known to fit the data well in many cases.... The trend variable is there to reflect an institutional phenomenon, namely, the growing bargaining strength of labor. Not only will labor's income fluctuate with the fluctuations of output as determined by strict profit maximization, but it will also increase gradually as the strength of the organized labor movement grows. Increasing unionization means a persistent, gradual shift of the demand function, and this shift is reflected in the variable, t. [12]

Before obtaining statistical estimates of his model, Klein found it desirable to modify Eq. (9–33) in order to take into consideration the role of the government in production. The government's contribution to total output, which is considered to be exogenously determined rather than to result from utility-maximizing or profit-maximizing considerations, is measured by the total amount of wages paid by the government to its employees. Hence the total wage bill, W, is divided into two components:

$$W = W_1 + W_2, \tag{9–34}$$

where W_1 is the total amount of wages paid by business firms to their employees and W_2 is the total amount of wages paid by the government to its employees. In the revised form of Eq. (9–33), W_2 is subtracted from the Y terms on the right-hand side. Klein also observed that national output valued at market prices exceeds national income valued at factor costs by T, the total amount of business taxes. Hence in the revised form of Eq. (9–33), T is added to the Y terms on the right-hand side. After these modifications are made, Eq. (9–33) is replaced by the following equation expressing the demand relationship by business firms for human labor power:

$$W_1 = \gamma_0 + \gamma_1(Y + T - W_2) + \gamma_2(Y + T - W_2)_{-1} + \gamma_3 t + u_3. \tag{9–35}$$

Three additional definitional equations which are not subject to random terms and which contain no unknown parameters are included in Klein's model. These are:

$$Y + T = C + I + G. \tag{9–36}$$

$$Y = \Pi + W. \tag{9–37}$$

$$K - K_{-1} = I. \tag{9–38}$$

The only new variable introduced in these equations is G, the total amount of output demanded by the government and by foreigners (the foreign

---

[12] *Ibid.*, pp. 61–62.

demand is considered to be net of imports). Equation (9–36) indicates that the national output valued at market prices is divided into three components: consumer demand, business demand, and government plus net foreign demand. According to Eq. (9–37), national income valued at factor costs is the sum of profits and wages. Finally, Eq. (9–38) states that the net change in the value of the capital stock during the year equals the aggregate amount of net investment expenditures.

Equations (9–31)–(9–32) and (9–34)–(9–38) constitute a simplified model of the economy of the United States. Although highly aggregated, it is derived from a general equilibrium framework. This simple model is a purely real system, since all economic variables are measured in constant dollar terms, rather than in current dollar terms. Using annual data for the American economy for the period 1921–41, Klein obtained the statistical estimates for the parameters of his model which are shown in Table 9–5.

TABLE 9–5

KLEIN'S STATISTICAL ESTIMATES OF THE PARAMETERS*

Equation	Parameter	Variable that the Parameter is the Coefficient of	Statistical Estimate of the Parameter
(9–31)	α_0	Constant Term	16.78
	α_1	W	0.80
	α_2	Π	0.25
(9–32)	β_0	Constant Term	17.79
	β_1	Π	0.23
	β_2	Π_{-1}	0.55
	β_3	K_{-1}	−0.15
(9–35)	γ_0	Constant Term	1.60
	γ_1	$Y + T - W_2$	0.42
	γ_2	$(Y + T - W_2)_{-1}$	0.16
	γ_3	$(t - 1931)$	0.13

* All variables except t are measured in billions of 1934 dollars. The time trend, t, is measured by the years, i.e., $t = 1921, 1922, \ldots, 1941$.

SOURCE: Lawrence R. Klein, *Economic Fluctuations in the United States*, Cowles Commission Monograph 11 (New York: John Wiley & Sons, Inc., 1950), p. 68. There is an apparent misprint in Klein's presentation of the statistical estimates of the consumption function. In his Eq. (3.1.23), p. 68, he includes both Π and Π_{-1} terms, contrary to the way in which he writes the corresponding equation elsewhere [e.g., Eq. (3.1.16), p. 65; Eq. (3.1.16*), p. 66; Eq. (3.1.31), p. 71, and Eq. (3.1.37), p. 75]. We have summed the estimates Klein gives on p. 68 for the coefficients of Π and Π_{-1} to obtain the estimate shown in Table 9–5 for α_2.

Although Klein intended this simple model to be used for illustrative purposes only, his interpretation of the statistical estimates is that: "All the point estimates of the parameters ... look very reasonable; i.e., they seem not to contradict the general evidence that would be based on experience other than that contained in the data used, and all have the signs that we should expect on the basis of economic theory."[13]

Klein has stated that since the foregoing model was intended as only an illustration of the way in which macroeconometric models could be developed on the basis of general equilibrium considerations, many undesirable aggregations have been performed in order to keep the number of variables small.

> The variable I includes several categories of investment that could well be separated. More information would be gained from such separations, but at the same time new computational problems would be created. We might split investment, for example, into (1) expenditures on business plant and equipment, (2) expenditures on net additions to inventories, (3) expenditures on residential construction. Introducing the first category may make it necessary to introduce the price of output and the price of capital goods as separate variables; hence new equations would be required to explain price determination. The second category may also entail prices and the third category, rents and construction costs, as new variables for which additional equations would be needed. Similarly, the expenditures on consumer goods could be segregated into such classes as services, nondurables, and durables, but the demand for each class of consumer goods would probably depend upon the price ratios between the several classes. Again we would need more equations to determine these prices.[14]

Klein and other economists have developed a number of macroeconometric models for the United States and other countries which include complexities of these types. Because of the ways in which prices enter, these more complex models are even closer to the spirit of general equilibrium analysis than the simple model described earlier.[15]

III. Summary

In this chapter we have introduced another approach to the analysis of economic problems. Chapters 4–8 used a partial equilibrium approach which enables the economist to treat a particular market in isolation. In the general equilibrium approach it is possible to focus on the interrelationships among markets.

---

[13] *Ibid.*, p. 68.

[14] *Ibid.*, pp. 62–63.

[15] For examples of these more complex macroeconometric models, see *ibid.*, pp. 84–114; L. R. Klein and A. S. Goldberger, *An Econometric Model of the United States* (Amsterdam: North-Holland Publishing Company, 1955); and L. R. Klein, R. J. Ball, A. Hazlewood, and P. Vandome, *An Econometric Model of the United Kingdom* (Oxford: Basil Blackwell & Mott, Ltd., 1961).

Our exposition of general equilibrium analysis was made in terms of a two-sector economy. We assumed an economy composed of a household sector and a business firm sector. In this simplified model all production is done by firms and all productive services are supplied by households. There are no inventories and no unemployment in the model. For this model it was possible to write down all the equations which described the functions of the households and the firms. The six types of equations that were specified are:

1. Household demand equations for commodities.
2. Household supply equations for productive services.
3. Firm demand equations for factors.
4. Firm supply equations for commodities.
5. Clearing of the commodity market equations.
6. Clearing of the factor market equations.

As a first step in determining whether a solution exists, we analyzed the system of equations for redundancy. We showed that one of the equations in Eq. (9–4) was redundant. On counting variables and equations we found that we had one more variable than we had independent equations. This meant that our system was underdetermined, in the sense that we could not find a unique set of values which would constitute a solution to the system. By arbitrarily selecting one commodity as a *numéraire* we were able to transform the system into an exactly determined one which has a unique solution.

We then went on to consider two applications which utilize general equilibrium theory. The first, input-output analysis, was an explicit attempt to make general equilibrium analysis operational. We took as an example of input-output analysis a simple model based on data from the Italian economy. There were four sectors in the model: services, agriculture, basic industry, and finished goods. Production coefficients were specified for each sector. We assumed a set of consumer demands (measured in monetary units at constant prices) for each of the four sectors. With this set of demands we then solved for the total output required in each sector. The solution utilized the production coefficients and included the goods and services which each sector furnished for use in the other sectors. For example, 120 units of agriculture were demanded by consumers but a total production of 300 units was required in agriculture. Of the 180 units produced for intermediate use, 30 were required by the agricultural sector itself and 150 by the finished goods sector. We then went on to discuss briefly the stability of the production coefficients and the way in which prices can be incorporated into input-output analysis.

The second application of general equilibrium theory is the formulation of macroeconometric models for an entire economy. This can be done in terms of variables which represent two stages of aggregation on the variables used in general equilibrium analysis. The first stage of aggregation, which was discussed in Section II.A, consists in defining market aggregates for the amounts supplied or demanded of any commodity or factor by summing over all households or over all firms the quantities supplied or demanded by them. The second stage of aggregation consists in multiplying the market aggregates by appropriate prices and then summing over several commodities or factors to obtain composite commodities or factors. Thus an aggregate variable, such as total consumption expenditures, can be derived from the quantities of each commodity demanded by every household by a two-stage aggregation process. When suitable aggregations are performed on a general equilibrium model, a macroeconometric model containing a relatively small number of equations and formulated in terms of a relatively small number of aggregate variables can be obtained.

We used a simple model of the American economy between 1921–41 which Klein developed to illustrate how macroeconometric models can be developed from a general equilibrium framework. The demand relationship for consumer goods relates total consumption expenditures to income received from wages and income received from profits. The demand relationship for producer goods relates total net investment expenditures to profits during the current and the previous years and to the stock of capital at the beginning of the year. The demand relationship by business firms for labor relates the total private wage bill to privately produced output during the current and the previous years and to a time trend reflecting increased unionization in the economy. Four identities are also included in Klein's model. Statistical estimates of the parameters were presented. Some of the ways in which more complex and more realistic macroeconometric models could be formulated from a general equilibrium framework were also indicated.

SUGGESTED READINGS

These recommendations are in addition to the footnote references cited in this chapter.

Arrow, K. J., "The Firm in General Equilibrium Theory," in *The Corporate Economy*, Robin Morris and Andrian Wood, eds., chap. 3. London and Basingstoke: Macmillan & Co., Ltd., 1971.

Dorfman, Robert, Paul A. Samuelson, and Robert M. Solow, *Linear Programming and Economic Analysis*, chaps. 9, 10, 13. New York: McGraw-Hill Book Company, 1958.

Friedman, Milton, "The 'Welfare Effects' of an Income Tax and an Excise Tax," in *Essays in Positive Economics*, pp. 100–13. Chicago: University of Chicago Press, 1953. (For some comments on the methodology introduced in Friedman's paper, see James M. Buchanan,

Fiscal Theory and Political Economy, chap. 7. Chapel Hill: University of North Carolina Press, 1960.)

JONES, R. W., "Distortions in Factor Markets and the General Equilibrium Model of Production," *Journal of Political Economy*, LXXIX (May/ June, 1971), 437–59.

KLEIN, LAWRENCE R., *Introduction to Econometrics*, pp. 129–39 and chap. 5. Englewood Cliffs, N.J.: Prentice-Hall, Inc., 1962.

MUSGRAVE, RICHARD, *The Theory of Public Finance*, chap. 10. New York: McGraw-Hill Book Company, 1959.

RICHARDSON, G. B., "Equilibrium, Expectations and Information," *Economic Journal*, LXIX (June, 1959), 223–27.

WELLS, PAUL, "General Equilibrium Analysis of Excise Taxes," *American Economic Review*, XLV, No. 3 (June, 1955), 345–59. (For some modifications of Wells' paper, see Harry G. Johnson, "General Equilibrium Analysis of Excise Taxes: Comment," *American Economic Review*, XLVI, No. 1 [March, 1956], 151–56.)

Chapter Ten

Monopoly

We have now examined in detail the nature and implications of a perfectly competitive market. In this chapter we shall discuss monopoly, which, in terms of the number of firms in the market, is at the opposite end of the spectrum from perfect competition. In a monopoly market one firm accounts for the total supply of the commodity. We continue to assume, however, that there are large numbers of buyers in the market and that no buyer is large enough to influence price by his purchasing behavior.

I. The Basic Monopoly Model

A. Definition of Monopoly

There are two aspects to the definition of a monopoly market. First, as already noted, a monopoly market has only one seller of a product. Second, the demand for the product must be reasonably independent of the price of other products. The dependence of demand between products can be measured by the cross-elasticity of demand. This is a generalization of the price elasticity of demand which was defined in Chapter 3, Section III. The cross-elasticity of demand between products i and j is a measure of the relative responsiveness in the demand for product i to changes in the price of product j. More precisely, the cross-elasticity of demand between products i and j is

$$\eta_{ij} = \frac{\text{relative change in the demand for } i}{\text{relative change in the price of } j} = \frac{dq_i}{dp_j}\frac{p_j}{q_i}. \tag{10-1}$$

We will call a product i which has only one seller a monopolized product if

$$\eta_{ij} \leq \epsilon \qquad \text{for all } j \neq i, \tag{10-2}$$

where ϵ is some arbitrarily small positive number.[1] The case where Eq. (10–2) is valid except for a small subset of products is known as "oligopoly" and will be discussed in Chapter 12.

B. THE DEMAND CURVE

Since a monopolist is the sole seller of a particular product, the market demand curve for that product is the same as the monopoly firm's demand curve. In contrast, in a perfectly competitive market the individual seller's demand curve is a horizontal line at the prevailing market price, but the market demand curve is downward sloping. Thus the monopolist cannot sell any quantity that he wishes at any given price; in order to increase his sales, the monopolist must reduce his average price.

The total revenue for the monopolist is

$$TR(q) = pq. \tag{10-3}$$

It follows immediately on dividing both sides of Eq. (10–3) by q that average revenue equals price:

$$AR(q) = \frac{TR(q)}{q} = p, \tag{10-4}$$

i.e., the average revenue curve for the monopolist coincides with the market demand curve. The marginal revenue curve is the rate of change in total revenue with respect to changes in the rate of output:

$$MR(q) = \frac{d}{dq}(pq) = p + q\frac{dp}{dq}. \tag{10-5}$$

---

[1] Note that when $\eta_{ij} > 0$, then product j must be a substitute for product i. We are defining a monopoly market as one in which there is a single seller of a product for which there are no close substitutes. When $\eta_{ij} < 0$, then products i and j are called *complements*. Examples of complementary products are automobiles and tires, cameras and films, and ham and eggs. By our definition a monopolized product may have complements, but it will not have any close substitutes.

It is convenient to develop a relationship between marginal revenue and price elasticity of demand which will be used later in this chapter. This relationship is

$$MR(q) = p\left(1 + \frac{1}{\eta}\right). \tag{10-6}$$

To establish Eq. (10-6), rewrite Eq. (10-5) in the form:

$$MR(q) = p\left(1 + \frac{q}{p}\frac{dp}{dq}\right). \tag{10-7}$$

From the definition of price elasticity of demand, Eq. (10-6) immediately follows from Eq. (10-7).[2]

C. PRICE AND OUTPUT DECISION RULES[3]

We assume that the monopolist maximizes profits in the short run. His profits are

$$\pi(q) = pq - TC(q). \tag{10-8}$$

To maximize profits, differentiate Eq. (10-8) with respect to q and equate the result to zero:

$$\frac{d\pi}{dq} = \frac{d}{dq}(pq) - \frac{d}{dq}[TC(q)] = 0. \tag{10-9}$$

Solving Eq. (10-9) and using the definitions of marginal revenue and marginal cost, we have:

$$MR(q) = MC(q). \tag{10-10}$$

Equation (10-10) is a necessary condition for the monopoly firm to maximize profits; it states that marginal revenue must equal marginal cost.

A sufficient condition for maximizing profits is that the second derivative of profits with respect to output be negative. This is equivalent to the condition:

$$\frac{d}{dq}[MR(q)] < \frac{d}{dq}[MC(q)]. \tag{10-11}$$

---

[2] Note that from Eq. (10-6) the relationship established in Theorem 4 of Chapter 3 follows by substituting the appropriate values for η. It is also useful to note that for a linear demand curve, $p = a - bq$, the marginal revenue curve is also linear, with the same intercept but a slope twice as steep: $MR(q) = a - 2bq$.

[3] For convenience of exposition, in this section we shall assume that the monopolist produces only a single product. The modifications in the analysis which are necessary when a firm possesses monopoly power in the sale of two or more products should become obvious after the analysis of market discrimination and multiple plants in Sections II.A and II.B.

Since a monopolist's marginal revenue curve is downward sloping, Eq. (10–11) will be satisfied if the marginal cost curve intersects the marginal revenue curve from below.

The optimal rate of output for the monopoly is determined by finding that value of q which satisfies both Eq. (10–10) and (10–11). Let $\bar{q}$ denote this optimal output.[4] The firm's optimal selling price, $\bar{p}$, is then found by substituting $\bar{q}$ for q in the demand curve, Eq. (10–4), i.e.,

$$\bar{p} = AR(\bar{q}). \tag{10–12}$$

From our discussion it should be clear that a monopoly firm has no supply curve. The concept of a supply curve is defined by determining the output that would be produced at a given market price. Since a monopolist sets market price rather than accepting it as a given datum, it is meaningless to ask what quantity the monopolist would produce if market price were given.

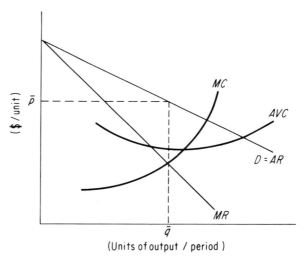

FIGURE 10–1.   Monopoly price and output decision.

The optimal price and output decision for a monopolist is illustrated graphically in Figure 10–1. This figure corresponds to the mathematical analysis of Eq. (10–8)–(10–12). It should be noted that our analysis in this section is a short-run analysis, since short-run cost curves corresponding to a given size of plant are used.

---

[4] Implicit here is the assumption that the resulting revenues cover at least the firm's resulting total variable costs, i.e., $TR(\bar{q}) \geq TVC(\bar{q})$. Otherwise, the firm should produce nothing in the short run despite the fact that it has a monopoly.

D. Long-Run Equilibrium

In a perfectly competitive industry in long-run equilibrium there are no economic profits and each firm operates an optimum-sized plant. Neither of these conditions will necessarily prevail in monopoly. The size of plant for the monopolist will be determined by the intersection of his long-run marginal cost curve and marginal revenue curve, as shown in Figure 10–2.

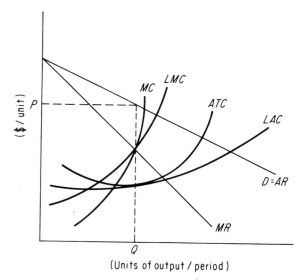

FIGURE 10–2.   Long-run monopoly price and output decision.

The short-run marginal cost curve, MC, corresponding to the plant that is most profitable, cuts both the long-run marginal cost curve, LMC, and the marginal revenue curve, MR, at their point of intersection indicating the optimal long-run rate of output, Q.[5] The optimal long-run selling price is P. This analysis assumes that the monopolist has a stable long-run demand curve, which implies that there are restrictions preventing new firms from entering the industry. In the example portrayed in Figure 10–2, there will be long-run monopoly profits, since the demand curve, D, is above the long-run average cost curve, LAC, at an output Q.

When the monopolist is in long-run equilibrium and is operating the size of plant corresponding to the ATC and MC curves shown in Figure 10–2, then the most profitable short-run price and output decision is to produce Q

---

[5] Note that in Section I.C of Chapter 8, we proved that MC and LMC intersect at the same rate of output Q for which ATC and LAC are tangent.

units and charge a price of P. Thus the most profitable short-run and long-run decisions of the firm are identical when long-run equilibrium is attained. This must necessarily be true, because otherwise the monopolist would have some incentive to alter either his price and output decision or else his scale of plant.[6]

As Figure 10–2 is drawn, the monopolist has a plant which is larger than the optimum size. Thus his average costs are higher than the minimum attainable, but the intersection of the long-run marginal cost and marginal revenue curves indicate that this is a more profitable scale of plant for the monopolist than the optimum size of plant. Conceptually the most profitable plant for the monopolist could correspond to any point on the long-run average cost curve. For example, if the marginal revenue curve intersects the long-run average cost curve at the minimum point, then the most profitable plant for the monopolist is the optimum sized plant. Similarly with appropriate shifts in the demand curve the most profitable scale of plant would be smaller than the optimum sized plant. In each case the monopolist's average costs are higher than the minimum attainable except when the most profitable scale of plant coincides with the optimum size of plant.

II. Some Extensions of the Basic Model

A. MARKET DISCRIMINATION

Since a monopolist is the only seller of the product, it may be possible for him to increase his profits by discriminating among the consumers and selling the same product to various customers at different prices. Effective discrimination becomes possible only when one consumer cannot resell the product to another. Resale becomes difficult when the commodity is not transferable, such as an appendectomy, or when transportation costs between consumers are so high as to make resale unprofitable, such as milk in Pittsburgh and milk in Denver. Discrimination also becomes possible if some customers are unwilling to buy in particular markets for reasons of status. For example, it is possible for a department store to discriminate between customers of the basement and patrons of other floors because some people are unwilling to be seen in the basement.

---

[6] We have assumed in this analysis that the demand curve is the same in both the short run and the long run. An argument can be made for distinguishing between the demand curves in the two cases. If this were done, then our discussion about the consistency of the most profitable short-run and long-run price and output decisions has no meaning.

Arguments for distinguishing between the short-run and the long-run demand curves are contained in George J. Stigler, *Theory of Price*, rev. ed. (New York: The Macmillan Company, 1954), pp. 45–47, 210–13.

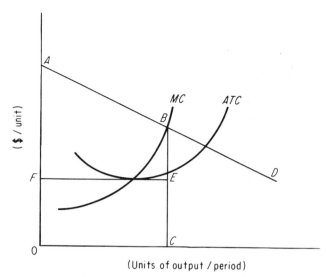

FIGURE 10–3. Monopoly output: complete price discrimination.

The ultimate in price discrimination, complete discrimination, occurs when it is possible to sell each unit of the product for the maximum price that the consumer is willing to pay for it. For example, the first unit will be sold at a price close to OA in Figure 10–3, the second unit at a slightly lower price, etc. As shown in Figure 10–3, the discriminating monopolist's most profitable output is OC. This output is determined by the intersection of the marginal cost curve with the demand curve at B. The marginal revenue of the OCth unit is CB, since that is precisely the increase in revenue due to the sale of that unit.[7] Thus the monopolist is still following his decision rule of operating where marginal cost equals marginal revenue. Total revenue is $ABCO$, total costs are $FECO$, and profits are $ABEF$.

Complete price discrimination, however, is extremely difficult to attain. A more common case found in the real world is two-market discrimination. In this case, the monopolist is able to divide his total market demand curve into two demand curves with different elasticities of demand at each price. If the two demand curves are independent, which is the case that we shall analyze, then there can be no "leakage" between markets; i.e., consumers

[7] This analysis essentially assumes that the market for the product consists of a large number of individuals, each of whom wishes to buy at most a single unit of the product. The downward-sloping market demand curve, D, in Figure 10–3 results when the maximum price at which an individual is willing to buy the product differs from person to person. With complete price discrimination, the demand curve D in Figure 10–3 is the *marginal* revenue curve rather than, as in the usual case, the *average* revenue curve. The average revenue curve is above D when there is complete price discrimination.

in the market with the lower price cannot resell the product in the other market. A common example of two-market discrimination occurs in foreign trade, since firms sometimes sell their products at a higher price in the domestic market than in the foreign market.

The decision rule for determining the optimal selling prices in each market and the optimal total output is similar to the marginal revenue equals marginal cost rule derived in Section I. Let q_1 and q_2 be the monopolist's sales in the two markets. The monopolist's total output, q, equals the sum of his sales in both markets:

$$q = q_1 + q_2. \tag{10-13}$$

The prices at which the firm can sell its output in each market are determined by the separate average revenue curves for these markets:

$$p_i = AR_i(q_i) \qquad i = 1, 2. \tag{10-14}$$

Assuming that the monopolist produces his total output in a single plant, his profits are

$$\pi = p_1 q_1 + p_2 q_2 - TC(q). \tag{10-15}$$

In Eq. (10–15), q_1 and q_2 can be regarded as the basic decision variables, with p_1, p_2, and q being determined by Eq. (10–13) and (10–14). Therefore to find the monopolist's maximum profits we can equate the partial derivatives of Eq. (10–15) with respect to q_1 and q_2 to zero:[8]

$$\frac{\partial \pi}{\partial q_1} = \frac{d}{dq_1}(p_1 q_1) - \frac{d}{dq} TC(q) = 0. \tag{10-16}$$

$$\frac{\partial \pi}{\partial q_2} = \frac{d}{dq_2}(p_2 q_2) - \frac{d}{dq} TC(q) = 0. \tag{10-17}$$

Equations (10–16) and (10–17) can be usefully rewritten in the following form:

$$MR_1(q_1) = MR_2(q_2) = MC(q). \tag{10-18}$$

---

[8] Equations (10–16) and (10–17) were obtained by making use of the relations:

$$\frac{\partial}{\partial q_1}[TC(q)] = \frac{dTC(q)}{dq}\frac{\partial q}{\partial q_1} = \frac{dTC(q)}{dq}.$$

$$\frac{\partial}{\partial q_2}[TC(q)] = \frac{dTC(q)}{dq}\frac{\partial q}{\partial q_2} = \frac{dTC(q)}{dq}.$$

The left-hand equalities follow from the chain rule for differentiation. The right-hand equalities follow from Eq. (10–13), since

$$\frac{\partial q}{\partial q_1} = \frac{\partial q}{\partial q_2} = 1.$$

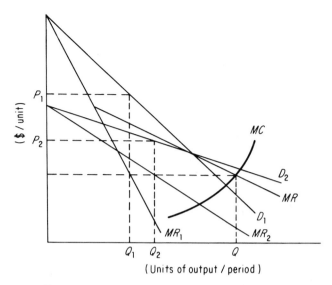

FIGURE 10–4. Two-market price discrimination.

The conditions in Eq. (10–18) can be interpreted as stating that if a monopolist can divide his market into two independent submarkets, then he should divide his over-all output between the two markets in such a way that he equalizes the marginal revenue he obtains in each market, and that this common marginal revenue should be equal to the marginal cost of his over-all output. The prices charged in each market are determined by substituting q_1 and q_2 into the average revenue curves, Eq. (10–14).

A graphical analysis of two-market discrimination is shown in Figure 10–4. As a first step, it is necessary to add laterally the marginal revenue curves for each market, MR_1 and MR_2, to form an over-all marginal revenue curve, MR. The intersection of this over-all marginal revenue curve with the marginal cost curve determines the optimal output of the firm, Q. This output is then allocated to each market to equalize the marginal revenue of the last unit sold in each market. Q_1 and Q_2 are the amounts sold in each market. The prices charged, P_1 and P_2, are determined by the demand or average revenue curves for each market.

It is possible to determine which market will have the higher price by comparing the price elasticities for each demand curve. By substituting Eq. (10–6) into (10–18) we can obtain:

$$MR_1\,(q_1) \;=\; p_1\!\left(1 + \frac{1}{\eta_1}\right) \;=\; MR_2\,(q_2) \;=\; p_2\!\left(1 + \frac{1}{\eta_2}\right). \qquad (10\text{–}19)$$

Since for a downward-sloping demand curve the price elasticity is negative, we can rewrite Eq. (10–19) in the following form:

$$\frac{p_1}{p_2} = \frac{1 - (1/|\eta_2|)}{1 - (1/|\eta_1|)}. \qquad (10\text{--}20)$$

From Eq. (10–20), it follows that p_1 will be less than p_2 if $|\eta_1| > |\eta_2|$, and p_2 will be less than p_1 if $|\eta_2| > |\eta_1|$. That is, the market having the more elastic demand at the chosen output will have the lower price.[9]

B. Multiple Plants

Under some circumstances it may be desirable for a monopolist to have more than one plant. In general, multiple plants will increase the monopolist's profits if the weighted average of the long-run average costs for the several plants at the outputs they will produce is less than the long-run average cost for the same total output produced by a single plant. If this condition holds, then the firm should have more than one plant unless there are severe transportation diseconomies.

Let us consider the case of a monopolist who has two plants but is selling in only one market. His problem is to determine how much to produce in each plant. The solution is analogous to the two-market discrimination solution. In the present case, there are two marginal cost curves, MC_1 and MC_2. These must be added laterally to obtain an over-all marginal cost curve, MC, as shown in Figure 10–5. The common marginal cost of the last unit produced in each plant is then equated to the marginal revenue of the last unit sold in the market. Thus the most profitable total output is Q, of which Q_1 is produced in the first plant and Q_2 in the second plant. The most profitable price is P for each unit sold, regardless of whether it was produced in the first or the second plant. The implicit assumption in Figure 10–5 that the two plants have different marginal cost curves is not essential to the analysis.

This analysis could easily have been carried out mathematically instead of graphically. It is also possible to consider the case of a monopolist producing in several plants. The solution is analogous to the solution obtained for the two-plant case: compute the over-all marginal cost curve by adding laterally the marginal cost curves of each plant and then equate the over-all marginal cost to marginal revenue. The general case in which a monopolist discriminates among several markets and produces in several plants can be handled by combining the methods of analysis used in this and the pre-

---

[9] The two-market discrimination analysis becomes considerably more complex in case leakage is permitted between the two markets. The demand curve in each market then becomes a function of the prices charged in both markets.

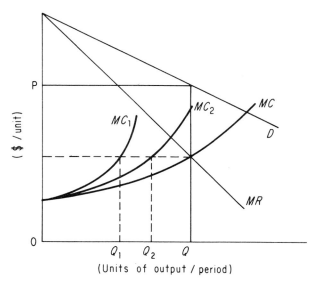

FIGURE 10–5. Monopoly output: two-plant monopolist.

ceding section. The general solution is to allocate sales among the markets
so that the marginal revenues of the last units sold are equal for all markets,
to allocate production among the plants so that the marginal costs of the
last units produced are equal for all plants, and to equate the common
marginal revenue with the common marginal cost.

C. Limit Price Analysis

For any monopoly to prevail, there must be some method for restricting
entry into the industry. Commonly the restrictive device is complete control
of a critical material or process. At some point in the life of the monopoly,
however, the danger of entry by other firms may arise if the restrictions on
entry have been weakened.[10] In such a situation, the monopolist has the
choice of continuing to reap monopoly profits for a short time (i.e., until
new firms enter the industry) or else of reducing its rate of profits to a level
where the industry is not attractive to new firms. If the latter policy is
followed, the monopolist attempts to achieve its objective by a self-imposed
scheme of price control. The problem then becomes one of deciding on the
optimum price and output under such conditions. This analysis can be most
conveniently made by graphical methods, as shown in Figure 10–6.

---

[10] For a discussion of this and related cases, see Joe S. Bain, "A Note on Pricing in
Monopoly and Oligopoly," *American Economic Review*, 39, (1949), 448–64.

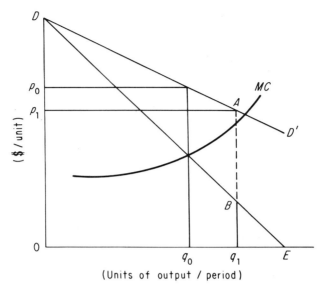

FIGURE 10–6.   Limit price analysis.

In Figure 10–6 it can be seen that the regular monopoly solution would be
to produce an output of q_0 (where the marginal revenue curve DBE intersects the marginal cost curve MC) to be sold at a price of p_0. Suppose that
the firm decides that it should never sell at a price higher than p_1, in order
to discourage the entry of new firms. Then the segment DA of the market
demand curve DAD' is replaced by p_1A, and the segment DB of the marginal revenue curve DBE is also replaced by p_1A (for when average revenue
is horizontal, marginal revenue coincides with it). The resulting marginal
revenue curve is discontinuous, consisting of the two segments p_1A and BE.
Since the marginal cost curve "intersects" the marginal revenue curve at
the output q_1 where the marginal revenue curve is discontinuous, the
monopoly should produce and sell an output q_1 at a price of p_1.

This type of analysis is appropriate for a monopolist who makes long-run
calculations. Such a firm in effect forgoes some of its opportunities for short-
run monopoly profits in order to maintain its monopoly position in the
long run. If the firm always equates its short-run marginal revenue with its
marginal cost, then competitors will attempt to enter the industry in
response to the high profits which are present. This will be the better
course for the firm to follow only if the present value of the declining profits
stream obtained by equating short-run marginal revenue with marginal
cost exceeds the present value of the constant profits stream obtained by
always charging the limit price p_1.

III. Some Effects of Monopoly on Resource Allocation

We can utilize the theory of monopoly behavior that has been developed to examine the effects of monopoly on the pattern of resource allocation. One fundamental distinction between a perfectly competitive firm and a monopoly is that the former has no ability to affect market prices, whereas the monopolist can set the selling price of his product. The power of any one firm to affect market prices has sometimes been attacked on political, social, and ethical grounds. We shall, however, restrict our attention to some economic comparisons of the different patterns of resource allocation that result from perfect competition and monopoly. In order to make these comparisons definite, we assume that the long-run average cost curve of a monopoly firm is the same as the long-run average cost curve for any of the firms in the same industry if it were organized under perfect competition. In particular, this implies that any economies of large-scale production which may exist in this industry occur at relatively small rates of output, so that the monopoly firm would be operating many plants. We shall indicate in Chapter 20 the manner in which our conclusions must be modified when a monopolist is able to take advantage of economies of scale unattainable under perfect competition.

We have seen in Chapter 8 that, in the long run, a perfectly competitive industry will reach equilibrium at a market price which is equal to the minimum height of the long-run average cost curve for all firms in the industry. At this long-run equilibrium market price, firms in the industry are earning a zero rate of profits, and price is equal to long-run marginal cost.

In contrast, we have seen in Section I.D. that, for a monopoly, the long-run equilibrium price will be established by the intersection of the marginal revenue curve and the long-run marginal cost curve. Since the corresponding price will be higher than this marginal revenue, the long-run market price which is charged by a monopolist is greater than the long-run equilibrium price which would prevail if the industry were perfectly competitive (where the same long-run average cost curve applies). Since the market demand curve is downward sloping, this means that a smaller rate of output is sold under monopoly conditions than would be the case under perfect competition. Hence under monopoly, consumers pay a higher price for, and receive less of, the product than they would under perfect competition. This is one of the alleged "evils" of monopoly.

The existence of monopoly can also be shown to lead to a less efficient utilization of productive resources than perfect competition. In Chapter 7 we saw that a perfectly competitive firm uses an input up to the point at which the price of that factor, say w_i, is equal to the marginal cost of output, MC, times the marginal product of that factor, which we denote by G_i:

$$w_i = (MC)G_i. \tag{10–21}$$

Since in perfect competition a firm's marginal cost equals the selling price of the product, p, we can rewrite Eq. (10–21) in the form:

$$w_i = pG_i. \tag{10–22}$$

Equation (10–22) can be interpreted as stating that in a perfectly competitive industry, pG_i, the value of the marginal product of factor i, equals the price, w_i, which is paid for this factor. For a monopoly, however, marginal cost equals marginal revenue. Therefore Eq. (10–21) becomes

$$w_i = (MR)G_i. \tag{10–23}$$

Equation (10–23) can be interpreted as stating that for a monopoly, the *marginal revenue product* of input i, $(MR)G_i$, equals the price which is paid for this factor.

Let us compare the effects of monopoly versus competition by assuming the same demand curve for the monopoly as for the competitive industry. Assume also that the marginal cost curve of the monopoly is the supply curve for the competitive industry. This implies that there are no economies or diseconomies of scale, so that the monopoly could be replaced by a large number of firms without affecting costs.

By comparing Eq. (10–22) and (10–23), we can see the effects of monopoly on the utilization of productive resources. Assuming a positively sloping market supply curve (marginal cost curve for the monopolist), the monopolist's marginal revenue, MR, must be less than price, p, for the competitive industry. If we assume that the factor price, w_i, remains constant, then for w_i to be equal in both Eq. (10–22) and (10–23), the marginal product, G_i, must be larger in Eq. (10–23) than in Eq. (10–22). Assuming that conditions of diminishing marginal returns prevail, this means that a monopoly uses less of any factor than would a perfectly competitive industry. Thus the existence of monopoly leads to the underutilization of productive resources. The value of the marginal product of an input (valued at the market price) is greater than the marginal revenue product for the monopolist. This is another major criticism often made of monopoly in comparison with perfect competition.

IV. A Case Study of a Monopoly

From the date of its formation in 1888 until World War II, the Aluminum Company of America was the only manufacturer of virgin aluminum ingot in the United States.[11] We shall examine the behavior of Alcoa during this period to determine how closely the theoretical analysis developed in this chapter applies to a monopoly in the real world.

The initial basis for Alcoa's monopoly position was control of the basic production process secured by patents. This patent protection expired in 1909. Alcoa secured protection of its monopoly position for three more years by two different means. First, it entered into a cartel agreement with foreign manufacturers of aluminum. Alcoa agreed not to export aluminum to certain foreign countries in return for an agreement by the foreign companies either not to export aluminum to the United States or else to do so under certain restrictions which included the fixing of prices. Second, Alcoa signed long-term contracts with three American companies which controlled important sources of raw materials necessary for the manufacture of aluminum. These contracts contained restrictive covenants which prevented the companies from selling the raw materials to any firm other than Alcoa which might have wished to begin manufacturing aluminum. Both these types of agreements were annulled by court decree in 1912.

After 1912, how was Alcoa able to maintain its position of being the sole American producer of virgin aluminum ingot until World War II? It no longer had patent protection; it did not enter into any further restrictive agreements; and it did not have complete control over essential raw materials.[12] Although the government alleged that Alcoa controlled a substantial amount of the raw material sources (e.g., 90 per cent of all known economically suitable sources of bauxite in the United States and Canada were allegedly owned by Alcoa in 1912), the Department of Justice did not feel that this constituted an effective barrier to entry because of the economic feasibility of importing bauxite from foreign sources.

Apparently the most effective means that Alcoa used to maintain its monopoly position was by constantly increasing its productive capacity,

---

[11] More detailed information about the history of the aluminum industry is contained in Robert F. Lanzillotti, "The Aluminum Industry," in *The Structure of American Industry*, 3rd ed., chap. 6, ed. Walter Adams (New York: The Macmillan Company, 1961); and Donald H. Wallace, *Market Control in the Aluminum Industry* (Cambridge, Mass.: Harvard University Press, 1937). Extensive excerpts from the two major antitrust decisions involving Alcoa are contained in Andreas G. Papandreou and John T. Wheeler, *Competition and Its Regulation* (Englewood Cliffs, N.J.: Prentice-Hall, Inc., 1954), chap. 17.

[12] Although Alcoa did not explicitly enter into further cartel agreements after the 1912 consent decree, international cartel agreements were signed by all other major aluminum companies in 1912, 1926, and 1931. Alcoa did not itself sign these agreements, but Alcoa's Canadian subsidiaries, Northern Aluminum Company and Aluminium, Limited of Canada, were formal signatories. Alcoa apparently conformed to the policies contained in these cartel agreements, and in turn Alcoa apparently received some protection from foreign competition in the United States. (See Lanzillotti, *op. cit.*, pp. 190–93.)

enabling it always to meet the growing market demand without raising prices. In the words of Judge Learned Hand's 1945 decision in an antitrust suit against Alcoa:

> It was not inevitable that it should always anticipate increases in the demand for ingot and be prepared to supply them. Nothing compelled it to keep doubling and redoubling its capacity before others entered the field. It insists that it never excluded competitors; but we can think of no more effective exclusion than progressively to embrace each new opportunity as it opened, and to face every newcomer with new capacity already geared into a great organization, having the advantage of experience, trade connections and the elite of personnel.[13]

In its pricing policy, Alcoa followed a policy of restraint which is comparable to the limit price analysis presented in Section II.C. It did not attempt to exploit its monopoly position in the short run by pricing without regard for potential entrants to the market. In particular, Alcoa's pricing policy seems to have been sensitive to the threat of foreign imports. Judge Learned Hand argued that " ... it is hard to resist the conclusion that potential imports did put a 'ceiling' upon those prices."[14]

Another view of Alcoa's pricing policy is:

> Alcoa recognized very early the advantages accruing to the company from an orderly reduction of aluminum prices over the years as necessary to penetrate new markets, coupled with a policy of stabilized prices between price reductions.... Orderly price reductions, coupled with unfair methods of competition (price discrimination, delivery delays, etc.), were all a part of the company's policy of market penetration and broadening the uses of aluminum. This policy also served to discourage potential competitors.[15]

Although the courts and most economists have viewed Alcoa as a monopolist until World War II, the company has never agreed that its being the sole producer of virgin aluminum ingot in the United States gave it a monopoly position. Alcoa pointed out that, in selling virgin aluminum ingot in the United States, it faced competition from secondary aluminum ingot (i.e., ingot produced from scrap aluminum), from foreign producers of aluminum, and from the producers of other materials which (in some uses) are substitutes for aluminum. Judge Hand, however, ruled that secondary aluminum ingot and other materials are irrelevant and that, since foreign producers supplied less than 10 per cent of the virgin aluminum ingot market in the United States, Alcoa had a monopoly position because of its control of over 90 per cent of the domestic market. As a side issue, it is interesting to note that Judge Hand said: "Dissolution is not a penalty but a remedy; if the industry will not need it for its protection, it will be a

---

[13] Papandreou and Wheeler, *op. cit.*, p. 318.

[14] *Ibid.*, p. 315.

[15] Lanzillotti, *op. cit.*, pp. 209–211.

disservice to break up an aggregation which has for so long demonstrated its efficiency."[16]

V. Summary

We defined a monopoly market as one in which there is a single seller and the product being sold has a low cross-elasticity of demand with all potentially competitive products. In such a market the firm will maximize profits in the short run by producing an output where marginal revenue equals marginal cost. The most profitable price is determined by substituting this output in the demand curve.

In the long run the monopolist may be able to increase his profits by building a new plant. The most profitable long-run output is determined by the intersection of the long-run marginal cost curve and the marginal revenue curve. That plant on the long-run average cost curve corresponding to this output is the most profitable plant for the monopolist. It was noted that this most profitable plant can be anywhere on the long-run average cost curve, not just at the point representing the optimum-sized plant.

The basic monopoly model was first extended to show that a monopolist may increase his profits by practicing price discrimination, i.e., by selling the same product to various customers at different prices. The extreme case of this is complete discrimination, in which it is possible to sell each unit of the product at the maximum price that anybody is willing to pay for it. In two-market discrimination the monopolist divides his total market into two submarkets having different elasticities of demand.

When he can practice two-market discrimination, it is most profitable for the monopolist to divide his over-all output between the two markets in such a way that he equalizes the marginal revenue obtained in each market and equates this common marginal revenue to the marginal cost of the over-all output. A higher price will be charged in the market having the more inelastic demand.

When the weighted average of the long-run average costs for several plants at the output they will produce is less than the long-run average cost for the same total output produced by a single plant, then the monopolist will find it more profitable to operate several plants rather than a single plant. A monopolist operating multiple plants should equate the marginal costs in each plant, and then determine over-all output by equating the

---

[16] Papandreou and Wheeler, *ibid.*, p. 320.

In a subsequent antitrust case, it was ruled in 1950 that there should be no dissolution of Alcoa. This decision was based on the fact that Reynolds Metals Company and Kaiser Aluminum Company had become domestic producers of virgin aluminum ingot with the help of plants which had been built by the government during World War II. The court did not exclude the possibility of a later dissolution order if the new competitors proved ineffective.

common marginal cost with marginal revenue. Regardless of where the output is produced, it should be sold at the same price unless the monopolist is able to practice price discrimination. In the general case when a multiple-plant monopolist can discriminate among several markets, he should allocate sales among the markets so that the marginal revenues of the last unit sold are equal for all markets, allocate production among the plants so that the marginal costs of the last units produced are equal for all plants, and equate the common marginal revenue with the common marginal cost.

If the barriers to entry have been weakened, then a monopolist may have to choose between continuing to exploit his monopoly position for a short time or reducing his rate of profits to a level which will discourage new firms from entering the industry. If the latter policy is followed, then the limit-price analysis becomes relevant. When there is a maximum price the monopolist can charge if he is to avoid attracting new firms to the industry, then the effective marginal revenue curve becomes discontinuous. One segment of the effective marginal revenue curve is a horizontal line from the limit price to the demand curve; the other segment is the original marginal revenue curve for outputs greater than that which can be sold at the limit price. When the marginal cost curve passes through the gap between the two discontinuous segments of the effective marginal revenue curve, the firm will charge only the limit price. The firm then forgoes some of its opportunities for exploiting short-run monopoly profits in order to maintain its long-run monopoly position.

In comparing the different patterns of resource allocation that would result under monopoly or perfect competition, we assumed that the long-run average cost curve of a monopoly is the same as the long-run average cost curve for any firm if the industry were organized under perfect competition. We then showed that under monopoly the consumers pay a higher price for, and receive less of, the product than they would under perfect competition. A perfectly competitive firm uses any factor up to the point where the value of the marginal product of that factor equals its price. In contrast, a monopolist uses any factor only up to the point where the marginal revenue product of that factor equals its price. This means that a monopoly uses less of any factor than would be used if the industry were perfectly competitive.

To compare the theoretical analysis of this chapter with the real-world behavior of a monopoly firm, we examined the history of the Aluminum Company of America. Until World War II, Alcoa was the sole producer of virgin aluminum ingot in the United States. The patents which were the original basis for Alcoa's monopoly position expired in 1909. From 1909 to 1912 a cartel agreement and a restrictive agreement with raw material suppliers protected Alcoa's market position. After 1912 Alcoa maintained its monopoly position by constantly increasing its productive capacity so that it was always able to meet the increasing market demand without raising prices; such a policy made the industry unattractive to potential entrants. As a result of an antitrust decision in 1945, Alcoa's monopoly position was ended. Rather than accomplishing this by breaking Alcoa into several smaller companies, the government sold most of its war surplus aluminum plants to two new producers of virgin aluminum ingot.

SUGGESTED READINGS

These recommendations are in addition to the footnote references cited in this chapter.

BACON, D. P., "Limit Pricing, Potential Entry, and Barriers to Entry," *American Economic Review*, LXIII (September, 1973), 666–74.

CRANDALL, R. W., "The Economic Effect of Television Network Program Ownership," *Journal of Law and Economics*, XIV (October, 1971), 385–412.

GROSSACH, I. M., "The Concept and Measurement of Permanent Industrial Concentration," *Journal of Political Economy*, LXXX, No. 4 (July/August, 1972), 745–60.

HICKS, J. R., "Annual Survey of Economic Theory: The Theory of Monopoly," in *Readings in Price Theory*, George J. Stigler and Kenneth E. Boulding, eds., chap. 18. Homewood, Ill.: Richard D. Irwin, Inc., 1952.

PHELPS BROWN, E. H., AND J. WISEMAN, *A Course in Applied Economics*, chaps. 4, 5. London: Sir Isaac Pitman & Sons, Ltd., 1964.

SCHWARTZMAN, D., "The Effect of Monopoly on Price," *Journal of Political Economy*, LXVII (August, 1959), 352–62.

Session on "The Monopoly Problem as Seen by Social Scientists," *American Economic Review, Papers and Proceedings*, XLVII, Part 2 (May, 1957), 293–327. (Papers by Edward H. Levi, Earl Latham, and Carl Kaysen; discussion by Corwin D. Edwards, Ward S. Bowman, Jr., and Charles E. Lindblom.)

STIGLER, GEORGE J., "The Statistics of Monopoly and Merger," *Journal of Political Economy*, LXIV (February, 1956), 33–40.

ZERBE, R. O., "Monopoly, the Emergence of Oligopoly and the Case of Sugar Refining," *Journal of Law and Economics*, XIII (October, 1970), 501–15.

Chapter Eleven

Monopolistic Competition

For some time economists thought that the two extreme models of perfect competition and monopoly were adequate tools for analyzing any market. Although it was recognized that some markets may not empirically conform to either model, it was assumed that some combination of the two models would be adequate to analyze such cases. In the latter part of the 1920's, beginning with an article by an English economist, P. Sraffa, more vigorous activity to develop models to handle the "middle ground" was apparent.[1] This activity culminated in the publication in the early thirties of two books: Joan Robinson's *Imperfect Competition* and Edward Chamberlin's *Monopolistic Competition.*[2] In this chapter we shall explore the model

---

[1] P. Sraffa, "The Laws of Returns under Competitive Conditions," *Economic Journal,* 36 (December, 1926), 535–50.

[2] Joan Robinson, *The Economics of Imperfect Competition* (London: The Macmillan Company, 1933). Edward Hastings Chamberlin, *The Theory of Monopolistic Competition* (Cambridge, Mass.: Harvard University Press, 1933); the quotations which follow are taken from Chamberlin's sixth edition, 1948.

211

developed by Chamberlin. After a detailed exposition, we shall examine some of the criticisms that have been levied against the model of monopolistic competition.

I. The Nature of Monopolistic Competition

In Chapter 4 we specified five assumptions to define the perfectly competitive model. All these assumptions except the assumption of homogeneous product are used to define the model of monopolistic competition. The perfectly competitive model assumes that the product is completely homogeneous in every possible dimension, so that at a given price no buyer has any reason to favor any seller. The monopolistically competitive model, on the other hand, assumes that each firm has a product which is differentiated in the minds of the consumers. Thus it is possible to have wide differences among the firms in price, output, and profits, at least in the short run. As we shall soon see, however, the major concern of the theory is with the long-run equilibrium position of the firms.

Monopolistic competition is a market structure in which there are many firms selling products which are close, but not perfect, substitutes for each other. This type of market structure combines the characteristics of perfect competition and monopoly.

Chamberlin defined *product differentiation* as follows:

> A general class of product is differentiated if any significant basis exists for distinguishing the goods (or services) of one seller from those of another. Such a basis may be real or fancied, so long as it is of any importance whatever to buyers, and leads to a preference for one variety of the product over another....
> Differentiation may be based upon certain characteristics of the product itself, such as exclusive patented features; trade-marks; trade names; peculiarities of the package or container, if any; or singularity in quality, design, color, or style. It may also exist with respect to the conditions surrounding its sale.[3]

When we say that a monopolistically competitive industry has many sellers, we mean not only that there are a large number of sellers of the many varieties of the product, but also that each seller is small enough so that no one either presently supplies or has sufficient capacity to supply a significant proportion of the total market. This means that each seller will pursue independent policies with respect to pricing, advertising, and product variation without any explicit regard for the behavior of his competitors and without any concern for retaliatory measures from his competitors. According to Chamberlin,

> ...any adjustment of price ... by a single producer spreads its influence over so many of his competitors that the impact felt by any one is negligible

---

[3] *Ibid.*, p. 56.

and does not lead him to any readjustment of his own situation. A price cut, for instance, which increases the sales of him who made it, draws inappreciable amounts from the markets of each of his many competitors, achieving a considerable result for the one who cut, but without making incursions upon the market of any single competitor sufficient to cause him to do anything he would not have done anyway.[4]

A seller under monopolistic competition can undertake three different types of actions in order to influence his rate of sales. First, he can change his selling price. Second, he can vary the nature of his product. Third, he can alter his expenditures for advertising and other methods of product promotion. The first type of action represents a movement along the demand curve he is facing, whereas the latter two types of action represent shifts of the demand curve confronting him. Chamberlin explained the possibility of a firm influencing the demand curve for its product in the following manner:

> The adjustment of his product is likewise a new problem imposed upon the seller by the fact of differentiation. The volume of his sales depends in part upon the manner in which his product differs from that of his competitors. . . . Under pure competition a producer may, of course, shift from one field of activity to another, but his volume of sales never depends, as under monopolistic competition, upon the product or the variety of product he chooses, for he is always a part of a market in which many others are producing the identical goods. . . .
> Thirdly, the seller may influence the volume of his sales by making expenditures, of which advertising may be taken as typical, which are directed specifically to that purpose. Such expenditures increase both the demand for his product, and his costs; and their amount will be adjusted, as are prices and "products," so as to render the profits of the enterprise a maximum. This third factor is likewise peculiar to monopolistic competition, since advertising would be without purpose under conditions of pure competition, where any producer can sell as much as he pleases without it.[5]

II. Pricing Decisions under Monopolistic Competition

In examining the behavior of monopolistically competitive firms, it is convenient first to look at pricing decisions assuming that the firms have already determined their most profitable varieties of product and selling expenses. This is the approach taken in the present section. In Sections III and IV we shall consider the manner in which firms reach product differentiation and selling expense decisions. Finally, in Section V we shall attempt an evaluation of the model of monopolistic competition, both from the standpoint of economic methodology and social welfare.

---

[4] *Ibid.*, p. 83.
[5] *Ibid.*, pp. 71–72.

A. THE SHORT RUN

Following Chamberlin, we present a graphical analysis which is based
upon the simplifying assumption that all firms have essentially identical
demand and cost functions. We can then analyze the marketwide behavior
in terms of a "representative firm." This assumption will later be relaxed,
although it is convenient for the moment.

Two different demand curves are used in the model. The first, following
Chamberlin, we designate as *DD*. It is based on the assumption that
competitors' prices are always the same as the price of the firm being
analyzed. The second, *dd*, is based on the assumption that competitors'
prices remain fixed. Thus *DD* shows the quantity that will be purchased at
each price from the firm when its price is always matched by its competitors. The other curve, *dd*, shows the amount that will be purchased at
each price from the firm when the firm's price is either lower or higher than
its competitors' (except for the one point of price equality which is the point
of intersection of the two curves).[6] Using these two demand curves, it is
possible to determine the short-run equilibrium position for the firm.

In Figure 11–1 the market price is *OP* and the firm is selling an output
OA. Now let the firm assume that any change in its price will not be followed
by the other firms. The *dd* curve then becomes the relevant demand curve

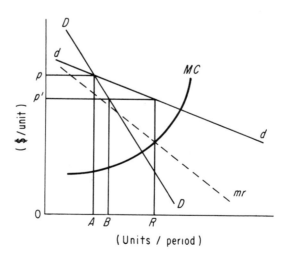

FIGURE 11–1.   Initial price and output decisions.

---

[6] As already indicated, product characteristics and advertising expenditures are
assumed fixed.

for the firm, and it attempts to operate as a monopolist given this demand curve. To maximize its profits, the firm will produce an output *OR* to sell at a price *OP'*, since *OR* is the output determined by the intersection of the marginal cost curve, *MC*, with *mr*, the marginal revenue curve derived from the *dd* demand curve. The new output and price would increase the firm's profits, if the assumption that competitors do not change their prices is accurate. In fact, however, all firms must follow the same logic and take the same action, since by assumption they all have the same information and the same motivation. As a result the actual movement of price is downward on the *DD* curve rather than the *dd* curve, since when all firms change price together, the *DD* curve is the relevant demand curve. The result is that at the new price *OP'* the output which is sold by each firm is only *OB*.

Figure 11–2 shows the resulting situation. Since all firms are now selling at the price *OP'*, the *dd* demand curve, which represents the amounts which any one firm can sell if it alone changes its price, has slid downward along the *DD* demand curve until it now intersects *DD* at the price *OP'*. The reasoning employed in the preceding paragraph can now be repeated. Again assuming that it can behave as a monopolist with the *dd* demand curve, the representative firm now tries to sell an output *OR'* at the price *OP''*. (Note that *OR'* is the output for which *MC* = *mr*.) Since this new decision is most profitable for the representative firm, all firms will choose to make the same move because we have assumed that all firms have identical demand and cost functions. As a result, when all firms cut their prices to *OP''*, it is the *DD* demand curve, rather than the *dd* demand curve, which is relevant. Each firm then sells only *OB'* units at the price *OP''*.

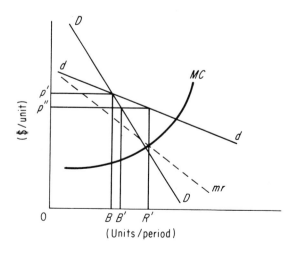

FIGURE 11–2. Results of initial decision.

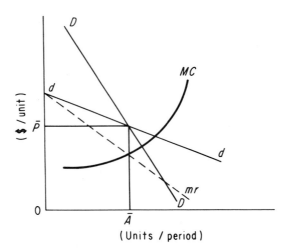

FIGURE 11–3. Short-run equilibrium.

A situation analogous to that in Figure 11–2 will again prevail, except that now the *dd* curve will have moved downward along the *DD* curve until it reaches the price OP''. Will this process ever stop? Under what circumstances will a short-run equilibrium position be reached, i.e., a position at which no firm has any incentive to alter its selling price? This position can be reached when the conditions shown in Figure 11–3 are realized. In Figure 11–3 the representative firm produces an output $O\bar{A}$ and sells it at a price $O\bar{P}$. This represents the short-run equilibrium position for the representative firm, since $O\bar{A}$ is the output for which the perceived marginal revenue, *mr*, equals the marginal cost, *MC*. Under the simplifying assumption that all firms have identical demand and cost functions, Figure 11–3 represents the short-run equilibrium position for all firms in the monopolistically competitive industry.

In the short-run equilibrium position, the representative firm does not necessarily earn positive profits. The firm's profit position depends upon the relationship between the average total cost of producing $O\bar{A}$ and the selling price $O\bar{P}$. In the next section we shall show that the long-run equilibrium position necessitates zero economic profits for the representative firm.

B. THE LONG RUN

In the long run, firms can vary the scale of plant and enter or leave the industry. We saw in Chapter 8 that the assumption of free entry and exit in a perfectly competitive market leads to a long-run equilibrium solution in which all firms in the industry have zero profits; i.e., a situation in which

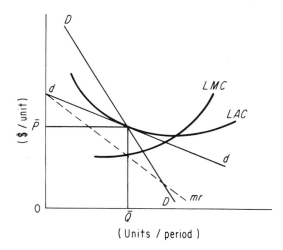

FIGURE 11–4. Long-run equilibrium.

profits are competed away. We shall show that a similar result holds for monopolistic competition given free entry and exit.

The long-run equilibrium solution is shown in Figure 11–4. In contrast to the preceding analysis, long-run rather than short-run cost curves are used. In the long-run equilibrium position, the long-run average cost curve LAC is tangent to the dd curve at the output $\bar{Q}$ and price $\bar{P}$ where the dd and DD curves intersect.

There are many ways by which long-run equilibrium can be attained. The actual dynamic process through which any particular equilibrium position is reached depends upon the position from which the industry starts. The adjustments required to reach equilibrium can be described in general, however, by looking at the movements of the DD and the dd curves, the principal actors.

From Figure 11–4, it can be seen that DD must intersect dd and the long-run average cost curve at the point of their tangency. This means that the entry of new firms or the exit of existing firms may be necessary before the long-run equilibrium position is obtained, since this is the way in which DD is moved. As new firms enter or as existing firms leave the market, the position of the DD curve changes. The DD curve confronting the representative firm moves to the left as the number of firms in the market increases, since there are now more sellers to share in a relatively constant total market. Similarly, as the number of firms in the market decreases, the DD curve facing the representative firm shifts to the right, since now fewer sellers divide the relatively constant total market among themselves. As

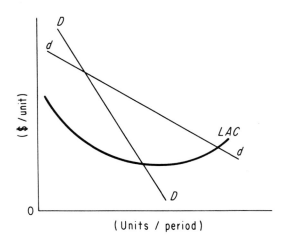

FIGURE 11–5.   Intersection of *DD* and *dd* above *LAC*.

long as entry and exit are free, *DD* can reach its long-run equilibrium position.

The other important curve, *dd,* reaches its long-run position by the same types of movements described earlier in analyzing the short-run equilibrium. So long as the point of intersection of *dd* with *DD* is above the long-run average cost (Figure 11–5), it is possible to earn profits in the industry. These profits can be earned from existing plants if their short-run average

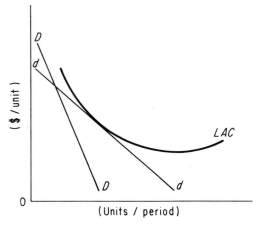

FIGURE 11–6.   Intersection of *DD* and *dd* to the left of the point of tangency.

total costs are below the intersection of dd and DD or with new plants that can be built so that their short-run average total costs are below the intersection. In each case, however, as long as the intersection is compatible with profits, the dd curve will move as each firm tries to gain more profits by changing output. This movement continues to take place until the dd curve is tangent to the long-run average cost curve. If at that time the DD curve does not pass through the point of tangency, movement of dd will still continue as firms attempt to minimize losses. If the intersection is to the left of the point of tangency (Figure 11–6), then losses will occur as firms attempt to expand along the dd curve to the point of tangency. These losses will drive firms out of the industry and move DD to the right. If the intersection is to the right of the point of tangency (Figure 11–7), profits will result as firms attempt to reduce output to the point of tangency. New firms will enter as a result and DD will move to the left. Thus the movement in the long run will be toward the point of equilibrium portrayed in Figure 11–4.[7]

Let us compare the long-run equilibrium positions under monopolistic competition, perfect competition, and monopoly. Monopolistic competition and perfect competition are similar in that long-run economic profits are

---

[7] We can show that the long-run marginal cost curve LMC intersects the marginal revenue curve mr at the same output $\bar{Q}$ for which dd is tangent to LAC. This is necessary to prove that the conditions portrayed in Figure 11–4 are consistent. Let the dd demand curve be represented by

$$p = f(q). \tag{11-1}$$

Since in long-run equilibrium dd is tangent to LAC at $q = \bar{Q}$, then

$$f(\bar{Q}) = LAC(\bar{Q}) \tag{11-2}$$

and

$$\frac{df(q)}{dq}\bigg|_{q=\bar{Q}} = \frac{dLAC(q)}{dq}\bigg|_{q=\bar{Q}}. \tag{11-3}$$

Multiplying both sides of Eq. (11–3) by $\bar{Q}$ and adding the result to Eq. (11–2), we have

$$f(\bar{Q}) + \bar{Q}\left[\frac{df(q)}{dq}\right]_{q=\bar{Q}} = LAC(\bar{Q}) + \bar{Q}\left[\frac{dLAC(q)}{dq}\right]_{q=\bar{Q}}. \tag{11-4}$$

The left-hand side of Eq. (11–4) is the value of marginal revenue at $q = \bar{Q}$, because

$$mr(\bar{Q}) = \frac{d}{dq}[qf(q)]_{q=\bar{Q}} = f(\bar{Q}) + \bar{Q}\left[\frac{df(q)}{dq}\right]_{q=\bar{Q}}. \tag{11-5}$$

The right-hand side of Eq. (11–4) is the value of long-run marginal cost at $q = \bar{Q}$, since

$$LMC(\bar{Q}) = \frac{d}{dq}[qLAC(q)]_{q=\bar{Q}} = LAC(\bar{Q}) + \bar{Q}\left[\frac{dLAC(q)}{dq}\right]_{q=\bar{Q}}. \tag{11-6}$$

Thus Eq. (11–4), (11–5), and (11–6) together imply

$$mr(\bar{Q}) = LMC(\bar{Q}), \tag{11-7}$$

which is the result we wanted to establish.

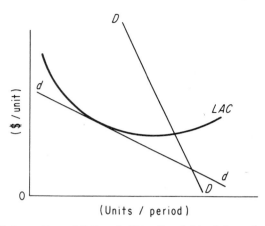

FIGURE 11–7.   Intersection of *DD* and *dd* to the right of the point of tangency.

zero, because of freedom of entry and exit.[8] In monopolistic competition, however, firms are producing smaller rates of output and incurring higher average costs (and hence selling their products at higher prices) than are identical firms in perfect competition. Since the *dd* curve is downward sloping, it is necessarily tangent to the long-run average cost curve to the left of the latter's minimum point. This means that from the standpoint of society, firms are not operating at the optimum scale of plant, and hence there is excess capacity in the industry. This property of monopolistic competition has received a great deal of attention in the literature; we shall

---

[8] It is, however, possible that there may be some immobility of resources which prevents long-run profits from being entirely competed away for all firms. As Chamberlin (*op. cit.*, pp. 111–13) writes:

"It has been argued, under the assumption of uniform curves, that, where profits are above the competitive level, multiplication of producers will reduce them, so that, although monopoly prices remain, profits are competitive and uniform for every one. The argument rested upon the implicit assumption that the production of substitutes within the general field and any portion of it was sufficiently possible to bring about this result. However, in so far as substitutes of such a degree of effectiveness may not be produced, the conclusions are different—demand curves will lie to the right of the point of tangency with cost curves, and profits will be correspondingly higher. This is the explanation of *all* monopoly profits, of whatever sort . . . .

"To sum up this phase of the matter, our statement of the group problem must be modified by recognizing that the demand curves are not adjusted uniformly to a position tangent to the cost curves. In so far as profits are higher than the general competitive level in the field as a whole or in any portion of it, new competitors will, *if possible*, invade the field and reduce them . . . . In fact, it is only partially possible. As a result, some (or all) of the [*dd*] curves may lie at various distances to the right of the point of tangency [with the long-run average cost curves], leaving monopoly profits scattered throughout the group—and throughout the price system.''

further consider the excess capacity "theorem" in Section V.B. Even though in the long run under monopolistic competition firms do not earn any excess profits, they do incur higher costs than would prevail under perfect competition, leading to higher selling prices for the product.

In comparison with monopoly, it is apparent from Figure 11–4 that monopolistically competitive firms have lower profits than would a monopoly firm in similar circumstances. If all the firms in a monopolistically competitive market were to behave as a single monopoly seller, i.e., if they were to collude, they could earn positive profits by raising their prices and restricting output since the *DD* curve is above the long-run average cost curve for some outputs less than $\bar{Q}$ in Figure 11–4. Although the firms would be more profitable, the monopoly type of market structure would definitely lead to lower levels of consumer utility because higher prices would be charged for smaller amounts of finished goods.

III. Product Variation Decisions under Monopolistic Competition

In addition to price variations, Chamberlin assumes that product quality and selling expenses can also vary. The long-run equilibrium conditions depicted in Figure 11–4 must continue to prevail even though other variations are allowed. Thus in investigating other variables we are showing how they may change as the firm moves toward its long-run equilibrium position.

Let us first consider product variation. It seems reasonable to approach the problem by assuming the price and product quality of the competitors fixed. Then by allowing price to vary for each possible product of the representative firm, we can find the most profitable price for each product given the prices and products of competitors. There will be one product which will be the most profitable of all the possible products. The representative firm will select this product, together with the price that makes it most profitable. As competitors then change their products and prices, the representative firm may then find further adaptation to be necessary. Changes in product will shift the long-run average cost curve. [9] Allowing changes in the product, therefore, means that in the process of attaining long-run equilibrium three curves move, the *DD* curve, the *dd* curve, and the *LAC* curve. In long-run equilibrium, however, the relative positions of all three curves must be the same as shown in Figure 11–4, since the analysis in Section II.B applies no matter which product is chosen.

---

[9] Changes in product will also shift the *dd* curve, and they may even conceivably shift the *DD* curve. Since in Section II we have seen how to analyze shifts in the *dd* and the *DD* curves, in this section we concentrate on shifts in the *LAC* curve.

Some generalizations can be made about the effects of product differentiation on consumer welfare.

> The conclusion seems to be warranted that just as, for a given "product," price is inevitably higher under monopolistic than under pure competition, so, for a given price, "product" is inevitably somewhat inferior. After all, these two propositions are but two aspects of a single one. If a seller could, by the larger scale of production which is characteristic of pure as compared with monopolistic competition, give the same "product" for less money, he could, similarly, give a better "product" for the same money.[10]

Chamberlin essentially assumes that all firms perceive the market in the same way, and that although they act independently they in fact pursue similar actions and achieve products of similar quality.

If, however, firms perceive the composition of the market differently, then they may not pursue similar product differentiation policies. According to Bain:

> For example, the market may be made up in part of buyers who are strongly quality-conscious and not especially price-conscious—being willing to pay substantially more for higher quality—and in part of buyers who are more price-conscious, or willing to accept substantially lower quality to get a somewhat lower price. In this case some sellers may see increased profits in policies of product improvement and relatively high price, whereas the very fact that they pursue such policies tends to make it more profitable for others to emphasize lower quality, cost, and price. . . . with buyers able to choose among a wide range of alternative product qualities, costs, and prices, there will tend to be a much better balance of the cost of product improvement against the resulting increment to buyer satisfaction than where uniform product improvement policies are pursued.[11]

Bain has relaxed the assumption that the demand and cost curves are the same for all firms in a monopolistically competitive industry. Under these conditions we must determine whether any essential aspects of the long-run equilibrium analysis must be modified. It is easy to see that differences in the product and differences in the cost curves of the firms can make the long-run equilibrium positions differ from firm to firm. Hence larger firms can exist alongside of smaller firms, higher-priced firms can exist alongside of lower-priced firms, and higher-quality firms can exist alongside of lower-quality firms. This diversity is consistent with each firm having a long-run equilibrium position similar to the one portrayed in Figure 11–4.

IV. Selling Expense Decisions under Monopolistic Competition

The analysis required when selling expenses are allowed to vary is similar to the analyses made in Sections II and III. We begin by assuming that

---

[10] Chamberlin, *op. cit.*, p. 99.

[11] Joe S. Bain, *Pricing, Distribution, and Employment*, rev. ed. (New York: Holt, Rinehart & Winston, Inc., 1953), pp. 371–72.

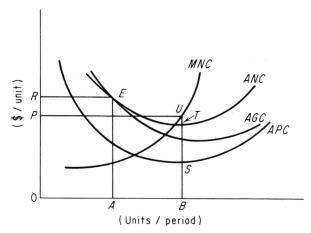

FIGURE 11-8. Initial selling expense decision.

price and product quality are given and that each of the firms is incurring a certain amount of selling expense.

The starting point of the analysis is E in Figure 11–8. For the representative firm, the selling price is OP, output is OA, and the firm is losing PR per unit. The APC curve is the long-run average cost curve of the firm when only *production* costs are considered. The AGC curve is the APC curve to which the actual amount of selling expense currently being incurred by the representative firm has been added. Thus the AGC curve approaches the APC curve as output increases.

Now the same process that operated in the case of price will operate in the case of selling expense. The firm can improve its profit position by increasing its selling expense if all other firms maintain their selling expenses at the previous level. In Figure 11–8 ANC is the APC curve to which has been added, for each output, the amount of selling expense necessary to sell that output, assuming that all other firms maintain constant selling expenses. Since selling expense must increase to sell additional output, the ANC curve does not approach the APC curve as output increases. In Figure 11–8 MNC is the marginal cost curve corresponding to the ANC average cost curve.[12] Since this analysis of selling expense assumes that price and marginal revenue are constant and equal to OP, the most profitable output for the representative firm is OB units where MNC intersects the price line. At this output, average production costs are BS per unit, selling costs are ST per unit, and profits are TU per unit.

---

[12] The total cost curve corresponding to the ANC average cost curve is $qANC(q)$. Hence the corresponding marginal cost curve is

$$MNC(q) = \frac{d}{dq} [qANC(q)].$$

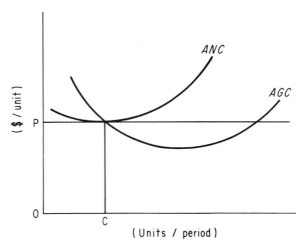

FIGURE 11–9.   Equilibrium position for selling expense.

Let us now determine whether the representative firm will be able to reach this position. Assume, for ease of analysis, that (a) increased selling expenses will not increase the market demand curve; (b) no firms leave or enter the market. Further assume that all firms make similar increases in their selling expenses in the hope of improving their profit positions. With these assumptions, the sales of the representative firm will remain OA, but the average total costs will be higher because of the increased selling expense.

This process will continue until the ANC curve, which is drawn on the assumption that all other firms keep selling expenses constant, is tangent to the price line. At this point the representative firm has no further incentive to change its selling expense. Each firm may be incurring losses at this point, however.

If we now relax assumption (b) and allow firms to leave the industry, the output of each remaining firm will increase. The process will continue until the remaining firms are no longer incurring losses and there is no longer any perceived gain from one firm increasing selling expense assuming that the selling expenses of other firms are constant. The situation at this point, when selling expenses are in equilibrium, is portrayed in Figure 11–9.

The complete long-run equilibrium solution when all variables (price, product quality, and selling expense) are considered is a combination of Figures 11–4 and 11–9. The dd curve is tangent to AGC (which corresponds to the LAC curve of Figure 11–4) at a price $O\bar{P}$ and an output $O\bar{A}$ for the representative firm, and the DD curve intersects dd and AGC at the point of tangency. This solution is shown in Figure 11–10. At this equilibrium position, zero profits are being made and there is no incentive for firms to

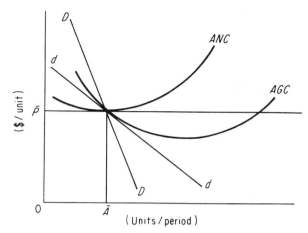

FIGURE 11–10. Long-run equilibrium position allowing adjustments in price, product quality, and selling expense.

enter or leave the industry. There is no way that an individual firm can expect to gain by changing price, product quality, or selling expense, assuming that all other firms keep their prices, product qualities, and selling expenses constant.

The analysis of selling expense has, of course, been simplified. Other assumptions are possible; e.g., we could analyze the effects of an increase in the market demand curve *DD* as a result of increased selling expense. The basic mechanisms in the model operate in the same fashion, however, and the resulting equilibrium conditions are the same as shown in Figure 11–10.

V. Evaluation of Monopolistic Competition

Although the first edition of *The Theory of Monopolistic Competition* appeared in 1933, there is still controversy among economists as to the significance of Chamberlin's theory. The criticisms are of two kinds: the first is a challenge on methodological grounds; the second is a challenge to the excess capacity implications which follow from the equilibrium conditions.

A. METHODOLOGICAL CRITICISMS

In the process of developing the methodological criticisms, we shall call attention to three assumptions that Chamberlin made which have been implicit in our exposition. The first is the concept of the "group." In defining the perfectly competitive model, we assumed a homogeneous product, so that price is the only reason a buyer might prefer one seller to any other. Thus under perfect competition the firms in an industry are considered to be those selling the homogeneous product.

In monopolistic competition, however, there is difficulty in determining the precise boundaries of an industry because of the lack of homogeneity in the product. Chamberlin uses the term "group" as an approximate equivalent to an industry. He defines the group thus:

> The group contemplated is one which has *ordinarily* been regarded as composing one imperfectly competitive market: A number of automobile manufacturers, of producers of pots and pans, of magazine publishers, or of retail shoe dealers. From our point of view, each producer within the group is a monopolist, yet his market is interwoven with those of his competitors, and he is no longer to be isolated from them.[13]

Stigler, the most severe critic of Chamberlin's methodology, has argued that the definition of the group is ambiguous. He focuses on three implications of the definition:

1. It is perfectly possible, on Chamberlin's picture of economic life, that the group contain only one firm, or, on the contrary, that it include all of the firms in the economy. This latter possibility can readily follow from the asymmetry of substitution relationships among firms: taking any one product as our point of departure, each substitute has in turn its substitutes, so that the adjacent cross-elasticities may not diminish, and even increase, as we move farther away from the "base" firm in some technological or geographical sense.
2. The picture of diversity and unsystematism also makes it very likely, if the group contains several firms, that the products be heterogeneous from the technological viewpoint.
3. The picture also dictates that often, and perhaps usually, a large or dominant role is played by firms outside the group in determining prices and profits within the group.[14]

Chamberlin's problem in defining the group is unavoidable. On the one hand he assumes that each firm is a monopolist, which implies that there is a low cross-elasticity of demand among the products of the group. On the other hand he assumes that the group is closely interdependent, which implies that there is a high cross-elasticity of demand among the products of the group.

Chamberlin attempts to simplify the analysis by assuming " ... that both demand and cost curves for all the 'products' are uniform throughout the group."[15] He refers to this as the *uniformity* assumption; it is one that we have used throughout the exposition. A second simplifying assumption introduced by Chamberlin is that the impact of changes by one firm in any of its three decision variables affects such a large number of firms that

---

[13] Chamberlin, *op. cit.*, p. 81.

[14] George J. Stigler, *Five Lectures on Economic Problems* (London: Longmans, Green and Co., 1949), p. 15.

[15] Chamberlin, *op. cit.*, p. 82.

it does not evoke retaliation by any firms. Stigler calls this the *symmetry* assumption.

These two assumptions, in Stigler's view, do not save the concept of the group. The basic criticisms are twofold. For the uniformity assumption to make sense, the firms in the group must be selling physically homogeneous products, and it is then not clear why each firm should have a negatively sloping demand curve. With the further introduction of the symmetry assumption, Stigler argues that " . . . now we have utterly abandoned the picture with which our analytic technique was designed to deal: there is no variety and there is only one possible type of interrelationship [substitution] between products."[16]

Further criticisms can be made of the analysis if one relaxes the uniformity assumption and allows the possibility of certain firms having monopoly profits at equilibrium, as Chamberlin did. Stigler's conclusion is that " . . . in the general case we cannot make a single statement about economic events in the world we sought to analyze. It is true that many such statements are made by Chamberlin, but none follows rigorously from the ambiguous apparatus."[17]

B. Excess Capacity Criticisms

The equilibrium conditions under the model of monopolistic competition lead to an output that is less than the output for which long-run average costs are minimum. Thus it was concluded that monopolistic competition leads to firms having excess productive capacity as compared with perfect competition where in long-run equilibrium the firm is operating at the minimum point on the long-run average cost curve.

In recent years the proposition of excess capacity has come under attack. A more careful appraisal of the proposition has resulted, although there is not complete agreement on its present status.

---

[16] Stigler, *op. cit.*, p. 17.

[17] *Ibid.*, pp. 18–19.

Chamberlin has replied to Stigler's criticisms in an essay, "The Chicago School." Referring to the uniformity assumption, Chamberlin says: "No one outside the Chicago School has to my knowledge interpreted the 'uniformity assumption' to mean homogeneity of the products involved; and since it is clearly explained what is meant by it and why this is not so, there is no excuse for anyone to proclaim such an absurdity." *Towards a More General Theory of Value* (New York: Oxford University Press, 1957, p. 300.)

Archibald has attempted to review the arguments on both sides of the controversy. He concludes that monopolistic competition yields very few empirically testable propositions. He summarizes the reasons for this as follows: " . . . in the case of the individual firm, with advertising and quality variation, the reason is that significant predictions cannot be obtained without more information than is usually assumed or readily available. In the case of the group, even without advertising and quality variation, the reason is that the demand relations of the theory are inadequately specified." G. C. Archibald, "Chamberlin *versus* Chicago," *Review of Economic Studies*, 29 (1961–62), 2.

The most comprehensive statement has come from Harrod. His argument utilizes long-run considerations. In particular, Harrod believes that the excess capacity "theorem" implies that the entrepreneur acts in an inconsistent manner. The inconsistency arises because the entrepreneur uses a short-run marginal revenue curve and a long-run marginal cost curve to determine his optimal output and scale of plant. He then sets his price at such a level that competitors enter and thereby shift his marginal revenue curve downward. In other words the model of monopolistic competition assumes that the entrepreneur is highly rational but extremely short-sighted; as Harrod puts it, "Apparently it is impossible to be an entrepreneur and not suffer from schizophrenia!"[18]

Harrod's own analysis uses the intersection of the long-run marginal revenue curve with the long-run marginal cost curve to determine the firm's optimal output and scale of plant. The long-run marginal cost curve intersects the long-run marginal revenue curve at a greater output than it intersects the short-run marginal revenue curve, because the demand curve is assumed to be more elastic in the long run. Further, Harrod argues that the entrepreneur will charge a price that will yield only normal profits, even though the short-run marginal revenue for that price and output is less than the short-run marginal cost; the entrepreneur's purpose in foregoing some potential short-run profits is to discourage new firms from entering the market. Harrod summarizes his argument by saying:

> Consequently we may conclude that imperfect competition does not usually tend to create excess capacity. Economists should therefore discard the "generally accepted" doctrine to the contrary effect [19]

It should be noted that so long as the long-run equivalent of *dd* is downward sloping, Harrod's solution still contains some excess capacity, since the point of tangency between any downward-sloping demand curve and a U-shaped long-run average cost curve must be above and to the left of the cost curve's minimum point. Since, however, the long-run demand curve is assumed to have a flatter slope than the short-run demand curve, the amount of excess capacity is less under Harrod's analysis than under Chamberlin's analysis.

Harrod's discussion of the excess capacity issue has stimulated several articles on the subject which have resulted in a variety of answers.[20] These

---

[18] R. F. Harrod, *Economic Essays* (New York: Harcourt, Brace and Company, 1952), p. 149.

[19] *Ibid.*, p. 152.

[20] See especially H. R. Edwards, "Price Formation in Manufacturing Industry and Excess Capacity," *Oxford Economic Papers*, new ser., 7, No. 1 (February, 1955), 94–118; F. H. Hahn, "Excess Capacity and Imperfect Competition," *Ibid.*, 7, No. 3 (October, 1955), 229–40; Paul Streeten, "Two Comments on the Articles by Mrs. Paul and Professor Hicks," *Ibid.*, 259–64; and H. F. Lydall, "Conditions of New Entry and the Theory of Price," *Ibid.*, 300–11.

answers differ because each author introduces somewhat different assumptions to supplement those made by Chamberlin. It is only by adding the further assumption that the entrepreneur is able to foresee the effects of his policies on the entry of potential competitors that Harrod is able to obtain a somewhat different result regarding excess capacity than Chamberlin. Later writers have reached still different results only by further modifying Chamberlin's assumptions. Therefore when they quarrel with the excess capacity implications of monopolistic competition, Harrod and the other critics are really developing their own models of imperfect competition rather than analyzing the properties of Chamberlin's model.

C. FINAL APPRAISAL

Our basic position is that the model of monopolistic competition is not a useful addition to economic theory because it does not describe any market in the real world. We take this position on both empirical and theoretical grounds.

Let us first examine the empirical considerations. Those markets containing a large number of relatively small firms in which there are no barriers to entry are generally markets in which the firms sell a standardized product. Examples of this type of market are wheat and lumber. Such markets are most appropriately analyzed using the model of perfect competition. Even if there were a moderate degree of product differentiation in these markets, the individual firms would possess such a limited power to set their own prices (i.e., their demand curves would be so nearly horizontal) that the marketwide implications derived on the basis of the perfectly competitive model would be reasonable approximations to reality.

Markets in which brand preferences among consumers are strong, however, generally have a relatively small number of firms in them, even though each firm may sell several different brands. Examples of this type of market are automobiles and cigarettes. These markets are most appropriately analyzed using the framework of oligopoly (to be discussed in Chapter 12), since, when there are only a few firms, the interdependencies among them become paramount and explicitly recognized.

Third, markets in which a firm sells a product for which there are no close substitutes are most appropriately analyzed using the monopoly model. Examples of this type of market are telephone services and electric power.

Finally, the most frequently cited class of markets for which monopolistic competition is allegedly appropriate is the retail sector in any large city. Thus the retail groceries, retail shoe stores, gasoline stations, automobile dealers, and drug stores are often regarded as examples of monopolistically competitive markets. Monopolistic competition can be shown to be inapplicable in even these cases. Chamberlin's symmetry assumption will not be valid when applied to all the retailers of a given product in a large city, since the impact of a price change by any one retailer will be greatest on those few retailers in his immediate marketing area. Therefore the recognized interdependencies which characterize oligopoly must be present in these retail markets, and they must be analyzed as oligopolies.

We thus cannot find any examples of markets in the real world for which the model of monopolistic competition is relevant. Even if some examples could be found, however, we would not change our basic position. On theoretical grounds we would not expect monopolistic competition to be anything more than a transitory phenomenon. We hold this position for two reasons. First, from a behavioral standpoint, we would expect the firms eventually to learn that their actions in fact induce reactions from competitors and that recognition of these interdependencies can lead to greater profits for all firms. Such a situation would eventually lead to a market most appropriately analyzed by oligopoly or by perfectly competitive models, depending upon the conditions of entry. Second, if the firms in the market do not recognize their interdependence and continue to compete as though they were independent, then we would expect the number of firms in the market to decrease as the more successful firms "win out." Thus an oligopoly model would eventually become appropriate when there are few enough firms so that they cannot avoid recognizing the interdependencies among them. A typical example of this is provided by automobile manufacturers in the United States, where the number of active producers of automobiles has decreased from a high of 88 firms in 1921 to less than one-tenth that number today.[21]

In developing the model of monopolistic competition, Chamberlin attempted to introduce greater realism into the theory of the firm. In general we are sympathetic to such an attempt, as our discussion of several new approaches to the theory of the firm in Part III of this book indicates. It is unfortunate, however, that Chamberlin succeeded in creating only an empirically empty economic model.

VI. Summary

In this chapter we have examined Chamberlin's model of monopolistic competition. This model combines some features of perfect competition with some features of monopoly. All five of the assumptions defining perfect competition except for the assumption of homogeneous products apply to monopolistic competition, where each firm is assumed to sell a differentiated product in which it has a partial monopoly position.

---

[21] Data on the entrances, exits, and numbers of active automobile producers in the United States in each year between 1902 and 1926 are found in Lawrence H. Seltzer, *A Financial History of the American Automobile Industry* (Boston: Houghton Mifflin Company, 1928), table 5, p. 65.

Chamberlin assumes that because of the large number of firms in the market, each pursues pricing, product quality, and selling expense policies without any explicit concern about retaliatory measures from its competitors. We looked first at pricing decisions. For this purpose, Chamberlin uses two different demand curves for the representative firm. The *DD* curve is based on the assumption that competitors' prices are always the same as the price of the firm being analyzed; the *dd* curve is based on the assumption that competitors' prices remain fixed.

Since the firm sets its prices on the assumption that its actions do not induce any retaliation by its competitors, the *dd* curve is assumed relevant. In the short run, the representative firm attempts to operate at the most profitable point determined by its short-run cost curves and the *dd* curve. All firms will be similarly motivated, however, with the result being that the *DD* curve is actually followed, instead of the *dd* curve. As a result, each firm may again attempt to alter its selling price to improve its short-run profits. A short-run equilibrium position is reached only when the intersection of the marginal revenue curve with the short-run marginal cost curve occurs at the same rate of output for which the *dd* and *DD* curves intersect.

In the long run when firms can vary the scale of plant and enter or leave the industry, equilibrium will be established only when profits are zero for all firms in the industry and no firm perceives that any improvement in its profits can occur from changes in its output or scale of plant. In the long-run equilibrium position, the long-run average cost curve is tangent to the *dd* curve at the output and price where the *dd* and *DD* curves intersect. This long-run equilibrium solution implies that there is excess capacity in the industry, since firms are not operating at the optimum scale of plant.

The possibility of product variation does not change the nature of the long-run equilibrium solution, although it means that the *LAC* curve, as well as the *DD* and the *dd* curves, may shift in the process of reaching equilibrium. Similarly, adding selling expense as a decision variable further enriches the adjustments which can occur in the movement toward an equilibrium position without changing the nature of the solution. In long-run equilibrium, zero profits are being made and there is no incentive for firms to enter or leave the industry; there is no way that an individual firm perceives any increase in its profits by unilaterally changing price, product quality, or selling expense.

To conclude this chapter, we briefly reviewed some criticisms that have been made of Chamberlin's theory. Stigler has argued that many of Chamberlin's assumptions are ambiguous, and that as a result there are no empirically testable propositions implied by the theory of monopolistic competition. Harrod has attempted to gain greater realism by introducing further assumptions, the result being a weakening of the excess capacity implications of monopolistic competition. In our opinion, monopolistic competition is an empirically empty economic model.

SUGGESTED READINGS

These recommendations are in addition to the footnote references cited in this chapter.

AZARIADIS, C., K. J. COHEN, AND A. PORCAR, "A Partial Utility Approach to the Theory of the Firm," *Southern Economic Journal*, XXXVIII, No. 4 (April, 1972), 485–94.

BAIN, J. S., "Changes in Concentration in Manufacturing Industries in the United States, 1954–1966: Trends and Relationships to the Levels of 1954 Concentration," *Review of Economics and Statistics*, LII (November, 1970), 411–16.

BREMS, H., "Employment, Prices and Monopolistic Competition," *Review of Economics and Statistics*, XXXIV (November, 1952), 314–25.

DEMSETZ, HAROLD, "The Welfare and Empirical Implications of Monopolistic Competition," *The Economic Journal*, LXXIV (September, 1964), 623–41.

HARROD, R. F., "Imperfect Competition, Aggregate Demand and Inflation," *The Economic Journal*, LXXXII (March, 1972), 392–401.

KALDOR, NICHOLAS, "Market Imperfection and Excess Capacity," in *Readings in Price Theory*, George J. Stigler and Kenneth E. Boulding, eds., chap. 19. Homewood, Ill.: Richard D. Irwin, Inc., 1952.

QUALLS, D., "Concentration, Barriers to Entry and Long Run Economic Profit Margins," *Journal of Industrial Economics*, XX (April, 1972), 146–58.

Session on "The Theory of Monopolistic Competition After Thirty Years," *American Economic Review, Papers and Proceedings*, LIV, No. 3 (May, 1964), 28–57. (Papers by Joe S. Bain, Robert L. Bishop, and William J. Baumol; discussion by Jesse W. Markham and Peter O. Steiner.)

TRIFFIN, ROBERT, *Monopolistic Competition and General Equilibrium Theory.* Cambridge: Harvard University Press, 1941.

Chapter Twelve

Duopoly and Oligopoly

In this chapter, the third of four dealing with various types of imperfect market structures, we shall discuss duopoly and oligopoly. An oligopolistic market is characterized by the existence of a relatively small number of sellers. The key feature is recognized interdependence among the sellers. Each oligopolist realizes that changes in its price, advertising, product characteristics, etc., may stimulate responses by rivals.

The single-seller market, monopoly, has been discussed in Chapter 10. When there are exactly two sellers in the market, this is a special case of oligopoly called *duopoly*. Because the key features and resulting problems of oligopolistic interdependence are seen most easily in the two-seller case, a large part of our discussion in this chapter will be devoted to duopoly. Markets with three, four, or five firms are clear examples of oligopoly. It is impossible to state precisely the maximum number of sellers that there can be in a market before we no longer would call it oligopoly. Whether or not there is recognized interdependence among the sellers depends primarily upon the number and relative size of the firms, the degree of product differentiation, and geographical dispersion. Most economists would call the primary steel industry in the United States an oligopoly, even though there are over one hundred American producers of basic steel; in fact, no more than the ten largest steel producers seem to be important in pricing decisions. Other examples of oligopoly markets in the American economy are automobile tires, cigarettes, heavy electrical equipment, dynamite, plate glass, sulfur, refrigerators, and automobiles.

If an oligopoly is to persist over a long period of time, there must usually be some types of barriers to entry which tend to keep new sellers from entering the market. Otherwise in any highly profitable oligopolistic industry, new firms will enter and the market will eventually become competitive. Some possible barriers to entry are economies of scale (which may make it unprofitable for more than a few firms of optimal size to exist in an industry), control over indispensable resources, exclusive franchises (such as patents, licenses, and copyrights), high capital requirements (whether due to plant costs, distribution network costs, or advertising costs), and the existence of unused capacity (which makes the industry appear unattractive to potential entrants).

The rival firms in an oligopoly may sell either identical or differentiated products. When their products are considered by the buyers to be virtually identical, then in any period the oligopoly sellers will charge the same prices. When the sellers have differentiated products, however, then they each may charge different prices. Both types of oligopoly markets, those with identical as well as those with differentiated products, will be considered in this chapter. Dynamite, plate glass, and sulfur are examples of oligopoly markets where the sellers all have virtually the same products. Typical oligopoly markets with differentiated products are automobile tires, cigarettes, refrigerators, and automobiles.

I. Conjectural Variations and Duopolistic Interdependence

The easiest framework within which to examine the nature of oligopolistic interdependence is the special case of duopoly, where there are only two sellers. In this section we shall develop several alternative models of price and output behavior in duopoly markets. The fundamental notions behind each of these models could be generalized to apply equally well to oligopoly markets containing more than two sellers. For analytical convenience, however, we shall consider here only the two-firm case.

A. Duopolists Selling Undifferentiated Products

Let us start by considering a duopoly market in which the two firms sell a standardized product at the same market price. Let p denote the common selling price, and let q_1 and q_2 denote the output of the first and second firms, respectively. The demand function of the market expresses price as a function of total output, Q, which is the sum of q_1 and q_2:

$$p = F(q_1 + q_2) = F(Q). \tag{12-1}$$

The demand curve is negatively sloping:

$$F' < 0. \tag{12-2}$$

The total revenues received by each firm, R_1 and R_2, are

$$R_i = q_i F(q_1 + q_2) = R_i (q_1, q_2) \qquad i = 1,2. \tag{12-3}$$

The profits of each firm, π_1 and π_2, are

$$\pi_i = R_i (q_1, q_2) - C_i(q_i) \qquad i = 1,2 \tag{12-4}$$

where C_1 and C_2 are the total production costs of each firm.

Differentiating Eq. (12–4) with respect to each firm's decision variable (its own output), and equating the resulting derivatives to zero, to find the profit-maximizing output for each firm:

$$\frac{d\pi_1}{dq_1} = \frac{\partial R_1(q_1, q_2)}{\partial q_1} + \frac{\partial R_1(q_1, q_2)}{\partial q_2}\frac{dq_2}{dq_1} - \frac{dC_1(q_1)}{dq_1} = 0. \tag{12-5}$$

$$\frac{d\pi_2}{dq_2} = \frac{\partial R_2(q_1, q_2)}{\partial q_1}\frac{dq_1}{dq_2} + \frac{\partial R_2(q_1, q_2)}{\partial q_2} - \frac{dC_2(q_2)}{dq_2} = 0. \tag{12-6}$$

In order to solve Eq. (12–5) and (12–6), we need to know either the values of, or else functional forms for, dq_2/dq_1 and dq_1/dq_2. These two derivatives are called *conjectural variations*. They represent one firm's conjecture (or expectation) of how the other firm's output will alter as a result of its own change in output. More specifically, dq_2/dq_1 represents firm 1's conjecture about the response of firm 2 to a change in firm 1's output. Note that the conjectural variations are *ex ante* concepts which need not necessarily correspond to *ex post* reality.

A variety of different duopoly models result, all of which have somewhat different solution characteristics, depending on what economic assumptions are made regarding the conjectural variations. We shall now examine four specific duopoly models, each of which results from different behavioral assumptions about the conjectural variations.

B. The Cournot Model

The first formal duopoly model to appear in the literature was published in 1838 by a French mathematician, Augustin Cournot.[1] He assumed that the conjectural variation terms are both zero, i.e., that in setting its own

---

[1] Augustin Cournot, *Researches into the Mathematical Principles of the Theory of Wealth*, Nathaniel T. Bacon, trans. (New York: The Macmillan Company, 1897), chap. vii.

output each firm assumes that the other firm's output will not change:

$$\frac{dq_2}{dq_1} = 0. \qquad (12\text{--}7)$$

$$\frac{dq_1}{dq_2} = 0. \qquad (12\text{--}8)$$

Substituting Eq. (12–7) and (12–8) into Eq. (12–5) and (12–6), the Cournot duopoly solution implies that each firm equates its own marginal revenue and marginal cost:

$$\frac{\partial R_1(q_1,\, q_2)}{\partial q_1} = \frac{dC_1(q_1)}{dq_1}. \qquad (12\text{--}9)$$

$$\frac{\partial R_2(q_1,\, q_2)}{\partial q_2} = \frac{dC_2(q_2)}{dq_2}. \qquad (12\text{--}10)$$

The specific situation discussed by Cournot was that of two proprietors who were selling mineral water taken from the same spring. Solely as a matter of convenience, Cournot assumed there were no costs in taking the water from the spring and putting it in a form to be sold:

$$C_i(q_i) = 0 \qquad i = 1,2. \qquad (12\text{--}11)$$

If the market demand curve is linear, we have

$$p = a - bQ \qquad (12\text{--}12)$$

where
$$Q = q_1 + q_2 \qquad (12\text{--}13)$$

is the total output of both proprietors. Under the Cournot assumptions, Eq. (12–9) and (12–10) become:

$$\frac{\partial R_1(q_1,\, q_2)}{\partial q_1} = a - 2bq_1 - bq_2 = 0. \qquad (12\text{--}14)$$

$$\frac{\partial R_2(q_1,\, q_2)}{\partial q_2} = a - bq_1 - 2bq_2 = 0. \qquad (12\text{--}15)$$

From Eq. (12–14) and (12–15), the profit-maximizing outputs for each firm are

$$q_1 = \frac{a}{2b} - \frac{q_2}{2} \qquad (12\text{--}16)$$

and
$$q_2 = \frac{a}{2b} - \frac{q_1}{2}. \qquad (12\text{--}17)$$

For most values of q_1 and q_2, Eq. (12–16) and (12–17) are not mutually consistent. There is, however, one pair of output values for which Eq. (12–16) and (12–17) both hold. Solving these two equations simultaneously, we get

$$q_1 = q_2 = \frac{a}{3b}. \qquad (12\text{–}18)$$

Equation (12–18) is an equilibrium solution, since there is no tendency for either firm to change its output. If the equilibrium solution is attained, then the *ex ante* conjectural variations, Eq. (12–7) and (12–8), are also valid *ex post* relations.

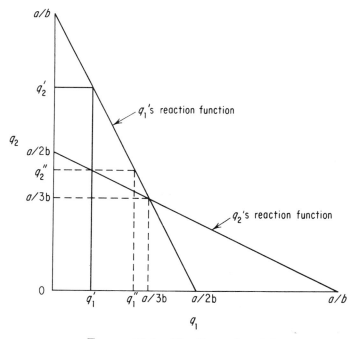

FIGURE 12–1. The Cournot model.

The Cournot model implicitly defines a dynamic process. This is easily seen by graphing Eq. (12–16) and (12–17), which are called the *reaction functions* for proprietors 1 and 2. In Figure 12–1, suppose that the second proprietor begins producing an output of q_2'. Then q_1' becomes the output which maximizes profits for the first proprietor, if he assumes the other proprietor will keep his output at q_2'. When the first proprietor changes his output to q_1', however, the best output for the second proprietor becomes q_2'', under the assumption that the first proprietor will not alter his output. But now the first proprietor will change his output to q_1'', and so on. This process will continue until both firms are producing at the equilibrium output, $a/3b$.

The proprietors in the Cournot model behave in a peculiar manner when they are not in equilibrium. At each point each proprietor assumes that his rival's output will be unchanged when his own output is changed. Although this assumption is repeatedly shown to be false, each proprietor continues to make it. In other words, the Cournot firms have no capacity for learning. Eventually, however, if equilibrium is reached the proprietors will find that their conjectural variations are fulfilled.

Let us consider a numerical example where the costs of each firm are non-zero. Suppose that the total costs of each firm are

$$C_1 = 10q_1 \qquad\qquad (12\text{--}19)$$

and
$$C_2 = q_2^2. \qquad\qquad (12\text{--}20)$$

Suppose that the market price is determined by

$$p = 200 - q_1 - q_2. \qquad\qquad (12\text{--}21)$$

The profit functions for the two firms are

$$\pi_1 = 190\, q_1 - q_1^2 - q_1 q_2 \qquad\qquad (12\text{--}22)$$

and
$$\pi_2 = 200 q_2 - q_1 q_2 - 2q_2^2. \qquad\qquad (12\text{--}23)$$

Differentiating Eq. (12–22) and (12–23) with respect to q_1 and q_2 respectively, and equating the results to zero, we obtain

$$\frac{d\pi_1}{dq_1} = 190 - 2q_1 - q_2 = 0 \qquad\qquad (12\text{--}24)$$

and
$$\frac{d\pi_2}{dq_2} = 200 - q_1 - 4q_2 = 0. \qquad\qquad (12\text{--}25)$$

Firm 1's reaction function is obtained by solving Eq. (12–24) for q_1:

$$q_1 = 95 - 0.5q_2. \qquad\qquad (12\text{--}26)$$

Similarly, firm 2's reaction function is obtained by solving Eq. (12–25) for q_2:

$$q_2 = 50 - 0.25q_1. \qquad\qquad (12\text{--}27)$$

The Cournot equilibrium solution results from simultaneously solving these two reaction functions. This results in

$$q_1 = 80 \text{ units/period}$$
$$q_2 = 30 \text{ units/period}$$
$$p = \$90/\text{unit} \qquad (12\text{-}28)$$
$$\pi_1 = \$6,400/\text{period}$$
$$\pi_2 = \$1,800/\text{period}$$
$$\pi = \pi_1 + \pi_2 = \$8,200/\text{period}.$$

C. THE COLLUSION MODEL

Instead of assuming that the two duopoly firms act independently, let us suppose that they act in concert to maximize their joint profits. Analytically this is equivalent to assuming that the two firms merge, in effect becoming a monopoly. The solution is the same as the two-plant monopoly solution discussed in Chapter 10. It can be obtained by maximizing $\pi_1 + \pi_2$ with respect to both q_1 and q_2. This is equivalent to assuming the same conjectural variations shown in Eq. (12–7) and (12–8), but with a different objective function (total industry profits) being maximized (as opposed to the Cournot case where each firm attempts to maximize its own profits).

To see how the collusion solution differs from the Cournot solution, let us find the optimal collusive solution for the duopoly market defined by Eq. (12–19)–(12–21). The total profits in the industry, π, can be obtained by adding Eq. (12–22) and (12–23):

$$\pi = \pi_1 + \pi_2 = 190q_1 + 200q_2 - q_1^2 - 2q_2^2 - 2q_1q_2. \qquad (12\text{-}29)$$

Differentiating Eq. (12–29) with respect to both q_1 and q_2, and equating the results to zero, we obtain

$$\frac{\partial \pi}{\partial q_1} = 190 - 2q_1 - 2q_2 = 0. \qquad (12\text{-}30)$$

$$\frac{\partial \pi}{\partial q_2} = 200 - 4q_2 - 2q_1 = 0. \qquad (12\text{-}31)$$

Solving Eq. (12–30) and (12–31) simultaneously results in

$$q_1 = 90 \text{ units/period}$$
$$q_2 = 5 \text{ units/period}$$
$$p = \$105/\text{unit} \qquad (12\text{-}32)$$
$$\pi_1 = \$8,550/\text{period}$$
$$\pi_2 = \$500/\text{period}$$
$$\pi = \$9,050/\text{period}.$$

Comparing Eq. (12–32) with (12–28), we see that total industry profits are \$850/period higher when the duopolists collude. The profits of firm 2 have *decreased*, however, by \$1,300/period. In order for firm 2 to agree to collude, it will have to receive a side-payment from firm 1 of at least \$1,300/period. Since firm 1's profits are \$2,150/period higher under collusion, however, it can afford to make the required side-payment to firm 2 and still be better off. Although the market results (total output and price) are entirely determinate under the collusion model, the amount of the side-payment from firm 1 to firm 2 is not uniquely determined. Our analysis shows only that the side-payment will be somewhere between \$1,300/period and \$2,150/period.

D. The Stackelberg Model

The German economist, Heinrich von Stackelberg, developed a leadership-followership analysis of the duopoly model.[2] A firm which is a follower behaves exactly as the Cournot firm. A leader takes advantage of the assumption that the other firm is behaving as a follower.

More specifically, if firm 1 is a follower, then firm 1 will attempt to choose q_1 to maximize $\pi_1(q_1, q_2)$, on the assumption that $dq_2/dq_1 = 0$. If firm 2 is a follower, then firm 2 will attempt to choose q_2 to maximize $\pi_2(q_1, q_2)$, on the assumption that $dq_1/dq_2 = 0$. If firm 1 is a leader, then firm 1 will attempt to choose q_1 to maximize $\pi_1[q_1, \psi_2(q_1)]$, where $\psi_2(q_1)$ is firm 2's reaction function, that is, $\psi_2(q_1)$ is the optimal value of q_2 when firm 2 is a follower. This means that firm 1 assumes

$$\frac{dq_2}{dq_1} = \frac{d\psi_2(q_1)}{dq_1}.$$

Finally, if firm 2 is a leader, then firm 2 will attempt to choose q_2 to maximize $\pi_2[\psi_1(q_2), q_2]$, where $\psi_1(q_2)$ is firm 1's reaction function, that is $\psi_1(q_2)$ is the optimal value of q_1 when firm 1 is a follower. This means that firm 2 assumes

$$\frac{dq_1}{dq_2} = \frac{d\psi_1(q_2)}{dq_2}.$$

Four possible situations can arise in the Stackelberg analysis. If both firms act as followers, the result will be exactly the same as in the Cournot model. If one firm wishes to act as the leader and the other firm wishes to act as the follower, then a stable equilibrium will result. When both firms wish to be leaders, however, the resulting situation will be unstable. This type of *Stackelberg disequilibrium* situation is one for which no specific outcome can be predicted in advance. Until one or both duopolists alter

---

[2] Heinrich von Stackelberg, *The Theory of the Market Economy*, Alan T. Peacock, trans. (New York: Oxford University Press, 1952), pp. 194–204.

their behavior patterns (e.g., by one succumbing to the leadership of the other, or by a collusive agreement being reached), no stable pattern of prices and outputs will emerge in this market. The period when the market is in a Stackelberg disequilibrium state can be regarded as a situation of economic warfare, with each duopolist trying to take advantage of the other.

According to Stackelberg's analysis, each firm determines the maximum profits it can attain both by being a leader and by being a follower. It will then choose to play whichever role will result in greater profits. Stackelberg believed that most of the time both firms want to be leaders, so that economic warfare is the typical result.

For concreteness, let us apply the Stackelberg analysis to the duopoly market defined by Eq. (12–19)–(12–21). Firm 1 can determine the maximum profits it can attain as a leader by substituting firm 2's reaction function, Eq. (12–27), into firm 1's profit function, Eq. (12–22). Doing so results in the following expression:

$$\pi_1 = \pi_1\left[q_1,\ \psi_2(q_1)\right] = 190q_1 - q_1^2 - q_1(50 - 0.25q_1)$$

$$= 140q_1 - 0.75q_1^2. \tag{12-33}$$

Differentiating Eq. (12–33) with respect to q_1 and equating the result to zero:

$$\frac{d\pi_1}{dq_1} = 140 - 1.5q_1 = 0. \tag{12-34}$$

Solving Eq. (12–34), we find that the optimal leadership output for firm 1 is

$$q_1 = 93\tfrac{1}{3} \text{ units/period.} \tag{12-35}$$

Substituting Eq. (12–35) into (12–33), we find that the maximum profits that firm 1 can obtain as a leader are

$$\pi_1 = \$6,533\tfrac{1}{3}/\text{period.} \tag{12-36}$$

In an analogous manner, firm 2 can determine the maximum profits it can attain as a leader by substituting firm 1's reaction function, Eq. (12–26), into firm 2's profit function, Eq. (12–23). Doing so results in

$$\pi_2 = \pi_2\left[\psi_1(q_2),\ q_2\right] = 200q_2 - (95 - 0.5q_2)q_2 - 2q_2^2 = 105q_2 - 1.5q_2^2. \tag{12-37}$$

Differentiating Eq. (12–37) with respect to q_2 and equating the result to zero,

$$\frac{d\pi_2}{dq_2} = 105 - 3q_2. \tag{12-38}$$

Solving Eq. (12–38), the optimal leadership output for firm 2 is

$$q_2 = 35 \text{ units/period}. \qquad (12\text{–}39)$$

Substituting Eq. (12–39) into (12–37), the maximum profits that firm 2 can obtain as a leader are

$$\pi_2 = \$1,837.5/\text{period}. \qquad (12\text{–}40)$$

Firm 1 can determine the maximum profits it can attain as a follower by substituting into its own reaction function, Eq. (12–26), the optimal leadership output of firm 2, Eq. (12–39). Thus, if firm 1 acts as a follower, its output would be

$$q_1 = 95 - 0.5(35) = 77.5 \text{ units/period}. \qquad (12\text{–}41)$$

By substituting Eq. (12–39) and (12–41) into firm 1's profit function, Eq. (12–22), the followership profits for firm 1 are

$$\pi_1 = 190(77.5) - (77.5)^2 - (77.5)(35) = \$6,006.25/\text{period}. \qquad (12\text{–}42)$$

In an analogous manner, firm 2 can determine the maximum profits it can obtain as a follower by substituting into its own reaction function, Eq. (12–27), the optimal leadership output of firm 1, Eq. (12–35). Thus if firm 2 acts as a follower, its output will be

$$q_2 = 50 - 0.25 \ (93\tfrac{1}{3}) = 26\tfrac{2}{3} \text{ units/period}. \qquad (12\text{–}43)$$

By substituting Eq. (12–35) and (12–43) into firm 2's profit function, Eq. (12–23), the followership profits for firm 2 are

$$\pi_2 = 200(26\tfrac{2}{3}) - (93\tfrac{1}{3}) \ (26\tfrac{2}{3}) - 2(26\tfrac{2}{3})^2 \qquad (12\text{–}44)$$
$$= \$1,422\tfrac{2}{9}/\text{period}.$$

The maximum profits that firm 1 can obtain as a leader ($6,533$\tfrac{1}{3}$/period) are greater than the maximum profits it can obtain as a follower ($6,006.25/period). Therefore, firm 1 will wish to act as leader. Similarly, the maximum profits that firm 2 can obtain as a leader ($1,837.5/period) are greater than the maximum profits it can obtain as a follower ($1,422$\tfrac{2}{9}$/period). Thus firm 2 will also wish to act as a leader. It is not possible, however, for both firms 1 and 2 to act as leaders and for both to have the anticipated higher profits at the same time. When firms 1 and 2 both produce their optimal leadership outputs, the resulting profits each firm attains can be determined by substituting Eq. (12–35) and (12–39) into the profit functions Eq. (12–22) and (12–23):

$$\pi_1 = 190 \ (93\tfrac{1}{3}) - (93\tfrac{1}{3})^2 - (93\tfrac{1}{3}) \ (35)$$
$$= \$5,755\tfrac{5}{9}/\text{period}. \qquad (12\text{–}45)$$
$$\pi_2 = 200 \ (35) - (93\tfrac{1}{3}) \ (35) - 2(35)^2$$
$$= \$1,283\tfrac{1}{3}/\text{period}. \qquad (12\text{–}46)$$

Note that when both firms try to act as leaders (the Stackelberg disequilibrium case), the profits that each actually attains are less than their anticipated profits. In fact, when both firms try to act as leaders, each receives profits less than it would if it were to act as a follower. If the firms are capable of learning from their experience, the leader-leader case will not prevail, and some other mode of behavior will be adopted.

TABLE 12-1. THE STACKELBERG MODEL

Firm 1's Profits ($ period)

| | | *Firm 2's Policy* | |
		Leader	*Follower*
Firm 1's	*Leader*	5,755 5/9	6,533 1/3
Policy	*Follower*	6,006 1/4	6,400

Firm 2's Profits ($ period)

| | | *Firm 2's Policy* | |
		Leader	*Follower*
Firm 1's	*Leader*	1,283 1/3	1,422 2/9
Policy	*Follower*	1,837 1/2	1,800

The profits to each firm under all possible combinations of leadership-followership behavior are conveniently summarized in Table 12-1. A glance at this table reveals that the leader-leader behavior, which each firm is led to adopt by the Stackelberg analysis, is the worst possible combination of policies for both firms.

E. THE MARKET SHARES MODEL

The market shares solution to the duopoly problem assumes that one firm always wishes to maintain a fixed share of the total market, regardless of the short-run effect this has on its profits.[3] This may be reasonable when the firm is primarily interested in the long-run advantages it may gain by having a particular market share. Suppose, for example, that firm 2 always wishes to maintain a market share of k. This means that

$$\frac{q_2}{q_1 + q_2} = k. \tag{12-47}$$

---

[3] An analogous market-shares model, in which the desired share of market is expressed in terms of revenues rather than physical units, and in which prices rather than quantities are the decision variables of the firms, has been presented by A. Heertje, "La Théorie de l'Oligopole de Baumol," *Economia Internazionale*, XIV, No. 4 (November, 1961), 3–10.

Solving Eq. (12–47), the output produced by firm 2 is

$$q_2 = \frac{kq_1}{1 - k}. \tag{12–48}$$

In determining its output from Eq. (12–48), firm 2 acts as though firm 1's output is fixed, i.e., $dq_1/dq_2 = 0$.

In maximizing its profits, firm 1 utilizes the knowledge that firm 2 wishes to maintain a fixed market share. Substituting Eq. (12–48) into its own profit function, firm 1 will then choose q_1 to maximize $\pi_1[q_1, (kq_1/1 - k)]$. The conjectural variation of firm 1, from Eq. (12–48), is

$$\frac{dq_2}{dq_1} = \frac{k}{1 - k}.$$

The market shares model will have a stable equilibrium solution if only one firm tries to attain a fixed market share and the other firm is willing to let it do so. If both duopolists attempt to maintain fixed market shares, and if these market shares do not sum to unity, then there will not be a stable equilibrium solution.

Returning to the duopoly market defined by Eq. (12–19)–(12–21), suppose that firm 2 attempts to maintain a market share of 50 per cent, i.e., that $k = 0.5$. From Eq. (12–48), this means that

$$q_2 = q_1. \tag{12–49}$$

Substituting Eq. (12–49) into firm 1's profit equation, (12–22), we obtain

$$\pi_1 = 190q_1 - 2q_1^2. \tag{12–50}$$

The profit-maximizing output for firm 1 is found by setting the derivative of Eq. (12–50) with respect to q_1 equal to zero. Doing so, firm 1's optimal output is

$$q_1 = 47\tfrac{1}{2} \text{ units/period.} \tag{12–51}$$

Substituting Eq. (12–51) into (12–50), the maximum profits firm 1 can attain are

$$\pi_1 = \$4,512.5/\text{period.} \tag{12–52}$$

The output of firm 2, according to Eq. (12–49) and (12–51), is

$$q_2 = 47\tfrac{1}{2} \text{ units/period.} \tag{12–53}$$

Substituting Eq. (12–51) and (12–53) into firm 2's profit function, Eq. (12–23), we find that firm 2's profits will be

$$\pi_2 = \$2,731.25/\text{period.} \tag{12–54}$$

As long as firm 2 insists on attaining 50 per cent of the market, and as long as firm 1 is willing to permit it to do so, the resulting market shares solution will be a stable equilibrium.

F. Empirical Limitations of These Models

In the preceding sections, we have seen that as soon as specific values or functional forms are assigned to the conjectural variation terms, the duopoly model may be solved. Many different solutions are possible, however, depending upon the assumptions made regarding the conjectural variations. What duopoly solution is the most realistic? This is an empirical question for which there is not yet enough evidence for a definitive answer. Hence, many economists prefer to approach the oligopoly problem in entirely different ways, and to develop oligopolistic market analyses in which it is not necessary to focus specific attention on the conjectural variation terms. In the rest of this chapter, we shall pursue some of these alternative developments.

II. Price Leadership

A. The Dominant-Firm Model

1. THE FORMAL MODEL. One way of avoiding an assumption about the values of the conjectural variation terms is to create a model in which one of the firms is clearly so powerful that it is the leader. Such is the case in the dominant-firm model. The model is alleged to describe behavior in industries having one large firm and a number of smaller ones. Frequently steel and cement are cited as prototypes for the model.

The basic operating assumption is *the dominant firm sets the price and allows the minor firms to sell all they can at that price; the dominant firm sells the rest.* Given this assumption, the market demand curve, the supply curve of the minor firms, and the marginal cost curve of the dominant firm, a determinate solution can be derived, as shown in Figure 12–2.

In Figure 12–2 DD' is the market demand curve, S_m is the supply curve of the minor firms, and MC is the marginal cost curve of the dominant firm. The first problem is to determine the demand curve of the dominant firm under the operating assumption just stated. The procedure is to assume a particular price, compute the amount the minor firms would sell at that price, and then subtract that amount from the total demand at the assumed price. The remainder is the amount the dominant firm can sell.

Assume a price of OA in Figure 12–2. At that price, the minor firms will supply the whole market and the dominant firm will supply nothing. At higher prices the minor firms will also supply the total demand. Therefore, the point A is the vertical intercept of the dominant firm's demand curve. Next assume a price of OC. The amount that will be supplied by the minor firms is CG. The total demand is CF. Therefore the dominant firm's demand at this price is GF. Thus E is a point on the dominant firm's demand curve since $CE = GF$. Other points can be developed in a similar manner, and the dominant firm's demand curve can be shown to be $AEBD'$.

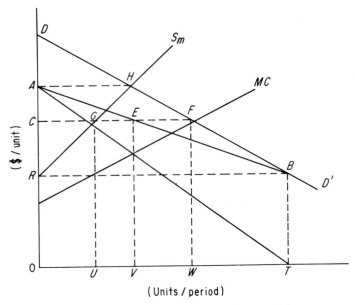

FIGURE 12–2. The dominant firm model.

Given this demand curve, the dominant firm will then proceed to operate as a monopolist. The relevant portion of the marginal revenue curve for the dominant firm is AT, and the output is determined by the intersection of the marginal cost and marginal revenue curves. The dominant firm's output will be OV. The price for this output is determined from the dominant firm's demand curve to be OC. Given a price of OC the minor firms will produce OU. The total demand in the market is OW, where $OW = OU + OV$.

The total market demand will be satisfied, and a solution is obtained. Note that this solution was attained without explicitly introducing conjectural variation terms. The reason this omission was possible goes back to the original assumption of the model in which the minor firms were placed in a completely dominated position. The assumption in effect removed the minor firms from consideration as rivals in the usual sense.

2. DOMINANT-FIRM PRICE LEADERSHIP IN PRACTICE. In this section, we present evidence suggesting that there are some oligopolistic industries which appear to behave according to the dominant-firm model. Specifically we consider three industries: beryllium, retail groceries, and steel.

a. Beryllium. In hearings held during 1939 before the Temporary National Economic Committee, substantial evidence was presented indicating that price leadership was prevalent among the fabricators of beryllium alloy products. The largest of these firms was the American Brass Company, which supplied approximately 25 per cent of the market. The price lists published by American Brass generally became the prices which other beryllium alloy fabricators charged. On May 9, 1939, the president of the Riverside Metal Company, a small fabricator of beryllium alloy products with about 1.5 per cent of the market, presented the following testimony:

MR. COX: Mr. Randall, would it be correct to say that there is a well-crystallized practice of price leadership in the industry in which you are engaged?

MR. RANDALL: I would say so.

MR. COX: And what company is the price leader?

MR. RANDALL: I would say the American Brass Company holds that position.

MR. COX: And your company follows the prices which are announced by American Brass?

MR. RANDALL: That is correct.

MR. COX: So that when they reduce the price you have to reduce it too. Is that correct?

MR. RANDALL: Well, we don't have to, but we do.

MR. COX: And when they raise the price you raise the price.

MR. RANDALL: That is correct.

. . .

MR. ARNOLD: You exercise no individual judgment as to the price you charge for your product, then, in a situation?

MR. RANDALL: Well, I think that is about what it amounts to; yes, sir.[4]

b. Retail Groceries. In a study of pricing practices in large business firms published in 1958, it was found " . . . that A. & P. is generally the price leader in the territory in which it operates. Where this coincides with Kroger territory, e.g., in the East Central States, it is clear that Kroger is usually a follower . . . . Its pricing is, as for so many operators, largely a matter of finding out what A. & P. charges on the most important food items and then coming very close to A & P's prices."[5]

c. Steel. During most of the twentieth century, the United States Steel Corporation has been the dominant firm in the steel industry. Throughout this period its share of market steadily declined as its competitors increased their capacities. When it was formed in 1903, U.S. Steel controlled 75 per cent of the market. In 1920, it controlled 50 per cent of the market. In the 1960's, its share of total industry capacity was only 25 per cent. For over sixty years, however, U.S. Steel " . . . remained 'Big Steel,' the giant of the industry, the only truly national steel manufacturer, and the traditional price leader."[6]

---

[4] As quoted in Marshall R. Colberg, Dascomb R. Forbush, and Gilbert R. Whitaker, Jr., *Business Economics: Principles and Cases*, 3rd ed. (Homewood, Ill.: Richard D. Irwin, Inc., 1964), pp. 236–37.

[5] A. D. H. Kaplan, Joel B. Dirlam, and Robert F. Lanzillotti, *Pricing in Big Business: A Case Approach* (Washington, D.C.: The Brookings Institution, 1958), p. 206.

[6] Colberg, Forbush, and Whitaker, *op. cit.*, p. 246.

In June, 1955, Mr. Ernest Weir, who was then president of the National Steel Corporation, presented the following testimony to the Celler Committee:

> MR. MCCULLOCH: In recent years has this uniform price [for tin plate] been the price as fixed by the United States Steel Corporation, for instance?
> MR. WEIR: I would say in the majority of cases, yes. But there is no necessity, except that it would be a normal, natural price.
> MR. MCCULLOCH: Does your company ever fix prices or announce prices that are lower than your competitors' by reason of your more efficient operations?
> MR. WEIR: Well, we have made prices that differ from our competitors' based on reasons that we thought were good reasons.
> MR. MCCULLOCH: Does that happen often?
> MR. WEIR: No, it doesn't. [7]

B. THE BAROMETRIC FIRM

1. DEFINITION. So far we have used the term *price leadership* to refer to the situation where a dominant firm sets the price and supplies what is left of the market after the minor firms have supplied all they can. Another pattern of price leadership, the so-called *barometric price leadership*, occurs when one firm conventionally is the first to announce price changes which are usually followed by the other firms in the industry. Often the barometric price leader is not the dominant, or even the largest, firm in its industry. "For example, International Paper was for a long period the price leader in newsprint although it produced less than one-seventh of the output, and it was succeeded in this role by Great Northern, a smaller firm." [8]

In their study of pricing in large business firms, Kaplan, Dirlam, and Lanzillotti state that barometric price leadership often develops as a reaction to a period of economic warfare in which all firms in the industry suffer (e.g., the Stackelberg disequilibrium case discussed in Section I.D.):

> The development of price leadership in large-scale industry has roots in the earlier experience of violent price fluctuation and cut-throat competition, which culminated in consolidation of competitors, as in steel, copper, oil production, tin cans, and farm equipment. Such experience has generated a distinct predisposition on the part of managements to avoid price changes except through periodic, well-considered, and well-publicized alterations in recognized base prices. By relating price changes to such formalized bases as changes in direct costs or style and quality changes, the firm attempts to avoid the extreme fluctuations in return on investment that were attributed to frequent, uncontrolled disturbances of the price structure. [9]

---

[7] As quoted in Kaplan, Dirlam, and Lanzillotti, *op. cit.*, p. 205.

[8] George J. Stigler, "The Kinky Oligopoly Demand Curve and Rigid Prices," in *Readings in Price Theory*, ed. George J. Stigler and Kenneth E. Boulding (Homewood, Ill.: Richard D. Irwin, Inc., 1952), p. 431.

[9] Kaplan, Dirlam, and Lanzillotti, *op. cit.*, p. 271.

2. PETROLEUM. The petroleum industry provides a clear example of barometric price leadership. All the suppliers in a marketing territory pay attention to the same set of facts. They all consider such statistical measures as crude oil and gasoline production, sales, and inventories. They all watch the attempts of competitors to increase market share, judging these primarily by salesmen's reports. When secret price concessions by dealers in some areas break into the open as a reduction in the posted prices, all suppliers are faced with demands by the dealers for a reduction in their tank-wagon prices. Whether these demands are met depends upon the suppliers' judgments regarding the underlying state of the market and competitive conditions. In the words of Mr. S. A. Swensrud, of Standard Oil of Ohio:

> In summary, therefore, the so-called price leadership in the petroleum industry boils down to the fact that some company in each territory most of the time bears the onus of formally recognizing current conditions .... In short, unless the so-called price leader accurately interprets basic conditions and local conditions, it soon will not be the leading marketer. Price leadership does not mean that the price leader can set prices to get the maximum profit and force other marketers to conform.[10]

C. COLLUSION AND CARTELS

1. DEFINITION. There have been occasions in the American economy when all firms in an industry have agreed to establish prices at levels which are most profitable for the industry as a whole, rather than to set their prices by individual actions. This results in the same levels of price and output for the industry which would exist were the industry a single-firm monopoly (see Section I.C.). When this collusive arrangement is openly accomplished through formal agreement, it is called a *cartel.* Most collusive agreements in manufacturing and trade, whether of the secret or cartel variety, have been illegal in the United States since the Sherman Anti-Trust Act was passed in 1890. Before then, price-fixing agreements were common in many American industries, and even since 1890, illegal collusive agreements have frequently been discovered and successfully prosecuted by the Department of Justice. In many European countries formal cartel agreements are a common (and legal) form of market organization.

Cartels and secret collusive agreements can be regarded as an extreme form of price leadership, in which agreements among the firms are explicit, rather than implicit. In order for such agreements to prevail for a long period, there must be some types of sanctions which most of the firms can invoke against any firm wishing to pursue an independent pricing course. Since a small price concession below the official cartel price can frequently

---

[10] As quoted in Stigler, *op. cit.,* p. 432.

result in an increased market share for the lower-priced firm, there often is an incentive for firms individually to "chisel" on the cartel. For the cartel to hold together, the larger firms must be able to supply economic sanctions against the "chiselers," or there must be legal actions which can be taken against the price cutters, or all firms must realize that it is to their long-run interests to maintain the cartel agreement.

2. ELECTRICAL EQUIPMENT MANUFACTURERS.[11] In February, 1960, the Department of Justice obtained indictments against forty companies and eighteen individuals on charges of fixing prices and dividing the market on seven electrical products: switchgears, oil circuit breakers, low-voltage power circuit breakers, insulators, open-fuse cutouts, lightning arresters, and bushings. Additional indictments followed. At the end of the resulting trial, in February, 1961, the United States District Court in Philadelphia handed down guilty verdicts against most of the defendants. A total of $1,924,500 in fines was levied against twenty-nine guilty companies. These ranged from fines of $437,500 against General Electric Company and $372,000 against Westinghouse Electric Corporation to $7,500 apiece against Carrier Corporation and Porcelain Insulator Corporation. Seven guilty executives were sent to prison, and twenty-four others received suspended jail sentences.

The price-fixing agreements on these electrical products were reached through meetings, telephone calls, and written memoranda among sales executives of the companies involved. Although these collusive agreements were in clear violation of the antitrust laws, the executives involved participated in them for the sake of greater profits to their companies, personal rewards to themselves (in the form of salaries, bonuses, and promotions), and an easier life (less "worry" about competition). To keep these agreements as secret as possible, the participants, among other precautions, did not use their companies' names when registering in the hotels where meetings were held; they did not eat breakfast together in public dining rooms; they disguised their expense account records; they used code numbers to represent the companies; they rotated the companies who were given the privilege of submitting the lowest bids in competitive bidding.

As an example of how the electrical equipment conspiracy worked, let us consider the case of circuit breakers. In 1951, there were only four circuit-breaker manufacturers in the United States. They all entered into a conspiracy to rotate the sealed-bid business among them, with G. E. receiving 45 per cent, Westinghouse 35 per cent, Allis-Chalmers 10 per cent, and Federal Pacific 10 per cent. Roughly every ten days or two weeks, secret meetings were held to decide whose turn it was to submit the lowest sealed

---

[11] For a detailed account of the price-fixing agreements among the electrical equipment manufacturers, see Richard Austin Smith, "The Incredible Electrical Conspiracy," *Fortune* (April, May, 1961).

bids. Based upon the business each company had obtained in recent weeks and the target market shares, it was decided who would be permitted to submit the lowest bids, and at what prices. This form of behavior persisted for several years, but eventually overcapacity in the industry led the participating companies secretly to "chisel" on the collusive agreement and to pursue independent pricing patterns. Sporadic attempts were made to revive the price-fixing agreements. For example, in 1958 there was again a formal market-sharing arrangement established, with G. E. getting 40.3 per cent, Westinghouse 31.3 per cent, Allis-Chalmers 8.8 per cent, Federal Pacific 15.6 per cent, and I-T-E (which by then had begun manufacturing circuit breakers) 4 per cent.

In switchgears, an elaborate system, called the "phases of the moon" pricing formula, was established to facilitate collusive actions on sealed bids. Secret records were found consisting of sheets of paper containing columns of numbers. The bidding order for the seven switchgear manufacturers was recorded in one set of columns. Every two weeks (hence the term, *phases of the moon*) a different firm's code number would reach the priority position. The amounts which each manufacturer were to bid below the agreed-upon book prices were recorded in a second set of columns, keyed into the company code numbers. Thus, for example, when it was Westinghouse's (#2's) turn to be low bidder at a certain differential below book price, all that G. E. (#1) or Allis-Chalmers (#3) had to do to determine how much they should bid *above* #2 was to find their code numbers in the second set of columns. The companies would then slightly alter the indicated differentials in order to eliminate any overt indications that the winning bids had been collusively determined.

3. IDENTICAL SEALED BIDS. The electrical equipment manufacturers took some care that their collusive actions should not result in identical sealed bids on any potential contract. Frequently firms in other industries have submitted identical sealed bids for contracts, creating a *prima facie* impression that collusion, whether implicit or explicit, had occured. For example, in a bid for furnishing and delivering 6,000 barrels of cement, on April 23, 1936 the United States Engineer at Tucumcari, New Mexico received sealed bids from eleven different companies. Each of these bids was for a delivered price of $3.286854 per barrel, with a discount of $0.10 per barrel if payment was received within fifteen days.[12]

Some awareness of the extent to which identical sealed bids arise in the American economy can be obtained by consulting a report of the Joint Economic Committee. This report consists of a sample which " ... shows that Federal procurement agencies have reported to the Attorney General instances of suspected bid rigging in every major product and service

[12] Vernon A. Mund, *Government and Business*, 2nd ed. (New York: Harper & Row, Publishers, Inc., 1955), p. 381.

category."[13] The industries included in the sample cover such diverse products and services as rock salt, weed control chemicals, towel service, corrugated metal pipe and couplers, and care of remains of Navy dead. The report merely lists the identical bids without indicating whether there were any actual violations of the antitrust laws.

4. CARTELS WITH GOVERNMENT SANCTIONS. Not all formal cartel agreements in the United States violate the Federal antitrust laws. Many types of cartels in fact have obtained official sanction from the American government. Thus, for example, the Export Trade Act (more commonly known as the Webb-Pomerene law) was passed by Congress in 1918 to permit cartels to be formed for international trade purposes, so long as this does not lead to collusive actions by the participants in the domestic market. Federal government policy permits the operation of specific types of cartels, such as labor unions, agricultural cooperative marketing or producing associations, common carriers, and manufacturers and handlers of hog-cholera serum and hog-cholera virus. We now consider in somewhat more detail two other cartels which have received Federal government sanction: the NRA and the IATA.

a. The NRA. As one of its weapons to fight the Great Depression, in 1933 Roosevelt's New Deal administration set up the National Recovery Administration (NRA) in an attempt to introduce stable market conditions in many American industries. In effect, the NRA codes for various industries permitted the formation of government-sponsored cartels to establish price levels higher than those which had prevailed under free-market conditions.

Immediately after the NRA codes were adopted, there were marked price increases in the affected industries. Many firms did not agree that the NRA-established prices were individually to their best interests, however. As a result there were widespread evasions of the cartel prices, either directly or through various forms of nonprice competition. "Under the N.R.A., when prices were controlled by code provisions, a retail druggist in California, unable to cut prices, employed a medium to give free psychic readings to his customers! An automobile dealer was accused of price cutting because he bought six suits of clothes from a tailor to whom he sold a car."[14]

The Federal government's largest-scale attempt at the compulsory cartelization of industry ended in 1935 when the Supreme Court ruled that the National Recovery Act was unconstitutional.

b. The IATA. Most airlines flying transatlantic routes are members of the International Air Transport Association (IATA). This is a voluntary organization which, among other things, permits its members to agree on

---

[13] Joint Economic Committee, *93 Lots of Bids Involving Identical Bids Reported to the Department of Justice by the Federal Procurement Agencies in the Years 1955–1960*, 87th Cong., 1st sess. (Washington, D.C.: Government Printing Office, August, 1961), p. xiv.

[14] Marshall R. Colberg, William C. Bradford, and Richard M. Alt, *Business Economics: Principles and Cases*, rev. ed. (Homewood, Ill.: Richard D. Irwin, Inc., 1957), p. 223.

uniform tariffs for transatlantic flights. If the IATA members unanimously agree on a tariff schedule, and if their respective governments approve, then this set of tariffs becomes binding upon the air lines. Fines of up to $25,000 may be imposed by the IATA on any members failing to abide by the agreed-upon tariff schedules. When the IATA members cannot agree upon a uniform tariff schedule, then the airlines are free to set their own rates unilaterally.

The only regularly scheduled airline offering transatlantic service which is not a member of IATA is Icelandic Airlines (Loftleider). Icelandic's fares generally average 20 per cent less than the established IATA tariffs. Since it flies no jets, however, its transatlantic flight time is considerably longer than that of the IATA members. Because Icelandic has been able to obtain only a small share of market (2 per cent), the IATA has not attempted to cut its members' fares to Icelandic's level. Thus, the cartel has permitted a recalcitrant firm to exist because so little business is lost to it. Icelandic's underpricing has been profitable however: "Icelandic is reported to have a load factor of about 70 per cent compared to the 50 per cent load factor of the IATA members."[15]

III. The Kinked Demand Curve Model

A. The Formal Model

In 1939, Paul M. Sweezy published his now-famous *kinked demand curve* analysis to rationalize the price rigidities allegedly observed in oligopolistic markets.[16] He assumed that if an oligopolist were to cut his selling price, then his rivals would quickly match the price reduction; if, however, the oligopolist were to increase his selling price, then his rivals would not change their prices. In this situation, the oligopolist's demand curve would be much more elastic for price increases than for price decreases, and it might appear as the curve DKD' in Figure 12–3, where OP is the current market price.

Because of the kink or corner in the demand curve at K, the marginal revenue curve is discontinuous, consisting of the two segments MRA and BMR'. The usual profit-maximizing condition, marginal revenue equals marginal cost, must be reinterpreted, since in Figure 12–3 the marginal cost curve, MC, nowhere intersects the marginal revenue curve. By considering the incremental effects on profits of small shifts in output in either direction from OQ, however, it is clear that OQ is the most profitable output for the firm. Given the perceived demand curve, DKD', the firm will sell its output, OQ, at the prevailing market price, OP.

---

[15] Colberg, Forbush, and Whitaker, *op. cit.*, p. 355.

[16] Paul M. Sweezy, "Demand Under Conditions of Oligopoly," *Journal of Political Economy*, 47 (1939), pp. 568–73. This is reprinted in Stigler and Boulding, *op. cit.*, pp. 404–409.

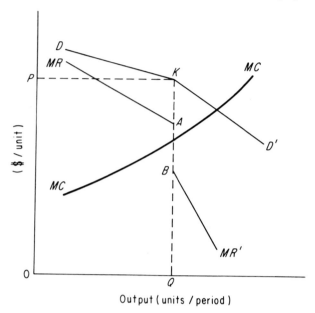

FIGURE 12–3.   The kinked demand curve model.

For a wide range of vertical shifts in the oligopoly firm's marginal cost curve, *OQ* and *OP* remain the optimal output and selling price. Similarly, for a wide range of lateral shifts in demand (as long as the kink, point *K*, remains at the price level *OP*), the optimal selling price remains *OP*, although the optimal output will change.

The sulfur industry illustrates the type of price rigidities the kinked demand curve model attempts to explain. From 1926 to 1938, the price of sulfur "remained absolutely stationary at $18 per ton except for 2 years. In one of those years the price varied by 3 cents per ton from $18; in the other year it varied by 2 cents per ton."[17] This remarkable price stability persisted during a period when there were great shifts in demand as well as many changes in production costs. During this period 94 per cent of the sulfur produced in the United States came from two companies, Freeport Sulphur Company and Texas Gulf Sulphur Company.

B. Stigler's Empirical Tests

In his empirical tests of the kinked demand theory, Stigler first analyzed the sequence of price changes in seven oligopolies.[18] He showed that rival

---

[17] Colberg, Bradford, and Alt, *op. cit.*, p. 276.

[18] George J. Stigler, "The Kinky Oligopoly Demand Curve and Rigid Prices," *Journal of Political Economy*, 55 (1947), pp. 432–49. This is reprinted in Stigler and Boulding, *op. cit.*, pp. 410–39. All page references are to the reprinted version.

firms follow price increases as readily as they match price cuts, so that there is in fact no objective basis to believe that any kink exists in the oligopolist's demand curve. On the basis of his examination of cigarettes (where there has been a strong pattern of price leadership) automobiles (where without a strong pattern of price leadership, price increases were more nearly synchronous than were price reductions), anthracite coal (where prices are flexible and usually change simultaneously), steel (where U.S. Steel is a recognized price leader, and there is no evidence of price rigidity), dynamite (where prices change simultaneously both upwards and downwards), and gasoline (where price increases are more nearly synchronous than are price reductions), Stigler concludes that " . . . there is little historical basis for a firm to believe that price increases will not be matched by rivals and that price decreases will be matched."[19]

When the kinked demand theory was first proposed, a number of textbook writers treated it as though it were a general theory of oligopoly. Stigler's article, which is one of the few attempts in the literature of economics to confront a part of oligopoly theory with empirical evidence, clearly demonstrated that the kinked theory cannot be a general theory. At the same time, however, Stigler's data revealed instances when the firms did behave according to the kink assumption, and casual empiricism suggests that there have been additional instances in oligopoly markets. Thus it may be that the kinked demand theory does have some role in the battery of oligopoly models applicable to the real world. We now propose to examine the conditions under which kinked demand curves might be appropriate.

C. STATUS OF THE KINKED DEMAND CURVE IN OLIGOPOLY THEORY

Our position is that the kink is clearly not a stable long-run equilibrium explanation of oligopoly price. Stigler's data cast strong doubt on the kink's long-run validity. An analysis of the kinked theory, however, does lead to the likelihood of the kink assumptions having validity when interfirm knowledge is at a low level. When firms, for whatever reason, have no knowledge of how their rivals will react, our hypothesis is that the kink may reasonably explain the behavior of firms.

The difficulty with this hypothesis is, of course, the development of the conditions under which interfirm knowledge is low. Unless this can be done we have nothing more than a tautological statement. Two instances where the kink might be appropriate because of low interfirm knowledge are (1) a new industry in its early stages, (2) an industry in which new and previously unknown rivals enter the market. We shall discuss an example of the latter case shortly.

---

[19] *Ibid.*, p. 425.

First we will show briefly why we have constructed the hypothesis that the kink may be appropriate when interfirm knowledge is low. The chain of reasoning is short and simple. An analysis of the kinked demand theory leads to the conclusion that each firm assumes that its rival will always behave so as to inflict the worst possible damage on the firm. Thus if the firm raises prices, its rivals will keep theirs constant and reduce the demand for the firm's product; but if the firm lowers prices, the rivals will immediately match it so that the firm will gain no significant increase in demand. This assumption may be the best the firm can make when it has no knowledge of its rivals. It would be expected, however, that firms would move quickly to acquire the necessary knowledge as Stigler has indicated:

> The kink is a barrier to changes in prices that will increase profits, and business is the collection of devices for circumventing barriers to profits. That this barrier should thwart businessmen—especially when it is wholly of their own fabrication—is unbelievable. There are many ways in which it can be circumvented.... In the multidimensional real world there are many ways to teach a lesson, especially when the pupil is eager to learn.[20]

An interesting example of a situation in which the kink prevailed because of the lack of knowledge of rivals is revealed by a brief period from the history of the potash industry. In 1933 substantial amounts of Spanish potash were sold abroad, and active competition in the important Dutch market caused sharp price reductions following failure of negotiations to stabilize price between the Franco-German potash syndicate and the Spanish producers. Shipments from the U.S.S.R. appearing in small amounts in various markets occasioned speculation regarding Soviet policy in relation to their growing production of potash and further uncertainties in the outlook for 1934. The 1934–35 season found sellers unwilling to commit themselves to a price policy by publication of the usual seasonal schedules. Earlier fears were realized as increased offerings from Spain and substantial shipments from the U.S.S.R. combined with other disturbing factors to demoralize world markets and bring about price concessions.[21]

This is the background of the price situation in potash during 1934. On June 1, 1934 a price list was announced by American Potash and Chemical Corporation. The price was 50 cents per unit of K_2O, with other conditions on discounts and delivery dates. This price was apparently above the price which importers were ready to charge. "No other suppliers issued printed lists at that time, but it was rumored that importers were prepared to sell all forms of potash fertilizer salts except sulphate and double sulphate at the equivalent of 44 cents per unit of K_2O."[22] When other sellers failed to

---

[20] *Ibid.*, p. 435.

[21] This description of conditions in the potash market is based on discussion in the *Minerals Yearbook, 1934* (Washington, D.C.: Government Printing Office, 1934), p. 1031 and *Minerals Yearbook, 1935*, p. 1149.

[22] *Minerals Yearbook, 1935*, p. 1149.

follow their lead and no other price lists were published, the price list was withdrawn and canceled by American Potash and Chemical. It seems fairly clear from the situation that the price list was withdrawn because the announced list was above the market price. Other sellers were not prepared to commit themselves to a price higher than the rumored market price. Thus the price list, in fact, was a price increase which rivals would not follow. On July 27 a further price decrease by American Potash and Chemical to 40 cents per unit was quickly met by competitors. "Following the final slash in prices that was met by all sellers, the market steadied . . . . After the turn of the year interest focused on probable price levels for the coming season and the possibility of understandings between competing interests that would stabilize the market at reasonable levels."[23] Within a two-month period in 1934, there were two instances of the working of the kink in the American Potash and Chemical Corporation's demand curve.

Thus with the entry of new importers into the potash market, a situation developed in which firms had little or no information about several important rivals. This is the kind of situation in which we have argued the kink has a chance to be relevant. The observed behavior—in which most firms did not issue price lists, and in which one firm was forced to withdraw what was, in comparison with rumored actual prices, a price increase—is consistent with our expectations. Finally, the following type of behavior is consistent with an attempt to increase the amount of interfirm knowledge: "Evidence of cooperation between the principal suppliers of the American market is seen in the incorporation by the leading importers and the three chief domestic producers of the American Potash Institute, Inc., a research organization to promote efficient and profitable use of potash in crop production."[24]

D. The Kinked Demand Curve and Conjectural Variations

The kinked demand curve theory can be formulated in terms of particular assumptions about the conjectural variations. Instead of stating the conjectural variations in terms of quantity changes, as we did in Section I, however, it is most convenient to state them in terms of price changes.[25] In the duopoly version of kinked demand theory, dp_2/dp_1, firm 1's conjecture about the rate of change in firm 2's price with respect to changes in firm 1's price, is zero if dp_1 is positive (i.e. if firm 1 raises price) and it is unity if dp_1 is negative (i.e., if firm 1 lowers price). Similarly, dp_1/dp_2, firm 2's conjecture about the rate of change in firm 1's price with respect to changes in firm 2's price, is zero if dp_2 is positive and unity if dp_2 is negative.

---

[23] *Ibid.*, p. 1150.

[24] *Ibid.*, p. 1147.

[25] This simply amounts to regarding price, rather than output, as each firm's basic decision variable.

When viewed in this light, it is clear that kinked demand theory is only one of a large family of models that make special assumptions about the price conjectural variation terms.[26] Along with most of these models, the kinked demand theory suffers by following the static approach and not having any provision for learning by the firms. In addition, as we have pointed out, the implicit assumptions about interfirm information are so severe that the possible application of the kinked demand model is limited. From our analysis it would appear that the kink might be a relevant way to describe behavior in young industries, but for only a relatively short period of time until information sources within the industry developed. Another situation in which the kink may be applicable is where new sellers enter the market. The lack of information between new sellers and old may make the kink realistic, as in the potash case.

In summary, we suggest that under some circumstances, the kinked demand theory is an appropriate short-run model for oligopoly price behavior. By focusing on the means by which interfirm information is disseminated, we can eventually identify the conditions under which this theory is applicable. In the long run, learning by firms and the development of new information sources can remove the perceived kink in the demand curve.

IV. Implications for Resource Allocation

In this chapter we have examined a few of the many alternative oligopoly models which economists have developed. There is no general agreement at present that any existing oligopoly model is appropriate for analyzing behavior in a specific industry. Because of this lack of agreement, it is difficult to predict the equilibrium solution for a particular oligopolistic market. Therefore we cannot state with any degree of confidence the equilibrium levels of market price, output, and factor usage. Furthermore the comparative statics of oligopolistic markets are equally elusive. Thus we are on shaky ground when we try to indicate the expected reactions of market price, output, and factor usage to shifts in demand, shifts in supply, technological changes, factor price changes, variations in tax rates, etc.

Despite these problems, however, it is necessary to indicate the effects of oligopoly on the allocation of resources in an economy. To do so, we must at times go beyond the confines of the particular formal models developed in this chapter and use empirical knowledge about the behavior of large business firms in the American economy.

---

[26] For example, all the models discussed earlier, in Section I, could equally well have been formulated with price, rather than output, as the basic decision variable. Each model would then have arisen from a particular assumption about the price conjectural variation terms.

A. PRICES

The analytical models that we have examined generally lead to prices that are above the levels that would prevail under perfect competition. The amount by which an oligopoly price exceeds the competitive level is a function of the number of firms in the market and the degree of freedom of entry.

The greater the number of firms in the market, the higher the probability that price will move toward the competitive level. This proposition must be qualified slightly by stressing that the size distribution of the firms is critical. If this distribution is highly skewed, so that there are only one or two large firms and a group of minor firms, then the dominant-firm model is likely to apply. In this case price will be closer to the monopoly level.[27]

The second factor that is critical in judging the behavior of price in an oligopoly market is the entry problem. If entry is easy (i.e., if new firms meet no barriers, such as patents, lack of raw materials, shortage of technical knowledge, or high capital requirements), price will tend toward the competitive level. The possible entry of new firms is a constraint on the price policies of existing firms in the industry. Free entry exposes the industry to increased competition if profits become larger and the rate of return on capital higher than normal when risk is taken into account. New entrants may come from established firms in related industries or from entirely new combinations of resources.[28]

The oligopoly markets where prices are most likely to remain above the competitive level are those in which there are a small number of firms, a relatively small market, and great economies of scale. In these circumstances a new firm must build a relatively large plant to compete effectively, and this may mean potential excess capacity in the market at any given price level. This fact, plus the capital requirement that is necessary for a large plant, may present barriers to entry that will generate a protected oligopolistic market. Under such conditions price will tend to be closer to the monopoly level than to the competitive level.

There may be temporary periods (especially during price wars) when oligopoly market prices may be lower than the competitive level. If there are great economies of scale, however, the oligopolistic price may be

---

[27] There is evidence, however, that the dominant-firm model is not a long-run phenomenon. This is primarily because the minor firms are able to grow at a faster rate than the dominant firm. In this situation, there would be a long-run tendency for price to move toward the competitive level. See Dean A. Worcester, Jr., "Why 'Dominant Firms' Decline," *Journal of Political Economy*, 65 (August, 1957), 338–46.

[28] In general, the capital requirement may not be as significant an entry barrier as is commonly thought. The reason is that the expectation of a significant rate of return greatly facilitates raising new venture capital. Similarly, brand names developed by advertising will generally not build protected areas in the long run, since other firms can also advertise.

permanently less than the price that would be charged if there were many smaller firms in the industry. This type of result is dependent upon two conditions. First, there must be no collusion among the oligopolists. Second, a market structure consisting of many smaller firms could be maintained only if there were some external force, such as potential governmental intervention, preventing the firms from attaining the optimal-sized plants. There is evidence in several antitrust cases that the courts are concerned that the dissolution of a large company may result in the loss of economies of scale, and hence lead to higher prices for the public.

Prices in oligopoly industries are more stable than prices would be under perfect competition. Oligopolistic firms are more likely than competitive firms to keep prices constant despite great shifts in demand, and to adjust to these demand changes by varying the quantities supplied rather than by altering selling prices.

B. Outputs

The same types of reasoning that we used in comparing oligopoly and competitive prices may be applied to outputs. As long as the oligopolistic price is higher than the competitive price, for any given market demand curve the total output in the industry will be less under oligopoly than under competition. If, however, economies of scale are important, then oligopoly prices may be lower and outputs higher than would be the case if a large number of firms were to exist in the same industry.

Using the same market demand curve to compare oligopolistic and competitive market structures may not be reasonable in the real world. The extensive expenditures for advertising and new product development which are common in oligopolistic industries may shift the market demand curve to the right. Hence both output and price may be higher in an oligopoly market than if the same industry had perfectly competitive conditions.

Because of the tendency for price levels to be more rigid, over the course of a business cycle total output may vary more in oligopoly than under perfectly competitive conditions. This means that fluctuations in employment and the utilization of other productive factors may be more extreme with the existence of oligopoly, thus intensifying macroeconomic stabilization problems.

C. Nonprice Competition

Although the formal analytical models discussed in this chapter do not explicitly deal with various forms of nonprice competition, there is a great deal of empirical evidence which indicates that various forms of nonprice competition are much more important for oligopolies than for perfectly competitive markets. Nonprice competition primarily involves attempts to differentiate the oligopolist's product from its rivals' products by establishing in the consumers' minds through advertising real or imaginary differences in quality and style. In addition, other factors, such as accompanying sales and repair services, terms of trade, etc., may be used.

From the viewpoint of the consumer, the effects of using advertising to sell the products, rather than price reductions, may be undesirable. Evaluating the total social effects of advertising is a complex question which we do not intend to analyze in detail here. Assuming no economies of scale in production, it is clear that some consumers would be better off (on higher indifference curves) if they could buy the products alone rather than the products plus bundles of additional services, such as radio and television entertainment. The additional services are in fact provided by the advertising expenditures of the producers of the products. Thus when a housewife buys a box of detergent powder, she is not only paying for the product but also helping pay for the television program sponsored by the manufacturer. If she views this program, she may be getting a bargain, but if she does not, she is subsidizing others who do view the program, many of whom may not buy the detergent. If products and the services purchased by advertising were separately priced, then consumers would be able to choose the precise bundles which would give them the highest utility.

The importance of this problem becomes clear by examining the aggregate magnitude of advertising costs in the United States. According to the Internal Revenue service, $7.66 billion was spent on all types of advertising during 1957. The six industries with the largest total expenditures on advertising that year were department stores ($426 million), retail food stores ($233 million), drugs and medicine ($225 million), cigarettes ($210 million), beer ($209 million), and motor vehicles ($195 million).[29]

The aim of product differentiation is to establish a segment of the consumers with whom the firm has a monopoly position. This may be accomplished by the development of nationally advertised brand names. Once the monopoly position is established, the manufacturer can gain large profits by exploiting the market through a variety of means, including price discrimination. For example:

> A Federal Trade Commission investigation revealed that the Goodyear Tire and Rubber Company sold tires to Sears Roebuck under the brand name "Allstate" which were of the same quality as those marketed by Goodyear under its own "All Weather" brand. The difference in wholesale prices between these two brands ranged from 29 to 40 per cent in the period 1927–33. At retail, Allstate tires were sold at prices 20 to 25 per cent below those of All Weather tires.[30]

---

[29] These advertising expenditure figures for 1957 are from *The Source Book of Income* (Internal Revenue Service), as cited in Lester G. Telser, "Advertising and Cigarettes," *Journal of Business*, 36, (1963), 471.

[30] Colberg, Forbush, and Whitaker, *op. cit.*, p. 227.

Without the existence of its heavily advertised brand name, it is doubtful that Goodyear would have been able to price its own brand of tires so high and still sell a significant share of the market.

One effect of quality competition has been a genuine improvement in product quality, and in some oligopolistic industries this has been substantial. For example:

> According to tests made by the Procurement Division of the United States Treasury in 1931, the average consumption of five makes of 6-cubic-foot refrigerators was 44 kilowatt-hours per month. A test based on 14 makes in 1938 showed average electricity consumption to have declined to 35 kilowatt-hours per month. By 1954, this amount of current was sufficient to operate the average 8.3–9.6-cubic-foot refrigerators for a month, according to tests by Consumers Union.[31]

The total costs involved in quality competition may be high. For example, in a study of the costs of quality competition in the automobile industry, it was found that the cost of model changes by American automobile manufacturers during the 1950's was approximately $5 billion per year.

> Were such costs worthwhile? It is difficult to say. There is a presumption that consumer purchases are worth the money paid, yet one might argue that the fact that our figures for the late 1950's (about $700 in the purchase price per car, or more than 25 per cent, and $40 per year in gasoline expenses) will probably seem surprisingly high to consumers is an indication that the costs in question were not fully understood by the consuming public.[32]

D. Profits

The rates of return earned by oligopolists theoretically should be higher than the rates of return earned by perfectly competitive firms, as long as there are some barriers to entry in the oligopolies. There is a considerable amount of empirical evidence to indicate that in fact the average profit rate earned by American firms is an increasing function of the degree of concentration in the industry.[33] A typical result of the empirical studies is the following:

---

[31] *Ibid.*, pp. 225–26.

[32] Franklin M. Fisher, Zvi Griliches, and Carl Kaysen, "The Costs of Automobile Model Changes since 1949," *Journal of Political Economy*, 70, No. 5 (October, 1962), 450.

[33] Joe S. Bain, "Relation of Profit Rate to Industry Concentration: American Manufacturing, 1936–1940," *Quarterly Journal of Economics*, 65, No. 3 (August, 1951), 293–323. Victor Fuchs, "Integration, Concentration, and Profits in Manufacturing Industries," *Quarterly Journal of Economics*, 75, No. 2 (May, 1961), 278–91. Harold M. Levinson, "Post War Movements in Prices and Wages in Manufacturing Industries," Joint Economic Committee, *Study of Employment, Growth, and Price Levels*, Study Paper No. 21, 1960. Leonard W. Weiss, "Average Concentration Ratios and Industrial Performance," *Journal of Industrial Economics*, 11, No. 3, 237–54.

The major hypothesis to be tested was that the profit rates of firms in industries of high seller concentration should on the average be larger than those of firms in industries of lower concentration, although subject to a considerable dispersion of the profit rates of individual firms and industries. Our statistical study has suggested that this was very probably the case in the interval 1936 through 1940 in American manufacturing industry, and that the association of concentration to profits was such that there was a rough dichotomy of industries into those with more and less than 70 per cent of value product controlled by eight firms.[34]

As long as there is competition in the capital markets, the common stocks of oligopoly firms will be capitalized at a rate which takes into account the above-average earnings of these firms. Thus allowing for risk differentials, the common stocks of oligopoly firms will tend to be priced to yield their owners the same rates of return that they can obtain by holding the common stocks of any other firms. Therefore, you should not expect to receive any windfalls if you rush into the market to buy the stocks of oligopoly firms. For the same reason, it is not possible to use the price-earnings ratios of common stocks to test whether rates of return are higher in oligopolistic than in competitive industries.[35]

V. Summary

This is the third of four chapters on imperfect competition. Our analyses of monopoly and of monopolistic competition in Chapters 10 and 11 were considerably easier than our analyses of oligopoly, because the assumptions were more definite and less ambiguous. Oligopoly behavior is difficult to comprehend; witness the wide range of possible formal models that have been developed by economists. In the next chapter, some elements of oligopolistic interdependence, but on the buying side, will reappear when we analyze imperfectly competitive factor markets.

Despite the difficulty in easily representing oligopoly behavior in a generally accepted model, this form of market structure is extremely commonplace in the American economy, especially in manufacturing industries.[36]

---

[34] Bain, *op. cit.*, p. 323.

On the basis of different empirical evidence, Stigler reaches the conclusion that concentrated industries do not have rates of return which are always significantly higher (on a statistical basis) than the rates of return in unconcentrated industries. Stigler's evidence for 1938–40 is consistent with Bain's results; however, Stigler's data for 1947–54 do not reveal any statistically significant relationship between rates of return and concentration ratios. See George J. Stigler, *Capital and Rates of Return in Manufacturing Industries*, National Bureau of Economic Research (Princeton, N.J.: Princeton University Press, 1963), pp. 66–69.

[35] Hence the empirical studies referred to earlier all used rate of return on book value of assets, rather than rate of return on market value of equity.

[36] Joe S. Bain, *Industrial Organization* (New York: John Wiley & Sons, Inc., 1959), pp. 125–30.

Automobiles, primary aluminum, and primary copper are oligopolies in which there is a very high concentration of total output (over 85 per cent) in the hands of the largest three or four firms, and a small total number of firms. Cigarettes, electric light bulbs, gypsum products, and flat glass are oligopolies in which there is a very high concentration of output (over 85 per cent) in the hands of the largest three or four firms but a somewhat more numerous group of minor sellers. Rubber tires, distilled liquor, transformers, and laundry equipment are oligopolies in which the proportion of the market controlled by the four largest sellers is over 65 per cent and in which there is a competitive fringe of a fairly large number of small firms. Steel, pianos, and ball and roller bearings are oligopolies in which the largest four sellers control between 50 per cent and 65 per cent of the market and the largest eight sellers control between 70 per cent and 85 per cent, with the competitive fringe being fairly important. At the low end of the oligopoly scale are such industries as meat packing, greeting cards, wallpaper, and insecticides, in which the top four firms control between 35 per cent and 50 per cent of the market and the top eight firms between 45 per cent and 70 per cent, with a large number of small sellers.

The key feature which characterizes an oligopoly is the recognized interdependency among the sellers. Each oligopolist is acutely aware that his rivals will notice any changes in his own prices, advertising, product quality, etc., and that his rivals will swiftly change their own policies in response to his actions. We saw that the easiest way to examine the nature of oligopolistic interdependence was to consider the duopoly situation, where there are only two sellers. In the case of a duopoly market with an undifferentiated product, the conjectural variations play an important role. Formally the conjectural variations are derivatives, representing one firm's expectation of how the other firm's output will alter as a result of its own change in output. Depending upon the specific assumptions made regarding the conjectural variations, different duopoly models result. We analyzed four of these in detail: the Cournot model, the collusion model, the Stackelberg model, and the market shares model. Unfortunately there is no empirical evidence available to indicate the extent to which any of these models is particularly applicable to real-world behavior.

Thus we were led to consider some other forms of oligopoly models which do not focus specific attention on the conjectural variation terms. Two forms of price leadership behavior, the dominant-firm model and the barometric firm approach, were considered. Some illustrations of both of these types of price leadership behavior in the American economy were provided. Two other forms of market organization, collusion and cartels, were also considered. Illustrations of these structures, some illegal and some with government sanctions, were given.

The kinked demand curve theory was originally developed by Sweezy to explain observed price rigidities in oligopolistic industries. Stigler presented some empirical evidence which shows that this is not a generally valid oligopoly model. By focusing on the importance of interfirm knowledge, however, we have been able to suggest some circumstances in which this theory may be appropriate.

Finally, the implications of oligopoly for resource allocation were considered. Except for temporary price wars and for economies of scale, oligopoly prices will be somewhere between the price levels in monopolized and in perfectly competitive industries. If barriers to entry are weak, oligopolistic prices will tend toward the competitive level; if entry barriers are formidable, oligopolistic prices will be closer to the monopoly level. Since oligopoly prices are generally above the competitive levels, oligopoly outputs may be expected to be lower than the competitive levels. The possibility exists, however, that advertising and quality competition will shift the market demand curve to the right so that both price and output may be higher than would be expected under perfect competition. Nonprice competition will be prevalent in oligopolies, perhaps to excessive amounts from the viewpoint of consumer efficiency. Profit rates will tend to be higher in oligopolistic than in competitive industries.

SUGGESTED READINGS

These recommendations are in addition to the footnote references cited in this chapter.

Baumol, William J., "On the Theory of Oligopoly," *Economica*, XXV (August, 1958), 187–98.

Bhagwati, J. N., "Oligopoly Theory, Entry-Prevention and Growth," *Oxford Economic Papers*, XXII (November, 1970), 297–310.

Bishop, Robert L., "Duopoly: Collusion or Warfare?" *American Economic Review*, L, No. 1 (December, 1960), 933–61.

Cyert, R. M., and M. H. DeGroot, "Bayesian Analysis and Duopoly Theory," *Journal of Political Economy*, LXXVIII (September/October, 1970), 1168–84.

―――, "Interfirm Learning and the Kinked Demand Curve," *Journal of Economic Theory*, III (September, 1971), 272–87.

Frisch, Ragnar, "Monopoly-Polypoly—the Concept of Force in the Economy," in *International Economic Papers*, No. 1, Alan T. Peacock et al., eds., pp. 23–36. London: Macmillan & Co., Ltd., 1951.

Hurwicz, Leonid, "The Theory of Economic Behavior," in *Readings in Price Theory*, George J. Stigler and Kenneth E. Boulding, eds., chap. 25. Homewood, Ill.: Richard D. Irwin, Inc., 1952.

Sherman, Roger, *Oligopoly*. Lexington, Mass.: D. C. Heath & Co., 1972.

SHUBIK, MARTIN, *Strategy and Market Structure*. New York: John Wiley & Sons, Inc., 1959.

TELSER, LESTER G., *Competition, Collusion, and Game Theory*. Chicago, Ill.: Aldine-Atherton, Inc., 1972.

Chapter Thirteen

Imperfections in the Factor Markets

So far in this book we have assumed that firms purchase their factors of production in perfectly competitive markets. Hence we assumed that a firm could purchase any amount of a factor it desires at prevailing market prices. In this chapter we shall analyze the effects of various types of market imperfections on the firm's production decisions and on the allocation of resources. It is most convenient in this analysis to assume that any firm produces only a single product.

I. Types of Factor Market Imperfections

There are as many different types of market structures in the factor markets as in the product markets. At one extreme is perfect competition; perfectly competitive factor markets were analyzed in Chapter 7. The other extreme is *monopsony*, a market in which there is only one purchaser of a factor. Intermediate between these extremes is *oligopsony*, which is analogous to oligopoly on the product side.

There are a number of imperfect factor markets in the American economy. The type of "company town" which used to be prevalent in coal mining areas represents monopsony, since a single firm was the sole employer of labor in the town. These towns were in isolated areas, and the miners usually lacked the resources and knowledge to take advantage of employment opportunities elsewhere. A more common example of monopsony is found today in a situation in which a small firm sells its entire output to one large firm. The small firm in such a situation has usually designed its production facilities to produce a product meeting the specifications of the large firm. Hence without additional investment expenditures the small firm has no alternative purchaser other than the large firm. Examples of this type of situation are common among the suppliers of automobile manufacturers and giant retailing firms. Some examples of oligopsony are cigarette manufacturers purchasing leaf tobacco or meat packers purchasing livestock, since in each case there are only a small number of purchasers and a large number of sellers.

The crucial feature of any type of factor market imperfection is the dependence of purchase price on the quantity of the factor which is purchased by a firm. The general nature of this dependence is illustrated in Figure 13–1, where the firm is confronted with an upward-sloping factor supply curve. This means that when the firm expands its output, it pays a higher price for the additional units of factor it hires as well as for the quantity of factor previously used, since we are assuming that a single price is paid for all units of the factor. The supply curve, therefore, represents the average outlay curve of the firm for this factor. Letting w represent the price of the factor and letting v represent the quantity used of the factor,

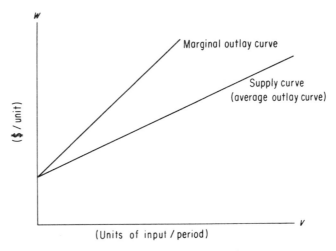

FIGURE 13–1.   The factor supply curve in monopsony.

we can represent the firm's average outlay curve by

$$w = AO(v) \tag{13-1}$$

where

$$\frac{dw}{dv} > 0 \tag{13-2}$$

for an imperfect market.

The total outlay curve of the firm for the factor is

$$TO(v) = vw = vAO(v). \tag{13-3}$$

The marginal outlay curve of the firm for the factor is

$$MO(v) = \frac{d}{dv}[TO(v)] = w + v\frac{dw}{dv}. \tag{13-4}$$

In view of Eq. (13-2), in an imperfect factor market the marginal outlay curve is above the average outlay curve for every positive value of v, as shown in Figure 13-1.

II. The Optimal Mix of Inputs

When the firm purchases some or all of its inputs in imperfect factor markets, then the analysis of the optimal mix of inputs presented in Chapter 7 is no longer valid. In this case the production function constraint which was introduced in Chapter 7 must continue to be observed. We now, however, must recognize that the prices which the firm pays for its inputs are functions of the quantities of inputs purchased.

A. GRAPHICAL ANALYSIS[1]

The one-output, two-input production function is considered first because it can be analyzed graphically. As in Chapter 7, the production function is

$$q = G(v_1, v_2). \tag{13-5}$$

Figure 13-2 is a graphical representation of this production function when the two factors are imperfect substitutes. Each isoproduct curve denotes a specific level of production, the level being higher the further the isoproduct curve is from the origin.

The firm's total cost when it uses v_1 and v_2 units of the two factors and pays the prices w_1 and w_2 for them is

$$TC = w_1v_1 + w_2v_2 + A \tag{13-6}$$

---

[1] This section illustrates that in some cases it is impossible to use graphical analysis in a rigorous fashion without employing some mathematics.

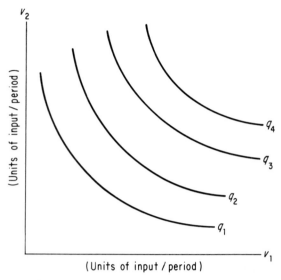

FIGURE 13–2. Isoproduct curves for a two-input production function.

where A is fixed cost. In Chapter 7 the analogous equation was graphed as a straight line, since it was assumed that w_1 and w_2 were given constants. Now, however, Eq. (13–6) no longer represents a straight line, since the prices are functions of the amounts purchased.

In order to see the nature of the isocost curves defined by Eq. (13–6), take the total differential of TC:

$$dTC = w_1\, dv_1 + v_1\, dw_1 + w_2\, dv_2 + v_2\, dw_2 = 0. \qquad (13\text{–}7)$$

Equation (13–7) is set equal to 0 because along an isocost curve, the total cost is constant. Solving Eq. (13–7) for the slope of an isocost curve, dv_2/dv_1, we obtain

$$\frac{dv_2}{dv_1} = -\,\frac{w_1 + v_1\,(dw_1/dv_1)}{w_2 + v_2\,(dw_2/dv_2)}. \qquad (13\text{–}8)$$

Since w_1, w_2, v_1, v_2, dw_1/dv_1, and dw_2/dv_2 are all nonnegative, it follows from Eq. (13–8) that the slope of any isocost curve is necessarily negative, that is,

$$\frac{dv_2}{dv_1} < 0. \qquad (13\text{–}9)$$

In order to determine whether an isocost curve is convex or concave to the origin, it is necessary to examine the algebraic sign of the isocost curve's second derivative. It can be shown that under fairly reasonable assumptions the second derivative is negative, so that an isocost curve is concave to the origin.[2] A representative set of isocost curves is shown in Figure 13–3. Along each isocost curve, the total cost of production for the firm is constant. The further from the origin an isocost curve is, the higher the level of total cost it represents.

Figure 13–4 shows the isoproduct curve corresponding to a particular level of output, q, and several possible isocost curves for the firm. The point of tangency between the isoproduct curve q and the isocost curve TC_2 represents the most efficient combination of productive factors. $\bar{v}_1$ units of the first input and $\bar{v}_2$ units of the second input can produce the desired level of output q at the lowest possible cost. Any other point on the isoproduct curve q will also result in the same level of output, but all other points intersect some isocost curve further from the origin than TC_2; that is, they represent higher levels of total cost. The isocost lines lying inside of TC_2, that is, closer to the origin than TC_2, represent lower total

---

[2] These assumptions are that the second derivatives of the supply curves for the factors are nonnegative. This is reasonable because a negative second derivative would indicate that the supply curve is increasing at a decreasing rate. This would mean that the firm could purchase an increasing number of units of the factor at a decreasing increment of price.

Another assumption is that the factor markets are independent of each other. This means, for example, that the supply curve of factor 2 is independent of the quantity purchased of factor 1, and vice versa.

The second derivative of an isocost curve is found by differentiating Eq. (13–8) with respect to v_1:

$$\frac{d^2v_2}{dv_1^2} = -\frac{1}{[w_2 + v_2(dw_2/dv_1)]^2}\left\{\left[\left(w_2 + v_2\frac{dw_2}{dv_2}\right)\left(\frac{dw_1}{dv_1} + v_1\frac{d^2w_1}{dv_1^2} + \frac{dw_1}{dv_1}\right)\right]\right.$$
$$\left. -\left[\left(w_1 + v_1\frac{dw_1}{dv_1}\right)\left(\frac{dw_2}{dv_2} + v_2\frac{d^2w_2}{dv_2^2} + \frac{dw_2}{dv_2}\right)\frac{dv_2}{dv_1}\right]\right\}.$$

Since we have already shown in Eq. (13–9) that the slope of an isocost curve is negative, we may rewrite this equation in the form:

$$\frac{d^2v_2}{dv_1^2} = -\frac{1}{[w_2 + v_2(dw_2/dv_1)]^2}\left\{\left[2\frac{dw_1}{dv_1}\left(w_2 + v_2\frac{dw_2}{dv_2}\right) + \left|\frac{dv_2}{dv_1}\right|\left(2\frac{dw_2}{dv_2}\right)\left(w_1 + v_1\frac{dw_1}{dv_1}\right)\right]\right.$$
$$\left. +\left[v_1\left(w_2 + v_2\frac{dw_2}{dv_2}\right)\frac{d^2w_1}{dv_1^2} + \left|\frac{dv_2}{dv_1}\right|v_2\left(w_1 + v_1\frac{dw_1}{dv_1}\right)\frac{d^2w_2}{dv_2^2}\right]\right\}.$$

Since we have assumed that the second derivatives of the supply curves for the factors are nonnegative, every term within the braces in the foregoing equation is nonnegative. Indeed, as long as either or both factors have upward-sloping supply curves, the entire expression within the braces is positive. It therefore follows that the right-hand side of the foregoing equation is negative; hence the second derivative of an isocost curve is negative.

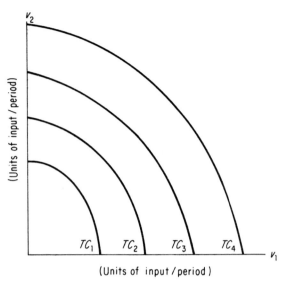

FIGURE 13–3.   Isocost curves for imperfect factor markets.

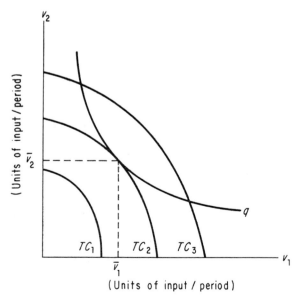

FIGURE 13–4.   Tangency condition for an efficient combination of input factors.

costs than TC_2, but along any of these cheaper isocost curves it is impossible to produce a level of output as large as q. Hence the point of tangency (with coordinates $\bar{v}_1$ and $\bar{v}_2$) is the best combination of input factors for producing a level of output q.

It is clear from Figure 13–4 that the optimal mix of inputs, $\bar{v}_1$ and $\bar{v}_2$, depends upon the particular level of output, q. Hence we can write the optimal input mix as $\bar{v}_1(q)$ and $\bar{v}_2(q)$. Substituting these values into Eq. (13–6), we obtain the firm's total cost function:

$$TC(q) = AO_1[\bar{v}_1(q)]\,\bar{v}_1(q) + AO_2[\bar{v}_2(q)]\,\bar{v}_2(q) + A. \qquad (13\text{–}10)$$

By writing Eq. (13–10) in the form shown, we have recognized that w_1 and w_2, the prices paid for the two factors, depend upon the amounts used of each factor; this dependence is expressed through the firm's average outlay curve for each factor.

B. MATHEMATICAL ANALYSIS

The graphical analysis can be used when there are only two inputs in the production function. By using mathematics, however, similar results can be obtained for more general production functions. We shall consider the following production function with N inputs:

$$q = G(v_1, \ldots, v_N). \qquad (13\text{–}11)$$

The firm's total cost when it uses v_i units of input i purchased at a price w_i to produce a specified level of output q is

$$TC = A + \sum_{i=1}^{N} w_i v_i. \qquad (13\text{–}12)$$

To find the most efficient combination of factors to produce an output q, it is necessary to determine the values of $v_1, \ldots, v_N$ which minimize the total cost in Eq. (13–12), subject to the production function constraint, Eq. (13–11). This constrained minimization problem differs from the analogous problem under perfect competition because now the prices $w_1, \ldots, w_N$ depend upon the amounts of the factors used.

Form the Lagrangian function:

$$L = A + \sum_{i=1}^{N} w_i v_i - \lambda[G(v_1, \ldots, v_N) - q]. \qquad (13\text{–}13)$$

Equating all of the partial derivatives of L to zero,

$$\frac{\partial L}{\partial v_i} = w_i + v_i \frac{dw_i}{dv_i} - \lambda \frac{\partial G}{\partial v_i} = 0 \qquad i = 1, \ldots, N. \qquad (13\text{–}14)$$

The solution of Eq. (13–14) is

$$\frac{1}{\lambda} = \frac{G_i}{w_i + v_i \, (dw_i/dv_i)} \qquad i = 1, \ldots, N, \qquad (13\text{–}15)$$

where $\qquad G_i = \dfrac{\partial G}{\partial v_i} \qquad\qquad\qquad i = 1, \ldots, N \qquad (13\text{–}16)$

is the marginal productivity of input i. The system of equations (13–15) can be written in the form:

$$\frac{G_1}{w_1 + v_1 \, (dw_1/dv_1)} = \frac{G_2}{w_2 + v_2 \, (dw_2/dv_2)} = \cdots = \frac{G_N}{w_N + v_N \, (dw_N/dv_N)} = \frac{1}{\lambda}.$$

$$(13\text{–}17)$$

Equations (13–17) can be interpreted as stating that the marginal productivity of a factor divided by the marginal outlay on that factor must be the same for all factors.

The N independent equations in (13–17), together with the production function constraint, Eq. (13–11), can be solved for the $N + 1$ values $\bar{v}_1, \ldots, \bar{v}_N$ and $\bar{\lambda}$. $\bar{v}_i$ is the optimal amount of input i in producing a specified amount of output, q. The total cost function is determined by substituting these values into Eq. (13–12):

$$TC(q) = A + \sum_{i=1}^{N} AO_i[\bar{v}_i(q)] \, \bar{v}_i(q). \qquad (13\text{–}18)$$

We now show that the Lagrange multiplier λ equals marginal cost. This is done by using the ratio of the total differentials of Eq. (13–12) and (13–11):

$$dTC = \sum_{i=1}^{N} (w_i \, dv_i + v_i \, dw_i) = \sum_{i=1}^{N} [w_i + v_i \, (dw_i/dv_i)] \, dv_i. \qquad (13\text{–}19)$$

$$dq = \sum_{i=1}^{N} \frac{\partial G}{\partial v_i} \, dv_i = \sum_{i=1}^{N} G_i \, dv_i. \qquad (13\text{–}20)$$

$$MC = \frac{dTC}{dq} = \frac{\displaystyle\sum_{i=1}^{N} [w_i + v_i \, (dw_i/dv_i)] \, dv_i}{\displaystyle\sum_{i-1}^{N} G_i \, dv_i}. \qquad (13\text{–}21)$$

From Eq. (13–15),

$$w_i + v_i \frac{dw_i}{dv_i} = \lambda G_i \qquad i = 1, \ldots, N. \qquad (13\text{–}22)$$

Therefore, substituting Eq. (13–22) into (13–21) and simplifying,

$$MC = \frac{\sum_{i=1}^{N} \lambda G_i \, dv_i}{\sum_{i=1}^{N} G_i \, dv_i} = \lambda. \tag{13–23}$$

Since λ is marginal cost, it is clear from Eq. (13–4) and (13–22) that the marginal outlay by a firm for any factor must equal the marginal cost of the firm's output multiplied by the marginal product of the factor:

$$MO_i = w_i + v_i \frac{dw_i}{dv_i} = (MC)G_i \qquad i = 1, \ldots, N. \tag{13–24}$$

III. The Effects of Factor Market Imperfections on a Firm's Utilization of Resources

So far in this chapter we have considered only the factor markets in which a firm purchases inputs, but we have not considered the product market in which the firm sells its output. The effects of factor market imperfections on a firm's utilization of resources are similar whatever the nature of the market in which the firm's output is sold. We shall show that the existence of monopsony leads to the utilization of a smaller amount of the factor at a lower purchase price than would be the case under a perfectly competitive factor market.

From Chapters 6 and 10, we know that both perfectly competitive firms and monopolies produce at rates of output for which marginal revenue equals marginal cost. Therefore Eq. (13–24) can be written in the form:

$$MO_i = w_i + v_i \frac{dw_i}{dv_i} = (MR)G_i = \left(p + q \frac{dp}{dq} \right) G_i. \tag{13–25}$$

Equation (13–25) is general enough to apply to perfectly competitive product or factor markets, monopoly, or monopsony. dp/dq equals zero if there is perfect competition in the product market, but dp/dq is negative if there is a monopoly in the product market. Similarly, dw_i/dv_i equals zero if factor market i is perfectly competitive, but if it is a monopsony, then dw_i/dv_i is positive.

In order to consider how the firm's utilization of input i depends upon the market structure in which this input is purchased, it is necessary to assume that the firm utilizes input i under conditions of diminishing marginal productivity:

$$\frac{\partial G_i}{\partial v_i} < 0 \qquad i = 1, \ldots, N. \tag{13–26}$$

Diminishing marginal productivity necessarily exists under perfect competition. We shall assume that it exists in general, an assumption which is realistic except for unusual and extreme cases.

First consider that the output is sold under monopolistic conditions. Then Eq. (13–25) can be solved for w_i, the price paid for the factor:

$$w_i = \left(p + q\frac{dp}{dq}\right)G_i - v_i\frac{dw_i}{dv_i}. \tag{13–27}$$

From Eq. (13–27), we can compare the effects of monopsonistic buying versus competitive buying on the price of the factor. In this comparison we must assume that the buying conditions do not change either the market structure or the demand curve for the product.

It is clear from Eq. (13–27) that w_i^M, the price paid for factor i by a firm which is a monopsonist, is lower than w_i^C, the price the firm would pay under competitive buying conditions, since

$$w_i^M = \left(p + q\frac{dp}{dq}\right)G_i - v_i\frac{dw_i}{dv_i} < \left(p + q\frac{dp}{dq}\right)G_i = w_i^C. \tag{13–28}$$

Note that the result in Eq. (13–28) is also valid when the output is sold under perfectly competitive conditions. In this case Eq. (13–28) becomes:

$$w_i^M = pG_i - v_i\frac{dw_i}{dv_i} < pG_i = w_i^C. \tag{13–29}$$

Thus, whether the product market is competitive or monopolistic, the effect of monopsony is to lower the price paid for the monopsonized factor. Since we have assumed an upward-sloping supply curve for input i and diminishing marginal productivity, it therefore follows that v_i^M, the quantity of factor i purchased under monopsony, is less than v_i^C, the quantity of factor i that would be purchased under competitive buying. These results are illustrated in Figure 13–5.

Note that if the output is sold under perfect competition, then the derived demand curve in Figure 13–5 should be interpreted as the value of the marginal product of factor i; if the output is sold under monopoly conditions, then the derived demand curve should be regarded as the marginal revenue product of factor i. The assumption of diminishing marginal productivity made in Eq. (13–26) is sufficient to insure that the derived demand curve is downward sloping under either type of market structure. Under monopoly the curvature of the derived demand curve would be even sharper than it is under perfect competition, since both marginal productivity and (for a monopoly) marginal revenue decrease as the amount used of the factor increases.

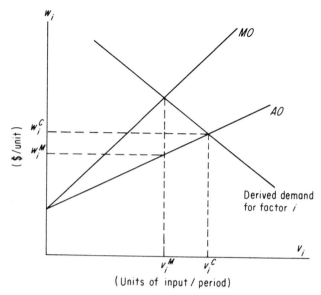

FIGURE 13–5.   Effects of monopsony on the utilization of a factor.

An alternative derivation of the effects of monopsony on factor price and utilization is suggested by Figure 13–5. Since the derived demand curve for input i is downward sloping, the intersection of the derived demand curve with the marginal outlay curve occurs to the left of the intersection of the derived demand curve with the average outlay curve. Hence v_i^M is necessarily less than v_i^C, and w_i^M must also be less than w_i^C. Thus monopsony reduces the utilization of a factor and depresses the price received by the suppliers of the factor, compared with perfect competition in the factor market.

An interpretation of Eq. (13–25) is that, under monopsony, factor i is utilized up to the point where the marginal outlay for the factor equals the value of the marginal product or the marginal revenue product (depending upon whether the output is sold under competition or under monopoly). The corresponding result when factor i is purchased in a perfectly competitive market is that the factor is utilized up to the point where the price of the factor equals the value of the marginal product or the marginal revenue product (depending upon whether the output is sold under competition or under monopoly). It will be demonstrated in Chapter 20 that this difference between monopsony and perfect competition leads to an inefficient pattern of resource allocation for the economy as a whole whenever monopsony is present.

IV. Bilateral Monopoly and Bargaining

The existence of monopsony buying power may sometimes be partially or entirely negated by the existence of countervailing monopoly selling power. A market structure consisting of a monopsony buyer of a factor and a monopoly seller of the factor is called *bilateral monopoly*. When there are several buyers of the factor possessing oligopsony power confronting several sellers of the factor having oligopoly power, the market structure is called *bilateral oligopoly*. The general nature of the analysis which we present for bilateral monopoly also applies to bilateral oligopoly, but the specific details of solution and the range of uncertainty are even greater in bilateral oligopoly than they are in bilateral monopoly.

A graphical analysis is most convenient for examining bilateral monopoly. In Figure 13–6, D is the derived demand curve for the factor. As noted in the preceding section, D is either the value of the marginal product of the factor or the marginal revenue product of the factor, according to whether the final output is sold under conditions of perfect competition or monopoly. S is the relevant portion of the marginal cost curve of the monopoly seller of the factor. Although in Chapter 10 we showed that a monopoly has no supply curve, if a monopoly were constrained to sell at fixed prices (rather than where marginal cost equals marginal revenue), then the upward-sloping portion of the monopoly's marginal cost curve above its average

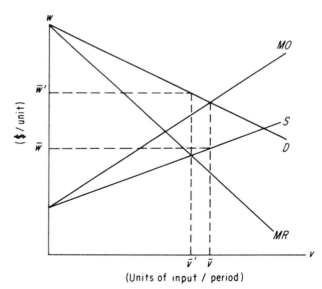

(Units of input / period)

FIGURE 13–6.   Bilateral monopoly.

variable cost curve would indicate the amounts that would be supplied. Thus when the monopoly power of the seller is ignored, S is the supply curve for the factor and MO is the monopsonist's marginal outlay curve for the factor.

For the moment, let us ignore the fact that the seller of the factor has monopoly power. Then the conventional monopsony solution is that $\bar{v}$ units of the factor would be purchased at a price $\bar{w}$ per unit, since the monopsonist's marginal outlay curve intersects his derived demand curve at $\bar{v}$, and the height of the average outlay curve at $\bar{v}$ is $\bar{w}$.

Now let us ignore the monopsony power of the buyer and consider only the monopoly power of the seller of the factor. D is the average revenue curve for the monopolist, and the corresponding marginal curve, MR, is the monopolist's marginal revenue curve. The intersection of this marginal revenue curve with his marginal cost curve, S, indicates that $\bar{v}'$ is the most profitable amount of factor for the monopolist to sell, at a price $\bar{w}'$.

Since there is only one buyer and one seller of the factor, they will have to reach some agreement about the factor price. There will be an inherent conflict in this bargaining situation, since we have shown that the monopsonist prefers a price $\bar{w}$, whereas the monopolist prefers a higher price $\bar{w}'$. It is impossible to determine the actual price that will be established without making assumptions about the bargaining strengths and skills of each firm. The actual position of the price within the possible range between $\bar{w}$ and $\bar{w}'$ provides a measure of the relative bargaining abilities of the

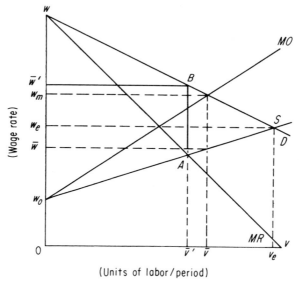

FIGURE 13–7. Effects of unionization on a monopsony.

monopsonist and the monopolist. Because it is possible to determine only a range of possible prices rather than a unique price which will prevail in bilateral monopoly, the solution to this type of market structure is said to be indeterminate.

The analysis of bilateral monopoly may provide some insights into the effects of labor unions on wage rates and employment levels. Some of the possible effects are illustrated in Figure 13–7. As a reference point, we suppose that initially there is a monopsony buyer of labor services confronting a large number of independent sellers of these services. The market supply curve of labor, S, is drawn positively sloping, indicating that a higher wage rate must be paid to obtain a larger quantity of labor. The monopsony solution is for the firm to hire $\bar{v}$ units of labor at a wage rate $\bar{w}$.

Now suppose that a union is organized and becomes the sole seller of labor services to the monopsonist. Assume that the union is powerful enough to enforce any wage rate that is established. This means that although there may be an excess supply of labor at the established wage rate, the unemployed workers are unable to obtain employment by their willingness to work at a lower wage rate.

The preceding analysis of bilateral monopoly suggests that $\bar{w}'$ is the wage rate the union would seek to establish, at which the level of employment would be $\bar{v}'$. This wage rate would maximize the difference between the total wages received by the employed workers and the total expenditures that would be required to provide that level of labor services if each unit of labor were purchased at exactly that rate necessary to bring it onto the market.[3] This difference is analogous to the profits of the monopoly seller of a factor in Figure 13–6.

The union may have other objectives, however.[4] If the union prefers to obtain the highest possible wage rate consistent with the initial level of employment $\bar{v}$, then it would attempt to establish the wage rate w_m. If the union prefers to obtain the highest possible level of employment, then it would attempt to establish the wage rate w_e. If the supply curve of labor is in fact positively sloping, then the union would never seek a wage rate lower than w_e, since on the basis of the derived demand curve for labor the firm can afford to pay at least that wage rate for any quantity of labor that it can employ.

---

[3] In Figure 13–7, the total wages received by the employed workers are represented by the area $\bar{w}'B\bar{v}'0$. The total wages demanded to provide an amount $\bar{v}'$ of labor services (i.e., the total of the minimum offer prices) is represented by the area $w_0A\bar{v}'0$. Therefore the difference between these two areas is the area $\bar{w}'BAw_0$. No wage rate other than $\bar{w}'$ can provide a larger area determined in an equivalent manner.

[4] For an extended discussion of other possible union objectives, see John T. Dunlop, *Wage Determination under Trade Unions* (New York: The Macmillan Company, 1944) pp. 32–44.

Whatever the objective of the union may be, the firm still wishes to establish a wage rate as close to $\bar{w}$ as possible, in order to obtain some monopsony profits. The actual wage rate that will be established as a result of the bargaining process is indeterminate, depending upon the relative bargaining ability of the two sides. Our analysis shows. however, that the introduction of a labor union into a previously monopsonized labor market may possibly result in a higher level of employment as well as in a higher wage rate.

V. Discrimination in the Factor Markets

In addition to the types of factor market imperfections which stem from the existence of monopsony or oligopsony power, market imperfections in the real world may arise from discrimination based on noneconomic considerations. The treatment of this type of discriminatory behavior was first formalized by Becker.[5]

Becker's approach to economic discrimination is characterized by the concept of a *discrimination coefficient* (*DC*). This serves to modify actual market prices so that the result reflects the combined economic and psychic costs to the discriminator of a potential transaction. If an employer, because of his own prejudice, discriminates against a particular group of potential employees (e.g., members of some minority group), then the combined economic and psychic costs to that employer of hiring these employees would be $w(1 + d_i)$, where w is the money wage rate paid for employees of this type and d_i is the employer's *DC* against this type of employee. If $d_i > 0$, the employer is *prejudiced against* this type of employee; if $d_i < 0$, the employer shows *favoritism toward* this type of employee.

Suppose that B and W are two different groups of employees. We consider the employees to be homogeneous within each group, although there may be real differences between the groups. Let v_B and v_W be the amounts of labor employed from these two groups by a firm, and let w_B and w_W be the money wage rates paid to members of each group.

In determining the optimal mix of inputs for a discriminating employer, Becker assumes that the employer defines the total cost function in terms of the combined monetary and psychic production costs. If d_B and d_W are the employer's *DC*'s against workers from groups B and W, then the combined costs of using v_B and v_W units of labor from each group are

$$TC = w_B(1 + d_B)v_B + w_W(1 + d_W)v_W + A. \qquad (13\text{--}30)$$

By introducing a one-output, two-input production function as a constraint and finding the mix of inputs which minimizes Eq. (13–30), the

---

[5] Gary S. Becker, *The Economics of Discrimination* (Chicago: University of Chicago Press, 1957).

amounts of labor which will be hired from each group can be determined by the type of analysis used in Chapter 7 and in Section II of this chapter. Assume that the employer discriminates more against workers from group B than from group W—that is, that $d_B > d_W$. Then it can be shown that workers from group B are not employed to the point where the value of their marginal product equals their wage rate. Workers from group.W are employed beyond the point where the value of their marginal product equals their wage rate. The conclusion which emerges from Becker's model is that discriminatory behavior by an employer will alter both the relative and absolute levels of resource utilization and the amounts of final products which are produced.

Becker has shown that an extended version of his model can provide insights on the mechanisms and extent of economic discrimination against blacks in the United States. He concludes

> ... that tastes for discrimination would produce—via the workings of a competitive economic system—effective discrimination against Negroes. There is evidence not only that effective discrimination occurs against Negroes but also that [the amount of discrimination in the market place] is quite large. Negroes in the United States have owned an extremely small amount of capital, while whites have had a more balanced distribution of resources; a substantial decline in the amount of white capital available to Negroes would greatly reduce the absolute and relative incomes of Negroes. [6]

Becker provides some rough estimates of the economic loss to blacks and whites in the United States which results from market discrimination. He warns that these estimates are highly tentative, because they depend upon assumptions about the actual quantity of discrimination, the nature of the production functions, and the amounts of labor and capital supplied by these groups. Becker's results indicate that discrimination in the market place by whites against blacks reduces black incomes by approximately 13 per cent. Viewed in another way, this means that the average black income would increase by about 16 per cent if market discrimination were to cease. Because whites gain relatively little from trading with blacks, Becker estimates that discrimination reduces the incomes of whites by a fairly small amount.

Because of the uneven distribution of resources, even if there were no market discrimination against blacks the per capita income of blacks in the United States would be only about 66 per cent of the per capita income of whites. With complete segregation (i.e., no white capital employed with black labor) black per capita income would average about 39 per cent of the white per capita income.

Becker estimates that the actual amount of discrimination in the United States causes the equilibrium per capita black income level to be approx-

---

[6] *Ibid.*, pp. 19–20.

imately 57 per cent of the per capita white income in the United States. This estimate falls within the 39 per cent to 66 per cent range stated in the preceding paragraph. "White labor and Negro labor lose from it; but, since the net loss of Negroes is greater than that of whites, total market discrimination occurs against Negroes."[7]

Becker's analysis shows that substantial market discrimination against blacks in the United States could easily result from the manner in which individual tastes for discrimination influence the allocation of resources within a competitive, free-enterprise economy. There is no need to assume that political discrimination, monopolies or other forms of market imperfections, or social class warfare are the causes of discrimination in this country. Although these may be secondary determinants of market discrimination, Becker concludes that the primary determinant is the result of individual tastes for discrimination within a competitive economy.

VI. Summary

There are several types of imperfect factor markets. A *monopsony* is a market in which there is only one purchaser of a factor. An *oligopsony* is a market in which there are a small number of purchasers of a factor. The crucial feature of these types of factor market imperfections is the dependence of purchase price on the quantity of a factor purchased by a firm. The factor supply curve which a monopsonist faces is upward sloping. The corresponding marginal outlay curve lies above the factor supply curve in an imperfect factor market.

In determining the optimal mix of inputs when a firm purchases some or all of these inputs in imperfect factor markets, the dependence of purchase price on the quantity used of a factor must be recognized. This means that in solving the constrained minimization problem involved in determining the lowest-cost method for producing a stated amount of output, the prices of the factors must be treated as variables rather than as constants. The nature of the optimal input mix was first explored using a one-output, two-input production function which was analyzed graphically. The isocost curves were shown to be negatively sloping and concave to the origin. The point of tangency between an isoproduct curve and some isocost curve represents the most efficient combination of input factors for producing a specified level of output. The prices paid can then be determined by substituting the indicated amounts of inputs in the supply curves. Using mathematical analysis to derive the optimal mix of inputs for the more general production function with N inputs, we showed that the marginal outlay on each factor should be proportional to its marginal productivity, the factor of proportionality being marginal cost.

---

[7] *Ibid.*, pp. 21.

We next considered the effects of factor market imperfections on a firm's utilization of resources. These effects are the same whether the firm sells its output under conditions of monopoly or perfect competition. The existence of monopsony leads to the utilization of a smaller amount of the factor at a lower purchase price than would be the case under a perfectly competitive factor market. Under monopsony, any factor is utilized up to the point where the marginal outlay for the factor equals the value of the marginal product or the marginal revenue product (depending upon the nature of the product market). When a factor market is perfectly competitive, the factor is utilized up to the point where the price of the factor equals the value of the marginal product or the marginal revenue product. This difference between monopsony and perfect competition leads to an inefficient pattern of resource allocation from the viewpoint of the economy as a whole whenever monopsony is present.

Bilateral monopoly is a market structure consisting of a monopsony buyer of a factor confronting a monopoly seller of that factor. The price which will be established in such a market is indeterminate on the basis of conventional economic analysis, since the monopsonist prefers one price and the monopolist prefers a higher price. The relative bargaining abilities of the two parties will determine where within the possible range the actual price will be established. The bilateral monopoly analysis was applied to bargaining over wage rates between a firm and its union. We observed that the preferred wage rate for the union depends upon the nature of its goals. Whatever its exact goals, however, the union will attempt to establish a higher wage rate than the firm wishes to grant. Instead of a unique solution, there is a range established within which the actual wage rate will fall. Without adding a theory of bargaining behavior to the analysis of bilateral monopoly, it is impossible to remove the indeterminateness of the wage rate in this situation. Our analysis did show, however, that, when a union is introduced into a previously monopsonized labor market, it may be possible for the union to obtain a higher level of employment as well as a higher wage rate.

To conclude this chapter, we briefly reviewed Becker's analysis of factor market imperfections which arise from discrimination against members of a minority group. A discrimination coefficient is used to modify actual market prices to indicate the combined economic and psychic costs to a discriminator of a market transaction. Becker has shown that discriminatory behavior by an employer alters both the relative and absolute levels of resource utilization and the amounts of final products which are produced. Becker extended this type of analysis to show that discrimination against blacks in the United States may be produced by individual tastes for discrimination within a competitive economy. Whites lose relatively little economically from this discrimination, but the economic loss to blacks is substantial.

SUGGESTED READINGS

These recommendations are in addition to the footnote references cited in this chapter.

ADELMAN, M. A., "Steel, Administered Prices and Inflation," *Quarterly Journal of Economics*, LXXV, No. 1 (February, 1961), 16–40.

BISH, R. L., AND P. D. O'DONOGHUE, "A Neglected Issue in Public Goods Theory: The Monopsony Problem," *Journal of Political Economy*, LXXVIII (November/December, 1970), 1367–71.

CARTTER, ALLAN M., *Theory of Wages and Employment*, chaps. 5–6. Homewood, Ill.: Richard D. Irwin, Inc., 1959.

KELLEY, WILLIAM T., "Specification Buying by the Large-Scale Retailer," *Journal of Marketing*, XVIII, No. 3 (January, 1954), 255–65.

MALKIEL, B. G., AND J. A. MALKIEL, "Male-Female Pay Differentials in Professional Employment," *American Economic Review*, LXIII (September, 1973), 693–705.

MEYERS, FREDERIC, "Price Theory and Union Monopoly," *Industrial and Labor Relations Review*, XII (April, 1959), 434–45. (Also see the comment on this paper by J. R. O'Connor and the reply by Meyers, *ibid.*, XIII [October, 1959], 90–95.)

Part 3

New Approaches to the
Theory of the Firm

Chapter Fourteen

Decision Making for an Uncertain Future

The analysis of microeconomics assumes rational behavior by individual economic agents. The usefulness of this analysis for answering questions involving the allocation of resources among broad economic sectors, such as markets or industries, does not necessarily depend upon the extent to which consumers actually do maximize their utilities and business firms actually do maximize their profits. We saw in Chapter 2 that even though the assumptions of a model may not be exact and complete representations of reality, if they are realistic enough for the purposes of the analysis, then we may be able to derive from them conclusions which are applicable to the world.

So far in this book we have primarily formulated models of rational economic behavior within the context of a static and certain world. It is now time to consider the extent to which the results we presented remain broadly applicable to the real world even though we admit that economic agents do not necessarily always behave rationally, and that they must make decisions over many time periods under changing conditions in the absence of complete certainty. In this chapter we shall consider some alternative models for decision making. These models in varying degrees relax the assumptions of rational behavior in a static, certain world.

I. General Characterization of Decision Problems

In order to provide a framework which will enable us to contrast our previous analyses of rational behavior in a static world of certainty with the alternative models of economic decision making which are developed in this chapter, it is useful to characterize in relatively abstract terms the general features which are common to all decision problems.[1] Whenever an economic agent is faced with a decision problem, the following elements will all be present:

1. There is a set of two or more *possible behavior alternatives* which represents the range of different decisions which an economic agent can conceivably make.

2. There is a set of two or more *behavior alternatives that the economic agent actually considers*. These alternatives will generally be discovered as a result of overt search behavior by the agent. The search behavior may discover only a subset of the set of possible behavior alternatives specified in (1), although in some decision problems the set of behavior alternatives actually considered may coincide with the set of possible behavior alternatives.

3. There is a set of two or more possible future states of affairs which represent the *possible outcomes* which can conceivably result from the economic agent's actions in this decision situation. At this time we will not specify whether the outcomes exist objectively or whether they exist subjectively in the mind of the economic agent.

4. There is a *pay-off function* which represents the subjective value or the utility which the economic agent places upon each possible future state of affairs. This pay-off function defines a partial ordering on the set of possible future states of affairs. In some cases, the pay-off function may be represented by a cardinal function, in other cases, by an ordinal function.

5. The economic agent possesses some degree of *information about which of the possible outcomes may actually occur* if he chooses any particular behavior alternative. This information may either be complete, in which case each of the agent's behavior alternatives will correspond to a unique outcome; or this information may be incomplete, in which case there is at

---

[1] This general characterization of decision problems was developed by Herbert A. Simon, "A Behavioral Model of Rational Choice," *Quarterly Journal of Economics*, 69 (1955), 99–118. This article is reprinted in Herbert A. Simon, *Models of Man: Social and Rational* (New York: John Wiley & Sons, Inc., 1957).

least one behavior alternative to which there correspond two or more possible outcomes. When this information is incomplete, there may be *information as to the probability that a particular outcome will occur* if the economic agent selects a particular alternative.

These five characteristics can be conveniently summarized. A decision problem exists only when there are at least two different alternative courses of action among which the economic agent must choose. These alternative courses of action must be different not only in that they represent different choices by the agent, but also in that they might conceivably result in different outcomes. The alternative courses of action which are discovered by the economic agent may be narrower than the action alternatives which actually exist. Each course of action the agent might take corresponds to one or more outcomes. The agent may possess varying degrees of information about this correspondence. Finally, there is some pay-off function which orders the possible outcomes according to the agent's preferences.

II. Classification of Economic Decision Models

We can characterize a variety of economic decision models in terms of the five preceding characteristics. To start with, decision models may be either *static* or *dynamic.* If the alternative courses of action among which the economic agent must choose and the possible future states of affairs which might result all pertain to a single time period, and if the pay-off function which defines the agent's preference ordering on the set of outcomes depends only upon events of this same time period, then the decision model is static. In contrast, if both the alternative courses of action and the possible resulting outcomes involve considerations pertaining to more than one time period, then the decision model is dynamic.[2]

A second dimension according to which economic decision models can be classified is the type of information possessed by the economic agent about the correspondence between the alternative courses of action he might take and the states of affairs which will result. Depending upon the type of information that is assumed, we have models of *certainty, objective risk, subjective risk,* or *uncertainty.* In a certainty model it is assumed that the economic agent possesses complete information which relates a unique outcome to an alternative course of action.

In the absence of certainty, multiple outcomes may result from at least some actions the decision maker can take. If the agent is able on an ob-

[2] This usage of the terms *static* and *dynamic* follows that of J. R. Hicks, *Value and Capital,* 2nd ed. (London: Oxford University Press, 1946), p. 115: "I call Economic Statics those parts of economic theory where we do not trouble about dating; Economic Dynamics those parts where every quantity must be dated." According to this definition, a dynamic decision model would be a theory of how economic agents make decisions in a changing world; it would not necessarily be a theory of how the world changes.

jective basis to compute the probability that a particular outcome will result if any given action is taken, then the decision model is an objective risk model. When the economic agent has no objective basis for determining these probabilities but nevertheless feels that he knows them, then the decision model is a subjective risk model. Finally, if the economic agent is unwilling or unable to formulate, either on objective or subjective grounds, the probabilities that specific outcomes will correspond to particular actions, but instead is able only to indicate the range of outcomes which might follow from any action, then the decision model is an uncertainty model.[3]

The final criterion used in classifying the various types of economic decision models is the degree of rationality in the behavior of the economic agent. There are three types: *objectively rational, subjectively rational,* or *nonrational* models. Either of the first two models assumes that the economic agent chooses that course of action from the discovered alternatives which maximizes the value of his pay-off function.[4] If the set of discovered alternatives from which the best action is chosen is the set of all possible behavior alternatives, then the model is objectively rational. If the set of discovered alternatives from which this "best" action is chosen is a subset of all possible behavior alternatives, then the model is subjectively rational.[5] In contrast, the agent's behavior will be called nonrational if he selects an action from among the discovered alternatives which does not maximize his pay-off function.

Each of the three dimensions used to classify economic decision models, namely the time dimension, the degree of information dimension, and the degree of rationality dimension, represent independent considerations which can be combined in twenty-four different ways. There are two different time models (static or dynamic), four different information models (certainty, objective risk, subjective risk, or uncertainty), and three different rationality models (objective rationality, subjective rationality, or nonrationality). The economic decision model on which most of the analysis in this book has been based is a static, certainty, objectively rational model. For

---

[3] Sometimes the word "uncertainty" is used to refer to any noncertainty type of decision situation, instead of in the narrower sense defined here. The title of this chapter, "Decision Making for an Uncertain Future," uses the word "uncertain" in this broader sense. The distinction between risk and uncertainty in terms of whether the probabilities of the alternative outcomes are known (or at least can be estimated) was developed by Frank H. Knight, *Risk, Uncertainty and Profit* (Boston: Houghton Mifflin Company, 1921; reprinted by the London School of Economics, Reprints of Scarce Tracts in Economics Series No. 16, 1933).

[4] In the absence of certainty, the pay-off function must be of a type which establishes preference orderings between "outcome bundles" to which either probability distributions or ranges of possibility are attached. We shall see later some of the ways in which this might be done.

[5] In some cases, subjectively rational and objectively rational behavior may coincide, as when the set of discovered and possible behavior alternatives is the same.

the remainder of this chapter we shall consider several alternative economic decision models which can be formulated.

III. The Role of Anticipations and Plans in Economic Decision Making[6]

We can draw a distinction between two different types of economic variables: *ex ante* variables and *ex post* variables. *Ex ante* variables are *anticipated* future actions of economic agents or *anticipated* future states of the economic environment. In contrast, *ex post* variables are *actual* actions of economic agents or *actual* states of the economic environment. This distinction between *ex ante* and *ex post* variables is the distinction between subjective expectations and objective realizations. Thus we can speak of past *ex ante* variables, which are anticipations and plans held at any point in the past.

Ex ante variables can be classified as (a) anticipations or forecasts, and (b) decisions and plans. Anticipations relate to the future course of variables outside the direct control of the agent; they include forecasts of prices, demand conditions, availability of labor, population, general business activity, etc. Decisions and plans relate to the future course of action of the agent himself; they include production schedules, budgets, investment programs, etc. Whenever we use the words "expectations" or "*ex ante* variables," we intend to refer to anticipations as well as to decisions and plans.

A. REVIEW OF THE STATIC CERTAINTY MODEL OF ECONOMIC DECISION MAKING

The traditional static certainty model which we have hitherto used to analyze the effects of decisions by consumers and business firms on the marketwide allocation of resources is of little value in analyzing the role that expectations play in economic decision making. Anticipations and plans play no role in the model, since the variables all pertain to the same time period. In a static, certainty model the problem of the economic agent is typically visualized as that of choosing a single course of action from an available set of alternatives. A course of action is determined by specifying a particular value for each of a number of variables. Not just any set of values may be chosen, however, because the variables are subject to certain constraints which may be broadly classified as demand constraints, supply constraints, budget constraints, and transformation or production-function constraints. The specific form of these constraints is determined both by

---

[6] The material in this section is largely drawn from Franco Modigliani and Kalman J. Cohen, "The Role of Anticipations and Plans in Economic Behavior and Their Use in Economic Analysis and Forecasting," *Studies in Business Expectations and Planning*, No. 4 (Urbana: University of Illinois, Bureau of Economic and Business Research, 1961), pp. 12–26. Extensive excerpts from these pages have been paraphrased or reproduced verbatim in this section.

the physical and by the social environment, including the behavior of other units. Among the alternatives open, the economic agent is supposed to choose the one most conducive to the achievement of his goal. This goal is generally assumed to be for firms the maximization of profit, which is regarded as a known function of the possible values of the decision variables, and for households the maximization of utility, which is similarly regarded.

The static model provides an explanation of a wide range of phenomena. It is, however, quite inadequate as an explanation of anticipatory and planning activity and many other features of observed behavior, including such phenomena as the holding of terminal inventories of goods or money, the existence of debt, and the expenditure of resources to create "good will." In order to understand such phenomena, economists have developed dynamic models. The starting point of such models is the assumption that decision makers recognize that their present actions may influence the conditions which will confront them in the future.

In reality the current actions of consumers and businessmen are influenced by awareness that the future is uncertain and that the future is relevant. It is possible to examine the implications of each of these considerations separately. Thus the effects of uncertainty *per se* on behavior can be studied by a static, uncertainty model in which some of the constraints facing the decision maker are of a stochastic nature. With stochastic constraints any course of action may correspond to a set of mutually exclusive outcomes with varying degrees of likelihood rather than to a certain unique outcome. A model incorporating such constraints may explain *some* important aspects of economic behavior which cannot be accounted for by the static certainty model.

Similarly, the fact that the future is relevant may be analyzed by assuming that the future is known with certainty. Such an analysis shows that *other* important aspects of behavior can be explained by a dynamic certainty model. Thus whether or not uncertainty has to be introduced explicitly into the analysis depends on the kinds of behavior we are interested in explaining. If the behavior in question can be understood without the complications of uncertainty, it is better not to introduce uncertainty since a simpler model is always preferable to a more complicated model.

B. Hick's Dynamic Theory of the Firm

Hicks has developed a dynamic model of entrepreneurial decision making under certainty which is a generalization of the static model.[7] Just as in the static theory, the firm chooses the course of action which maximizes the value of its pay-off function. This pay-off function depends upon both the future and the current actions of the firm.

It is convenient to divide the prospective history of a firm into discrete time periods, say T in number. Since the life span of a corporate firm is

---

[7] Hicks, *op. cit.*, especially chaps. 9, 15.

potentially unlimited, T may be an indefinitely large number. To preserve in a clear fashion the useful distinction between present and future, we regard only the first one of the T time intervals as "the present", whereas the remaining $T - 1$ periods comprise "the future." We refer to T as the *horizon* at date zero, where "date zero" denotes the beginning of the first period.

During each of the T intervals, the firm decides on some course of action. This decision corresponds to assigning numerical values to a set of components, which we call the firm's *decision variables*, for that period. We call the action carried out by the firm in any period its *move* in that period. The implementation of the firm's decision consists in making effective the numerical values assigned by the firm to all of its decision variables for that period.

There are a large number of different courses of action which the firm can choose over the entire horizon, and the firm is not indifferent about the consequences of choosing different paths. The Hicksian model assumes that the firm has a well-defined set of goals in terms of which it is able to decide when it prefers the results which follow from one course of action to the consequences resulting from another pattern of behavior. This set of goals is summarized in terms of the firm's "payoff function." The value of the pay-off function depends upon the particular moves chosen by the firm during each time period comprising the horizon, and it is assumed that the firm attempts to maximize its pay-off function. In the Hicksian model, the pay-off function is the present value of profits over the horizon.[8]

As in the static analysis, the firm's decision variables are subject to demand, supply, and transformation constraints. In the Hicksian formulation, which is basically built on assumptions of perfect competition, the demand and supply constraints merely state that the purchase or selling price of each commodity is equal to some constant entirely outside the firm's control, i.e., completely determined by the environment, and the transformation conditions take the form of a *single* constraint relating the inputs and outputs of every period. These very special assumptions can, however, be considerably broadened without affecting the essence of the model. The basic points to keep in mind are that the decision variables are subject to various constraints, and that the constraints relating to the variables of *future* periods are largely determined by the *future* behavior of the environment.

From this formulation, and by exact analogy to the static case, Hicks draws the conclusion that the decision problem confronting the firm at any given point of time is the selection of the entire best course of action over

---

[8] In other models of the firm the pay-off function may be more general than assumed in the Hicksian model. The only properties required of the pay-off function are that it be a partial ordering of prospective histories of the firm according to the decision maker's preferences.

the horizon. "Just as the static problem of the enterprise is the selection of a certain set of quantities of factors and products, so *the dynamic problem is the selection of a certain production plan* from the alternatives that are open";[9] and again, " ... the decision which confronts any particular entrepreneur at any date ... may be regarded as the establishment of a *production plan*."[10] In other words, the firm is assumed to solve a T-period constrained maximization problem and determine the optimal values of all components of all moves over the entire horizon. Solving this constrained maximization problem requires knowing the specific form of every future constraint. The firm acts in the first period in accordance with the solution obtained for the components of the first move. The remaining portion of the solution, the values assigned to the components of the last $T - 1$ moves, represents the *plan* for future operations.

Thus on the basis of the Hicksian analysis, we would expect to find that firms at all times have explicit plans—formal or informal—covering at least the major aspects of their operations over some definite horizon, and that underlying these plans are definite estimates of the parameters of all future constraints over the horizon. These implications are definitely not supported by available empirical evidence. This is not surprising, for even introspection and casual observation suggest that economic agents do not generally behave in the way implied by the Hicksian model. One possible explanation is that the empirical evidence relates to a world of uncertainty, and the existence of uncertainty tends to shorten considerably the horizon over which it is useful to formulate anticipations and plans. Although this explanation may have some validity, it is far from complete. It may be pointed out, for instance, that plans seldom cover every aspect of operations even for the very near future, whereas, with respect to some aspects of operations, plans may extend fairly far into the future, being supported by definite anticipations about future conditions. Similarly uncertainty *per se* appears inadequate to account for various other observed aspects of the planning and anticipation horizon. Another possible explanation is that actual behavior cannot adequately be accounted for in terms of a model which assumes rational behavior on the part of business firms, as does the Hicksian model.

C. The Decision Problem of the Firm as the Selection of the "Best" First Move

We propose to show that many important aspects of anticipatory and planning behavior can, in fact, be adequately understood and analyzed within the basic framework of the Hicksian model of rational decision making under certainty. To do this, however, we are required to make some

---

[9] Hicks, *op. cit.*, p. 194 (italics ours).
[10] *Ibid.*, p. 193.

relatively minor modifications of the basic assumptions in the direction of greater "realism" and to adopt a major change of viewpoint.

1. REVISIONS OF THE HICKSIAN MODEL. The assumption of certainty usually involves, explicitly or implicitly, the notion that information about the future is single-valued, is known to be correct, and is "inborn" in the agent or can be acquired and exploited by him without significant cost or effort. We propose to modify this assumption in three major directions:

(a) Although we continue to regard anticipations as single-valued, we assume that the agent recognizes that his single-valued expectations are not entirely reliable, i.e., they may turn out to be wrong.

(b) We further recognize that at a particular date, more reliable information about the future can be acquired only at the cost of devoting scarce resources to this task. The cost of acquiring this information decreases as the future draws nearer.

(c) We recognize that problem solving, decision making, and planning are all costly activities, since they absorb scarce resources. These activities, therefore, should be avoided unless the expected return from them is greater than their cost.

Let us next consider the suggested change of viewpoint. We must first note that in the Hicksian analysis, the analogy between the dynamic and the static problems is carried one step too far. It is perfectly true that in terms of the pay-off function the single current move of the static model is replaced by the entire set of moves over the horizon, but it does not necessarily follow that, as in the static model, the firm must choose now its entire course of action. The only choice that *must* be made at a given point of time (such as date zero) and which *cannot* be postponed is the choice of the first move.[11] We suggest, therefore, that the decision problem confronting the entrepreneur at a given point of time is most usefully regarded not as that of selecting the best possible plan of operations over the horizon, but, rather, as that of *selecting only the best possible first move.* By "best possible" we mean, of course, the move that is best, not merely with reference to the first period, as though it were the only period, but with reference to the entire constrained maximization problem over the horizon. We suggest that the entrepreneur's proper concern is the determination and the enforcement of the first-move components belonging to the optimal course of action over the firm's entire prospective history.

It is evident that this way of viewing the firm's decision problem is operationally feasible, since the choice of the first move is the only decision that *must* be made at date zero. In order to make this choice optimally, the firm may have to consider some aspects of the future. The firm must take into account the manner in which its first move will affect future constraints.

---

[11] Note that our concept of "move" is broad enough to include any failure to act as itself being part of the move that is made.

2. THE NATURE OF THE DYNAMIC CONSTRAINTS—RELEVANT AND IR-RELEVANT ANTICIPATIONS. To understand the relationship between the first move and future constraints, it is useful to examine the nature of these constraints. Consider, for example, the constraints on the firm's move in period t. These constraints consist, in part, of demand, supply, and production functions. As seen at the beginning of period t, these constraints depend upon both initial conditions—size and location of plants, state of productive facilities, established connections in buying and selling markets, inventories in the hands of customers, etc.—and the behavior of the environment during the course of period t—general business conditions, competitors' behavior, consumer incomes, etc. It is clear that these initial conditions are in part the results of the firm's own moves in previous periods.

These considerations indicate why a firm may have to form anticipations about some aspects of the future in order to make an optimal choice of the first move. If some components of the first move enter directly or indirectly into some future constraint, and thus limit the firm's future freedom of action, then the optimum value of the first move may depend on the specific form of that constraint, or, as we shall say hereafter, upon the parameters of that constraint. When this is the case, we say that these parameters are *relevant* as of date zero.

We can also see, however, why at date zero it may not be necessary to consider some aspects of the future. Suppose, for example, that the components of the first move, whatever values they might take, do not affect the freedom of choice with respect to some components of, say, the tth move. Then any constraint involving only these later components is of no relevance for deciding the first move—that is, the constraints and the parameters thereof can be said to be *irrelevant* as of date zero.

The concepts of relevance and irrelevance introduced in the preceding two paragraphs can be usefully formalized as follows: An "aspect of the future"—or more specifically, a future constraint or a parameter thereof—is irrelevant as of date zero if the optimum value of the first move is the same, no matter what might be the specific form of the constraint (or the specific value of the parameter). Anticipations relating to irrelevant constraints or parameters are called irrelevant anticipations.

It follows from our formulation of the decision problem that the firm *need not* estimate totally irrelevant parameters at date zero. From our assumption that the cost of obtaining information about conditions in a future time period decreases as that period draws near, it further follows that at date zero the firm *should not* devote scarce resources to this task.[12]

---

[12] A parameter is *totally* irrelevant if it is irrelevant no matter what its value might turn out to be; it is *conditionally* irrelevant when it is irrelevant provided that its value falls within some stated range. If a parameter is conditionally irrelevant, then no more effort should be devoted to estimating it than is required to ascertain that the conditions for irrelevance are satisfied.

In order to illustrate the selective nature of relevant anticipations, a number of examples can be constructed in which aspects of the future which are obviously relevant to the choice of some moves are still irrelevant as of date zero, since they do not affect the *first* move. We shall only summarize here some of the major features and implications of these examples.[13]

An obvious situation in which the relevant horizon does not extend beyond the current period is one characterized by a Hicksian-type pay-off function and constraints that are independent of earlier decisions. A reasonable approximation to this type of situation is a firm dealing in a nonstorable commodity which must be produced (or purchased) and disposed of within the same period in a perfectly competitive market and employing little fixed capital. If the pay-off function is of the Hicksian type, decisions within each period depend exclusively on actual and anticipated conditions within that period. Knowledge about conditions in future periods is of little value, since such knowledge does not lead to current decisions different from those taken in its absence.

Situations in which commodities cannot be stored are rare with present-day technology. True, the possibility of storage may make the future relevant, but this is not always the case. This point is illustrated by a simple example involving a two-period problem. Consider a firm producing a single product. Its marginal cost is constant in each period, but not necessarily the same in the two periods. In each period the quantity demanded depends only on the price in that period, although the position of the demand curve may be different in each period. Suppose that the product can be carried over from the first period to the next at a constant storage cost per unit. It can readily be seen that as long as the second-period marginal cost is no larger than the first-period marginal cost plus the storage cost, then the optimum course of action is to produce no more in the first period than can be profitably sold in this period—*regardless* of the demand conditions of the second period. Hence the parameters of the second-period demand curve are irrelevant, and the only relevant information about the second-period marginal cost is that it does not exceed the first-period marginal cost plus the storage cost.

The third illustration allows a T-period horizon, where T can be indefinitely large. The problem considered is scheduling the production of a commodity in such a way that the quantity demanded in each of the T periods is provided at the lowest possible total cost over the horizon. It can be shown that even if storage were costless, unless demand is expected to exhibit forever a steadily increasing trend, there will be some date t such that the actual demand beyond t is irrelevant. The presence of storage tends to shrink the relevant horizon. In particular, if demand exhibits seasonal variation, then at any point within a given seasonal cycle, the

---

[13] The interested reader can find the full details of these examples in Modigliani and Cohen, *op. cit.*, pp. 36–42.

relevant horizon extends to the peak of the given cycle or shortly beyond it. All further seasonal cycles are irrelevant. This result agrees with certain characteristics of observed planning and anticipations horizons; namely, that the length of the horizon is frequently a periodic function of time, linked with the seasonal cycle.

In general, the length of the relevant horizon may itself depend on certain strategic parameters. In particular, there are a number of considerations which suggest that the relevant horizon may tend to grow when economic activity is high and expected to rise.

3. THE NATURE OF PLANNING ACTIVITY. If there are components of future moves which have the property that no matter what their optimum values are, the best first move is the same, then these components are *irrelevant components* as of date zero. All remaining components of future moves are relevant at date zero. *Irrelevant plans* are plans relating to irrelevant components. The firm should not devote scarce resources to making irrelevant plans.

What does relevance of a component imply with respect to the advisability of planning, i.e., selecting a value for the component at date zero? Our fundamental proposition that the problem of the firm is ·to select the best first move might seem to imply that no components of future moves are worth planning, even if the components are relevant. A number of considerations, however, suggest that this conclusion is not warranted and help us understand why relevant components will frequently—although not necessarily—be worth explicit planning. In essence, relevant components are interrelated with the components of the current move, in the sense that the optimal values of these various components depend on each other. Stated in more formal terms, the constrained maximization problem that needs to be solved in selecting the first move involves finding the solution to a system of simultaneous relations. Relevant components— in contrast to irrelevant ones—appear as variables in this system of simultaneous relations. All the information required to solve for the relevant future components is already available at no extra cost, since it is required in the solution for the first move. Furthermore, once a system has been solved for some of its unknowns, the remaining ones can frequently be computed at a low marginal cost. Finally—and this is probably the most important consideration from the empirical point of view—the most economical or "natural" way of solving for the first move may well involve solving first for certain components of future moves. Indeed the promulgation of a plan may be a convenient way of providing information to various parts of an organization as to what actions they are expected to take in the current period.

We may conclude, therefore, that relevant components of future moves may be worth explicit planning for two reasons. First, they may be a by-product of the most convenient way of solving the first-period decision problem. Second, the marginal cost of making these plans is not large; although part of the plan may eventually be discarded, the value of the rest of the plan may still be greater than the cost of making it explicit. We must remember, however, that plans are not decisions about the future course of action. Decisions refer to planned moves not subject to replanning, and therefore only to components of the current or first move. Plans should preferably be regarded as representing the best forecast that can be made by the firm at date zero about the values that certain components of future moves will eventually take; this forecast is made for the purpose of deciding the *first* move, *not* for the purpose of deciding *later* moves.

IV. Decision Making under Conditions of Subjective Risk

A model of subjective risk assumes that a decision maker can attach probabilities to the various possible outcomes which may result from a particular course of action. To develop such models we need to determine how a decision maker evaluates outcomes which are less than certain but to which he can attach probability beliefs. Given a scheme of evaluation for these outcome bundles, we then assume that the decision maker chooses that action leading to the most preferred outcome bundle. Unfortunately there is no single model of rational behavior under conditions of subjective risk to which all economists subscribe. We shall, however, outline a model, based on *expected utility maximization*, which we believe has potential significance.

Starting from some basic postulates of rational behavior, the expected utility maximization model shows (a) that the information available to the decision maker concerning an uncertain event—such as the value of an unknown parameter—can be represented by a subjective probability distribution, (b) that there exists a (cardinal) utility function such that the decision maker acts as though he were endeavoring to maximize the expected value of his utility.[14] To illustrate the applicability of this model, we shall consider a particular decision: whether it is worthwhile to pay the necessary cost to determine the actual value of a relevant parameter.

We must now regard the pay-off function as a cardinal measure of utility. When uncertain about the value of one or more relevant parameters, it is assumed that the decision maker chooses the course of action that maximizes the expected value of the pay-off. For this purpose, it is necessary to include in the pay-off function the cost of obtaining information.

The decision maker's payoff, if he incurs the cost to obtain information about the parameter's value, is a function of the actual value of the parameter. Before actually acquiring the information, the decision maker can compute only an expected pay-off based on his subjective probability

[14] For an elaboration of these postulates see L. J. Savage, *The Foundations of Statistics* (New York: John Wiley & Sons, 1954), pp. 27–67.

distribution. This calculation considers all possible values of the parameter, the corresponding optimal actions, and the likelihood that each of these parameter values will be realized. He then compares the expected pay-off which is based on his incurring the cost of obtaining information with the expected pay-off which assumes he does not incur the cost (or benefits from) obtaining the information. On the basis of this comparison, the decision maker determines whether the information is worth the cost of obtaining it.

To make these somewhat abstract ideas more concrete, consider a specific decision problem facing a monopolist. Suppose that his total cost function is

$$TC(q) = 90q + 25 \qquad (14\text{–}1)$$

and that his demand function is

$$p = 100 - \frac{B}{2} q. \qquad (14\text{–}2)$$

The monopolist does not know the actual value of B, but he has a subjective probability distribution which indicates that the probability is $\frac{1}{2}$ that B equals 1 and the probability is $\frac{1}{2}$ that B equals 0.5.

Assuming that the monopolist's utility function is equivalent to his profit function and that the cost of determining the exact value of B is 10, we can apply the subjective risk model outlined earlier to solve the monopolist's problem. Let us first consider the monopolist's optimal output if he does not determine the exact value of B. The profit function is

$$\pi = \left(100 - \frac{B}{2}q\right) q - 90q - 25 = 10 q - \frac{B}{2} q^2 - 25. \qquad (14\text{–}3)$$

The expected profit function is obtained by substituting each possible value of B in Eq. (14–3), multiplying the result by the probability of obtaining that value of B, and summing,

$$E\pi = (10q - \tfrac{1}{2} q^2 - 25)\tfrac{1}{2} + (10q - \tfrac{1}{4}q^2 - 25)\tfrac{1}{2} = 10q - \tfrac{3}{8}q^2 - 25. \qquad (14\text{–}4)$$

To find the output q which maximizes the expected profits, equate the derivative of Eq. (14–4) to zero and solve for q:

$$\frac{dE\pi}{dq} = 10 - \frac{3}{4}q = 0. \qquad (14\text{–}5)$$

$$q = 13\tfrac{1}{3}. \qquad (14\text{–}6)$$

The resulting maximum value of expected profits is found by substituting Eq. (14–6) into Eq. (14–4):

$$E\pi = 41\tfrac{2}{3}. \qquad (14\text{–}7)$$

Next consider the possibility that the monopolist incurs the cost of 10 to determine the value of B before choosing his output. Then the profit functions net of the information cost for the two possible values of B are

$$\pi_N(B = 1) = (100 - \tfrac{1}{2} q)q - 90q - 25 - 10 = 10q - \tfrac{1}{2}q^2 - 35. \tag{14-8}$$

$$\pi_N(B = 0.5) = (100 - \tfrac{1}{4} q)q - 90q - 25 - 10 = 10q - \tfrac{1}{4}q^2 - 35. \tag{14-9}$$

The optimal output for the monopolist when he has determined the actual value of B is found by equating the derivatives of Eq. (14–8) and (14–9) to zero and solving for the resulting values of q:

$$\frac{d\pi_N (B = 1)}{dq} = 10 - q = 0. \tag{14-10}$$

$$q = 10. \tag{14-11}$$

$$\frac{d\pi_N (B = 0.5)}{dq} = 10 - \tfrac{1}{2} q = 0. \tag{14-12}$$

$$q = 20. \tag{14-13}$$

The maximum profits that are obtained in either case are found by substituting Eq. (14–11) into (14–8) and Eq. (14–13) into (14–9):

$$\pi_N(B = 1, q = 10) = 15. \tag{14-14}$$

$$\pi_N(B = 0.5, q = 20) = 65. \tag{14-15}$$

The expected profits when the monopolist determines the value of B before choosing his output are

$$E\pi_N = \tfrac{1}{2} (15) + \tfrac{1}{2} (65) = 40. \tag{14-16}$$

Comparing Eq. (14–7) and (14–16), the conclusion is that it is not profitable to incur the cost of 10 to determine the exact value of B. Hence the monopolist should produce $13\tfrac{1}{3}$ units of output. In terms of our more abstract discussion of whether it is worthwhile to pay the necessary cost to determine the value of a relevant parameter, Eq. (14–16) represents the expected pay-off when the decision maker incurs the cost of estimating the value of the parameter and then acts optimally under certainty, and Eq. (14–7) represents the expected pay-off if the decision maker does not ascertain the true value of the parameter and acts in the absence of certainty.

Those economists who do not subscribe to the expected utility maximization model frequently reject the assumption that the decision maker is always able to formulate a meaningful subjective probability distribution regarding possible values of the outcomes resulting from any course of action. Without such probability distributions it is impossible to define the expected value of the pay-off function, let alone to maximize this expected value. In the preceding example, if the monopolist has little confidence in his subjective probability distribution of the values of B, then he might see his choice as acting in complete uncertainty (rather than under subjective risk) or else incurring the necessary cost to obtain certainty.

V. Decision Making under Uncertainty

When the decision maker cannot formulate meaningful subjective probability distributions, he must nevertheless make some decision. In this section we investigate the nature of rational decision making in such circumstances. This discussion will be conducted in the context of the monopoly example introduced earlier.

Suppose that the monopolist is certain that in his demand function, Eq. (14–2), B will equal either 1 or 0.5, but that he is unable to attach meaningful subjective probability estimates to these two possible values. Since we are analyzing behavior under conditions of uncertainty, in this section we assume that there is no cost that the monopolist can incur to ascertain the value of B with certainty.

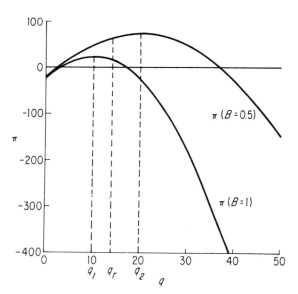

FIGURE 14–1.   Profit curves.

Using this example we can illustrate a number of possible decision rules. The profits that will result from any output for the two possible values of B are shown in Figure 14–1. These profit curves were obtained from Eq. (14–3). The values $q_1 = 10$ and $q_2 = 20$ are the values of output that maximize profits for the two possible values of B. These optimal outputs under certainty were derived in Eq. (14–11) and (14–13), because, except for the difference in fixed costs, the profit functions Eq. (14–8) and (14–9) correspond to (14–3).

Under conditions of uncertainty it is not necessarily the case that either q_1 or q_2 is the optimal output for the monopolist. It is clear from Figure 14–1, however, that no output smaller than q_1 or larger than q_2 could be optimal. This follows because one of the two profit curves will in fact be realized, and no matter which value B has, an output q_1 is more profitable than any smaller output and an output q_2 is more profitable than any larger output.[15] The precise output selected from the range q_1 through q_2 inclusive will depend upon the criterion used to define an optimal decision under conditions of uncertainty. We shall discuss three possible criteria.[16]

One possible criterion can be rationalized by the pessimistic view that the world is malicious; in this case the decision maker assumes that the worst possible outcome will always occur. In Figure 14–1, this means that the lower profit curve will materialize, i.e., that B will equal 1. The optimal output for the monopolist in this case is q_1 (10 units). This assures the monopolist a profit of at least 25 regardless of the actual value of B.

A second possible criterion can be derived from the optimistic view that the world is benign; in this case the decision maker assumes that the best possible outcome will always occur. In Figure 14–1, this means that the upper profit curve will materialize, i.e., that B will equal 0.5. The optimal output for the monopolist in this case is q_2 (20 units). If the optimistic assumption that B equals 0.5 is wrong, then the monopolist will incur a loss of 25.

The third possible criterion that we shall discuss is characterized by a different psychological viewpoint. It is based on the notion that the de-

---

[15] There is a single range within which increasing levels of output result in higher profits under one profit curve and lower profits under the other profit curve because of the parabolic shapes of the two profit curves defined by Eq. (14–3). If the two profit curves had more complicated shapes, there might be two or more ranges within which increasing levels of output result in higher profits under one profit curve and lower profits under the other profit curve. It is irrational to choose an output which does not fall within, or on the boundary of, such a range, since it can be shown that some different output is more profitable regardless of which profit curve materializes.

[16] For a more extensive discussion of these three possible criteria for an optimal decision under conditions of uncertainty, see the comment by Franco Modigliani which appeared in *American Economic Review, Papers and Proceedings*, 39, No. 2 (May, 1949), 201–208. This comment was made during a session on "Liquidity and Uncertainty" at the December, 1948, meetings of the American Economic Association.

cision maker will experience pangs of remorse, i.e., *regret*, if he finds that his decision did not produce the maximum profit after he sees the profit curve which actually occurs. This regret is measured by the difference between the maximum profit that could have been attained with the optimal decision and the actual profit obtained. If it turns out that B equals 1, then the maximum profit the monopolist could attain is 25; subtracting Eq. (14–3) from 25 the regret function is

$$R(B = 1) = 25 - 10q + \tfrac{1}{2}q^2 + 25 = 50 - 10q + \tfrac{1}{2}q^2. \qquad (14\text{–}17)$$

If it turns out that B equals 0.5, then the maximum profit the monopolist could attain is 75; subtracting Eq. (14–3) from 75 the regret function is

$$R(B = 0.5) = 75 - 10q + \tfrac{1}{4}q^2 + 25 = 100 - 10q + \tfrac{1}{4}q^2. \qquad (14\text{–}18)$$

These two regret functions are shown in Figure 14–2.

The intersection of the two regret functions occurs at an output of q_r. By equating the right-hand sides of Eq. (14–17) and (14–18), it can be seen that

$$q_r = \sqrt{200} \cong 14.1. \qquad (14\text{–}19)$$

This is the output for which the maximum possible value of regret is minimized. For example, if an output of 10 were chosen and the actual value of B turns out to be 1, the monopolist would have zero regret, but if B turns out to be 0.5, the monopolist would have more regret than he does for an output of q_r. Thus the maximum possible regret is less for q_r

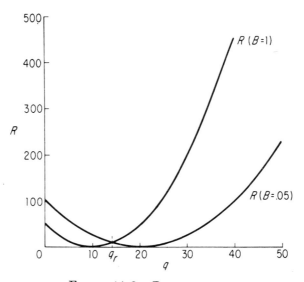

FIGURE 14–2.   Regret curves.

than for an output of 10. Analogous statements could be made for an output of 20.

We thus see that the monopolist is led to three different output decisions, depending upon the criterion he uses for optimal decision making under uncertainty. We are not prepared to state that q_1, q_r, q_2, or any other output within the range of q_1 through q_2 should in fact be chosen, because we do not think that any one of these possible criteria for decision making under uncertainty is particularly convincing. Empirical evidence suggests that a firm will not make an important decision under conditions of complete uncertainty, but rather, that it will attempt through search activity to obtain greater knowledge or that it will redefine its decision problem so that uncertainty is no longer critical. A more convincing alternative model of behavior is discussed in the next section and in Chapter 17.

VI. Subjectively Rational Decision Models

To conclude this chapter, we consider a model of subjectively rational decision making developed by Simon.[17] This model assumes that the decision maker's pay-off function can have only a few discrete values. When there are only two values, these may be interpreted as "satisfactory" or "unsatisfactory." For convenience in exposition, we shall consider only two-valued pay-off functions.

Suppose that a decision maker must choose a particular course of action from a number of possible alternatives. Initially he may not actually consider all possible alternative courses of action, but he may be aware of only a subset of the alternatives. This may be a decision problem under conditions of uncertainty, since there may be more than one possible outcome corresponding to any course of action. The decision maker's two-valued pay-off function indicates which of the possible outcomes are satisfactory and which are unsatisfactory.

If any of the alternative courses of action in the initially considered set of alternatives corresponds only to satisfactory outcomes, then the decision problem is solved, since Simon's model assumes that one of these satisfactory alternative courses of action will be chosen. Otherwise the decision maker will undertake search behavior in an attempt to enlarge the set of alternative courses of action actually considered. This search behavior will cease if a satisfactory course of action is discovered; i.e., a course of action which corresponds only to satisfactory outcomes. It is assumed that the decision maker adopts the first satisfactory course of action he discovers.

It is not at all obvious, however, that a satisfactory course of action necessarily exists in every decision problem, let alone that it will actually be discovered by the decision maker. Simon introduces the concept of

---

[17] Simon, *op. cit.*

aspiration level as one mechanism for increasing the likelihood that a satisfactory alternative will eventually be found in any decision problem, although the existence of a solution still cannot be guaranteed. The aspiration level defines the boundary between satisfactory and unsatisfactory outcomes.

When instead of a static, once-and-for-all decision problem there is a sequence of similar decision problems which a decision maker must solve, then Simon hypothesizes that the aspiration level is a function of the ease with which satisfactory courses of action have been discovered in the past. Thus if the decision maker fails to discover a satisfactory course of action after an extended period of search behavior, his aspiration level is lowered so that a broader range of possible outcomes is now considered to be satisfactory. Similarly, if the decision maker finds a satisfactory course of action after only a small amount of search behavior, his aspiration level is increased so that a narrower range of possible outcomes is now considered to be satisfactory. Through such changes in the aspiration level, it is likely that satisfactory solutions will eventually be found in any sequence of similar decision problems.

Subjectively rational decision models of the type proposed by Simon represent a promising alternative to the usual models of economists which implicitly assume that great knowledge and computational ability are possessed by decision makers. Evidence suggests that Simon's approach to economic decision making is likely to provide good explanations and predictions of the actual decision-making behavior of consumers and businessmen. Chapter 17 provides further elaboration of this point of view.

VII. Summary

The objective of this chapter has been to explore some ways of extending the decision-making models of business firms and consumers beyond the static, certainty framework which has primarily been assumed thus far in this book. Any decision problem is characterized by five general features:

1. The set of possible behavior alternatives
2. The set of behavior alternatives actually considered
3. The set of possible outcomes
4. The decision maker's pay-off function
5. Information about the correspondence between the alternative courses of action and the possible outcomes

Depending upon the specific assumptions made regarding the features of a decision problem, a number of different types of decision models result. We showed that there are twenty-four possible types of decision models corresponding to two different views of time (static or dynamic), four different states of information (certainty, objective risk, subjective risk, or uncertainty), and three different degrees of rationality (objectively rational, subjectively rational, and nonrational).

In order to explain the role of anticipations and plans in economic decision making, it was necessary to introduce dynamic considerations into models of the firm. We first examined Hicks' dynamic model of the firm. This model assumes a T-period pay-off function, and it views the firm as determining the course of action throughout all T periods necessary to maximize its pay-off function. Since the firm does not have unlimited freedom of action, it must solve a constrained maximization problem to determine its optimal course of action. The constraints consist, for example, of demand functions, supply functions, and production functions. In the first period the firm implements its solution for the components of the first move; the rest of the solution pertaining to the components of the last $T - 1$ moves represents the firm's plan for future operations. The major criticism made of Hicks' model is that its implications for anticipatory and planning behavior do not seem to agree with available empirical evidence.

Some revisions of Hicks' model were made in order to explain certain aspects of the planning behavior of firms. The assumptions were modified in three ways:

1. The agent recognizes that his single-valued anticipations may prove to be wrong.
2. Information about the future is not free.
3. Problem solving, decision making, and planning are not free.

A major change of viewpoint adopted was that at any point of time the firm's decision problem consists of choosing only the best possible first move. What is meant by the best first move is the first step of an optimal solution to the T-period constrained maximization problem. With this reformulation of Hicks' model, it was shown that many types of anticipations and plans are irrelevant, since they do not affect the choice of the best first move. Several examples were given to illustrate the manner in which irrelevance may arise. Firms should not devote scarce resources to formulating irrelevant anticipations and plans.

A model of subjective risk, the expected utility maximization model, was analyzed in terms of the problem of obtaining information about the value of a relevant parameter. By paying some appropriate cost, it was assumed that the decision maker could determine the actual value of the unknown parameter and then choose his action in the light of this knowledge. His alternative was to avoid incurring this information cost and then choose his action under conditions of uncertainty. In analyzing this problem by the expected utility maximization model, it was necessary to assume that the decision maker possesses a subjective probability distribution indicating the likelihood that various values would be the true value of the parameter. In this situation the decision maker compared the expected pay-off with, and without, the information in order to determine whether the information is worth acquiring. In general, the expected utility maximization model asserts that a person chooses that course of action which maximizes the expected value of his utility function.

Since it is not clear that a decision maker always possesses subjective probability distributions, we investigated some criteria for rational decision making under conditions of uncertainty. Three specific criteria were considered in the context of a situation in which either of two possible profit functions might prevail. The first criterion led to the decision which maximized profit on the pessimistic assumption that the lower profit function prevailed. The second criterion led to the decision which maximized profit on the optimistic assumption that the higher profit function prevailed. The third criterion led to an intermediate decision which minimized the maximum possible value of regret. Regret was defined as the difference between the maximum profit obtainable and the actual profit attained. We did not consider any one of these three possible criteria satisfactory, but instead we suggested that, rather than make an important decision under conditions of complete uncertainty, a firm would redefine its decision problem in such a way that uncertainty is no longer critical.

One way of redefining decision problems to eliminate critical uncertainties is suggested by Simon's model of subjectively rational behavior. This model assumed a two-valued pay-off function, so that any possible outcome was viewed as being either satisfactory or unsatisfactory. The set of alternative courses of action actually considered by a decision maker was regarded as a small subset of the set of all possible alternative courses of action. A satisfactory course of action was defined as a course of action which corresponds only to satisfactory outcomes. It was assumed that the first satisfactory course of action discovered was actually selected. To increase the likelihood that a satisfactory course of action will actually be discovered by the decision maker, the aspiration level was introduced. As a result of past success or failure in discovering satisfactory courses of action, the aspiration level rises or falls, thereby changing the set of satisfactory outcomes. This type of model seems consistent with the process by which firms actually make decisions, a view which will be further developed in Chapter 17.

SUGGESTED READINGS

These recommendations are in addition to the footnote references cited in this chapter.

DAY, R. H., D. J. AIGNER, AND K. R. SMITH, "Safety Margins and Profit Maximization in the Theory of the Firm," *Journal of Political Economy*, LXXVI (November/December, 1971), 1293–1301.

FRIEDMAN, MILTON, AND L. J. SAVAGE, "The Utility Analysis of Choices Involving Risk," in *Readings in Price Theory*, George J. Stigler and Kenneth E. Boulding, eds., chap. 3. Homewood, Ill.: Richard D. Irwin, Inc., 1952.

GRUNBERG, E., AND F. MODIGLIANI, "The Predictability of Social Events," *Journal of Political Economy*, LXII (December, 1954), 465–78.

HARING, JOSEPH E., AND GORMAN C. SMITH, "Utility Theory, Decision Theory, and Profit Maximization," *American Economic Review*, XLIX, No. 4 (September, 1959), 566–83.

KAMIEN, M. I., AND N. L. SCHWARTZ, "Uncertain Entry and Excess Capacity," *American Economic Review*, LXII, No. 5 (September, 1972), 918–27.

Session on "Frontiers in Uncertainty Theory: the Evidence of Futures Markets," *American Economic Review*, Papers and Proceedings, LI, No. 2 (May, 1961), 160–62. (Papers by Holbrook Working, Hendrik S. Houthakker, and Paul H. Cootner; discussion by Warren J. Bilkey and Reavis Cox.)

SHERMAN, R., AND R. TOLLISON, "Technology, Profit Risk and Assessments of Market Performance," *Quarterly Journal of Economics*, LXXXVI (August, 1972), 448–62.

SIMON, H. A., "Theories of Decision-Making in Economics and Behavioral Sciences," *American Economic Review*, XLIX, No. 3 (June, 1959), 253–83.

TELSER, LESTER G., "Futures Trading and the Storage of Cotton and Wheat," *Journal of Political Economy*, LXVI (June, 1958), 233–55. (Also see the discussion of this article by Paul H. Cootner and Lester G. Telser, *ibid.*, LXVIII [August, 1960], 396–418.)

Chapter Fifteen

The Cost of Capital
and Investment Decisions

We saw in Chapter 8 that a firm may need to purchase long-lived productive factors as part of the process of attaining its long-run profit-maximizing equilibrium position. Purchases of capital inputs, such as plant and equipment, result from investment decisions of business firms. In this chapter we shall analyze the considerations relevant to a firm's capital investment decisions in considerably greater detail than was possible in Chapter 8. The reason this more thorough analysis of business investment decisions had to be postponed to this stage of the book is that we must utilize some of the insights obtained in Chapter 14 when we explored some approaches to decision making over time and under uncertainty. As we shall see, a typical investment decision represents a sacrifice of some cash now in return for a promise of more cash at one or more future dates. Future prospects are, moreover, often uncertain.

The market rate of interest was referred to in Chapter 8 as one determinant of the cost of using a long-lived input factor during any production period. Although we then simply regarded the rate of interest as a given parameter, we shall see in this chapter that the rate of interest is a market price. In particular, the rate of interest is the market price for using money now rather than later. In the discussion of general equilibrium analysis in Chapter 9, we did not specifically refer to the rate of interest as one of the prices being determined by the market mechanism. As we shall see, however, the general equilibrium solution simultaneously determines the market rate of interest as well as the prices of all commodities and productive services.

For convenience in analysis, the subjects of Sections I and II of this chapter will be investigated assuming conditions of certainty. This simplifies the analysis, permitting us to gain some insights into the issues involved in the determination of the market rate of interest and the investment decision-making behavior of business firms. A more complete understanding, however, requires the analysis to be broadened to include conditions of uncertainty, which is done in Section III. We shall then see that determining the cost of capital for a business firm is considerably more complex than just observing the market rate of interest.

I. Perfect Capital Markets under Certainty

A major reason for beginning the analysis of the cost of capital and its impact on business investment decisions with perfect capital markets under certainty is that these conditions greatly simplify the types of financial transactions which need be considered. A "perfect capital market" is a market for funds (e.g., loans) for which all of the assumptions of the perfectly competitive model (see Section I.D in Chapter 4) are valid.

A. BORROWING AND LENDING OPPORTUNITIES

If an economic agent (i.e., a household or a firm) has excess funds during any time period (i.e., funds available beyond the funds required for the immediate purchase of consumption goods or the immediate purchase of productive factors in its optimal consumption or production plan over time), it should lend these funds to other economic agents, thereby earning the market rate of interest on these funds. By postponing some consumption from one period to a future period, a household will gain additional resources which permit it to consume at a higher level in the future period. This is one of the considerations determining the optimal level of consumption expenditures during any period for a household. Similarly, profit-maximization behavior of a firm over time may result in the firm utilizing only a portion of its available cash resources for the purchase of input factors during the current production period. By lending the excess resources (i.e., otherwise idle funds) to other economic agents, the firm will earn an interest return which contributes to its profits.

Just the opposite situation may, of course, occur. A household may find it optimal to consume more during this period than is permitted by the resources that it currently has available. In order to do so, it can borrow the required additional funds from other economic agents. Similarly, in maximizing the value of its profits over time, a firm may find it optimal to spend more funds in the purchase of inputs during this period than it has available. It finances the deficit by borrowing the additional required funds from other economic agents.

In the real world, there are many ways in which households and firms can borrow and lend funds. The hypothetical model of perfect capital markets under certainty permits a vast reduction in the number of possible borrowing and lending opportunities. In a world of certainty, no lender will provide funds to any borrower unless he knows for sure that the borrower will pay him the principal amount and accumulated interest upon maturity of the loan. In such a world of perfect certainty, the interest rate on a loan would represent a pure time value of money, rather than also reflecting some allowance for uncertainty.

In the real world, of course, there are varying degrees of uncertainty inherent in alternative ways of borrowing or lending funds, resulting in some of the differences in rates of return that we observe. In the American financial markets, loans that come closest to being risk-free are securities issued by the U.S. government. Because of its ultimate power to create new money, it seems unlikely that the U.S. government would ever default on the interest or principal obligations it has incurred by issuing securities.[1]

It is a convenient simplification in this chapter to assume that the time horizon is divided into discrete time periods of equal length. We shall also assume that all borrowing and lending occurs for only a single time period. Thus all loans can be considered as being made at the beginning of a decision period, to be repaid, along with accumulated interest, at the end of that decision period. When a firm borrows money for N periods, we can formally regard this as being accomplished by a sequence of N successive one-period

---

[1] The reason the nominally quoted rate of interest on U.S. government securities is higher than that on state and local government obligations is that these rates of interest are most typically quoted in terms of pre-tax market rates of return. Under U.S. Federal income tax laws, most dividend and interest income received is subject to ordinary income tax rates. However, interest income received from state and local government obligations is, with minor exception, wholly exempt from U.S. Federal income tax. If one made appropriate adjustments for these tax effects, the after-tax interest returns on U.S. government securities are typically the lowest rates of interest prevailing in American financial markets.

Because of uncertainties regarding future interest rates and future rates of inflation in the real world, even U.S. government securities are not really risk-free loans. They are essentially free of default risks, but they are not free of market price risks and inflation risks. Thus the notion that there are "risk-free" securities earning the "pure" rate of interest must be regarded as an analytical convenience rather than as a description of actual securities traded in real-world financial markets.

loans. The major simplification that we obtain by treating all borrowing and lending activities as being only one period in duration (with renewals being the formal way of representing longer maturities) is that we thereby avoid complications connected with the term structure of interest rates.

In reality, there tends to be a systematic relationship between the interest rate on a security and the maturity of that security. This relationship is what is referred to as "the term structure of interest rates." An important part of financial management in the real world involves the development of an optimal schedule of maturities for various assets and liabilities. Thus, considerations of the term structure of interest rates become significant for financial managers in firms. Because we focus primary attention in this book on the marketwide pattern of resource allocation rather than on decision making within actual firms, we can ignore the complications (and greater realism) that result from considering the possibilities of borrowing and lending funds with different maturities.[2]

Another aspect of the model of perfect capital markets under conditions of certainty is the assumption that in any period, both households and firms face a market rate of interest over which they have no control. In other words, any household or firm can borrow or lend as much as it wishes at a constant market rate of interest for that period. Because we are dealing with conditions of certainty, both borrower and lender are confident that any loan made will be fully repaid, along with accumulated interest, at the end of that period. Under these stringent assumptions there is no reason for the amount borrowed to affect the interest rate paid.[3]

B. Compound Interest as a Market Transformation Process

Suppose that at the start of period 1 an amount of money, P, is lent for one period to earn a rate of interest r per period. Note that r should be regarded as a fraction—e.g., 0.05—so that the percentage rate of interest per period is $100r$ (e.g., 5 per cent). The amount of interest earned on the

---

[2] For an example of the way in which the analysis of Section I in this chapter would be modified by consideration of various maturities for lending and borrowing, see J. Hirshleifer, *Investment, Interest and Capital* (Englewood Cliffs, N.J.: Prentice-Hall, Inc., 1970), pp. 109–13 and 129.

[3] In reality, of course, the capital markets do not behave in this way. The main reason is not so much that the markets are imperfect but that the world is uncertain. Other things being equal, the greater the amount of a loan, the less certain it is that the loan will be repaid without any delay or default. Thus, the empirical observation that in general there may be a systematic relationship between the relative amounts of funds borrowed and the costs of loans may be explained because of the presence of uncertainty, without the need to stress the presence of market imperfections (which, of course, may also be present in real financial markets). To put it another way, loans of the same maturity but with different degrees of default risk are really not the same commodity, and hence in equilibrium they should not be expected to have the same price.

loan during the first period would be Pr. The total amount repaid to the lender at the end of the first period, which we can denote by S_1, would be

$$S_1 = P + Pr = P(1 + r). \tag{15-1}$$

Suppose now that this amount S_1 is lent again at the same rate of interest of r per period for period 2. At the end of period 2, the total amount repaid to the lender, consisting of the amount of the loan plus accumulated interest, will be S_2 as shown in the following formula:

$$S_2 = S_1 + S_1 r = S_1(1 + r) = P(1 + r)^2. \tag{15-2}$$

Generalizing, we can see that if this loan is continually renewed at the start of each period, then at the end of period N the total accumulated amount, S_N, to which the loan will have grown will be:

$$S_N = P(1 + r)^N. \tag{15-3}$$

The term $(1 + r)^N$ can be defined as the "single-payment compound amount factor." Tables are available which show the values of the single-payment compound amount factor for various sets of values of r and N. By using these tables, we can readily convert any present sum P into an equivalent accumulated amount S on the assumption that P is continually lent at the interest rate r per period for N periods.

The computations inherent in the preceding paragraphs may, of course, be logically inverted. Thus if one wishes to determine how much money (P) has to be lent at the start of period 1 in order to obtain a designated amount of money (S_1) at the end of period 1 when the loan is repaid, Eq. (15-1) need only be solved for P as a function of S_1 and r, yielding

$$P = S_1[1/(1 + r)]. \tag{15-4}$$

More generally, to find the amount of money P that needs to be lent at the constant rate of interest r in order to accumulate an amount of money S_N at the end of N periods, Eq. (15-3) is solved for P as a function of S_N and r, yielding

$$P = S_N[1/(1 + r)^N]. \tag{15-5}$$

In Eq. (15-5), the term $[1/(1 + r)^N]$ is known as the "single-payment present worth factor." Tables are available which show the values of the single-payment present worth factor for various sets of values of r and N.

There are many additional types of compound interest formulas that could be developed. One way of generalizing the previous formulas would be to consider that the rate of interest may vary from period to period. Another generalization would be to consider multiple payments rather than single payments. If the payment made in each series were the same amount, the various types of level-payment annuity formulas would result. Another way of generalizing these compound interest formulas would be to consider the compounding of interest at shorter intervals within the time periods, the ultimate limit being that interest could be compounded continuously. It is beyond the scope of this book to derive any of these types of generalizations of the compound interest formulas.[4]

In following portions of this chapter, we shall indicate some ways in which various types of compound interest formulas can be utilized in analyzing investment decisions. For now, however, it is important to stress the economic meaning of these formulas. Too many people have learned to apply compound interest formulas in a mechanical fashion without really understanding the economic assumptions lying behind them. As a result, it is easy to misuse compound interest formulas and, accordingly, to draw erroneous conclusions.

The perceptive reader will notice that in deriving Eq. (15–1) through (15–5) we have been explicitly dealing with financial markets in which there are market opportunities for borrowing and lending funds. These markets, moreover, are assumed to operate under conditions of certainty, so that there is no default risk inherent in the loans. Hence the formulas relating an initial amount of money P to a terminal amount of money S_N are expressing market opportunities for transforming funds at the start of period 1 into funds at the end of period N. In other words, the so-called "time value of money" arises in this context because of market opportunities. The only reason that \$1.00 today is viewed as being equivalent to \$$(1 + r)$ at the end of one period is the existence of a market opportunity (lending funds for one period) that will permit the holder of \$1.00 to obtain the amount \$$(1 + r)$ at the end of one period. If such market opportunities did not exist, then the compound interest formulas as they have been presented and derived above would not necessarily be valid.

To summarize, in this subsection we have developed some of the basic compound interest formulas that are useful for analyzing investment decisions. On the assumption that there are market opportunities for borrowing and lending funds for any one period and that these one-period loans may be renewed upon maturity for any desired number of periods, we have shown how one can transform an amount of money at one date into an equivalent amount of money at an earlier or later date. Note that these transformations reflect objective market opportunities rather than subjective preferences for "consumption now" rather than "consumption later." Regardless of any subjective time rates of preference that households or owners of firms may have regarding consumption now versus con-

---

[4] The interested reader can find these formulas and their derivations in many finance textbooks. For an elementary exposition, see J. Fred Weston and Eugene F. Brigham, *Managerial Finance*, 4th ed. (New York: Holt, Rinehart & Winston, Inc., 1972), chap. 6. For a more advanced derivation, see D. E. Peterson, *A Quantitative Framework for Financial Management* (Homewood, Ill.: Richard D. Irwin, Inc., 1969), appendix A.

sumption later, as long as there are perfect capital markets under certainty in which any desired amounts of funds can be borrowed or lent at constant market rates of interest, it is the market rates of interest (rather than any subjective time rates of preference) that should be utilized for transforming funds from one date to another date. We have only briefly alluded to the fact that many people, in mechanically applying compound interest formulas, often derive erroneous conclusions as a result of not understanding the economic assumptions inherent in these formulas.[5]

C. The Present Value of an Investment Project

An "independent" investment project is defined as a project whose net after-tax cash flows do not depend on other investment projects which might or might not be undertaken by the firm. Under the set of assumptions that have been made thus far in this chapter, it can be demonstrated that for a firm to maximize the present value of its profits, it should undertake an independent investment project if and only if the present value of the net after-tax cash flows associated with that project, when discounted at the market rate of interest, is positive. The reason is that the market rate of interest represents an opportunity cost to the firm, for it can obtain any required additional funds at the market rate of interest, and it can invest any excess funds to earn a return equal to the market rate of interest. In this context, the "market rate of interest" should be interpreted as being on an after-tax basis. Thus if the pre-tax nominal rate of interest is 6 per cent per period and the marginal rate of taxation applicable to the business firm is 40 per cent, then 3.6 per cent would be the relevant after-tax market rate of interest to use in the compound interest formulas for discounting the net after-tax cash flows associated with an investment project.

When a firm is choosing in which, if any, of a set of independent projects it should invest, the present-value rule implies that it should accept each investment project for which the present value of net after-tax cash flows,

---

[5] One common fallacy is the mechanical application of compound interest formulas to determine present values or future values under conditions of uncertainty. Thus, suppose that a household lends a business firm P dollars at the start of period 1, in return for a promise to repay the household $S_N = P(1 + r)^N$ dollars at the end of period N. Under uncertainty, the household is not absolutely confident of receiving this amount, but it has some subjective probability distribution regarding its receipt. For example, suppose it envisions a probability q of receiving S_N dollars at the end of period N, and a probability $(1 - q)$ of receiving nothing at the end of period N (or any time thereafter). Many people would mechanically apply a formula of the form (15–5) to determine the present value of this uncertain future sum of money. In doing so, they might use a so-called "risky interest rate" rather than a riskless interest rate in the single-payment present value factor. For a discussion of the pitfalls inherent in this naive approach, see Alexander A. Robichek and Stewart C. Myers, *Optimal Financing Decisions* (Englewood Cliffs, N.J.: Prentice-Hall, Inc., 1965), pp. 79–86.

discounted at the after-tax market rate of interest, is positive. In particular, let C_t be the net after-tax cash inflow associated with an investment project during period t. In keeping with the discrete time-period mode of analysis, we can regard the net cash inflow C_t as occurring at the end of period t. The project may be assumed to have a lifetime of L periods. Thus there will be $L + 1$ net after-tax cash inflows, $C_0, C_1, C_2, \ldots, C_L$, associated with this investment project. Of course C_0 will generally be negative, since it represents the initial after-tax cash outlay for the investment project. More generally, any particular value of C_t may be negative, representing a net after-tax cash outflow during period t. For the project to be at all worthwhile, of course, some other values of C_t (for different values of t) will be positive, representing net cash inflows during period t.

For simplicity (although this assumption is not essential and can be eliminated by employing more cumbersome notation), assume that the market rate of interest will be constant over the planning horizon, and that on an after-tax basis it equals r per period. Then the present value of this investment project will be

$$PV = \sum_{t=0}^{L} C_t/(1 + r)^t. \qquad (15\text{--}6)$$

For some purposes it is convenient to transform the present value, PV, of an investment project to its horizon value, HV, at the end of the lifetime of the project—i.e., period L—by multiplying Eq. (15–6) by the single-payment compound amount factor for L periods $(1 + r)^L$. Doing so, Eq. (15–6) becomes

$$HV = \sum_{t=0}^{L} C_t(1 + r)^{L-t}.$$

As an example, consider the net after-tax cash flows associated with two hypothetical projects A and B, as shown in Table 15–1. This example assumes that each project has a lifetime of three periods. The after-tax rate of interest, r, is assumed to be 5 per cent per period. As Table 15–1 indicates, project A has positive present and horizon values, and hence would be desirable for the firm to undertake. In contrast, project B has negative present and horizon values, and hence would be undesirable for the firm to undertake.

One modification of the preceding result must be made. When evaluating possible investments in a set of interrelated projects, it may not be feasible to invest in more than one project from this set. This represents a situation in which at most one of a set of mutually exclusive projects can be chosen. For example, one project may be to build a steel mill in a given location utilizing the open-hearth process, and a second project might be to build a steel mill in the same location utilizing basic oxygen furnaces. At most, one of these two projects can be undertaken, although both could be

TABLE 15-1

POSSIBLE INVESTMENT PROJECTS

Period	Project A Net After-Tax Cash Inflow	Project B Net After-Tax Cash Inflow
0	−$4,815.92	−$5,500.00
1	+$1,000.00	+$1,000.00
2	+$2,000.00	+$1,500.00
3	+$3,000.00	+$3,500.00
	Project A	Project B
Present value at a 5% interest rate	+$542.04	−$163.63
Horizon value at a 5% interest rate	+$627.59	−$189.30

rejected. It could turn out that each of these projects, evaluated separately, has a positive present value, and hence each would be desirable on an individual basis. Since the firm can undertake at most one of these projects, it should choose to invest in the one having the higher present value.

Other types of project interrelationships are possible, leading to the need to make appropriate modifications in the comparison of present values. Some additional examples of such project interrelationships are considered in Chapter 16.

D. THE INTERNAL RATE OF RETURN

It is evident from Eq. (15–6) that r, the after-tax market rate of interest, is a parameter that must be specified when computing the present value of an investment project. While there are sound economic reasons in the model of perfect capital markets under certainty to use the after-tax market rate of interest, r, as the discount rate, from a mathematical viewpoint we could regard the present value of an investment project, as specified in Eq. (15–6), as a function of the discount rate, r. Thus, for example, in Table 15–2 we show the results of computing the present value of the net after-tax cash flows associated with project A (from Table 15–1) for several different rates of interest, r. This relationship between the present value of project A and the rate of interest used in computing that present value has been presented graphically in Figure 15–1. It is evident that for this particular project, the higher the rate of interest used in computing the present value, the lower will be the resulting present value. In fact, for rates of interest greater than 10 per cent, the present value of the cash flows asso-

TABLE 15–2

PRESENT VALUE OF PROJECT A AS A FUNCTION OF THE INTEREST RATE

Rate of Interest per Period	Present Value of Project A
0%	+$1,184.08
5%	+$542.04
10%	$0.00
15%	−$461.51
20%	−$857.61
25%	−$1,199.92
30%	−$1,497.74

ciated with project A will be negative, whereas for interest rates smaller than 10 per cent the present value is positive.

The rate of interest for which the present value of the net after-tax cash flows associated with an investment project equals 0 is defined as "the internal rate of return" (this concept is also sometimes called "the rate of return," "the yield," "the marginal efficiency of investment," or "the

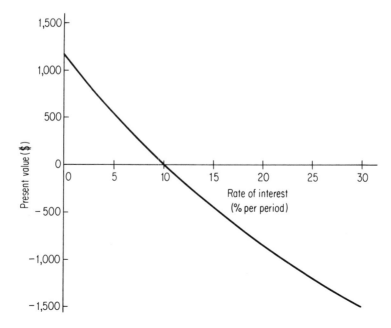

FIGURE 15–1.   Present value of project A as a function of the interest rate.

marginal efficiency of capital"). Letting I denote the internal rate of return, we can regard Eq. (15–6) as the mathematical definition of I, as follows:

$$\sum_{t=0}^{L} C/(1 + I)^t = 0. \tag{15-7}$$

It should be noted that the internal rate of return, I, as defined in Eq. (15–7), may not be uniquely defined and it may not even necessarily exist. The example project A defined in Table 15–1 was conveniently chosen so that the graph of its present value in Figure 15–1 is monotonically decreasing and has a single intersection with the interest-rate axis. To show that this need not necessarily be the case, however, consider the hypothetical investment projects C and D defined in Table 15–3. Table 15–4 and Figure 15–2 show the present value of the net after-tax cash flows associated with project C as a function of the interest rate. It is evident that there are two different interest rates, 10 per cent and 25 per cent, for which this present value equals 0. Table 15–5 and Figure 15–3 show the present value of the net after-tax cash flows of project D as a function of the interest rate. Note that there is no real interest rate for which this present value equals 0.

TABLE 15–3

POSSIBLE INVESTMENT PROJECTS

Period	Project C Net After-Tax Cash Inflow	Project D Net After-Tax Cash Inflow
0	−$72,727	+$100,000
1	+$170,909	−$200,000
2	−$100,000	+$150,000

TABLE 15–4

PRESENT VALUE OF PROJECT C AS A FUNCTION OF THE INTEREST RATE

Rate of Interest per Period	Present Value of Project C
0%	−$1,818
5%	−$660
10%	$0
15%	+$276
20%	+$253
25%	$0
30%	−$431

TABLE 15–5

PRESENT VALUE OF PROJECT D AS A FUNCTION OF THE INTEREST RATE

Rate of Interest per Period	Present Value of Project D
0%	+$50,000
5%	+$45,579
10%	+$42,150
15%	+$39,507
20%	+$37,500
25%	+$36,000
30%	+$34,912
50%	+$33,332
100%	+$37,500
150%	+$44,000

In order to see why such possibilities can arise, let us multiply Eq. (15–7) by the factor $(1 + I)^L$. This results in

$$\sum_{t=0}^{L} C_t(1 + I)^{L-t} = 0. \qquad (15\text{--}8)$$

It is convenient to introduce the abbreviation

$$X = 1 + I. \qquad (15\text{--}9)$$

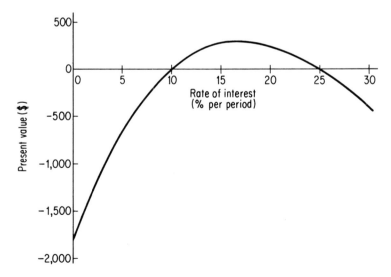

FIGURE 15–2.   Present value of project C as a function of the interest rate.

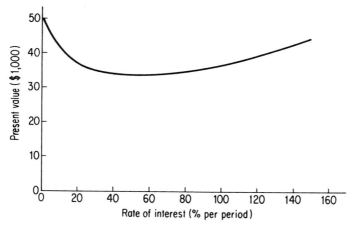

Present value ($1,000) — Rate of interest (% per period)

FIGURE 15–3. Present value of project D as a function of the interest rate.

By substituting Eq. (15–9) in (15–8) and writing out the terms involved in the summation, we obtain the following polynomial equation of degree L:

$$C_0 X^L + C_1 X^{L-1} + C_2 X^{L-2} + \cdots + C_{L-1} X + C_L = 0. \quad (15\text{–}10)$$

We have already observed that for the types of investment projects that one expects to encounter in the real world, some of the net after-tax cash flows will be negative and some will be positive. That is to say, some of the coefficients will be negative and some will be positive in the polynomial equation of degree L represented by Eq. (15–10).

The paradigm investment project that one normally encounters in textbooks is one in which C_0 is negative and all of the remaining C_i are positive. This, by definition, is called a "simple project." According to some well-known results in the theory of equations, the polynomial equation of degree L corresponding to any simple project will have exactly one real root.[6] That is to say, there is only one real value of X which will satisfy Eq. (15–10) when the net cash flows correspond to a simple project. Somewhat more generally, this same result will be true if there is some value of n for which

$$\left. \begin{array}{l} C_i \leq 0 \text{ for } i < n \\ C_j \geq 0 \text{ for } j \geq n \end{array} \right\} . \quad (15\text{–}11)$$

---

[6] There are many standard textbooks dealing with the theory of equations which discuss the number and types of roots that polynomial equations possess. The reader unfamiliar with these properties should consult an appropriate textbook in this area. For example, see J. V. Uspensky, *Theory of Equations* (New York: McGraw-Hill Book Company, Inc., 1948).

In the case of an independent investment project, unless the sum of the net after-tax cash flows over the entire lifetime of the project is positive, we would never accept it. The combination of conditions (15–11) and the property that the sum of the net after-tax cash flows over the lifetime of the project is positive are sufficient to insure that there will exist a unique positive value of I satisfying Eq. (15–7). That is, for such an investment project there will be a uniquely defined positive internal rate of return.[7]

In many real-world cases, however, conditions (15–11) will not be satisfied for some investment projects. Consider, for example, a project involving the opening of a mine for removing some particular mineral. There will initially be net after-tax cash outflows for the first several years of the project until the mine reaches full-scale production. There will then follow a period of positive net after-tax cash inflows while the mine is earning economic profits. Finally, as the useful lifetime of the mine nears an end, it may be necessary to incur net after-tax cash outflows to pay for the expense of removing equipment from the mine, sealing it, etc. Some well-known mathematical results from the theory of equations indicate that when the sequence of coefficients in Eq. (15–10) has more than one alternation in algebraic sign, then the possibility of multiple real routes (corresponding to multiple internal rates of return) arises.[8]

Some businessmen utilize the internal rate of return as a criterion for determining whether or not an investment opportunity should be undertaken.[9] More specifically, they use a decision rule which states that any investment project whose internal rate of return is greater than the after-tax market rate of interest should be accepted. Conversely, any investment project whose internal rate of return is less than the after-tax market rate of interest should be rejected.

In the case of investment projects whose cash flows satisfy conditions

---

[7] Note that project A (as defined in Table 15–1) is a simple project. For project A, Eq. (15–10) becomes

$$-4{,}815.92X^3 + 1{,}000.00X^2 + 2{,}000.00X + 3{,}000.00 = 0.$$

The reader can verify that the only real root of this equation is $X = 1.10$.

[8] Note that neither project C nor D (as defined in Table 15–3) is a simple project. For project C, Eq. (15–10) becomes

$$-72{,}727X^2 + 170{,}909X - 100{,}000 = 0.$$

The reader can verify that this equation has two real roots, $X = 1.10$ and $X = 1.25$. For project D, Eq. (15–10) becomes

$$100{,}000X^2 - 200{,}000X + 150{,}000 = 0.$$

The reader can verify that this equation has no real roots.

[9] The pioneering publication to advocate this approach is Joel Dean, *Capital Budgeting* (New York: Columbia University Press, 1951).

(15–11) so that a unique internal rate of return is defined, this rule leads to exactly the same accept-reject decisions as does the present-value criterion. There are, however, other cases in which the internal rate of return criterion leads to decisions which are different from, and less desirable than, the decisions implied by the present-value criterion. Obvious difficulties arise when a particular investment project possesses either multiple internal rates of return or no internal rate of return. Furthermore, when comparing two (or more) mutually exclusive projects, it is not necessarily the case that the project with the greater internal rate of return should be preferred over the project with the smaller internal rate of return. A correct approach would involve a comparison of the present values of the two projects computed using the after-tax market rate of interest.

A graphical explanation of the differences that can arise between the internal rate of return and the present-value criteria is presented in Figure 15–4, which is based on two mutually exclusive projects, F and G. In Figure 15–4, the curve GG' is a graph of the present value of project G computed for various interest rates. The curve FF' shows the present value of project F computed for various interest rates. It is evident that the in-

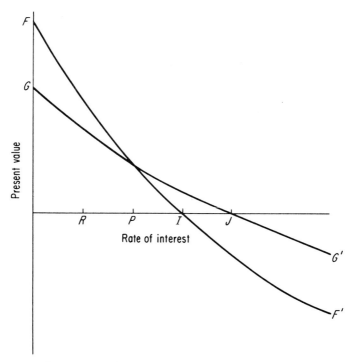

FIGURE 15–4. Comparison of the present-value and the internal rate of return criteria.

ternal rate of return for project G, which is represented by point J, is greater than the internal rate of return for project F, which is represented by point I. Thus if one were to choose between the two mutually exclusive projects F and G on the basis of the internal rate of return criterion, project G would be chosen over project F. If the after-tax market rate of interest is less than the rate of interest P for which the present values of projects F and G are equal, however, then this would be exactly the wrong choice. Suppose that the after-tax market rate of interest is R. Then the present value of project F is greater than the present value of project G when computed at the market interest rate, R. Hence for the firm to maximize the present value (discounted at the after-tax market rate of interest R) of its stream of future profits, it should choose project F rather than project G. Thus in the case of mutually exclusive projects, use of the internal rate of return as a project ranking device can lead to erroneous results.[10]

Despite the various shortcomings of the internal rate of return criterion, when it is used with independent projects whose cash flow patterns satisfy conditions (15–11), no difficulties arise. In such cases, in order to determine the volume of investment that a firm should undertake, a particularly simple graphical analysis can be made.

Suppose there are a large number of potential investment projects available to a firm and that funds can be invested in them on a continuous basis. Such assumptions avoid the "lumpiness" characteristics of many real-world investment projects and provide a framework in which the firm can invest any desired volume of funds. In keeping with the general economic notion of diminishing marginal efficiency, we shall suppose that the firm can construct an internal rate of return schedule that is monotonically decreasing, as shown in Figure 15–5. In this case, the optimal volume of investment for the firm to undertake is determined by the point at which the internal rate of return is equal to the after-tax market rate of interest, r. In Figure 15–5, this results in the volume of investment y.

In simplest terms, the traditional neoclassical economic analysis of the determinants of the volume of investment by a business firm is illustrated in Figure 15–5. In particular, the firm's internal rate of return schedule and the market rate of interest determine the firm's optimal volume of investment.

The after-tax market rate of interest, r, is itself determined as part of the general equilibrium framework that we discussed in Chapter 9. The full details of this extended analysis are too extensive to develop in this textbook, but the general idea that the market rate of interest is a price (the

---

[10] For a more complete discussion of difficulties inherent in the use of the internal rate of return criterion and for a comparison of the present-value and the internal rate of return criteria as the basis for investment decision rules, see Peterson, *op. cit.*, pp. 317–22.

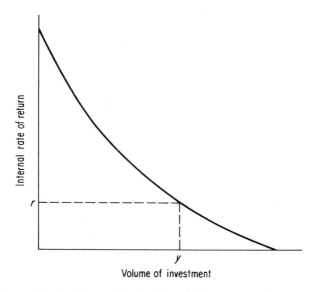

FIGURE 15–5.   The optimal volume of investment for a firm.

price for the use of money for some specified time period) is a central concept that will reappear later in this chapter.

E. The Joint Determination of Investment and Consumption Decisions

Thus far in this chapter we have analyzed the investment decisions of business firms from the perspective of the firms themselves, without paying explicit attention to the impact of these investment decisions on the people (individuals or households) who are the owners of the firms. We are now ready to consider the manner in which the investment decisions within a business firm may interact with the consumption decisions of the owners of that firm. In keeping with the general framework developed in Chapter 5, we assume that the personal consumption decisions of the owners of firms are based upon a utility-maximizing framework. We will now consider how an individual who owns a business firm makes the investment decisions within that firm in order to maximize utility.

For convenience of exposition, we assume that the planning horizon of the individual and of the firm consists of two discrete time periods. The major results obtained can be generalized to a multiperiod planning horizon consisting of more than two periods.[11]

---

[11] Although the terminology and notation has been changed, our analysis in this section closely parallels that found in J. Hirschleifer, *op. cit.*, pp. 59–64. For a more extensive presentation that indicates how the analysis would be modified to handle more complex types of investment opportunities as well as more general multiperiod horizons, see Hirshleifer, *op. cit.*, chap. 3.

Let us first consider the optimal two-period consumption choices of a woman who has a predetermined amount of income that she will receive in each of these two periods. A graphical analysis is presented in Figure 15–6, where y_1 and y_2 denote the income levels in periods 1 and 2, respectively (corresponding to the point Y). This woman has opportunities to borrow or lend funds in a perfect capital market under conditions of certainty. In the absence of such opportunities, she would consume her income in each period as she receives it. Because of the market opportunities available, however, any combination of consumption expenditures in periods 1 and 2 represented by the points on the straight line connecting W_1^Y and W_2^Y can be attained. This line represents the market transformation opportunities available in a perfect capital market when she can borrow or lend any amount of funds at an interest rate of r per period. The slope of this line, W_2^Y/W_1^Y, is equal to $1 + r$.

In Figure 15–6, UU' is an indifference curve derived from the woman's utility function, as shown in Chapter 5. One important difference is that the analysis in Chapter 5 was static, so that the indifference curves there represented combinations of consumption patterns *of different commodities* which would result in equal levels of utility for an individual. In contrast, the present analysis is intertemporal, so that the indifference curves here represent combinations of consumption patterns *in different periods* which would result in equal levels of utility for an individual.

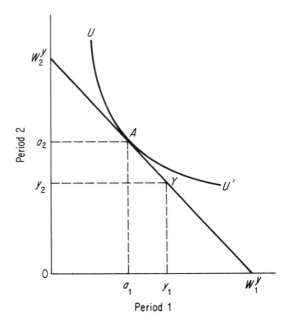

FIGURE 15–6.   Individual with market opportunities only.

Solutions along the straight line southeast of the point Y represent situations in which the woman will borrow funds in period 1 in order to consume more in that period, recognizing that she will then have less funds available for consumption in period 2. Points on the straight line northwest of the point Y represent situations in which the woman consumes less than her income in period 1, lending the excess funds in the capital market, in order to be able to consume more than her income in period 2. The optimal solution, clearly, is point A in the diagram, where the indifference curve UU' is tangent to the market opportunities line $W_2^Y W_1^Y$. At this point, the optimal solution is for the woman to consume a_1 in period 1 and a_2 in period 2. She will lend an amount $y_1 - a_1$ in the capital market in period 1, at an interest rate r, in order to achieve this desired result.

Let us next consider the situation of a man who does not have any market opportunities for borrowing or lending funds, but instead has some investment (and disinvestment) opportunities that he can exploit through his ownership of a firm. Suppose that the firm is entirely owned by the one man. This firm can be regarded as having some investment opportunities which utilize funds during period 1 and produce a greater amount of funds in period 2. The situation confronting this man is shown diagrammatically in Figure 15–7.

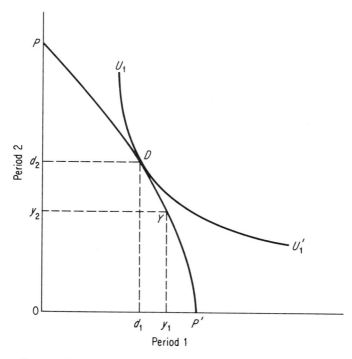

FIGURE 15–7. Individual with investment opportunities only.

In this diagram, the man has incomes of y_1 and y_2 during periods 1 and 2, corresponding to the point Y. The investment opportunities open to him through his ownership of the firm are represented by the curved line PP' in the diagram. Points along the investment opportunities curve PP' to the southeast of the point Y represent disinvestment in period 1—i.e., withdrawals of funds from the firm in order to increase consumption in period 1. Points to the northwest of point Y represent new investment in the firm during period 1, in order to increase consumption in period 2.

The man will attain his optimal consumption equilibrium at the point D in Figure 15–7, where his indifference curve $U_1 U_1'$ is tangent to the investment opportunities curve PP'. In order to attain this point, $y_1 - d_1$ in new funds are invested by the man in his firm during period 1. This permits him to have consumption expenditures of d_1 and d_2 in periods 1 and 2, respectively. No other feasible combination of consumption expenditures will give him a higher level of utility than d_1 and d_2.

To briefly review what we have just done, Figures 15–6 and 15–7 provide graphical analyses of the utility-maximizing two-period consumption decisions of an individual. In each case, the individual possesses predetermined amounts of externally available income y_1 and y_2, during periods 1 and 2. In Figure 15–6, the woman can take advantage of borrowing and lending opportunities in the perfect capital market in order to develop a pattern of consumption that differs from her pattern of income, thus increasing her utility. In Figure 15–7, the man can utilize his ownership of a firm and the physical investment and disinvestment opportunities available in the firm to develop a pattern of consumption that is different from the pattern of his income, again increasing his utility.

The next step is to combine the two analyses and consider the case of an individual who possesses both capital market opportunities (through lending and borrowing) and physical investment opportunities (through his ownership of a firm) for transferring funds between the two periods. This analysis is graphically presented in Figure 15–8, which is a combination of Figures 15–6 and 15–7. In Figure 15–8, point Y, corresponding to incomes of y_1 and y_2 in periods 1 and 2, represents the externally available income for a woman. As in Figure 15–6, if she has only capital market opportunities to borrow and lend funds at a constant interest rate of r per cent per period, then the equilibrium position that would maximize her utility would be point A. The physical investment (and disinvestment) opportunities available to her through ownership in a firm are represented by the curved line PP'. If she possessed only these physical investment opportunities and not any capital market opportunities, then, as we saw in Figure 15–7, her utility-maximizing equilibrium position would be point D. However, since she possesses both physical investment opportunities and capital market opportunities, her utility-maximizing equilibrium solution is point E, corresponding to consumptions of e_1 and e_2 in periods 1 and 2.

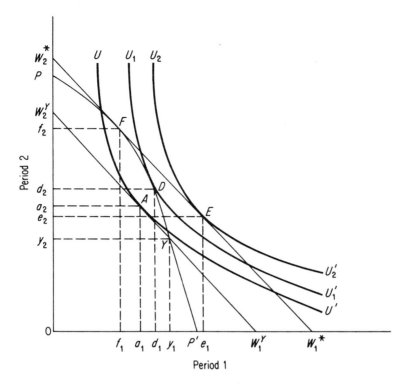

FIGURE 15–8.   Individual with investment and market opportunities combined.

The equilibrium solution E can be thought of as being reached in two stages. First, the woman undertakes new physical investments in her firm in order to reach the point F on the investment opportunities curve. This is the point at which the investment opportunities curve is tangent to the highest attainable market line—i.e., the line $W_2^* W_1^*$. Note that the slopes of all market opportunities lines are the same, since borrowing and lending are assumed always to take place at the same market rate of interest, r per cent per period. Thus, the market opportunities line $W_2^* W_1^*$ is parallel to the original market opportunities line $W_2^Y W_1^Y$.

The total opportunities set open to the woman is bounded by the market line $W_2^* W_1^*$. The equilibrium solution, then, is the point at which the boundary of this opportunities set is tangent to the indifference curve $U_2 U_2'$—i.e., the point E in Figure 15–8.

In this two-stage mode of analysis, we can think of the movement along the investment opportunities curve from point Y to point F as representing the investment solution which maximizes the present value of the firm's investment opportunities, represented by point F. The woman then in effect borrows (i.e., gives up some consumption in period 2 in order to obtain more consumption in period 1) in order to move along the market opportunities line from point F to point E.

Some aspects of the solution depend, of course, upon the particular shapes and locations of the various curves and lines drawn in Figure 15–8. In general, either physical investment or disinvestment would be possible, and either one could be combined with capital market borrowing or lending, depending upon the shapes of the various relevant opportunity and preference functions. What is important, however, is to note that the availability of market borrowing and lending opportunities has shifted the optimal investment solution away from point D to point F. The capital market opportunities in effect permit the woman (or the managers of the firm which she owns) to ignore her time rate of preference for consumption (i.e., the slope of her indifference curve) in order to attain for the firm the present-value maximizing position at point F.

The analysis portrayed in Figure 15–8 has, for simplicity, supposed that a woman is the sole owner of a firm through which she may undertake

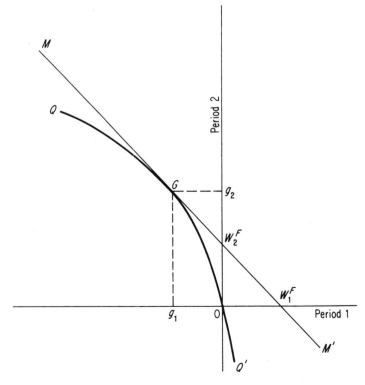

FIGURE 15–9.   Firm with investment opportunities.

physical investment opportunities. This convenient assumption is not necessary for similar conclusions to hold, as can be shown in Figures 15–9 and 15–10. In Figure 15–9 we consider a typical firm which might be owned by a collection of individuals rather than by a single individual. The firm in effect is viewed as an agent of its individual owners, whereby these individual owners have banded together to undertake investment and production activities. The firm itself is not viewed as having any income aside from that which it generates through investment and production activities. Therefore, the investment opportunities curve for this firm, QQ', passes through the origin in Figure 15–9. In effect, QQ', the investment opportunities curve in Figure 15–9, can be thought of as resulting from a translation of PP', the investment opportunities curves in Figures 15–7 and 15–8, downward and to the left so that the point Y becomes the origin.

The same types of assumptions inherent in the investment opportunities curves in Figures 15–7 and 15–8 are also present in Figure 15–9. In particular, it is assumed that the investment opportunities of the firm are independent, so that adopting any individual project does not affect the stream of net payments associated with other projects. This type of independence in the case of a two-period planning horizon makes it possible to make a unique

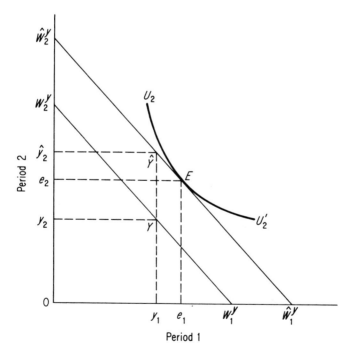

FIGURE 15–10. Individual with income augmented by pro-rata distribution of earnings from partially owned firms.

ranking of investment projects in order of their ratio of net cash inflow in period 2 to net cash outflow in period 1. Moreover, it has been assumed that the projects are infinitesimal in scale, so that any amount whatever can be invested in the firm. These assumptions result in the "regular" investment opportunities curve such as PP' or QQ' shown in the above diagrams. Thus they have been drawn as continuous curves whose slopes continually become flatter as one moves toward the northwest; i.e., diminishing marginal returns prevail as the scale of investment increases.

Because the investment opportunities curve, QQ', passes through the origin in Figure 15–9, the firm must borrow in the capital market to undertake any real investment it makes during period 1. As before, we assume that all such borrowing occurs at the market rate of interest, r per period. When the firm borrows and invests an amount g_1 in period 1 in order to produce g_2 in period 2, the present value of this investment, which is the same as the wealth of the firm, is as follows:

$$-g_1 + \frac{g_2}{1 + r} = W_1^F. \qquad (15\text{–}12)$$

The firm will maximize its present value—i.e., attain a maximum wealth position—when it invests at the point G—i.e., where the market opportunities line is tangent to the firm's investment opportunities curve.

From Eq. (15–12) we can readily derive:

$$g_2 = (1 + r)W_1^F + (1 + r)g_1. \qquad (15\text{–}13)$$

In Eq. (15–13), the first term on the right-hand side is equal to W_2^F, the intercept of the market opportunities line with the vertical axis. Therefore, the remaining term, which is the amount of loan plus accumulated interest which the firm must repay in the capital market during period 2, is equal to the vertical distance from W_2^F to g_2. Therefore, we may rewrite Eq. (15–13) in the form

$$g_2 = W_2^F + (g_2 - W_2^F). \qquad (15\text{–}14)$$

Since the firm is viewed as an agent for its individual owners, we can assume that all of the net income produced by the firm will be distributed to its owners in a pro rata manner. It is immaterial whether this distribution of income by the firm is undertaken entirely in period 1, in period 2, or in some combination of them. For convenience of analysis, we shall suppose that the income of the firm is distributed entirely in period 2. Therefore, in Figure 15–9 the vertical distance from the origin to W_2^F represents the net income of the firm which will be distributed to its owners.

Let us assume that k_i^f represents the fraction of firm f that individual i owns. Therefore, the income of individual i, after augmentation by the distributions of net income from firms, can be represented as:

$$\left.\begin{aligned} \hat{y}_1^i &= y_1^i \\ \hat{y}_2^i &= y_2^i + \sum_{f=1}^{F} k_1^f W_2^f \end{aligned}\right\} . \tag{15-15}$$

Let us now turn to Figure 15-10. This shows that an individual whose initial income was represented by the point Y now has an augmented income represented by the point $\hat{Y}$. Because of the assumption made in connection with Figure 15-9 and Eq. (15-15) that all net income of the firm is distributed in period 2, the augmented income is shown as a point directly above the original income point in Figure 15-10. The original market opportunities line that this individual faced is $W_2^Y W_1^Y$, the same as in Figure 15-6. Because of the augmented income of this individual, taking into consideration the net income distributed from his pro rata ownership in various firms, however, his new market opportunities line is $\hat{W}_2^Y \hat{W}_1^Y$. The optimal solution is, of course, at the point E in Figure 15-10 where the individual's utility is maximized. This results from his indifference curve $U_2 U_2'$ being tangent to his market opportunities line $\hat{W}_2^Y \hat{W}_1^Y$ at point E.

We thus see that the assumption that we made solely for convenience in connection with Figures 15-7 and 15-8, that an individual entirely owned a firm, is unnecessary to derive the desired result. The analysis of Figures 15-9 and 15-10 in effect leads us to the same type of solution that we obtained in Figure 15-8. In the real world, of course, firms are owned in varying proportions by different individuals. Thus, the analysis of the type undertaken in Figures 15-9 and 15-10 is somewhat closer to reality than that undertaken in Figure 15-8. The point, however, is that the nature of the optimal solution remains the same in either case.

In Figures 15-8 and 15-9 the optimal investment solution for the firm is the point at which the present value of the firm will be maximized. When firms and individuals face perfect capital markets, the maximization of the present value of the firm can take place independent of the owners' time preferences for consumption. The reason is that once their wealth has been maximized as a result of the investment decisions of the firm, the individual owners can rearrange their pattern of consumption to suit their own time preferences by borrowing or lending in the perfect capital market, as illustrated in Figure 15-10.

The discussion in this section has dealt with a two-period world under conditions of perfect certainty and perfect capital markets. As already indicated, the restriction to time horizons of only two periods is not at all essential, and similar analyses can readily be performed for more general horizons.[12] The assumptions of perfect capital markets and perfect certainty are, however, essential to this analysis. In Sections II and III these assumptions are relaxed, and the essential nature of the conclusions are modified as a result.

F. Determination of the Market Rate of Interest

Throughout Section I of this chapter, we have regarded the market rate of interest as a parameter while conducting various analyses of the firm's investment decisions (and, where relevant, of related consumption decisions of the owners of firms). As far as any individual consumer or any single business firm operating in a perfect capital market is concerned, the rate of interest is a given parameter beyond its control. It should be recognized, however, that the rate of interest is itself a market price which is determined in the capital market. Specifically, the market rate of interest is the price of using money now rather than using an appropriately larger amount of money later. We can now consider the process by which the market rate of interest is determined in a perfect capital market under certainty.

Supply and demand considerations analogous to our discussion in Chapter 4 are equally relevant regardless of whether we are considering a product or factor market (as has been the case in most of the earlier discussions in this book) or a capital market. At any point of time, there will be short-run demand curves and short-run supply curves for capital, as shown in Figure 15–11.

In a two-sector economy, both the demand and supply curves for loans shown in Figure 15–11 would result from the maximizing behavior of consumers and business firms. We have seen in Section I.E that consumers may sometimes wish to borrow money in order to reallocate their incomes to obtain an optimal consumption pattern over time. Other things being equal, the lower the market rate of interest, the greater will be the demand by consumers for loans for this purpose. Depending upon the relative time rates of preference for consumption of individuals (i.e., the shapes of their indifference curves), as well as upon the relative distributions of income that they expect to obtain in various time periods within their planning horizons, in any given time period some individuals may wish to lend while others may wish to borrow in the capital market. Those individuals wishing to lend during a given period will contribute to the supply curve for loans in that period, whereas those individuals wishing to borrow funds during a period will contribute to the demand curve for loans in that period. It is assumed that the higher the market rate of interest, the fewer loans will consumers demand and the more loans will they supply, other things being equal.

---

[12] See Hirshleifer, *op. cit.*, chap. 3.

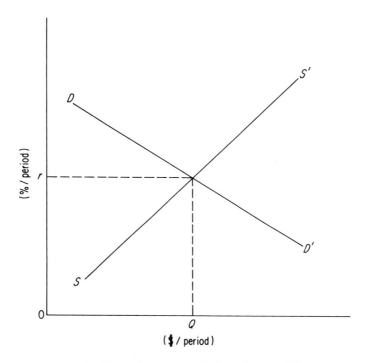

FIGURE 15–11. Short-run capital market equilibrium.

Some business firms, as a result of the types of analyses discussed earlier in Section I, may generate a demand for loans during any time period to support their desired investment expenditures. Other business firms may during the same period be net suppliers of loans to the capital market. It is assumed that the higher the market rate of interest, the fewer loans will business firms demand and the more loans will they supply, other things being equal.

In a two-sector economy (where there are no banks or other financial institutions), the demand and supply curves for loans in the capital market will be determined by consumers and business firms in the manner sketched above. The point at which the market demand curve and the market supply curve for loans intersect (see Figure 15–11) determines the short-run capital market equilibrium rate of interest, r, and the total volume of funds that will be borrowed and lent, Q, in any time period. Note that since every dollar which is borrowed by a person or firm must be similarly lent by some other person or firm, the total volume of funds lent and funds borrowed during any time period must be the same.

We shall briefly indicate the nature of the additional considerations that would be relevant when there are more than two sectors in the economy.

Additional sectors that could be added to the analysis (and which of course exist in the real world) would include the financial sector and the government sector. The financial sector consists of such institutions as commercial banks, insurance companies, mutual funds, etc. Although based on different considerations, each of these financial institutions would generate particular net demands for or supplies of loans at any given market rate of interest during any time period. The demands for and supplies of loans by financial institutions, in a perfect capital market under certainty, could be analyzed entirely on the basis of profit-maximizing behavior by these institutions. The shape and position of the market demand and supply curves for loans portrayed in Figure 15–11 might well change, but the essential property would remain that the demand curve would be downward sloping and the supply curve would be upward sloping.

When the government sector is included, the relevant considerations become considerably more complex. The government's financial behavior (and its impact on the capital market) tends to be influenced far more by aggregate economic considerations, especially those of monetary and fiscal policy, than by microeconomic considerations. It is theoretically possible to develop a normative analysis of governmental policies to optimize a social welfare function which includes economic stabilization and economic growth goals. One might thus develop the contributions of the government sector to the demand for and supply of loans in the capital market on the basis of a suitable economic optimizing model. Such a model is more within the province of macroeconomics than of microeconomics, however, and hence we shall not discuss it any further.

To sum up, during any time period there will be market demand and market supply functions for loans that result from the optimizing behavior of various economic agents. The intersection of these demand and supply curves for loans determines both the short-run equilibrium market rate of interest and the volume of funds that will be borrowed and lent in the capital market during that time period.

The long-run equilibrium relationships in the capital markets differ from the short-run considerations not so much because of the entry and exit of firms (although to some extent when the financial sector is included this will be the case), but more so from the actions of the government sector in pursuing macroeconomic objectives. Since our interest is in microeconomics, we focus attention solely on the short-run equilibrium solution in the capital market, both in one time period and as it may be altered from one time period to another.

The notions of general equilibrium analysis were explored in Chapter 9 within the confines of a two-sector economy. In that chapter, we saw that there would be a simultaneous determination of equilibrium prices in all of the product and factor markets. The same is true when we add the capital market to the general equilibrium system. The market rate of interest is determined jointly along with the market prices of all factors and products. We shall not repeat the formal presentations that were developed in Chapter 9 with the addition of loans as another "commodity" and with the market rate of interest as an additional price. Instead, we shall conclude by pointing out some reasons why changes in the market rate of interest might be expected to affect prices of various products and factors in the economy.

As we have already indicated, when the market rate of interest falls, firms will generally increase their desired volume of investment expenditures. Suppose this increase does occur. Remember that in order for firms to undertake physical investment activities, they must purchase or produce a variety of goods and services. Many forms of investment expenditures, for instance, involve the acquisition by firms of machine tools. These machine tools in turn are made from steel and other materials. Hence, an increased investment by automobile manufacturers to expand their own plants and equipment would increase the demand for machine tools and the demand for steel. The increased demands for these products would tend to raise the prices of them. Thus, we can see that a whole round of general equilibrium adjustments would be initiated by a decline in the market rate of interest, which would lead to greater physical investment activities by business firms.

As we mentioned in Section I.E, the market rate of interest is a key parameter in determining the manner in which a price system, functioning in a perfectly competitive economy, allocates real economic resources to satisfy present consumption desires rather than investing them to provide for economic growth and, hence, greater consumption possibilities in the future. When consumers decide what products to buy in order to maximize their utility, taking account of their current incomes and future expected incomes, these households are simultaneously deciding how much of their income to save for increased future consumption. Business firms are making analogous decisions. When managers decide to accumulate capital to build larger plants or purchase new types of equipment, they do so because they feel that they can earn sufficiently greater profits in the long run to more than repay the opportunity costs of investing funds right now. This may occur, for example, when a firm foresees an increase in the future market demand for its product or in response to basic technological change. The more households and firms decide to save from their current income, the easier it will be for entrepreneurs to obtain funds for new investment expenditures. As we have seen, the market rate of interest is a key price in determining how much households and firms will consume today rather than save for future use. In a perfect capital market under certainty, this interest rate is the same as the cost of capital for a business firm. As we shall see in Sections II and III, however, the analysis becomes considerably more complex when we consider the types of imperfections and the uncertainties that exist in real-world capital markets.

II. Imperfect Capital Markets under Certainty

Throughout Section I of this chapter, we analyzed a world of perfect capital markets under conditions of certainty. In this section and in Section III, we shall successively relax these assumptions. This section retains the assumption of certainty, but it considers that there may be imperfections in the capital market and briefly discusses their impact on investment decisions. In Section III, we shall drop the assumption of certainty and consider some implications of uncertainty on investment decisions.

Although many different types of capital market imperfections may exist, we shall specifically analyze only one of the most common types. This discussion will be sufficient to indicate the manner in which some of the conclusions we reached in Section I must be modified in the presence of imperfect capital markets. The type of capital market imperfection that we shall specifically consider is the existence of different market rates of interest for borrowing than for lending.

A. Differences in the Rates of Interest for Borrowing and Lending

The easiest way of analyzing the case in which individuals or firms pay different interest rates when they borrow funds than they earn when they lend funds is to indicate how the analysis in Section I.E would be modified in these circumstances. In that section we considered the manner in which the investment decisions within a business firm interact with the consumption decisions of the owners of that firm.

We say in Figure 15–8 that an individual who possessed both investment opportunities (through a firm that he owned) and market opportunities (through his ability to borrow or lend funds in the capital market) could develop an opportunity set bounded by the points 0, W_1^*, and W_2^*. This opportunity set is determined by the investment opportunities curve, PP', and the highest attainable capital market opportunities line, denoted $W_2^*W_1^*$. The slope of any market line is determined by the market rate of interest, which in Figure 15–8 was assumed to be the same for both borrowing and lending. That this was the highest attainable market line arose from the fact that it was tangent to the investment opportunities set at the point F. Any other attainable market line would lie closer to the origin than $W_2^*W_1^*$, Any market line lying further from the origin than $W_2^*W_1^*$ would not be attainable by the individual as a feasible solution. With this determination of the individual's opportunity set, his optimal equilibrium solution is clearly at the point E, where his highest indifference curve, U_2U_2', is tangent to the opportunity set.

One extreme case of capital market imperfection would be a situation in which the individual had no access to the capital market for either borrowing or lending. This in fact was the situation analyzed in Figure 15–7. In such circumstances, the individual's optimal consumption pattern is determined solely by his own subjective tastes and his investment opportunities, but not by any capital market considerations.

We are now ready to consider the situation in which an individual possesses both investment and capital market opportunities, but in which he must pay a higher rate of interest when he borrows funds than he receives when he lends funds. A graphical portrayal of this situation is shown in Figure 15–12.

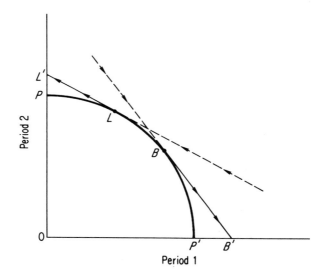

FIGURE 15–12.   Individual with investment opportunities in an imperfect capital market in which the borrowing interest rate is higher than the lending interest rate.

In this diagram, PP' represents the investment opportunities curve of the individual resulting from his ownership of a firm. There are now two types of capital market lines, depending upon whether the individual is borrowing or lending funds. It is assumed that the individual borrows funds at an interest rate r_B, and that he lends funds at an interest rate r_L. These interest rates are assumed to be constant, regardless of how much the individual borrows or lends. However, the rate of interest paid when the individual borrows, r_B, is assumed to be higher than the rate of interest received when the individual lends funds, r_L. Therefore, the market lines associated with borrowing funds have a steeper slope than the market lines associated with lending funds.

In Figure 15–12, the highest attainable lending market line is drawn tangent to the investment opportunities line at the point L; this is the lending market line LL'. Similarly, the highest attainable borrowing market line is drawn tangent to the investment opportunities line at the point B; this is the borrowing market line BB'. The dashed lines which extend LL' and BB' are drawn only for convenience of analysis, because it is not feasible for the individual to attain any points on the dashed extensions of these market lines.

The entire feasible opportunity set of the individual now consists of the area bounded by the points 0, L', L, B, and B'. The individual's indifference curves relating consumption in period 2 and consumption in period 1 have not been drawn. The solution occurs where the feasible opportunity set is tangent to the highest indifference curve. Such a point of tangency could occur either along the line $L'L$, along the arc LB, or along the line BB', depending upon the particular shape of the utility function.

If the highest attainable indifference curve is tangent to the opportunity set in the range $L'L$, the optimal solution would involve an investment optimum for the firm at point L, combined with lending transactions to move the consumer toward his consumption optimum northwest of L. Similarly, a tangency of the highest attainable indifference curve in the range BB' would involve an investment optimum at the point B, combined with borrowing transactions leading to the attainment of the optimal consumption pattern at a point southeast of B. The third possibility, for which the highest indifference curve is tangent to the opportunity set within the range LB, would mean that the investment optimum is also the consumption optimum; in this situation neither lending nor borrowing by the consumer would take place.

B. THE IMPACT OF CAPITAL MARKET IMPERFECTIONS

In the situation portrayed in Figure 15–8, the firm could determine its optimal investment policy, point F, by employing a present-value decision rule with the market rate of interest, r, used as the interest rate in discounting future net after-tax cash flows. As we already noted in Section I.E, the firm's optimal investment position was independent of the subjective tastes (i.e., utility functions) of the firm's owner. Depending upon the exact shape of the owner's utility function, the point of tangency between his indifference curve and the opportunity set could have occurred either northwest or southeast of point F. No information concerning the owner's utility function was required, however, for the manager running the firm on behalf of the owner to determine the optimal investment position for the firm. In particular, a present-value decision rule utilizing the market rate of interest was adequate for this purpose. This property critically depends upon the assumption of a perfect capital market.

When the assumption of a perfect capital market is dropped, and the particular type of imperfection analyzed in Figure 15–12 is introduced, we see that the manager running the firm on behalf of an owner cannot determine the optimal investment expenditures of the firm without knowing the owner's utility function; i.e., his time rates of preference for consumption in period 2 relative to consumption in period 1. Depending upon this time rate of preference—i.e., the individual owner's utility function for consumption in different periods—the optimal investment position of the firm could be at point L, at point B, or at any point in between. Note that when point L is the optimal investment solution for the firm, this position could be reached by discounting net cash flows associated with investment projects at the lending market rate of interest, r_L. Similarly, when point B is the optimal investment solution for the firm, this position could be reached by discounting net cash flows associated with investment projects at the borrowing rate of interest, r_B. When the point of optimal investment expenditures for the firm lies between points L and B, however, there is no obvious market rate of interest that could be used to discount future net cash flows in order for the net present-value decision rule to lead to the optimal amount of investment expenditures for the firm. Thus, the operational usefulness of the present-value decision rule for investment expenditures may break down in the presence of particular types of capital market imperfections—in particular, when there are different rates of interest at which borrowing and lending occur.

III. The Impact of Uncertainty

So far in this chapter we have analyzed investment decisions and the role that market interest rates play in investment (and in consumption) decisions under the assumption that firms and households have complete knowledge about all relevant aspects of the present and future. In particular, we have assumed that all economic agents possess complete information concerning the consequences of choosing any particular decision alternative. Thus, for example, when considering an investment alternative, the firm was assumed to know with certainty the net after-tax cash flows that would result if that investment were undertaken, the present and future market rates of interest, etc.

In the real world, of course, firms and consumers do not possess complete information concerning all their relevant decision alternatives. As we frequently observed earlier in this book, the analysis of economic behavior under the assumptions of certainty can provide many insights into market processes and market behavior in the real world. Nonetheless, we found in Chapter 14 that it was worthwhile to consider the manner in which economic agents might make decisions under various types of uncertainty. Similarly, we shall now find it useful to consider how the analyses of business investment decisions and the determination of the market interest rate may be affected when explicit recognition is given to uncertainty.

A. The Cost of Capital for a Firm

A simplifying assumption made in previous sections of this chapter is that the only loans which could be made are those that mature in one period. This assumption was not a necessary accompaniment of the certainty assumption, but it proved to be convenient for expository purposes. Together with the assumption of perfect certainty, it meant that the cost of capital for a firm was simply the market rate of interest. In such a situation, a firm can obtain whatever volume of funds it requires by borrowing at a constant rate of interest. If a firm requires funds for more than a single period of time, then by continually repaying last period's loan (together with accumulated interest) and borrowing an appropriate amount of funds in the form of a new one-period loan, it can effectively obtain loan funds for any desired length of time. When the rate of interest on one-period loans is expected to change from period to period, the cost of capital to the firm is an appropriately weighted average of the rates of interest during the various relevant time periods.

1. MATURITIES AND TYPES OF SECURITIES REPRESENTING SOURCES OF CAPITAL. When the assumption that all loans mature in one period is dropped but the assumption of complete certainty retained, a firm that must borrow to finance its investment expenditures would choose that particular pattern of debt maturities which minimizes its net interest cost during the planning horizon for the required volume of external funds. In a perfect capital market, loans of different maturities may carry different interest rates. An economic agent would, however, be able to borrow at a constant rate of interest any desired volume of funds of a particular maturity. Given the assumption of certainty concerning present and future interest rates and present and future net flows of funds, a firm could choose an optimal mix of loan maturities that would minimize its total borrowing cost and, hence, minimize its cost of capital. This cost of capital would itself be an appropriately weighted average of the costs of the different types of loans that the firm obtains during various time periods.

When the assumption of complete certainty is dropped, it then becomes necessary to distinguish between two major sources of capital funds that a firm may utilize. First, there are debt (or loan) funds, the only source of capital that we have explicitly discussed so far in this chapter. Second, there are equity (or owners') funds, which we have not yet considered. In a world of perfect certainty, no sharp distinction is meaningful between debt and equity funds. When debt is issued (e.g., in the form of a long-term issue of bonds) with some designated maturity (e.g., twenty years), the issuer promises to pay interest on the bonds periodically (e.g., every six months) throughout the lifetime of the bond issue and to repay the principal amount of the bonds upon their maturity. In a world of complete certainty, both the issuers and the holders of bonds are absolutely certain that the promised streams of interest and principal payments will be made; no defaults on interest or principal are envisioned. Equity can be viewed in a world of certainty as being similar to a bond issue having an infinite maturity—i.e., for which the principal is never repaid. Instead of interest payments, the holders of an issue of common stock in a corporation will periodically receive dividend payments (typically, every three months). In a world of complete certainty, there is no less certainty inherent in an issue of common stock than there is in an issue of bonds. The owner of either type of security is assumed to know with certainty the exact amount and pattern of cash payments that he will receive throughout the lifetime of this issue (or throughout his own planning horizon, whichever is shorter).

When the assumption of complete certainty is dropped, however, a major distinction must be made between debt and equity financing. The supplier of equity funds to a corporation is far less certain about the stream of future returns that he will receive from the corporation than is the supplier of debt funds to the corporation. Furthermore, not all types of debt issues are completely certain regarding their future payments of interest and principal. Corporations that have poor business prospects and an over-burdened debt structure are less likely to pay their contractual interest and principal obligations than are corporations with relatively little debt and promising future economic prospects.

In the real world, market prices of various types of security issues adjust so that they reflect the varying degrees of uncertainty associated with future payments on those securities. The more risky or uncertain are the prospects for the future payment stream of a particular security, the lower will its market price be; this results in the higher average or expected return needed to induce people to buy and hold that security. Thus, other things being equal, an investor in equity securities can, on average, expect a higher return on his funds than an investor in debt securities. Similarly, an investor in high-grade (i.e., less risky and more certain) debt securities would receive, on average, a lower return on his funds than would an investor in low-grade (i.e., more risky and less certain) debt securities.

2. TYPES OF DEBT FUNDS. We shall now briefly mention a few of the major types of securities that a corporation might issue in order to obtain capital funds. We have already noted that bonds, or long-term debt obligations, may be issued in different maturities.

Debt issues may be either secured or unsecured. When a debt issue is secured, specific designated assets of the corporation are pledged as collateral to the holders of that debt issue. In the event of default by the corporation on its obligations, the holders of a secured debt issue have first claim to funds realized from sale of those assets pledged as collateral against that secured debt issue. In contrast, the holders of unsecured debt issued by the corporation have no prior or special claim against the assets of the corporation, but instead have the same legal status as other general creditors of the firm. In the event of bankruptcy of a corporation, however, the holders of all types of debt must have their claims entirely satisfied before the holders of equity securities issued by the corporation are legally entitled to receive any funds generated by liquidation of the corporation's assets.

Corporate bonds may be issued as straight bonds or as convertible bonds. A straight bond issue carries with it a promise to pay interest on the bond periodically throughout the maturity of the issue and to repay the principal amount of the bond upon maturity. In contrast, a convertible bond issue has the same features, but in addition it gives the holder a right to convert these bonds into some specified number of shares of common stock in the corporation. Thus convertible bonds can be viewed as providing on the one hand the high degree of certainty (or safety) that bonds generally possess, a feature of importance when the corporation has a mediocre record of profits. In addition, if the corporation should have an excellent record of profits, so that the price of its common stock were to rise, then the holder of a convertible bond could obtain some of the benefits of higher equity returns by converting his bonds into common stock.

As might be expected, the prices at which various types of debt issues sell, and hence the interest costs that they represent to the corporation, depend upon many different factors. First, the general level of interest rates in the economy are a key determinant of the cost of any type of corporate debt issue. Second, such features as whether the bonds are secured or unsecured, straight bonds or convertible bonds, etc., will also be reflected in their price. In general, convertible bonds sell at a higher price than do equivalent straight bonds, because of the option to participate in equity returns that convertible bonds carry. Similarly, secured bonds will sell at a higher price than unsecured bonds, because of the greater default protection that secured bonds offer.[13]

3. TYPES OF EQUITY FUNDS. As is the case with debt, there are many different forms in which equity capital may exist in a corporation. One major source of equity capital is retained earnings. A corporation generates retained earnings when the dividends paid to stockholders are less than the net after-tax profits earned by the corporation. Most corporations adopt a policy of paying less than 100 per cent of their earnings as dividends, and hence they may accumulate substantial amounts of retained earnings as sources of equity funds.

---

[13] The reader interested in a detailed discussion of the various types of debt funds that are available to a corporation should consult a standard textbook in finance. See, for example, James C. Van Horne, *Financial Management and Policy*, 2nd ed. (Englewood Cliffs, N.J.: Prentice-Hall, Inc., 1971), chaps. 11, 12, and 14; or Weston and Brigham, *op. cit.*, chaps. 15–17 and 21.

The other main source of equity funds is new issues of stock. In general there are two different types of common stock which may be issued by corporations: preferred stock and common stock. The holders of common stock do not have any contractual right to receive dividends from the corporation. It is up to a corporation's board of directors to decide when and in what amount dividends will be paid to the common-stock holders. There is no explicit contract between a corporation and its common-stock holders that promises any specific amount of dividends. In practice, however, most corporations develop a stable dividend policy which results in a relatively predictable pattern of dividends over time. In such cases, stockholders are able to anticipate what future dividend payments will be, although these anticipations are not certain and at best can be held with some reasonable degree of probability.

The situation concerning dividend payments to holders of preferred stock is intermediate between that of interest payments to bondholders and dividend payments to common-stock holders. The holder of a preferred stock issue receives a certificate stating a specific rate at which dividends are to be paid on the preferred stock of the corporation. This rate represents the maximum amount of dividends that may be paid rather than the minimum or required amount of dividends that must be paid. If the corporation's profit performance has not been adequate to enable it (in the judgment of its board of directors) to make the promised dividend payments to the preferred-stock holders, these dividends may be waived or passed. However, no dividends may be paid to the holders of common stock until all of the required dividends to preferred-stock holders have been paid. Thus, while the holders of preferred stock are not absolutely guaranteed the right to receive their promised dividends, they have a greater degree of certainty of doing so than do the holders of common stock.

We already noted that in the event of bankruptcy of a corporation, debt holders must have their claims fully satisfied before stockholders have any right to receive funds generated by liquidation of the corporation's assets. In this case a precedence ordering is also established with respect to the stockholders themselves. In particular, preferred-stock holders have a claim on the assets of a corporation in the event of liquidation which takes priority over the claim of common-stock holders. In essence, common-stock holders are the last group of suppliers of funds to a corporation to receive any return of their funds from the corporation in the event of its liquidation.[14]

4. THE COSTS OF VARIOUS TYPES OF CAPITAL. We are now ready to consider the costs associated with various sources of capital funds. Let us first discuss

---

[14] Those readers interested in a more complete discussion of various types of equity capital should consult a standard introductory finance textbook: for example, either Van Horne, *op. cit.*, chap. 13 or Weston and Brigham, *op. cit.*, chap. 14.

the costs associated with straight (i.e., nonconvertible) bonds. If the bonds are issued at their par or face value, and if there are no underwriting or flotation costs associated with the issue, the coupon interest rate on the bonds is the pre-tax cost of this debt issue to the corporation. Since interest payments on debt are legitimate tax deductions in determining corporate income tax payments, the after-tax cost to the firm of a debt issue is the product of (a) its pre-tax interest rate and (b) one minus the corporate income tax rate. For example, if a corporation issues bonds at par carrying a 6 per cent annual interest rate, if it has no significant flotation costs, and if the marginal corporate income tax rate for this firm is 40 per cent, then the after-tax interest cost of this debt issue is 3.6 per cent.

More generally, there may be substantial underwriting or flotation costs connected with debt issues, and the bonds may be issued at a discount or at a premium rather than at par. With a proper understanding of the corporate income tax laws (especially with respect to the manner in which flotation costs and bond premiums and discounts are treated for tax purposes), it is possible to determine the net after-tax cash flows on a period-by-period basis that will be associated with the debt issue over its lifetime. Then by properly applying the compound interest formulas— in particular, finding that discount rate which equates the net funds realized from the debt issue with the present value of the future after-tax cash payments that the firm thereby contractually incurs—it is possible to determine accurately the net after-tax interest cost to the firm of any straight debt issue.

The costs of issues of convertible bonds are more complex to determine. If present expectations are such that the bonds will never be converted into common stock, then one can use the procedures outlined above to compute the after-tax interest cost of these bonds. However, if expectations are such that one would anticipate these bonds being converted into common stock at some future time, it is necessary to compute the after-tax interest cost on these bonds for the length of time that they remain bonds, by the procedure outlined above, and to compute the costs of the resulting common stock from the time of conversion according to the procedures outlined below for equity capital. These two costs are then combined using the present-value formulas to determine the cost of a convertible bond issue.

Let us now consider the costs of equity capital. Neither dividends paid nor flotation costs incurred on preferred stock or common stock are tax-deductible expenses. The only effect of flotation costs is to reduce the net proceeds received by a corporation on a new stock issue.

The cost of a straight (i.e., nonconvertible) issue of preferred stock is simply the annual dividend rate on the preferred stock divided by the net proceeds received from issuing this stock. Since the dividend obligations on an issue of straight preferred stock are a perpetual obligation, this simple computation immediately gives the after-tax cost of a new issue of straight preferred stock. The cost of an issue of convertible preferred stock is determined in a manner analogous to the cost of convertible bonds, except that the difference in the tax treatment of bond interest and preferred-stock dividends must be taken into consideration.

In discussing the cost of equity funds supplied by new issues of common stock or by retained earnings, we come to an area where there is a great deal of controversy among financial theorists. In principle the cost of funds provided 'by common stock could be regarded as the minimum rate of return that a corporation must earn on these funds in order to leave unchanged the market price per share of common stock. It is difficult, however, to implement this theoretical notion operationally. It is first necessary to know what determines the price of common stock. Theoretically, one could say that the present market price of a share of common stock, from an investor's viewpoint, is the present value of the future stream of dividends that the investor will receive from this share of common stock. From the corporation's viewpoint, the discount rate which equates the present market price per share of common stock with the present value of this future stream of dividends can be regarded as the cost of common stock.

From an operational viewpoint, in a world of uncertainty the major difficulty with this approach comes in trying to estimate the future dividend stream that will be paid on a share of common stock. There is no contractual obligation for the corporation to pay any particular amount of dividends, and hence there is no simple basis for trying to estimate the future dividend payment stream. In companies which are in favorable economic circumstances and expected to prosper and grow over time, investors would anticipate a growing stream of future dividends. Hence, one would seriously underestimate the cost of common-stock financing if one were simply to divide the current annual dividend rate being paid on that stock by the market price of the stock. A more accurate estimate of the cost of common stock would be the sum of the expected annual growth rate in dividends and the ratio of current annual dividends to current market price. This would provide a reasonable approximation to the cost of retained earnings (i.e., equity funds resulting from previously issued common stock), although there is much controversy as to how one might best estimate the expected growth rate in dividends.

New issues of common stock are generally sold for less than the current market price of the outstanding stock. This underpricing is necessary in order to induce the marketplace to absorb more shares of that common stock. The effect of a new issue is to shift the supply curve of that common stock to the right, without any corresponding change in the demand curve, thus lowering its equilibrium price. Underwriting or flotation costs are also incurred when new common stock is issued (these costs are not tax-deductible). The effect of underpricing and of flotation costs is to reduce the net amount of funds that the corporation receives from the new stock issue to an amount that is less than the product of (a) the current market price per share of the common stock and (b) the number of new shares issued. That discount rate which equates the net proceeds received from the new stock issue with the present value of the aggregate amounts of dividends that the corporation will pay on the new shares in each future period is the corporation's cost for the funds it receives from a new issue of common stock. This will be higher than the cost of retained earnings, because of the underpricing and flotation costs that accompany the new common-stock issue.

There is considerable controversy among financial theorists concerning some aspects of the cost of equity (and the cost of capital) of a firm. In particular, this controversy concerns the extent and manner in which the use of debt will affect the firm's cost of equity (and cost of capital). Another aspect of this controversy surrounds the extent to which the firm's dividend policies have any direct impact on the firm's cost of equity (and cost of capital).[15]

5. THE OVERALL COST OF CAPITAL. Now that we have considered the manner in which the cost of each source of capital funds for a corporation may be determined, we are ready to indicate how these various costs can be combined to produce an over-all cost of capital for the firm. The firm's over-all cost of capital is the weighted average of the costs of the various sources of capital funds that it utilizes. The weights to be employed in computing this weighted average are the relative proportions of each source of funds in the firm's capital structure. When the firm plans in the future to maintain its existing capital structure, the proportions of different sources of capital funds both in the present and in the future are identical. However, if the firm plans to alter its capital structure in the future, its desired future capital structure, rather than its present capital structure, should be used to determine the relative weights to apply to the cost of each different type of capital funds. Current market values, rather than accounting book values, are generally recommended for use in measuring the proportions of various capital funds in the firm's capital structure; there is not complete agreement on this point, however.

It is beyond the scope of this book to discuss the considerations involved in determining what is the optimal capital structure for a firm. This would require extended examination of some of the controversies we have briefly noted concerning the effect of debt policy and dividend policy on the firm's cost of equity and cost of capital.

---

[15] Readers interested in a discussion of these controversies should consult any of a number of finance textbooks: for example, either Van Horne, *op. cit.*, chaps. 7 and 9, or Robichek and Myers, *op. cit.*

B. ANALYZING BUSINESS INVESTMENT DECISIONS UNDER UNCERTAINTY

In Section I.C, we saw that in a perfect capital market under conditions of certainty, a reasonable decision criterion that could be used to determine whether a proposed investment project should be accepted or rejected by a firm was the present value of the net after-tax cash flows associated with that investment project, with the market rate of interest being used to discount future cash flows when computing the net present value. In a world of uncertainty, the consequences of adopting an investment alternative will generally not be known with complete certainty. In attempting to develop some analogue of the present-value decision criterion to use under conditions of uncertainty, one might naturally consider (a) replacing the certain projections of future net cash flows with the expected values of the probability distributions of net cash flows, and (b) replacing the after-tax market rate of interest with the after-tax cost of capital of the firm.

Such an approach would make most sense when the general riskiness (i.e., the degree of uncertainty) of the investment alternative being considered is the same as the over-all business risk of the firm. For example, if the firm manufactures small household appliances and sells them in the United States, then an investment alternative which consists of expansion of factory capacity so that more appliances of the same type could be produced and sold in the United States would generally have the same degree of risk that the firm as a whole possesses. Hence, the above-mentioned approach might be considered as suitable. However, an investment alternative that consists of the introduction of some very different product into the firm's existing product line, or another investment alternative that consists of introducing the firm's products into some new and different markets, would be likely to have very different degrees of risk and, hence, not be suitable to analyze in this way.

It should be noted that the general business risk of the firm is already reflected in the capital market prices of the firm's debt and equity securities. Investments which shift the firm into different degrees of business risk will, in turn, cause feedback effects on the prices of the firm's securities and, hence, on its over-all cost of capital. Such a change in the cost of capital of the firm would mean that the wrong discount rate had been used to evaluate any proposed investment alternative having a degree of risk different from that of the firm as a whole.

We have already noted in our discussion of security prices that rational investors must receive higher expected returns to induce them to hold more risky securities. There is an analogue of this property in the analysis of investment projects by business firms. In general, the more risky a prospective investment alternative seems to the managers of a firm, the higher the promised rate of return must be before that investment will be undertaken.

We will not discuss any further the various normative approaches to the analysis of business investment projects under conditions of uncertainty. A variety of generalizations of the decision aids and models presented in Sections I and II and in Chapter 16 have been developed, and some of them are utilized in practice. Some of these techniques are modifications of the decision-rule criteria that we have discussed in this chapter for analyzing projects on a piecemeal (or one-at-a-time) basis. Others are techniques for analyzing interdependent sets of investment alternatives in a portfolio context, representing generalizations of the approaches discussed in Chapter 16.

For our present purposes, it is sufficient to state a few general observations concerning the determinants of business investment behavior in a world of uncertainty. First, the higher the cost of capital of a firm, the less likely will it be to undertake any specific investment project and the lower will be its over-all volume of investment expenditures. A firm's cost of capital will increase if there is a general increase in market rates of interest and if, on an over-all basis, the firm encounters higher degrees of business risk. Note, however, that some investment projects which on an individual basis may appear to be highly risky may in fact serve to reduce the over-all business risk of the firm if such projects are negatively correlated with the firm's main business activities; such projects would be expected to contribute relatively high profits to the firm in time periods in which other parts of the firm's business have relatively low profits.

C. General Equilibrium in the Capital, Product, and Factor Markets

In Section I.F, we outlined the manner in which the market rate of interest is determined in a perfect capital market under certainty both in terms of a partial equilibrium analysis of the capital market itself and, more broadly speaking, in terms of a general equilibrium analysis involving the capital market and the various product and factor markets. Under uncertainty, there are many different sets of equilibrium prices to be determined in the capital markets. Market prices must be established for each of the different types of securities issued by various business firms. Although a partial equilibrium analysis could in principle be developed for each specific security, one must recognize that there are high degrees of interdependence among the markets for various types of securities. For example, the demand function for the common stock of one particular corporation is affected by the prices of other securities issued by that corporation, by the prices of common stock issued by other corporations, etc. Thus, nothing short of a general equilibrium analysis of the capital markets as a whole would seem to make economic sense.

Even this would stop short of capturing the real essence of economic interactions that take place. As we have already observed in connection with the determination of the market rate of interest (in Section I.F), there are many important interactions that take place between the capital markets on the one hand and the product and factor markets on the other. Thus, capital market price changes which generally lower the cost of capital for funds as a whole will tend to increase business investment expenditures. Such an increase, in turn, leads to increased demand by business firms for machine tools, steel, etc. The increased demand for the factors that are included in business investment expenditures will raise prices in the relevant markets and increase the earnings prospects of the companies producing these factors of production. Such developments will, in turn, have some further impact on the capital markets, changing the relative equilibrium prices of various types of securities and differentially affecting the cost of capital of various business firms. Without a complete general equilibrium analysis (which is beyond the scope of this book to formulate), it is impossible to trace all the various ramifications that could occur in response to equilibrium price adjustments in the capital markets as they have their interactions and feedbacks through the product and factor markets.

The essential message we have attempted to convey in this chapter is that there are important interactions and interconnections among the various markets that comprise a free-enterprise economy. In studying the processes by which the behavior of firms affects the allocation of resources in the economy, it is necessary to consider at least briefly the manner in which the capital markets function and the impact they have on business investment decisions. The investment decisions of firms help answer the fundamental resource allocation question of how much of society's resources will be devoted to meeting present consumption desires rather than being invested to provide for increased consumption goods in future years. We have seen that the answer to this question is determined by a general equilibrium analysis of the capital markets together with the product and factor markets.

IV. Summary

In this chapter, we have attempted to gain an understanding of the relevant considerations when business firms decide whether or not to undertake particular capital investment projects. As we saw in Chapter 8, the choice of technique and scale of production will affect the long-run production and cost functions of a firm and, ultimately, the long-run equilibrium of the marketplace. During any particular period of time, the fixed plant and equipment to which the firm has committed itself determines its short-run production function and, in conjunction with market demand conditions, its current output decisions. Over time, however, the firm may invest in projects which will change its scale of plant and the nature of its technology, thus inducing modifications in its production function, its cost functions, and its output decisions.

One prerequisite for analyzing investment decision making is a framework which permits us to reduce to some common basis arbitrary sequences of cash flows which occur during various periods of time. One dollar today is worth more than one dollar a year from now. Compound interest formulas can be developed to provide a computational means of transforming sums of money (or cash flows) at particular dates to equivalent sums of money (or cash flows) at other points in time. For the compound interest formulas to make economic sense, there must be market opportunities that permit sums of money at one date to be transformed into the equivalent sums of money at other dates.

Using the compound interest formulas, the present value of the net after-tax cash flows associated with an investment project, computed at the market rate of interest, was defined. This can serve as a decision criterion for a firm to use under perfect capital markets and conditions of complete certainty. In the context of perfect capital markets under certainty, we also considered how a firm could order a set of independent investment alternatives to develop its internal rate of return schedule. This schedule, in conjunction with the market rate of interest, could be used to determine the over-all volume of expenditures on investment activities that a business firm should undertake.

We also considered, primarily by means of graphical analyses, the interactions that exist between the consumption decisions of individuals and the investment decisions of firms that are owned by these same individuals. We saw that such individuals can increase the utility of their consumption expenditures over time by undertaking investment opportunities through the firms they own and by undertaking capital market transactions (i.e., borrowing or lending funds). Such activities permit these individuals to achieve an optimal consumption pattern which may be different from the intertemporal pattern of their income receipts.

We discussed the manner in which the market rate of interest, which is the price of money now rather than money later, is determined in a perfect capital market under certainty. Although a partial equilibrium analysis of the capital market could be made to analyze the determinants of the market rate of interest, it is more realistic to consider a general equilibrium analysis which shows the interrelationships between the capital market on the one hand and the product and factor markets on the other.

In Section II we considered the impact of capital market imperfections on business investment behavior while retaining the assumption of complete certainty. We saw that when there are differences between the rates of interest for borrowing and for lending, some of the preceding types of analyses would no longer be valid. In particular, the present-value decision criterion is no longer applicable in all cases, because there may be no way of knowing (without first obtaining a solution for the optimal investment expenditures) which rate of interest should be used to discount future cash flows in computing present values.

Finally, in Section III we considered how dropping the assumption of complete certainty might modify the preceding analyses. No longer can we retain the simplifying assumption that all borrowing and lending take place in the form of one-period loans. Furthermore, it becomes essential to distinguish between debt and equity sources of capital. The suppliers of debt funds to a firm have far more certainty regarding the stream of future payments that they will receive from the firm than do the suppliers of equity funds. We briefly discussed the manner in which the after-tax cost to a firm of various types of debt and equity funds could be determined. By taking a suitably weighted average of the various costs of different types of debt and equity funds, with the weights being the proportions of funds stemming from these various sources of capital, we can determine the over-all cost of capital for a firm.

The over-all cost of capital of a firm is useful in analyzing, under conditions of uncertainty, specific alternative investment projects and the optimal total volume of investment expenditures. Although we did not describe in detail the procedures that might be utilized for analyzing investment projects under conditions of uncertainty, we did indicate some general properties that would result from a more complete discussion. In particular, the higher the firm's over-all cost of capital, the less likely it is to select any particular investment project and the lower its total volume of investment expenditures will be. Under uncertainty, firms are generally more willing to invest in projects having low degrees of risk than in projects having high degrees of risk. One major exception, however, occurs if a particular project is negatively correlated with the over-all business activity of a firm. In such a case it may be worthwhile for a firm to undertake this type of risky investment, because it could decrease the over-all business risk of the firm.

We concluded this chapter by briefly reviewing the nature of price determination in the capital markets themselves and the general equilibrium interrelationships between the capital markets and the various product and factor markets. The capital markets provide an important linkage between physical and financial variables. In a predominantly private enterprise economy, such as we have in the United States of America, it is through the capital markets that business firms obtain funds to invest in capital projects and to expand their productive capacities. Such investments require an expenditure of real economic resources which could otherwise be devoted to satisfying the current consumption desires of consumers. However, such sacrifices of current consumption are made in order to increase future consumption in a growing economy. One of the fundamental resource allocation questions, deciding between current and future needs, is answered through the functioning of the capital markets and their interactions with the product and factor markets. The decisions made by business firms concerning investment projects, combined with the time preferences of consumers, permit the question of the choice between present and future needs to be answered in a decentralized manner through means of the market process.

SUGGESTED READINGS

These recommendations are in addition to the footnote references cited in this chapter.

BIERMAN, HAROLD, JR., AND SEYMOUR SMIDT, *The Capital Budgeting Decision*, second ed. New York: The Macmillan Company, 1966.

HAMADA, ROBERT S., "Portfolio Analysis, Market Equilibrium and Corporation Finance," *Journal of Finance*, XXIV, No. 1 (March, 1969), 13–31.

JENSEN, MICHAEL C., "Risk, the Pricing of Capital Assets, and the Evaluation of Investment Portfolios," *Journal of Business*, XLII, No. 2 (April, 1969), 167–247.

JOHNSON, ROBERT W., *Capital Budgeting*. Belmont, Calif.: Wadsworth Publishing Company, Inc., 1970.

LINTNER, JOHN, "The Valuation of Risk Assets and the Selection of Risky Investments in Stock Portfolios and Capital Budgets, *Review of Economics and Statistics*, XLVII (February, 1965), 13–37.

MILLER, MERTON H., AND FRANCO MODIGLIANI, "Some Estimates of the Cost of Capital to the Electric Utility Industry," *American Economic Review*, LVI (June, 1966), 333–91.

QUIRIN, G. DAVID, *The Capital Expenditure Decision*. Homewood, Ill.: Richard D. Irwin, Inc., 1967.

SHARPE, WILLIAM F., *Portfolio Theory and Capital Markets*. New York: McGraw-Hill Book Company, 1970.

Chapter Sixteen

Linear Programming Approaches to Investment Decisions

Our discussion of investment decision making in Chapter 15 was focused on decision-rule criteria for accepting or rejecting specific investment projects and for determining the over-all amount of investment expenditures to be undertaken by a firm. Most of our analysis of decision-rule criteria considered individual investment projects on a piecemeal or "one-at-a-time" basis, but we did briefly consider the applicability of these criteria to sets of mutually exclusive projects. Our discussion of determination of the over-all amount of investment expenditures by a firm assumed that the various investment projects being considered were independent of each other.

In this chapter, we shall consider in some detail two different models for the analysis of interrelated sets of investment projects. The types of possible physical interrelationships among projects can be considerably more complex than sets of mutually exclusive projects. By using the types of models discussed in Sections II and III, we can determine an optimal portfolio of investment projects which a firm should undertake. This portfolio implicitly determines the over-all amount of funds the firm should devote to investment expenditures.

The models for selecting an optimal set of investment projects in a firm that we present in this chapter utilize a mathematical technique known as linear programming (LP). Since some readers may be unfamiliar with this area of mathematics, Section I is devoted to a brief exposition of the essentials of LP, together with an extended economic interpretation of an LP model that could be considered as an alternative approach to the analysis of production decisions developed in Chapter 7.

I. Linear Programming[1]

Linear programming is a term that describes constrained optimization problems in which the objective function and the constraints are linear in nature. Typical objective functions are to minimize costs or maximize profits. The constraints reflect the existence of scarce resources and minimum requirements of activity levels.

The Lagrange multiplier approach[2] for solving constrained optimization problems is inappropriate for LP problems for two reasons: (1) equating derivatives to zero does not yield meaningful results with linear functions, and (2) the constraints are typically inequalities rather than equalities.

A. MATHEMATICAL FORMULATION OF THE LP PROBLEM

The general LP problem can be stated mathematically as follows:

Maximize:
$$z = \sum_{j=1}^{n} c_j x_j \tag{16-1}$$

Subject to:
$$\sum_{j=1}^{n} a_{ij} x_j \begin{Bmatrix} \leq \\ = \\ \geq \end{Bmatrix} b_i, \qquad \text{for } i = 1, 2, \ldots, m \tag{16-2}$$

$$x_j \geq 0, \qquad \text{for } j = 1, 2, \ldots, n. \tag{16-3}$$

Given n competing activities, the decision variables x_j are the activity levels. For example, if the activities were levels of production, then x_j could be interpreted as the number of units of product j produced. The objective function Eq. (16–1) is a measure of effectiveness when the decision

---

[1] The authors wish to thank Randall G. Chapman, a Ph.D. student at the Graduate School of Industrial Administration, Carnegie-Mellon University, for his assistance in initially drafting this section.

[2] See Section IV of the Appendix.

variables assume a specified set of values. If one more unit of x_j is produced, then c_j will be added to the previous effectiveness measure.

LP problems can be either minimization or maximization problems. It is important to note that only one class of problem need be considered, since maximizing the negative of a function is equivalent to minimizing the function. Hence, minimization problems can be expressed in maximization terminology, and vice versa.

There are $m + n$ constraints in the general LP problem specified above. The first m constraints Eq. (16–2) represent the scarce resources or the minimum requirements (depending on the direction of the inequality). The available level of resources or the minimum requirement for the ith constraint is b_i. The coefficient a_{ij} indicates the units of resource i consumed or the units of output i produced per unit of x_j. The remaining n constraints Eq. (16–3) are termed nonnegativity restrictions. Typically, negative levels for the decision variables are difficult to interpret (for example, it would be difficult to interpret a production level of -5 units of a given product). If it were desirable to permit negative values for some decision variable, however, the transformation $x_j = x_j^+ - x_j^-$, with x_j^+ and x_j^- being restricted to be nonnegative, may be incorporated as a constraint. This transformation would have the effect of allowing for negative x_j values.

B. An Illustrative Example: Formulation

Consider a profit-maximizing firm producing small and large widgets, where the profit contribution per unit is $2.00 and $5.00 for the small and large widgets, respectively. The widgets must undergo several operations during production. Specifically, they must be stamped, bolted, and painted. Each of these operations requires a set amount of time, and there are established capacity levels for available time (because of manpower and machine limitations). Table 16–1 indicates the time required for each operation and the total time available.

TABLE 16–1

TIME REQUIREMENTS

	Stamping	Bolting	Painting
Small widgets (hours per unit)	1	2	1
Large widgets (hours per unit)	3	1	1
Maximum time available (hours per day)	24	16	10

From Table 16–1 it can be seen that each small widget produced requires one hour of stamping time, two hours of bolting time, and one hour of painting time; while each large widget requires three hours of stamping time, one of bolting time, and one of painting time. The total availability of stamping, bolting, and painting time is twenty-four, sixteen, and ten hours per day. We will assume that the firm is in a perfectly competitive market where it can sell all the products it makes. The question facing management is how many of each product should be produced in order to maximize daily profits.

This problem may be formulated mathematically as follows:
Maximize:

$$z = 2x_1 + 5x_2 \qquad \text{(objective function)} \qquad (16\text{--}4)$$

Subject to:

$$x_1 + 3x_2 \leq 24 \qquad \text{(stamping time constraint)} \qquad (16\text{--}5)$$

$$2x_1 + x_2 \leq 16 \qquad \text{(bolting time constraint)} \qquad (16\text{--}6)$$

$$x_1 + x_2 \leq 10 \qquad \text{(painting time constraint)} \qquad (16\text{--}7)$$

$$x_1, x_2 \leq 0 \qquad \text{(nonnegativity constraints)} \qquad (16\text{--}8)$$

The variables x_1 and x_2 indicate, respectively, the number of small and large widgets produced. The objective function, z, is a measure of the performance generated by the decision variables, x_1 and x_2, expressed in terms of daily dollar profit.

C. FUNDAMENTAL ASSUMPTIONS

In applications of linear programming, the following conditions must be present if the model is to be properly formulated and the results obtained meaningful:

1. *Divisibility.* Fractional levels of the decision variables must be allowed in the optimal solution.
2. *Additivity.* There cannot be joint interactions between some of the activities such that the sum of the joint interactions would be greater than if the activities were carried out individually.
3. *Proportionality.* Marginal measures of effectiveness and of resource consumption must be constants over all possible levels of each activity.

Even when all these properties are not present in a problem, an LP model can still be a useful tool for analysis. For example, nonlinearities can often be approximated by piece-wise linear functions.

D. EXAMPLE (CONTINUED): ASSUMPTIONS

The basic LP assumptions of fixed input and output costs, constant returns to scale, divisibility of activity levels, and additivity of returns are present in the example problem introduced in Section B. The values for all the a_{ij}, c_j, and b_i parameters are given in the problem description. Constant returns to scale are present in that, for example, replacing x_2 by $x_2/2$ results in one-half the original profit of x_2 being generated in the objective function and one-half the original hours being required in each of the constraints for x_2. Divisibility of activity levels is present since fractional values for the x_j values can be interpreted as work in progress or widgets partially completed. There are no joint effects because terms involving the product of x_1 and x_2 are not present.

E. THE SIMPLEX SOLUTION PROCEDURE

The simplex method, as developed by George Dantzig in the early 1950's, is one of the standard computational algorithms available for the solution of linear programming problems.[3]

The simplex method is based on some fundamental properties.

1. The collection of feasible solutions (a set of values, $\{x_j\}$, for $j = 1, 2, \ldots, n$, such that all the constraints are satisfied) must be a convex set. A set is *convex* if, for any two points in the set, the straight line between them consists only of points in the set (see Figure 16–1 for examples of convex and nonconvex sets).

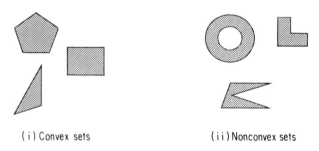

(i) Convex sets   (i i) Nonconvex sets

FIGURE 16–1.　Convex and nonconvex sets.

2. If a feasible solution exists, a basic feasible solution, corresponding to an extreme point of the set of feasible solutions, exists. A point is an extreme point (i.e., a corner point) of a set if that point is not in the interior of any line segment connecting two distinct points of that set.

3. Only a finite number of basic feasible solutions exist (because there is a finite number of constraints, and each extreme point of the set of feasible solutions is determined by the intersection of two or more constraints).

4. If the objective function has a finite maximum, then there is at least one basic feasible solution that is optimal.

[3] See G. B. Dantzig, *Linear Programming and Extensions* (Princeton, N.J.: Princeton University Press, 1963).

In general, the simplex procedure starts with a basic feasible solution and moves to an adjacent extreme point for which the value of the objective function is increased. The simplex method allows the user to "step around" the feasible convex region, from one corner point to another, always improving the value of the objective function until the optimum is achieved.

In order to obtain solutions to large-scale LP problems, commercially available computer codes, such as IBM's Mathematical Programming System/360, are typically used.[4]

F. Example (Continued): Geometrical Solution

A solution to our example problem can be obtained via a two-dimensional graph. The shaded section in Figure 16–2 is the feasible region; every

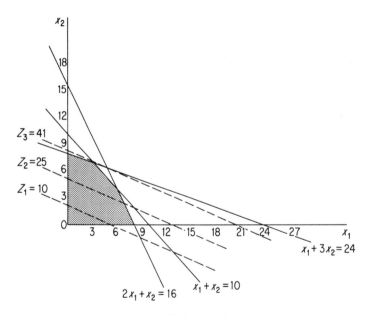

Figure 16–2. Geometrical solution to the example *LP* problem.

point within it satisfies the constraints. The dashed lines are combinations of x_1 and x_2 that yield equal profits. For line z_1, every feasible combination of outputs x_1 and x_2 yields \$10 in profits to the firm. The profit lines are drawn parallel to one another with slope $-2/5$. As we move from profit line z_1 to z_3, profit increases from \$10 to \$41. The optimal values of the

---

[4] See IBM, "Mathematical Programming System/360–Linear and Separable Programming," Application Program Manual No. H20-0476-1, International Business Machines Corporation, 1968.

decision variables will always lie on an extreme point of the region of feasible solutions (i.e., the optimal value will be a basic feasible solution) because the profit line will be "tangent to" the feasible region here, and any additional parallel shifts of the profit line would not allow any point on it to intersect the feasible region.

In this case, the optimal levels of x_1 and x_2 are 3 and 7 units, respectively, yielding a profit of \$41 per day to the firm. (Fractional optimal values could have been interpreted as work in progress or as units only partially completed.)

The graphical method of solution is only usable in two or three dimensions; when more than three variables are present, the simplex procedure may be invoked.

G. Example (Continued): Simplex Solution

The simplex procedure depends heavily on the theory of solving simultaneous linear equations.

The initial set of equations for this example problem is:

$$\left.\begin{array}{rl} z - 2x_1 - 5x_2 & = 0 \\ x_1 + 3x_2 + v_1 & = 24 \\ 2x_1 + x_2 + v_2 & = 16 \\ x_1 + x_2 + v_3 & = 10 \end{array}\right\} . \qquad (16\text{-}9)$$

Note that the inequality constraints have been converted to equalities by the addition of slack variables (v_1, v_2, v_3). *Slack variables* (or *surplus variables* in the case of "$\geq$" constraints) effectively "make up" the difference between the sum of the coefficients of the decision variables times the values of the decision variables and the value of the right side of the inequality. As in the case of the decision variables, slack variables are restricted to nonnegative values.

In the initial set of equations (16-9), if $z = x_1 = x_2 = 0$, $v_1 = 24$ $v_2 = 16$, and $v_3 = 10$, the equations are satisfied. (This solution corresponds to the corner point $(0, 0)$ in Figure 16-2.) For this set of equations, x_1 and x_2 are called *nonbasic* variables, while v_1, v_2, and v_3 are termed *basic* variables.

The final set of equations is:[5]

---

[5] We have not attempted to describe the computational procedures utilized in deriving the final set of Eq. (16-10) from the initial set of Eq. (16-9). Readers interested in the computations involved when the simplex procedure is used to solve a linear programming problem should see, for example, either Edward H. Bowman and Robert B. Fetter, *Analysis for Production and Operations Management*, 3rd ed. (Homewood, Ill.: Richard D. Irwin, Inc., 1967), chap. 3, or A. Charnes and W. W. Cooper, *Management Models and Industrial Applications of Linear Programming* (New York: John Wiley & Sons, Inc., 1961), Vol. I, chap. 5.

$$\left.\begin{array}{l} z \qquad + \tfrac{3}{2}v_1 \qquad + \tfrac{1}{2}v_3 = 41 \\[4pt] \quad x_2 + \tfrac{1}{2}v_1 \qquad - \tfrac{1}{2}v_3 = \ 7 \\[4pt] \qquad \tfrac{1}{2}v_1 + v_2 - \tfrac{5}{2}v_3 = \ 3 \\[4pt] x_1 \qquad - \tfrac{1}{2}v_1 \qquad + \tfrac{3}{2}v_3 = \ 3 \end{array}\right\}. \qquad (16\text{--}10)$$

In the set of Eq. (16–10), the equations are satisfied if $x_1 = 3$, $x_2 = 7$, $v_2 = 3$, $z = 41$, $v_1 = v_3 = 0$. [This solution, the optimal one, corresponds to the corner point $(3, 7)$ in Figure 16–2.] The basic variables are x_1, x_2, and v_2, while v_1 and v_3 are the nonbasic variables. This set of values can be seen to be optimal by examining the objective function. If either v_1 or v_3 were increased from 0 to some positive value (recall that the decision and slack variables are restricted to be nonnegative), the value of z would have to decrease because the equality must be satisfied.

H. DUALITY: FORMULATION

Every linear programming problem has associated with it another closely related LP problem. Either one of these LP problems may be called the *primal* problem, with the other then being called the *dual*. The simplex maximization procedure can therefore be applied to the dual of minimization problems, since the primal maximization problem has associated with it a dual minimization problem, and vice versa.

The relationship between the primal and dual problems is indicated below (the "primal" and "dual" labels are arbitrary insofar as they could have been interchanged):

Primal Problem

Maximize: $$z = \sum_{j=1}^{n} c_j x_j \qquad (16\text{--}11)$$

Subject to: $$\sum_{j=1}^{n} a_{ij} x_j \le b_i, \qquad i = 1, 2, \ldots, m \qquad (16\text{--}12)$$

$$x_j \ge 0, \qquad j = 1, 2, \ldots, n \qquad (16\text{--}13)$$

Dual Problem

Minimize: $$z' = \sum_{i=1}^{m} b_i y_i \qquad (16\text{--}14)$$

Subject to: $$\sum_{i=1}^{m} a_{ij} y_i \ge c_j, \qquad j = 1, 2, \ldots, n \qquad (16\text{--}15)$$

$$y_i \le 0, \qquad i = 1, 2, \ldots, m. \qquad (16\text{--}16)$$

The relationship between the primal and dual problems is as follows:

1. The jth column of coefficients in the primal becomes the jth row of coefficients in the dual.

2. An n-variable, m-constraint primal problem has an m-variable, n-constraint dual problem.

3. The right-hand side coefficients in the primal become the objective-function coefficients in the dual, and the objective-function coefficients in the primal become the right-hand side coefficients in the dual.

4. The direction of the inequalities is reversed.

5. If the primal is a maximization problem, the dual is a minimization problem, and vice versa.

6. If the ith row of the primal is an equality, the ith variable in the dual is unconstrained in sign.

I. EXAMPLE (CONTINUED): FORMULATION OF THE DUAL

The dual formulation of our example problem would be:

Minimize: $\qquad\qquad z' = 24y_1 + 16y_2 + 10y_3$ $\qquad\qquad$ (16–17)

Subject to: $\qquad\qquad y_1 + 2y_2 + y_3 \geq 2$ $\qquad\qquad$ (16–18)

$\qquad\qquad\qquad 3y_1 + y_2 + y_3 \geq 5$ $\qquad\qquad$ (16–19)

$\qquad\qquad\qquad y_1, y_2, y_3 \geq 0.$ $\qquad\qquad$ (16–20)

J. DUALITY: INTERPRETATION

The basic theorem of duality states that if either the primal or the dual problem has a finite optimal solution, then the other problem possesses a finite optimum, and the optimal values of the objective functions are equal.

There is a completely symmetrical relationship between the primal and dual LP problems: the dual of the dual is the primal. The primal simplex algorithm solves both the primal and the dual problems simultaneously in that the optimal value of the ith dual variable equals the coefficient of the ith slack variable in the final objective function equation.

Shadow prices or *dual evaluators* are terms used to describe the optimal values of the dual variables. Each shadow price indicates the incremental change in the optimal value of the objective function that would occur if the right-hand side of the corresponding constraint were increased by one unit.

K. EXAMPLE (CONTINUED): INTERPRETATION OF THE DUAL

The final set of equations for the dual problem is:

$$\left. \begin{aligned} z' \quad - 3y_2 \quad\quad - 3w_1 - 7w_2 &= 41 \\ \tfrac{5}{2}y_2 + y_3 - \tfrac{3}{2}w_1 + \tfrac{1}{2}w_2 &= \tfrac{1}{2} \\ y_1 - \tfrac{1}{2}y_2 \quad\quad + \tfrac{1}{2}w_1 - \tfrac{1}{2}w_2 &= \tfrac{3}{2} \end{aligned} \right\} \qquad (16\text{–}21)$$

where w_1 and w_2 are the dual "slack" (or surplus) variables. These equations are satisfied if $z' = 41$, $y_1 = \tfrac{3}{2}$, $y_3 = \tfrac{1}{2}$, and $y_2 = w_1 = w_2 = 0$.

The values of the dual variables are interpreted as shadow prices. If the stamping-time constraint were increased by 1 unit from 24 hours to 25 hours, then the maximum profit would increase by $\frac{3}{2}$, as indicated by $y_1 = \frac{3}{2}$. Similarly, if the painting-time constraint were increased by 1 unit from 10 hours to 11 hours, then the maximum profit would increase by $\frac{1}{2}$, as indicated by $y_3 = \frac{1}{2}$. However, because $y_2 = 0$, increasing the bolting-time constraint by 1 unit would not result in an increase in profit because not all of the bolting time is being used at the optimal solution [$v_2 = 3$ in the primal Eq. (16–10), indicating 3 available unused hours of bolting time]. This slackness is illustrated in Figure 16–2 by the nonbinding constraint $2x_1 + x_2 \leq 16$.

The total profit in the primal case is analogous to the total worth of all the resources (stamping, bolting, and painting time) in scarce supply in the dual case. Recall that a_{ij} is the consumption of the ith resource by the jth activity. Note that $\sum_{i=1}^{m} a_{ij}y_i$ indicates the economic cost of activity j in terms of the shadow prices. For the first constraint in the dual problem (i.e., for $j = 1$), for example, $(1)(\frac{3}{2}) + (2)(0) + (1)(\frac{1}{2}) = 2$, which equals the profit per unit of x_1. The dual problem's constraints ensure that the profit of an activity cannot exceed its economic worth at the optimum. Furthermore, an activity will not be used unless its profit equals its economic worth.

Finally, note that the primal method also solves the dual variables. The coefficients of the slack variables in the objective function in Eq. (16–10) are $\frac{3}{2}$, 0, and $\frac{1}{2}$. These are also the optimal values of the dual variables [see Eq. (16–21)].

L. DUALITY: COMPLEMENTARY SLACKNESS

An interesting corollary to the basic theorem of duality is the theorem of complementary slackness. This theorem states that whenever a constraint in either the primal or dual problem holds with a strict inequality (i.e., there is some available slack in the constraint), the corresponding variable in the other problem equals zero. More formally, if x_j^o, for $j = 1, 2, \ldots, n$, and y_i^o for $i = 1, 2, \ldots, m$ are feasible solutions to the primal and dual problems, respectively, then both are optimal if and only if

$$x_j^o \left[\sum_{i=1}^{m} a_{ij}y_i^o - c_j \right] = 0, \qquad \text{for } j = 1, 2, \ldots, n \qquad (16\text{--}22)$$

$$y_i^o \left[\sum_{j=1}^{n} a_{ij}x_j^o - b_i \right] = 0, \qquad \text{for } i = 1, 2, \ldots, m. \qquad (16\text{--}23)$$

M. Example (Continued): Complementary Slackness

For the optimal values of x_1 and y_1, complementary slackness indicates that

$$x_1 \left[\sum_{i=1}^{3} a_{i1} y_i - c_1 \right] = 3[(\tfrac{3}{2})(1) + (0)(2) + (\tfrac{1}{2})(1) - 2] = 3 \cdot 0 = 0 \tag{16-24}$$

and

$$y_1 \left[\sum_{j=1}^{2} a_{1j} x_j - b_1 \right] = \tfrac{3}{2}[(3)(1) + (7)(3) - 24] = \tfrac{3}{2} \cdot 0 = 0. \tag{16-25}$$

II. An LP Model for Investment Project Selection

We are now ready to consider one approach to a business firm's problem of selecting an optimal portfolio of investment projects from a larger set of potential investment alternatives. Under conditions of certainty, Weingartner has shown that this problem can be formulated as a linear programming model.[6] Throughout most of this section we shall assume the existence of perfect capital markets, although this assumption is relaxed in Section II.J.

A. Individual Investment Projects

Suppose that there are N capital investment projects which the firm is considering. We shall let the variable x_j denote whether or not investment project j is accepted (i.e., undertaken) by the firm, for $j = 1, 2, \ldots, N$. In particular, $x_j = 0$ means that project j is rejected, whereas $x_j = 1$ means that project j is accepted.

The variables x_j in the LP model being formulated should, strictly speaking, be restricted to the integer values 0 and 1, to denote that any particular project is either rejected or accepted. In technical terms this requires that the model be regarded as a mixed integer programming model rather than as an ordinary linear programming model. For now, however, let us conveniently regard the x_j as linear variables subject to the following ordinary inequality constraints:

$$0 \leq x_j \leq 1 \qquad j = 1, 2, \ldots, N. \tag{16-26}$$

---

[6] The pioneering research exploring the application of linear programming to the analysis of capital projects is reported in H. Martin Weingartner, *Mathematical Programming and the Analysis of Capital Budgeting Problems* (Englewood Cliffs, N.J.: Prentice-Hall, Inc., 1963). The material presented in this section is adapted from that book, especially chaps. 3, 8, and 9. The reader interested in more detail should refer to Weingartner's book.

Suppose that the planning horizon consists of T discrete time periods. For simplicity, we can regard the periods as each being one year long, so that the entire planning horizon covers T years. The first decision interval for which decisions need to be made is period 1.

Acceptance of project j will give rise to a sequence of net after-tax cash outflows in the firm. Let c_{tj} denote the net after-tax cash outflow that will occur in the firm during period t if project j is accepted. Each c_{tj} may be either positive or negative. A positive value of c_{tj} denotes a net after-tax cash outflow (i.e., expenditure). Similarly, a negative value for c_{tj} denotes a net after-tax cash inflow (i.e., revenue) for the firm.

The actual investment projects may generate streams of net after-tax cash flows beyond the end of period T, which is the assumed planning horizon. Let a_j denote the value of all net after-tax cash inflows to the firm, if any, subsequent to the horizon at the end of period T, discounted (i.e., present-valued) to the horizon date by some appropriate market rate of interest, r. The convention regarding the algebraic sign of the a_j is opposite to that associated with the c_{tj}. Hence a positive value of a_j denotes that project j has a positive net present value at the horizon date. In contrast, a negative value of a_j indicates a negative net present value for the project at the horizon date, for example, as might stem from required costly demolition at the end of the asset's life. In terms of the previously defined notation,

$$a_j = \sum_{t=T+1}^{\infty} \frac{-c_{jt}}{(1+r)^{t-T}}. \tag{16–27}$$

Each particular capital investment project implicitly carries with it a starting date. The N different investment projects should not all be interpreted as projects that could be undertaken only during the first decision interval. Some of these projects can start during period 1, other projects can start during period 2, others might start in period 3, etc. There is no need explicitly to add a second (i.e., a time) subscript to the project acceptance decision variable, x_j, because the values of the net after-tax cash flows associated with that project (the c_{tj}) implicitly indicate the starting date of the project. Thus, for example, if project j actually begins in period 3, then c_{1j} and c_{2j} will both be 0 and c_{3j} will be non-zero (and, for most projects, positive to indicate that a net after-tax cash outflow occurs at least during the first year of the project).

B. Interrelationships among Investment Projects

A particular capital investment project—e.g., building a bridge across a river which separates two plants belonging to the same firm—could conceivably be undertaken in any one of several periods during the planning horizon. This can be mathematically represented within the model in the following fashion. Starting in period 1 to build the bridge across the river to connect the plants is defined as one particular project. Starting in period

2 to build the same bridge is defined as a second (and different) investment project. Similarly, starting in period 3 to build the same bridge is defined as a third investment project, etc. We then must introduce a constraint into the linear programming model to prevent us from accepting more than one of these projects—i.e., from starting to build the bridge in two or more different periods. The following constraint will accomplish this:

$$\sum_{j \in J} x_j \leq 1. \tag{16-28}$$

In Eq. (16–28) the summation over the index numbers corresponding to the set J runs over all possible elements in a set of mutually exclusive investment alternatives. This constraint can be satisfied by all of the x_j being set equal to 0. In this case none of the mutually exclusive investment alternatives will be undertaken. It also may be satisfied by $x_j = 1$ for one particular j in the set J, with all of the other $x_i = 0$ for $i \in J$ and $i \neq j$. If, as suggested above, each x_j is restricted to the integer values 0 or 1, then these are the only ways in which Eq. (16–28) can be satisfied. Should fractional solutions for the x_j be permitted, there are additional possible ways of satisfying Eq. (16–28); we shall, however, postpone consideration of how to interpret solutions which involve fractional investment projects until later.

There are other types of logical interrelationships among projects besides mutual exclusiveness. We also need to consider contingent projects and compound projects. Two investment projects are contingent if one of them cannot be logically accepted without prior acceptance of the other. For example, suppose that project k is the purchase of a Cadillac limousine for the company president, and that project m is the installation of a two-way radio telephone in that executive limousine. Clearly the Cadillac limousine can be purchased for the president without its being equipped with a two-way telephone, but it would be ridiculous to buy a two-way telephone for the president's limousine if he does not already have (or simultaneously obtain) the limousine itself. This would be an example in which the feasibility of project m is contingent upon the acceptance of project k (but not vice versa). This type of project interrelationship can be introduced into the model by the following constraint:

$$x_m \leq x_k. \tag{16-29}$$

Because of constraint (16–29) (in conjunction with Eq. [16–26], of course), project m cannot be accepted without project k also being accepted (i.e., $x_m = 1$ implies $x_k = 1$). The opposite is, of course, possible, since project k can be accepted with project m being rejected (i.e., $x_k = 1$ is consistent with $x_m = 0$). Again the possibility of fractional values for the project acceptance variables could cause some difficulty, but this will be discussed later.

There is an alternative procedure for handling contingent projects in the LP model which sometimes may be preferable. This involves transforming the two contingent projects so that they instead become two mutually exclusive projects. Thus, for example, we could suppose that project c is a compound project involving the purchase for the company president of a Cadillac limousine which is equipped with a two-way radio telephone. In effect, project c is the compound project obtained by accepting both projects k and m. Rather than introducing the constraint to express the contingent nature of project k and m, an alternative would be to formulate the model in terms of projects k and c and to introduce the following constraint:

$$x_k + x_c \leq 1. \tag{16-30}$$

Although more elaborate conditions on contingent and mutually exclusive projects can arise, they can be handled by combinations of the procedures already presented. Consider the following example. Suppose that project a is building a bowling alley. If a bowling alley is built, it need not necessarily be equipped with automatic pinsetters; instead pin boys can be utilized. Hence suppose project a is merely the building of the bowling alley without installation of automatic pinsetters. Suppose project b is installation of Brunswick automatic pinsetters and project d is installation of AMF pinsetters. Clearly, no automatic pinsetters whatever need be installed, but if any are installed, they should all be either Brunswick or AMF rather than mixing the two brands. The following set of restrictions which combines contingent projects with mutually exclusive projects will handle this situation:

$$x_b \leq x_a, \quad x_d \leq x_a, \quad x_b + x_d \leq 1, \quad x_a \leq 1. \tag{16-31}$$

C. FINANCIAL CONSTRAINTS

In order to complete the specification of the LP model, we need to introduce some additional parameters and decision variables. We shall let D_t denote the net after-tax cash inflow which the firm will generate during year t from the existing resources which the firm controls in the absence of any of the investment projects $1, 2, \ldots, N$ being undertaken. Thus the D_t are the exogenous future after-tax net cash inflows generated by continuation of the firm as a going concern in the absence of any of the new investments which the model is being formulated to analyze.

In keeping with the assumptions of perfect capital markets and certainty, we shall suppose that the firm may lend and borrow any desired amounts of funds at the market rate of interest, r. Let w_t denote the amount of funds borrowed by the firm during period t. It is convenient to assume that all lending and borrowing be done with one-year contracts, and that all interest is paid or received at the end of the year. We can, therefore, denote the financial restrictions on the firm's investment activities in the following ways:

$$\sum_{j=1}^{N} c_{1j}x_j + v_1 - w_1 \leq D_1 \qquad (16\text{--}32)$$

$$\sum_{j=1}^{N} c_{tj}x_j - (1+r)v_{t-1} + v_t + (1+r)w_{t-1} - w_t \leq D_t \qquad t = 2, \ldots, T.$$
$$(16\text{--}33)$$

Note that any outstanding lending or borrowing that took place before the beginning of the planning horizon is implicitly included in the values of $D_1, D_2, \ldots, D_T$ (in particular, if lending and borrowing is permitted for only one period, all of these effects will be included in the value of D_1). The reason Eq. (16–33) contains the additional terms that are not contained in Eq. (16–32) is that provision must be made for the repayment of lending and borrowing activities undertaken within the planning horizon.[7]

D. OBJECTIVE FUNCTION

The objective function to be maximized in the LP model is the value on the horizon date of the firm's financial and physical assets. The value of the firm's financial assets on the horizon date can be regarded as the net funds lent by the firm at that time; this is represented in the objective function as

$$v_T - w_T. \qquad (16\text{--}34)$$

We should discuss the reason that the amounts lent and borrowed by the firm during the final period of the horizon, v_T and w_T, are not multiplied (i.e., compounded) by the factor $(1 + r)$. Even though the firm will receive $v_T(1 + r)$ dollars during period $T + 1$ as a result of lending v_T dollars in period T, in order to obtain the value as of the horizon date of this amount, the $v_T(1 + r)$ dollars to be received one period later must be discounted—i.e., multiplied by the discount factor $1/(1 + r)$. Hence, v_T, rather than $v_T(1 + r)$, represents the present value as of the horizon date of the post-horizon flows associated with the loans made by the firm in period T. Similarly, even though the firm will experience a cash outflow of $w_T(1 + r)$ dollars in period $T + 1$ in order to repay the w_T dollars it

---

[7] It is apparent that the objective function to be maximized that is specified in Eq. (16–35) implicitly assumes repayment of any lending and borrowing activities during the final period T.

borrowed during period T, the present value as of the horizon date of this post-horizon commitment is only w_T.[8]

The value of the firm's physical assets on the horizon date can be represented by the present value (as of the horizon date) of the discounted streams of net after-tax cash inflows to the firm accruing from its investment projects. For investment project j, this concept has already been denoted by a_j.

Hence the objective function to be maximized can be written as

$$\sum_{j=1}^{N} a_j x_j + v_T - w_T. \tag{16-35}$$

Before continuing further, it is desirable to consider how the objective function of the present LP model, Eq. (16–35), relates to the general presumption of the multiperiod theory of the firm that under conditions of certainty, the firm should maximize the present value of its net after-tax profits. When the discount rate used to discount future profits is the market rate of interest, r, this is essentially equivalent to the objective function expressed in Eq. (16–35). In particular Eq. (16–35) is the present value of the firm's assets as of the horizon date (i.e., the end of period T).[9] In the absence of any new investment opportunities that are not considered in the model, Eq. (16–35) is equivalent to the present value as of the horizon date of the firm's post-horizon net after-tax profit stream.[10] The reason that no explicit consideration need be given to the stream of profits that the firm will earn within the horizon date is that the model is being developed

---

[8] This discussion is assuming, of course, that the appropriate interest rate to use in discounting post-horizon flows is the same as the interest rate at which the firm can borrow and lend during the horizon. This requires not only the assumptions of perfect capital markets and certainty but also the additional assumption that the market rate of interest remains unchanged.

[9] For this statement to be strictly true, it would be necessary to add to Eq. (16–35) a term that represents the present value as of the horizon date of the assets which the firm controls as of date zero (the beginning of the planning horizon). In terms of the symbols already defined, this term would be

$$\sum_{t=T+1}^{\infty} \frac{D_t}{(1+r)^{t-T}}.$$

Because this term is an exogenously determined constant, its omission does not change the optimal values of the decision variables to be determined by the LP model.

[10] This statement implicitly assumes that the firm's accounting system defines net after-tax profits in any year to be identical to the firm's net after-tax cash flow in that year. In reality, of course, neither standard accounting practices nor Internal Revenue Service regulations permit profits to be determined strictly on a cash-flow basis. It is beyond the scope of this discussion to consider the modifications of the LP model that are required when accounting practices and tax regulations are more realistically taken into consideration.

under conditions of perfect capital markets. Any profits (remember that this term is assumed to be equivalent to cash funds available) that are generated within the horizon date will be utilized by the optimal solution to the LP model either to allow additional investment projects to be undertaken by the firm, to lend outside the firm at the market rate of interest, or to reduce the external funds borrowed by the firm at the market rate of interest. In other words, there is no opportunity-cost reason to separately value funds generated by the firm's operations within the horizon date other than as these funds affect the optimal solution values to the decision variables x_j, v_t, and w_t. All potentially profitable uses of cash funds generated within the horizon date are included as potential decision variables in the model.

The situation is different, however, with respect to profitable ways of the firm using funds beyond the horizon date. In particular, the LP model does not explicitly contain any decision variables whatever pertaining to post-horizon considerations. The only way in which any post-horizon considerations enter the model is in terms of the horizon date values of the various investment projects that the firm might undertake before the horizon date—i.e., the a_j.

E. Summary of the LP Model

In order to recap in a convenient way the LP model that has been developed, let us for now ignore all consideration of mutually exclusive and contingent projects and assume that we are considering only a set of independent investment projects. The LP model that we have formulated then takes the following form:

Maximize:
$$\sum_{j=1}^{N} a_j x_j + v_T - w_T$$

Subject to:

(a) $\displaystyle\sum_{j=1}^{N} c_{1j} x_j + v_1 - w_1 \leq D_1$

(b) $\displaystyle\sum_{j=1}^{N} c_{tj} x_j - (1 + r)v_{t-1} + v_t + (1 + r)w_{t-1} - w_t \leq D_t$
$$t = 2, \ldots, T$$

(c) $x_j \leq 1 \quad j = 1, \ldots, N$

(d) $x_j \geq 0 \quad j = 1, \ldots, N$

$v_t \geq 0$ and $w_t \geq 0 \quad t = 1, \ldots, T$

$\left.\begin{array}{c}\\\\\\\\\\\\\\\\\\\\\end{array}\right\} \cdot (16\text{--}36)$

As already indicated, we should in principle add restrictions that require the x_j to take on only integer values, so that the programming model is a mixed integer programming problem. If ordinary linear programming techniques are used to solve Eq. (16–36), it is possible that some fractional projects will appear in the optimal solution.

The major result we shall derive later in Section G is that under the conditions of certainty, perfect capital markets, and project independence that were assumed in the formulation of Eq. (16–36), the optimal solution to the LP problem Eq. (16–36) is exactly equivalent to selecting or rejecting the independent investment proposals on a piecemeal basis according to whether their present value is positive or negative when discounted at the market rate of interest, r. In order to demonstrate the equivalence of these two approaches under the assumed conditions, it is necessary to utilize the dual problem to the primal problem defined in Eq. (16–36). In order to analyze the dual problem, it is first convenient to represent the LP model defined in Eq. (16–36) in the tableau form shown in Table 16–2.

Ignore for the moment the left-hand column in Table 16–2, headed "Dual Variables." Let us then consider the LP problem determined by reading across Table 16–2. The column headings contain the decision variables of the primal problem: $x_1, x_2, \ldots, x_N$; $v_1, v_2, \ldots, v_T$; $w_1, w_2, \ldots, w_T$. The rows in the main body of the table correspond to the constraints in Eq. (16–36). In order to see this, the variable names shown at the tops of the columns are assumed to be multiplied by the coefficients entered in the body of the columns, with the resulting products then summed across rows. Thus the first row in Table 16–2 can readily be seen to correspond to constraint (a) in Eq. (16–36). The right-hand side of this constraint is, of course, shown in the final column of Table 16–2 labeled "Requirements."

In a similar fashion, the next $T - 1$ rows in Table 16–2 correspond to constraints (b) in Eq. (16–36). The next N rows in Table 16–2 correspond to constraints (c) in Eq. (16–36). The nonnegativity constraints in (d) of Eq. (16–36) are not explicitly shown in Table 16–2 but instead are implicitly assumed. The computational procedures used for solving LP problems will automatically insure that the nonnegativity constraints on variables are satisfied, and hence they need not be explicitly entered in the tableau.

The objective function in Eq. (16–36) to be maximized can be seen in Table 16–2 by associating the coefficients in the bottom row labeled "Objective" with the names of the variables at the heads of the columns. With this interpretation, by reading across Table 16–2 the primal problem encompassed in Eq. (16–36) may readily be seen.

F. FORMULATION OF THE DUAL PROBLEM

The dual problem corresponding to Eq. (16–36) can be formed by reading down Table 16–2. Refer now to the first column headed "Dual Variables." Variable names appear here corresponding to each of the constraints in the primal problem. These variable names in the dual problem are often called the "dual evaluators" or the "shadow prices" of the con-

TABLE 16–2

PRIMAL (READ ACROSS) AND DUAL (READ DOWN) LINEAR PROGRAMS CORRESPONDING TO EQ. (16–36)

Dual Vbles \ Primal Vbles	x_1	x_2	$\cdots$	x_j	$\cdots$	x_N	v_1	v_2	$\cdots$	v_{t-1}	v_t	$\cdots$	v_{T-1}	v_T	w_1	w_2	$\cdots$	w_{t-1}	w_t	$\cdots$	w_{T-1}	w_T	Objective	Requirements
ρ_1	c_{11}	c_{12}	$\cdots$	c_{1j}	$\cdots$	c_{1N}	1								-1								$\le$	D_1
ρ_2	c_{21}	c_{22}	$\cdots$	c_{2j}	$\cdots$	c_{2N}	$-(1+r)$	1							$(1+r)$	-1							$\le$	D_2
$\cdots$	$\cdots$	$\cdots$		$\cdots$		$\cdots$			$\ddots$								$\ddots$							$\cdots$
ρ_t	c_{t1}	c_{t2}	$\cdots$	c_{tj}	$\cdots$	c_{tN}				$-(1+r)$	1							$(1+r)$	-1				$\le$	D_t
$\cdots$				$\cdots$		$\cdots$					$\ddots$	$\ddots$							$\ddots$	$\ddots$				$\cdots$
ρ_T	c_{T1}	c_{T2}	$\cdots$	c_{Tj}	$\cdots$	c_{TN}							$-(1+r)$	1							$(1+r)$	-1	$\le$	D_T
μ_1	1																						$\le$	1
μ_2		1																					$\le$	1
$\cdots$			$\ddots$																					$\cdots$
μ_j				1																			$\le$	1
$\cdots$					$\ddots$																			$\cdots$
μ_N						1																	$\le$	1
Objective	$\ge$	$\ge$	$\cdots$	$\ge$	$\cdots$	$\ge$	$\ge$	$\ge$	$\cdots$	$\ge$	$\ge$	$\cdots$	$\ge$	$\ge$	$\ge$	$\ge$	$\cdots$	$\ge$	$\ge$	$\cdots$	$\ge$	$\ge$		
Requirements	a_1	a_2	$\cdots$	a_j	$\cdots$	a_N	0	0	$\cdots$	0	0	$\cdots$	0	1	0	0	$\cdots$	0	0	$\cdots$	0	-1		

377

straints in the primal problem. The dual variables $\rho_1, \rho_2, \ldots, \rho_T$ correspond to the funds availability constraints, and the dual variables $\mu_1, \mu_2,$
$\ldots, \mu_N$ correspond to the upper-bound restrictions preventing us from
choosing to undertake more than 100 per cent of any investment project.

In reading the dual problem down Table 16–2, this time the column
headings in the row labeled "Primal Variables" must be ignored. For the
reader's convenience, the conventional algebraic formulation of the dual
problem is also shown in Eq. (16–37). The first N columns in the main
body of Table 16–2, when read downward, correspond to constraints (a) in
Eq. (16–37). The next $T - 1$ columns in Table 16–2 correspond to constraints (b) in Eq. (16–37). The next column in Table 16–2 corresponds to
(c) in Eq. (16–37). Constraints (d) in Eq. (16–37) correspond to the next
$T - 1$ columns in Table 16–2. Finally, the last column in the main body of
Table 16–2 corresponds to constraint (e) of Eq. (16–37). The objective
function to be minimized in Eq. (16–34) may be read in Table 16–2 by
associating the coefficients in the right-hand column of the table with the
dual variable names shown in the first column of the table.

$$
\left.
\begin{aligned}
&\text{Minimize:} && \sum_{t=1}^{T} \rho_t D_t + \sum_{j=1}^{N} \mu_j \\
&\text{Subject to:} \\
&\text{(a)} \ \sum_{t=1}^{T} \rho_t c_{tj} + \mu_j \geq a_j && j = 1, \ldots, N \\
&\text{(b)} \ \rho_{t-1} - (1+r)\rho_t \geq 0 && t = 2, \ldots, T \\
&\text{(c)} \ \rho_T \geq 1 \\
&\text{(d)} \ -\rho_{t-1} + (1+r)\rho_t \geq 0 && t = 2, \ldots, T \\
&\text{(e)} \ -\rho_T \geq -1 \\
&\text{(f)} \ \rho_t \geq 0 && t = 1, \ldots, T \\
&\quad \text{and} \\
&\quad \mu_j \geq 0 && j = 1, \ldots, N
\end{aligned}
\right\} . \qquad (16\text{–}37)
$$

Let us adopt the convention of attaching an asterisk to a variable to
denote its value in an optimal solution to the LP problem. Let us assume
that we have found an optimal solution to Eq. (16–36); i.e., an optimal set
of values $x_1^*, x_2^*, \ldots, x_N^*; v_1^*, v_2^*, \ldots, v_T^*; w_1^*, w_2^*, \ldots, w_T^*$. Given a set of
optimal solution values for the primal problem, we automatically can
obtain an associated optimal solution to the dual problem: $\rho_1^*, \rho_2^*, \ldots, \rho_T^*;$
$\mu_1^*, \mu_2^*, \ldots, \mu_N^*.$

G. Analysis of the Dual Problem

We are now ready to analyze the dual problem in Eq. (16–37). Constraints (c) and (e) of Eq. (16–37) together imply that

$$
\rho_T = 1. \qquad (16\text{–}38)
$$

In similar fashion it can be seen that (b) and (d) of Eq. (16–37) together imply that

$$\rho_{t-1} = (1 + r)\rho_t \qquad t = 2, \ldots, T. \qquad (16\text{–}39)$$

From Eq. (16–39), we readily obtain the following relations:

$$\left.\begin{array}{l} \rho_1 = (1 + r)^{T-1} \\ \rho_2 = (1 + r)^{T-2} \\ \qquad \vdots \\ \rho_t = (1 + r)^{T-t} \\ \qquad \vdots \\ \rho_T = 1 \end{array}\right\} . \qquad (16\text{–}40)$$

The economic reasonableness of Eq. (16–40) stems from our assumption of perfect capital markets. Clearly, one way of utilizing one extra dollar first received by the firm during period t is to lend it at the market rate of interest r for period t; then to re-lend the principal and interest for period $t + 1$; and so forth throughout the remaining periods in the planning horizon. By doing so, the incremental dollar brought into the firm during period t will grow to an horizon value of $(1 + r)^{T-t}$ dollars. Hence we can interpret ρ_t as the future value compound interest factor based on the market rate of interest indicating the yield at the end of the planning horizon (i.e., at the end of period T) of an additional dollar initially available to the firm in period t.

In order to interpret constraints (a) in the dual problem in Eq. (16–37), let us rewrite them in the following form:

$$\mu_j \geq a_j - \sum_{t=1}^{T} \rho_t c_{tj}. \qquad (16\text{–}41)$$

The left-hand side of Eq. (16–41) is the shadow price of the constraint that prevents us from undertaking more than 100 per cent of project j. The first term on the right-hand side of Eq. (16–41), i.e., a_j, is the present value as of the horizon date of all net cash inflows resulting from project j subsequent to the horizon date. The remaining term on the right-hand side of Eq. (16–41), $-\sum_{t=1}^{T} \rho_t c_{tj}$, is the horizon value of the net cash inflows associated with the project j before the end of the planning horizon (recall that c_{tj} is negative when project j produces a net cash inflow during period T). This can be seen more clearly by utilizing Eq. (16–40) to obtain:

$$-\sum_{t=1}^{T} \rho_t c_{tj} = \sum_{t=1}^{T} (-c_{tj})(1 + r)^{T-t} = \sum_{t=1}^{T} \frac{-c_{tj}}{(1 + r)^{t-T}}. \qquad (16\text{–}42)$$

Let us now substitute Eq. (16–27) and (16–42) into Eq. (16–41) to obtain:

$$\mu \geq \sum_{t=T+1}^{\infty} \frac{-c_{tj}}{(1+r)^{t-T}} + \sum_{t=1}^{T} \frac{(-c_{tj})}{(1+r)^{t-T}} \tag{16-43}$$

or, more simply,

$$\mu_j \geq \sum_{t=1}^{\infty} \frac{-c_{tj}}{(1+r)^{t-T}}. \tag{16-44}$$

The interpretation of Eq. (16–44) becomes easier if we divide both sides of the inequality by the positive constant $(1+r)^T$, obtaining

$$\frac{\mu_i}{(1+r)^T} \geq \sum_{t=1}^{\infty} \frac{(-c_{tj})}{(1+r)^t}. \tag{16-45}$$

Since we have assumed that positive values of c_{tj} represent net after-tax cash *out*flows associated with project j during period t, it follows that the right-hand side of Eq. (16–42) is simply the present value as of the beginning of period 1 of the after-tax cash *in*flows of project j computed on the basis of the market rate of interest, r.

$$NPV_j = \sum_{t=1}^{\infty} \frac{(-c_{tj})}{(1+r)^{t-1}}. \tag{16-46}$$

Combining Eq. (16–45) and (16–46), we have

$$\mu_j \geq (1+r)^T (NPV_j). \tag{16-47}$$

It follows from the theorem of complementary slackness (see Section I.L above) that when any inequality constraint in the primal problem is not tightly binding as a strict equality in an optimal solution, then the corresponding optimal value of the shadow price must be zero. In particular, whenever project j is not (entirely) included in an optimal solution, i.e., when $x_j^* < 1$, then $\mu_j^* = 0$. Combining this result with Eq. (16–47), we see that when a project is not (entirely) accepted in the optimal set of investments, its present value cannot be positive.

Suppose, however, that the present value of project j is positive, i.e., $NPV_j > 0$. It then follows from Eq. (16–47) that $\mu_j^* > 0$. Another implication of the theorem of complementary slackness is that when the value of a dual variable in an optimal solution of the dual problem is positive, the corresponding inequality constraint of the primal problem must be tightly binding as a strict equality in an optimal solution. Therefore, $x_j^* = 1$ and project j will be accepted whenever the present value of project j is positive.

One further property that follows from the theorem of complementary slackness is that when project j is fully accepted, i.e., when $x_j^* = 1$, the corresponding inequality constraint in the dual problem must be tightly binding as an equality. Writing the jth constraint in (a) of Eq. (16–37) as a strict equality and repeating the derivation of Eq. (16–41) through (16–47) (but now formulated as an equality), we find that

$$\mu_j^* = (1 + r)^T (NPV_j) \qquad (16\text{–}48)$$

must hold for (entirely) accepted projects. We also know, of course, that both sides of Eq. (16–48) will be positive for fully accepted projects. In this case the shadow price of an accepted project is proportional to the present value of that project, where the factor of proportionality is the compound amount factor that transforms a present value to a horizon value. It follows that the horizon value of a project could be used as an alternative to the present value to determine whether a project will be accepted or rejected in the LP model Eq. (16–36).

There is one potentially ambiguous situation that remains, however. When the present value of project j is exactly equal to zero, then it cannot be determined on the basis of the preceding line of reasoning whether project j will be accepted or rejected. It turns out that under the assumed conditions, it is a matter of indifference to the firm whether it accepts or rejects projects whose present values equal zero; the optimal value of the firm at the horizon date is unchanged in either case.

When ordinary linear programming is used to solve the primal problem in Eq. (16–36), it is possible that one or more projects appear fractionally in the optimal solution (i.e., $0 < x_j^* < 1$ for one or more values of j). Any such project, however, will necessarily have a present value exactly equal to zero, and it can be shown that there are alternative optimal solutions to the primal problem possessing the same maximal value of the criterion function but not involving any fractional projects.[11]

H. Summing up the Main Results

Let us now sum up the main results obtained so far. We have used the primal problem expressed in Eq. (16–36) and its associated dual problem expressed in Eq. (16–37) to derive a powerful conclusion. Under conditions of perfect capital markets and certainty, when a firm is choosing from a set of completely independent investment projects, the optimal set of projects consists of those projects having positive present values of net cash inflows discounted at the market rate of interest. Any project with a positive present value should be accepted, and any project with a negative present value should be rejected. Exactly the same results would be obtained if future value rather than present value were used as the figure of merit for a project. Thus in this particular case there is no difference in the optimal solutions obtained from a piecemeal (or one-at-a-time) mode of

---

[11] The proof is presented in Weingartner, *op. cit.*, pp. 143–47.

project analysis and a portfolio analysis which simultaneously focuses on an entire set of independent projects.

I. Modifications Required for Interdependent Projects

This striking conclusion must be modified, however, when there are physical or logical interrelationships among various projects. Without going into the mathematical details, we shall indicate the essential nature of the results.[12]

Let us first consider a set of projects which are mutually exclusive. At most, one of these projects can be accepted. If it is optimal to accept any project from this set, the accepted project must have a positive present value, and its present value must be at least as high as that of any other project in the mutually exclusive set. This means that some rejected projects (from a set of mutually exclusive projects) may have positive present values when discounted at the market rate of interest.

In the case of contingent projects, the following modification of the present value rule is required. It is possible that the independent project of a pair of contingent projects might have a negative present value even though that project is accepted in an optimal solution. This can happen if the dependent project (which cannot be accepted without acceptance of the independent project) of the pair of contingent projects has such a high present value that both projects together are desirable.

To amplify on this discussion of contingent projects, suppose that projects f and g are a pair of contingent projects. In particular, project f cannot be accepted without also accepting project g, although project g may be undertaken independently. We then refer to project g as the "independent" project and project f as the "dependent" project.

If in an optimal solution to the appropriately formulated LP model the independent project is accepted and the dependent project is rejected, or both projects are rejected, the present-value rule that we have already derived (accept if $NPV > 0$ and reject if $NPV < 0$) continues to apply. However, it may turn out that in an optimal solution to the LP model both projects are accepted, even though the independent project may have a negative present value. The reason is that the present value of the compound project, which consists of the independent project plus the associated dependent project, may be positive even though the present value of the independent project itself is negative. When considered as a compound project, it turns out to be optimal to accept both the independent and the associated dependent project, although if it were possible (which it is not), it would be even more desirable to accept only the dependent project and to reject the independent project.

---

[12] The reader interested in the detailed derivations of these modified results is referred to Weingartner, *op. cit.*, pp. 147–52.

J. MODIFICATIONS REQUIRED FOR IMPERFECT CAPITAL MARKETS

When the assumption of perfect capital markets is relaxed (even though the assumption of certainty is retained), the present-value rule, with the market rate of interest used to determine the discount factors, may no longer lead to correct investment decisions. In particular, the one-project-at-a-time approach to evaluating projects, even when only independent projects are considered, is likely to be suboptimal in imperfect capital markets. The reasons this may be so can be clearly seen by analyzing the particularly simple case of capital market imperfection which is generally known as *capital rationing*.

Capital rationing exists when there are absolute upper limits on the amounts of funds that a firm may borrow in particular time periods. We shall analyze the impact of capital rationing by introducing a slight modification to the linear programming model for investment project selection developed above for the case of a perfect capital market. This model was compactly formulated in Eq. (16–36).

In order to introduce capital rationing into this model, we shall let B_t denote the maximum amount of debt that the firm is permitted to have during period t. Then the following constraints must be added to the LP model already presented in Eq. (16–36):

$$w_t \leq B_t \qquad t = 1, \ldots, T. \tag{16-49}$$

If some of these new constraints are binding in an optimal solution to the new LP model, their impact will be to increase the effective rates of interest that should be used in computing the present values or the horizon values of the projects. In order to see this, we have constructed Table 16–3 to portray both the primal and dual problems corresponding to Eqs. (16–36) and (16–49). We have retained the same notation that we used in Table 16–2, with the addition of β_t to denote the dual variables associated with the new constraints in Eq. (16–49). An algebraic representation of the new dual problem is given in Eq. (16–50).

$$\text{Minimize:} \quad \sum_{t=1}^{T} \rho_t D_t + \sum_{j=1}^{N} \mu_j + \sum_{t=1}^{T} \beta_t B_t$$

Subject to:

$$
\left.
\begin{aligned}
&\text{(a) } \sum_{t=1}^{T} \rho_t c_{tj} + \mu_j \geq a_j && j = 1, \ldots, N \\
&\text{(b) } \rho_{t-1} - (1+r)\rho_t \geq 0 && t = 2, \ldots, T \\
&\text{(c) } \rho_T \geq 1 \\
&\text{(d) } -\rho_{t-1} + (1+r)\rho_t + \beta_{t-1} \geq 0 && t = 2, \ldots, T \\
&\text{(e) } -\rho_T + \beta_T \geq -1 \\
&\text{(f) } \rho_t \geq 0 \text{ and } \beta_t \geq 0 && t = 1, \ldots, T \\
&\qquad \text{and } \mu_j \geq 0 && j = 1, \ldots, N
\end{aligned}
\right\} \quad (16-50)
$$

TABLE 16–3

PRIMAL (READ ACROSS) AND DUAL (READ DOWN) LINEAR PROGRAMS CORRESPONDING TO EQ. (16-36) AND (16-49)

Dual Vbles \ Primal Vbles	x_1	x_2	$\cdots$	x_j	$\cdots$	x_N	v_1	v_2	$\cdots$	v_{t-1}	v_t	$\cdots$	v_{T-1}	v_T	w_1	w_2	$\cdots$	w_{t-1}	w_t	$\cdots$	w_{T-1}	w_T	Requirements / Objective
ρ_1	c_{11}	c_{12}	$\cdots$	c_{1j}	$\cdots$	c_{1N}	1								-1								$\le D_1$
ρ_2	c_{21}	c_{22}	$\cdots$	c_{2j}	$\cdots$	c_{2N}	$-(1+r)$	1							$(1+r)$	-1							$\le D_2$
$\cdots$	$\cdots$	$\cdots$	$\ddots$	$\cdots$		$\cdots$			$\ddots$								$\ddots$						$\cdots$
ρ_t	c_{t1}	c_{t2}	$\cdots$	c_{tj}	$\cdots$	c_{tN}			$\cdots$	$-(1+r)$	1	$\cdots$					$\cdots$	$(1+r)$	-1	$\cdots$			$\le D_t$
$\cdots$					$\ddots$							$\ddots$								$\ddots$			$\cdots$
ρ_T	c_{T1}	c_{T2}	$\cdots$	c_{Tj}	$\cdots$	c_{TN}						$\cdots$	$-(1+r)$	1						$\cdots$	$(1+r)$	-1	$\le D_T$
μ_1	1																						≤ 1
μ_2		1																					≤ 1
$\cdots$			$\ddots$																				$\cdots$
μ_j				1																			≤ 1
$\cdots$					$\ddots$																		$\cdots$
μ_N						1																	≤ 1
β_1															1								$\le B_1$
β_2																1							$\le B_2$
$\cdots$																	$\ddots$						$\cdots$
β_t																			1				$\le B_t$
$\cdots$																				$\ddots$			$\cdots$
β_T																						1	$\le B_T$
Objective	a_1	a_2	$\cdots$	a_j	$\cdots$	a_N	0	0	$\cdots$	0	0	$\cdots$	0	1	0	0	$\cdots$	0	0	$\cdots$	0	-1	
Requirements	$\ge$	$\ge$	$\cdots$	$\ge$	$\cdots$	$\ge$	$\ge$	$\ge$	$\cdots$	$\ge$	$\ge$	$\cdots$	$\ge$	$\ge$	$\ge$	$\ge$	$\cdots$	$\ge$	$\ge$	$\cdots$	$\ge$	$\ge$	

From (c) and (e) in Eq. (16–50):

$$1 \leq \rho_T \leq 1 + \beta_T. \tag{16-51}$$

Hence if $\beta_T^* > 0$, i.e., the debt limit constraint is binding in period T, then $\rho_T^* > 1$ is possible (and, in fact, will necessarily result).

From (b) and (d) in Eq. (16–50):

$$(1 + r)\rho_t \leq \rho_{t-1} \leq (1 + r)\rho_t + \beta_t \text{ for } t = 2, \ldots, T. \tag{16-52}$$

From Eq. (16–52), we can derive the following recursive relation:[13]

$$\rho_t^* = (1 + r)^{T-t} + \sum_{\tau=t}^{T} (1 + r)^{\tau-t}\beta_\tau^* \text{ for } t = 1, \ldots, T. \tag{16-53}$$

Note that if all $\beta_t^* = 0$—i.e., if none of the debt limit constraints are binding—then Eq. (16–53) reduces to Eq. (16–40). When, however, some of the debt-limit constraints are binding, then $\beta_t^* > 0$ for these values of t and Eq. (16–53) no longer reduces to Eq. (16–40). In such a situation the shadow price of the funds-available constraint in year t not only depends upon the market rate of interest by means of the conventional compound interest formulas, but it also depends upon the opportunity costs associated with various debt ceilings. Hence the opportunity cost of funds will be greater than the market rate of interest.

For an (entirely) accepted project, $x_j^* = 1$ and constraint (a) of Eq. (16–50) holds as an exact equality. Thus

$$\mu_j^* = a_j - \sum_{t=j}^{T} \rho_t^* c_{tj} \tag{16-54}$$

expresses the value of an accepted project. By substituting Eq. (16–53) into (16–54), we obtain

$$\mu_j^* = a_j + \sum_{t=1}^{T} (-c_{tj}) \left[(1 + r)^{T-t} + \sum_{\tau=t}^{T} (1 + r)^{\tau-t}\beta_\tau^* \right]. \tag{16-55}$$

After substituting Eq. (16–27) into (16–55), by rearranging terms and by interchanging the order of the double summation we can obtain

$$\mu_j^* = \sum_{t=1}^{\infty} (-c_{tj})(1 + r)^{T-t} + \sum_{t=1}^{T} \beta_t^* \sum_{\tau=1}^{t} (-c_{tj})(1 + r)^{t-\tau}. \tag{16-56}$$

According to Eq. (16–56), the value of an accepted project is the horizon value of the project computed at the market rate of interest, r, plus an additional complicated term which must be explained more fully.

To simplify notation, let us define the variable S_{tj} as the future value in year t, compounded at the market rate of interest r, of all net *inflows*

---

[13] The proof is presented in Weingartner, *op. cit.*, p. 163.

associated with project j during year t and all earlier years. Symbolically,

$$S_{tj} = \sum_{\tau=1}^{t} (-c_{\tau j})(1 + r)^{t-\tau}. \tag{16-57}$$

Substituting Eq. (16–57) into (16–56), we have

$$\mu_j^* = \sum_{t=1}^{\infty} (-c_{tj})(1 + r)^{T-t} + \sum_{t=1}^{T} \beta_t^* S_{tj}. \tag{16-58}$$

In terms of the notation introduced above, we now see that the second term in both expressions (16–56) and (16–58) for the value of an accepted project involves the opportunity costs of the debt ceilings as they interact with the net cash flows associated with a project. When the debt-ceiling opportunity cost is positive in year t, i.e., when $\beta_t^* > 0$, then an opportunity cost adjustment may be required in evaluating project j even though this project may not have any non-zero net cash flows during year t itself; the reason is that S_{tj} can still be non-zero to reflect the non-zero net cash flows of project j during earlier years. "For example, a project may become more valuable because it generates revenues in earlier years and hence reduces the pressure of the borrowing constraint in the later year. Alternatively, the value of a project is lowered because its costs in earlier years are a drain on resources which could, had they been preserved, have lessened the pinch on funds in the given year."[14]

One important consequence of Eq. (16–58) is that a project may be accepted even though its associated net cash flows have a negative present value (and a negative horizon value) when computed using only the market rate of interest, r. There can be a positive value of μ_j^* (implying that $x_j^* = 1$) and, hence, project j is entirely accepted even though

$$\sum_{t=1}^{\infty} (-c_{tj})(1 + r)^{T-t} < 0 \tag{16-59}$$

as long as

$$\sum_{t=1}^{T} \beta_t^* S_{tj} > \sum_{t=1}^{\infty} c_{tj}(1 + r)^{T-t}. \tag{16-60}$$

Thus, in the presence of capital market imperfections, "the reason for possible acceptance of a project with net negative present values at [the] market rate [of interest], r, becomes clear. It may generate inflows (that is, revenues) at times when these are most needed. Hence such an alternative can become attractive even though it would never be acceptable in the absence of borrowing limits. The converse is also likely to occur. A project may be rejected even though its present value at the market rate of interest is positive."[15]

[14] *Ibid.*, p. 165.
[15] *Ibid.*, p. 166.

We thus have seen that even the relatively simple type of capital market imperfection represented by capital rationing can lead to the nonoptimality of the present-value criterion (based on the market rate of interest) as a guide to the acceptance or rejection of investment projects. An analogous result was derived in Section II.A of Chapter 15, where we analyzed a different type of capital market imperfection—i.e., differences in the rates of interest for borrowing and lending.

Perceptive readers might feel that the general form of the present-value rule remains a theoretically valid guide to piecemeal project evaluation, but that it requires values other than market interest rates to be used in computing the present values of projects' net after-tax cash flows. For example, Eq. (16–56) in principle determines an appropriate accept or reject signal for a project. Unfortunately, this would not be an operationally feasible approach to selecting investment projects in a one-project-at-a-time mode of analysis. The reason is that under various types of capital market imperfections, it is often impossible to determine the proper interest rates to use in computing a theoretically valid present value for a project without first obtaining an optimal solution to the relevant LP model formulated for analyzing the investment projects in a portfolio context. In such circumstances the proper interest rates to use in computing the correct present value of a project are partly determined by the optimal values of shadow prices of constraints in the LP model rather than directly corresponding to market rates of interest.[16]

III. An LP Model of the Interactions between Investment Decisions and Current Operations

Although the LP models discussed thus far in this chapter have all been developed under the assumptions of perfect certainty (and sometimes perfect capital markets), they nonetheless are relevant and applicable to real business situations. In order to see this more clearly, we shall now describe in some detail a multiperiod linear programming model initially formulated by Rapoport and Drews. This is a prototype of a class of models that has been extensively used for physical investment analyses in

---

[16] The interested reader can find a detailed analysis of investment project selection under various types of capital market imperfections in Weingartner, *op. cit.*, chap. 9. Another feature of the LP models under imperfect capital markets is that fractional projects may appear in an essential manner in the optimal solution (*essential* in the sense that the elimination of fractional projects lowers the maximal value of the LP model's objective function). In such circumstances, either ways must be found to make it meaningful to accept fractional projects or else mixed-integer programming solution techniques must be utilized.

the Exxon Corporation and its various affiliated and subsidiary companies.[17]

Because it also utilizes the mathematical tool of multiperiod linear programming, the Rapoport and Drews model to be described below has some similarities to the LP model of Weingartner considered in Section II. The major difference between these two models is in their treatment of the net cash flows that will result from the acceptance of various physical investment projects. In the Weingartner model, as we have seen, these net cash flows, c_{tj}, are exogenously forecasted inputs. As we shall see, in the Rapoport and Drews model these net cash flows are endogenously determined (implicit) outputs. In this respect the Rapoport and Drews approach is more realistic, because the net cash flows that will result from any capital investment project in reality depend not only upon the capital investment projects that are selected but also upon the manner in which current operations are conducted. Although these decisions are endogenously determined in an explicit manner in the Rapoport and Drews model, they are implicitly assumed when determining the exogenous cash flow forecasts provided as inputs to the Weingartner model (although the notion of compound projects can be used to deal with a limited number of project interactions in the Weingartner approach).

The Rapoport and Drews model, which has been formulated in terms of a vertically integrated oil company, analyzes the implications of any particular set of physical facilities for the various operating decisions that must be made. The types of operating decisions encompassed in this model are the amounts of crude oil to be pumped from various oil fields, the allocations of oil to various refineries, the products to be blended in various refineries, etc. The model in effect examines how these various operating decisions should be changed in order to reflect different configurations of physical assets, such as oil wells, pipelines, etc. In this way, the model can determine when it is profitable to drill new oil wells, expand pipeline networks, increase refinery capacities, etc. Many types of extensions of this prototype Rapoport and Drews model, often involving mathematical programming techniques that exceed linear programming in sophistication and power, have been usefully applied in the investment planning process of integrated oil companies.

---

[17] A nontechnical description of this prototype model can be found in Leo A. Rapoport and William T. Drews, "Mathematical Approach to Long-range Planning," *Harvard Business Review*, 40, No. 3 (May–June, 1962), 75–87. Our discussion in this section is based on this article by Rapoport and Drews. Our assertion that more elaborate models of this type have in fact "been extensively used for physical investment analyses in the Exxon Corporation and its various affiliated and subsidiary companies" is based upon personal contacts with executives involved in these analyses.

A. Current Operations during Period t

We can consider a vertically integrated oil company as consisting of four main stages of activities: (1) production of crude oil, (2) transportation of crude oil from wells to refineries, (3) refining operations, and (4) sales of finished products. For each time period t in the model, Table 16–4 defines some relevant operational variables and parameters.

Using the notation in Table 16–4, we can formulate a set of constraints on the integrated oil company's operations during period t. The first of these, Eq. (16–61), indicates that the total amount of heavy crude oil transported to the gathering station during period t is the sum of the heavy crude oil pumped from the three different oil fields where heavy crude oil is produced. Similarly, Eq. (16–62) indicates that the total amount of light crude oil transported to the gathering station during period t is the sum of the amounts of light crude oil pumped from the two different oil fields capable of producing light crude oil:

$$X_{1t} + X_{2t} + X_{3t} = X_{6t} \tag{16–61}$$

$$X_{4t} + X_{5t} = X_{7t}. \tag{16–62}$$

Let us consider the transportation operations of the company, as indicated in the following two relationships:

$$X_{6t} = X_{8t} + X_{9t} + X_{12t} \tag{16–63}$$

$$X_{7t} = X_{10t} + X_{11t} + X_{13t}. \tag{16–64}$$

Equation (16–63) indicates that the heavy crude oil received at the gathering station will be transported to refinery A, to refinery B, or to the sales terminal from which outside sales are made. Similarly, Eq. (16–64) reflects the stipulation that the light crude oil received at the gathering station will be transported either to refineries A or B for further processing or else to the sales terminal for sale outside of the company.

Let us next consider the operating relationships in the refinery. In refinery A these are expressed by Eq. (16–65) through (16–67):

$$a_g X_{8t} + \alpha_g X_{10t} = X_{14t} \tag{16–65}$$

$$a_k X_{8t} + \alpha_k X_{10t} = X_{16t} \tag{16–66}$$

$$a_f X_{8t} + \alpha_f X_{10t} = X_{18t}. \tag{16–67}$$

The amounts of gasoline, kerosene, and industrial fuel produced at refinery A are related to the amounts of heavy and light crude oils used in refinery A on the basis of particular yield coefficients. This is an oversimplification, for purposes of this example, of the actual physical relationships existing in a refinery. In practice a larger and more complicated system of linear and piecewise linear relationships could be substituted in

TABLE 16–4

Operational Variables and Parameters for Period t

Operational Variables Pertaining to Production

$\left.\begin{array}{c} X_{1t} \\ X_{2t} \\ X_{3t} \end{array}\right\}$ Amount of heavy crude oil pumped from different oil fields

$\left.\begin{array}{c} X_{4t} \\ X_{5t} \end{array}\right\}$ Amount of light crude oil pumped from different oil fields

Operational Variables Pertaining to Transportation and Sales of Crude Oil

X_{6t} Amount of heavy crude oil transported to the gathering station
X_{7t} Amount of light crude oil transported to the gathering station
X_{8t} Amount of heavy crude oil allocated to refinery A
X_{9t} Amount of heavy crude oil allocated to refinery B
X_{10t} Amount of light crude oil allocated to refinery A
X_{11t} Amount of light crude oil allocated to refinery B
X_{12t} Amount of heavy crude oil allocated to outside sales
X_{13t} Amount of light crude oil allocated to outside sales

Operational Variables Pertaining to Refining

X_{14t} Amount of gasoline produced at refinery A
X_{15t} Amount of gasoline produced at refinery B
X_{16t} Amount of kerosene produced at refinery A
X_{17t} Amount of kerosene produced at refinery B
X_{18t} Amount of industrial fuel produced at refinery A
X_{19t} Amount of industrial fuel produced at refinery B

Capacity Limits on Operational Variables

$\left.\begin{array}{c} K_{1t} \\ K_{2t} \\ K_{3t} \\ K_{4t} \\ K_{5t} \end{array}\right\}$ Capacity limits on the production of various heavy crudes and light crudes at different oil fields

K_{6t} Capacity limit on pipeline connecting the gathering station with the sales terminal
K_{7t} Capacity of refinery A
K_{8t} Capacity of refinery B

Demands for Various Products in the Market

D_{Ht} Demand for heavy crude oil
D_{Lt} Demand for light crude oil
D_{Gt} Demand for gasoline
D_{Kt} Demand for kerosene
D_{Ft} Demand for industrial fuel

Refinery Yield Coefficients

$\left.\begin{array}{c} a_g \\ a_k \\ a_f \end{array}\right\}$ Yield coefficient for light crude oil in refinery A

$\left.\begin{array}{c} b_g \\ b_k \\ b_f \end{array}\right\}$ Yield coefficient for light crude oil in refinery B

$\left.\begin{array}{c} \alpha_g \\ \alpha_k \\ \alpha_f \end{array}\right\}$ Yield coefficient for heavy crude oil in refinery A

$\left.\begin{array}{c} \beta_g \\ \beta_k \\ \beta_f \end{array}\right\}$ Yield coefficient for heavy crude oil in refinery B

place of Eq. (16–65) through (16–67) in order to represent the actual physical relationships more realistically.

A similar set of refinery-yield relationships is defined for refinery B in Eq. (16–68) through (16–70):

$$b_g X_{9t} + \beta_g X_{11t} = X_{15t} \tag{16–68}$$

$$b_k X_{9t} + \beta_k X_{11t} = X_{17t} \tag{16–69}$$

$$b_f X_{9t} + \beta_f X_{11t} = X_{19t}. \tag{16–70}$$

For any particular time period t in the model, Eq. (16–61) through (16–70) represent the most important interrelationships among the operating variables. There would be a similar set of such relationships formulated for each of the periods within the planning horizon.

B. CAPACITY RESTRICTIONS DURING PERIOD t

Let us now consider the capacity restrictions in the model to which the various operating variables must conform during each time period t. We first have the following set of capacity restrictions on the production of heavy and light crude oil from the different oil fields:

$$X_{it} \leq K_{it} \qquad i = 1, \ldots, 5. \tag{16–71}$$

We next have a restriction which prevents the total amount of crude oil sent through the pipeline connecting the gathering station with the sales terminal from exceeding the capacity of that pipeline:

$$X_{12t} + X_{13t} \leq K_{6t}. \tag{16–72}$$

Finally, we have capacity restrictions which limit the total amount of crude oil processed through each refinery:

$$X_{8t} + X_{10t} \leq K_{7t} \tag{16–73}$$

$$X_{9t} + X_{11t} \leq K_{8t}. \tag{16–74}$$

The inequality relationships in Eq. (16–71) through (16–74) would be repeated for each time period in the planning horizon. In addition, there would be some market demand relationships limiting the outside sales of heavy and light crude oils and finished products in the marketplace. These are represented by the inequality relationships expressed in Eq. (16–75) through (16–79):

$$X_{12t} \leq D_{Ht} \tag{16–75}$$

$$X_{13t} \leq D_{Lt} \tag{16–76}$$

$$X_{14t} + X_{15t} \leq D_{Gt} \tag{16–77}$$

$$X_{16t} + X_{17t} \leq D_{Kt} \tag{16–78}$$

$$X_{18t} + X_{19t} \leq D_{Ft}. \tag{16–79}$$

C. Investment Decisions

It should be noted that the market demand constraints (16–75) through (16–79) appear at first glance to be analogous to the physical capacity constraints (16–71) through (16–74), in that both portray inequality relationships with a "fixed" right-hand side. Further reflection indicates, however, that they are different in that the market demand, i.e., the capacity limits on external sales, are viewed as truly fixed in this model, whereas the physical capacity limits are fixed in any particular time period but can be changed over time by means of physical investments undertaken by the firm. Thus, for each successive pair of periods within the planning horizon of the model, there would be a set of relationships indicating how physical capacity can be changed by means of the firm's physical investment activities. In order to portray this, we must first define the set of physical investment variables shown in Table 16–5.

Table 16–5

Investment Variables Representing Increments to Capacity during Period t

$\left.\begin{array}{l} Y_{1t} \\ Y_{2t} \\ Y_{3t} \end{array}\right\}$ Additions during period t to the capacity for producing heavy crude oil at different oil fields

$\left.\begin{array}{l} Y_{4t} \\ Y_{5t} \end{array}\right\}$ Additions during period t to the capacity for producing light crude oil at different oil fields

Y_{6t} Addition during period t to the capacity of the pipeline connecting the gathering station with the sales terminal

Y_{7t} Addition during period t to the capacity of refinery A

Y_{8t} Addition during period t to the capacity of refinery B

With the aid of these physical investment variables, Eq. (16–80) indicates the manner in which investment activities in any one time period of the model will increase related operating capacities in the next time period of the model:

$$K_{i,t+1} = K_{it} + Y_{it} \qquad i = 1, \ldots, 8. \qquad (16\text{–}80)$$

Equations (16–61) through (16–80) constitute all of the constraints in the intertemporal linear programming model describing an integrated system of operating and investment activities for an oil company over a multiperiod planning horizon. The operating conditions during any one time period are specified by a set of values for the current operating variables. Their values must be chosen in conformance with existing capacity restrictions. By undertaking investment activities, however, these physical capacities can be altered over time.

D. OBJECTIVE FUNCTION

Now that we have specified the complete set of structural constraints in the model, it is necessary to discuss the objective function to be optimized in the LP model. The model is formulated to maximize the present value of the net after-tax profits associated with the various decision variables. Within any particular time period, the net after-tax profit coefficients associated with each operating variable can be determined by subtracting an appropriate unit-cost coefficient from a corresponding unit-revenue coefficient (either or both of which could be zero).

Only cost coefficients (which will be negative numbers because they are subtracted from zero revenue coefficients) will be associated with many of the internal operating variables in any particular period. For example, it will cost c_{1t} dollars to produce one barrel of heavy crude oil from oil field 1 during period t; similarly, it will cost c_{6t} dollars to transport one unit of heavy crude oil to the gathering station, etc.

Those operating variables which represent the sales of crude oil or refined products to the outside market will have net-profit coefficients in any time period that represent the difference between the sales revenue per unit and the selling cost per unit. Thus, for example, the coefficient of X_{12t}, the amount of heavy crude oil allocated to outside sales during period t, would represent the difference between the net after-tax revenues received and the net out-of-pocket marketing costs of selling heavy crude to the outside market.

For the investment variables which represent expansions of capacity, it is more complex to determine the appropriate unit cost to associate with an incremental unit of capacity added in any particular time period. An argument much like that presented in Section I.A of Chapter 8 can be utilized to let us develop the opportunity cost per period of any addition to capacity. As we discussed in Chapter 8, this per-period opportunity cost for an incremental unit of capacity will depend upon the purchase cost of the incremental capacity, the lifetime of the incremental capacity, and the market rate of interest. Without going into details at this time, it is sufficient to state that we can then adjust the resulting opportunity cost of any incremental capacity to reflect the residual value of that incremental capacity at the end of the planning horizon. Since we are dealing with a finite horizon model, it is necessary to recognize that capacity increments may well have substantial residual values to the firm at the end of the planning horizon. In order to avoid developing a view that is too short-run in the model, it is necessary to make some adjustment of this type to reflect the value to the firm of the remaining capacity at the end of its planning horizon.

With this understanding, we can now let U_{it} represent the opportunity cost to the firm of adding one incremental unit of capacity of type i in period t, where this opportunity cost appropriately reflects the residual salvage value of the incremental unit of capacity at the end of the planning horizon.

The objective function to be maximized by the firm, the discounted value of profits during the planning horizon, can then be readily expressed in the following manner:

$$\pi = \sum_{t=1}^{T} \frac{1}{(1+r)^t} \left[\sum_{i=1}^{19} c_{it} X_{it} + \sum_{j=1}^{8} U_{jt} Y_{jt} \right]. \qquad (16\text{--}81)$$

As Eq. (16–81) has been written, it is assumed that there are T time periods in the planning horizon and that the market discount rate is r per cent per period in each period of the planning horizon.

E. SUMMARY OF THE MODEL

To summarize, the linear programming model relating current operations to physical investment decisions that has been outlined in Eq. (16–61) through (16–81) is a simplified, prototype version of a class of models that has been extensively applied in investment planning at the Exxon Corporation and its various affiliated and subsidiary companies. This type of framework has proved to be a practical, useful tool for determining when and where physical investments should be undertaken. In many ways it is considerably richer than the LP model outlined in Section II. One important way in which the Rapoport and Drews model goes beyond the Weingartner model is that the net cash flows associated with any investment alternative —i.e., any increment to capacity—are not exogenously specified or forecasted. Instead, these net cash flows associated with an investment alternative indirectly emerge as part of the optimal solution to the over-all LP model.

The extensions of the Rapoport and Drews model that have been successfully implemented represent good examples of useful management-science models. *Management science* may be defined as the application of scientific concepts and quantitative techniques to help executives analyze the planning, decision-making, and control problems of large, complex organizations. When the organizations are business firms, microeconomics is one of the key areas from which relevant scientific concepts are drawn in formulating management science models for analyzing complex business problems. Linear programming is often a useful mathematical technique for modelling real-world resource allocation problems. It is clear from the formulation of even the prototype Rapoport and Drews model that a considerable degree of relevant descriptive detail may be incorporated in LP models intended for practical implementation.[18] All three of these ingredients (micro-

---

[18] In this regard, contrast the general short-run production function presented in Eq. (7–1) of Chapter 7 with the short-run production function of the integrated oil company which in effect is represented by the set of Eq. (16–61) through (16–74).

economic concepts, quantitative techniques, and relevant descriptive detail) are generally present in those management-science models that in fact prove helpful to executives in analyzing complex problems in business firms. LP models of the type described in this chapter have been usefully applied to a broad spectrum of business problems.

IV. Summary

This chapter has considered the manner in which linear programming models may be formulated to aid in the analysis of investment decisions. The use of LP models permits the simultaneous analysis of an interrelated set of investment alternatives. This can identify the optimal portfolio of investment projects which a firm should undertake.

Linear programming is a mathematical technique for dealing with particular types of constrained optimization problems. In a typical LP problem, the objective function is a linear function of the decision variables, the constraints are a set of linear inequality relations involving the decision variables, and the decision variables must assume nonnegative values.

An example problem was used to illustrate some essential aspects of LP. This illustrative LP model involved a firm which produces multiple products (small widgets and large widgets). Each unit of product requires specific amounts of several operations (stamping, bolting, and painting). There are capacity limits to the amounts of time available for the various operations. The firm operates under perfect competition, and its objective is to maximize profits.

Some fundamental conditions required for the applicability of an LP model are divisibility, additivity, and proportionality. The example LP problem was shown to satisfy all of these conditions.

The profit-maximizing numerical solution to the example problem was obtained using both the geometrical and the simplex solution techniques. The simplex technique is based upon the theory of simultaneous linear equations.

The concept of duality in linear programming was discussed. We saw that any LP problem (which may be regarded as the primal problem) has associated with it another closely related LP problem (called the dual problem). The rules for obtaining the dual problem from the primal problem were stated. The simplex technique simultaneously provides solutions to both the primal and dual problems.

The optimal values of the dual variables are called shadow prices (or dual evaluators). Each shadow price indicates the incremental change in the optimal value of the objective function resulting from an incremental change in the right-hand side of the corresponding constraint. An interesting relationship between the optimal values of the primal and dual problems follows from the theorem of complementary slackness: Whenever a constraint in either the primal or dual problem is satisfied as a strict inequality, then the corresponding variable in the other problem must equal zero.

After this brief exposition of the essentials of linear programming in Section I, the rest of this chapter described two different types of LP models for the analysis of investment projects. Both these models were multiperiod (or intertemporal) linear programming models.

Weingartner's model, outlined in Section II, provides a convenient way of expressing complex types of physical interrelationships among the projects, and it is useful for investigating interactions between the firm's investment project selection and its financial market transactions. Under conditions of perfect capital markets, this model shows that the present-value decision criterion is adequate for analyzing independent investment projects and could be suitably modified to analyze interdependent investment projects. In the presence of capital market imperfections, however, the present-value decision rule based on market rates of interest may no longer lead to optimal investment decisions. In such circumstances a suitably formulated LP model will determine the optimal investment portfolio.

The linear programming model of Rapoport and Drews, outlined in Section III, focuses on interactions between current operating decisions and investment decisions which expand physical capacities. This model is a simplified version of a class of mathematical programming models that have been extensively used for physical investment analyses in major petroleum companies. The net cash flows associated with any investment project are endogenously determined by the Rapoport and Drews model rather than being exogenously forecasted, as in the Weingartner model.

The Rapoport and Drews approach contains an LP submodel which depicts the current operations of the firm during each time period within the planning horizon. Among the constraints on the operating decision variables during period t are some physical capacity restrictions. During any operating period (i.e., in the short run), capacities are fixed, but there are physical investment decision variables which permit changes in the capacities of physical facilities for future operating periods (i.e., in the long run). The objective function to be maximized is the present value of the net after-tax profits associated with the various decision variables. The optimal solution to the LP model indicates the set of physical investments that the firm should undertake, as well as how the firm should operate, in each period.

Because of the importance of understanding the impact of capital market imperfections on investment decisions, we shall conclude by summarizing some relevant results based upon the analyses in both Chapters 15 and 16. In models dealing with perfect capital markets under conditions of certainty, it is possible to determine the optimal investment expenditures of the firm by means of appropriate compound interest formulas (the present-value criterion) utilizing market rates of interest. The optimal investment expenditures of a firm do not depend upon the utility functions (i.e., consumption preferences) of the owners of the firm, but only upon the state of technology, current market information, and expectations about future market information. Given the same degree of knowledge and the same set of expectations, two different managers in a firm would undertake the same investment decisions on behalf of the firm even though these two managers had very different utility functions. With perfect capital markets under certainty, there is only a single rate of interest at which borrowing and lending for a specified maturity will take place during a time period. The present-value decision rule, based on market rates of interest, is generally adequate as an investment decision rule for project selection. Where there are physical interdependencies among projects, some direct modifications of this present-value rule based on market rates of interest will be sufficient to yield correct decision criteria for the firm.

When any one of a number of types of capital market imperfections is introduced, these results no longer remain valid. The sharp separation between the optimal volume of investment expenditures by a firm and the utility functions of the owners of the firm can no longer be made. In some circumstances under capital market imperfections, the managers operating a firm cannot determine the optimal volume of investment expenditures that the firm should undertake without knowing the utility functions of the owners of the firm. Although sometimes a present-value decision rule can be employed, it is often impossible to determine the proper rate of interest to use in discounting future net after-tax cash flows without already having obtained an optimal investment solution (e.g., by solving a suitably formulated mathematical programming problem). Thus, although the present-value decision rule may be theoretically correct in such circumstances, it is operationally impossible to utilize it without already having determined the optimal investment expenditures that the firm should undertake.

A properly formulated mathematical programming model could be used in such circumstances to determine the set of investment projects that a firm should undertake. As a by-product of this solution, information is generated which indicates the correct discount rates to use in computing the present values of investment projects. These correct discount rates may not coincide with observed market rates of interest, since they are determined by the shadow prices of appropriate constraints in the linear programming model.

SUGGESTED READINGS

These recommendations are in addition to the footnote references cited in this chapter.

COHEN, KALMAN J., AND EDWIN J. ELTON, "Inter-Temporal Portfolio Analysis Based on Simulation of Joint Returns," *Management Science,*

Theory Series, XIV, No. 1 (September, 1967), 5–18.

DORFMAN, R., "Mathematical or 'Linear' Programming," *American Economic Review*, 43 (December, 1953), 797–825.

GAVER, DONALD P., AND GERALD L. THOMPSON, *Programming and Probability Models in Operations Research*. Monterey, Calif.: Brooks/Cole Publishing Company, 1973.

PHILIPPATOS, GEORGE C., *Financial Management: Theory and Techniques*. San Francisco: Holden-Day, Inc., 1973.

SIMMONARD, M., *Linear Programming*. Englewood Cliffs, N.J.: Prentice-Hall, Inc., 1966.

WAGNER, H. M., *Principles of Operations Research with Applications to Managerial Decisions*. Englewood Cliffs, N.J.: Prentice-Hall, Inc., 1969.

WEINGARTNER, H. MARTIN, "Capital Budgeting of Interrelated Projects: Survey and Synthesis," *Management Science*, Series A, XII, No. 7 (March, 1966), 485–516.

Chapter Seventeen

New Considerations in the
Theory of the Firm[1]

Up to this point we have assumed that the firm is attempting to maximize profits. We have implicitly taken the point of view that only market considerations determine the decisions of the firm. We have assumed that the internal organizational structure of the firm has no effect on the decisions that the firm makes. Now we shall look at the firm from a different viewpoint. In particular, we should like to rely on some of the results derived from a behavioral approach to the firm. The nature of the behavioral approach will become clear as we proceed.

---

[1] This chapter draws heavily from Richard M. Cyert and James G. March, *A Behavioral Theory of the Firm* (Englewood Cliffs, N.J.: Prentice-Hall, Inc., 1963), chaps. 3–5. Some of this material has been used directly without explicit indication of quotation; other material has been paraphrased.

I. Motivation of the Behavioral Theory

Periodically in the history of the theory of the firm in economics, there have been attacks on the assumption of profit maximization. In particular, as one looks closely at the behavior of actual firms, the justification for the assumption of profit maximization seems to weaken. When one adds uncertainty to the firm's decision-making process, even defining the meaning of profit maximization becomes difficult to do in an empirically meaningful way. The behavioral theory of the firm takes the position that arguments over motivation are somewhat fruitless. The critical issue is not whether one assumes profit maximizing instead of satisficing behavior. Instead, it is fruitful to develop an understanding of the process of decision making within the firm.

The behavioral theory is viewed as supplementing the conventional theory of the firm. The traditional theory is essentially one in which certain broad questions are asked. Specifically, the conventional theory of the firm is designed to explain the way in which the price system functions as a mechanism for allocating resources among markets; relatively little is said about resource allocation within the firm. For the purposes of the classical theory, the profit maximization assumption may be perfectly adequate. It is clear, however, that as one asks a different set of questions, specifically questions designed to uncover the way in which resources are allocated within the firm, the profit maximization assumption is neither necessary nor sufficient for answering these questions. Therefore the behavioral theory of the firm should be viewed as focusing on a different set of questions, questions concerning the internal decision-making structure of the firm. Thus, with this theory we are interested in answering such questions as

1. How does the allocation of resources within the firm's budget relate to the organizational goals?
2. How do objectives change over time?
3. What happens to information as it flows through the organization?
4. Are there biases in the information?
5. How do these biases affect the decisions that are finally made?
6. What is the relationship between decisions made by management and the final form of the decision as it is implemented by the organization?

In general the behavioral theory is most applicable to those firms whose decisions are not completely determined by the market. These firms have some freedom to develop decision strategies or rules that become part of the decision-making system within the firm.

II. Key Concepts of the Behavioral Theory

A. ORGANIZATIONAL GOALS

The phrase, "organizational goals," is slightly misleading, since an organization as such cannot have goals. Only the individuals within the organization can have goals. When we speak of organizational goals, however, we mean essentially that there is agreement among some group responsible for the direction of the organization on the nature of the goals. In particular, this group (which we shall call a *coalition* within the organization) is an interacting group, and the goals will be modified by discussions and pressures within the group. Thus the decision on the final set of goals of the organization is in some sense a political decision. The coalition within the organization for a business firm may include managers, workers, stockholders, customers, and so on. In other words, all the individuals who have some stake in that particular organization may in one way or another affect the goals of the organization.

The concept of a coalition assumes a different type of firm than we have been dealing with in the preceding chapters of this book. Hitherto, the firm was implicitly regarded as controlled by an entrepreneur, and the goals of the entrepreneur were the goals of the organization. He purchased conformity to these goals by payments in the forms of wages to workers, interest to capital sources, and profits (when they existed) to himself.

To understand organizational goals it must be realized, first of all, that all resolutions of goals within the coalition are not made by money. Rather, many side-payments to members in an organization are made in the form of policy commitments. For example, in order to get the vice-president of marketing to stay within the organization, it may be necessary to commit resources to research on new products. It may well be that some of the policy demands are inconsistent with the side-payments that are made. Thus, every organization is continually undergoing the test of new demands, the test to see how these new demands conform to existing policy and, in general, pushing the policy toward new dimensions. In some sense, therefore, the goals of the organization are never completely consistent at any particular point in time.

The second point that must be understood about goals is that some objectives are stated in the form of a normative dictum. For example, we must have 46 per cent of the market, or we must expend 6 per cent of our gross revenue in advertising. Third, some objectives are stated in a nonoperational form. In other words, they are not necessarily in a form to have any effect on decisions. Thus, a nonoperational goal may be that the firm desires to be a leading innovator in the industry. In and of itself, this goal does not lead to a particular set of actions. A goal in nonoperational form may, however, be a guide in making certain sets of decisions on personnel or may more broadly affect the allocation of resources. In general, nonoperational demands are encouraged by the coalition, since these nonoperational objectives are consistent with virtually any other set of objectives.

Given a set of goals, an interesting question arises as to how these goals change over time. It is believed that an important phenomenon is the aspiration level mechanism. The aspiration level concept is taken from psychology. It assumes, first, that goals are stated in operational form, such as "our profit goal for this year is $5,400,000." The organization then periodically compares its performance with its aspiration level.

The following propositions describe the way in which we would expect goals in the form of aspiration levels to change:

1. In a steady state, i.e., one where the external environment in the form of the demand curve is constant, we would expect the aspiration level to be higher than actual performance by a small amount.

2. Where the performance is improving at an increasing rate, the aspiration level will generally lag in the short run behind achievement.

3. When performance is decreasing in quality, the aspiration level will tend to be above achievement.

These three propositions have not been empirically verified for a wide range of business firms. They are essentially based on a set of assumptions which postulate that current aspirations are an optimistic extrapolation of past achievements and past aspirations. The model does seem to be consistent with a wide range of human goal-setting behavior which has been observed in experiments reported in the psychological literature. We would expect the demands of the individual participants in the coalition to change over time, partly as a function of the achievement of the individual, and also as a function of the individual's achievement in relation to others that he deems comparable to him both in this and in other organizations. Thus, we would expect that aspirations with respect to salary would vary as a function of the payments actually received. Similarly, aspirations regarding advertising budget, volume of sales, capital investment, etc., will vary as a function of achievement. Unfortunately, until we know a great deal more about the nature of the relationship between achievement and aspiration, we can make only weak predictions. Even so, some of these predictions are still useful. as we shall see.

B. Organizational Slack

In terms of the present framework, a coalition is viable if the payments made to the various coalition members are adequate to keep them in the organization. If enough resources exist to meet all demands, the coalition is a feasible one. Since demands adjust to actual payments and alternatives external to the organization, there is a long-run tendency for payments and demands to be equal. In this sense, what we have called *coalition demands* are analogous to the factor prices of the more conventional view of the firm.

There is a critical difference, however. In the behavioral theory we focus on the short-run relation between payments and demands and on the imperfections in factor markets. The imperfections, in fact, dominate behavior, for three primary reasons:

1. As we have already noted, payments and demands are in a variety of forms: monetary payments, perquisites, policies, personal treatments, and private commitments. As a result, information on actual factor "prices" is hard to obtain, easily misinterpreted, and often unreliable.

2. Information about the "market" is not obtained automatically; it must be sought. Typically, the participants in the organization do not seek this information until stimulated to do so by some indication of failure.

3. Adaptations in demands are slow—even in the face of strong pressure.

Because of the frictions in the mutual adjustment of payments and demands, there is ordinarily a disparity between the resources available to the organization and the payments required to maintain the coalition. This difference between total resources and total necessary payments is called *organizational slack*. Slack consists in payments to members of the coalition in excess of what is required to maintain the organization. Many interesting phenomena within the firm occur because slack is typically not zero.

In conventional economic theory slack is zero (at least in equilibrium). In discussions of managerial economics, specific attention is generally paid to only one part of slack—payments to owners—and it is generally assumed that other slack is maintained at zero. Neither view is an accurate portrayal of an actual firm. Many forms of slack typically exist: stockholders are paid dividends in excess of those required to keep stockholders (or banks) within the organization; prices are set lower than necessary to maintain adequate income from customers; wages in excess of those required to maintain labor are paid; executives are provided with services and personal luxuries in excess of those required to keep them; subunits are permitted to grow without real concern for the relation between additional payments and additional revenues; public services are provided in excess of those required.

From time to time virtually every participant in any organization obtains slack payments. Some participants, however, ordinarily obtain a greater share of the slack then do other participants. In general, we would expect that those members of the coalition who are full-time, in a position to perceive potential slack early, or have some flexibility in the unilateral allocation of resources will tend to accumulate more slack than will other members.

In most cases we use the organizational slack concept not to explain differential payments but as a hypothetical construct for explaining overall organizational phenomena. In particular, it seems to be useful in dealing with the adjustment of firms to gross shifts in the external environment. For example, consider what happens when the rate of improvement in the environment is great enough so that it outruns the upward adjustment of aspirations. In a general way, this seems to be the situation that faces business firms during strong boom periods. When the environment outruns the aspiration-level adjustment, the organization secures, or at least has the potential of securing, resources in excess of its demands. Some of these resources are simply not obtained—although they are available. Others are used to meet the revised demands of those members of the coalition whose demands adjust more rapidly—usually those most deeply involved in the organization. The excess resources would not be subject to general bargaining because they do not involve allocation in the face of scarcity.

When the environment becomes less favorable, organizational slack represents a cushion. Resource scarcity brings on renewed bargaining and tends to cut heavily into the excess payments introduced during plush times. It does not necessarily mean that precisely those demands that grew abnormally during better days are pruned abnormally during poorer ones, but in general we would expect this to be approximately the case. More important, the cusion provided by organizational slack permits firms to survive in the face of adversity. Under the pressure of a failure (or impending failure) to meet some set of demands on the coalition, the organization discovers some previously unrecognized opportunities for increasing the total resources available. For example, it was reported that after losses of about $50 million for the first three quarters of 1946, the Ford Motor Company "announced that it had found methods of reducing operating costs (on a given volume of output) by about twenty million dollars per year."[2]

Organizational slack absorbs a substantial share of the potential variability in the firm's environment. As a result, it plays both a stabilizing and an adaptive role. We have already noted that the demands of participants adjust to achievement. Aspiration-level adjustment, however, tends to be a relatively slow process—especially downward adjustment. If the only adaptive devices available to the organization were adjustments in aspirations of the members of the coalition, the system would be quite unstable in the face of an environment with even moderate fluctuations. Slack op-

---

[2] M. W. Reder, "A Reconsideration of Marginal Productivity Theory," *Journal of Political Economy*, 55 (1947), 450–58.

erates to stabilize the system in two ways: (1) by absorbing excess resources, it retards upward adjustment of aspirations during relatively good times; (2) by providing a pool of emergency resources, it permits aspirations to be maintained (and achieved) during relatively bad times.

This is not to argue that slack is deliberately created for such a stabilizing purpose; in fact, it is not. Slack arises from the bargaining and decision process we have described, without conscious intent on the part of the coalition members to provide stability to the organization. In a sense, the process is reinforced because it "works" and it "works" partly because it generates slack, but we have seen no significant evidence for the conscious rationalization of slack in business firms. From the point of view of a behavioral theory of the firm, however, the critical question is whether predictions based on the concept can be verified. For example, we would predict that the costs of firms that are successful in the market place will, *ceteris paribus*, tend to rise. Such predictions are susceptible to direct test.[3] They also may be tested within the context of more complicated models of the behavior of firms.

III. Business Goals and Price and Output Decisions

Suppose we wish to use the foregoing general considerations to construct a model of organizational decision making by a business firm determining price, output, and general sales strategy. As we have already noted, we are not yet in a good position to develop a theory that focuses intensively on the formation of objectives through bargaining and coalition making (rather than on the revision of such objectives and selective attention to them). As a result, when we look at price and output determination in business firms, we do three things:

1. We assume a small set of operational goals. In making such an assumption we suggest that the demands of many parts of the coalition are not operative for this class of decisions most of the time or are substantially satisfied when the set of goals assumed is satisfied.

2. We assume that this set of goals is fixed in the sense that no other classes of goals will arise within the coalition. Such an assumption does not exclude changes in the levels of the goals nor in the attention directed at specific goals within the set.

3. We attempt to determine by empirical investigation what specific goals ordinarily enter into the price and output decisions. In general, we have observed that we can represent organizational goals reasonably well by using five different goals. In any organization, other considerations sometimes arise. For example, governmental demands occasionally become

---

[3] R. M. Cyert and J. G. March, "Organizational Factors in the Theory of Oligopoly," *Quarterly Journal of Economics,* 70 (1956), 44–46.

of prime importance. In a few organizations other considerations are as important as those we have identified. For example, in some organizations considerations of prestige or tradition are major goal factors. For most decisions concerning price, output, and general sales strategy in business firms, we think we can limit our primary attention to five goals.

We list the five goals here in an arbitrary order without attempting to establish any necessary order of importance; most of the time no order of importance is required. All goals must be satisfied. It should be clear in the model we shall present in Section V that there is an implicit order reflected in the way in which search activity takes place and in the speed and circumstances of goal-level change. These latent priorities appear to vary from organization to organization in a way that is not clear. It seems most probable that their variation should be explainable in terms of differences in either the current or historical bargaining position of the several participants in the coalition, but at present we treat the implicit priorities simply as organizational parameters.

A. PRODUCTION GOAL

We assume that an organization has a complex of goals surrounding the production operation. These can be summarized in terms of a production goal, with two major components. The first is a smoothing goal: we do not want production to vary more than a certain amount from one time period to another. The second is a level-of-production goal: we want to equal or exceed a certain production level. These two components can be summarized in terms of a production range: we want production to fall within a range of possible production.

The production goal represents in large part the demands of those coalition members connected with production. It reflects pressures toward such things as stable employment, ease of scheduling, development of acceptable cost performance, and growth. Thus, the goal is most frequently evoked in the production part of the organization and is most relevant to decisions (e.g., output) made in that part.

B. INVENTORY GOAL

We assume certain aspirations with respect to finished-goods inventory levels. As in the case of the production goal, the inventory goal summarizes a number of pressures, most conspicuously the demands of some participants to avoid runouts in inventory and to provide a complete, convenient source of inventoried materials. We summarize these demands in terms of either an absolute-level-of-inventory goal or an inventory range (in which case we also attend to demands to avoid excessive inventory costs).

The inventory goal reflects the demands of those coalition members connected with inventory. Thus it is affected by pressures on the inventory department from salesmen and customers. Since inventory essentially serves as a buffer between production and sales, the inventory goal is most frequently invoked and is most relevant to decisions in the output and sales areas.

C. Sales Goal

We assume that most participants in business firms believe the firm must sell the goods or services it produces in order to survive. Thus, various members of the coalition demand that the organization meet some general criteria of sales effectiveness. The sales goal and the market-share goal (Section III.D) summarize these demands. In addition, the sales department itself (and the personnel in it) link subunit goals with sales. The sales goal is simply an aspiration with respect to the level of sales. It may be stated in terms of dollars, units, or both.

The sales goal represents primarily the demands of those members of the coalition closely connected with sales and secondarily those members of the coalition who view sales as necessary for the stability of the organization. The goal is most frequently evoked and is most relevant to decisions with respect to sales strategy.

D. Market-Share Goal

The market-share goal is an alternative to the sales goal insofar as the concern is for a measure of sales effectiveness. Either or both may be used, depending on the past experience of the firm and the traditions of the industry. In addition, the market-share goal is linked to the demands of those parts of the organization that are primarily interested in comparative success (e.g., top management, especially top sales management) and to the demands for growth.

Like the sales goal, the market-share goal is most frequently evoked and most relevant to sales strategy decisions.

E. Profit Goal

We assume that the business firm has a profit goal. This goal is linked to standard accounting procedures for determining profit and loss. It summarizes the demands for two things: (1) demands for accumulating resources in order to distribute them in the form of capital investments, dividends to stockholders, payments to creditors, or increased budgets to subunits; (2) demands on the part of top management for favorable performance measures. In general, we assume that the profit goal is in terms of an aspiration level with respect to the dollar amount of profit. In principle, of course, this goal might also take the form of profit share or return on investment.

The profit goal reflects the pressure of those parts of the coalition that share in the distribution of profits and in the distribution of credit for profitability. Thus, in general, this pressure comes from top-level managers throughout the firm, from stockholders, creditors, and from those parts of the organization seeking capital investment. The goal is usually most closely linked to pricing and resource allocation decisions.

Although our fivefold specification of goals deviates substantially from the conventional theory of the firm, it will not necessarily satisfy anyone who would like to reflect all the goals that might conceivably be of relevance to price, output, and sales strategy decisions. Without insisting on the necessary efficacy of five goals, we think a strong case can be made for expanding the set of goals beyond the single profit goal of the conventional theory, and even beyond the elaboration to include a sales goal which was suggested by Baumol.[4] We think, however, that expanding the list of assumed goals much beyond the present list of five rapidly meets a point of diminishing returns.

IV. Organizational Expectations

Just as the theory of the firm requires some understanding of goals and goal formation within the organization, it also requires an understanding of the generation and handling of information within the firm and the ways in which information about the environment enters into the decision process of the firm. As already indicated, we consider the organization to be a coalition, and that members of this coalition make decisions affecting the organization's resources. These decisions depend upon information and expectations formed within the organization.

On the basis of a number of empirical studies certain conclusions can be tentatively drawn. In particular, resource allocation within the firm reflects only gross comparisons of the marginal advantages of alternatives. Rules of thumb for evaluating alternatives provide some constraints on resource allocation, and there is no conscious comparison of specific alternative investments. Any alternative that satisfies the constraints and secures suitably powerful support within the organization is likely to be adopted. This means that decision making is likely to reflect heavily a response to local problems of pressing need.

Search activity is stimulated when a problem area is recognized. At the first stage, however, only rough expectational data are used to screen obviously inappropriate actions. In general the early search is stopped after a few suitable alternatives are generated. These alternatives are then considered in greater detail. In most cases studied, a rather firm commit-

---

[4] William J. Baumol, *Business Behavior, Value and Growth* (New York: The Macmillan Company, 1959).

ment to an action was taken before the search for information proceeded very far.

Computation by the organization of anticipated consequences seems to be quite simple. There appear to be two main reasons for the simplicity. First the major initial question about a proposed action was not how it compared with alternatives but whether it was feasible. There are two varieties of feasibility. The first is the budgetary constraint: Is money available for the project? The second is an improvement criterion: Is the project clearly better than existing procedures? The second reason relates to the difficulty of measuring all the relevant considerations on a single dimension. In the studies referred to, many factors, such as speed and accuracy of work, safety of personnel, and convenience of location, were not viewed by the firm as reducible, in a meaningful way, to dollars. As a result such variables were treated as independent constraints and as irrelevant to cost estimation.

Expectations in the firm seem to be related to the hopes and wishes of the decision maker. In each of the studies made there is some suggestion of unconscious or semiconscious adjustment of perceptions to hopes. Thus there is a tendency to bias estimates of costs, revenues, and other important variables in the direction desired. It would be a mistake to think of these biases as great or the result of dishonesty. They are no different from the biases a scientist has in reviewing the evidence for a favored hypothesis.

V. A Partial Model of Price and Output Determination

Much of what has been said here may be difficult for the reader to make operational in the form of a model; therefore, as a way of illustrating some of the points which have been made and as a way of demonstrating that models other than the classical models can be constructed we are going to describe a duopoly model which summarizes some of the implications of the concepts of goals and expectations that have been discussed. The model itself is solved by simulation. This is a methodology which economists are beginning to use for developing and analyzing complex formal models. The model is developed for a duopoly situation, the product is homogeneous and, therefore, only one price exists in the market. The major decision that each of the two firms makes is an output decision (this is similar to the duopoly models discussed in Chapter 12, Section I). In making this decision each firm must estimate the market price for varying outputs. When the output is sold, however, the actual selling price will be determined by the market. No discrepancy between output and sales is permitted, so there are no inventory problems in the model.

We assume the duopoly to be composed of an ex-monopolist and a firm developed by former members of the established firm. We shall call the latter the *splinter* and the former the *ex-monopolist*. Such a specific case is

TABLE 17–1

PROCESS MODEL FOR OUTPUT DECISION OF FIRM

1. *Forecast* Competitor's reactions	Compute conjectural variation term for period t as a function of actual reactions observed in the past.
2. *Forecast* Demand	Keep slope of perceived demand curve constant but pass it through the last realized point in the market.
3. *Estimate* Average unit costs	Cost curve for this period is the same as for last period. If profit goals have been achieved two successive times, average unit costs increase.
4. *Specify objectives* Profit goal	Specify profit goal as a function of the actual profits achieved over last periods.
5. *Evaluate* Examine alternatives	Evaluate alternatives within the estimate space. If an alternative which meets goal is available, go to (9). If not, go to (6).
6. *Reexamine* Cost estimate	Search yields a cost reduction. Go to (5). If decision can be made after evaluation there, go to (9). If not, go to (7).
7. *Reexamine* Demand estimate	Estimate of demand increased after search. Go to (5). If decision can be made after evaluation, go to (9). If not, go to (8).
8. *Reexamine* Profit goal	Reduce profit goal to a level consistent with best alternative in the estimate space as modified after (6) and (7).
9. *Decide* Set output	Selection of alternative in original estimate space to meet original goal, in modified estimate space to meet original goal, or in modified estimate space to meet lowered goal.

formulated so that some rough assumptions can be made about appropriate functions for the various processes in the model. The assumptions are gross but, hopefully, not wholly unreasonable. To demonstrate that the model as a whole has some reasonable empirical basis, we will compare certain outcomes of the model with data from the can industry in the United States, where approximately the same underlying conditions hold.

We can describe the specific model at several levels of detail. In Table 17–1 the over-all skeleton of the model is indicated.

The decision-making process postulated by the theory begins with a forecast phase (in which competitor's reactions, demand, and costs are estimated) and a goal specification phase (in which a profit goal is established). An evaluation phase follows, in which an effort is made to find the "best" alternative, given the forecasts. If this "best" alternative is inconsistent with the profit goal, a reexamination phase ensues, in which an effort is made to revise cost and demand estimates. If reexamination fails to yield a new best alternative consistent with the profit goal, the immediate profit goal is abandoned in favor of "doing the best possible under the circumstances."

The specific details of the model will now be presented, following the framework in Table 17-1.

A. Forecasting Competitor's Behavior

Since we deal with a duopoly, an estimate of the rival firm's output is a significant factor in each firm's output decision. These estimates are essentially the same as the conjectural variation terms introduced in Chapter 12, Section I.[5] Our model assumes that these depend upon the actual reactions of the rival observed in previous periods.

To express this dependence, let $V_{m,t}$ denote the ratio of the actual change in the splinter's output between periods t and $t-1$ to the actual change in the ex-monopolist's output between periods t and $t-1$:[6]

$$V_{m,t} = \frac{Q_{s,t} - Q_{s,t-1}}{Q_{m,t} - Q_{m,t-1}} \tag{17-1}$$

where $Q_{s,t}$ is the splinter's actual output during period t and $Q_{m,t}$ is the ex-monopolist's actual output during period t. Analogously, let $V_{s,t}$ denote the ratio of the actual change in the ex-monopolist's output between periods t and $t-1$ to the actual change in the splinter's output between these same periods:[7]

$$V_{s,t} = \frac{Q_{m,t} - Q_{m,t-1}}{Q_{s,t} - Q_{s,t-1}} \tag{17-2}$$

We assume that the *ex-monopolist* estimates the ratio of the change in the splinter's output to his own change, that is, $V_{m,t}$, on the basis of the splinter's behavior during the past three time periods. Specifically, we assume that the ex-monopolist's estimate, $V'_{m,t}$, is a weighted average:

$$V'_{m,t} = V_{m,t-1} + [4(V_{m,t-1} - V_{m,t-2})$$
$$+ 2(V_{m,t-2} - V_{m,t-3}) + (V_{m,t-3} - V_{m,t-4})]/7 \tag{17-3}$$

where $V'_{m,t} = $ the ex-monopolist's estimate of $V_{m,t}$.

---

[5] The only difference is that in Chapter 12, where a continuous time dynamic analysis was implicit, the conjectural variations were treated as partial derivatives. Here, where we explicitly use a discrete time dynamic analysis, the conjectural variations are formulated as the ratios of finite differences.

[6] In case $Q_{m,t} = Q_{m,t-1}$, we arbitrarily define $V_{m,t} = 1$.

[7] In case $Q_{s,t} = Q_{s,t-1}$, we arbitrarily define $V_{s,t} = 1$.

The ex-monopolist's estimate of the splinter's output, $Q'_{s,t}$, is

$$Q'_{s,t} = Q_{s,t-1} + V'_{m,t} (Q_{m,t} - Q_{m,t-1}). \tag{17-4}$$

We expect the *splinter* firm to be more responsive to recent shifts in its competitor's behavior and less attentive to ancient history than the ex-monopolist, both because it is more inclined to consider the ex-monopolist a key part of its environment and because it will generally have less computational capacity as an organization to process and update the information necessary to deal with more complicated rules. Our assumption is that the splinter will simply use the information from the last two periods in obtaining $V'_{s,t}$, its estimate of $V_{s,t}$. In particular,

$$V'_{s,t} = V_{s,t-1} + (V_{s,t-1} - V_{s,t-2}). \tag{17-5}$$

The splinter's estimate of the monopolist's output is

$$Q'_{m,t} = Q_{m,t-1} + V'_{s,t} (Q_{s,t} - Q_{s,t-1}). \tag{17-6}$$

B. FORECASTING DEMAND

We assume that the actual market demand curve is linear; i.e., the market price is a linear function of the total output offered by the two firms. We also assume that the firms forecast a linear market demand curve, which is not necessarily the same as the actual demand curve. There has been considerable discussion in the literature of economics concerning the alleged discrepancy between the "imagined" demand curve and the actual demand curve; and it is the former concept that is incorporated in the model. The values we assign to the parameters of the imagined demand curve are based on rough inferences about the nature of the two firms.

We assume that, because of its past history of dominance and monopoly, the *ex-monopolist* will be overly pessimistic with respect to the quantity that it can sell at lower prices; i.e., we assume its initially perceived demand curve will have a somewhat steeper slope than will the actual market demand curve. On the assumption that information about actual demand is used to improve its estimate, we assume that the ex-monopolist changes its demand estimate on the basis of experience in the market. The firm assumes that its estimate of the slope of the demand curve is correct and it re-positions its previous estimate to pass through the observed demand point.

We posit that the *splinter* firm will initially be more optimistic with respect to the quantity that it can sell at low prices than the exmonopolist. We further assume that initially the splinter firm perceives demand as increasing over time. Thus, until demand shows a downward turn, the splinter firm estimates its demand to be 5 per cent greater than that found by re-positioning its perceived demand through the last point observed in the market place.

C. Estimating Costs

We do not assume that the firm has achieved optimum costs. We assume, rather, that the firm has a simplified estimate of its average cost curve, i.e., the curve expressing cost per unit as a function of output. It is horizontal over most of the range of possible outputs; at high and low outputs (relative to capacity) average costs are perceived to be somewhat higher.

Further, we make the assumption that these cost estimates are "self-confirming"; i.e., the estimated costs will, in fact, become the actual per-unit cost. The concept of organizational slack as it affects costs is introduced at this point. Average unit cost for the present period is estimated to be the same as the last period, but if the profit goal of the firm has been achieved for two consecutive time periods, then costs are estimated to be 5 per cent higher than "last time." The specific values for costs are arbitrary.

The *ex-monopolist's* initial average unit cost is assumed to be $800 per unit in the range of outputs from 10 per cent to 90 per cent of capacity. Below 10 per cent and above 90 per cent the initial average unit cost is assumed to be $900.

It is assumed that the *splinter* will have somewhat lower initial costs because its plant and equipment will tend to be newer and its production methods more modern. Specifically, initial average costs are $760 in the range of outputs from 10 per cent to 90 per cent of capacity. Below 10 per cent and above 90 per cent costs are assumed to average $870 per unit produced.

D. Specifying Objectives

The multiplicity of organizational objectives is a fact which will not be considered in this model. For simplicity, we limit ourselves to a single goal defined in terms of profit. In this model the function of the profit objective is to restrict or encourage search as well as to determine the actual decision made. If, given the estimates of rival's output, demand, and cost, there exists a production level that will provide a profit that is satisfactory, we assume the firm will produce at that level. If there is more than one satisfactory alternative, the firm will adopt that quantity level which maximizes profit.

We assume that the *ex-monopolist*, because of its size, substantial computational ability, and established procedures for dealing with a stable rather than a highly unstable environment, will tend to maintain a relatively stable profit objective. We assume that the objective will be a moving average of the realized profit over the last ten time periods. Initially the ex-monopolist seeks to achieve a profit level that is in the same proportion to the profit level achieved during its monopoly period as its current capacity is to total industry capacity.

The *splinter* firm will presumably be inclined to consider a somewhat shorter period of past experience, for reasons indicated earlier. We assume that the profit objective of the splinter will be the average of experienced profit over the past five time periods and that the initial profit objective will be linked to the experience of the former monopolist and the relative capacities of the two. Thus, we specify that the initial profit objective of the two firms will be proportional to their initial capacities.

E. REEXAMINATION OF COSTS

We assume that when the original forecasts define a satisfactory plan, there will be no further examination of them. If, however, such a plan is not obtained, we assume an effort to achieve a satisfactory plan in the first instance by reviewing estimates and finally by revising objectives. We assume that cost estimates are reviewed before demand estimates and that the latter are reexamined only if a satisfactory plan cannot be developed by the revision of the former. The reevaluation of costs is a search for methods of accomplishing objectives at lower cost than appeared possible under less pressure. We believe this ability to revise estimates when forced to do so is characteristic of organizational decision making. It is, of course, closely related to the organizational slack concept previously introduced. In general, we have argued that an organization can ordinarily find possible cost reductions if forced to do so and that the amount of the reductions will be a function of the amount of slack in the organization.

It is assumed that the reexamination of costs under the pressure of trying to meet objectives enables each of the organizations to move in the direction of the "real" minimum cost point. For purposes of this model it is assumed that both firms reduce costs 10 per cent of the difference between their estimated average unit costs and the "real" minimum.

F. REEXAMINATION OF DEMAND

The reevaluation of demand serves the same function as the reevaluation of costs. In the present model it occurs only if the reevaluation of costs is not adequate to define an acceptable plan. It consists of revising upward the expectations of market demand. The reasoning is that some new alternative is selected that the firm believes will increase its demand. The new approach may be changed advertising procedure, a scheme to work salesmen harder, or some other alternative that leads the firm to an increase in optimism. In any event, it is felt that the more experienced firm will take a slightly less sanguine view of what is possible. As in the case of estimating demand, we assume that both firms persist in seeing a linear demand curve and that no changes are made in the perceived slope of that curve. In the case of the *ex-monopolist*, it is assumed that as a result of the reexamination of demand estimates, the firm revises its estimates of demand upward by 10 per cent. In the case of the *splinter*, the assumption is that the upward revision of demand is 15 per cent.

G. Reexamination of Objectives

Because our decision rule is one that maximizes among the available alternatives and our rule for specifying objectives depends only on outcomes, the reevaluation of objectives does not, in fact, enter into our present model in a way that influences behavior. The procedure can be interpreted as adjusting aspirations to the "best possible under the circumstances."

Table 17–2

Initial Conditions for Model

Initial market demand (unknown to firms)	$p = 2000 - q$
Ex-monopolist's initial perception of demand schedule	$p = 2200 - 3q$
Splinter's initial perception of demand schedule	$p = 1800 - q$
Ex-monopolist's average unit cost	
$\begin{cases} 0.1q_{max,m} < q_m < 0.9q_{max,m} \\ q_m > 0.9q_{max,m}, q_m < 0.1q_{max,m} \end{cases}$	$800 \\ 900
Splinter's average unit cost	
$\begin{cases} 0.1q_{max,s} < q_s < 0.9q_{max,s} \\ q_s > 0.9q_{max,s}, q_s < 0.1q_{max,s} \end{cases}$	$760 \\ 870
"Real" minimum average unit cost	$700
Ex-monopolist's capacity	400
Splinter's capacity	50
Market quantity	233
Market price	$1500
Ex-monopolist's profit goal	$163,100
Splinter's profit goal	$20,387
Conjectural variations ($V'_{m,t}$ and $V'_{s,t}$)	All 0 initially
Splinter's overoptimism of demand in forecast phase	5%
Splinter's raise of demand forecast upon reexamination	15%
Ex-monopolist's raise of demand forecast upon reexamination	10%
Cost reduction achieved in M's and S's search for lower costs (percentage of costs above "real" minimum average unit cost)	10%
Cost rise attributable to increase in "internal slack"	5%
Shift of actual demand schedule to right each time period	8%
Constraint on changing output from that of the last period	$\pm 25\%$
Percentage of capacity at which firm must be producing before it may expand (subject to other conditions)	90%
Change in capacity, upon expansion	20%

TABLE 17–3
VALUES OF SELECTED VARIABLES AT TWO-PERIOD INTERVALS

	I	III	V	VII	IX	XI	XIII	XV	XVII	XIX	XXI	XXIII
Market												
Price	1420	1710	2196	2763	3283	3927	4430	4942	5425	3722	2785	2573
Output	290	311	262	205	209	195	303	466	713	914	855	534
Ex-monopolist												
Aspiration level	163,100	165,671	169,631	176,800	173,221	178,385	203,693	246,746	319,561	348,006	247,455	182,580
Conjectural variations	0	0	0.74	−22.4	1.09	0.74	0.26	0.35	0.28	0.30	−0.38	0.05
Costs (A.U.C.)	826	813	881	944	1041	1106	1219	1344	1482	1634	1801	1986
Output	240	251	206	153	161	150	233	363	566	703	658	369
No. reexam. steps	2	0	0	3	0	0	0	0	0	0	0	0
Splinter												
Aspiration level	20,387	27,107	31,448	39,763	46,218	39,684	54,245	79,090	113,595	121,973	86,083	60,742
Conjectural variations	0	0	9.2	−1.78	−6.58	8.72	3.39	3.96	4.76	3.91	6.3	−17.1
Costs	760	798	865	954	1023	1057	1166	1285	1417	1562	1623	1790
Output	50	60	56	52	48	45	70	103	147	211	197	165
No. reexam. steps	0	0	0	3	3	0	0	0	0	0	0	3
Profit ratio												
Splinter's profit ÷ ex-monopolist's profit	0.19	0.21	0.26	0.34	0.30	0.30	0.30	0.28	0.26	0.30	0.34	0.68
Share of market												
Ex-monopolist's output ÷ total output	0.83	0.81	0.79	0.75	0.77	0.77	0.77	0.78	0.79	0.77	0.77	0.69

416

TABLE 17-3 (continued)

	XXV	XXVII	XXIX	XXXI	XXXIII	XXXV	XXXVII	XXXIX	XLI	XLIII	XLV
Market											
Price	2229	1719	2286	2970	3355	3742	4099	4546	5463	6730	7294
Output	360	335	250	140	218	340	529	735	777	727	1126
Ex-monopolist											
Aspiration level	157,664	148,648	154,010	158,120	159,060	179,859	203,892	239,045	280,940	260,501	340,745
Conjectural variations	0.64	−1.07	28.4	−1.40	0.85	0.95	0.96	0.65	3.77	1.91	1.35
Costs (A.U.C.)	2085	1710	1609	1436	1363	1502	1656	1826	2013	2071	2283
Output	207	193	143	80	125	195	303	432	342	320	500
No. reexam. steps	1	3	0	3	0	0	0	0	0	0	0
Splinter											
Aspiration level	37,977	19,272	28,402	37,123	38,627	53,005	77,001	109,136	164,566	266,512	396,911
Conjectural variations	2.21	−0.32	2.43	50.7	1.32	1.31	1.32	2.3	−0.8	3.16	0.79
Costs	1853	1821	1608	1669	1840	2029	2237	2466	2719	2771	3055
Output	153	142	107	60	93	145	226	303	435	407	626
No. reexam. steps	0	1	0	0	0	0	0	0	0	0	0
Profit ratio											
Splinter's profit ÷ ex-monopolist's profit	0.98	0.74	0.75	0.64	0.49	0.49	0.49	0.47	0.90	0.97	0.95
Share of market											
Ex-monopolist's output ÷ total output	0.57	0.58	0.57	0.57	0.57	0.57	0.57	0.59	0.44	0.44	0.44

If our decision rule were different or if we made objectives at one time period a function of both outcomes and previous objectives, the reevaluation of objectives would become important to the decision process.

H. Decision

We have specified that the organization will follow traditional economic rules for maximization with respect to its perception of costs, demand, and competitor's behavior. The specific alternatives selected, of course, depend on the point at which this step is invoked (i.e., how many reevaluation steps are used before an acceptable plan is identified). The output decision is constrained in two ways:

1. A firm cannot produce, in any time period, beyond its present capacity. Both models allow for change in plant capacity over time. The process by which capacity changes is the same for both firms. If profit goals have been met for two successive periods and production is above 90 per cent of capacity, then capacity increases 20 per cent.

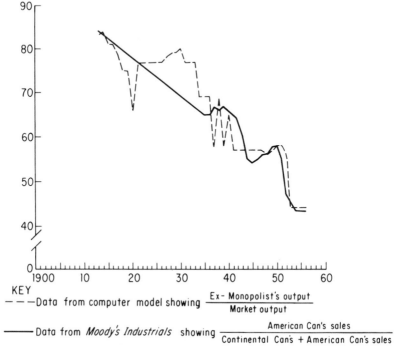

KEY

— — —Data from computer model showing $\dfrac{\text{Ex- Monopolist's output}}{\text{Market output}}$

———— Data from *Moody's Industrials* showing $\dfrac{\text{American Can's sales}}{\text{Continental Can's + American Can's sales}}$

FIGURE 17–1.   Comparisons of share-of-market data.

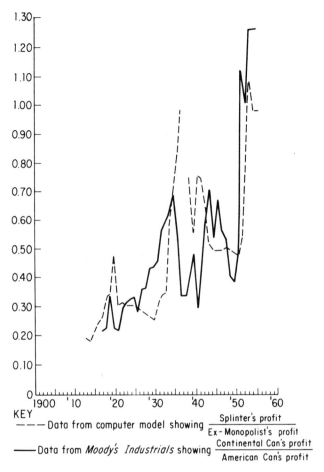

KEY

– – – Data from computer model showing $\dfrac{\text{Splinter's profit}}{\text{Ex-Monopolist's profit}}$

——— Data from *Moody's Industrials* showing $\dfrac{\text{Continental Can's profit}}{\text{American Can's profit}}$

FIGURE 17–2.   Comparisons of profit-ratio data.

2. A firm cannot change its output from one time period to the next more than ± 25 per cent. The rationale behind the latter assumption is that neither large cutbacks nor large advances in production are possible in the very short run, since there are large organization problems connected with either.

The various initial conditions specified previously are summarized in Table 17–2, along with the other initial conditions required to program the models.

We have now described a decision-making model with a large ex-monopolist and a splinter competitor. Table 17–3 shows some of the results of the model for selected periods.[8] By examining Table 17–3 we can determine the time paths of such variables as cost, conjectural variation, and output for each firm.

We also have compared the shares of market and profit ratio results with actual data generated from competition between an ex-monopolist, the American Can Company, and its splinter competitor, Continental Can Company, between 1913 and 1956. These results are shown in Figures 17–1 and 17–2. In general, we are encouraged by the surprisingly good fit of the behavioral model to real-world data, although we do not feel that this result *per se* constitutes a validation of our new approach to the theory of the firm.

VI. Summary

In this chapter we have considered a new, behavioral approach to the theory of the firm. This involves detailed consideration of the decision-making processes within a firm. Our major aim has been to show that the traditional theory is not the only way in which the economics of the firm can be analyzed. In order to acquire a complete understanding of the business firm as an institution it is necessary to analyze the effects of such variables as goal setting, goal adjustment, information flow, search patterns, and other internal organizational characteristics on the firm's decisions.

In general, the behavioral approach assumes that the firm is essentially an adaptively rational system. An adaptive system, as we use the term, has the following properties:

1. There exist a number of states of the system. At any point in time, the system in some sense "prefers" some of these states to others.

2. There exists an external source of disturbance or shock to the system. These shocks cannot be controlled.

3. There exist a number of decision variables internal to the system. These variables are manipulated according to some decision rules.

4. Each combination of external shocks and decision variables in the system changes the state of the system. Thus, given an existing state, an external shock, and a decision, the next state is determined.

5. Any decision rule that leads to a preferred state at one point is more likely to be used in the future than it was in the past; any decision rule that leads to a nonpreferred state at one point is less likely to be used in the future than it was in the past.

---

[8] Market demand was varied in the following way during this simulation: (1) The slope of the actual demand curve was held constant. (2) In each time period the intercept of the actual demand curve, I_t, was set equal to aI_{t-1}. The value of a was 1.08 for periods 1–16, 0.90 for periods 17–20, 1 for periods 21–26, and 1.08 from period 27 onward.

With this general assumption the behavioral approach then investigates effects of variables internal to the firm on price and output decisions. This approach is in sharp contrast to the traditional theory which ignores the internal structure of the firm. The latter approach assumes that market considerations dominate the internal structure of the firm in price and output decisions. This seems to be a valid position in the case of perfect competition. In the case of oligopoly, however, the firm can affect the market by its behavior and it is not completely dominated by market considerations. Thus a study of the internal factors affecting decisions can increase our understanding of firm behavior, especially in imperfect markets. Although the elaborations of the behavioral theory necessary for this have just begun, this seems a highly fruitful area for further research.

SUGGESTED READINGS

See the end of Chapter 18.

Chapter Eighteen

New Considerations in the
Theory of the Firm (Continued)

This chapter continues the exploration of attempts to develop new models of the firm which we began in Chapter 17. We shall consider three particular models. Williamson's managerial discretion model is an attempt to embody some notions of the behavioral theory of the firm into a model which can be treated analytically rather than requiring simulation. The nonmaximizing monopoly model is an example of a simplified dynamic model for which simulation techniques are necessary; it is an illustration of a model which does not assume maximization but relies instead upon an aspiration-level mechanism to determine when satisfactory performance is attained. Finally, Baumol's revenue-maximization model assumes that firms attempt to maximize sales revenues, subject to a minimum profits constraint.

I. A Managerial Discretion Model

A. RATIONALE FOR THE MANAGERS' UTILITY FUNCTION

Williamson has developed a model of business behavior which focuses on the self-interest-seeking behavior of corporate managers.[1] This emphasis is reasonable once we acknowledge that the modern corporate enterprise is a complex organization far different from the traditional economic notion of a single entrepreneur running his own small firm.

One of the striking attributes of the typical large firm in the American economy is the separation of the ownership and the management functions which has become increasingly prevalent.[2] The owners of the firm, i.e., the stockholders, generally have little interest in, and even less direct knowledge of, the day-to-day operations of the firm. It is the owners, however, who have contributed the capital with which the firm operates and who receive the dividends which are paid by the firm. The actual power of the stockholders to influence the firm's plans and operations resides in the board of directors, who are elected by stockholder vote. In practice, however, because of the widespread custom of voting by means of proxies, which are generally solicited by managment, the board tends to be a self-perpetuating group, over which the stockholders individually—and even sometimes collectively—exert little power.

The top management of the firm is appointed by, and responsible to, the board of directors. In many firms, however, top management is represented by membership on the board of directors and may play a dominant role on the board. Even where the board is predominantly made up of outside directors, top management usually possesses a great deal of freedom of action if the results of the firm's operations are satisfactory.

This separation of ownership and management functions permits the managers of a firm to pursue their own self-interest, subject only to their being able to maintain effective control over the firm. In particular, if profits at any time are at an acceptable level, if the firm shows a reasonable rate of growth over time, and if sufficient dividends are paid to keep the stockholders happy, then the managers are fairly certain of retaining their power.

---

[1] O. E. Williamson, "A Model of Rational Managerial Behavior," in Richard M. Cyert and James G. March, *A Behavioral Theory of the Firm* (Englewood Cliffs, N.J.: Prentice-Hall, Inc., 1963), chap. 9. A more extensive development of this model is contained in Oliver E. Williamson, *The Economics of Discretionary Behavior: Managerial Objectives in a Theory of the Firm* (Englewood Cliffs, N.J.: Prentice-Hall, Inc., 1964).

[2] See A. G. Papandreou, "Some Basic Problems in the Theory of the Firm," in *A Survey of Contemporary Economics*, ed. B. G. Haley (Homewood, Ill.: Richard D. Irwin, 1952), Vol. 2, pp. 197–200; R. A. Gordon, *Business Leadership in the Large Corporation* (Berkeley: University of California Press, 1961), chaps. 2, 8; A. A. Berle, Jr., and G. C. Means, *The Modern Corporation and Private Property* (New York: Macmillan, 1932).

What might the management group's self-interest depend upon? As is the case in the traditional theory of household behavior, we can postulate a utility function which incorporates those goals in which management is interested. We can regard the managers' utility as dependent primarily upon

1. The salaries (and other forms of monetary compensation, such as bonuses, stock options, etc.) which the managers receive from the firm.

2. The number and quality of staff personnel who report to the managers.

3. The extent to which the managers are able to direct the investment of the firm's resources.

4. The type and amount of perquisites (such as expense accounts, lavishly furnished offices, chauffeur-driven limousines, etc.) which the managers receive from the firm and which are beyond the amount strictly necessary for the firm's operations.

There can be little disagreement that salaries are a major factor affecting the well being of managers, since monetary compensation from their jobs provides them the means for financing their private life expenditures. Money alone, however, is not the entire reward which a manager obtains from his job.

The staff personnel commanded by managers are important both as a mark of status and as a measure of power.

Discretionary spending for investments is primarily important because it represents in tangible form the command over resources which a manager possesses. By directing the flow of new investment, the manager is able to exert an influence on the future development of the firm. The larger the amount of discretionary investment spending the manager controls, the more easily can he further his own personal interests (and pet projects).

The perquisites of management represent a form of economic rent that the managers obtain from the firm. If management's perquisites go beyond the amount strictly necessary for efficient and effective operations of the firm, the extra perquisites are a return to management's privileged (and sheltered) position.

Williamson argues that there is a close relationship between the size of staff reporting to a manager and the level of monetary compensation that the manager receives. Therefore Williamson simplifies his formal model without distorting its realism by using a single variable, dollar expenditures on staff, in place of separate salary and staff variables.

Williamson treats the nonessential management perquisites, which are beyond the level required for effective operations of the firm, as "management slack"; management slack becomes part of the firm's cost function. This distinction focuses attention on that portion of managerial perquisites which functions as economic rent.

The concept of discretionary spending for investments is not intended to include those investments which are strictly necessary on the basis of economic considerations. The expenditures on those investments which are essential for a firm's survival (such as periodic replacement of equipment) are regarded as part of the minimum required profits which a firm must generate for the managers to retain effective control of the firm.

B. The Formal Model

In order to formalize his model, Williamson introduces four different types of profits: maximum profits, actual profits, reported profits, and minimum required profits. The concept of *maximum profits* π^*, refers to the profits which the firm would obtain if it behaved as a profit-maximizing agent. π^* is thus the maximum value of the criterion function in traditional theories.

Actual profits, π_A, differ from maximum profits by the amount of excess expenditures for staff. Not all staff expenditures are excess, of course, especially since the managers' salaries are included in them. If, however, we let MS represent the amount of management slack absorbed as staff expenditures, we can write

$$\pi_A = \pi^* - MS. \tag{18-1}$$

Reported profits, π_R, are less than actual profits by the amount of management slack which is absorbed as a cost. Reported profits are the same as taxable profits; they are used to pay taxes and dividends and to finance some investment. Letting M denote the amount of management slack absorbed as a cost, we have

$$\pi_R = \pi_A - M. \tag{18-2}$$

Minimum required profits (after taxes), π_0, are the lowest level of profits consistent with the managers' retaining effective control over the firm. This minimum level must be high enough to enable the firm to pay normal dividends to the stockholders (and perhaps to allow for gradual growth in dividends) and to provide for any economically necessary investments (which are not included in the discretionary investment spending). If there exists an expectation that profits will generally grow over time (with due allowance, of course, for cyclical fluctuations), the minimum required profit level may increase from year to year. Letting t denote the tax rate on (reported) corporate profits and letting T denote the total taxes of the firm, we have

$$T = t\pi_R. \tag{18-3}$$

The minimum required profits constraint can be expressed most simply as

$$\pi_R \geq \pi_0 + T. \tag{18-4}$$

An equivalent form for expressing this constraint is

$$\pi_R \geq \frac{\pi_0}{1 - t}. \tag{18-5}$$

The amount of slack in the minimum required profits constraint, i.e., the difference between reported profits and minimum required profits and taxes, represents the amount of discretionary investment spending which the firm's managers may undertake. Letting I_D be discretionary spending for investments, we have

$$I_D = \pi_R - \pi_0 - T. \tag{18-6}$$

Since a firm's investment expenditures are not tax deductible at the time they are undertaken (although over a sufficient period of time they are deductible, in the form of depreciation), I_D as here defined is close to an "availability of funds" notion. The larger I_D is, the more funds will the managers have at their disposal to invest as they see fit. Although these funds will always be invested in projects which are said to be sound and useful to the firm's well-being, they do not have the same economic function as those investments which are part of π_0.

In Williamson's formal model, the utility function that managers are trying to maximize may be represented as a function of three variables: (1) dollar expenditures on "staff," S; (2) management slack absorbed as cost, M; and (3) discretionary investment spending, I_D. Letting U denote the utility function, we have

$$U = U(S, M, I_D). \tag{18-7}$$

The managers attempt to maximize the value of the utility function in Eq. (18-7) subject to three constraints. The first is the minimum required profits constraint, Eq. (18-4). Note from Eq. (18-6) that (18-4) is equivalent to requiring I_D to be nonnegative. Two additional constraints must be imposed to insure that S and M are also nonnegative. By adopting the reasonable assumption that U exhibits diminishing marginal utility in all its components and that, as any of its components approaches zero, the marginal utility of that component becomes unbounded, then these nonnegativity constraints will be automatically satisfied whenever U is maximized.

We shall regard the firm's decision variables as X, its output level in the period; S, its staff expenditures in the period; and ρ, which we define as the ratio of reported to actual profits:

$$\rho = \frac{\pi_R}{\pi_A}. \tag{18-8}$$

Let R denote total revenue in the period and let P denote price during the period. Then,

$$R = PX. \tag{18-9}$$

Price is regarded by Williamson as a function of X, S, and a demand shift parameter, ϵ. Hence,

$$P = P(X, S, \epsilon). \tag{18-10}$$

The demand function is assumed to be negatively sloping:

$$\frac{\partial P}{\partial X} < 0. \tag{18-11}$$

Staff expenditures help increase demand for the firm's product:

$$\frac{\partial P}{\partial S} > 0. \tag{18-12}$$

Increases in the demand shift parameter, ϵ, are interpreted as raising demand:

$$\frac{\partial P}{\partial \epsilon} > 0. \tag{18-13}$$

Letting C denote total production costs

$$C = C(X). \tag{18-14}$$

We can now write the firm's actual profits as the difference between its revenues and its production and staff costs:

$$\pi_A = R - C - S. \tag{18-15}$$

In view of Eq. (18–8),

$$\pi_A - \pi_R = \left(1 - \frac{\pi_R}{\pi_A}\right) \pi_A = (1 - \rho)\, \pi_A. \tag{18-16}$$

Eq. (18–2), (18–15), and (18–16) imply that the second component of the managers' utility function can be written

$$M = \pi_A - \pi_R = (1 - \rho)\, (R - C - S). \tag{18-17}$$

To obtain a more convenient expression for the third component of the managers' utility function, I_D, from Eq. (18–3) and (18–6) we have

$$I_D = \pi_R - \pi_0 - t\pi_R = (1 - t)\pi_R - \pi_0. \tag{18-18}$$

From Eq. (18–18), (18–8), and (18–15),

$$I_D = (1 - t)\rho\pi_A - \pi_0 = \rho(1 - t)\, (R - C - S)\ - \pi_0. \tag{18-19}$$

Substituting Eq. (18–17) and (18–19) into (18–7), the managers' utility function becomes

$$U = U[S, (1 - \rho)(R - C - S), \rho(1 - t)(R - C - S) - \pi_0]. \quad (18\text{–}20)$$

In order to find the values of X, S, and ρ which maximize the managers' utility function, equate the partial derivatives of Eq. (18–20) with respect to these three variables to zero:

$$\frac{\partial U}{\partial X} = U_2 (1 - \rho) \left(\frac{\partial R}{\partial X} - \frac{\partial C}{\partial X} \right) + U_3 \rho (1 - t) \left(\frac{\partial R}{\partial X} - \frac{\partial C}{\partial X} \right) = 0. \quad (18\text{–}21)$$

$$\frac{\partial U}{\partial S} = U_1 + U_2 (1 - \rho) \left(\frac{\partial R}{\partial S} - 1 \right) + U_3 \rho (1 - t) \left(\frac{\partial R}{\partial S} - 1 \right) = 0.$$

$$(18\text{–}22)$$

$$\frac{\partial U}{\partial \rho} = U_2 (-1)(R - C - S) + U_3 (1 - t)(R - C - S) = 0. \quad (18\text{–}23)$$

The only way for Eq. (18–21) to be satisfied in general is for

$$\frac{\partial R}{\partial X} = \frac{\partial C}{\partial X}. \quad (18\text{–}24)$$

Solving Eq. (18–22) for $\partial R/\partial S$, we obtain

$$\frac{\partial R}{\partial S} [U_2(1 - \rho) + U_3 \rho (1 - t)] + U_1 - U_2(1 - \rho) - U_3 \rho (1 - t) = 0$$

$$(18\text{–}25)$$

or
$$\frac{\partial R}{\partial S} = \frac{-U_1 + U_2(1 - \rho) + U_3 \rho (1 - t)}{U_2(1 - \rho) + U_3 \rho (1 - t)}. \quad (18\text{–}26)$$

From Eq. (18–23),
$$U_2 = U_3(1 - t). \quad (18\text{–}27)$$

The three equations (18–24), (18–26), and (18–27) jointly determine the optimal values of X, S, and ρ for the firm. From Eq. (18–27), we can see that the marginal utility of discretionary investment must be proportional to the marginal utility of management slack absorbed as cost, the proportionality factor being $1/(1 - t)$. To spend one dollar on discretionary investment, which is not immediately tax deductible, $1/(1 - t)$ dollars of profits before taxes must be used. Thus unless the marginal utility of the last dollar spent on discretionary investment equals the marginal utility of the last $1/(1 - t)$ dollars allocated to management slack, which is tax deductible, a reallocation between these expenditures will increase the value of the utility function.

C. Comparisons with the Profit-Maximizing Model

A comparison of Williamson's model with the traditional model can be made by examining the necessary conditions for profit maximization. For the profit-maximizing firm, π^*, π_A, and π_R are all equal; hence, in this case,

$$\rho = 1. \tag{18-28}$$

In order to find the values of X and S which maximize

$$\pi^* = R - C - S \tag{18-29}$$

we can differentiate Eq. (18–29) partially with respect to both X and S and equate the results to zero:

$$\frac{\partial \pi^*}{\partial X} = \frac{\partial R}{\partial X} - \frac{\partial C}{\partial X} = 0. \tag{18-30}$$

$$\frac{\partial \pi^*}{\partial S} = \frac{\partial R}{\partial S} - 1 = 0. \tag{18-31}$$

The resulting necessary conditions are

$$\frac{\partial R}{\partial X} = \frac{\partial C}{\partial X}. \tag{18-32}$$

$$\frac{\partial R}{\partial S} = 1. \tag{18-33}$$

The first necessary condition for the utility-maximizing firm, Eq. (18–24) has exactly the same form as Eq. (18–32), the corresponding necessary condition for the profit-maximizing firm. This does not mean that the resulting optimal output levels are the same, however, since $\partial R/\partial X$ is implicitly a function of S and the optimal values of S are generally different in the two models.

Let us now consider the differences in the second necessary conditions, Eq. (18–26) and (18–33), for the utility-maximizing and the profit-maximizing firms. As long as there is a positive marginal utility from staff expenditures (that is, as long as $U_1 > 0$), then Eq. (18–26) implies that

$$\frac{\partial R}{\partial S} < 1. \tag{18-34}$$

Thus the implications of Eq. (18–26) and (18–33) for staff expenditures are clearly different for the two firms.

It is reasonable to assume that continually higher staff expenditures have a diminishing marginal effectiveness on the firm's ability to raise prices, i.e.,

$$\frac{\partial^2 P}{\partial S^2} < 0 \tag{18-35}$$

and

$$\frac{\partial^2 R}{\partial S^2} < 0. \tag{18-36}$$

Equation (18-36) means that $\partial R/\partial S$ is monotonically decreasing, implying that expenditures for staff will be higher for the utility-maximizing firm than for the profit-maximizing firm.

In summary, we can state that a utility-maximizing firm has higher staff expenditures and more management slack than a profit-maximizing firm. No general statement can be made about the relative output levels for the two firms.

If we examine the comparative static properties of Williamson's model, we can find additional ways in which its implications differ from the profit-maximizing model. In particular, let us consider how changes in demand (represented by shifts in ϵ), change in the profits tax rate, t, and changes in a lump sum tax (which we shall denote by $\bar{T}$) affect the optimal values of X, S, and ρ. Since the mathematical manipulations involved in deriving these results are both lengthy and fairly complicated, we shall merely present the results which Williamson has obtained. Table 18-1 shows the direction in which each of the decision variables changes as a result of an increase in any one parameter. Thus, for example, Table 18-1 indicates that $\partial X/\partial \epsilon > 0$, $\partial S/\partial \bar{T} < 0$, etc.

The import of these comparative static results for Williamson's model is best seen by contrasting them with the corresponding results for the profit-maximizing model. The latter are presented in Table 18-2.

TABLE 18-1

RESPONSES TO DISPLACEMENTS FROM EQUILIBRIUM FOR WILLIAMSON'S MODEL

Variable	Parameter		
	ϵ	t	$\bar{T}$
X	+	+	−
S	+	+	−
ρ	−	−	+

SOURCE: O. E. Williamson, "A Model of Rational Managerial Behavior," in Richard M. Cyert and James G. March, *A Behavioral Theory of the Firm* (Englewood Cliffs, N.J.: Prentice-Hall, Inc., 1963), table 9.1, p. 248.

TABLE 18–2

RESPONSES TO DISPLACEMENTS FROM EQUILIBRIUM
FOR THE PROFIT-MAXIMIZING MODEL

Variable	Parameter		
	ϵ	t	$\bar{T}$
X	$+$	0	0
S	$+$	0	0

SOURCE: O. E. Williamson, "A Model of Rational Managerial Behavior," in Richard M. Cyert and James G. March, *A Behavioral Theory of the Firm* (Englewood Cliffs, N. J.: Prentice-Hall, Inc., 1963), table 9.2, p. 248.

A first major difference between these two models is that the profit-maximizing firm always reports the entire amount of actual profits. In Williamson's model the fraction of actual profits reported is generally less than unity, and this fraction itself changes in response to parameter changes.

The responses of firms to tax changes under the two models are also strikingly different. The output behavior of a profit-maximizing firm is not affected by changes in either the corporate profits tax rate or in a lump sum tax. This is to be expected, since the firm which is maximizing profits must necessarily also be maximizing any fraction of these profits (such as profits remaining after taxes). In Williamson's model, on the other hand, all the decision variables of the firm are affected by changes in either tax rates or in lump sum taxes. Increases in the profits tax rate, t, will cause the utility-maximizing·firm to increase both its output and its staff expenditures and to decrease the fraction of actual profits which are reported; increases in a lump sum tax, $\bar{T}$, cause just the opposite types of changes in the decision variables.

The output and staff expenditure responses of these two models are the same for an increase in demand. Management slack is never supposed to exist for the profit-maximizing firm. For the utility-maximizing firm, however, there is both an absolute and a relative increase in management slack as the environment becomes more favorable (i.e., when there is an increased demand for the firm's products). Just the opposite takes place in a hostile environment: a decline in demand leads both to an absolute and a relative reduction in the amount of management slack. When it is realized that management slack includes such items as travel, office improvements, expense accounts, executive yachts and limousines, etc., casual empiricism suggests that this aspect of Williamson's model is realistic.

An increase in the corporate profits tax rate can be regarded as a higher penalty imposed on reported profits. That the utility-maximizing firm responds to an increase in this penalty by shifting away from reported profits and obtaining a larger proportion of its satisfaction from higher staff expenditures and increased management slack, seems eminently reasonable. Increases in advertising expenditures, customer services, public relations activities, etc., as well as general increases in managerial perquisites, usually accompany a rise in the profits tax rate. A profit-maximizing firm would not respond in this way to changes in the tax rate; its optimum combination of factors is unaffected by changes in the percentage of profits retained after payment of corporate taxes.

A profit-maximizing firm cannot avoid a lump sum tax except by going out of business. As long as such a tax does not force the firm to suspend its operations, it does not affect the firm's behavior. The Williamson-type of firm, however, is not maximizing profits, and thus it has some latitude to modify its behavior in order partially to compensate for any increases in a lump sum tax. In Williamson's model, a firm will generate a minimum required amount of after-tax profits. An increase in the lump sum tax thus raises the necessary amount of before-tax profits which this firm must generate. Hence the utility-maximizing firm must modify some of its decisions to generate more reported profits before taxes. Thus expenditures on staff and management slack will decrease in response to the imposition of a lump sum tax. (The decrease in output which also accompanies the imposition of a lump sum tax follows because, with lower staff expenditures, the demand curve is shifted downward.) Since a lump sum tax is effectively a fixed cost, Williamson's model predicts that changes in fixed costs will affect the short-run decisions of the firm, a different result than implied by the short-run profit-maximizing model of the firm.

The frequently observed phenomenon of a newly appointed executive achieving striking cost reductions by cutting down on managerial perquisites and by removing "excess" staff is consistent with Williamson's model. The manager who is trying to reduce cost can be interpreted as having a low preference for staff expenditures, relative to other components of his utility function. Since some of the staff expenditures in Williamson's model are devoted to management's utility maximization, rather than to profit maximization, any marked change in management taste will be accompanied by significant changes in staff.

II. A Nonmaximizing Monopoly Model

A. Rationale

The model of a monopoly firm which we present in this section illustrates how a firm may behave in the absence of a well-defined objective function which it is trying to maximize.[3] This model assumes behavior by the firm

---

[3] The authors developed this model for illustrative purposes in this book. The computer program used to explore the properties of this model was written by R. Dale McDowell.

which is characterized by an aspiration level mechanism defining when satisfactory performance has been attained and by the existence of organizational slack which allows members of the firm to absorb part of the profits as costs.

The model embodies a simple type of dynamic behavior: it is a sequence of one-period decisions in which the environment at the start of each period is affected by the firm's past behavior. The internal climate of the firm, and its mechanism for making decisions, are also affected by past behavior. The firm makes its decisions on a one-period basis, however, ignoring any implications for the future which may be implicit in its present behavior.

The demand function facing the monopolist is the same each period, except for the addition of a random term which varies over time. The firm's aspiration level equals its profits last period. Over time the firm tries to increase its profits. If it succeeds, organizational slack increases and it becomes less precise in determining output. Thus in good times there is less pressure on the managers of the firm, and they have more freedom to pursue their own aims independent of the firm's profit goal. During any period that the firm fails to increase its profits, the reverse effect occurs. Organizational slack decreases and the managers become more attentive to business and set the firm's output more precisely.

B. The Formal Model

Let us present the model in formal terms. In any period the demand function facing the monopolist is

$$p = d_1 - d_2 q + r_p \qquad (18\text{–}37)$$

where p is selling price, q is output (which is assumed equal to the number of units sold in the current period, so that there is no inventory carry-over), d_1 and d_2 are positive constants, and r_p is an independently distributed uniform random variable, drawn from the range $[-u_p, u_p]$.[4] Given the firm's output decision, q, the market price is determined by Eq. (18–37). From period to period, the monopolist's selling price may vary both because of changes in the random variable r_p and because of changes in the firm's output decisions.

The firm's total cost function in any period is

$$C = c_1 + c_2 q + c_3 q^2 + S \qquad (18\text{–}38)$$

---

[4] In principle each variable should be followed by parentheses indicating the time period to which it pertains. Thus, for example, $p(t)$ denotes selling price in period t, whereas $p(t-1)$ denotes selling price in period $t-1$, etc. Where no confusion can result, for the sake of simplicity we omit specific time period indications from the variables; in such cases the variables always refer to their current values, i.e., to their values in period t. Those parameters which we label as *constants* do not change in value from period to period.

where C is total cost, c_1, c_2, and c_3 are positive constants, and S is organizational slack.

Organizational slack is a function of the firm's profits during the preceding two periods. Letting $\pi(t)$ denote the firm's profits in period t, organizational slack is determined in period t by

$$S(t) = S(t - 1) + r_S \qquad \text{if } \pi(t - 1) > \pi(t - 2).$$

$$S(t) = S(t - 1) - r_S \qquad \text{if } \pi(t - 1) \leq \pi(t - 2). \qquad (18\text{--}39)$$

However, $0 \leq S(t) \leq S_M$.

In Eq. (18–39), r_S is an independently distributed uniform random variable, drawn from the range $[0, u_S]$; u_S is a positive constant; S_M, a positive constant, is the maximum organizational slack cost permitted during any period.

At the start of any period, let us consider what the firm's optimal output would be if it were to ignore the random component in its demand function (that is, if it were to assume that $r_p = 0$, which is its expected value). Let π_c denote the monopolist's profits if its demand function had no random perturbation:

$$\pi_c = [(d_1 - d_2 q_c)q_c] - [c_1 + c_2 q_c + c_3 q_c^2 + S]. \qquad (18\text{--}40)$$

q_c is the firm's optimal output when the demand function contains no random term:[5]

$$q_c = \frac{d_1 - c_2}{2(d_2 + c_3)}. \qquad (18\text{--}41)$$

We assume that the firm's actual output, q, is a random perturbation of q_c:

$$q = r_q q_c \qquad (18\text{--}42)$$

where r_q is an independently distributed uniform random variable. The range from which r_q is drawn is

$$r_q \,\epsilon[1 - u_1 - u_2 S, \, 1 + u_1 + u_2 S] \qquad (18\text{--}43)$$

where u_1 and u_2 are positive constants. This range allows r_q to vary symmetrically around 1. The larger the organizational slack, S, the bigger is the range around 1 in which r_q varies. Thus an increase in organizational slack can lead to greater discrepancies between q and q_c.

During period t, the firm's profits are

$$\pi(t) = p(t)\, q(t) - C(t). \qquad (18\text{--}44)$$

---

[5] q_c is determined just as the optimal output for a monopolist was determined in Chapter 10. Equate the derivative of Eq. (18–40) with respect to q_c to zero, and solve for q_c.

C. Analysis of the Model

Equations (18–37)–(18–44) constitute the nonmaximizing monopoly model. Because the actual behavior which results from this model depends upon the ways in which its several random variables interact over time, it is not easy to examine its properties analytically. It is possible, however, to simulate the behavior of this model on an electronic computer.

Since organizational slack is a relatively new concept, we are interested in determining its effect on the firm's profits in this model. We therefore simulated the same model with organizational slack constantly equal to zero, instead of the values determined by Eq. (18–39). It can be seen by inspection of Eq. (18–38), (18–42), and (18–43) that this modification reduces the firm's total costs in some periods and alters its output decisions.[6]

Using the parameter values and initial conditions shown in Table 18–3, the behavior of the monopoly model was simulated for 10,000 periods. To illustrate the general nature of the results, Table 18–4 and Figures 18–1–5 show the values generated for five of the major variables of interest during a particular fifty-period sequence of this simulation. The average and standard deviation of these five variables over all 10,000 periods are shown

---

[6] The same sequence of random terms was generated in simulating both versions of the model. Hence any differences in profits between the two versions of the model in any period are due only to the presence of organizational slack.

Table 18–3
Parameter Values and Initial Conditions for the Model

Parameter	Value
c_1	200,000
c_2	10
c_3	0.002
u_S	20,000
S_M	100,000
u_1	0.01
u_2	0.000005
d_1	150
d_2	0.005
u_p	5

Initial Condition	Value
$\pi(0)$	500,000.
$\pi(-1)$	500,000.
$S(0)$	50,000.
q_c	10,000.

TABLE 18–4

SAMPLE HISTORY

t	f	π	S	q	p
Period	Foregone Profit Due to Organizational Slack (dollars)	Profit (dollars)	Organizational Slack Cost (dollars)	Output	Price (dollars)
8,301	72,037	405,162	69,865	10,421	95.62
8,302	87,741	375,793	63,483	7,866	107.00
8,303	91,906	378,213	54,745	12,110	86.49
8,304	97,654	419,451	73,682	11,974	91.84
8,305	119,247	331,755	90,345	7,594	107.10
8,306	106,660	384,146	83,437	8,113	108,52
8,307	99,553	379,431	97,885	9,343	101.18
8,308	110,254	427,908	87,796	12,077	93.42
8,309	138,002	376,210	100,000	12,432	89.26
8,310	96,486	451,146	89,350	11,395	97.77
8,311	108,634	407,178	96,192	11,448	94.33
8,312	91,513	397,202	91,481	10,025	98.75
8,313	114,271	343,410	80,842	7,497	108.26
8,314	121,033	398,414	74,446	7,552	114,20
8,315	212,853	240,381	90,246	13,875	75.99
8,316	106,192	350,535	85,843	11,431	88.53
8,317	101,910	396,888	97,234	9,174	104,01
8,318	153,140	355,748	100,000	12,819	86.79
8,319	94,799	423,860	93,169	10,630	98.71
8,320	205,739	265,254	97,062	5,849	117.83
8,321	94,517	439,869	79,858	8,773	109.58
8,322	215,769	266,705	99,541	13,956	78.49
8,323	116,652	422,947	88,473	8,252	112.72
8,324	98,618	450,718	89,505	9,153	109.18
8,325	98,482	390,446	90,277	11,008	93.85
8,326	168,405	355,751	74,851	13,828	83.26
8,327	78,836	420,423	59,583	11,654	91.66
8,328	70,500	381,770	66,379	10,505	92.71
8,329	101,084	363,247	50,961	12,446	84.24
8,330	40,851	440,745	31,381	8,703	104.63
8,331	80,421	401,889	43,195	12,192	87.29
8,332	32,291	497,303	27,908	9,381	106.07

TABLE 18–4 (continued)

t	f	π	S	q	p
Period	Foregone Profit Due to Organizational Slack (dollars)	Profit (dollars)	Organizational Slack Cost (dollars)	Output	Price (dollars)
8,333	43,214	449,147	32,993	11,160	93.44
8,334	36,917	482,414	31,434	9,235	105.77
8,335	55,093	473,110	40,148	11,666	94.47
8,336	27,047	445,331	26,416	10,169	96.40
8,337	13,969	466,814	12,070	10,420	95.99
8,338	25,375	442,549	20,972	8,964	101.95
8,339	1,540	475,598	1,371	10,116	97.15
8,340	14,137	447,932	13,854	9,442	98.97
8,341	0	467,290	0	9,920	97.11
8,342	20,313	451,652	17,272	9,130	101.53
8,343	4,226	520,695	3,540	9,771	103.66
8,344	24,309	495,565	18,554	9,210	105.96
8,345	5,317	460,826	5,506	9,719	98.00
8,346	5,281	537,436	5,046	9,933	104.62
8,347	10,861	458,686	11,038	9,711	98.39
8,348	2,921	457,039	3,109	9,898	96.49
8,349	0	520,781	0	10,086	101.64
8,350	390	507,112	378	9,949	101.01

in Table 18–5. It is clear that the particular form of nonmaximizing behavior which results from organizational slack in this model led to a substantial decrease in the monopolist's profits; if there were no organizational slack the monopoly firm's profits would have been 18 per cent higher, on the average.

We have frequently used the calculus to determine the comparative static properties of particular economic models. Since the nonmaximizing monopoly model has not been analytically solved, the same procedure is not possible here. By means of repeated simulation runs, however, it is possible to determine some of the comparative static properties of this model. For example, let $\bar{f}$ denote the average value (computed over 10,000 periods) of profits which the monopoly firm foregoes because of the existence of organizational slack. From the model specified by Eq. (18–37)–(18–44), the average value of foregone profits, $\bar{f}$, depends upon all the parameters shown in Table 18–3. For convenience, let k denote any particular param-

TABLE 18–5

AVERAGE VALUES AND STANDARD DEVIATIONS OVER 10,000 PERIODS FOR
THE MAJOR VARIABLES

Variable	Average Value	Standard Deviation
Foregone profits due to organizational slack (f)	\$75,232.11	\$56,751.00
Profits (π)	\$425,588.11	\$63,782.22
Organizational slack (S)	\$52,119.50	\$30,068.89
Price (p)	\$100.20	\$9.59
Output (q)	9,976.90	1,812.38

eter. Then we write $\bar{f}(k)$ to show that the average value of foregone profits is a function of the particular value of the parameter k, when all the other parameters are held constant at the values specified in Table 18–3. The value of the parameter k in Table 18–3 is k_0.

We can approximate the partial derivative of average foregone profits with respect to variations in the parameter k by the following relationship:

$$\left. \frac{\partial \bar{f}(k)}{\partial k} \right|_{k=k_0} \cong \frac{\bar{f}(1.01\ k_0) - \bar{f}(k_0)}{0.01\ k_0}. \tag{18–45}$$

The approximate partial derivatives of average foregone profits with respect to selected parameters are shown in Table 18–6. They were obtained by using computer simulation runs of 10,000 periods to obtain the values of $\bar{f}(1.01\ k_0)$ and $\bar{f}(k_0)$ needed in Eq. (18–45). In an analogous way, we have determined the partial derivatives of the average values of the other four major variables of interest with respect to changes in each of the selected parameters. These are also shown in Table 18–6.

Most of the results shown in Table 18–6 are in accord with our theoretical expectations, and none of them are contrary to our expectations. c_1 is the fixed cost of the monopolist. As shown in Table 18–6, increasing the value of c_1 by \$1 merely reduces the firm's profits by \$1, without changing the values of any of the other major variables.

c_2 is the intercept in the monopolist's marginal cost function. Increasing the value of c_2 moves the intersection of the marginal cost curve with the marginal revenue curve further to the left, and hence reduces the firm's target output—see Eq. (18–41). The actual effects of an increase in c_2 are consistent with this reasoning, as shown in Table 18–6. Average output decreases, and hence average price increases. Average profits decrease, because of the increase in total costs. Although not necessarily expected on theoretical grounds, average organizational slack and average foregone profits due to organizational slack both decrease.

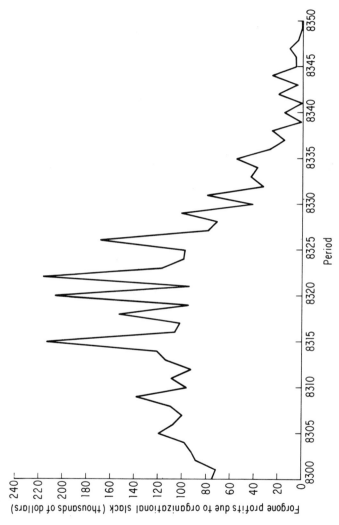

FIGURE 18–1. Forgone profits due to organizational slack.

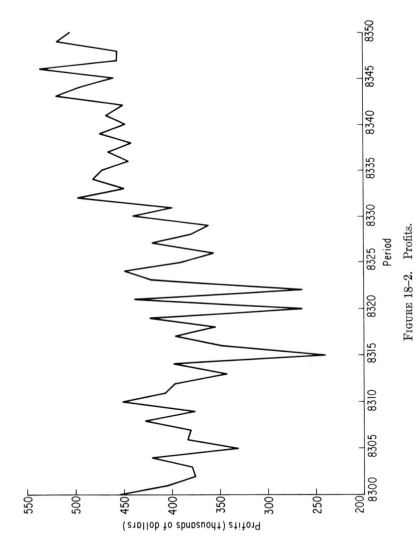

FIGURE 18-2. Profits.

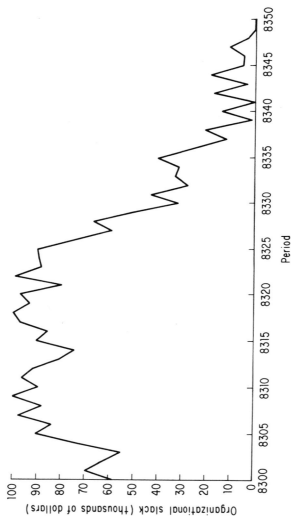

FIGURE 18–3. Organizational slack.

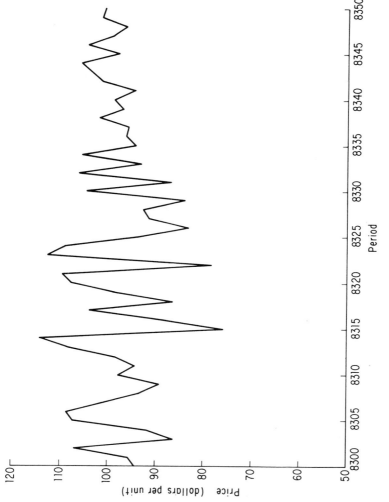

FIGURE 18–4. Price.

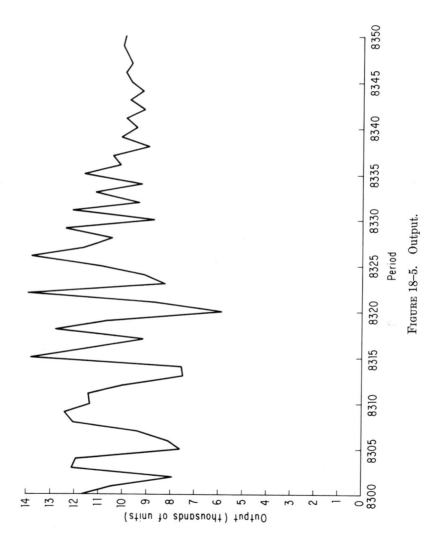

FIGURE 18–5. Output.

TABLE 18–6

APPROXIMATE PARTIAL DERIVATIVES OF THE AVERAGE VALUES OF THE MAJOR
VARIABLES WITH RESPECT TO SELECTED PARAMETERS
(Computed over 10,000 Periods)

Parameter	Variable				
	$\bar{f}$	$\bar{\pi}$	$\bar{S}$	$\bar{p}$	$\bar{q}$
c_1	0	−1.00	0	0	0
c_2	−299	−9,700	−21.4	0.354	−71
d_1	−187	10,200	−306	0.645	71
S_M	1.54	−1.54	0.910	0	0
u_S	−2.85	2.85	−0.352	0	0

d_1 is the intercept of the monopolist's demand curve and also of his marginal revenue curve. Increasing the value of d_1 moves the intersection of the marginal revenue curve with the marginal cost curve further to the right, and hence increases the firm's target output—see Eq. (18–41). The actual effects of an increase in d_1 are consistent with this reasoning, as shown in Table 18–6. Average output increases. Since the demand curve is shifted upward by the increase in d_1, the increased output does not necessarily lead to a price decrease; in fact, as shown in Table 18–6, the price increases. Average profits increase as a result of the upward shift in the demand curve. From theoretical considerations alone the effect of an increase in d_1 on average organizational slack and average profits foregone cannot be predicted; in fact, both decrease.

S_M is the maximum value permitted for organizational slack. Increasing the value of S_M should, on the average, lead to higher values of organizational slack, lower values of profits, and higher values of foregone profits due to organizational slack. There is no reason to expect the average values of output and price to change, however. Table 18–6 shows that in fact these expected results were obtained when the value of S_M was increased.

Finally, u_S is the maximum change permitted during any one period in organizational slack. Increasing the value of u_S should not alter the average values of output or price. The expected effect on the average values of profits, organizational slack, and foregone profits due to organizational slack are not known from theoretical considerations. Table 18–6 shows the actual results of increasing the value of u_S; as expected, the average values of output and price were unchanged.

In conclusion, we have developed a model to show how a firm may behave in the absence of a well-defined objective function. Because of organizational slack, which both increases the firm's costs and leads to less precision in determining output levels, the firm foregoes a considerable amount of profits. The effects of shifts in parameters of the firm's demand and cost functions on the average values of price, output, and profits are qualitatively the same as in the conventional monopoly model. There are other aspects of behavior in the nonmaximizing monopoly model which are, however, not present in the conventional model. Thus it is possible to analyze the effects of parameter shifts on organizational slack and on foregone profits resulting from organizational slack.

This nonmaximizing monopoly model is a further illustration of the power of computer programing languages for model building. Although this model has been considerably simplified for expository purposes, it is possible to use the same technique to formulate models which could give us good predictions of the actual behavior of firms. The binding restriction at the moment is the lack of detailed empirical knowledge about the decision processes actually followed by firms. Further research should provide more realistic specifications of these decision processes. No matter how complex these specifications may be, we can incorporate them into new models of the firm formulated in a computer programing language, and we can use simulation techniques to analyze the properties of the resulting models. In this way we hope eventually to obtain models of the firm which can provide accurate predictions of the behavior of individual firms or industries.

III. A Revenue-Maximization Model

Baumol has proposed a third variant of a maximization model in which it is assumed that firms attempt to maximize total revenues rather than profits or the value of a utility function.[7] Profits are not ignored altogether in Baumol's model, however, since a minimum profits level is imposed as a constraint.

A. Rationale for the Revenue-Maximization Hypothesis

Several reasons are presented to justify the revenue-maximization hypothesis. Some are based on a casual type of empiricism:

> Surely it is common experience that, when one asks an executive, "How's business?" he will answer that his *sales* have been increasing (or decreasing), and talk about his profit only as an after-thought, if at all. And I am told the requirements for acceptance to membership in the Young Presidents Organization (an honorific society) are that the applicant be under 40 years of age and president of a company whose annual volume is over a million dollars. Presumably it makes no difference if this firm is in imminent danger

---

[7] William J. Baumol, *Business Behavior, Value and Growth* (New York: The Macmillan Company, 1959), chaps. 6–8.

of bankruptcy.... Almost every time I have come across a case of conflict between profits and sales the businessmen with whom I worked left little doubt as to where their hearts lay. ... a program which explicitly proposes any cut in sales volume, whatever the profit considerations, is likely to meet a cold reception.[8]

Other evidence cited by Baumol essentially suggests that short-run revenue maximization may be consistent with long-run profit maximization. Baumol states, however, that revenue maximization, rather than profit maximization, can be regarded as the long-run goal of the management in many oligopoly firms.[9]

The minimum acceptable level of profits which serves as a constraint on a firm's attempts to maximize its revenues is not regarded as purely arbitrary. Baumol feels that this constraint is determined by the capital market:

> The typical oligopolistic firm, while large in the market for its own product, is relatively small in the capital market. This means that, in obtaining capital by the issue of stocks, it must be prepared to meet competitive pricing conditions—the yield on its stocks will be determined by the forces of competition.... The firm which hopes to have more securities to sell in the future, and wishes to pay what it may consider proper regard to the interests of its current stockholders, must take this into consideration. Its minimum earnings must supply funds sufficient to pay dividends, and to reinvest in such amounts that the combination of dividend receipts and stock price rises can remunerate stockholders adequately. If this is so, each company's minimum rate of profits is set competitively in terms of the current market value of its securities.[10]

B. THE FORMAL MODEL

For simplicity in formalizing Baumol's model, we assume that the firm produces only one product and that the minimum profits constraint is stated in terms of an absolute profit level.[11] Furthermore, we shall use Williamson's variable S, staff expenditures, in place of Baumol's variable A, advertising expenditures. As long as we interpret staff expenditures to include advertising, which Williamson himself did, no distortions result from this change of notation.

Using the same notation as in Williamson's model, Baumol's firm attempts to select values for its decision variables, X and S, which maximize

$$R = PX \tag{18–46}$$

---

[8] *Ibid.*, pp. 47–48.

[9] "I believe that sales maximization is management's objective in the long run as well as in the short." *Ibid.*, p. 52.

[10] *Ibid.*, pp. 50–51.

[11] Neither of these simplifications changes in any essential manner the implications derived from Baumol's model. Procedures for handling the multiple product case and other forms of the profit constraint are presented by Baumol, *op. cit.*, pp. 68–71.

subject to the constraint

$$\pi = (1 - t)(R - C - S - \bar{T}) \geq \pi_0. \qquad (18\text{-}47)$$

Note first that the minimum profits constraint, Eq. (18–47), can be replaced by an equality,

$$(1 - t)(R - C - S - \bar{T}) = \pi_0 \qquad (18\text{-}48)$$

because increasing expenditures on staff (e.g., increasing advertising) will permit any given level of output to be sold at a higher price, since

$$\frac{\partial P}{\partial S} > 0. \qquad (18\text{-}49)$$

Equations (18–46) and (18–49) imply that

$$\frac{\partial R}{\partial S} > 0 \qquad (18\text{-}50)$$

i.e., increases in staff expenditures raise revenues. If the minimum profits constraint Eq. (18–47) would be satisfied at any profit level, say $\bar{\pi}$, which is above the required minimum, π_0, then staff expenditures can be increased by the amount $\bar{\pi} - \pi_0$ without violating the constraint. In view of Eq. (18–50), however, this increase in staff expenditures will increase revenues. Therefore the values of X and S which maximize R subject to Eq. (18–47) also maximize R subject to Eq. (18–48).

In order to maximize Eq. (18–46) subject to the constraint Eq. (18–48), form the Lagrangian function:

$$L = R + \lambda[(1 - t)(R - C - S - \bar{T}) - \pi_0]. \qquad (18\text{-}51)$$

Setting the partial derivatives of Eq. (18–51) with respect to X and S equal to zero, we obtain the following necessary conditions:

$$\frac{\partial L}{\partial X} = \frac{\partial R}{\partial X} + \lambda(1 - t)\left(\frac{\partial R}{\partial X} - \frac{\partial C}{\partial X}\right) = 0. \qquad (18\text{-}52)$$

$$\frac{\partial L}{\partial S} = \frac{\partial R}{\partial S} + \lambda(1 - t)\left(\frac{\partial R}{\partial S} - 1\right) = 0. \qquad (18\text{-}53)$$

Solving Eq. (18–52) and (18–53) for $\partial R/\partial X$ and for $\partial R/\partial S$, we have

$$\frac{\partial R}{\partial X} = \frac{\lambda(1 - t)}{1 + \lambda(1 - t)}\frac{\partial C}{\partial X}. \qquad (18\text{-}54)$$

$$\frac{\partial R}{\partial S} = \frac{\lambda(1 - t)}{1 + \lambda(1 - t)}. \qquad (18\text{-}55)$$

In determining the implications of the necessary conditions for revenue maximization, Eq. (18–54) and (18–55), we shall first show that

$$\frac{\partial R}{\partial S} < 1. \tag{18–56}$$

The proof is by contradiction. If $\partial R/\partial S \geq 1$, then an extra dollar spent on advertising would increase revenues more rapidly than it increases costs. Thus increasing S would increase revenues without decreasing profits. Hence $\partial R/\partial S \geq 1$ means that X and S have not been optimally chosen. Therefore at the optimal point for the firm Eq. (18–56) must hold.

Another implication of the necessary conditions for revenue maximization is that

$$\frac{\partial R}{\partial X} < \frac{\partial C}{\partial X}. \tag{18–57}$$

This result follows from Eq. (18–54), (18–55), and (18–56).

C. Comparisons with Other Models

It is useful to contrast the decisions of a revenue-maximizing firm with the decisions stemming from a utility-maximizing model and from a profit-maximizing model. Equation (18–57) shows that a revenue-maximizing firm produces at an output level at which its marginal revenue is less than its marginal cost—in other words, the firm is giving up some profits in order to increase its revenues. Equations (18–24) and (18–32) show that this is not true for either of the other models.

We saw in Eq. (18–33) that the profit-maximizing firm carries staff expenditures only to the point where the marginal revenue generated by the last dollar spent on staff equals its marginal cost (which is \$1). Both a Williamson-type firm and a Baumol-type firm carry staff expenditures beyond the profit-maximizing point, as Eq. (18–34) and (18–56) show. However, the basic determinants of staff expenditures differ in these two models.

In Baumol's model, Eq. (18–54) and (18–55) imply

$$\frac{\partial R/\partial S}{1} = \frac{\partial R/\partial X}{\partial C/\partial X}. \tag{18–58}$$

Remembering that the 1 in the denominator of the left-hand side of Eq. (18–58) is really the marginal cost of staff expenditures, we can interpret Eq. (18–58) as stating that the firm combines its two "productive factors," staff and output, in such a way that the incremental amounts of revenue per dollar spent on staff or output are equal. This is precisely analogous to the results obtained in Chapter 7 when we considered the production decisions of a profit-maximizing firm. Here the "cost" of staff or output expenditures is measured in terms of the minimum-profits constraint, and the "benefits" derived are in terms of revenue. Equation (18–58) indicates that the Baumol-type firm is essentially neutral with regard to expenditures on staff or on production, each being judged solely in terms of its relative contributions to the revenue criterion. In Williamson's model, on the other hand, the managers display a positive preference toward staff expenditures. This is reflected in the result:

$$\frac{\partial R/\partial S}{1} < \frac{\partial R/\partial X}{\partial C/\partial X} \tag{18–59}$$

which follows from Eq. (18–34) and (18–24).

Comparative static properties which indicate the ways in which a firm in Baumol's model modifies its output and staff decisions in response to changes in demand, the corporate profits tax rate, and a lump sum tax can be derived. These are presented in Table 18–7.

A comparison of Tables 18–1, 18–2, and 18–7 reveals that Baumol's model yields the same qualitative predictions as Williamson's model and the traditional model about the ways in which changes in demand will affect output and staff expenditures. The qualitative effects of a lump sum tax on output and staff are the same in Baumol's and in Williamson's model; but these are different effects than the traditional theory implies. The corporate tax rate is the one parameter for which distinctly different qualitative predictions arise in all three models. When the corporate tax rate is raised, Baumol's firms reduce their output and staff expenditures (i.e., reduce revenues because of the more stringent profits constraint, which is phrased in after-tax terms); Williamson's firms increase their output and staff expenditures (because on an after-tax basis, staff expenditures—to which output will optimally adjust—are now relatively cheaper, compared to investment spending); profit-maximizing firms do not change their behavior (since the same output and staff decisions which maximize profits will also maximize any proportion of profits).

TABLE 18–7

RESPONSES TO DISPLACEMENTS FROM EQUILIBRIUM FOR BAUMOL'S MODEL

Variable	Parameter		
	ϵ	t	$\bar{T}$
X	+	−	−
S	+	−	−

SOURCE: Oliver E. Williamson, *The Economics of Discretionary Behavior: Managerial Objectives in a Theory of the Firm* (Englewood Cliffs, N.J.: Prentice-Hall, Inc., 1964), table 4, p. 80.

IV. Summary

In this chapter we have presented three models which attempt to develop new approaches to the theory of the firm: a managerial discretion model, a nonmaximizing monopoly model, and a revenue-maximization model.

Williamson's managerial discretion model assumes that the managers of the firm are trying to maximize a utility function which depends upon three components: (1) the level of staff expenditures; (2) the amount of management slack absorbed as cost (i.e., the amount of managerial perquisites); (3) the amount of discretionary spending available for investment.

The implications of Williamson's model appear to be plausible on the basis of casual empiricism. These implications include predictions that expenditures on both staff and managerial perquisites will increase as the environment becomes favorable (e.g., as demand increases or as competition in the market weakens), and that spending on both will decrease when the environment becomes more hostile. There are also predictions about how the firm will respond to changes in corporate tax rates and to changes in fixed costs.

Since in many respects the predictions of Williamson's model differ from those of the traditional profit-maximizing model, empirical tests can be devised which should discriminate between these two models. Williamson has presented some empirical evidence based both on field studies and statistical analyses which tends to support his model of management behavior.[12] This empirical evidence does not constitute a complete refutation of profit-maximizing behavior by the firms, but it at least suggests that in certain types of markets, namely where competitive forces are weak, Williamson's model may have more empirical relevance than the traditional profit-maximizing models.

The nonmaximizing monopoly model was presented to illustrate that it is possible to formulate and analyze a model which does not assume that the firm tries to maximize the value of some well-defined objective function. A simple type of aspiration level mechanism is used to define when satisfactory performance has been attained. Organizational slack increases or decreases according to whether the aspiration level is met. The existence of organizational slack not only increases the firm's costs but it also leads to reduced precision in determining the firm's output.

Because the behavior of the nonmaximizing monopoly model critically depends upon the interactions of several random components, computer simulation, rather than mathematical analysis, was used to determine the

---

[12] Williamson, *The Economics of Discretionary Behavior*, chaps. 6–7.

model's properties. The nonmaximizing behavior which results from organizational slack leads to substantial decreases in the firm's profits. The actual time paths, the average values, and the standard deviations of all major variables in the model have been determined by simulation techniques. Simulation was also used to determine the comparative static properties of the model. Although the effects of changes in the parameters of the firm's demand and cost functions on the average values of price, output, and profits are qualitatively the same as in the conventional monopoly model, the nonmaximizing monopoly model comprises other aspects of behavior which are not contained in the conventional model.

Baumol's revenue-maximization model assumes that a firm attempts to maximize its total revenues subject to a constraint that it earn some specified minimum amount of profits. The implications of Baumol's model differ in many respects from the implications of both Williamson's model and the traditional profit-maximization model. A revenue-maximizing firm produces at an output where its marginal revenue is less than its marginal cost; both a utility-maximizing and a profit-maximizing firm equate marginal revenue with marginal cost. A profit-maximizing firm equates the marginal revenue generated by the last dollar spent on staff to the marginal cost of this last dollar; both a revenue-maximizing and a utility-maximizing firm carry staff expenditures beyond this point. The comparative static properties of these models were also analyzed. Changes in the corporate tax rate produce distinctly different responses in all three models. When the corporate tax rate increases, a revenue-maximizing firm reduces its output and staff expenditures; a utility-maximizing firm increases its output and staff expenditures; a profit-maximizing firm does not alter its output and staff expenditures.

SUGGESTED READINGS

These recommendations are in addition to the footnote references cited in Chapter 17 and in this chapter.

ALCHIAN, ARMEN A., "Uncertainty, Evolution, and Economic Theory," in *Readings in Industrial Organization and Public Policy*, R. B. Heflebower and G. W. Stocking, eds., pp. 207–19. Homewood, Ill.: Richard D. Irwin, Inc., 1958.

BALDWIN, WILLIAM L., "The Motives of Managers, Environmental Restraints, and the Theory of Managerial Enterprise," *Quarterly Journal of Economics*, LXXVIII (May, 1964), 238–56.

BAUMOL, WILLIAM J., AND RICHARD E. QUANDT, "Rules of Thumb and Optimally Imperfect Decisions," *American Economic Review*, LIV, No. 2, Part 1 (March, 1964), 23–46.

BROWN, M., AND N. REVONKAI, "A Generalized Theory of the Firm: An Integration of the Sales and Profit Maximization Hypotheses," *Kyklos*, XXIV (1971), 427–41.

COHEN, K. J., R. M. CYERT, J. G. MARCH, AND P. O. SOELBERG, "A General Model of Price and Output Determination," *Symposium on Simulation Models: Methodology and Applications to the Behavioral Sciences*, A. C. Hoggatt and F. E. Balderston, eds., pp. 260–89. Cincinnati: South-Western Publishing Co., 1963.

CYERT, RICHARD M., AND CHARLES L. HEDRICK, "Theory of the Firm: Past, Present, and Future; An Interpretation," *The Journal of Economic Literature*, X, No. 2 (June, 1972), 398–412.

JOSKOW, PAUL L., "Pricing Decisions of Regulated Firms: A Behavioral Approach," *The Bell Journal of Economics and Management Science*, IV (Spring, 1973), 118–40.

KORNAI, JANOS, *Anti-Equilibrium*. Amsterdam: North-Holland Publishing Co., 1971.

LATSIS, SPIRO J., "Situational Determinism in Economics," *British Journal of Philosophy of Science*, XXIII (1972), 207–45.

MARGOLIS, JULIUS, "The Analysis of the Firm: Rationalism, Conventionalism, and Behaviorism," *Journal of Business*, XXXI (July, 1958), 189–99.

McGUIRE, JOSEPH W., *Theories of Business Behavior*. Englewood Cliffs, N.J.: Prentice-Hall, Inc., 1964.

ROSEN, S., "Learning by Experience as Joint Production," *Quarterly Journal of Economics*, LXXXVI (August, 1972), 366–82.

Session on "Research on Theory of the Firm," *American Economic Review, Papers and Proceedings*, L, No. 2 (May, 1960), 526–64. (Papers by Julius Margolis, Kalman J. Cohen, Jacob Marschak, Thomas M. Whitin, and Martin Shubik; discussion by Michael J. Farrell.)

SIMON, H. A., "New Developments in the Theory of the Firm," *American Economic Review*, LII, No. 2 (May, 1962), 1–15. (Also see the discussion of this paper by W. Allen Wallis, Paul F. Lazersfeld, and John Lintner, *ibid.*, pp. 16–27.)

WINTER, SIDNEY G., JR., "Economic 'Natural Selection' and the Theory of the Firm," *Yale Economic Essays*, Vol. 4, No. 1 (Spring, 1964), 225–72.

———, "Satisficing, Selection, and the Innovating Remnant," *Quarterly Journal of Economics*, LXXXV (May, 1971), 237–61.

Chapter Nineteen

Bayesian Analysis
and Economic Theory[1]

During recent years there has been work underway that applies the concept of organizational learning from both the behavioral theory of the firm and recent developments in Bayesian statistics to some aspects of economic theory. In particular the analysis has concentrated on duopoly theory and has resulted in the construction of a dynamic model that demonstrates a process by which firms can move from one position to another without making unrealistic assumptions of the type noted in Chapter 12.

---

[1] This chapter draws heavily on two articles by Richard M. Cyert and Morris H. DeGroot: "Multiperiod Decision Models with Alternating Choice as a Solution of the Duopoly Problem," *Quarterly Journal of Economics*, 84 (1970), 410–29, and "An Analysis of Cooperation and Learning in a Duopoly Context," *The American Economic Review*, 63, No. 1 (March, 1973), 24–37. Some of this material has been directly used without explicit indication of quotation; other material has been paraphrased.

I. Framework for Application of Adaptive Models

An adaptive model is one from which a firm can learn and thereby modify its previous behavior. This learning can take place with regard to other firms, with regard to the environment, or both. More will be said later about the concept of learning, but at this point we wish to concentrate on the nature of adaptive models. The important point in relation to conventional theory is that an adaptive model is not restricted to a fixed reaction function. In an adaptive model, for example, the firm is able to change its assumption about the way its rival will respond to any changes the firm will make in the decision variable. This means that for each decision period the firm can have a different value for the conjectural variations term and, therefore, a different reaction function chosen on the basis of the rival's decisions over earlier periods of the process.

For example, the firm may have a simple rule for shifting its conjectural variations term, or equivalently, its reaction function, from period to period in accordance with its changing expectations of the rival's behavior. One approach is for the firm to assign subjective probabilities to various modes of behavior of the rival. The firm might then use a given value for the conjectural variations term over several periods. Then, if the weight of evidence led to a substantial subjective probability in favor of one of the other modes of behavior, the firm might change the value of the conjectural variations term accordingly.

Another class of adaptive models can be developed by weakening the usual assumption that the precise form of the demand curve is known. This approach has not generally been taken in duopoly theory, but it is possible to derive the interaction between firms through conjectures relating to the rival's perception of the demand curve. We have, in the models that follow, generally taken this approach, partly because of greater ease in exposition but primarily because of the greater simplicity in achieving analytic answers while demonstrating some new approaches to the problems of duopoly. In some cases we have relied on behavioral rules that are different from those usually associated with economic models. Various other behavioral rules might have been presented here. However, the ones we have used serve our basic purpose of introducing the analytic treatment of learning and adaptive behavior in duopoly problems.

II. Firm Learning

Learning is a psychological concept, and it is natural to examine the literature in that discipline for an understanding of learning. As might be expected, there is a division of opinion on the exact process by which learning takes place. In recent years a mathematical approach to learning theory has been followed, and the definitions used are compatible with usage in economic theory. For example, Bush and Mosteller, who pioneered in this area with their book on stochastic learning models, define learning as follows: "We consider any systematic changes in behavior to be learning whether or not the change is adaptive, desirable for certain purposes, or in accordance with any other such criteria."[2] A probabilistic view of behavior is followed in which the subject (in a psychological experiment) is treated as having some probability p of making a particular response. The effect of the experiment on learning is measured by the change in probability of the subject's making a particular response. The completion of learning would be represented by a stable (obviously needing an operational definition) value for this probability of response. In other words, the learning has ceased when there is no longer any change in the probability of occurrence of the particular response.

In duopoly theory, learning concerns the behavior of rivals. More specifically, it is learning that enables a firm to predict how a rival will respond in the next decision period to an action that the firm takes in this period or to predict the value that a rival will set for its decision variable during a given period of simultaneous decision making. Our concept of learning involves the following three assumptions: (1) The entrepreneur (manager) of the firm starts with an *a priori* probability that his rival is going to behave in a particular way with respect to his decision making. (2) He observes the actual behavior of his rival in making a decision either in response or simultaneously. (3) He incorporates the results of his experience by modifying his original *a priori* probability, and the process is then repeated. The utilization of the observation of the rival's behavior to set new *a priori* probabilities is an act of learning by our definition, and the differences between the original and the new probabilities can be used to define a measure of the amount of learning. We shall not, however, consider that question further.

The specific process by which individuals learn—a learning theory or model—is an area of vigorous activity and disagreement in psychology. The most widely used theory for experimental purposes is the stimulus-response theory. In recent years both mathematical and computer models have been constructed to describe the learning process. It is accurate to say that much is known about the learning process in individuals. At the same time there is no well-established set of propositions that can be immediately transferred to units of analysis other than the individual.

In any event it would be foolish to assume that the learning process in business firms is the same as that observed in individuals. Nevertheless, it

[2] R. R. Bush and F. Mosteller, *Stochastic Models for Learning* (New York: John Wiley & Sons, Inc., 1955), p. 3.

is also obvious that firms exhibit adaptive behavior over time, a type of behavior included in the definition of learning given by Bush and Mosteller. As a first approach, it is useful to deal with this adaptive behavior at the aggregate level of the firm without referring to the individual members of the firm. The learning that takes place within the firm can be viewed as falling into two categories. First is the adaptation in the internal processes of the firm with respect to such factors as goals, attention rules, and search processes. The second relates to interfirm learning and is the area directly relevant to the problems of this chapter. More specifically, the problem is to exhibit the process by which firms are able to follow the Bayesian process in making decisions in an oligopolistic market. In economic theory, the approach followed has been one in which the firm is assumed to know nothing about its rivals and is unable to learn, or it knows everything and the collusive solution is appropriate.

We are advocating the development of models in which firms make decisions and take actions in the market and then are able to learn from their experiences. The learning process takes place in the first instance through observation of the reactions of the firm's rivals to its actions, and the storing of this information. These actions then become the basis for the computation of the new prior probabilities for the firm. These probabilities represent the firm's estimates, on the basis of its learning, of the reactions of its rivals for particular actions of the firm in the next decision period. Thus one aspect of learning as used here is the ability to develop enough knowledge of rivals to enable predictions of their behavior to be made. Increases in learning imply improvements in the accuracy of the predictions.

The learning process in the organization involves the gathering of information from the environment of the form and quantity necessary to make the appropriate inferences. Within the organization it requires the information to be processed and presented in such a manner that judgments can be made about the significance of the information.

The information comes from participants in the organization who are interacting with the environment either in their official organizational roles or as individuals. This information is generally about rival firms' plans and market behavior. Salesmen and managers are an especially fruitful source of information of this kind. Their information comes from interactions with customers who have been in contact with salesmen of other firms, and from direct interaction with rival salesmen. The information is most frequently about price or related selling conditions of the product such as credit terms. Any price changes, including attempts at secret price cuts, will generally be picked up in this information net. This information will not be without bias, because salesmen, influenced by their pay-off function, tend to press for changes in selling conditions that will increase sales. This bias in information is a factor that the organization must learn to evaluate and compensate for in the use of its information system.

III. Some Concepts for Analysis

The work we will describe introduces some new concepts from statistics and mathematics. All the concepts will not be used in this chapter, but they are concepts that are necessary to understand this area of analysis.

A. BAYES' THEOREM

It will be useful in understanding some of the work that will follow to have a little background in Bayesian analysis. The basic for the famous Bayes' Theorem (perhaps better called a formula) stems from the concept of a compound event—that is, two events occurring together.[3]

Suppose, for example, that the event A can happen only if events B_1 or B_2 occur. The events B_1 and B_2 cannot both occur at the same time but one of them must occur (that is, they are mutually exclusive and collectively exhaustive). The occurrence of events B_1 or B_2 is independent of the occurrence of event A. In other words, when B_1 or B_2 occur it is not necessary for A to occur. When A does occur, however, it means that B_1 or B_2 has occurred. The objective, as we shall see, of Bayes' theorem is to make an inference when A has occurred as to which event—B_1 or B_2—has occurred. The latter events can be viewed as hypotheses, and Bayes' theorem is sometimes known as the "formula for probabilities of hypotheses."[4]

The events (AB_1) or (AB_2) would be called compound events. The second concept that must be noted is that of a conditional probability, $P_R(A \mid B_1)$. This symbol translates to the probability of A given the occurrence of B_1. The probability of the compound event (AB_1) can be written as

$$P_R(AB_1) = P_R(B_1)P_R(A \mid B_1), \tag{19-1}$$

or

$$P_R(AB_1) = P_R(A)P_R(B_1 \mid A). \tag{19-2}$$

The expressions on the right-hand side can be equated and we can solve for $P_R(B_1 \mid A)$,

$$P_R(B_1 \mid A) = \frac{P_R(B_1)P_R(A \mid B_1)}{P_R(A)}. \tag{19-3}$$

Because the event A can occur only with B_1 or B_2 we have

$$P_R(A) = P_R(B_1)P_R(A \mid B_1) + P_R(B_2)P_R(A \mid B_2). \tag{19-4}$$

Bayes' formula thus will be

---

[3] Morris H. DeGroot, *Optimal Statistical Decisions* (New York: McGraw-Hill Book Company, 1970), pp. 11–12. Also, J. V. Uspensky, *Introduction to Mathematical Probability* (New York: McGraw-Hill Book Company, 1937), pp. 60–64.

[4] Uspensky, *op. cit.*, p. 61.

$$P_R(B_1 \mid A) = \frac{P_R(B_1)P_R(A \mid B_1)}{P_R(B_1)P_R(A \mid B_1) + P_R(B_2)P_R(A \mid B_2)} . \quad (19\text{--}5)$$

The idea is to be able to determine the probability of B_1 or B_2 having occurred, knowing that A has happened.

A simple example with the traditional urns containing white and black balls can clarify this point. Suppose we have urn 1 and it contains 2 white balls and 1 black ball. Urn 2 contains 1 white ball and 5 black balls. One ball is transferred from urn 1 to urn 2 and then one ball is drawn from urn 2. The ball happens to be white. What is the probability that the transferred ball was black?

In this case event A is the drawn ball that is white. We can let B_1 stand for the transfer of a black ball and B_2 for the transfer of a white ball. Thus we want to find $P_R(B_1 \mid A)$. In order to apply Bayes' formula we need the following:

$$P_R(B_1) = \tfrac{1}{3}$$
$$P_R(B_2) = \tfrac{2}{3}$$
$$P_R(A \mid B_1) = \tfrac{1}{7}$$
$$P_R(A \mid B_2) = \tfrac{2}{7}.$$

The answer then is

$$P_R(B_1|A) = \frac{(\tfrac{1}{3})(\tfrac{1}{7})}{(\tfrac{1}{3})(\tfrac{1}{7}) + (\tfrac{2}{3})(\tfrac{2}{7})} = \tfrac{1}{5}$$

Obviously the formula can be generalized for as many Bs as exist.

B. Subjective Probability

One of the revolutions that has occurred in statistics is the recognition of subjective probabilities having relevance, particularly in decision-making situations. In the previous example we were utilizing objective probabilities, but in some of the work we will do in economic theory the subjective probabilities of managers of firms will be used in exactly the same way.[5]

The terms *prior* and *posterior probability distributions* will be used at times. The *prior* is the probability distribution of an event, B_1, before an additional event (which gives more information) happens. *Posterior* refers to the probability distribution after the event has occurred.

---

[5] William Fellner, *Probability and Profit* (Homewood, Ill.: Richard D. Irwin, Inc., 1965); and R. D. Luce and P. Suppes, "Preference, Utility, and Subjective Probability," *Handbook of Mathematical Psychology*, Luce, Bush, and Golanter, eds. (New York: John Wiley & Sons, Inc., 1965), pp. 249–410.

C. BACKWARD INDUCTION

One of the useful techniques for developing an optimal procedure is backward induction. In backward induction the decision maker moves to the end of the series of decision periods and chooses the best decision for that period—for example, the output that maximizes profits for that period. He then moves to the next to the last period and makes the best decision for that period, knowing the decision in the last period, and so on. In this way the decision in each period will be optimal.

We will illustrate the procedure by an example in which there are n periods, where n is a fixed positive integer ($n \geq 2$), and we shall suppose that the two firms choose their outputs in alternating periods as follows: In the first period, firm 1 chooses its output q_1. In the second period, firm 2 chooses its output r_2 while firm 1 must hold its output at the same level q_1 as in the preceding period. In the third period, firm 1 can choose a new output q_3, while firm 2 must hold its output at the same level r_2 as in the preceding period. In the fourth period, firm 2 chooses a new output r_4, while firm 1 again retains the same output q_3 as in the preceding period. In general, in each odd period j ($j = 3, 5, 7, \ldots$), firm 1 chooses a new output q_j, while firm 2 must produce the same output r_{j-1} as in period $j - 1$. In each even period k ($k = 2, 4, 6, \ldots$), firm 2 chooses a new output r_k, while firm 1 must produce the same output q_{k-1} as in period $k - 1$. To be specific, we shall assume that the total number of periods n is even. Hence, firm 2 will choose its output r_n in the final period of the process.

For $i = 2, \ldots, n$, we shall let f_i denote the profit function of firm 1 in period i and shall let g_i denote the profit function of firm 2 in period i. Since firm 1 chooses its initial output q_1 before firm 2 has chosen its first output, we shall assume for simplicity that neither firm realizes any profit in the first period. Hence, the total profit Q for firm 1 over the entire process will be

$$Q = f_2(q_1, r_2) + f_3(q_3, r_2) + f_4(q_3, r_4) + \cdots + f_n(q_{n-1}, r_n). \quad (19\text{--}6)$$

Similarly, the total profit R for firm 2 will be

$$R = g_2(q_1, r_2) + g_3(q_3, r_2) + g_4(q_3, r_4) + \cdots + g_n(q_{n-1}, r_n). \quad (19\text{--}7)$$

There is no assumption as yet that the q's or r's are chosen in an optimal fashion. Equations (19–6) and (19–7) are merely definitional.

We assume that the total profits Q and R for the two firms are specified by Eq. (19–6) and (19–7). We assume that each firm wishes to maximize its own profit and that each firm will choose its own sequence of outputs in order to accomplish this goal. The implications of this assumption with regard to the method of backward induction are as follows.

Suppose all outputs $q_1, r_2, \ldots, q_{n-1}$ for periods 1 to $n - 1$ have been chosen, and that firm 2 must now choose its final output r_n. Because firm 2 wishes to maximize the value of R, it follows from Eq. (19–7) that r_n should be chosen in order to maximize the value of $g_n(q_{n-1}, r_n)$. That is, firm 2 will choose r_n so as to maximize its profits in the nth period, knowing firm 1's output q_{n-1}, which was chosen in the previous period $n - 1$. We shall suppose that this maximum value is finite and is attained by the choice

$$r_n^* = r_n^*(q_{n-1}). \tag{19–8}$$

Then the profit for firm 2 in period n will be

$$G_n(q_{n-1}) = g_n(q_{n-1}, r_n^*) \tag{19–9}$$

and the corresponding profit for firm 1 in period n will be

$$F_n(q_{n-1}) = f_n(q_{n-1}, r_n^*). \tag{19–10}$$

We shall now move back one period. Suppose that the outputs q_1, r_2, $q_3, \ldots, r_{n-2}$ for periods 1 to $n - 2$ have been chosen, and that firm 1 must now choose its output q_{n-1} in period $n - 1$. Since firm 1 knows that firm 2 will respond in period n in accordance with Eq. (19–8), it follows from Eq. (19–6) that firm 1 should choose q_{n-1} to maximize the value of

$$f_{n-1}(q_{n-1}, r_{n-2}) + F_n(q_{n-1}). \tag{19–11}$$

We shall suppose that this value is maximized by the choice

$$q_{n-1}^* = q_{n-1}^*(r_{n-2}). \tag{19–12}$$

Then the total profit for firm 1 from periods $n - 1$ and n will be

$$F_{n-1}(r_{n-2}) = f_{n-1}(q_{n-1}^*, r_{n-2}) + F_n(q_{n-1}^*), \tag{19–13}$$

and the corresponding total profit for firm 2 from periods $n - 1$ and n will be

$$G_{n-1}(r_{n-2}) = g_{n-1}(q_{n-1}^*, r_{n-2}) + G_n(q_{n-1}^*). \tag{19–14}$$

Similarly, firm 2 should choose its output r_{n-2} in period $n - 2$ in order to maximize the value

$$g_{n-2}(q_{n-3}, r_{n-2}) + G_{n-1}(r_{n-2}). \tag{19–15}$$

The optimal choice r_{n-2}^* will be a certain function of the output q_{n-3} of firm 1 at the preceding period.

By continuing backward in this way, the entire sequence of optimal choices can be determined. It is, of course, assumed that in each period the maximum value which is involved is finite and is actually attained at some finite value of the output which is being chosen at that period.

We have used G and F without defining them formally because that could not be done easily until now. In general for any even period k $(k = 2, 4, \ldots, n)$, $G_k(q_{k-1})$ denotes the total profit of firm 2 in periods k to n when the output of firm 1 in period $k - 1$ was q_{k-1} and the output

r_k and all subsequent outputs are optimal outputs for the period in which they are chosen. $F_k(q_{k-1})$ denotes the total profit of firm 1 in periods k to n under the same conditions. For any odd period $F_j(r_{j-1})$ and $G_j(r_{j-1})$ have analogous meanings.

In less rigorous terms backward induction is a technique that attempts to solve the problem of making an optimal decision in each period of a multiperiod problem. The technique works by starting at the end of the process and determining the optimal decision for that period. It then works backward to determine the optimal decision in each period that will be consistent with that of the previous period. Ultimately it enables the decision maker to determine the optimal decision in the beginning period. In short, knowing where you want to be at the end, you can work backward to determine where you should be at each prior period.

IV. A Duopoly Model with Learning

As we have seen in Chapter 12, the models of duopoly and oligopoly that have definite solutions assume some form of fixed behavior on the part of one or more of the firms—the Cournot model, the dominant-firm model, and the kinked demand curve being examples. In reality, of course, firms are learning, as we have pointed out earlier in this chapter, about their rivals' behavior. Our aim in this chapter is to demonstrate a model in which the firms can change their behavior toward their rivals and also change the assumptions made about their rivals. More specifically, we will show that firms can begin a process in which there is no cooperation between them and end the process at a position in which a joint maximum (the collusive position—i.e., the monopoly solution) is attained. The firms cannot move directly to such a position because of lack of trust in each other. The danger of one firm making a cooperative move is that it can be hurt (suffer losses) if the other does not follow.

In the process of constructing this model, we will introduce the notions of a coefficient of cooperation and of mutually optimal reaction functions. We will derive such mutually optimal reaction functions for various coefficients of cooperation. We will also utilize the concept of Bayesian learning.

A. Coefficient of Cooperation

Consider a duopoly problem in which the demand function in any given period is $p = f(q, r)$, where q is the output of firm 1 in that period and r is the output of firm 2. If $c_1(q)$ denotes the cost function of firm 1 in each period and $c_2(r)$ denotes the cost function of firm 2, then the profit π_i of firm i $(i = 1, 2)$ will be

$$\pi_1(q, r) = qf(q, r) - c_1(q), \tag{19--16}$$

$$\pi_2(q, r) = rf(q, r) - c_2(r). \tag{19-17}$$

Thus, in a process with n periods in which q_j and r_j denote the outputs in period j ($j = 1, \ldots, n$), the total profit of firm i over the n periods will be

$$\sum_{j=1}^{n} \pi_i(q_j, r_j).$$

The basic goal of each firm is to maximize its total profit. It is well known that this total profit will be higher for both firms when they cooperate with each other than it will be when each firm attempts to maximize its own profit without considering its rival. We propose, therefore, to introduce a utility function for each firm that will encompass the degree of cooperation the firm is prepared to demonstrate toward its rival.

We shall assume that there exists a constant $\gamma (0 \leq \gamma \leq 1)$ such that firm 1 desires to maximize the sum

$$V_1 = \sum_{j=1}^{n} [\pi_1(q_j, r_j) + \gamma \pi_2(q_j, r_j)]. \tag{19-18}$$

In other words, it is assumed that V_1 represents the utility function for firm 1. If $\gamma = 0$, then the sum in Eq. (19-18) is simply the total profit of firm 1 over the n periods. However, if $\gamma \neq 0$, then the sum in Eq. (19-18) is a linear combination of the total profit of firm 1 and that of firm 2. The number γ will be called the coefficient of cooperation of firm 1. If $0 < \gamma < 1$, firm 1 is interested in cooperating with firm 2 and desires to maximize its own total profits plus a fraction of the profits of firm 2. If $\gamma = 1$, firm 1 is interested in cooperating with firm 2 to the extent of desiring simply to maximize the total profits of the two firms. Although values of γ outside the interval $0 \leq \gamma \leq 1$ are conceptually possible, such values do not seem to be of practical interest and will not be considered further here.

Similarly, we shall assume that there also exists a constant $\partial (0 \leq \partial \leq 1)$ such that firm 2 desires to maximize a utility function V_2 of the following form:

$$V_2 = \sum_{j=1}^{n} [\pi_2(q_j, r_j) + \partial \pi_1(q_j, r_j)]. \tag{19-19}$$

Thus, ∂ is the coefficient of cooperation of firm 2.

It should be emphasized that in the theory to be presented here, there is a rational reason why each firm attempts to maximize a linear combination such as V_1 or V_2 rather than simply trying to maximize its own profits. The firms recognize that for certain pairs of positive values of γ and ∂, their profits will actually be larger when they try to maximize V_1 and V_2 than when each firm tries to maximize its own profits directly. The joint maximum is attained when $\gamma = \partial = 1$. We have called V_1 and V_2 the utility functions of the firms because they choose their outputs in order to maximize these functions. This terminology is slightly inappropriate, however, since the firms ultimately evaluate the usefulness of given coefficients, γ and ∂, not in terms of how large the values of V_1 and V_2 are, but in terms of how large their individual profits are.

B. Mutually Optimal Reaction Functions

Ignoring the values of the coefficients of cooperation for the moment, we define two reaction functions to be mutually optimal if the intersection point of the two is also the point of maximum profit for each firm relative to the reaction function of the rival. This concept can be made clearer by looking at the traditional Cournot model where the reaction functions are not mutually optimal. If firm 1 knows that firm 2 is using the Cournot assumptions, then firm 1 can use this information to develop a new reaction function that will intersect the reaction function of firm 2 at a point that is more profitable for firm 1.[6] On the other hand, two reaction functions, one vertical and one horizontal, that intersect at the Cournot equilibrium point are mutually optimal. With this preface we undertake a more complete definition and analysis.

Consider now a duopoly problem in which the number of periods n is large. We shall assume that the two firms choose their outputs in alternating periods, that firm 1 chooses its output q according to a reaction function $q = \alpha(r)$, and that firm 2 chooses its output r according to a reaction function $r = \beta(q)$. In other words, if firm 2 has just chosen its output in a given period to be r_0, then firm 1 will choose its output in the next period to be $q_1 = \alpha(r_0)$ while firm 2 holds its output at r_0. In the following period, firm 2 will then choose its output to be $r_2 = \beta(q_1)$ while firm 1 holds its output at q_1. The choices continue to be made in this alternating fashion through successive periods.

If the curves $q = \alpha(r)$ and $r = \beta(q)$ intersect at the point $y^* = (q^*, r^*)$, then as indicated in Figure 19–1, the sequence of successive points

$$y_1 = (q_1, r_0), \qquad y_2 = (q_1, r_2),$$

$$y_3 = (q_3, r_2), \qquad y_4 = (q_3, r_4), \ldots$$

will typically converge to the point y^*. This convergence to the point of intersection y^* will take place for any reaction functions α and β satisfying the following three properties.

1. Both the curves $q = \alpha(r)$ and $r = \beta(q)$ are decreasing (or nonincreasing).

2. The curve $q = \alpha(r)$ lies above the curve $r = \beta(q)$ for all points (q, r) such that $q < q^*$.

---

[6] R. G. D. Allen, *Mathematical Analysis for Economists* (London: Macmillan & Company, Ltd., 1938), pp. 345–47.

3. The curve $q = \alpha(r)$ lies below the curve $r = \beta(q)$ for all points (q, r) such that $q > q^*$.

Thus, under these conditions, if the two firms repeatedly use the reaction functions $q = \alpha(r)$ and $r = \beta(q)$, their outputs will converge to q^* and r^*, regardless of the initial outputs at which the process starts.

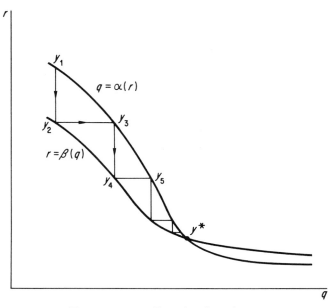

FIGURE 19–1. Reaction functions.

Suppose now that the coefficients of cooperation of firms 1 and 2 are γ and ∂, respectively, and that each firm knows the rival's cost and reaction functions. In any given period, firm 1 knows that corresponding to any value that it chooses for its output q, firm 2 will react in the next period by choosing the value $r = \beta(q)$. The profits of firms 1 and 2 will then be:

$$\pi_1[q, \beta(q)] = qf[q, \beta(q)] - c_1(q) \tag{19-20}$$

and

$$\pi_2[q, \beta(q)] = \beta(q)f[q, \beta(q)] - c_2[\beta(q)]. \tag{19-21}$$

Since the coefficient of cooperation of firm 1 is γ, firm 1 is interested in maximizing the value of the utility function

$$P_1 = \pi_1[q, \beta(q)] + \gamma\pi_2[q, \beta(q)]. \tag{19-22}$$

Suppose that this utility function is maximized at the value $q = q_M$. Because of the convergence which we have described, we know that in the long run, the output of firm 1 will be close to the value $q = q^*$ in every period. It follows, therefore, that from the point of view of firm 1, the most desirable value of q^* is $q^* = q_M$.

For this reason, we shall say that the reaction function $q = \alpha(r)$ is optimal against the reaction function $r = \beta(q)$ of firm 2 if $q^* = q_M$. In other words, the reaction function $q = \alpha(r)$ of firm 1 is optimal against the reaction function $r = \beta(q)$ of firm 2 if the point of intersection (q^*, r^*) of the two reaction functions, toward which the outputs of the two firms converge, is also the point on the curve $r = \beta(q)$ at which the utility function P_1 of firm 1 is a maximum.

Similarly, for any choice of output r by firm 2 the reaction of firm 1 will be $q = \alpha(r)$ and the profits of the two firms will be $\pi_1[\alpha(r), r]$ and $\pi_2[\alpha(r), r]$. The utility function of firm 2 is

$$P_2 = \pi_2[\alpha(r), r] + \partial \pi_1[\alpha(r), r] \tag{19-23}$$

and we shall let r_M denote the value of r for which this utility is maximized. Then we say that the reaction function $r = \beta(q)$ of firm 2 is optimal against the reaction function $q = \alpha(r)$ of firm 1 if $r^* = r_M$.

Finally, we say that the two reaction functions are mutually optimal if both $q_M = q^*$ and $r_M = r^*$. In other words, the two reaction functions are mutually optimal if the preferred position of firm 1 along the curve $r = \beta(q)$ is at the point (q^*, r^*) and the preferred position of firm 2 along the curve $q = \alpha(r)$ is also at the point (q^*, r^*). It should be emphasized that the coefficients of cooperation γ and ∂ are assumed to have given values in this definition and that two reaction functions are considered to be mutually optimal relative to the given values of γ and ∂.

When the two reaction functions are mutually optimal, neither firm will desire to change the point of intersection toward which the outputs are converging by changing its own reaction function as long as the rival firm does not change.

C. Optimal Strategies in Multiperiod Decision Problems with Alternating Choice

We shall now consider again a process with n periods and assume that the two firms choose their outputs in alternating periods as described earlier in this chapter. We apply the method of backward induction to a problem in which the coefficients of cooperation γ and ∂ of the two firms are fixed, firm 1 desires to maximize the utility V_1 given by Eq. (19-18), and firm 2 desires to maximize the utility V_2 given by Eq. (19-19).

For each different pair of values γ and ∂, the method of backward induction specifies a different sequence of outputs for the two firms which, in turn, yield a different sequence of profits for the firms over the n periods. Thus, the choice of γ and ∂ by the firms fixes their profit stream over the n periods. Suppose, for example, that $\gamma = \partial$, so the firms are using the same coefficients of cooperation, and suppose that K_1 and K_2 are numbers such that $0 \leq K_1 < K_2 < 1$. Then in general, the profits of both firms will be higher when $\gamma = \partial = K_2$ than they will be when $\gamma = \partial = K_1$. In other words, it will be mutually profitable for the firms to use a common coefficient of cooperation that is as large as possible.

We shall assume for convenience that the total number of periods n is even and that firm 2 must choose its output r_n in the final period n. After the output q_{n-1} of firm 1 in period $n - 1$ is known, firm 2 will choose r_n to maximize its utility $\pi_2(q_{n-1}, r_n) + \partial \pi_1(q_{n-1}, r_n)$. Thus when firm 1 chooses its output q_{n-1} in period $n - 1$, it knows the output r_{n-2} of firm 2 in period $n - 2$ as well as the reaction function that firm 2 will use in period n. Hence, subject to these conditions, it can choose q_{n-1} to maximize its utility over the final two periods.

$$[\pi_1(q_{n-1}, r_{n-2}) + \gamma \pi_2(q_{n-1}, r_{n-2})] + [\pi_1(q_{n-1}, r_n) + \gamma \pi_2(q_{n-1}, r_n)]. \tag{19-24}$$

By moving backward through the process in this way, it is seen that at any given period, the firm which must choose its output in that period will know the reaction functions that will be used by the rival firm and by itself in all later periods. Hence, for any given output of the rival in the preceding period, it can choose its own output to maximize the sum of its utilities over all the remaining periods. The sequences of reaction functions for the two firms constructed in this way are called the pure duopoly strategies relative to the given coefficients of cooperation γ and ∂.

If this process of backward induction is continued indefinitely and the reaction functions for the firms are derived for earlier and earlier periods, then these reaction functions will typically converge to certain limiting reaction functions.

D. CHANGING COEFFICIENTS OF COOPERATION

Up to this point we have established the following conclusions:

1. For each fixed pair of coefficients of cooperation γ and ∂, there exists an equilibrium point obtained from mutually optimal limiting reaction functions.

2. There exists a unique pair of paths leading to each such equilibrium point established by a process of backward induction in which each firm wants to be in the optimal position vis-à-vis its competitor at the final point.

3. When $\gamma = \partial = 0$, the equilibrium point is the noncooperative solution. When $\gamma = \partial$ and their common value increases toward the value 1, the equilibrium point yields higher profits for both firms.

These conclusions mean that each firm can be viewed as facing a decision set consisting of an infinite number of pairs of multiperiod decision paths.

Each of these pairs of paths leads to an equilibrium point established from mutually optimal reaction functions. Each pair is identified by the values of the coefficients of cooperation held by each firm. On each path the alternating decisions assumption holds. In each decision period the firm making the decision in that period makes the optimum decision, given the rival's decision in the previous period, for maximizing its utility over the infinite horizon. This entire process is, of course, based on the assumption that neither demand nor cost conditions are changing.

It is not, however, necessary to assume that the coefficients of cooperation are fixed throughout the entire process. Each firm can change its coefficient of cooperation at any time. Hence, no firm need stay on a fixed path.

In order to illustrate the model's potential, let us start with a situation in which both firms are on the paths consistent with the values $\gamma = \partial = 0$. Assume that through the process of learning, one of the firms develops a probability distribution on the rival's likelihood of cooperating with a larger value for the coefficient of cooperation. Specifically, let firm 1 have a uniform prior distribution for firm 2's coefficient of cooperation ∂ on the interval $0 \leq \partial \leq d$, where 0 is the current value of ∂ and d is the highest level of cooperation to which firm 1 believes firm 2 will implicitly consent. Let us further assume that if d is less than the value of γ that firm 1 uses, then firm 2 will keep $\partial = 0$, and that if $\gamma \leq d$, firm 2 will match its coefficient of cooperation and choose $\partial = \gamma$.

If we assume a two-period analysis, then it is possible to determine an optimal value for γ, the value that firm 1 should set. Let $W_1(\gamma \mid 0, d)$ stand for the expected utility of firm 1 over the two periods for a given value of $\gamma (0 \leq \gamma \leq d)$. The expression for W_1 must take into account the fact that decisions are made in alternating periods. We assume a process in which each firm is proceeding along its optimum path for $\gamma = \partial = 0$. In the period appropriate for firm 1 to make its output decision, it does so on the basis of the previous output r_o of firm 2, but with a new choice of γ. By choosing an output q^* that is consistent with r_o and a new value of $\gamma > 0$, firm 1 indicates to firm 2 that it is prepared to operate at a higher level of cooperation than previously. Firm 2 then has the opportunity to respond positively—that is, to choose an r_1^* based on q^* and $\partial = \gamma > 0$, or to continue to hold $\partial = 0$ and choose an r_2^* based on $\partial = 0$ and q^*. On this basis, firm 1 must choose γ to maximize the following expected utility:

$$W_1(\gamma \mid 0, d) = [\pi_1(q^*, r_o) + \gamma\pi_2(q^*, r_o)]$$

$$+ \frac{d - \gamma}{d} [\pi_1(q^*, r_1^*) + \gamma\pi_2(q^*, r_1^*)]$$

$$+ \frac{\gamma}{d} [\pi_1(q^*, r_2^*) + \gamma\pi_2(q^*, r_2^*)]. \tag{19-25}$$

Because q^*, r_1^*, and r_2^* are also functions of γ, the maximization process becomes messy although straightforward. The question is whether there is a value of $\gamma > 0$ such that $W_1(\gamma \mid 0, d) > W_1(0 \mid 0, d)$. Some economic insight can be gained by regrouping the terms in $W_1(\gamma \mid 0, d)$ and examining the resulting expression. We have

$$W_1(\gamma \mid 0, d) = [\pi_1(q^*, r_o) + \pi_1(q^*, r_1^*)]$$

$$+ \gamma[\pi_2(q^*, r_o) + \pi_2(q^*, r_1^*)]$$

$$+ \frac{\gamma}{d} \left\{ [\pi_1(q^*, r_2^*) - \pi_1(q^*, r_1^*)] \right.$$

$$\left. + \frac{\gamma^2}{d} [\pi_2(q^*, r_2^*) - \pi_2(q^*, r_1^*)] \right\}. \quad (19\text{--}26)$$

It is reasonable to assume that the first two expressions are positive. The third one should be negative since we would expect firm 1 to make more profit when firm 2 cooperated by making $\partial = \gamma$. The fourth term should be positive since we would expect firm 2 to make more profit by being un-cooperative (while firm 1 is being cooperative) than by being cooperative. Thus, the impact of firm 2's noncooperative action on firm 1 becomes decisive in determining whether the expected utility is increasing and in determining the size of the optimum γ if W_1 is positive. The larger the absolute value of the third term, the smaller the optimum value of γ will be. This result, of course, is not surprising, because it is the response of firm 2 to firm 1's action that is the uncertain element in the situation.

Though this analysis is for the two-period case, it illustrates the process by which the firms can move from one track leading to a mutually optimal equilibrium to another. It is possible in this way for the firm to move from the uncooperative track $\gamma = \partial = 0$ to the higher profits corresponding to $\gamma = \partial = 1$. Once learning takes place and the optimal value of γ becomes $\gamma^* > 0$, firm 1 can rationally attempt to move to the new track—namely the one for which both $\gamma = \partial = \gamma^*$. Firm 2 then has two alternatives. It can refuse to follow and make larger profits than it did previously. How-ever, it can expect firm 1 to come back eventually to the track represented by $\gamma = \partial = 0$. Under such a situation firm 2 is back to its original profit position. If firm 2, on the other hand, moves to the new track by making $\partial = \gamma^*$, its profits will be greater than they were for $\partial = \gamma = 0$.

An interesting question arises with respect to the problem of communica-tion in a market. More specifically, we need to amplify the process by which one firm knows the other has changed its coefficient of cooperation. We have assumed that this communication takes place through output changes and that each firm is capable of knowing when the other has changed. This assumption is not too far at variance with the real world. In a number of industries this information or similar information is published (automobile registrations, per cent of capacity at which steel companies are producing). Where a model is based on differentiated products with different prices, the problem of communication is obviously simpler.

It is possible to extend the analysis for the optimum new coefficient of cooperation to more periods than the two assumed. It is possible to view the expected utility over n periods and to solve for the optimum decision horizon as well as the optimum coefficient of cooperation. It is also possible to postulate a different decision rule for the firm initiating the move to the higher level of cooperation. We assumed that firm 1 determined its output q^* based on the γ and the current output of firm 2, r_o. Many other decision rules might have been used by firm 1. The main point is that firm 1 wants to behave in such a way that firm 2 clearly understands that firm 1 is signalling a change in the level of cooperation.

The process just described continues to occur over time. If firm 1's efforts succeed and firm 2 increases its ∂ to make it equal to γ, then both firms are on a track leading toward a new mutually optimal equilibrium point. Both firms are making more profits than they were when each was on the uncooperative track. Both firms continue to learn and form priors about the new values toward which the other firm will raise its coefficient of cooperation. At some point when the decision rule being used shows that the expected gain in utility is worth the risk of increasing the coefficient of cooperation, one of the firms will make the move and eventually the firms will move to another pair of tracks where the profit is higher. In this model either firm may initiate the movement.

Even if the first move should fail to stimulate the rival to match the new coefficient of cooperation, eventually the process will succeed. The temporary gains from not matching will be lost as soon as the firm initiating the upward movement reduces its coefficient of cooperation back to the old. Punishment is as effective a stimulus for learning for real firms in the real world as it is for subjects in an experiment in a laboratory.

We argue, therefore, that this model demonstrates the kind of behavior that many economists have speculated does occur in duopoly and oligopoly. We have shown how firms progress from a noncooperative solution to situations of increasing profit and ultimately to the tracks characterized by $\gamma = \partial = 1$.

Making the duopoly model dynamic has been accomplished by the introduction of the concept of firm learning, by the formalization of the learning through Bayesian analysis, and by utilizing the concept of mutually optimal equilibria all within the format of multiperiod analysis. We believe this pattern of concepts can also be used to extend and improve other duopoly and oligopoly models.

V. Summary

The purpose of this chapter has been to bring the reader closer to the frontier of current research in the field of duopoly and oligopoly. It had the further purpose of demonstrating the manner in which some techniques that have not been used extensively in economics prior to this work can help bring models closer to the behavior observed in the real world.

The thrust of this chapter can be classified in the category of developing models that are adaptive. By "adaptive" we mean the ability to learn and change to behavior that will better achieve the objectives of the firm. We developed the concept of firm learning by starting with some psychological concepts of learning. We concentrated on the area in which firms learn about each other's behavior and called this "interfirm" learning. Because this learning involved the process of modifying probabilities on the basis of observed behavior, we were lead to the area of Bayesian analysis.

Bayes' theorem is a process by which the probability can be calculated as to which of a set of mutually exclusive and collectively exhaustive set of events, $B_1, B_2, \ldots, B_n$, has taken place when it is known that a specific event A has occurred. It is particularly useful when combined with the concept of subjective probability. The combination of concepts enables us to introduce a process whereby a firm can make a subjective probability estimate of its rival's behavior and on the basis of the observed behavior modify this "prior."

A second concept that is crucial to this new work is backward induction. This concept is a method for making a "system" of optimal decisions where the system consists of n periods of decisions. By starting with the end optimal decision, it is possible to work backward and derive optimal decisions for each of the periods.

On the basis of these concepts and the introduction of the coefficient of cooperation, we were able to develop a new type of duopoly model that is truly adaptive. The model assumes that each firm is trying to maximize a function that consists of its profits and the profits of its rival. The weight given to the latter is dependent on the degree of cooperation the firm wishes to exhibit, the largest weight being a value of one. The model as developed is composed of a series of tracks (or paths), each leading to an equilibrium position for the two firms. Each path is characterized by a different combination of the coefficients of cooperation for the two firms. The path with the greatest joint profit (the sum of the profit of each firm) is the one for which the two coefficients of cooperation are each equal to one.

We show within the operation of the model how the firms, through a Bayesian learning and decision process, can adapt their behavior and move from one path to another. It is thus possible for the two firms to begin in an uncooperative posture and ultimately reach a joint maximum equilibrium.

SUGGESTED READINGS

These recommendations are in addition to the footnote references cited in this chapter.

CYERT, RICHARD M., AND MORRIS H. DEGROOT, "Bayesian Analysis and Duopoly Theory," *The Journal of Political Economy*, LXXVIII, No. 5 (September/October, 1970), 1168–84.

DOLBEAR, F. T., et al., "Collusion in the Prisoner's Dilemma: Number of Strategies," *Journal of Conflict Resolution*, XIII (June, 1969), 252–61.

FERGUSON, CHARLES E., AND RALPH W. PFOUTS, "Learning and Expectations in Dynamic Duopoly Behavior," *Behavioral Science*, VII (April, 1962), 223–37.

FRIEDMAN, J. W., "Reaction Functions and the Theory of Duopoly," *Review of Economic Studies*, XXXV (July, 1968), 257–72.

LUCE, R. D., AND H. RAIFFA, *Games and Decisions*. New York: John Wiley & Sons, Inc., 1957.

Part 4

Implications of
Microeconomics for the
Economic System

Chapter Twenty

Economic Efficiency and
Welfare Economics

In Chapters 4 through 19, we have discussed the ways in which the decisions of households and business firms, interacting through a set of product and factor markets, determine the pattern of resource allocation in an economy. We are now ready to discuss the extent to which we can compare two different patterns of resource allocation and state that one is preferable to the other. We shall also consider the ways in which different types of market structures may lead to patterns of resource allocation which are not equally efficient.

I. The Economics of Efficiency

A *pattern of resource allocation* is a complete specification of the amounts of each commodity consumed by every household, the amounts of each productive service supplied by every household, the amounts of each product produced by every firm, the amounts of each resource used by every firm, and the amounts of every commodity and resource used and supplied by the government. Although market prices are not themselves part of the pattern of resource allocation, they influence the particular resource allocation pattern which emerges.

It should be evident from our discussion in Chapter 9 that the resource allocation pattern in an economy results from some type of general equilibrium system. The fundamental decisions in such a system are made by individual business firms and households. We have seen that firms make different decisions depending upon the types of markets in which they operate. Thus the particular market structure of the economy will influence the pattern of resource allocation.

The criterion ultimately used for determining whether one pattern of resource allocation is preferable to another is consumer well-being. As a fundamental ethical belief, most Western economists regard the general levels of satisfaction of consumers as the major criterion for social welfare judgments. Our discussion in this chapter is based on this ethical belief. It should be recognized, however, that some political-economic philosophies (e.g., fascism) start from a very different fundamental ethical premise, namely that the good of the state is more important than the satisfactions of the consumers.

A. Interpersonal Comparisons of Utility and the Social Welfare Function

The concept of an individual's utility function was introduced in Chapter 5, where it provided a basis for the derivation of individual and market demand curves. At that time, we assumed that every individual allocated his income among the various consumption goods in such a way as to maximize his own individual utility. This led to the construction of each individual's demand function, from which the market demand function was obtained by simple summation. At no time did we find it necessary to make an *interpersonal comparison of utility*, i.e., a comparison between the utility level achieved by one consumer and the level of utility attained by any other consumer.

The problem of making interpersonal comparisons of utility is analogous to the problem of making interpersonal comparisons of pain. It is meaningful for me to say that the pain I feel from my toothache today is less intense than the pain I felt from my toothache yesterday, but there is no way in which I can meaningfully state that the pain I feel from my toothache today is greater than the pain that you feel from your toothache today. The difficulty arises because there is no suitable measuring scale and measuring device for detecting levels of pain. Exactly the same problem exists with respect to utility.

The problems inherent in interpersonal comparisons of utility can be avoided by using a *social welfare function*. A social welfare function, as its name implies, is an aggregate measure of national well-being. It is a function of each individual's utility level, but is is not a sum of these individual utilities. If any one person's utility rises, everybody else's utility staying the same, then the value of the social welfare function increases. Because interpersonal comparisons of utility are not meaningful, we can, however, say nothing about the value of the social welfare function if one individual's utility rises while some other individual's utility falls. In essence, then, we can use the social welfare function to provide only a partial ordering of national economic well-being. We are capable of sometimes saying that one distribution of resources is better than some other distribution; but there will be some states of affairs among which we cannot make any relevant comparisons.

B. The Concept of Welfare Economics

In keeping with the notion that the social welfare function can provide only a partial ordering, economists generally think in terms of limited types of welfare comparisons. It is easiest to see how these comparisons are made by considering the circumstances in which people find it mutually advantageous to barter. The problems of barter are most readily explored in a simplified world consisting of two individuals possessing only two different commodities. The essential features of our discussion will generalize readily to more realistic situations involving numerous persons and many commodities.

Let us call our two commodities *apples* and *bananas*, and our two people *Xavier* and *Yerkes*. (Purists generally prefer to speak of commodities A and B and of individuals X and Y.) Suppose that initially Xavier possesses a_x apples and b_x bananas, and Yerkes has a_y apples and b_y bananas. **Figure 20–1 shows**

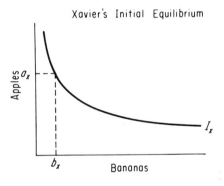

Xavier's Initial Equilibrium

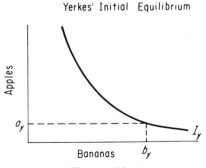

Yerkes' Initial Equilibrium

FIGURE 20–1.
Initial equilibrium conditions.

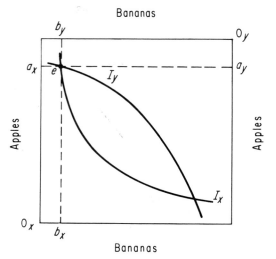

FIGURE 20–2.   Box diagram.

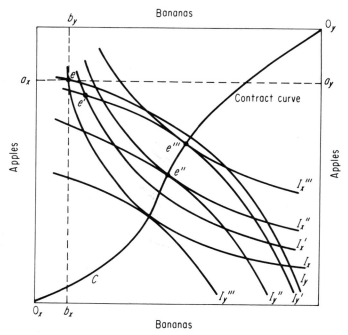

FIGURE 20–3.   Result of bartering.

the amounts of these commodities each individual has. I_x and I_y are indifference curves indicating the utility levels of each person.

A convenient graphical trick in determining the extent to which barter will take place between Xavier and Yerkes is to take the diagram for Yerkes in Figure 20–1, rotate it by 180°, and superimpose it on the diagram for Xavier. The resulting construction, called a *box diagram*, is shown in Figure 20–2. The quantity of apples is still measured vertically and the quantity of bananas is still measured horizontally. The origin for these measurements is in the southwest corner for Xavier (O_x) and in the northeast corner for Yerkes (O_y). The height of the box is the total quantity of apples possessed by both, $a_x + a_y$. The width of the box is $b_x + b_y$, the total quantity of bananas in our two-person world. The indifference curves I_x and I_y remain convex to their respective origins.

The initial positions of Xavier and Yerkes are represented by the point e in Figure 20–2. There are numerous positions which Xavier and Yerkes can achieve by bartering which are better for them both. In particular, any point inside the area between the two indifference curves I_x and I_y is preferred by both Xavier and Yerkes to the point e. For example, point e' in Figure 20–3 can be achieved if Xavier gives a few apples to Yerkes in return for some bananas. At e', Xavier is better off than he is at e, for I'_x is a higher indifference curve than I_x. But Yerkes is also happier at e' than he is at e, for I'_y is a higher indifference curve (relative to O_y) than I_y.

Once Xavier and Yerkes have moved from e to e', the same argument can again be repeated, since there is still an area between the indifference curves I'_x and I'_y. Thus some new exchange of apples for bananas between Xavier and Yerkes will enable each to attain a higher level of satisfaction. This process will continue until some position is reached from which no further movement is possible which will benefit both Xavier and Yerkes. One such point in Figure 20–3 is e''. Xavier and Yerkes both prefer e'' to either e' or e. No point can, however, be found which both individuals prefer to e''. Any movement from e'' which leads northeast of I''_x will improve the lot of Xavier, but it will make Yerkes less happy. Conversely, any shift from e'' going southwest of I''_y will increase Yerkes' satisfaction, but Xavier will be worse off. Finally any change of position from e'' which goes between I''_x and I''_y will be resisted by both Xavier and Yerkes. Thus when a point of tangency between two indifference curves (such as e'') has been reached, no further free trading between Xavier and Yerkes will take place.

There is nothing unique about the point e''. Within the area enclosed by the curves I_x and I_y, there are an infinite number of points where an indifference curve of Xavier is tangent to one of Yerkes' indifference curves. The curve C in Figure 20–3 (which we have labeled the *contract curve*, for reasons which will soon become apparent) represents the locus of all points of tangency between Xavier's and Yerkes' families of indifference curves. Any point on the contract curve which lies inside the original area is a possible equilibrium point which might be reached by bargaining between Xavier and Yerkes. The equilibrium point which is ultimately attained depends solely upon Xavier's and Yerkes' relative skills in bargaining.

If Xavier and Yerkes start from the point e, and both are approximately equal in bargaining skill, then a point on the contract curve around e'' will probably be reached. If, however, Xavier is considerably stronger in the bargaining process, some point such as e''' might be reached. At e''', both Xavier and Yerkes are still better off than they were at e. Xavier, however, is better off at e''' than he is at e'', whereas Yerkes is worse off.

In summary, as long as any two individuals possess an initial amount of any two commodities which is represented by some point not on the contract curve, both persons can simultaneously improve their positions by engaging in barter. Once they have arrived at any point lying on the contract curve, no further free trade will take place between them.

The contract curve is very closely related to the notion of the social welfare function. On the basis of the utility functions of both Xavier and Yerkes, the contract curve provides a partial ordering relation which can be used to evaluate various distributions of resources (apples and bananas) between them. Any point which is not upon the contract curve can be shown to be inferior (according to both Xavier's and Yerkes' utilities) to some point which is on this curve. Xavier and Yerkes cannot, however, reach agreement concerning the relative desirability of two different points which are both on the contract curve. In a world which consists only of Xavier and Yerkes, the social welfare function would depend only on the utility levels of Xavier and Yerkes.

In more realistic worlds, comprised of several commodities and many individuals, the notion of the contract curve remains equally valid. Its geometric representation becomes considerably more complex, however, because the number of dimensions in our geometric space must be greatly increased. In this N-dimensional space, the contract curve is defined as the locus of points of tangency between the indifference surfaces of various individuals. As long as any two individuals are not on the contract curve, both can improve their positions by trading with each other. Any movement between two different points on the contract curve, however, represents one person's gain but some other person's loss.

The notion of *economic efficiency* is readily defined in terms of the contract curve. A particular distribution of resources in the economy is said to be efficient if and only if it is not possible to make at least one person better off without making anybody else worse off. In other words, an efficient distribution of resources is represented by a point lying on the contract curve. Welfare economics can be interpreted as the economics of efficiency. Any state of society which is not economically efficient is undesirable because it is possible to increase the utilities of some people without decreasing the utilities of others.

C. Some Necessary Conditions for Economic Efficiency

It is easy to show that there are a number of *marginal conditions* which must be satisfied if we are to have an efficient economic system. These marginal conditions can be viewed both as ways of detecting when any economic system is not functioning optimally, as well as positive goals toward which we can strive in our efforts to establish economic efficiency. An elegant mathematical derivation of these marginal conditions can be obtained by using the differential calculus to maximize the social welfare function.[1] Geometrical diagrams can also be used to establish these results.[2] We shall employ simple algebraic arguments to show that unless all these marginal conditions are simultaneously satisfied, we cannot have an efficient economic system.[3]

> *Theorem 1. The marginal rates of substitution between any two commodities should be the same for any two consumers.*

To prove Theorem 1, consider two arbitrary commodities, H and K, and any two consumers, A and B. Let H_A and H_B be the initial stocks of commodity H possessed by A and B, and let K_A and K_B be the initial quantities of commodity K in the hands of A and B. Let A_{KH} be A's marginal rate of substitution of commodity K for commodity H (that is, A's utility level would be unchanged if, at the margin, he were to exchange 1 unit of H for A_{KH} units of K); similarly, B_{KH} is B's marginal rate of substitution of K for H.[4]

First, suppose that $A_{KH} < B_{KH}$. Then we shall show that for some suitably small but positive value Δ, B's utility will be increased but A's utility will not be decreased if A gives Δ units of H to B in exchange for $A_{KH} \Delta$ units of K. After this trade, A has $H_A - \Delta$ units of H and $K_A + A_{KH} \Delta$ units of K. Since A_{KH} was defined as A's marginal rate of substitution of commodity K for commodity H, A's utility level has not changed as a result of this exchange. However, B now has $H_B + \Delta$ units of H and $K_B - A_{KH} \Delta$ units of K. To maintain the same utility level that he had initially

---

[1] The details of this approach can be found in Paul Anthony Samuelson, *Foundations of Economic Analysis* (Cambridge, Mass.: Harvard University Press, 1947), chap. 8.

[2] For example, see Melvin Warren Reder, *Studies in the Theory of Welfare Economics* (New York: Columbia University Press, 1947), chap. 2.

[3] This discussion, and the numerical examples used, are adapted from Kenneth E. Boulding, "Welfare Economics," in *A Survey of Contemporary Economics*, Vol. II. ed. Bernard F. Haley (Homewood, Ill.: Richard D. Irwin, Inc., 1952), chap. 1.

[4] In general the marginal rates of substitution vary from point to point, as we saw in Chapter 5. Thus in principle instead of A_{KH} we should write $A_{KH}(H_A, K_A)$, and instead of B_{KH} we should write $B_{KH}(H_B, K_B)$. For convenience, we shall merely write A_{KH} and B_{KH}, but it should be understood that these marginal rates of substitution are evaluated at particular points.

Similar remarks apply to the notation for the various marginal rates used in Theorems 2–5.

with $H_B + \Delta$ units of H, B should have only $K_B - B_{KH} \Delta$ units of K. Since by assumption $A_{KH} < B_{KH}$, B has more units of K than he needs to maintain his old utility level. This extra $(B_{KH} - A_{KH})\Delta$ units of K moves B to a higher indifference curve, and hence B's utility is increased by this exchange.

Second, suppose $A_{KH} > B_{KH}$. Then reasoning precisely analogous to that used in the preceding paragraph shows that if B gives Δ units of H to A in return for $B_{KH} \Delta$ units of K, then A's utility level will be increased while B's utility level will remain unchanged. Since we have shown that when $A_{KH} < B_{KH}$ or when $A_{KH} > B_{KH}$, some reallocation of resources between A and B will increase the utility of one person without decreasing the utility of the other person, $A_{KH} = B_{KH}$ is a necessary condition for economic efficiency, thus proving Theorem 1.[5]

For a numerical example illustrating Theorem 1, take $A_{KH} = 2$, $B_{KH} = 3$, $H_A = 20$, $K_A = 10$, $H_B = 5$, $K_B = 20$, and $\Delta = 1$. Suppose that A gives 1 unit of H to B, in return for 2 units of K. A now has 19 units of H and 12 units of K, and his utility level is unchanged, since his marginal rate of substitution of K for H is 2 units of K for 1 unit of H. B, however, has 6 units of H and 18 units of K. Since B's marginal rate of substitution is 3 units of K for 1 unit of H, B would be indifferent between 5 units of H and 20 units of K and 6 units of H and 17 units of K. Therefore, the trade between A and B increases B's utility, since B prefers 6 units of H and 18 units of K to 5 units of H and 20 units of K.

Theorem 2. The marginal rates of transformation between any two products should be the same for any pair of producers.

To prove that Theorem 2 is a necessary condition for economic efficiency, we shall show that whenever it is violated a reallocation of production between the producers will increase the total output of one product without decreasing the total output of the other. Let H and K again be two arbitrary commodities, and now let A and B represent any producers of both of these commodities. A is initially manufacturing H_A units of H and K_A units of K; B is initially making H_B and K_B units of H and K. Together, they are initially making $H_A + H_B$ units of H and $K_A + K_B$ units of K. Let A_{KH} be the marginal rate of transformation by producer A between commodities K and H (that is, if A produces 1 more unit of H, he must decrease his production of K by A_{KH} units, holding constant the amount of productive

---

[5] For this argument to be completely rigorous, Δ must be chosen small enough so that the assumed inequalities between A_{KH} and B_{KH} continue to hold in the same directions. In particular, when $A_{KH}(H_A, K_A) < B_{KH}(H_B, K_B)$ is assumed, then Δ must be small enough so that $A_{KH}(H_A - \Delta, K_A + A_{KH} \Delta) < B_{KH}(H_B + \Delta, K_A - A_{KH} \Delta)$. In the limit, as Δ approaches zero, this algebraic argument becomes a differential calculus argument.

Similar remarks apply to the proofs of Theorems 2–5, although they will not be explicitly repeated.

factors used). B_{KH} is B's marginal rate of transformation of commodity K for commodity H.

Suppose first that $A_{KH} < B_{KH}$. For some suitably small but positive value Δ, let A's production of H be increased by Δ units, and let B's production of H be reduced by Δ units. If the amount of factors used by each producer is held constant, A's production of K must then be decreased by $A_{KH} \Delta$ units while B's production of K may be increased by $B_{KH} \Delta$ units. The total amount of H made by these two producers remains unchanged, but the total amount of K they produce is increased from $K_A + K_B$ to $K_A + K_B + (B_{KH} - A_{KH})\Delta$.

Conversely, if $A_{KH} > B_{KH}$, the total production of K will be increased while the total production of H remains constant if B produces Δ more units of H while A produces Δ fewer units of H. In this case, the total production of K would be $K_A + K_B + (A_{KH} - B_{KH})\Delta$.

A numerical example illustrating Theorem 2 is $A_{KH} = 2$, $B_{KH} = 3$, $H_A = 15$, $K_A = 25$, $H_B = 5$, $K_B = 10$, and $\Delta = 1$. Initially, 20 units of H are being produced, while 35 units of K are being made. Keeping the employment of productive factors constant, when A changes his production of H to 16 units, he can then produce only 23 units of K; if B cuts his output of H to 4 units, he will be able to make 13 units of K. This results in a total production of H of still 20 units, but now 36 units of K are being produced.

Theorem 3. The marginal physical products of a given factor for a given product should be the same for any pair of producers.

Let f be the factor of production, K the product, and A and B the two producers. Let A_{Kf} be the marginal physical productivity of factor f in product K for producer A (that is, if A uses 1 more unit of f, he can produce A_{Kf} additional units of K); let B_{Kf} be B's marginal physical productivity of factor f in product K. Suppose that initially A is using f_A and B is using f_B units of f to produce K_A and K_B units of K. Thus these two producers together are using $f_A + f_B$ units of f to produce $K_A + K_B$ units of K.

Suppose first that $A_{Kf} < B_{Kf}$. Then for some small but positive Δ, the total production of K will be increased by $(B_{Kf} - A_{Kf})\Delta$ units without changing the total utilization of f when Δ units of f are reallocated from A to B. Similarly if $A_{Kf} > B_{Kf}$, then shifting Δ units of f from B to A will increase the total production of K by $(A_{Kf} - B_{Kf})\Delta$ units.

For a numerical example illustrating Theorem 3, let $A_{Kf} = 2$, $B_{Kf} = 3$, $f_A = 20$, $K_A = 40$, $f_B = 20$, $K_B = 60$. Initially A and B together are using 40 units of factor f and making 100 units of product K. If 1 unit of f is reallocated from A to B, then A can produce only 38 units of K, but B will be able to produce 63 units of K, thus increasing total output of K to 101 units.

Theorem 4. The marginal rates of technical substitution between any two factors should be the same for any pair of producers.

Let f and g be the two different factors of production, and let A and B be the two producers who are using these factors to make the same product. Let A_{gf} be producer A's marginal rate of technical substitution between factors g and f (that is, A's total production would remain unchanged if he were to substitute A_{gf} units of factor g in place of 1 unit of factor f); let B's marginal rate of technical substitution between factors g and f be B_{gf}. Initially, suppose that A is using f_A and g_A units of factors f and g, and that B is using f_B and g_B units of these same factors. Together, A and B are thus using $f_A + f_B$ units of f and $g_A + g_B$ units of g.

Suppose first that $A_{gf} < B_{gf}$. Then by reallocating the usage of factors (giving more f to B and more g to A), the same total output can be produced from fewer units of g, while the amount used of f remains unchanged. If Δ units of f are shifted from A to B, A will then use only $f_A - \Delta$ units of f and B will use $f_B + \Delta$ units of f, the total usage of f remaining constant. If the output of each producer is held constant, then A will have to use $g_A + A_{gf}\Delta$ units of g, whereas B can use only $g_B - B_{gf}\Delta$ units of g. The total amount of g which is used is thus $g_A + g_B - (B_{gf} - A_{gf})\Delta$ units, a smaller amount than initially used as long as $A_{gf} < B_{gf}$.

In a precisely analogous manner, it can be shown that if $A_{gf} > B_{gf}$, then a shift of Δ units of f from B to A will allow the same total output to be made with $(A_{gf} - B_{gf})\Delta$ fewer units of g being used, total usage of f remaining unchanged.

For a numerical illustration of Theorem 4, suppose that for producer A the marginal rate of technical substitution is 2 units of g for 1 unit of f, and for B it is 3 units of g for 1 unit of f. Initially, suppose that A is using 20 units of f and 30 units of g, and B is using 10 units of f and 20 units of g. The total initial factor usage is 30 units of f and 50 units of g. If 1 unit of f is taken from A and given to B, A will be using 19 units of f whereas B will be using 11 units. To keep each producer's output constant, A will have to use 2 more units of g, that is, 32 units of g in all, while B can use only 17 units of g. Now the combined usage of g by both producers is only 49 units, 1 unit less than originally was used.

Theorem 5. The marginal rate of substitution between any two commodities should be the same as the marginal rate of transformation between these two commodities for any producer.

Consider an arbitrary consumer A, any two commodities H and K, and any producer B who makes both of these commodities. Initially suppose that A consumes H_A units of H and K_A units of K per period, and that B produces H_B and K_B units per period of H and K. Let A_{KH} be consumer A's marginal rate of substitution between commodities K and H, and let

B_{KH} be producer B's marginal rate of transformation between commodities K and H. Suppose that A's consumption of H and K is entirely supplied by B. Then $H_B - H_A$ and $K_B - K_A$ are the amounts of H and K from B's output which are available each period for other consumers besides A to use. To prove Theorem 5, we shall show that unless $A_{KH} = B_{KH}$, it is possible to make more goods available to other consumers without decreasing A's level of utility and without requiring B to use any additional productive resources.

Suppose first that $A_{KH} < B_{KH}$. Let us then reduce, by Δ units, both the amount of H which B produces and the amount of H which A consumes. For A to maintain the same utility level, he can be given $A_{KH} \Delta$ additional units of K to compensate for the loss of Δ units of H. With the productive resources made available by reducing his production of H by Δ units, B can produce an additional $B_{KH} \Delta$ units of K. After this adjustment has taken place, the same amount of H, that is, $(H_B - \Delta) - (H_A - \Delta) = H_B - H_A$ units, is still available from B's output for other consumers. However, a larger amount of K, that is, $K_B - K_A + (B_{KH} - A_{KH})\Delta$ units, is now available from B's output for other consumers.

Similarly, it can be shown that if $A_{KH} > B_{KH}$, then increasing by Δ units the amounts of H which A consumes and B produces will maintain A's utility level while at the same time making a larger amount of K, that is, $K_B - K_A + (A_{KH} - B_{KH})\Delta$ units, available from B's output for other consumers.[6]

For a numerical example illustrating Theorem 5, suppose that A is initially consuming 20 units of H and 30 units of K, while B is initially producing 20 units of H and 30 units of K. Suppose that consumer A's marginal rate of substitution is 2 units of K for 1 unit of H, and that producer B's marginal rate of transformation is 3 units of K for 1 unit of H. The original surplus amounts of H and K from B's output which are available each period for other consumers are zero. If A's consumption and B's production of H are each reduced by 1 unit, however, then B can produce 3 additional units of K, but A requires only 2 additional units of K to maintain his original utility level. Hence 1 additional unit of K is now available from B's production for other consumers.

Additional marginal conditions can also be stated which must be satisfied if we are to have an efficient pattern of resource allocation. We shall not go into further detail on these, since both their statements and proofs are analogous to the five theorems we have already proved. Samuelson has

---

[6] Note that our supposition that A's consumption of H and K is entirely supplied by B makes the interpretation of our argument simpler, but it is not essential to its validity. If A consumed more of H or K than B produced, $| H_B - H_A |$ or $| K_B - K_A |$ is the amount of H or K beyond that produced by B which A must obtain from other producers. Even though $H_B - H_A$ or $K_B - K_A$ is negative, the utilities of other consumers are increased by making $K_B - K_A$ algebraically larger without changing the value of $H_B - H_A$; this is what our preceding argument accomplishes whenever $A_{KH} \neq B_{KH}$.

pointed out that these five theorems, plus the others which could be stated, are embodied in a single rule:

Necessary Marginal Conditions for an Optimum. Between any two variables, the marginal rates of substitution must be (subjectively) equal for all individuals, and (technically) equal for all alternative processes, with the common technical and subjective ratios being equivalent; otherwise there exists a technically attainable position that makes everyone better off.[7]

II. Market Structures and Economic Efficiency

A. THE PRICE SYSTEM, PERFECT COMPETITION, AND ECONOMIC EFFICIENCY

It can be shown that the necessary conditions for an efficient pattern of resource allocation embodied in the theorems of the preceding section are satisfied in a perfectly competitive economy. The key properties of a perfectly competitive economy which lead to this result are the following:

1. All factors and commodities are sold at fixed prices which are the same for every buyer and seller and which no individual buyer or seller can change.

2. In the long run there is an equality of quantity supplied and quantity demanded for all products, with the prices at which this occurs being the minimum possible prices at which the producers would be willing indefinitely to supply these products.

We have seen in Chapter 5 that for a household to maximize its utility, the marginal rate of substitution between any two commodities for that household must equal the ratio of the prices of the two commodities. Since in perfect competition all households purchase commodities at the same (constant) set of market prices, the marginal rates of substitution between any two commodities are the same for all pairs of owners. This shows that the conditions of Theorem 1 are fulfilled in perfect competition.

In perfect competition the input prices and the output prices are the same for all producers. We have seen in Chapter 7 that when a producer maximizes profits, he will allocate his production so that the marginal rate of product transformation between any two outputs equals the ratio of their selling prices. Hence the conditions of Theorem 2 must necessarily be satisfied in perfect competition. In an analogous manner, it can be shown that profit-maximizing behavior by producers results in the conditions of Theorems 3 and 4 being satisfied in perfect competition.

The conditions of Theorem 5 are necessarily fulfilled in perfect competition. The consumer sets his marginal rate of substitution between

---

[7] Paul A. Samuelson, "Comment" [on Kenneth E. Boulding, "Welfare Economics"], in *A Survey of Contemporary Economics, op. cit.*, p. 38.

any two commodities equal to the ratio of their selling prices and the producer sets his marginal rate of product transformation equal to the ratio of the same selling prices.

In summary, these five theorems and others of a similar nature which are implicit in the Samuelson rule are all satisfied in perfect competition; both consumers and producers are setting subjective and technical marginal rates of substitution equal to price ratios which are the same for all buyers and sellers.

B. Losses in Efficiency from Market Imperfections

Since the essence of the types of market imperfections discussed in Chapters 10–13 is that some prices are not accepted as given constants by all households and firms in the market, it can be shown that these types of market structures violate some of the necessary conditions for economic efficiency. For example, suppose that commodities H and K are both produced by the same firm, and that the firm has a monopoly in producing H but produces K in a perfectly competitive market. Then the conditions of Theorem 5 will not be fulfilled. The firm equates the marginal rate of transformation between K and H to the ratio of the marginal revenue of H to the selling price of K, whereas consumers equate the marginal rate of substitution between K and H to the ratio of the selling price of H to the selling price of K. Since for the monopolist the marginal revenue of H is less than the selling price of H, it follows that the conditions of Theorem 5 are not fulfilled.

As another example, suppose that commodity H is produced by a monopolist who is able to practice price discrimination in two different markets. Then the conditions of Theorem 1 will not be fulfilled. Consider any commodity K which is sold under conditions of perfect competition. Each consumer equates his marginal rate of substitution between K and H to the ratio of the selling prices of H and K. Since consumers in the two different markets pay different prices for H but the same price for K, it follows that the marginal rates of substitution between K and H will not be the same for consumers in the different markets, thus violating the conditions of Theorem 1.

Similarly, it can be shown that any modification of market prices for products or factors will violate one or more of the necessary conditions for economic efficiency. The power of business firms or households to modify market prices stems from their ability to regard price as a decision variable rather than as a constant given by the market. Such economic power for private decision-making units stems from some form of market imperfections of the types described in Chapters 10–13. Governments also have the power to modify market prices by such acts as the establishment of quotas, the granting of subsidies, and the imposition of sales taxes or import duties.

Government quotas set maximum limits on either the amounts of output which may be produced and sold in the market or the amounts of inputs which may be used for some productive purpose. Quotas on output may lead to the nonfulfillment of our first, second, third, and fifth necessary marginal conditions for economic efficiency. Quotas on input may lead to the nonfulfillment of the third and fourth necessary conditions. In mathematical terms, either of these types of governmental quotas, if they are binding, means that in equilibrium the firms or the households are unable to equate certain marginal rates of substitution or transformation to market price ratios. The equilibrium position is then a corner-type solution, characterized by particular inequalities relating marginal rates to market prices, rather than the equality relationships which we have found are necessary for economic efficiency.

Subsidies, excise taxes, or import duties all lead to a violation of the fifth necessary condition for economic efficiency, because they prevent the marginal rates of substitution between two products for consumers from being equal to the marginal rates of transformation between the same products for producers. A producer who receives a subsidy for making some commodity will produce more of it relative to a nonsubsidized commodity than the consumption preferences of consumers would dictate. Similarly, an excise tax leads consumers to buy less of the taxed commodity relative to other commodities than they otherwise would. Since an excise tax has no effect upon the marginal rates of transformation for producers, the consumers' subjective and the producers' technical marginal rates of substitution between the taxed and untaxed products no longer will be equal.

C. Discrepancies Between Social and Private Benefits or Costs

It must be recognized that before we can call an economy efficient, certain marginal conditions relating social benefits and social costs must be satisfied. For example, if the marginal gain to society as a whole from expanding one particular activity exceeds the marginal loss to society as a whole which results when other activities are curtailed (a consequence of society's limited resources), then the first activity should be expanded. We have so far shown only that perfect competition fulfills the necessary conditions for economic efficiency which were stated in terms of private benefits and costs.

It is not at all clear that the equating of private marginal benefits with private marginal costs which occurs in a perfectly competitive economy results in similar equalities between social marginal benefits and social marginal costs. In fact it is easy to envision situations where this is not the case. For example, a farmer who dams a stream running across his land creates benefits to all landowners downstream. In a perfectly competitive economy a dam which is clearly beneficial to society as a whole may not be built because its private value to any individual is less than its cost of construction.

Another example of the divergence between social costs and private costs is the smoke nuisance. Smoke is sometimes a by-product which is produced by firms while they are manufacturing useful commodities. This smoke is indeed a cost to society as a whole (in terms of increased laundry and cleaning bills, increased incidence of respiratory diseases, etc.) and yet it is frequently not regarded as a private cost by any individual producer. Thus, the total amount of smoke which is produced as a by-product may be excessive from the standpoint of over-all economic efficiency.

Our two examples illustrate that where there are discrepancies between social benefits and private benefits or between social costs and private costs, the utility-maximizing decisions of households and the profit-maximizing decisions of business firms may not lead to an efficient pattern of resource allocation even in a perfectly competitive economy. In such circumstances, it is conceivable that some actions can be taken by the government to create the conditions under which each individual decision-making unit's pursuit of its self-interest will lead to an efficient pattern of resource allocation. Thus our first example, in which there was a discrepancy between the social benefits and the private benefits from a dam, illustrates the reason why in fact such projects as dams, highways, airports, schools, stadiums, etc., are frequently financed and operated by governments rather than by private firms. Our second example, in which there was a discrepancy between the social costs and the private costs of smoke, illustrates why such types of social legislation as smoke control laws, unemployment compensation insurance, compulsory vaccination laws, etc., may be passed by governments. Where the equating of private marginal benefits with private marginal costs does not lead to the equating of social marginal benefits with social marginal costs, it may be necessary to supplement the economic market process by the political governmental process in order to attain an efficient pattern of resource allocation.

III. Economic Efficiency, Social Welfare, and the Distribution of Wealth

In Section I.B. we defined the *contract curve* as the locus of points of tangency between the indifference surfaces of various individuals. An economy is efficient if and only if it results in a point lying on the contract curve. When the economy is not efficient, then the utility level of at least one individual can be increased without decreasing the utility levels of the rest of society. Thus economic efficiency is a necessary condition for maximizing the value of the social welfare function. Economic efficiency is not, however, a sufficient condition for maximizing the value of the social welfare function, since not all points on the contract curve are equally desirable. For example, a small percentage of the population might be receiving a high percentage of the economy's income (although no one individual might receive enough income to violate the assumption of atomistic competition) while a large percentage of the population might be receiving a small percentage of the economy's income. This might result in a society in which considerable economic resources were devoted to the production of yachts and caviar while many members of the society were living at a near-starvation level of subsistence. Such a society could satisfy all the conditions necessary for economic efficiency, and hence represent a point on the contract curve. It is likely, however, that few people would regard such a society as having the most socially desirable pattern of resource allocation.

At best, the arguments of Section II indicate that perfect competition may lead to an efficient pattern of resource allocation, especially when any required governmental actions are taken to remove discrepancies between social and private benefits or costs. It is not at all clear, however, that perfect competition leads to that particular point on the contract curve where the value of the social welfare function is maximized.

It can be shown that the initial distribution of wealth in a perfectly competitive economy is an important factor in determining the particular point on the contract curve which will be attained. Furthermore, it can be shown that movements from one point on the contract curve to any other point on the contract curve could be obtained under perfect competition if it were somehow possible to effect an appropriate redistribution of wealth among the members of society. Thus perfect competition may be viewed as being compatible with the attainment of maximum social welfare, but it does not inevitably lead to this result.

If the long-run equilibrium position attained under perfect competition does not maximize the value of the social welfare function, then it is possible for the government to redistribute wealth in an attempt to increase social welfare. This might be accomplished by the imposition of taxes, particularly income taxes and inheritance taxes. As long as such taxes are not strictly proportional to income or wealth, they result in some redistribution of wealth. The main justification which can be made for the type of progressive income and inheritance taxes which are frequently found in Western capitalistic economies is that the resulting redistribution of wealth (at least in the eyes of the proponents of such taxes) increases social welfare. If an economy in which such taxes are imposed were otherwise economically efficient, the effect of these taxes would be to move the economy from one point on its contract curve to another.

IV. Summary

Consumer well-being, as measured by the value of the social welfare function, is the criterion for determining whether one pattern of resource allocation is preferable to another. Although the social welfare function is a function of each individual's utility level, we generally stop short of making interpersonal comparisons of utility. Hence the social welfare function provides a partial, rather than a complete, ordering of national economic well-being.

Welfare economics can be interpreted as the economics of efficiency. A particular state of the economy is efficient whenever it is impossible to reallocate resources in a way which will increase the utility of at least one person without decreasing the utility of any other person. An efficient pattern of resource allocation is represented by a point lying on the contract curve, which is the locus of points of tangency between the indifference surfaces of various individuals.

Several necessary marginal conditions for economic efficiency were derived in this chapter. The first condition states that the marginal rates of substitution between two commodities should be the same for all consumers. Whenever this is not the case, a transfer of some of these commodities between the two individuals can increase the utilities of both.

The second necessary condition for economic efficiency states that the marginal rates of transformation between two products should be the same for all producers. If this is not the case, then production of at least one of the products can be increased without decreasing production of the other by shifting production of each commodity toward its relatively more efficient producer.

The third necessary condition for economic efficiency states that the marginal physical productivities of any factor in a specific product should be the same for all producers. Otherwise, the total output produced by any given amount of factor can be increased by shifting some of the factor from the low-productivity to the high-productivity firms.

The fourth necessary condition for economic efficiency states that the marginal rates of technical substitution between any two factors must be the same for all producers. If this is not the case, then fewer total amounts of factors can be used in producing the same final output if each factor is shifted toward that firm which, on relative terms, can use it more efficiently.

The fifth necessary condition for economic efficiency which we proved states that the marginal rates of substitution of two products for consumers must equal the marginal rates of transformation of the same two products for firms. Otherwise, consumers can be made better off without utilizing any more productive factors if the production of these two commodities is suitably reallocated.

Other necessary conditions for economic efficiency could be developed. These necessary conditions were all derivable from a single marginal rule: between any two economic variables (inputs or outputs), the marginal rates of substitution must be (subjectively) equal for all individuals, and (technically) equal for all alternative processes, with the common technical and subjective ratios being equivalent.

We showed that perfectly competitive markets lead to the fulfillment of the necessary conditions for economic efficiency previously stated. All these necessary conditions do not, however, necessarily constitute a set of sufficient conditions for maximizing the value of the social welfare function—or even for achieving economic efficiency.

Each household and each firm in perfect competition regards all market prices as given constants beyond their control. Given these market prices, the households and firms separately attempt to maximize their utility or their profit functions. These simultaneous attempts at utility and profit maximization lead, through the general equilibrium system, to the determination of a set of factor market and product market prices which simultaneously clears all markets—i.e., which simultaneously equates supply with demand for each product and each factor.

We have seen that the equilibrium conditions for the individual household or firm maximizing its own utility or profit function involve setting marginal rates of substitution between products, between factors, or between products and factors equal to ratios of product or factor prices. Since each individual household and firm is facing the same market prices in a perfectly competitive economy, these marginal rates of substitution must be equal for all firms and all households.

If any individual household or firm were able to control market prices for a product or a factor through its own actions, or if any two households and firms did not face the same market prices for products or for factors, then the individual utility- and profit-maximizing behavior of households and firms would not automatically lead to the equating of marginal rates of substitution for all individuals, for all alternative processes, and for all firms. Thus any type of market imperfection leads to violations of one or more of the necessary conditions for economic efficiency.

Although our analysis of the effects of market imperfections on economic efficiency has concentrated on distortions which arise from the pricing power of individual firms and households, we indicated that market imperfections may also arise through particular types of governmental actions which interfere with the free workings of a price system. Such governmental interferences include quotas, subsidies, and import duties or excise taxes.

We have seen that there may be discrepancies between private and social benefits or between private and social costs. Where such discrepancies exist, some actions by the government may be necessary to create the conditions under which each individual household's and business firm's pursuit of its self-interest will lead to an efficient pattern of resource allocation.

Since not all economically efficient points are equally desirable, perfect competition does not necessarily lead to that pattern of resource allocation which maximizes the value of the social welfare function. By redistributing wealth through income taxes and inheritance taxes, the government may attempt to increase social welfare by moving from one point on the contract curve to another.

SUGGESTED READINGS

These recommendations are in addition to the footnote references cited in this chapter.

BATOR, FRANCIS M., "The Simple Analytics of Welfare Maximization," *American Economic Review*, XLVII, No. 1 (March, 1957), 22–59.

DAVIS, O. A., AND A. WHINSTON, "The Economics of Urban Renewal," *Law and Contemporary Problems*, XXVI, No. 1 (Winter, 1961), 101–17.

FAIO, R. C., "The Optimal Distribution of Income," *Quarterly Journal of Economics*, LXXXV (November, 1971), 551–79.

FELDMAN, P., "Efficiency, Distribution, and the Role of Government in a Market Economy," *Journal of Political Economy*, LXXIX (May/June, 1971), 508–26.

FELDSTEIN, M. S., "Distributional Equity and the Optimal Structure of Public Prices," *American Economic Review*, LXII (March, 1972), 32–36.

KNIGHT, F. H., "Some Fallacies in the Interpretation of Social Cost," in *Readings in Price Theory*, George J. Stigler and Kenneth E. Boulding, eds., chap. 8. Homewood, Ill.: Richard D. Irwin, Inc., 1952.

LIPSEY, R. G., AND K. LANCASTER, "The General Theory of Second Best," *Review of Economic Studies*, XXIV, No. 1 (1956), 11–32.

PHELPS, EDMUND S., ed., *Private Wants and Public Needs*, pp. 102–46. New York: W. W. Norton & Company, Inc., 1962. (Articles by Francis M. Bator, O. H. Brownlee, Walter W. Heller, and George J. Stigler.)

SCHALL, L., "Technological Externalities and Resource Allocation," *Journal of Political Economy*, LXXIX (September/October, 1971), 983–1001.

TINBERGEN, JAN, "Welfare Economics and Income Distribution," *American Economic Review, Papers and Proceedings*, XLVII, Part 2 (May, 1957), 490–503.

Chapter Twenty-One

Some Guidelines for
Microeconomic Policy

In this book we have examined in detail various types of market structures and their implications for resource allocation. We have discussed the conditions for an efficient economy. In addition, we have considered a number of new approaches to analyzing the behavior of business firms. Our focus throughout this book has been on business firms and their role in the resource allocation process. We are now in a position to generate some guidelines for public policy. Many of these recommendations must be tentative because of the lack of empirical evidence on some critical issues, and many may stem from our personal values. Nevertheless, we think that it is useful for the student to see how public policy guidelines flow from the economic theory which has been developed.

I. Some Unsolved Problems in Welfare Economics

We have seen in Chapter 20 that the traditional analysis of welfare economics, based upon models of behavior under static, certainty conditions, makes at least a *prima facie* case for perfect competition as a socially desirable form of market structure. Under this pattern of industrial organization, the individual self-interest-seeking behavior of business firms and of consumers will lead to the fulfillment of the necessary marginal conditions for economic efficiency. Furthermore, we have seen that any type of market imperfection causes some of the necessary conditions for economic efficiency to be violated. We should, however, remember that the necessary conditions for economic efficiency discussed in Chapter 20 are *not* sufficient conditions for maximizing the value of the social welfare function. Perfect competition, even under static, certainty conditions, may not automatically lead to the best of all possible worlds. As a guide to public policy, the *prima facie* case for perfectly competitive markets becomes even more precarious when we recognize that actual business and consumer behavior takes place in a dynamic and uncertain world.

Even though imperfectly competitive markets can easily be shown to violate some of the necessary marginal conditions for economic efficiency, whether on balance these markets function less effectively from the standpoint of economic welfare than do perfect markets is not an easy question to answer. Static inefficiencies may still be compatible with desirable dynamic attributes. The case for perfect competition under static, certainty conditions assumes that consumer tastes (i.e., utility functions) are given and that the range of available products and productive techniques are themselves fixed and known to everybody. Since it is clear that the behavior of firms in the real world will in fact affect consumer tastes, the range and quality of available products, and the techniques of production, it is necessary to reassess the empirical relevance of the conclusions reached in Chapter 20.

In this section, we shall argue that, under some types of imperfectly competitive market structures, business firms allocate a larger percentage of their resources to activities which result in technological change, product variation, and changing consumer tastes than would be the case under perfect competition. Whether on balance these dynamic aspects of business behavior under imperfect competition contribute more to social welfare than the losses resulting from the static inefficiencies of imperfect competition is a difficult question to answer. We shall be able only to indicate the nature of the difficulties involved in trying to answer this question.

A. TECHNOLOGICAL CHANGE

Technological change will increase the set of products, resources, and techniques available to firms. Technological change, if it were to arise at no cost to society, would undeniably be desirable. There are clear benefits which can be derived if firms can choose from a wider range of products, resources, and techniques. Producers would not choose to use the new developments unless they led to higher profits, and consumers would not buy the new products unless they contributed to higher consumer satisfactions. As long as there are competitive forces present in the market place, technological change, if it were costless, would be beneficial.

Realistically, however, we must recognize that technological change cannot arise at no cost to society. In order to develop cheaper production methods, procedures for obtaining higher-quality output, new types of products, or new types of productive factors, real economic resources must be expended on research and development. Since some resources are devoted to research and development as a result of the profit-seeking decisions of individual business firms, it is necessary to consider how various types of market structures might encourage or discourage technological change.

Economists disagree on the ways in which size of firms and form of market structure affect technological progress. Strong statements on both sides of the question appear in the literature, but relatively little evidence has been presented. Table 21–1 illustrates Maclaurin's approach to this problem. It is a highly subjective approach in which the classification of industries was made primarily on the basis of Maclaurin's judgment; not all economists necessarily agree with the classifications. Table 21–1 appears to show that technological progress has been greatest in less competitive

TABLE 21–1

DEGREE OF MONOPOLY AND RATE OF TECHNOLOGICAL PROGRESS IN
THIRTEEN AMERICAN INDUSTRIES

Industry	Degree of Monopoly	Rate of Technological Progress
Chemical manufacturing (heavy)	High	Highest
Photographic manufacturing	High	Highest
Oil refining	High	Highest
Airplane manufacturing	Medium	Highest
Electric light manufacturing	High	High
Radio and television set manufacturing	Medium	High
Automobile manufacturing	High	Medium
Steel	High	Medium
Paper manufacturing (except newsprint)	Low	Medium
Food processing	Medium	Lower
Cotton textile manufacturing	Low	Lower
Coal mining	Low	Lower
House assembling in tracts	Lowest	Lower

SOURCE: W. Rupert MacLaurin, "Technological Progress in Some American Industries," *American Economic Review, Papers and Proceedings*, 44, No. 2 (May, 1954), tables 1 and 2; 180–81.

TABLE 21–2

RESEARCH AND DEVELOPMENT EXPENDITURES AS A PERCENTAGE OF SALES

Industry	Number of Employees			
	50–499	500–999	1,000–4,999	5,000 and over
Food and kindred products	Not available	0.04	0.16	0.19
Chemicals and allied products	1.16	1.77	1.79	2.90
Fabricated metal products and ordnance	Not available	0.79	0.54	0.40
Machinery	0.63	0.83	1.28	1.80
Electrical equipment	1.96	1.00	1.70	2.80
Professional and scientific instruments	1.65	2.64	1.66	3.00

SOURCE: Henry H. Villard, "Reply," *Journal of Political Economy*, 67 (1959), 634, table 1.

industries. Maclaurin himself felt " . . . that some degree of monopoly is essential to technological progress; on the other [hand] that some freedom of entry and the spirit of competition are stimulating to progress."[1]

A more recent approach to this problem has examined the research and development expenditures of business firms. Table 21–2 contains Villard's estimates of research and development expenditures as a percentage of sales for various sizes of firms in six different industries. Unfortunately it is not possible to reach any firm conclusions about the effects of market structure on research and development. Table 21–2 does indicate that in three of the six industries there is an increasing percentage spent on research and development from the smallest through the largest size classes of firms, and also that in five of the six industries the largest firms spent the highest percentages on research and development.[2] Since oligopolies are associated with "bigness," this latter conclusion establishes a tenuous relationship between market structure and research and development expenditures.

The status of the relationship between market structure and technological change is adequately summarized in the conclusion of a recent study: "Hence, though positive association between R and D intensity [i.e., the percentage of sales devoted to research and development expenditures] and industrial concentration apparently exists, it must be described as weak,

---

[1] W. Rupert Maclaurin, "Technological Progress in Some American Industries," *American Economic Review, Papers and Proceedings*, 44, No. 2 (May, 1954), 182.

[2] The data on which Table 21–2 is based have been interpreted in a different fashion by Jacob Schmookler, "Bigness, Fewness, and Research," *Journal of Political Economy*, 67 (1959), 628–32.

as must also be the case for industrial concentration as a stimulus to R and D, both in absolute and relative terms."[3]

We have already indicated that under static, certainty conditions, the existence of oligopoly leads to a reduction in economic welfare. If in fact the evidence that oligopoly firms play an important role in technological change is valid, then we may be caught on the horns of a dilemma. Do the desirable effects of the increased technological change which oligopoly firms promote outweigh the loss in social welfare which results from the pricing power of the oligopolies?

Perhaps as a guide to public policy we should not try to measure these opposing effects quantitatively and thereby approve or disapprove of oligopoly depending upon which effect appears stronger. Instead, we might ask whether there are alternative methods by which technological change can be encouraged other than through the creation of oligopoly. The possible role of government must be considered in this respect. Since World War II the American government directly has undertaken a great deal of research and development which has resulted in important technological benefits for the civilian economy. The ability of the government to encourage technological change is great, both through direct payments to business firms for conducting research and development and through research grants to universities and other nonprofit organizations. It is by no means clear whether governmental encouragement of technological change is in the long run more or less efficient than having the business sector organized in such a way that a similar amount of research and development activity would be conducted entirely by private firms without any government subsidization.[4]

---

[3] D. Hamberg, "Size of Firm, Oligopoly, and Research: The Evidence," *Canadian Journal of Economics and Political Science*, 30, No. 1 (February, 1964), 75.

Additional evidence that oligopoly markets may be particularly conducive to the encouragement of technological change is provided in a study of the fur industry by Fuchs. He has shown that the major technological changes which have occurred in the fur industry, i.e., the development of new mutations of fur-bearing animals and the dying of pelts, have been initiated by the breeders and tanners, those sectors of the fur industry which most nearly have an oligopoly market structure. Those sectors of the industry which are most nearly perfectly competitive, the manufacturers of fur coats and the retail stores which sell them, have contributed virtually nothing to technological change. See Victor R. Fuchs, *The Economics of the Fur Industry* (New York: Columbia University Press, 1957), especially pp. 35–36; 81–82.

A recent article by Mansfield presents additional empirical evidence on technological progress, although it by no means answers the question raised in the text. See Edwin Mansfield, "Size of Firm, Market Structure, and Innovation," *Journal of Political Economy*, 71, No. 6 (December, 1963), 556–76.

[4] In 1956, of an estimated $9 billion spent for research and development in the United States, almost 60 per cent of the total was financed by the government, even though almost 75 per cent of the total represented research actually performed by industry. See Henry H. Villard, "Competition, Oligopoly, and Research," *Journal of Political Economy*, 66 (1958), 486.

Another problem in assessing the impact of technological change on economic efficiency and social welfare is the possibility that technological change is occurring too rapidly. It is possible that technological change has resulted in many products and production techniques being scrapped because of obsolescence long before their physical usefulness had ended. Especially suspect in this regard is the type of built-in product obsolescence which some large oligopoly firms are alleged to have introduced into consumer products to expand the replacement market. Do some firms design automobiles, refrigerators, and other products in a way which prevents their lasting as long as possible, in order to create the need for replacement sales within a few years? If there is any truth to this charge, it is clear that more vigorous competition in-the product markets would tend to reduce this undesirable practice. With relatively free entry, new producers would enter the industry and capture a large share of the market by building more durable products. If anything, recent developments in automobiles (longer guarantee periods), razor blades (stainless steel blades), and light bulbs (long-life bulbs) seem to indicate that in the United States firms in fact try to improve the quality and longevity of their products.

B. PRODUCT VARIATION

The social welfare implications that we have derived in Chapter 20 rest upon the assumption that there exists a given set of products. We have seen in analyzing imperfect markets, however, that one strategy often employed by firms to increase their profits is the introduction of new varieties of a product, hoping that each new variety will shift the firm's demand curve upward. One of the assumptions of a perfectly competitive market is that all firms produce a homogeneous product. When this is the case, there is no reason, other than price alone, for consumers to prefer one firm's product to another. As we have seen in Chapter 4, product homogeneity leads to uniformity of prices in perfect markets.

Where markets are imperfect, however, and where firms possess a considerable degree of pricing power, there are incentives for firms to try to produce variants of the basic product in order to appeal to particular segments of the market. To the extent that the variations between products are real and correctly perceived by consumers, then the greater freedom of choice consequently available better enables consumers to select the exact assortment of commodities which will maximize their satisfactions.

In a dynamic economy, it is possible that imperfectly competitive market structures encourage firms to develop product variety, and thereby serve consumer interests better than perfectly competitive markets. Some of the inefficiencies of imperfect markets developed under a static analysis may be mitigated by dynamic considerations of product variation. It is necessary, however, to compare the relative magnitudes of the increased consumer satisfactions resulting from greater product variety with the losses in economic welfare which arise from the pricing policies of imperfectly competitive firms. Furthermore, there may also be increased production costs and higher advertising and distribution costs arising from product variations. On balance, it is not clear whether those market imperfections which lead to product variation increase or decrease social welfare. Is a society in which consumers have smaller amounts of toothpaste and a smaller total number of automobiles, as a consequence of their being able to choose from among fifty different brands of toothpaste and twenty different brands of automobiles, better or worse than a society in which consumers have greater amounts of a single standard type of toothpaste and a larger total number of a single standard type of automobile? The answer is not obvious. It appears that the value system which characterizes most capitalist societies provides a different answer to this type of question than does the value system which characterizes most communist societies.

C. Advertising Which Changes Consumer Tastes

Some types of advertising serve a desirable economic function. When advertising primarily provides information to prospective buyers about the range of products available, their prices, and their characteristics, it increases the degree of knowledge which consumers have. The increased knowledge should enable consumers to make product choices which are more likely to increase their satisfactions. At least within moderate limits, there is probably little dispute about the merits of this type of advertising.

There are other forms of advertising, however, which do not disseminate information but which are aimed at changing the preference functions of consumers. This latter type of advertising is prevalent in some types of imperfect markets. In these markets, firms are likely to use advertising to create brand preferences, thus obtaining a partial monopoly position and some control over selling prices.

This type of advertising increases the demand for a particular product by changing tastes so that consumers have a relatively higher preference for the advertised product. When consumer tastes change, however, it is not clear how this affects social welfare. Welfare economics uses consumer tastes as the criterion for measuring social welfare. When these tastes themselves change, the measuring sticks of welfare economics also change.

In trying to compare two successive states of the economy, i.e., two different patterns of resource allocation, it is not clear whether the before-tastes or the after-tastes should be used as standards when these are different. An apparent paradox may arise when on the basis of preadvertising tastes one economic state is preferable, whereas on the basis of post-advertising tastes a different economic state is preferable. The criterion of consumer well-being, which is the heart of modern welfare economics, does not indicate who the economic arbitrator should be in this circumstance. To put the matter somewhat differently, who should assume the role of economic dictator to determine which resource allocation pattern is preferable? Economic activity which affects consumer tastes cannot be evaluated on the basis of these changing tastes.

II. Some Policy Guidelines

Let us now indicate how microeconomic analysis can provide some tentative guides to public policy. To place these recommendations in perspective, let us first summarize the present state of the American economy.

The American economy consists of a mixture of many types of market structures. Some markets satisfy reasonably closely the assumptions of perfect competition. Although other markets violate some of these assumptions, they still may produce similar results, i.e., prices which tend to equal marginal costs. A few industries are single-firm monopolies, and in these there are probably large gaps between prices and marginal costs, except where public regulation intervenes. Governmental regulation may be imperfect, however, so that even regulated monopolies do not necessarily equate selling prices with marginal costs. A large number of important American industries are organized as oligopolies, and here we are not able to say confidently how selling prices are related to marginal costs. Probably prices tend to exceed marginal costs in oligopolies, but by how much is not easily predictable. In many factor markets there are imperfections leading to gaps between factor returns and the values of marginal products. It is difficult to measure in any precise fashion the extent to which various types of market structures exist in the economy. Table 21–3 represents one economist's attempt to estimate this.

TABLE 21–3

PERCENTAGE OF NATIONAL INCOME IN THE UNITED STATES GENERATED IN
DIFFERENT MARKET STRUCTURES

Type of Market Structure	Percentage of National Income
Competition	55
Oligopoly	35
Monopoly	10

SOURCE: This is our interpretation of the data presented in G. Warren Nutter, "Competition: Direct and Devious," *American Economic Review, Papers and Proceedings*, 44, No. 2 (May, 1954), 75–76.

The extent of imperfections in the competitive pattern of the American economy, make it unlikely that any close approximation to the ideal static pattern of resource allocation exists. It is difficult to say how far our existing pattern of resource allocation departs from the social welfare ideal. Undoubtedly too much of some and too little of other goods and services are produced. Because of the competition that does exist between firms, and because of the possibility of new entrants in many markets, great departures from ideal output probably do not occur for many products for long periods of time. Furthermore, the government's antitrust policies keep some types of monopoly practices from attaining serious proportions. The government's regulation of those publicly licensed monopolies which are justified because of economies of scale, while far from perfect, probably prevents too large a marginal cost-price gap from developing.[5]

In addition to noting that the existing resource allocation pattern in the American economy is probably not ideal, we can provide some guides for public policy in this area. Increasing the extent of economic pressures felt by firms probably leads to greater economic efficiencies and increases in social welfare. One manner in which this might be furthered is by trying to insure the highest possible degree of competition in the market place. Barriers to entry, whether they arise because of private or public action, should be reduced as much as is consistent with economic freedom. Reducing international barriers to free trade may produce a double benefit for the American economy. Not only will the static efficiency considerations (which can easily be shown to favor free trade) be furthered, but the impact of increased competition in the market place on American oligopoly firms may also provide a spur toward increasing their productive efficiencies and reducing some of their monopoly profits.

We have pointed out a number of times that on balance it is difficult to evaluate the desirability of oligopoly. On the one hand, static analysis indicates that the existence of oligopolies is incompatible with the attainment of some of the necessary conditions for economic efficiency. At the same time, however, we have argued that because of economies of scale and the effects of oligopoly firms on technological progress and product variation, oligopoly may be a desirable form of market structure. There is a

---

[5] Harberger made an attempt to get a crude measure of the welfare losses resulting from a misallocation of resources due to monopoly elements in the American economy during 1924–28. He found that ". . . an estimate of by how much consumer welfare would have improved if resources had been optimally allocated throughout American manufacturing in the late twenties . . . is 59 million dollars—less than one-tenth of 1 per cent of the national income. Translated into today's national income and today's prices, this comes out to 225 million dollars, or less than $1.50 for every man, woman, and child in the United States." See Arnold C. Harberger, "Monopoly and Resource Allocation," *American Economic Review, Papers and Proceedings*, 44, No. 2 (May, 1954), 82.

clear role for antitrust policy to play in enforcing competition in oligopolistic industries. It would be undesirable to permit oligopolies to collude or to erect artificial barriers to entry. Because of the potentially desirable aspects of oligopoly, we do not advocate an unrestricted policy of dissolving oligopoly firms and replacing them with a number of smaller firms. The critical factor, we believe, is maintaining freedom of entry in oligopolistic industries. If this is accomplished, then the static inefficiencies of oligopoly will be minimized and the dynamic advantages will be attained.

In order to approximate more closely the assumption of perfect knowledge, any public actions which increase the knowledge possessed by economic agents are beneficial. Laws which enforce honest and fair labeling on textiles, drugs, processed food products, etc., are steps in this direction. Standardization of nomenclature and the development of governmental standards also make it possible for purchasers to buy with greater knowledge. Not all attempts to increase knowledge of the market need arise from governmental actions. Some private groups, such as trade associations and consumer organizations, are active in promoting economic knowledge in the market place.

Any measures which increase the mobility of resources lead to a more efficient economy. Long-run equilibrium adjustments may come too slowly (or never be attained at all) if resource-mobility barriers are too great. The ability of our economy to adjust efficiently to changes in consumer tastes and to changes in technology depends upon resource mobility. Some public policies aimed at increasing mobility are retraining displaced workers for new occupations and relocating workers from depressed areas to areas where there is a relative shortage of labor. Such devices as government guarantees on mortgages and other types of loans, making them more liquid and more marketable, can be regarded as attempts to increase the mobility of financial resources.

Discrimination based on race, religion, or sex decreases the mobility of economic resources. The refusal of some firms to hire Negroes forces them to work in occupations where the value of their marginal product is less than it otherwise could be. This violates some of the necessary conditions for an efficient pattern of resource allocation thereby reducing the aggregate amount of goods and services available for consumption in the entire economy. Thus such measures as the fair employment practices clause in the Civil Rights Act of 1964 can be recommended on the basis of microeconomic policy considerations as well as for ethical reasons.

The behavioral theory of the firm considerations in Chapter 17 and our analysis of Williamson's model in Chapter 18 suggest that it is desirable to try to align the interests of managers with the interests of stockholders. This will increase economic efficiency by reducing the amounts of resources which the managers of firms absorb in the pursuit of their private interests.

The market responses of firms to shifts in supply and demand will probably be smoother and more efficient if management is trying to maximize profits rather than to pursue its own interests, especially when the firms are in competitive or approximately competitive industries. Policies which increase external representation on boards of directors will reduce the power of managers to control the firms' resources for their own ends. Those forms of executive compensation which closely tie managers' financial gains to the stockholders' interests (e.g., profit-related bonuses and stock option plans) are also helpful in this regard.

An increase in the skills of managers will enable them to run business firms in a more efficient manner. One way of obtaining these increased skills is through the professional education of managers in graduate schools of business. The result of this type of training is to orient managers toward optimal decision making. Managers should therefore not only be technically able to make better decisions, but they will be more highly motivated to make those decisions which produce the greatest benefits to the firm. In general the more successful we are as a nation in management education, the more efficient will our pattern of resource allocation become.

In Chapter 20, we indicated that even when all the necessary conditions for economic efficiency are satisfied, social welfare may still not be maximized if social costs and benefits differ from private costs and benefits. Here we can only reiterate that public policies which help align private costs with social costs and private benefits with social benefits will lead to an improved economy. To some extent this may be possible through government taxes or subsidies. In other cases it may be necessary for the government to prohibit certain types of private actions. In still other cases the government may have to undertake some economic functions itself to insure that desirable public expenditures will be made.

Although microeconomic analysis is not yet at the point where it can provide a complete guide to public policy and unambiguous answers to all present-day economic issues, nonetheless we feel that it can be used to shed some light on a variety of important issues. In summary, we feel that desirable public policy measures should

1. Increase the economic pressures on firms
2. Increase freedom of entry into imperfect markets
3. Encourage technological change
4. Increase market knowledge of economic units
5. Reduce barriers to resource mobility
6. Eliminate discrimination which is based on race. religion, or sex
7. Align the interests of managers more closely with the interests of stockholders
8. Increase the skills of managers through improved academic training
9. Align social costs and benefits with private costs and benefits.

SUGGESTED READINGS

These recommendations are in addition to the footnote references cited in this chapter.

ADAMS, WALTER, "Public Policy in a Free Enterprise Economy," in *The Structure of American Industry*, 3rd ed., Walter Adams, ed., chap. 15. New York: The Macmillan Company, 1961.

ANDREWS, K. R., "Public Responsibility in the Private Corporation," *Journal of Industrial Economics*, XX (April, 1972), 135–45.

ECKSTEIN, O., AND J. V. KRUTILLA, "The Cost of Federal Money, Hells Canyon, and Economic Efficiency," Parts 1 and 2, *National Tax Journal*, XI (March/June, 1958), 1–20, 114–28.

VON FURSTENBERG, G. M., AND D. C. MUELLER, "The Pareto Optimal Approach to Income Redistribution: A Fiscal Application," *American Economic Review*, LXI (September, 1971), 628–37.

KAYSEN, C., AND D. F. TURNER, *Antitrust Policy*. Cambridge: Harvard University Press, 1959.

MANSFIELD, EDWIN, ed., *Monopoly Power and Economic Performance*, Parts 1 and 3. New York: W. W. Norton & Company, Inc., 1964. (Part 1 papers by G. J. Stigler, S. H. Slichter, T. Scitovsky, J. A. Schumpeter, J. K. Galbraith, J. Jewkes, D. Sawers, R. Stillerman, and E. Mansfield; Part 3 papers by C. Wilcox, T. Arnold et al., *Fortune*, A. E. Kahn, and E. S. Mason.)

PHELPS, EDMUND S., ed., *The Goal of Economic Growth*, pp. 94–152. New York: W. W. Norton & Company, Inc., 1962. (Articles by E. S. Phelps, T. W. Schultz, G. S. Becker, B. F. Massell and R. R. Nelson, and F. Machlup.)

SIMONS, HENRY C., *Economic Policy for a Free Society*, chap. 2. Chicago: University of Chicago Press, 1948.

STIGLER, GEORGE J., "The Goals of Economic Policy," *Journal of Business*, XXXI (July, 1958), 169–76.

STOIKOV, VLADIMER, "The Allocation of Scientific Effort: Some Important Aspects," *Quarterly Journal of Economics*, LXXVII, No. 2 (May, 1964), 307–23.

Appendix

Review of Optimization

by Marie-Thérèse Flaherty

I. Optimization of a Function of One Variable

Consider the real-valued function $f(x)$ defined on the real interval $[a, b]$ with a continuous second derivative, as pictured in Figure A–1, where the points labeled A through F are local maxima and minima.

A *local maximum* of the function $f(x)$ occurs at $x = y$ (points A, C, and E of Figure A–1) if there exists a $\partial > 0$ such that for all x in the interval defined by $|y - x| < \partial$, $f(y) \geq f(x)$. That is, $f(y)$ is greater than or equal to $f(x)$ for all x near y.

Similarly, define a *local minimum* of $f(x)$ at y (points B, D, and F of Figure A–1) if there exists $\partial > 0$ such that for all x in the interval defined by $|y - x| < \partial$, $f(y) \leq f(x)$. That is, $f(y)$ is less than or equal to $f(x)$ for all x near y.

The *global maximum* of $f(x)$ occurs at $x = y$ (point A of Figure A–1) if $f(y) > f(x)$ for all x in the interval $[a, b]$ on which $f(x)$ is defined.

Similarly, the *global minimum* of $f(x)$ occurs at $x = y$ (point D of Figure A–1) if $f(y) < f(x)$ for all x in the interval $[a, b]$ on which $f(x)$ is defined.

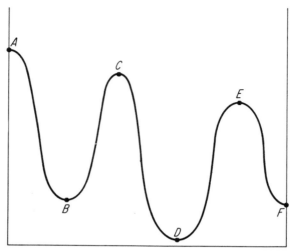

FIGURE A–1.

The following sections establish analytically necessary and sufficient conditions that a function $f(x)$ attain a local maximum or minimum at y if y is interior to the set X on which $f(x)$ is defined (local interior maxima or minima). Define x, an element of the set X, to be *interior to* X if there exists a $\partial > 0$ such that all x in the interval (set) defined by $|y - x| < \partial$ are elements of X. Points x which are not interior points of X may satisfy the definition of points at which $f(x)$ attains local maxima or minima but may not satisfy the analytic conditions derived for local maxima and minima; in such cases the definition must be applied directly. In particular, in a closed interval $[a, b]$ such as in Figure A–1, the end points of the interval must also be checked directly to see if they may be maximum or minimum points of the function. In Figure A–1, point A is both a local and global maximum of $f(x)$, while point F is a local minimum of $f(x)$.

Once the set of local maxima or minima is determined, iterative methods of comparison may be used to identify the global maximum or minimum value of $f(x)$.

II. Interior Local Optimization
of a Function of One Variable

Analytically, for a twice continuously differentiable function $f(x)$ defined on a set X to have a local interior maximum at a point y it is necessary that:

$$f'(y) = 0^1 \tag{A–1}$$

---

[1] $f'(x)$ denotes $df(x)/dx$ throughout this Appendix.

$$f''(y) \leq 0^2.$$ (A-2)

Intuitively, these conditions require that at y, (1) the function be neither increasing nor decreasing and (2) the slope of the function be nonincreasing. These necessary conditions may be quickly derived.[3]

Assume $f(x)$ has a *local interior* maximum at $x = y$. By the Mean Value Theorem:[4]

$$f(x) - f(y) = (x - y)f'[y + \theta(x - y)] \text{ for } 0 < \theta < 1.$$

Suppose $f'(y) > 0$. Then because $f(x)$ is continuously differentiable on X, there exists an interval in X defined by $|y - x| < m$ with $m > 0$ within which the following inequality holds everywhere: $f'(x) > 0$. So for all values of x greater than y in this interval $f(y) - f(x) < 0$. But this contradicts the hypothesis that $f(y)$ is a maximum. Similarly, the assumption $f'(y) < 0$ implies a contradiction. Thus equation (A-1) is a necessary condition for an interior local maximum of $f(x)$ at $x = y$.

In order to derive the second necessary condition, assume $f(x)$ has a local interior maximum at $x = y$. By Taylor's expansion with a remainder:

$$f(x) - f(y) = (x - y)f'(y) + \frac{(x - y)^2}{2} f''[y + \theta'(x - y)] \text{ with } 0 < \theta' < 1.$$

But $f'(y) = 0$. So:

$$f(x) - f(y) = \frac{(x - y)^2}{2} f''[y + \theta'(x - y)] \text{ with } 0 < \theta' < 1.$$

Suppose $f''(y) > 0$. Because $f(x)$ is twice continuously differentiable, $f''(x) > 0$ for all x in an interval defined by $|x - y| < m'$, for $m' > 0$. For such x, $f(x) - f(y) > 0$. But this contradicts our assumption that $f(y)$ is a local maximum. So $f''(y) \leq 0$.

Similarly, for $f(x)$ to have a local interior minimum at $x = y$ it is necessary that:

$$f'(y) = 0$$ (A-3)

$$f''(y) \geq 0.$$ (A-4)

It is necessary and sufficient for $f(x)$ to have a local interior maximum (minimum) at $x = y$ that:

$$f'(y) = 0$$ (A-5)

---

[2] $f''(x)$ denotes $d^2f(x)/dx^2$ throughout this Appendix.

[3] This proof is set out in Paul Anthony Samuelson, *Foundations of Economic Analysis* (New York: Atheneum, 1971), Appendix A, pp. 357–59.

[4] See R. Courant, *Differential and Integral Calculus* (New York: Interscience Publishers, Inc., 1953), I, 102–5. Or see George B. Thomas, *Calculus and Analytic Geometry* (Reading, Mass.: Addison-Wesley Publishing Company, 1968), p. 132.

$$f''(y) < (>) \ 0. \qquad\qquad (A\text{--}6)$$

EXAMPLE

$$\max f(x) = -x^2 \text{ on the interval } (-2, 2).$$

For $f(x)$ to have a local interior maximum, it is necessary that $f'(x) = -2x = 0$ and $f''(x) = -2 \leq 0$. Since $f''(x) = -2 < 0$, $f(x) = -x^2$ has a local interior maximum at $x = 0$.

III. Interior Local Optimization of a Function of Many Variables

The necessary and sufficient conditions for the interior local optimization of a function of many variables are an immediate extension of the conditions for the interior local optimization of a function of one variable. If $f(x_1, x_2, \ldots, x_n)$ is a twice continuously differentiable function defined on a set X, for $f(x)$ to attain a local interior maximum at $x = (y_1, \ldots, y_n)$ it is necessary that:[5]

$$\partial f(y_1, \ldots, y_n)/\partial x_i = 0 \qquad \text{for all } i = 1, \ldots, n \qquad (A\text{--}7)$$

$$\sum_{i=1}^{n} \sum_{j=1}^{n} [\partial^2 f(y_1, \ldots, y_n)/\partial x_i \, \partial x_j] h_i h_j \leq 0 \qquad (A\text{--}8)$$

where the h_k are arbitrary numbers not all zero. This condition is necessary and sufficient if (A–8) is a strict inequality.

Analogous to the development for functions of one variable, the previous conditions indicate an interior local minimum if (A–8) is greater than or equal to zero. In the succeeding sections all functions will be written as functions of one variable, x, but the extension to many, say n, variables is easily accomplished by considering x to be an n-tuple and formulating the results in vector or matrix notation.[6]

EXAMPLE

$$\min f(x_1, x_2) = x_1^2 + 3x_2^2 + x_1 \text{ over the area } \{-2 < x_1 < 2; -4 < x_2 < 3\}$$

It is necessary that:

$$\partial f(x_1, x_2)/\partial x_1 = 2x_1 + 1 = 0 \qquad \text{or } x_1 = -\tfrac{1}{2},$$

$$\partial f(x_1, x_2)/\partial x_2 = 6x_2 = 0 \qquad \text{or } x_2 = 0.$$

---

[5] This proof is developed in Samuelson, *op. cit.*, Appendix A, pp. 359–61.

[6] As in Samuelson, *ibid.*

Note that $[\partial^2 f(x_1, x_2)/\partial x_1^2](h_1 h_1) + [\partial^2 f(x_1, x_2)/\partial x_2^2](h_2 h_2) + 2[\partial^2 f(x_1, x_2)/\partial x_1 \partial x_2](h_1 h_2) = 2h_1^2 + 6h_2^2 + 0 > 0$ for all h_1, h_2 not all zero.

Thus $f(x_1, x_2) = x_1^2 + 3x_2^2 + x_1$ has an interior minimum at $(-\frac{1}{2}, 0)$.

IV. Interior Local Optimization
of an Equality-Constrained Function

Consider $f(x)$, a twice continuously differentiable function defined on a set X, and a set of n constraint functions indexed by i, $g_i(x) = b_i$, which are twice continuously differentiable and defined on X, and the problem:

$$\max f(x) \text{ subject to } \{g_i(x) = b_i\}. \qquad \text{(A–9)}$$

Let m be the dimension of x, with $m > n$.

In order that $f(x)$ attain an interior local maximum at $x = y$ subject to $\{g_i(x) = b_i\}$, it is necessary that:

$$\partial g_i(y)/\partial x_j \neq 0 \text{ for at least one value of } j \text{ for every value of } i; \qquad \text{(A–10)}$$

there exist a set of n constants λ_i such that if

$$L(x) = f(x) + \sum_{i=1}^{n} \lambda_i [g_i(x) - b_i],$$

then $\partial L(y)/\partial x = 0$ and $\partial L(y)/\partial \lambda_i = 0 \qquad$ for all $i = 1, \ldots, n$. (A–11)

Note that (A–9) is equivalent to (A–12):

$$\min \, [-f(x)] \text{ subject to } \{g_i(x) = b_i\}. \qquad \text{(A–12)}$$

This method of constrained functional optimization was originated by Lagrange, and the λ_i are called Lagrange multipliers.

EXAMPLE

Find a point x where the necessary conditions for maximizing $f(x)$ are satisfied when $f(x) = x_1^2 + 3x_2 + x_3^2$ subject to $3x_1 = 4$ and $4x_2 = 5$. Note that $m = 3$; $n = 2$. $\partial g_1(x)/\partial x_1 = 3$ and $\partial g_2(x)/\partial x_2 = 4$, so (A–10) is satisfied.

$$L(x) = f(x) + \lambda_1 [g_1(x) - b_1] + \lambda_2 [g_2(x) - b_2]$$
$$= x_1^2 + 3x_2 + x_3^2 + \lambda_1 (3x_1 - 4) + \lambda_2 (4x_2 - 5).$$

The following conditions must hold at the maximum points:

$$\frac{\partial L(x)}{\partial x_3} = 2x_3 = 0$$

$$\frac{\partial L(x)}{\partial x_1} = 2x_1 + 3\lambda_1 = 0 \qquad \frac{\partial L(x)}{\partial \lambda_1} = 3x_1 - 4 = 0$$

$$\frac{\partial L(x)}{\partial x_2} = 3 + 4\lambda_2 = 0 \qquad \frac{\partial L(x)}{\partial \lambda_2} = 4x_2 - 5 = 0.$$

Solving these equations simultaneously indicates the maximum is at:

$$x_1 = \tfrac{4}{3}, \qquad x_2 = \tfrac{5}{4}, \qquad x_3 = 0.$$

The Lagrange multipliers, λ_i, have economically meaningful interpretations, e.g., as prices or costs, depending on their context. A particular example of such an interpretation may be found in Section II.B of Chapter 13, where it is shown that when a firm purchases inputs in imperfect factor markets, the Lagrange multiplier in its production decision problem equals marginal cost.

V. Convexity, Concavity, and the Global Characteristics of Functions

Determining from a set of local optima the global optimum by iterative methods of comparison can be costly and time-consuming. In such cases knowledge that the function being optimized is concave (or convex) on X is sufficient to ensure that a local maximum (or minimum) is global on X.

A function $f(x)$ defined on a set X is *convex* on X if for each x' and x'' which are elements of X:

$$f[\lambda x'' + (1 - \lambda)x'] \leq \lambda f(x'') + (1 - \lambda)f(x') \text{ for } 0 \leq \lambda \leq 1. \quad \text{(A-13)}$$

Noting that a line segment in X joining the 2 points x' and x'' may be written analytically as:

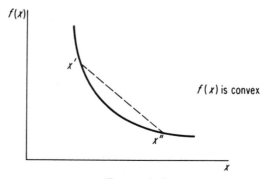

FIGURE A-2.

$$L = \{(x): x \text{ is in } X \text{ and } x = \lambda x'' + (1 - \lambda)x', 0 \le \lambda \le 1\}, \quad \text{(A–14)}$$

we may define convexity geometrically. $f(x)$ is *convex* on X if, for each pair of points, say x', x'' which are elements of X, on the graph of $f(x)$, the line segment joining these points lies entirely on or above the graph. See Figure A–2.

Concavity of a function $f(x)$ is analogously defined. $f(x)$ is *concave* on X if for all x', x'' in X:

$$f[\lambda x'' + (1 - \lambda)x'] \ge \lambda f(x'') + (1 - \lambda)f(x') \text{ for } 0 \le \lambda \le 1. \quad \text{(A–15)}$$

Geometrically, $f(x)$ is concave on X if, for each pair of points on the graph of $f(x)$, the line segment joining these points lies entirely on or below the graph. See Figure A–3. Note that a linear function is both concave and convex.

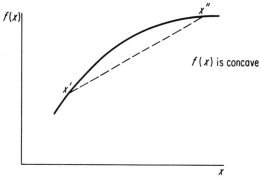

FIGURE A–3.

If $f(x)$ is concave (convex) on X, then a necessary and sufficient condition that $f(x)$ attain a global maximum (minimum) at $x = y$ is that $f(x)$ attain a local maximum (minimum) at $x = y$.

EXAMPLE

$$f(x) = x^2 \text{ is convex.}$$

$$\min f(x) = x^2.$$

It is necessary and sufficient for $f(x)$ to attain a global minimum at $x = 0$ for:

$$df(x)/dx = 2x = 0 \qquad \text{at } x = 0$$

$$d^2f(x)/dx^2 = 2 > 0 \qquad \text{at } x = 0.$$

SUGGESTED READINGS

COURANT, R., *Differential and Integral Calculus*, I and II. New York: Interscience Publishers, Inc., 1953.

HILLIER, FREDERICK S., AND GERALD J. LIEBERMAN, *Introduction to Operations Research*. San Francisco: Holden-Day, Inc., 1969.

SAMUELSON, PAUL ANTHONY, *Foundations of Economic Analysis*. New York: Atheneum, 1971.

THOMAS, GEORGE B., *Calculus and Analytic Geometry*. Reading, Mass.: Addison-Wesley Publishing Company, 1968.

Index